COGNITION

COGNITION
From Memory to Creativity

Robert W. Weisberg
Temple University

Lauretta M. Reeves
The University of Texas at Austin

WILEY

A JOHN WILEY & SONS, INC.

Library of Congress Cataloging-in-Publication Data:
Weisberg, Robert W.
  Cognition : from memory to creativity / Robert W. Weisberg and Lauretta M. Reeves.
    p. cm.
  Includes bibliographical references and index.
  ISBN 978-0-470-22628-5 (cloth)
  ISBN 978-1-118-25861-3 (e-bk)
  ISBN 978-1-118-23360-3 (e-bk)
  ISBN 978-1-118-22010-8 (e-bk)
  1. Cognition. I. Reeves, Lauretta. II. Title.
  BF311.W4155 2013
  153—dc23

                                                        2012032033

Printed in the United States of America

10 9 8 7 6 5 4 3 2 1

Without the support of my wife, Nancy, this book would never have been completed. I dedicate it to her.

—R.W.

I dedicate the book to my parents, my first educators.

—L.R.

CONTENTS

PREFACE

When authors set out to write a book, the first question they must answer is what the new book will add beyond related books that on the same topic. Once the book is published, that same question arises in the minds of those who might use it in courses: what does this book give us that is new and different? We believe that this book is a positive addition to the books available for courses in cognitive psychology, for two main reasons—a unique organization and expanded coverage. While many textbooks contain the words *cognition* or *cognitive psychology*, this book substantially alters the standard organization of cognition textbooks. In addition, this book covers a broader subject matter than most other cognitive texts through its inclusion of a separate chapter on creativity.

Most texts in cognition traverse the path set almost 50 years ago by Neisser in his pioneering textbook, *Cognitive Psychology* (1967): they follow information as it first comes into the system, is stored in memory, and then is used as needed to speak or solve problems or make decisions. Coverage usually begins with perception, attention, and related phenomena—the processes whereby information from the world "enters" the cognitive system, and is selected for further processing. Even though the organization of most books is thus "bottom-up," in that it begins with how material comes in from the environment, the authors acknowledge that perception and attention are influenced by "top-down" processes. That is, the authors often emphasize that our knowledge plays a critical role in even the early processes of perception and attention. For example, we are more efficient processors of information when we are familiar with the domain in which we are functioning. Although such discussions highlight the important role that memory—in the form of knowledge and expectancies—plays in perceptual processes, most standard textbooks cannot make too much of that connection, because memory is not discussed until *after* perception and attention. It is as if a promissory note has been given: we will be able to better understand the initial chapters later, when the discussion of memory is presented.

A similar disconnect is seen after the discussion of memory has been presented. The topic of memory is presented in the middle of the book, and is followed by discussions of processes that are assumed to be dependent on it—language, thinking and reasoning, problem solving. However in the typical text no explicit connection is made between memory and those higher processes.

The present book takes a different tack in organizing the phenomena that fall under the topic of cognitive psychology. If it is true, as most textbook writers emphasize, that memory is critical in all our functioning, including functioning of the "lower" mental processes such as perception and attention, then it seems to follow that the discussion of cognition should *begin* with the study of memory. If we understand first of all how information is encoded, stored, and retrieved (including information about what things look like), then not only will we have an understanding of memory, we will also have a conceptual base that we can use to understand other phenomena, such as visual recognition of objects, language, and decision making.

We also have used the discussion of memory as the organizing point for the discussion of the other "higher processes"—language; concepts; reasoning and decision making; and problem solving. We emphasize the close relation between memory and all the higher processes, and we make explicit the connections among them. For example, in our discussion of language development, we draw the connection between memory processes and the kinds of things children say when they are learning to speak. Similar connections are made in the discussion of language processing in adults, and of the role of memory in creativity.

There are also instructional benefits to beginning a cognitive psychology text with the study of memory: pedagogically it is a natural entry point for students in their engagement with the subject matter. After all, as students they are concerned with questions about memory—How can I better remember information? Why did I remember where an answer was on a textbook page, but not the answer itself? Why does my grandmother remember vivid details of her childhood experiences but not where she put her keys? Thus, memory processes are more familiar to us than almost any other cognitive activities (when was the last time you had a discussion about how you are able to recognize the machine in front of you as a computer?) Both authors have experimented over several years with beginning courses with the study of memory versus beginning with the usual perception and attention; students greatly prefer being introduced to the study of cognition starting with memory. It provides them with an accessible way to learn theoretical approaches to cognition, and to critically assess cognitive research. We have used drafts of this textbook in classes and have found that students like both the organization and the writing style, which one student described as feeling "like the authors are talking to us."

The main difference in content between the present book and other textbooks can be seen in the subtitle; the presence of the word *creativity* in the subtitle of our book indicates immediately that it is significantly different from other books. Most, but not all, cognitive texts have sections on creativity, but those discussions are often small sections within the Problem Solving chapter. In this book, creative thinking is presented in a separate chapter. It is our belief that research in problem solving and creativity are now mature enough to be covered on their own. It is also natural to cover both topics as arising out of the issues and themes discussed earlier in the book, especially memory. Thus, this textbook provides greater breadth than most other cognition texts. Again, our use of the book in classes and reviewers' responses, have demonstrated that people are fascinated by this material and by our approach of tying creativity to the "lower-level" processes discussed earlier in the book.

A final point of difference in our book is that we have tried to integrate neuroscience material into the presentation of key topics within each chapter. Rather than presenting neuroscience material in boxes or separate sections at the end of each chapter, neuroscience evidence—from both patients with brain damage and studies using PET scans or fMRI findings—is assimilated into each section where it is relevant.

In conclusion, we believe that *Cognition: From Memory to Creativity* provides instructors with a novel approach to the study of cognition, written in a highly accessible style. In addition, the book provides instructors and students with coverage of material that they will find nowhere else in the currently available texts.

ACKNOWLEDGMENTS

This book would never have seen the light of day if Tisha Rossi, Executive Editor for Psychology at John Wiley & Sons, had not casually asked whether I had been working on any other projects. I thank her for her support and encouragement. Kara Borbely, Editorial Program Coordinator for the Professional/Trade Division at Wiley, has also played an important role in the gestation of this book, and I thank her for her help. Several reviewers, including Yuhong Jiang, University of Minnesota, Department of Psychology; Tandra Ghose, UCLA, Department of Psychology; Yohan Delton, Brigham Young University, Department of Psychology; and Nadine Martin, Department of Communication Sciences and Disorders, Temple University, provided detailed feedback on an early draft of the manuscript, and I am grateful for their careful and helpful work.

A project of this magnitude inevitably encounters ups and downs during its production. I would like to thank my coauthor, not only for the knowledge and care that she brought to the project, but also for her dry sense of humor, which helped us get over the bumps.

R.W.

I would like to thank my husband and children for their forbearance during my physical and psychological absences throughout the writing process, and the many Austin take-out restaurants that have kept my family fed since this project was begun several years ago.

My gratitude goes to the following people and agencies who arranged for photos to be taken, or allowed us to borrow EEG or fMRI images: Dr. André Souza (Postdoctoral Fellow at Concordia University in Montréal, Canada), Dr. Logan Trujillo (Psychology Department of the University of Texas at Austin), and Dr. Jeffrey Luci (Imaging Research Center at the University of Texas at Austin). I am also grateful to those who served as models for many of the stimuli—Arian Mobasser, Claudia Tye, and members of the Anderson High School Little Theater Company (especially Connor Martin, Tristan McConnell, Catherine Pierce, Camilla Rivadenyra, Cecily Tye, and Hanna Tyson). Thanks to Cecily Tye, who helped with many of the drawings and graphic designs in the book, and to Claudia Tye, who assisted with photography and photo editing.

I would also like to thank my coauthor (and former dissertation advisor) Bob Weisberg, and Tisha Rossi, Kara Borbely, and Kim Nir of Wiley, for their help and patience during the writing (and re-writing, and re-re-writing) of this text. The reviewers have helped to make this a better book.

Many students and teaching assistants have provided informal feedback on assorted chapters; I appreciate both this feedback, and their enthusiasm for cognitive psychology, which has kept me inspired about teaching. Many thanks to colleagues and graduate students within the University of Texas Psychology Department, and to Michael Tye, for conversations that helped sharpen some of the ideas conveyed in the book.

L.R.

CHAPTER 1

INTRODUCTION TO THE STUDY OF COGNITION

Before you even arrived at your first class this morning, you had engaged in numerous cognitive acts: recognizing the sound of your alarm clock and the time depicted on its face, saying "good morning" to your roommate, and categorizing your cereal as a breakfast food. You also had to remember the day of the week so that you knew which classes to attend, you decided which clothes to wear, and you paid attention as you crossed the road to get to your first class. Perhaps you even engaged in some creative thinking as you doodled while waiting for class to start. These are all examples of the cognitive processes—the mental processes—at work. Cognition both allows us to operate in the real world, and makes life richer.

Humans are captivated by how the mind works, and this fascination makes its way into popular culture. Stories about cognitive functioning and the connection between the brain and the mind are in newspapers and on TV all the time. Films about memory—whether the loss of memory (*Memento*) or implanted memories (*Total Recall*, *Inception*)—have become top-grossing hits. Books about consciousness (Dennett, *Consciousness Explained*, 1991), intelligence (Herrnstein & Murray, *The Bell Curve*, 1994), language (Pinker, *The Language Instinct*, 1994), memory (Foer, *Moonwalking with Einstein: The Art and Science of Remembering Everything*, 2011), and the relation between talent, practice, and success (Gladwell, *Outliers: The Story of Success*, 2011) were bestsellers. Articles in popular magazines discuss insight in problem solving (Lehrer, "The Eureka Hunt," 2008) and creativity in business (Gladwell, "Creation Myth," 2011). The appeal of the mind holds even for scientists: Since 2001, psychological topics related to cognition or neurocognition have made the cover story of *Scientific American* magazine numerous times. The discipline of cognitive psychology has historically encompassed the study of the cognitive or mental processes, and provides the research upon which so many popular films and bestselling books are based. However, more recently, there has been a broadening of research on cognition to include neuroscience, computer science, linguistics, and philosophy, which has spawned a new discipline: cognitive science.

While much of the research on cognitive processes takes place in laboratories, for the cognitive scientist, life itself is an experiment in cognition: Everywhere one looks, it is possible to see evidence of mental processes at work. Dr. Weisberg's daughter used to be a competitive ice-skater, and every day she would go for practice sessions. The ice would be full of skaters, practicing the jumps, spins, and other moves they would need for their competitive programs. The practice sessions were not purely athletic endeavors; we can dissect what is happening at a cognitive level as each skater practices on a crowded ice rink.

First, *memory* is involved (Chapters 2–4). The main task facing those skaters is to master their material, so that they remember the correct sequence of jumps, glides, spins, and twists in their programs. Sometimes during a competition a skater begins to move in an erratic way, losing synchronization with the music: The skater has temporarily forgotten the program. The pressure of competition often causes skaters to forget or misremember a sequence of movements that was remembered easily many times during practice.

A second cognitive task facing the ice-skaters involves *visual* and *spatial processing* (Chapter 5): Each skater has to know the boundaries of the skating rink and the spatial configuration of their routine within those boundaries. They must also recognize other skaters as people to be avoided and determine their own and others' speed and direction, to determine if any collisions are likely. Sometimes younger skaters run out of space and cannot perform a jump because they are too close to the wall. Such skaters are not able to accurately calculate the space available for the move they hoped to carry out. This occurs much more rarely with experienced skaters, indicating that those visual-processing skills have developed over years of practice. This is one example of the general importance of knowledge in cognitive functioning.

Third, *attention* is involved in our skaters' practicing (Chapter 6). To a spectator, the scene on the ice has a chaotic quality, as all those youngsters zoom this way and that, each seemingly concentrating only on improving his or her own skills. And yet there are very few collisions; the skaters are typically able to practice their routines while avoiding each other. This requires both *selective* attention—each skater pays attention to his or her own skating routine while ignoring the practice routines of others—and *divided* attention (i.e., multitasking). As each skater is attending to his or her own routine, he or she must determine where other skaters are headed, so as not to be in the same place at the same time as anyone else. While watching a group of skaters of mixed levels of expertise, one quickly sees that the inexperienced skaters have problems with the multitasking demands of the practice session; they cannot concentrate on practicing their programs while at the same time attending to and avoiding the other skaters. The more-experienced skaters, in contrast, are able to avoid collisions while at the same time working on a jump or spin. So one of the consequences of the development of skill is an increase in the ability to multitask. Another way to put this is to say that the knowledge of the experienced skaters is useful in dealing with the attentional demands of the practice session.

Additional cognitive skills can also be seen in the skaters' practice sessions. Sometimes, one hears a coach give instruction to a skater: "Do you remember how crisply Jane does that tricky footwork at the end of her program? It would be good if you could move like that as you do yours." Presumably, the coach and the skater are able to communicate because both of them can recall Jane's appearance as she skates. They are able to use *imagery* (Chapter 7) to remember how Jane looked as she did her footwork. The coach can use the memory of how Jane looked as the basis for judging the quality of the skater's footwork, and the skater can use her memory of Jane's performance as the basis for her own attempt to do the footwork.

Other cognitive skills necessary for optimum ice-skating performance are the *acquisition and use of concepts* (Chapter 8) and *language processing* (Chapters 9 and 10). A coach may revise a routine by saying, "I'd like you to insert a Biellmann spin here—it's a layback where you pull your free leg over your head from behind." This example makes it evident that language is an important vehicle through which we *acquire concepts*. The skater will recognize a layback and use the coach's elaboration to understand what must be added to produce a Biellmann spin. In so doing, our hypothetical skater has just acquired a new concept. Also, the skaters' coaches constantly monitor the skaters' performance on the ice. One may hear a coach call out, "Keep that free leg up" while the skater spins, and one sees an immediate change in the posture of the skater. The skater processes the coach's linguistic message and adjusts his or her movements accordingly.

Finally, sometimes a coach and skater will change the routine during the practice session. The coach might decide that something more is needed in the way of jumps, for example, or that the choreography needs refinement. Or the skater might ask for some addition to the program, perhaps to make it more challenging. In these examples, the coach or skater has *made a decision under uncertainty* concerning the structure of the program (Chapter 11). Neither the coach nor skater is certain that the proposed changes will be helpful, but they have weighed the available information and decided that it would be beneficial to make a change. When changing the program, the coach and skater have identified *problems to solve* (Chapter 12) and *creative thinking* plays a role in producing changes in the program (Chapter 13).

These examples are by no means extraordinary. Surely each of us could compile, from any randomly selected day, a long list of phenomena in which cognitive processes are centrally involved: seeing a friend today, and picking up the thread of a conversation begun yesterday; using directions acquired online to drive to a new restaurant; being impressed with the creativity of a new song produced by your favorite group. Cognitive processes are at the core of everything we do.

In the past 30 years there has been an explosion in the study of human mental processes, and the momentum shows no signs of slowing down (Robins, Gosling, & Craik, 1999). New developments in the study of cognition have come from many disciplines, and are now best encompassed under the general term *cognitive science*. First, many areas which researchers had in the past studied only peripherally, if at all, such as imagery, language processing, and creative thinking, have come under investigation and have begun to yield their secrets. Second, in many areas, interdisciplinary cross-fertilization has occurred. Cognitive psychologists and neuroscientists regularly collaborate in the study of the relationship between the brain and cognitive processes, to determine the specific cognitive skills lost when a patient suffers a stroke or accident, or to discover, for example, which parts of the brain are most active when someone learns or recalls information. Those studies have increased our understanding of both normal and abnormal neurocognitive functioning. Linguists, cognitive psychologists, and computer scientists have made advances in our understanding of language processes. Philosophers of mind contribute to the study of cognition by clarifying the concepts and theoretical issues within cognitive psychology, including issues related to consciousness and the relation of mind and brain. Third, cognitive scientists have developed new ways of analyzing how we learn, organize information, and carry out cognitive tasks, most notably the computer-based information-processing perspective.

WHY DO WE NEED TO STUDY COGNITION SCIENTIFICALLY?

A psychologist once remarked that being considered an expert in the field of psychology is difficult because since everyone has psychological states, everyone thinks that they know everything there is to know about psychology. When students are introduced to the scientific study of cognition, including much new terminology and numerous new concepts, they sometimes wonder why it is necessary to study cognition scientifically. Don't we all know how memory functions, since we each use our memory all the time? Don't we know about attention, from our own experiences attending to events in the environment? We all possess what we could call a commonsense cognitive psychology. Why do we need to learn all this jargon to describe and explain phenomena with which we are already familiar?

The scientific study of cognition is of value is because, contrary to what laypeople believe, they do not know very much about their own cognitive processes. Nisbett and Wilson (1977) found that humans often are extremely bad at giving accurate explanations for their own behavior. A recent bestseller, *Blink*, begins with an example of art-history experts knowing that a supposedly ancient Greek sculpture is a fake, but even the experts could not explain how or why they could detect the fraud (Gladwell, 2005). Thus, even experts in a field cannot discern the processes that underlie their cognitive abilities.

In many places in this book, we discuss research findings that are surprising or counterintuitive. The dangers of texting while driving are well known, and 39 states have banned the practice (Governors Highway Safety Association, n.d.). However, one example of a nearly universal lack of knowledge about cognitive processes is seen in recent legislation in many states banning the use of hand-held cell phones while driving. Such laws seem totally reasonable: Statistics have shown that using a cell phone while driving increases the risk of accidents, and most people assume that the dangerous aspect of cell-phone use is taking one hand off the steering wheel to hold and dial the phone. Legislators then enact laws banning *hand-held* cell phones. However, experimental studies of people driving in a simulated vehicle while talking on a cell phone have found that hands-free cell phones are just as dangerous as hand-held phones (Strayer, Drews, & Crouch, 2006). Driving while talking on a cell phone—hands-on *or* hands-free—is as dangerous as driving drunk (Strayer et al., 2006; these findings are discussed further in Chapter 6), and increases the risk of a collision fourfold (Redelmeier and Tibshirani, 1997). The problem with talking while on a cell phone is not that your hands are occupied—it is that your *mind* is.

Only 10 states in the United States have passed laws prohibiting cell phones while driving for all drivers, but not a single state bans hands-free phones (as of 2012; http://www.ghsa.org/html/stateinfo/laws/cellphone_laws.html). That means that no state has a policy that is consistent with the research findings (several additional states ban all cell phone use by those under 18 only). The legislators' lack of knowledge about and/or understanding of the cognitive issues underlying cell-phone use could have tragic consequences (Redelmeier & Tibshirani, 1997). This real-life example illustrates why we have to study cognition scientifically; although we each possess the cognitive processes and use them all the time, in actuality most of us do not know very much about the finer points of how they work.

OUTLINE OF CHAPTER 1

This chapter has several purposes. We first examine two uses of the term *cognitive psychology*, to set the stage for discussion of the development of modern cognitive science over the past 150 years, culminating in the recent ascendance of cognitive psychology as a major area within contemporary psychology. Many disciplines contributed to what has been called "the Cognitive Revolution" in the 1950s and 1960s, in which the study of mental processes supplanted behaviorism, which had been opposed to the study of consciousness and mental events. As part of our discussion of the cognitive revolution, we will consider the question of how cognitive scientists can study mental processes, which cannot be seen, and which may not be accessible to us at a conscious level.

As we have already noted, the modern study of cognition is made up of many different domains of academic inquiry, ranging from traditional research in psychology, to modern techniques for the study of brain and behavior, as well as theories and methods from areas outside psychology, such as linguistics and computer science. The final major portion of the chapter provides a more detailed introduction to how those disciplines have come together in the contemporary study of cognition.

COGNITIVE PSYCHOLOGY: A SUBJECT MATTER AND A POINT OF VIEW

The term *cognitive psychology* has two uses: It describes a subject matter, and it also describes a point of view or philosophy concerning how one studies that subject matter. The *subject matter* of cognitive psychology is the *mental processes*. These include memory; perceptual processes, such as pattern recognition (e.g., recognition of objects, words, sounds, etc.), attention, and imagery; language, including comprehension and production, and related phenomena, such as conceptual knowledge; and the class of activities traditionally called thinking, or the "higher mental processes," including problem solving and creativity, and logical reasoning and decision making. *Cognitive psychology as a point of view*, or a scientific philosophy, refers to a set of beliefs concerning how those topics are to be studied (e.g., Neisser, 1967). According to the cognitive perspective, understanding behavior—such as remembering your mother's birthday, solving a math problem, or reading words on a page—requires that we analyze the mental processes that underlie that behavior. This perspective can be contrasted with behaviorism, which was based on the belief that behavior could be understood by determining the external stimulus conditions that brought it about, and not worrying about internal mental processes.

Studying Hidden Processes

Accepting the cognitive point of view raises a difficult question: How can one study cognitive or mental processes, which occur internally and therefore cannot be examined directly? Students often propose a simple method for studying internal processes: Have the person report on what he or she is thinking. That is, perhaps we can use *subjective reports* as the basis for studying hidden processes. This is a reasonable suggestion, but there is a basic difficulty with subjective reports. Suppose I tell you that right now I am imagining a dollar bill. How can you tell if my report is accurate? I may be lying about what I am thinking, or perhaps I am mistaken (and am really thinking about the candy bar I'd like to buy with that dollar). The fact that subjective reports cannot be *verified*—that is, the fact that we cannot tell whether they are accurate—means that they cannot be used as evidence for internal processes; other types of evidence must be found. Instead of subjective reports, we need objective data.

The question of whether and how one can study mental phenomena—which cannot be seen directly—had been a point of disagreement among psychologists for 100 years, until the advent of the cognitive revolution. We discuss this question in detail later in the chapter, after we place it in historical context. In our view, the cognitive scientist's study of hidden mental processes is no different than the activities carried out by scientists in many disciplines (e.g., biology, chemistry, physics) or, indeed, the activities carried out by ordinary folks in our understanding of events in the world. We deal with hidden processes all the time.

PSYCHOLOGY AS A SCIENCE

Wundt and Introspection

The beginning of psychology as a science is traced to Wilhelm Wundt's establishment of the first psychological laboratory in 1879, in Germany (Boring, 1953). Until that point, the sorts of phenomena now studied by psychologists were investigated by researchers in physics and biology, as well as in philosophy. Students from all over the world came to study with Wundt, and many of those new psychologists returned to their home countries and established their own laboratories. Wundt and his followers could be considered the first cognitive psychologists, because they were interested in several mind-related topics, including consciousness. However, there were a number of important differences between Wundt's psychology and modern cognitive psychology.

First, the specific topics of Wundt's research differ from the topics of contemporary cognitive-psychology experiments. Wundt and his followers were interested in determining the basic *elements* or *structure* of conscious experiences, in the same way that chemists of that era were attempting to determine the basic elements of chemical compounds. While many modern cognitive scientists are also interested in the study of consciousness, the subject matter of modern cognitive science encompasses many other phenomena, such as those outlined above. Second, the methods of studying cognitive processes have also changed significantly over the 125-plus years since Wundt, his students, and colleagues began their work. In those days, it was believed that one could study consciousness by training observers to analyze their own experiences into their basic components and to report on them. This method was called *introspection*, which means *looking inside*. An example of a task used in introspectionist investigations of consciousness would be to present the names of two animals, say *dog* and *cow*, and ask the participant to judge which animal is larger in size, and then to provide an introspective report of what occurred between the presentation of the task and the production of a response.

Introspection required more than a casual report, however. The observer had to be trained to avoid *the stimulus error*, which was reporting the unanalyzed conscious experience in terms of commonsense, everyday language, rather than analyzing it into more basic components (Mandler & Mandler, 1964). For example, if, after making the judgment that a cow is larger than a dog, the observer reported, "I imagined a cow standing next to a dog, and mentally compared their heights and lengths," that would be an example of the stimulus error. If the observer correctly engaged in introspection, he would convey more "raw" perceptual impressions, and might say something like: "An image of a large nonmoving bulk and smaller one. . . . A feeling of movement. . . . An image of one end of the small bulk, and then the other. . . . A verbal image 'the cow is bigger.' . . . Production of the verbal response."

The "Imageless Thought" Controversy

When introspection was applied to the study of conscious experience, several difficulties arose. First, the results obtained in different laboratories were not consistent. Some investigators, such as Titchener, one of Wundt's earliest students, insisted that virtually all thought relied on imagery, based on the results of his introspection studies, while others reported that their studies showed that thinking could also be carried out *without* imagery (see discussion in Mandler & Mandler, 1964). Those conflicting findings raised questions about the usefulness of introspection, since seemingly identical investigations had produced opposite results. Whether "imageless thought" could occur became a major controversy, and resulted in many psychologists becoming dissatisfied both with the focus of psychology being the "mind," and with the use of introspection as a scientific technique. One outcome of the imageless thought debate was the rise of a group of psychologists who wanted psychology to be a science of *behavior*—the behaviorists (Leahey, 1992).

Behaviorism and the Question of Consciousness

The strongest reaction against attempts to use introspection to analyze the structure of conscious experience came from John Watson (1913), the founder of American behaviorism. Watson wrote forcefully against the value of studying conscious experiences, because of the already-noted problems with verification of introspective reports. He proposed that psychology should follow the example of the established sciences, such as physics and chemistry, whose methods were only concerned with phenomena that were observable and directly measurable. When physicists studied the effects of gravity on falling objects, for example, they measured the height of the fall, weight of the objects, and time to fall. In his behaviorist manifesto—"Psychology as the Behaviorist Views It"—Watson (1913) advocated a similar perspective for psychology: "psychology must . . . never use the terms consciousness, mental states, mind, content, introspectively verifiable, imagery and the like . . ." (pp. 166–167) because the scientist cannot directly observe those things. Psychologists should study only observable events: environmental stimuli and behavior.

Watson promoted the now-familiar stimulus–response (S–R) approach to the analysis of behavior. He believed that there was a law-like relationship between environmental stimuli and behavioral responses, with every behavioral act being brought about by one measurable stimulus, and each stimulus producing only one response. Therefore, it should be possible to analyze behavior to such an exact degree that, for any response that occurred, the psychologist could know exactly what the stimulus had been; and if a given specific stimulus occurred, one could say exactly what the response would be. In Watson's view, the main task of psychology was to be able to predict and control behavior through presentation of environmental stimuli. One should not try to measure hypothesized internal psychological states, which might not even exist. Furthermore, Watson proposed that by strictly controlling the environment in which an organism grew up, he could determine the trajectory of a person's life:

> Give me a dozen healthy infants, well-formed, and my own specified world to bring them up in and I'll guarantee to take any one at random and train him to become any type of specialist I might select—doctor, lawyer, artist, merchant-chief and, yes, even beggar-man and thief, regardless of his talents, penchants, tendencies, abilities, vocations, and race of his ancestors. (Watson, 1930, p. 104)

Thus, Watson adopted a radical stance to the study of psychology, claiming that there are no mental processes that play any causal role in a behavioral chain.

The second major advocate of behaviorism was B. F. Skinner, who championed what is known as *operant conditioning*. Based on the ideas of Thorndike (1898, 1911), Skinner proposed that the consequences of behaviors—reinforcements and punishments—would determine whether those behaviors increased in frequency and intensity, or whether they decreased (Skinner, 1938). If a behavior was reinforced, it would become more likely to happen in the future; if punished, less likely. Like his predecessor Watson, Skinner rejected mentalistic explanations of behavior as unscientific. Skinner's principles of operant conditioning were derived from maze running and key pressing in animals. The book *Verbal Behavior* (1957) marked his attempt to apply conditioning principles to complex human behaviors, such as the development of language in a child. In Skinner's view, children acquire a language by mimicking what they have heard and by being reinforced for their utterances (e.g., by delighted parents or by more quickly receiving what they want). Thus, language learning is brought about by the same learning mechanisms that are evident in lower-level animals; there is no need in a scientific theory for mentalistic or cognitive explanations of any skill or behavior. As we shall see, the inability of the behavioristic framework to account for complex phenomena, such as language, problem solving, and creativity, would eventually lead to the paradigm's loss of favor (a paradigm is a theoretical framework that helps to guide research within a topic area).

TOWARD A NEW COGNITIVE PSYCHOLOGY

The development of behaviorism resulted in reduced interest in the study of cognition in the first half of the 20th century, particularly in America. However, even at this time there was still interest in cognitive processes among some psychologists and philosophers. As one example, William James, a philosopher with interests in the study of behavior, presented discussions of complex human psychological phenomena. Second, there were a number of centers of psychological research in Europe in which the full-fledged study of human cognitive processes went on. Thus, this work was available in books and journal articles when other psychologists began to become interested once again in cognition. Finally, developments in several areas outside of psychology, including linguistics and computer science, provided psychologists with new ways of analyzing complex psychological phenomena. Those new perspectives greatly stimulated the development of modern cognitive science.

Cognitive Stirrings in America

William James was an American philosopher who wrote a two-volume survey of psychology, *Principles of Psychology* (1890/1950), in which he addressed many issues that were to become important to modern cognitive psychologists (e.g., Estes, 1990). James provided detailed descriptions of his own *phenomenological* experiences, that is, his personal experiences of psychological phenomena. For example, he described the experience of selectively attending to some event or object at the expense of paying attention to others. Attention was "the taking possession of the mind, in clear and vivid form, of one out of what seems several simultaneously possible objects or trains of thought. . . . It implies withdrawal from some thing in order to deal effectively with others" (1890, pp. 403–404). James also described his phenomenological experiences of remembering, and presented descriptions of experiences, which led him to distinguish between *primary* and *secondary* memory (approximately corresponding to the distinction between short- and long-term memory that has been studied extensively by today's cognitive psychologists). Both these areas—attention and the question of the structure of memory—became foci of research in modern cognitive psychology.

It should be noted that James's use of phenomenological analysis is not the same as the introspection carried out by Wundt and his followers. James was not interested in analyzing his conscious experience into its component parts, but, rather, attempted to present a detailed and accurate description of the conscious experiences themselves. This work was important because James discussed complex cognitive phenomena, such as shifts in attention or remembering, not merely simple sensory experiences. James is also considered to be a *functionalist*, because his explanations often emphasized the purpose or function of psychological and mental phenomena (Leahey, 1992), and how they allow people to adapt to their environment: "Man, whatever else he may be, is primarily a practical being, whose mind is given him to aid in adapting him to this world's life" (James, 1898).

The Study of Cognition in Europe

A number of European investigators were engaged in research on topics within the realm of cognitive psychology, not only during the late 1800s, but even when behaviorism dominated American psychology during the first half of the 20th century.

Ebbinghaus and the Study of Memory

Hermann Ebbinghaus was a German psychologist who is credited with bringing scientific techniques to the study of memory. He insisted on using material that was not associated with any previously learned information, and thus devised *nonsense syllables*, meaningless consonant-vowel-consonant strings such as REZ and TOQ, to determine how many repetitions he needed to learn new lists of items, and how long he could retain the information after having learned it. He used the method of rote rehearsal—simply repeating the items again and again. With this method, he could objectively measure the amount of time needed to memorize a list. However, from a modern perspective, Ebbinghaus's analysis was lacking, as he did not make any inferences about the internal processes that accomplished remembering. Ebbinghaus also was the first researcher to systematically study forgetting. He retested his memory for the lists he had learned after 1, or 2, or 30 days. In this way, he was able to measure the amount of memory loss (or forgetting) as a function of time (Ebbinghaus, 1885/1964).

Ebbinghaus's work on memory had a great influence on the study of cognition many years after his death. Through the middle of the 20th century, a number of American psychologists who wanted to study human functioning without having to appeal to mental processes used Ebbinghaus's (1885/1964) research as their model, because of his rigorous scientific methods (see, for example, chapters in Cofer & Musgrave, 1961, 1963). Although Ebbinghaus's approach ignored the study of underlying mental processes, his work did demonstrate that one could study memory in the psychological laboratory. Ebbinghaus's research and that of those who followed him brought the study of memory to the attention of many experimental psychologists.

Donders's Subtractive Method

F. C. Donders, a researcher from Holland who was a contemporary of Wundt, developed techniques for *mental chronometry*—the measurement of the time to carry out basic operations within an act of cognition (Donders, 1868/1969). For example, Donders might seat a person in front of a light, and tell him to press a button whenever the light came on. Imagine that it takes, on average, 250 milliseconds (equal to $1/4$ sec.) for a person to *detect* the light and *respond* to it. The *reaction time* (RT) to the light is thus 250 milliseconds (msec). In another condition, the person would be told to press a button on the left if light A came on, but a button on the right if light B came on. This takes (hypothetically), on average, 400 msec. The second task requires *detection* of the light, *discrimination* of whether light A or light B has turned on, and the *response*. Let us say that the experimenter wants to determine the length of the discrimination stage in the second task. The *subtractive method* allows one to do that. The second task takes 400 msec; the first task takes 250 msec. The only difference between the tasks is *discrimination*, so that process must require the additional 150 msec. Thus, we have *decomposed* those tasks into their parts and measured the time needed to carry out one of them. (Note the similarity to Wundt's attempts to decompose conscious cognitive phenomena.)

The subtractive method provided a way of measuring mental processing that was based on objective measurement—that is, on the time needed to carry out various tasks. The subtractive method became important in modern cognitive psychology in the 1960s, when Sternberg (1966) used reaction time to measure how we recall information from memory. The logic of Donders's subtractive method has influenced the design of many cognitive psychology experiments, and RT is now a common measure used by many researchers. The subtraction method also plays an important role in neurocognitive research, as we shall see shortly.

Gestalt Psychology: Perception and Problem Solving

The Gestalt psychologists, who worked in Germany and then in the United States, mainly during the first half of the 20th century, carried out investigations of several areas of human cognition. They were interested in the study of perceptual situations in which the organization or form of the whole situation produced an experience that could not be anticipated from analysis of the elements or parts that made it up. The term *Gestalt*, German for *form*, has entered our ordinary vocabularies, as well as being a part of the technical vocabulary of psychology. An example of a situation of interest to the Gestalt psychologists is presented in Figure 1.1a: The perceptual experience of a triangle is accomplished by focusing on the organization, or Gestalt, of the elements (rather than the individual parts themselves). Thus, we impose an organization on the three Pac-Man–type figures by mentally filling in the lines between them.

The Gestalt psychologists also investigated reversible figures, such as the one shown in Figure 1.1b. When one studies such figures, it is common to see a sudden reversal, from a vase to two faces in profile (and back to a vase). Thus, a reversible figure is *one* stimulus that produces *two* responses. The existence of such figures disproves the behaviorists' belief, proposed by Watson (1913), that it would be possible to specify precisely a *single* response to any individual stimulus. Cognitive psychologists believe that the ambiguous faces/vase picture can produce two different responses because the person can cognitively analyze it in two different ways. Reversible figures are very simple illustrations of the necessity to analyze internal processes in order to understand observable behavior (e.g., the person first reports seeing a vase, then the two faces).

The Gestalt psychologists also carried out research on more complex human cognition, most notably problem solving and creative thinking (e.g., Duncker, 1945; Maier, 1930; Wertheimer, 1923, 1959). They believed that complex thought processes could not be broken down into simple elementary processes, and that the performance of

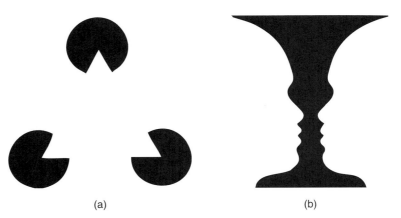

(a)   (b)

Figure 1.1   Gestalt demonstration: These figures illustrate how the perceiver is involved in the interpretation of a stimulus. (a) Kanizsa triangle. (b) Reversible figure: Vase/faces.

lower animals (e.g., pigeons, rats) on simplified versions of problem solving tasks would not shed light on human cognitive abilities. The Gestalt psychologists also emphasized the method of collecting *verbal protocols*, where participants were instructed to verbalize their thoughts, providing a stream-of-consciousness verbalization as they solved problems. Verbal protocols were different from the reports obtained by Wundt and Titchener during introspection, since the participants were not trying to break their conscious experiences into basic elements. Research has demonstrated that protocols can provide a useful record of thought processes that can be verbalized (Ericsson & Simon, 1980) and used as a supplement to other means of assessing cognitive activity.

Bartlett's Analysis of Memory

Sir Frederick Bartlett (1932, 1958), an English psychologist, carried out a long series of investigations of memory during the first half of the 20th century. Bartlett proposed that remembering information depends on more than the passive "stamping in" of the information in the person's memory. He suggested, instead, that people are *active* participants in cognitive processing and that they use their knowledge to interpret and remember information. Bartlett's view thus contrasted with Ebbinghaus's (1885/1964) adherence to rote rehearsal to memorize meaningless nonsense syllables. Bartlett theorized that much of what people remember consists of their interpretations of the material, rather than the material itself, and thus they actively *construct* their memory. He demonstrated that the person's interpretation of the material that is to be recalled plays a crucial role in remembering. When memorizing a verbal passage, for example, we most likely use a *schema*—a cognitive structure that helps us organize and make sense of the new material. Please perform the sample experiment in Box 1.1 before reading further.

BOX 1.1 BRANSFORD AND JOHNSON (1972) PASSAGE

Have a paper and pencil ready before going further. Please read the following passage once, at normal speed, and then try to recall it on paper.

The procedure is actually quite simple. First you arrange things into different groups depending on their makeup. Of course, one pile may be sufficient depending on how much there is to do. If you have to go somewhere else due to lack of facilities, that is the next step; otherwise you are pretty well set. It is better to do too few things at once than too many. Remember mistakes can be expensive. At first the whole procedure will seem quite complicated. Soon, however, it will become just another fact of life.

Write the passage as well as you can from memory. After you do that, go on reading the text.

Now read the passage again, with the hint that the passage is about *washing clothes*, and again try to write as much as you can from memory.

The passage in Box 1.1 is so designed that it is almost impossible to understand or to recall fully without being told what it is about. Bransford and Johnson (1972) asked participants to study the *washing clothes* passage and others like it for later recall. Half the people were given the title "Washing Clothes," to make the passage easier to understand. Presentation of the title *before* the passage made it much more comprehensible and also increased recall greatly. Providing the title *after* the passage did not facilitate either comprehension or recall. These results indicate that recall of the passage depended on activation of a schema (e.g., your knowledge about washing clothes), which improved comprehension of the passage as it was being read. Providing a framework for comprehension after the fact did not help. Bransford and Johnson's results are strongly supportive of Bartlett's view that one's interpretation of events plays a crucial role in memory for those events. Bartlett's emphasis on active processing of information became very important in psychologists' explanations of many cognitive phenomena, as we will see in Chapter 3.

Toward a New Cognitive Psychology: Summary

We have just seen that there were researchers—James, Donders, the Gestalt psychologists, Bartlett—interested in the study of cognition even when most American psychologists accepted the behaviorist viewpoint. The work of those individuals provided a foundation for the development of the cognitive revolution in psychology around the middle of the 20th century. Critical developments in psychology, linguistics, and computer science helped propel the study of cognitive processes to the forefront, as we will see in the next section.

THE COGNITIVE REVOLUTION

Despite European openness to the study of mental structures and processes, resistance toward mentalistic explanations of psychological phenomena remained high among many psychologists in the United States until the middle of the 20th century. At that time, dissatisfaction with strict behaviorism among psychologists, as well as developments in several disciplines outside psychology—most notably linguistics and computer science (Kendler, 1987)—culminated in a new orientation to the study of psychology, which Simon (1980) referred to as a "revolution," now known as the *cognitive revolution*.

Revolt Against Behaviorism

Many psychologists interested in understanding complex behaviors, such as language, memory, and problem solving, began to view strict behaviorism as inadequate to the task. Even from within the ranks of behaviorists, some suggested that mentalistic concepts and analyses of what was taking place internal to the learner might be critical in explanations of human (and even animal) behavior. For example, E. C. Tolman (1932) studied the behavior of rats in a maze similar to the one depicted in Figure 1.2. He first allowed the rats to explore the maze, then he put them in the Start Box, and reinforced them with food for running down the straight pathway (Path 1) to the Goal Box. Once they had learned that task, he blocked the pathway at Block Point A. The rats typically then avoided Block A by using the triangular Path 2. However,

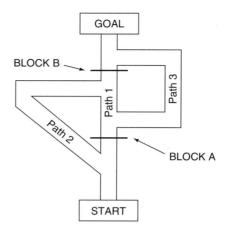

Figure 1.2 Tolman maze.

if Block Point B is used, only Path 3 will get the rats to the Goal Box (and to food). When they encountered Block B, the rats would run back and take Path 3 (ignoring Path 2). Behaviorism predicted that the rats' responses should be dependent only on the strength of pathway/reinforcement contingencies, but they were not. The rats chose pathways based on the most efficient way to the goal box. Tolman proposed that the only way to explain those results was to hypothesize that the rats had developed a "cognitive map" during their exploration of the maze, and that the internal map was being used to guide their behavior.

Given what we now know about how animals efficiently forage in the wild for food (MacArthur and Pianka, 1966) and find their way home after traveling long distances (Gould & Gould, 2012), the notion of a cognitive map does not seem revolutionary. However, during Tolman's time, it was a significant change in psychological theorizing, because it postulated a *mental representation*—an *internal* version of the environment—that played a critical role in an organism's response to a stimulus (such as the maze). Tolman and others working within a behaviorist framework (e.g., Woodworth, 1938) helped turn the tide to what became known as S-O-R psychology (stimulus-organism-response). In this "cognitive" elaboration of behaviorism, any law-like connections between environmental stimuli and behavioral responses are assumed to be filtered through the knowledge and habits of the organism. The door was opened in the United States for cognitive processing to become part of scientific inquiry.

Using Behavior to Infer Inner States

Behaviorism had what one could call two negative effects on early psychology: (1) a rejection of the study of consciousness and related mental phenomena, which had been the subject matter of interest to many of the founders of psychology; and (2) a shift away from the study of complex human activities, such as thinking, problem solving, and decision making. However, behaviorism also made a positive contribution to psychology through its emphasis on tying all concepts to observable behaviors. Although cognitive psychology considers the study of mental processes to be the key focus of scientific inquiry, it does use the behavior of people and animals as the basis for theorizing about cognitive processes. For example, if we are interested in studying whether a person bilingual in French and English has equal facility with both languages, we could ask her to read aloud identical words in either French or English, and measure her response time. If she was faster reading the French words, we could conclude that she was more facile with that language. Thus, her behavior in the word-reading task would shed light on her underlying cognitive processes and skills. We could also measure brain activity in areas known to be connected to language and word recognition, to determine if there is a difference in neural activity as our person reads French versus English words.

Most of the research detailed in this book uses behavioral responses as the basis for making inferences about underlying cognitive processes, and to develop theoretical models of cognitive abilities. A quick perusal of the graphs depicted within the book also shows that reaction time (RT) is a popular way to analyze the time sequence, and processing constraints, of cognitive processes.

Chomsky and Linguistics

The linguist Noam Chomsky became a major voice in the early years of the cognitive revolution. His work was important in two ways. First, he published a strongly negative review of Skinner's book *Verbal Behavior* (1957), in which Skinner had attempted to explain language acquisition using classical and operant conditioning principles (Chomsky, 1959). Within that review, Chomsky managed to present a negative critique of the whole enterprise of attempting to explain complex human behavior on the basis of conditioning. Second, he offered a view of the structure of language and of language development that had important implications for psychology. Chomsky argued that, contrary to Skinner, language development is based on innate language-specific principles, not on simple learning mechanisms that apply equally to a rat's learning how to run through a maze and a pigeon's learning how to peck a key to receive food. Furthermore, he considered those innate language abilities to be human-specific, since we are the only known species that possesses language.

In Chomsky's view, the most impressive aspect of human language was its creativity: We almost never say exactly the same sentence twice. Furthermore, we have no trouble producing new utterances as needed, and understanding the new sentences that others produce. As an example of the novelty in language, consider the following sentence: *George Washington was the King of England*. It is highly unlikely that anyone has ever spoken or written that sentence before, but it is a perfectly grammatical sentence, and you were able to read it and understand it (while recognizing it as false). Chomsky proposed that the ability to produce an unlimited number of grammatical sentences is due to human language being a rule-governed system; that is, we all learned a system of rules when we learned to talk. Furthermore, in discussing how children learn to speak, Chomsky concluded that the linguistic input to the developing child—the language that the child hears around her—is too simple to account for the complexity of the young child's speech. That is, an average 3-year-old's sentence-production abilities are too advanced to be accounted for purely on the basis of what she has heard. This idea has been called the argument of the *Poverty of the Input* (Pinker, 1994): The linguistic input to the developing child is, by itself, too "poor" to enable language to develop as richly as it does. If the environmental input is not sufficient to support the normal language development of children, then, Chomsky argued, nature must provide a language-specific set of guidelines or rules that are activated by hearing speech, and these help a child organize incoming speech.

Chomsky's theorizing had several important effects on psychology. If human language was rule-governed, and could not be understood in terms of conditioning, then many psychologists were led to question the basic assumptions concerning behavioristic explanations of *other* complex behaviors. In addition, since Chomsky's innate language-learning principles are specific to language, he introduced the concept of cognitive *modularity*—the rules for learning and carrying out one skill (in this case, language) are located in a specific *module*, or processing unit, separate from the rules for other skills (such as vision or problem solving; see also Fodor, 1983). To illustrate, learning the grammatical rules of a language does not help someone to develop the mathematical competence necessary to balance a checkbook.

The question of whether cognition depends on specific modules versus general processing mechanisms is one that has stimulated debate in modern cognitive science, and we will have occasion to address it numerous times in later chapters. Chomsky's concept of modularity and his view of language in particular (and cognition in general) as a rule-based system provided much of the basis of the information-processing model of human cognition.

The Computer Metaphor and Information–Processing Models

The invention of computers, and their increasing availability in academic circles in the 1950s and 1960s, had the indirect effect of changing many psychologists' beliefs about mental processes and whether they could be studied objectively. Computers were able to carry out tasks, such as arithmetic and problem solving, that require cognition (i.e., mental processes) when humans carry them out. Computer scientists used terms like *information processing* to describe what happens when a computer carries out a program. Programs specify the series of internal states that a computer undergoes between presentation of some input data and production of some output as it carries out some task, such as adding two numbers. A diagram of the processing components of a typical computer is presented in Figure 1.3. Let us say that the computer is running a program that gives you the phone number of a person whose name you enter using the keyboard. The computer's memory contains a database, listing people by name and phone number. When you type in a name, it is placed in the central processor, where the program uses it as input. The program takes the name and attempts to match it to items within the database in memory. If there is a successful match, the phone number is transferred from memory to the central processor, where it is then produced as output—either as a number on the screen, as printed output, or as spoken output.

Thus, in carrying out this simple task, the computer goes through a series of internal states (e.g., taking in information, scanning memory, transferring information from memory to the central processor, etc.). In theory, at least, those internal states could be specified, as long as you knew the design of the program that was running and the data that the program was using.

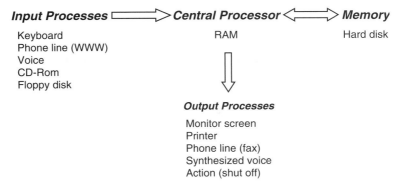

Figure 1.3   Information-processing components of a computer.

These facts led many to believe that we could study and interpret human mental processes as analogous to a computer carrying out a task by running through a program. Researchers in computer science, most notably Alan Newell and Herbert Simon (e.g., Newell, Shaw, & Simon, 1958; Newell & Simon, 1972), proposed that humans could also be described as information-processing devices, similar in some important respects to computers, although obviously made of different sorts of stuff. It is not that cognitive scientists believe that we have silicon chips in our heads; the analogy of the mind as a computer is at a *functional* level, or at the level of the software. Newell and Simon proposed that one should conceive of a human carrying out any task that involved cognition (i.e., thinking) as if he or she were a computer carrying out a program. If human mental processes are similar to the series of internal states produced as a computer carries out a program, then one should be able, in principle, to devise computer programs that mimic or *simulate* human thinking.

The concept of *modularity*, just introduced in the discussion of Chomsky's analysis of language as a cognitive module, is also illustrated in computers. Computers are not general, all-purpose machines. If you buy a new computer, you will be asked what types of software you want—word processing, a graphics package, statistical software, and so on. These will be loaded separately. Likewise, psychologists typically study cognitive skills in isolation from each other; it is assumed that the programmed rules for human mathematical computations are distinct from those for constructing sentences, or for imagining the face of a friend. The modularity seen in computer information-processing leads to the expectation that human cognition might also exhibit modularity. Although there have been challenges to the information-processing approach to cognition (such as parallel distributed processing models, which will be discussed later in this and other chapters), it has proved a useful framework for thinking about how people carry out various cognitive tasks.

Study of Cognition in Humans

Tolman's (1932) research on maze learning in rats, which led to the concept of a cognitive map, was an early attempt to study cognitive phenomena in lower organisms using objective methods. However, many psychologists interested in human cognition felt that Tolman's research was limited in its applicability to more complex cognitive processes that humans could carry out. To the new generation of cognitive psychologists (e.g., Miller, 1956; Miller, Galanter, & Pribram, 1960), human thinking was more than internal stimuli and responses. One early influential cognitive psychologist was Allan Paivio (e.g., 1971; 2006), a researcher interested in the effects of visual imagery on memory. An example of a study similar to those carried out by Paivio is given in Box 1.2; please carry out the demonstration before reading further.

BOX 1.2 DEMONSTRATION OF MEMORY FOR WORD PAIRS

Please get a pencil and paper before reading further. Below is a list of pairs of words. Each pair is followed by one of two words: REPEAT or IMAGE. If the word pair is followed by REPEAT, then repeat the pair five times to yourself, and then rate how hard it was to pronounce the pair, on a scale from 1 (very easy) to 5 (very hard). Write the rating in the space after the pair. If the word pair is followed by IMAGE, then take about five seconds to form an image of the words in the pair interacting, and then rate how hard it was to do that on a scale of 1 (easy) to 5 (hard). Write that rating in the blank. When you have finished, continue with the "Test for Word Pairs."

		Rating
diamond – coffee	IMAGE	_____
sauce – coin	REPEAT	_____
beggar – world	IMAGE	_____
factory – claw	IMAGE	_____
marriage – window	REPEAT	_____
cattle – stone	REPEAT	_____
money – slipper	IMAGE	_____
gem – hospital	REPEAT	_____
street – gift	IMAGE	_____
hotel – pepper	REPEAT	_____

Test for Word Pairs

Here are the first words from each pair in the top of the box. Without looking at the pairs, try to recall the second word and write it down. Then go back and check whether you recalled more of the words from the *imagery* pairs or the *repetition* pairs.

diamond –

sauce –

beggar –

factory –

marriage –

cattle –

money –

gem –

street –

hotel –

In a series of studies, Paivio (1971) demonstrated that people recalled information more easily when they used imagery as the basis for learning. Chances are that you, too, remembered more words in the imagery pairs than the repetition pairs in the demonstration in Box 1.2. In his research, Paivio first asked people to rate, on a 1–7 scale, how easily they could think of an image for the meaning of many concrete (e.g., *bell*) or abstract (e.g., *independence*) words (Paivio, Yuille, & Madigan, 1968). He then showed that words that had been ranked high in imageability (e.g., *car*) were recalled more easily than words that were low in concreteness (such as *idea*; for a review of many studies, see Paivio, 1971). Paivio proposed that participants could easily form images when they studied concrete words, thereby creating a *dual code*—both visual and verbal—for these words, and thus making them easier to recall. Paivio's research was important because it was an attempt to deal directly with cognitive processes and to use mentalistic concepts—in this case imagery—as a component part of the explanation of complex behavior.

THE COGNITIVE REVOLUTION: SUMMARY

By the early 1960s, many changes had taken place in psychology. There were criticisms raised about the adequacy of S–R analyses of behavior, both from within psychology and from outside. There were also a number of researchers who had embarked on research programs directed toward the understanding of cognitive processes. Several of these programs originated in Europe (e.g., Bartlett, the Gestalt psychologists), but there was also interest in human cognition among U.S. psychologists (e.g., Paivio, 1971) and linguists (Chomsky, 1959, 1965). In addition, the advent of computers provided a concrete example of a physical system that carried out processes that resembled human cognition. This raised the analogy of the mind as a computer, and the possibility that humans and computers were similar at a functional level. These streams of research came together in the 1960s to form the new discipline of cognitive psychology.

THE NEW COGNITIVE PSYCHOLOGY

Publication of the book *Cognitive Psychology*, by Ulric Neisser (1967), was evidence that the new cognitive viewpoint in psychology had become a dominant paradigm within psychological research. This book had several important effects, one of which was giving a name to the new developments. Neisser also used the computer metaphor to organize the presentation of material concerning human functioning. The organization of Neisser's book followed information as it worked its way into the organism, as outlined in Figure 1.4. According to his analysis, information passed through a series of stages, from perceptual processes to memory, from which it could be recalled when needed. Imagine the cognitive processes involved when we meet an old acquaintance, John, on the street. The first stage involves registering the parts or features of the stimulus, for example, the lines, angles, and curves of the stimulus, out of which a

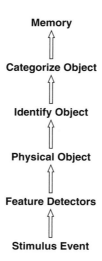

Figure 1.4 Information-processing model; bottom-up processing.

representation of John is constructed. The next stage might be recognizing that a visual object has been presented. The object would then be classified as a person, then as our friend John specifically, and finally stored in memory as a recent encounter with John. The information could then be used as needed, for example, as the basis for affirmative answer if someone asked, "Did you see John today?"

The coverage in Neisser's book was most heavily concentrated at the perceptual end of the information-processing sequence, such as pattern recognition and attention. Less than 10% of Neisser's book was concerned with the "higher mental processes," (e.g., memory, concept formation, and problem solving). Neisser acknowledged this lack of balance, and commented that at the time not very much was known about the higher processes. This book, on the other hand, will have about two-thirds of its pages devoted to the higher processes. This is because we have learned much about these topics over the years since Neisser's pioneering book was published. Another change from Neisser's book to the present one is an increase in emphasis on the role of knowledge in even the "lower-level" or perceptual processes. Neisser did discuss the role of knowledge in memory and perception, but we will place much more emphasis on the role of knowledge in all our cognitive functioning. That is why our book begins with memory, as information we have already stored in memory influences even lower-level processes such as perception.

An example of an information-processing model of human cognition that follows a *serial* path—outlining a *series* of stages in processing, as discussed by Neisser—is shown in Figure 1.5. The model deals with the visual processing of letters. The first stage of processing involves analysis of the letter into its important parts, or *features*, which are then used to identify the letter. When recognizing an A, for example, the features activated would be two slanted lines (/ and \) adjoined at the top, and a horizontal line (—). Once the features of the input have been identified, the bundle of features would first be identified as a physical object, and then identified as a specific letter. Finally, the results of this analysis can be stored in memory ("I saw an A").

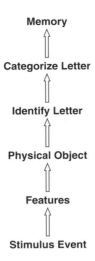

Figure 1.5 Letter-recognition model.

Posner, Boies, Eichelman, and Taylor (1969) conducted research using Donders's subtractive method to specify the stages that took place as people processed linguistic symbols, such as letters. The basic procedure involved presentation of pairs of upper- and/or lowercase letters to the participant, such as AA, aa, aA, or AB. In one condition, the participants were instructed to press one of two buttons, corresponding to whether two letters were *physically identical* (such as AA, aa) or physically different (Aa or AB). In a second condition, the judgment was based on whether the letters had the *same name* (AA, aa, and Aa) or different names (AB). People were faster to judge that physically identical letters are the same (AA, aa; average response time = 859 msec) than to judge that upper- and lowercase letters are (Aa; average response time = 955 msec).

The results of the Posner et al. (1969) study (as depicted in Figure 1.6) indicate that the first stage of letter recognition is based on the visual form of the letters; the second stage involves recall of the letter name from memory. On the basis of these results, Posner and his colleagues concluded that information about letters is processed through several stages, with each stage becoming more removed from the physical stimulus. Each stage thus utilized a different *code* to make the judgments: first a visual code (where AA has the advantage over Aa), then a name code (where AA and Aa judgments are equal). Thus, by carefully controlling the properties of the stimuli and the judgment that the participants were asked to make, it was possible to specify stages in the processing of the letter pairs.

The study of cognition has burgeoned since Neisser's classic book; Psychwatch.com lists over 60 scientific journals devoted to cognitive psychology and cognitive neuropsychology. Robins et al. (1999) provided a concrete measure of the development of the cognitive perspective over the end of the 20th century. They analyzed the number of times keywords such as "cognitive" or "cognition" were used in articles published in journals in psychology between 1950 and 1997, how often cognition-related articles were cited in those journals, and the number of dissertations that were related to cognitive psychology. As illustrated in Figure 1.7, the prevalence of articles, citations,

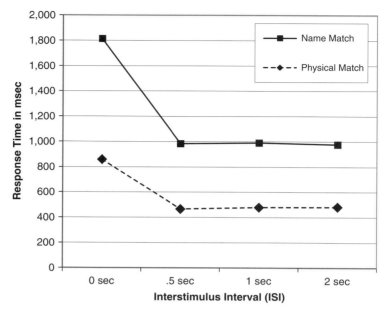

Figure 1.6 Posner et al. (1969) data illustrating the response time to whether two stimuli matched physically (A A) or in name (e.g., A a), per interstimulus interval (the time between when the second stimulus followed the first).

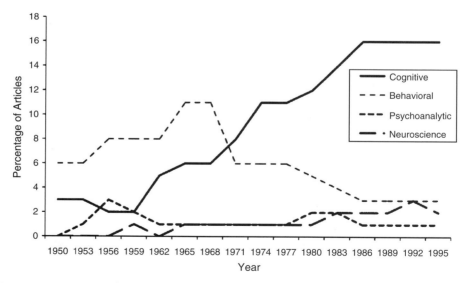

Figure 1.7 Robins et al. (1999) results, showing the increase in publications related to cognitive topics in recent history.
Adapted from Figure 4 in Robins et al., 1999.

and dissertations related to cognition continued to grow from the 1950s (surpassing the relative influence of the behavioral and psychoanalytic schools). Cognitive psychology citations, articles, and so on also surpassed those in neuroscience. However, Robins et al. (1999, Figure 4) also reported that membership in the Society of Neuroscience has increased dramatically in recent years. It is thus likely that neuroscience citations, articles, and dissertations will increase dramatically in future years as that field continues to grow.

FROM COGNITIVE PSYCHOLOGY TO COGNITIVE SCIENCE

The contributions from linguistics and computer science that helped spark the cognitive revolution guaranteed that the field of *cognitive science* would be interdisciplinary in its approach. Longuet-Higgins coined the term *cognitive science* in 1973, and it encompasses not only psychology, but also computer science, linguistics, philosophy, and neuroscience. Technological advances in the fields that fall under the cognitive science umbrella have also led to theoretical and empirical advances in the study of cognition. Notable contributions have come from computer science, with the advent of parallel distributed processing computer models, and from neuroscience, with the invention of neuroimaging techniques, which provide a window on the brain's activity.

DISTRIBUTED MODELS OF COGNITION

Parallel Distributed Processing Models

We have seen how the development of the computer served to stimulate research in cognitive psychology. An important modern development in the information-processing viewpoint has been the advent of what are called *parallel distributed processing* (PDP) models, also known as *connectionist* models (McClelland, Rumelhart, & the PDP Research Group, 1986; Rumelhart, McClelland, & the PDP Research Group, 1986). These models were stimulated by advances in computer theory, which led to the idea that efficient processing could be carried out by *parallel processors*, carrying out many activities at the same time, or in parallel. This sort of processing can be contrasted with the *serial* processing of information in the traditional information processing models, such as that in Figure 1.4, in which activities are carried out one at a time, or in a series of steps. As an example of parallel processing, when you see a word, you don't identify the letters separately left to right, but rather recognize all letters simultaneously (McClelland et al., 1986). Furthermore, information about the whole word plays a role in the recognition of the individual letters. That is, your knowledge about the whole word plays a role in your recognition of its parts. This is why word recognition is so rapid. This is a basic change from serial processing models such as those in Figures 1.4 and 1.5.

Connectionist models use an analogy of the nervous system in which multiple neurons operate in tandem, and each neuron may have tens of thousands of connections to other neurons. Furthermore, in PDP models, connections among neurons are built

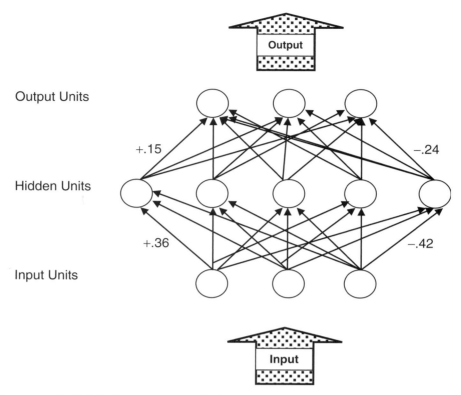

Figure 1.8 Parallel distributed processing (PDP) model.

up based on their working together in processing information; thus *learning* takes place with exposure to information or environmental stimuli.

The basic form of a PDP model is shown in Figure 1.8. Parallel distributed processing models differ from traditional information-processing models in that they are not divided into separate parts, such as the central processing unit and long-term memory storage (see Figure 1.3). Rather, parallel distributed processing models assume that the processing system works as one large unit. This means that there is no passing of information from one discrete component of the system to another, as in the information-processing model presented in Figure 1.4. Rather, the whole processing system works together. The typical parallel distributed processing model is built of several sorts of basic elements, called *units* or *nodes*. *Input* units (bottom row of Figure 1.8) respond to stimuli from outside, like sensory receptors in the nervous system. *Output* units (top row) produce output that can be connected to response systems, analogous to neurons that control muscles and glands. *Hidden* units (middle row) receive input from other units, rather than from the world, and send outputs to other units in the network, rather than to the outside world. They are considered hidden because they do not communicate with the external world in any way, and are comparable to neurons within the central nervous system.

As in the nervous system, the nodes or units of the network receive input, which can be *excitatory* (causing the unit to become active) or *inhibitory* (reducing the activity in the unit). The sum of the excitatory and inhibitory activity stimulating a node must be higher than the node's *threshold* for it to produce an output (and thereby send its message on to other connected units). The threshold of an individual node, and the strength of the connections among nodes, is based on learning. The past frequency with which a unit has been activated will determine its individual threshold; and units that have fired together in the past are correlated and thus develop stronger interconnections (again, in the same way as neurons in the brain).

The strengths of connections among some units are shown by the numbers in Figure 1.8. A higher number means that the unit sends a stronger message to those units to which it is connected, and the +/− signs indicate whether the message is excitatory or inhibitory. So, for example, a connection of +.15 is excitatory, while a connection of −.24 is inhibitory. Units that fire often will also have lower thresholds, and thus require less activation to fire. For instance, the set of nodes that represent your best friend's name probably has a low threshold because of how often you use that name.

One important component of parallel distributed processing models is that they can explain how knowledge is acquired and then is used to influence later cognitive functioning. For example, once a person has become proficient in reading and word recognition, connectionist models can explain how and why letters are recognized better in words than by themselves, and why highly familiar words are recognized more quickly than less-familiar words (we present an exposition of such a model in Chapter 5).

Bayesian Models of Cognitive Processes

Another type of computer model, based on conditional ("If . . . , then . . . ," or *Bayesian*) reasoning, has become popular in recent years in multiple areas, to explain topics as diverse as visual scene perception (Yuille & Kersten, 2006), inductive learning (Tenenbaum, Griffiths, & Kemp, 2006), and semantic memory (Steyvers, Griffiths, & Dennis, 2006). These models are called *Bayesian* models because they are based on an early theory of conditional reasoning that was developed by Thomas Bayes (c. 1701–1761; Bayes's work was published in 1763). As do connectionist models, these Bayesian models "learn" complex information from simpler data. Hierarchical Bayesian models (e.g., Gelman, Carlin, Stern, & Rubin, 2003; Good, 1980) permit learning at various levels of abstraction (e.g., learning complex grammatical rules) better than most connectionist models. However, explanatory differences between connectionist and Bayesian models have become less stark as connectionist models have become more sophisticated. Some PDP models are now capable of "learning" structured, abstract knowledge (Rogers & McClelland, 2004, 2008), and of allowing that structured knowledge to constrain later learning (McClelland et al., 2010).

Both types of distributed learning models have shown success in modeling aspects of visual perception, categorization, and language learning, and much work has been stimulated by this perspective. We review several parallel distributed processing and Bayesian models of cognition in later chapters.

Neurocognition

An important addition to modern cognitive science is the use of evidence from neurological research to understand cognitive functioning. Linking brain structures to cognitive functioning has a long history, dating back at least to Galen (129-199/217), a Roman physician of the second century. Historically, most of the knowledge concerning the functioning of the nervous system during cognitive processing was obtained indirectly—through studies of people and animals with brain damage. Modern advances have produced great increases in our knowledge, by allowing detailed mapping of brain structures in intact living organisms and direct measurement of brain activity as people are carrying out cognitive tasks.

Studies of Brain Structure and Function

The first great developments in the study of brain structure and cognitive functioning occurred almost two centuries ago. In the 1820s, Flourens showed that experimentally produced brain damage, or *lesions*, in certain areas of the brains of animals led to specific deficits in movements. Those results led to the *doctrine of localization*—the idea that specific brain areas controlled specific parts of the body (Gall & Spurzheim, 1809, 1810). Since it is not possible, due to ethical considerations, to experimentally induce brain damage in humans, much early information concerning human brain function during cognition was obtained from post-mortem examinations of the brains of individuals who had experienced various sorts of problems during their lives. For example, Broca (1861) studied a man who had lost the ability to speak (although he could understand speech perfectly well). Broca linked this language impairment to a relatively small area in the left hemisphere, in the frontal lobes adjacent to the motor cortex. This area now bears the name *Broca's area* (see Figure 1.9). People who have shown language-production deficits as the result of a stroke or accident have until

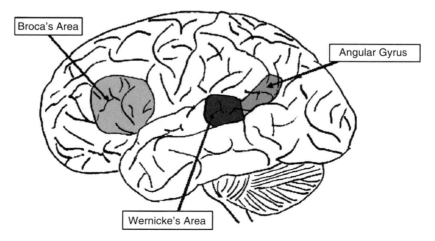

Figure 1.9   Diagram of Broca's area (and other speech areas) in left hemisphere.

recently been referred to as "Broca's aphasics" (*aphasia* means *without speech*); now the term *agrammatics—without grammar*—is often preferred, as we will see in Chapter 10. Broca's discovery also supported the *doctrine of lateralization*—the idea that each hemisphere is dominant for particular functions, with language largely controlled by the left hemisphere.

Almost all neuroscience research seeks to answer a basic question: Which part of the brain controls which psychological process? The answers to that question are sometimes referred to as brain:function correlates, or structure:function correlations. The methods of Flourens and Broca are still in use today, although modern research on *neurocognition* or *cognitive neuroscience* has provided more detailed evidence on the relation between the brain and cognitive processes than did their pioneering studies. Contemporary studies using animals and humans have yielded valuable information on the role of specific brain areas in particular behaviors. In some of the animal studies, brain areas are lesioned, and the effects on behavior are noted (although techniques for producing lesions and measuring the resulting brain damage are much more sophisticated than in Flourens's day). Following Broca, there have also been many detailed clinical studies of humans with brain damage caused by illness or injury. In addition, there have been studies of individuals who have had parts of their brains removed for medical reasons, such as to remove tumors, or to reduce the severity of life-threatening seizures. These studies have provided indirect evidence concerning the role of various brain structures in human cognition. Lastly, advanced technologies—to be reviewed shortly—have allowed neuroscientists a window into the normally functioning brain, to determine which brain parts are most active when it processes information. Figure 1.10 depicts the four lobes of the cerebral cortex (the wrinkled outer structure of the brain) and the functions associated with each, based on past neuroscience evidence.

The Dissociation Method

Unfortunately, nature often carries out neuropsychological "experiments" on humans that investigators are prevented from carrying out because of ethical concerns. Strokes, accidents, and surgery may all cause damage to the brain, resulting in specific cognitive deficits. Evidence exists that *physiological modularity* may apply to some cognitive skills: Damage to distinct brain areas causes distinct patterns of psychological malfunction. Imagine that a lesion in brain area A interferes with the person's ability to identify objects by sight (known as *visual agnosia*: *a-gnosia* comes from the Greek for *without knowing*). The person is not blind, since he or she can pick up the object if asked, and does not run into things, but he or she no longer recognizes the objects being picked up. However, if the object is put in the person's hand, he immediately tells you what it is. At a skill level, we have here a *dissociation* between identification based on vision and touch (*tactile* or *haptic* identification)—the two processes are separable, and the visual agnosia is based on a lesion in what we will call area A.

The symptoms of such a patient can tell us that area A is involved in visual identification of objects. However, there are at least two possibilities concerning how that area functions in recognition of objects. It might be that area A is necessary for only *visual* identification of objects, and that it has nothing to do with the identification of

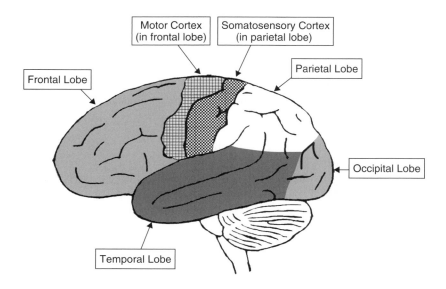

	FUNCTIONS
Frontal Lobe	Planning, selective attention, inhibition of responses, memory strategies, problem solving; contains motor cortex, speech production area (in left hemisphere)
Parietal Lobe	Contains somatosensory cortex; integration of senses, visual attention, and coordination of motor movement
Occipital Lobe	Visual processing
Temporal Lobe	Memory, object recognition, auditory processing, speech comprehension (in left hemisphere)

Figure 1.10   Lobes of the cerebral cortex and their functions.

objects by touch, say. That is, there might be two separate identification systems, one dealing with identification through vision and the other through touch. However, it could also be true that area A is part of a general *object-identification system* that affects *both* visual and tactile recognition of objects, but identification by vision is simply a more difficult task than tactile identification. Damage to area A might disrupt the general object-identification system enough to interfere with the hard task but not the easy one. Thus, finding a dissociation, by itself, does not tell the investigator exactly how the processing system in the brain is organized.

The gold standard for neuropsychologists is to find a *double dissociation*, which is exhibited if skill A is impaired in one patient, but skill B is intact, while another patient shows the opposite: impairment in skill B but normal performance in skill A. Such a pattern then suggests that, not only are skills A and B psychologically modular, but they are also neurologically distinct. In the agnosia example, we would need to find another brain region (call it area B) in which a lesion interferes with identification of objects by touch, but leaves visual identification unaffected. Since the person with the lesion in area B can do the visual task but cannot do the tactile identification, one can no longer say that the tactile task might simply be easier than the visual. It must be the case that the tasks are carried out separately, or else we could not find people who performed oppositely on them.

Anatomical Measures of Brain:Function Correlates

Several new techniques allow detailed mapping of damaged brain structures in living organisms. The CT scan (computerized tomography) is a sophisticated X-ray technique that produces cross-sectional pictures or slices of brain structure. CT scans cannot provide information on which part of the brain is most active in functioning during a given activity; they are limited to telling us the exact location of a person's brain damage. Magnetic resonance imaging (MRI) is another sophisticated technique that can be used to reveal the structure—but not the function—of any part of the body, including the brain. It is based on the fact that chemical molecules in living cells respond to magnetic fields (Huettel, Song, & McCarthy, 2004). The part of the body to be studied is placed in the center of a machine that generates a strong magnetic field. When the magnet is turned on, the molecules respond to the field by all turning in a specific direction; when the field is turned off, the molecules return to their normal state. As they go back to normal, they produce electromagnetic waves that can be measured and processed by a computer. Different types of molecules respond slightly differently to the magnetic field, so the pattern of responding can be used to determine the structure of the part being studied. This technique produces highly detailed structural cross-sections of the brain, much like CT scans (but without exposure to X-rays). Advances in MRI technology now allow measurements of brain function as well (see the following section).

Studies of Brain Function: Measures of Brain Activity

Recent development of a number of neuroimaging techniques have allowed investigators to go beyond studying the structure of the nervous system to examination of the functioning of the nervous system as people carry out cognitive tasks. Most of the techniques to be described in this section are noninvasive: The person does not have to be operated on in order to make the brain areas accessible to measurement. These techniques have resulted in great advances in our knowledge of how the brain functions online. We begin our discussion, however, with a method that is invasive, and so is limited largely to the study of animals.

Electrical Activity of Single Neurons

In animal studies, very thin wires, or *microelectrodes*, are placed in specified brain areas, and the brain activity of individual neurons is measured when the animal is carrying out some task (such as viewing visual stimuli on a screen). This was a technique used by

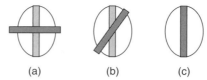

(a) (b) (c)

Figure 1.11 Receptive field of a single cell, from Hubel and Wiesel's (1959) research. (a) Little to no activation. (b) Moderate activation. (c) High activation.

The ovals depict the on-center receptive field of a cell, with inhibitory surround. The dark gray bar is a bar of light that falls within the receptive field of the cell. The degree of activation of the cell depends on the extent to which the stimulus bar falls on the receptive field, relative to the inhibitory surround.

the Nobel Prize–winning team of Hubel and Wiesel (1959) when they determined that individual neurons in the visual cortex of a cat processed lines of specific orientation in specific parts of the visual field (see Figure 1.11). Such experiments are especially enlightening when primates (monkeys, chimpanzees, gorillas) are used, as primate brains are very similar to human brains. However, since this technique cannot be carried out on humans for ethical reasons, this limits our ability to study electrical activity in single neurons during complex activities such as language or deductive reasoning, which are not carried out to the same degree in animals.

Electroencephalography (EEG)

An early recording technique that was used to obtain information about the relationship between brain function and cognitive processing is the electroencephalogram (EEG). Electrical recording devices, or *electrodes* (small discs of metal), are placed on the scalp, as shown in Figure 1.12a, and the electrical activity under the electrodes is recorded and displayed in graphic form, as shown in Figure 1.12b. The EEG provides a safe and easy way to gather information on which parts of the brain are electrically active during various tasks. In fact, it is now routinely used on human infants to gauge their information processing, such as when viewing faces (e.g., Bazhenova, Stroganova, Doussard-Roosevelt, Posikera, & Porges, 2007). Aside from the gel that is used to increase conductance, EEG's main methodological drawback is that it measures activity in very large brain areas at once. Figure 1.12b depicts the activity patterns of various regions of the brain, based on the set of electrodes shown in Figure 1.12a, each of which is measuring activity from a large number of neurons.

To obtain more specific information about brain functioning during cognitive processing, researchers sometimes measure *evoked potentials*, which are recordings of electrical activity *evoked* in response to specific stimuli. The electrical *potential* (electrical activity) is evoked, or stimulated, by the presentation of the stimulus. This procedure requires that the participant be repeatedly exposed to some stimulus, say a smiling or a neutral face (Bazhenova et al., 2007). As the infant (or adult) observes the stimulus face, brain activity is recorded, and the records are averaged. These responses are also called *event-related potentials* (ERPs).

Electrical Stimulation of Brain Areas

In the 1940s, neurosurgeon Wilder Penfield, working at McGill University in Montreal, developed a technique that became known as the Montreal procedure: Patients

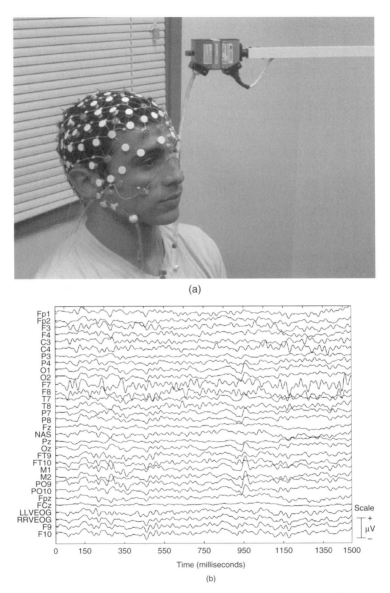

Figure 1.12   (a) Picture of a person in an electroencephalogram (EEG) cap and (b) EEG waves.
With thanks to the Langlois Social Development Lab at the University of Texas at Austin.

whose skulls had been opened because they were about to undergo brain surgery (typically for epilepsy) would have small electrical currents delivered to parts of their brain while conscious. Penfield could then determine which parts of the brain were most responsible for epileptic seizures, and thus only ablate (remove) those areas during surgery (Jasper & Penfield, 1951/1954). Using this method, he mapped the parts of the body related to subsections of the somatosensory cortex and motor cortex (see Figure 1.10, cortex map). Neurosurgeons still use the technique when removing tumors or conducting brain surgery (see cnn.com/2008/HEALTH/08/01/open .brain.surgery/index.html); by determining the specific regions of the brain responsible for speech and other important functions for an individual, doctors will try to avoid damaging critical areas during the surgery.

A similar but less invasive technique is transcranial magnetic stimulation (TMS). It was first used by Barker, Jalinous, and Freeston (1985) to test the relationship between brain structure and function. Magnets are placed on the skull, and magnetic fields are used to disrupt (or enhance) neural activity in the region of the brain under the magnets. The researcher can have the person engage in a task, say, reading a book aloud, then introduce TMS to see if it affects the person's reading performance. The advantage to this technique is that it is noninvasive; however, TMS cannot be used universally, as it has been shown to cause seizures, especially in people who may be prone to them.

PET Scans and Cerebral Blood Flow

Brains require three main things to survive and to carry out their functions: glucose, oxygen, and nutrients. All three of these substances are carried by blood. When a brain area is active, blood uptake at that area is enhanced. This knowledge forms the basis for both positron emission tomography (PET) scans and cerebral blood flow (CBF) measures, which provide information on brain functioning. During PET scans, a small amount of radioactive glucose (or oxygen) is injected into the bloodstream. When it reaches the brain, any areas that are active take up this glucose during metabolism and thereby become slightly radioactive. Sensitive recording devices allow researchers to measure the radioactivity, and thereby to determine which brain areas are active during different sorts of cognitive tasks.

Cerebral blood flow techniques operate the same way, but measure overall blood flow. A 2-D or 3-D picture of the brain can then show the most active areas of the brain during some cognitive activity, with red and yellow areas depicting higher levels of activity. The main drawback is that PET scans usually take 40 seconds or more for brain activity to translate into an image (www.nida.nih.gov/NIDA_notes/ NNVol11N5/Basics.html), whereas sometimes faster measurements are needed.

fMRI

As you read earlier, MRI uses magnetic fields to construct images of the brain (see Figure 1.13). More active parts of the brain require the blood to deliver more oxygen and glucose. *Functional magnetic resonance imaging* (*fMRI*) allows researchers to record brain activity as a person carries out various tasks, by measuring changes in the magnetic properties of blood as it undergoes changes in oxygenation levels. As active brain areas take up oxygen and glucose from the blood, the blood's response to a magnetic field changes. Thus, activity in various areas in the brain can be measured indirectly, by the response to the magnetic field of the blood in that area. Furthermore, since fMRI can provide an image every second, it gives a more real-time picture of the brain than PET scans. A quick Internet search will show you a color picture of activity levels depicted in an fMRI; highly active areas appear in red or yellow; moderate to low levels of activation will appear in blue or green.

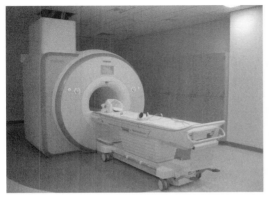
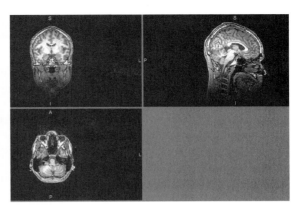

Figure 1.13 An fMRI machine and output depicting the structure of an individual's brain and skull from different perspectives.
With thanks to the Imaging Research Center at the University of Texas at Austin.

In using fMRI to measure brain areas active in carrying out some cognitive task, the simplest method involves a modern variation on Donders's (1868/1969) subtraction method for using reaction time measures to assess cognitive processes. In using the subtraction method for fMRI, two sets of brain recordings are compared: one obtained during the critical condition in which one is interested, and the other from a control condition that differs from the critical condition by one cognitive operation. In that way, any differences in brain activation are the result of the operation in which the two conditions differ. In other words, the critical condition differs from the control condition because of the *insertion* of the operation of interest in the critical condition. If a study of this sort is designed correctly, it results in what one could call *pure insertion*, which is important if the results are to be interpreted clearly. If pure insertion is not carried out, then the critical condition will differ from the control in more than one way, and it will be impossible to interpret the results, since any differences in brain activation might be due to any of those differences.

Conclusion

These new neuroimaging techniques have helped to supplement traditional studies of brain-damaged patients in determining brain:function correlates. Structural measures, such as CAT scans, take a picture of the brain, and areas of damage can be correlated with patient symptoms. Other measures, such as PET scans, CBF, and fMRI, measure the uptake of blood, glucose, or oxygen to determine which parts of the brain are most active as people perform a given task. These techniques have been useful tools in the study of a wide range of cognitive processes, including memory, pattern recognition, attention, imagery, unconscious processing, and decision making. Findings from neurocognitive studies will be discussed throughout many chapters in the book.

DEVELOPMENT OF MODERN COGNITIVE SCIENCE: SUMMARY

A number of research endeavors have come together to form modern-day cognitive science. In the late 1950s, there was a renewed interest in the study of consciousness and higher cognitive processes, such as language and problem solving. There was also a reaction against behaviorism, with its emphasis on external stimuli and responses, and its rejection of the study of mental phenomena. Developments in linguistics emphasized the structural complexity of human language, and stimulated psychologists to examine the rules by which other higher-level processes might be operating. The development of computers provided psychologists with a concrete example of a system that could carry out complex "mental" operations, without raising problems as to whether or not the internal states actually could be studied directly. Advances in neurocognitive research have also expanded cognitive psychologists' ideas of the kinds of evidence they could use to study cognitive phenomena in intact brains. All of these endeavors have led to a thriving and interdisciplinary science devoted to the study of cognition.

COGNITIVE SCIENTISTS' STUDY OF HIDDEN PROCESSES

As noted earlier in the discussion, the term cognitive psychology labels both a subject matter—the study of the cognitive processes—and a philosophy of science—the belief that cognition can be understood by analyzing the mental processes underlying behavior. This belief leads to a question that we touched on in passing earlier in this chapter: How can one apply scientific methods to the study of mental processes, which are by definition invisible and unobservable? Students sometimes wonder if we can ever say anything meaningful about those mysterious hidden processes. In the discussion of behaviorism, we noted that one lasting influence of the behavioristic perspective was the use of behavioral responses as the basis for drawing conclusions about hidden mental processes. We also mentioned that such a method is similar to the way we think about many phenomena in our ordinary day-to-day interactions with the world. That is, we ordinary folks think about hidden phenomena all the time. Furthermore, scientists in other disciplines have no problem dealing with phenomena that cannot be seen.

Because of the importance of this question, let us consider in some detail how cognitive scientists do in fact study hidden processes. We can begin considering a situation in everyday life in which people deal with phenomena for which they have no direct evidence.

Car Talk

On National Public Radio until recently there was a program called "Car Talk," where listeners called in with questions about problems with their cars. The two resident experts, mechanics with years of experience, provided a diagnosis of the problem, without ever seeing the caller's car. Furthermore, they sometimes made diagnoses concerning engine problems that they as mechanics had never before encountered. How could they make correct diagnoses without direct evidence for the phenomenon in question? The answer is obvious: They were using a listener's reported observations of the car's "behavior" (its performance problems) combined with their extensive knowledge of how cars work to draw conclusions about defective interior or hidden components. So we see a situation in which people formulate a hypothesis about what is happening inside a car from the available evidence, without being able to see the car itself or its presumably malfunctioning inner components. In a similar manner, scientists in many disciplines deal with phenomena that cannot be seen. One well-known example comes from molecular genetics: the discovery of the double helix of DNA.

The Double Helix

The discovery of the structure of DNA is a case in which scientists were able to discover the structure of a system without direct visual evidence. The hypothesis that the DNA molecule is in the shape of a double helix was proposed in 1953 by James Watson and Francis Crick (Weisberg, 2006a). No one had seen the double helix of DNA at the time it was proposed (and no one has seen it yet, as electron microscopes are not powerful enough to penetrate to that level of analysis). Thus, Watson and Crick did not have pictures of a helical structure on which to base their analysis of DNA. How then could they determine the structure of a molecule that they could not see? They began their work with an idea of what the structure might be, and they used this idea to interpret the results of experiments in biochemistry and biophysics. They built a model of the molecule that could explain the results of those experiments, which was presented to the scientific community in an article published in *Nature*, a scientific journal (Watson & Crick, 1953). Other scientists raised no crucial objections, and furthermore determined that Watson and Crick's proposed model was consistent with still other research findings. The scientific community thus accepted the double helix as the structure of DNA, although no one had ever seen it directly. Thus, if a scientist's model or theory can explain experimental results, and is useful in predicting future research findings, then one can say that the phenomenon described by the theory exists (even if one cannot see it).

Mental Processes

Cognitive scientists work in much the same way as the *Car Talk* mechanics and Crick and Watson: We use the available evidence—psychological and neuropsychological evidence based on reaction time and other behavioral data—to develop models of cognitive processes, such as object recognition, mathematical problem solving, and memory retrieval. We then use those models to derive hypotheses about other phenomena in the same domain, and we design experiments to collect data relevant to those hypotheses. Models are refined or altered in response to the data from the experiments, which then leads to new predictions and further experiments. As an example, let us consider the hypothesis that the ability to remember information sometimes depends on *rehearsal* of that information. Assume that rehearsal is an internal mental process that involves vocalizing the to-be-remembered items again and again to oneself. We predict that more rehearsal leads to better memory. How could one test that hypothesis? Before reading further, please carry out the demonstration experiment in Box 1.3.

BOX 1.3 REHEARSAL DEMONSTRATION: MEMORY SPAN FOR SHORT VERSUS LONG WORDS

Have a pencil and blank piece of paper ready. If you do not have them, please get them before reading further. Below are four columns of words. DO NOT LOOK AT THE WORDS YET. Your task is to read each word in the first column as many times as you can in an interval of about 10 seconds (cover columns 2, 3, and 4 with your hand as you do so). If you will not disturb anyone, read the words aloud. When you have read the words in the first column, try to write as many of them as you can *from memory*, in the order in which you read them. Do not look back at the list. When you have finished recalling the words in the first column, do the same for each of the other columns: Read each of the words as many times as you can in 10 seconds, write them in order from memory, and then go on to the next column.

disk	finger	picture	book
phone	bucket	sofa	glass
pen	package	berry	boat
head	number	tower	lamp
plant	electricity	buckle	nail
sound	fantasy	operation	paint

Box 1.3 presents a modified version of an experiment by Baddeley, Thomson, and Buchanan (1975), which tested the hypothesis that rehearsal is important for remembering certain kinds of information (such as words in a list). Experimental participants heard a string of unrelated words and then attempted to recall them in the order in which they had been presented. In some strings, all the words were short, only one syllable in length (as in the first and last columns in Box 1.3), while in others the words were longer, up to three syllables in length (as in the middle columns). Baddeley and coworkers reasoned that if the participants rehearsed the words by repeating them, then longer words would not receive as many rehearsals as shorter words in the same period of time (e.g., the 10-second interval for each list). Therefore, recall for longer words should be worse than for shorter words, and that was what the researchers found. If you recalled more words from the first and last columns than from the middle two, then you confirmed their results. This example shows how one can study hidden psychological processes through indirect methods, as in the examples discussed earlier from auto repair and the discovery of DNA. Cognitive scientists can obtain evidence and then formulate hypotheses about cognitive processes that can never be seen.

Neurophysiological Evidence for Mental Processes

Another possible type of evidence for mental processes comes from neurophysiological studies. Since cognitive skills are carried out by the brain, perhaps we can study memory processes (such as rehearsal), by recording brain activity while people study words. However, some caution is necessary in interpreting the results of neurophysiological studies alone. Let us assume that a researcher believes that people sometimes memorize information by internally rehearsing it, as Baddeley et al. (1975) tried to demonstrate in the experiment just discussed. The researcher decides to record brain activity as the participants try to remember strings of words. Assume that the participants report that they rehearsed the words to themselves in order to memorize them, and that the researcher detects activity in the same specific area in the brain for each participant. Would those brain records alone be useful in demonstrating that the words were remembered through the use of rehearsal? Not conclusively, because we have no way of knowing that the brain activity is indeed the record of *rehearsal*. We have the participants' reports that they rehearsed, but we know that such reports cannot be verified and so cannot serve by themselves as psychological evidence for rehearsal. Therefore, the records of brain activity simply indicate that some parts of the brain were active during the participants' attempts at memorizing; they do not tell us that the activity was internal rehearsal. For example, perhaps the people were using visual images instead of verbal rehearsal to remember the words. We need some independent *psychological* evidence that the participants were indeed rehearsing the words.

Instead of only relying on participants' reports that they were using rehearsal, a researcher could have a person engage in Baddeley et al.'s (1975) study from Box 1.3, with one small addition. The researcher could verify that rehearsal processes actually were taking place by having people rehearse *aloud*. Only then would it be legitimate to claim that the neurocognitive measures indicate that rehearsal (or any other process) is taking place in a particular part of the brain, and one would have to "subtract" the neural activity due just to vocalizing alone (but not rehearsal). The study of neural activity can then lead to further hypotheses about the psychological processes involved in various cognitive phenomena, so the investigation can work both ways. For example, if we give people stories to memorize, and the brain activity for that task is in an area different from that involved in studying lists of words, this could indicate that memorizing stories involves processes different from simple rehearsal. Thus, once we have provided support for an analysis of some phenomenon through cognitive methods, neurophysiological evidence can be very useful in expanding and enriching that analysis, as we shall see in many places throughout this book.

This completes our introduction to the study of cognitive processes. We now turn to an outline of the themes that will serve to organize the discussion in the book.

THEMES OF THE BOOK

There are several key themes that have guided the organization of this book, and our analysis of research connected to cognitive processes.

1. Cognitive processes are knowledge-based; cognition is a *constructive* and interpretive activity, not based only on incoming information.

2. Cognition is best explored via a functional approach.

3. Cognitive processes are often modular, but also involve significant integration to accomplish cognitive tasks.

4. Cognition is best understood via historical and contemporary coverage of research.

Next we explain each of these overarching themes and why we have found them useful in our thinking.

Cognitive Processes Are Knowledge-Based

We will emphasize the important role that our knowledge plays in virtually all cognitive processes. This emphasis on the constructive and interpretive nature of cognition was seen many years ago in the work of Bartlett, which was briefly discussed earlier (and which is considered in more detail in Chapter 3). Even when one examines the lower processes, such as pattern recognition and attention, one finds that experience plays a crucial role there as well, such as when we find it easier to read textbooks in our major field of study than textbooks outside our major. Those processes are constructive as well. In order to get a feeling for the role played by knowledge in cognition, we will briefly examine two ways of analyzing how people might carry out a low-level cognitive process: recognizing printed words.

One model of word recognition is shown in Figure 1.14a. As we discussed earlier, at an early sensory level, the person would engage in detection of the individual lines and angles—the *features*—making up each letter of the word. Then he would combine the features to recognize individual letters, and then combine the letters to recognize the whole word. In this way of looking at the process of recognition, a stimulus (e.g., the word) proceeds through the system by earlier stages feeding information into later stages. Information gets from the external world into the system in a *bottom-up process*, that is, it works its way into the organism's mind from outside. In this analysis, knowledge plays no role in the initial processing of information.

However, research in a number of domains indicates that our knowledge plays an important role in processing the stimuli in the environment. For example, when we are reading, common words are recognized more quickly than rare words (Paap, McDonald, Schvaneveldt, & Noel, 1987); and experts in a field (such as engineering) recognize words related to their profession more quickly than do nonexperts (Gardner, Rothkopf, Lapan, & Lafferty, 1987). Thus, in our Figure 1.14b model, in addition to the arrows going up from the bottom, there must also be arrows going from the top downwards. *Top-down processing* (as shown in Figure 1.14b) illustrates that what we know about the world influences how we process incoming information, even at the most basic levels of cognition.

It is easy to find examples of top-down processing in our ordinary activities. Anyone who has watched hockey on television knows that it is sometimes extremely difficult to follow the puck. One sees a tangle of players, with arms, legs, skates, and sticks going every which way at once, and suddenly the crowd is screaming and the puck is in the net. The commentator, usually a former player, gives a description of the puck's path, going from that player's stick, off that player's elbow, hitting another player's skate, through the goaltender's legs, and into the goal. The television audience

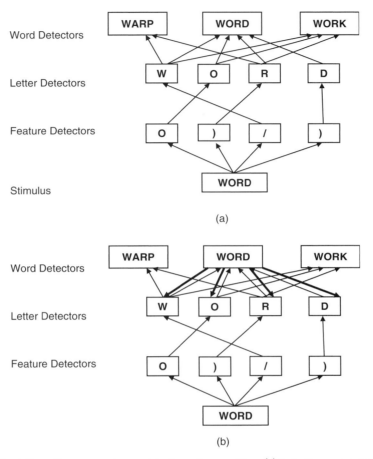

Figure 1.14 Information-processing model of word recognition. (a) In bottom-up processing, connections are one-way, from the stimulus to feature detectors to letter detectors to word detectors. (b) Top-down processing is illustrated by the bold arrows indicating feedback from the (higher) words level to the features level.

may respond with disbelief that the commentator was able to see the puck's multiple trajectories, until a slow-motion replay confirms the commentator's report. The reason that the analyst can see what untrained members of the audience cannot is due to his knowledge of the game. In fact, the effects of knowledge show up in virtually every cognitive endeavor—from pattern recognition and attention to problem solving and creative thinking (for examples, see Ericsson, Charness, Feltovich, & Hoffman, 2006).

The idea that all of our functioning depends on our knowledge will be expressed in several different ways throughout the book. In this chapter we have referred directly to the role in knowledge in cognitive functioning, but we have also talked about the *constructive* aspects of cognition, referring back to Bartlett (1932). We will also sometimes talk about cognitive processes as *active* processes, with the individual playing an active role in processing information. All those terms are different ways of saying the same thing.

If it is true that our mental functioning depends on what we already know (in other words, on top-down processing), then a logical place to begin the analysis of cognition is with memory—the processes involved in the acquisition, storage, and use of knowledge. We thus begin this book with three chapters on memory research and theory. Once we have an understanding of the basic factors underlying memory, we will use them as the basis for organizing the cognitive phenomena presented in the remainder of the book.

Functional Approach

As James (1890) pointed out more than a century ago, the real interest in cognitive skills is in their purpose or function. Discovering the subprocesses that one carries out when memorizing statistical equations or historical dates describes *what* people do; it is also important to find out *why* people memorize information or recognize objects. The functional approach assumes that there is some underlying logic or reason for why a particular skill is accomplished or structured the way it is. The reason may be based on that individual (a given strategy has worked well for her in the past), or species-based (some skills have evolved in all humans because they were adaptive). Sometimes, there is even a function for the systematic errors that people make, or for what on the surface seems to be a breakdown in processing. For example, in Chapter 4, we explore the possibility that there is an advantage even to forgetting information (Anderson & Schooler, 1991). We try to provide a functional analysis of each major cognitive skill throughout the book.

Modularity and Integration of Cognitive Processes

In cognitive psychology books such as this one, cognitive activities such as memory, mental imagery, and language are covered as discrete topics, and presented in separate chapters. In universities, those topics are studied in separate advanced seminars. This organization corresponds to the concept of modularity, which was a cornerstone of Chomsky's theory and the ensuing information-processing approach. Neuropsychological research also bears out the functional independence of various cognitive skills—some brain-damaged patients can lose one skill (e.g., the ability to recognize objects in agnosia) without losing other skills (e.g., the ability to speak, or to remember new information), whereas other patients may have the opposite set of symptoms (e.g., intact ability to recognize objects, but loss of the ability to speak). There is ample evidence for the general concept of modularity.

But we also want to stress that many cognitive skills are accomplished by interaction among modules, and that some skills, such as memory and attention, may play a role in carrying out the functions of many other modules. It is not always possible to specify precisely where one particular process ends and another begins. As an example, one important part of possessing the concept of a dog is the ability to recognize dogs (visual pattern recognition), and to retrieve an image of a favorite dog from your childhood (memory and mental imagery). Both pattern-recognition and mental imagery are based on visual stimuli stored in memory. Thinking of the concept "dog" may also activate the individual speech sounds necessary to say the word, thereby invoking language processing. Thus, conceptual knowledge is integrally tied to pattern recognition, visual imagery, memory, and language. Additional examples of the relations between cognitive abilities will be made explicit in many places throughout the text, and we provide cross-references from a given topic to related topics in other areas.

Historical and Contemporary Coverage of Research

As already demonstrated in this chapter, cognitive science, although relatively new as a paradigm, has a long and rich history. We use that history as the foundation for our presentation of material in all the chapters that follow. In each chapter, we present the pioneering research and theoretical development of each topic area, and then balance this approach with coverage of contemporary theories and experiments. This will allow you to see the evolution of thought within cognitive science. A historical approach also helps keep modern researchers humble, as one sees that many "new" ideas have been around for a long time. Each chapter also includes neuropsychological findings relevant to cognitive topics, which are often based on the latest technological advances in neuroscience.

Outline of the Book

The book is divided into several sections. As noted, we begin with the study of memory, in Chapters 2–4, because so many of our other cognitive skills are dependent on what we have already learned and can remember. Consistent with our historical orientation to the study of cognition, Chapter 2 begins with a discussion of one of the earliest cognitive models of memory, the multi-store model proposed by Atkinson and Shiffrin (1968), and a more current incarnation of short-term memory—Baddeley's concept of working memory (e.g., Baddeley, 1986). The second half of the chapter analyzes empirical support for the hypothesis that there are separate memory systems for storing factual information, autobiographical episodes, and skills we have learned. Chapter 3 examines the processes involved in the *encoding* of new information in memory and *retrieval* of that information when it is needed. Chapter 4 focuses on errors of memory—both when information is lost during forgetting and when we misremember details about events or facts.

The second section of the book is devoted to coverage of lower-level processes, including perception and attention, although, following our theme of top-down processing, we will consider the influence of knowledge on those processes. Chapter 5 examines visual pattern recognition—the recognition of words, objects, and people in the environment. Chapter 6 considers the closely related question of attention—how humans determine what aspects of the environment to which they attend, and whether there are limits on how much information we can pay attention to simultaneously. Chapter 7 examines research and theories related to imagery. The study of imagery brings together research in memory and pattern recognition, neurocognition, and the study of consciousness.

The third section of the book consists of three chapters concerned with concepts and language. Chapter 8 focuses on how our conceptual knowledge of diverse categories such as *odd numbers*, *fruits*, and *furniture* is represented in memory. Chapters 9 and 10 examine research and theory concerning language comprehension and production, respectively. The analysis will consider comprehension and production at various linguistic levels—sounds, words, and sentences. We will consider how language develops, why we make speech errors, and how we understand sentences. As mentioned earlier, Chomsky's theory of how language is structured and acquired was an important impetus in the development of modern cognitive psychology. We consider Chomsky's views and how psychologists have responded to him. In addition, Chapter 10 examines language impairments caused by damage to specific parts of the brain.

In the final section of the book, we focus on the topics in cognitive psychology that have traditionally been encompassed under thinking. Chapters 11–13 examine research and theorizing about logical thinking/decision making, problem solving, and creativity, respectively. Among the topics to be considered are whether humans are always able to think logically, how we make decisions in the face of less than complete information (Chapter 11), how we solve problems (Chapter 12), and the relationship between creative thinking and ordinary thinking (Chapter 13).

This has been enough in the way of background. We are now almost ready to begin our examination of human cognitive processes and their interrelations at the center: the functioning of memory. However, before we go there, it will be useful to review the material covered in this chapter.

REVIEW QUESTIONS

In order to help maximize the information obtained from each chapter, we have provided a set of review questions for each. Those questions, presented at the end of each chapter, will help you remember the information in the chapter if you use them in the right way. When you go over each question, the first thing to do is to try to answer it from memory, even if you are pretty sure that your answer is incorrect. Trying to remember the information, even if you are not successful, will increase the chances that you will remember the information after you learn the answer. Here are the review questions for Chapter 1.

1. Give an example of a situation in which our commonsense psychology is incorrect.

2. Why was Wundt an important figure in the development of modern cognitive psychology?

3. How did Wundt's methods differ from those of modern researchers?

4. What were behaviorism's main objections to the research on consciousness in early psychology?

5. What were the streams of research during the first half of the 20th century that helped pave the way for the development of modern cognitive psychology and how did each of them contribute?

6. How does modern cognitive science deal with the problem of studying hidden mental processes?

7. What is the relation between neuroscientific evidence and behavioral evidence in the development of theories of cognition?

8. Why was behaviorism rejected by many psychologists interested in the study of complex human functioning?

9. What developments in areas outside of psychology contributed to the cognitive revolution, and what were those contributions?

10. Why was Paivio's research significant in the development of modern cognitive psychology?

11. What changes have occurred in cognitive science between the publication of Neisser's groundbreaking book *Cognitive Psychology* and the one you are now reading?

12. How has the study of neurocognition contributed to our understanding of cognitive phenomena?

13. Briefly describe several techniques used to measure brain functioning related to cognitive processes.

14. What does it mean to say that cognitive processes are *constructive*?

15. What does it mean to say that cognitive functioning might be based on a *modular* system?

CHAPTER 2

MEMORY I: MODELS OF MEMORY AND MEMORY SYSTEMS

A WORLD-CLASS MEMORY

Imagine that you have been invited to observe a study on memory being carried out at your university. A researcher reads a string of digits to an undergraduate student, at a rate of 1 second per digit: "6, 2, 5, 9, 4, 3, 1, 8, 6, 7, . . . " She keeps reading, for about a minute and a half, while the student sits and listens. The researcher finally finishes, after reading 80 digits. A few seconds later, the student starts to speak. He repeats the numbers perfectly, all 80 of them, in the order in which they were read to him. He seems to have a photographic memory (or perhaps an MP3 memory, since he heard rather than saw the digits). Whatever we call it, there is no doubt that the student's performance is very impressive. Now the experimenter plays a video of the same student 20 months earlier, when he had first started the study. He listens to a string of 10 digits, but this time he can only remember 8 of them. It seems that the student did not start the experiment with a great memory: His impressive ability has developed over those 20 months.

This example of the development of an almost limitless memory comes from a study by Ericsson, Chase, and Faloon (1980; see also Chase and Ericsson, 1981), who gave one very cooperative college student, identified as S.F., large amounts of practice on the *memory-span* or *digit-span* task, as presented in Box 2.1. The memory-span task

---

BOX 2.1 MEMORY–SPAN DEMONSTRATION TASK

You will need a paper and pencil. Read the first string of digits, at a rate of about one second per digit. Then write the digits in order from memory. Then do the same for the second string.

    786194235
    618495372

To score yourself: Count how many digits you were able to remember in order. For example, if you recalled 7 8 6 1 9 4 2 x x (where each x denotes a forgotten number), your memory span would be seven.

constitutes part of most standardized IQ tests, and adults can typically remember from five to nine items, with an average of seven. S.F. began the study with a digit span of about eight, just about average, but after 20 months of practice, as we just saw, he was able to recall 80 digits in a row. Imagine how useful this skill would be before exams—to be able to memorize vast amounts of material on short notice.

The study was as simple as it could be: S.F. heard a series of strings of random digits and tried to repeat them in order. Each string was different. Presentation of one string and S.F.'s recall attempt made up one *trial*. If S.F.'s recall was correct on a given trial, the string for the next trial was lengthened by one digit; if he was incorrect, it was shortened by one. S.F. participated in one 1-hour session per day, 3 to 5 days per week, for 20 months (a total of 230+ hours of practice). By the end of that time, his digit span had reached 80 items, more than 10 times the average. S.F.'s final performance was comparable to that of several memory experts who have been studied by cognitive scientists (e.g., Luria, 1968). How could an otherwise average student become capable of remembering vast amounts of information in a short time? S.F.'s accomplishment was built upon his ability to use his knowledge as the basis for his recall. In other words, S.F.'s impressive memory was the result of active processing on his part.

S.F.'s remarkable memory performance will serve as the touchstone for the discussion of memory in this chapter and the next two. Elaborating the components of his skill will serve as the foundation for our analysis of recent research in memory. As we shall see, the processes carried out by S.F. have general relevance to the understanding of memory.

OUTLINE OF CHAPTER 2

The chapter begins with a brief examination of the functions of memory, centering on the importance of memory in our survival. We then turn to a discussion of the development of the processes underlying S.F.'s remarkable memory skill. Examining this student's performance will serve to introduce all of the concepts psychologists use to analyze memory and lay the groundwork for the discussion in this chapter and the next two. We then begin a survey of how psychologists have tried to understand and explain memory, with a consideration of the first information-processing theory of memory, the multi-store model developed by Atkinson and Shiffrin (1968, 1971). That model proposed that our memory systems are made up of three separate structures or memory stores: sensory store, short-term store, and long-term store. We examine research that has investigated the sensory store and short-term store components of the model. Then, we consider a more contemporary conceptualization of short-term store, known as *working memory* (Baddeley, 1986, 2000). Baddeley's analysis of working memory will illustrate a modern preference for considering the functions and processes (rather than the structures) involved in memory. The second half of the chapter examines long-term store, and considers how memories for facts, personal events, and new skills might be stored and organized. Throughout, we will discuss neuropsychological data from brain-recording techniques and brain-damaged patients to determine which brain areas control memory functions.

A Functional Account of Memory

What would happen if we had not evolved any mechanisms for storing information? Life would always be novel and exciting, but few of us would survive to adulthood. Parents would fail to care for their children, because parent–child attachment would be forgotten. We would walk out in front of cars, not remembering that we had been told of the dangers of doing so. And imagine our primitive ancestors trying to forage for food; not only would they forget the location where trees had had plentiful fruit last week, but they would be tempted to eat the same red berries that had made them feel sick the week before (having forgotten the dire consequences). In contemporary times, finding food at the grocery store would prove an impossible task. Assuming that we stumbled upon grocery stores as a source of food, it would take us hours to find things we wanted to eat (especially since we would be unable to recall what foods we *did* like), and then, if we ever reached the point of paying for our purchases, we would not know how to do it (because memory for the basic rules of addition and subtraction would be lost to us).

When we casually talk of memory, we use a single word, which can lead one to believe that *memory* is one thing—one capacity, one structure, or one set of processes (Baddeley, 1990). If we dig deeper, however, we uncover many different kinds of information that can be called memories, and many different activities that can be called remembering. The functions served by memory can by divided into two general classes. First, memory provides the basis for our adaptation to the environment. To do so, it must store a reasonably accurate record of our experiences, and this information must be available as it is needed. Memory also serves as a *work-space*, in which we carry out many of our moment-to-moment cognitive activities, such as keeping track of an ongoing conversation, determining how much of a tip to leave in a restaurant (Baddeley, 1986, 2000; Baddeley & Hitch, 1974, 1994), or deciding how to study material that we are trying to remember for a test.

Memory is central to almost everything we do, and we typically use memory without consciously thinking about it. Two sorts of situations make us stop and consider the role of memory in our lives. First, when our memory malfunctions (e.g., we forget an appointment, or search a parking lot for our missing car), we regret its occasional unreliability. *Why* did we forget that information? Could anything be done to ensure that we would not forget important information? Is it possible to improve one's memory performance, so that we can each function better? As we have already seen from the brief discussion of S.F.'s performance, the answer to that question is yes. As we work through the discussion in these chapters of research on memory, we will have occasion to consider how memory performance can be improved.

Second, we marvel when we hear about people with extraordinary memories, such as Chao Lu from China, who has memorized 67,890 digits of *pi* (a world record set in 2005, according to www.recordholders.org); or Stephen Wiltshire, a savant with a prodigious visual memory, who drew a picture of London with near photographic accuracy after taking a single relatively brief helicopter ride over the city when he was 11 years old (BBC News, 1987); or S.F. Although few of us can match those memory feats, and memory does sometimes fail us, our memories are remarkable nonetheless: Many of us know people in their 80s who easily recall incidents from their childhoods.

Let us now turn to an examination of how memory works, beginning with an analysis of S.F.'s impressive memory (also, see Foer [2011] for further discussion of how memory can be improved greatly).

BASIC PROCESSES IN MEMORY: S.F.'S METHOD FOR REMEMBERING

As you may remember, S.F. initially was able to recall only about eight random digits in order, but after 20 months of practice, his memory span had increased tenfold. In order to acquire information about the processes involved in memorizing, the researchers working with S.F. asked him to think out loud (i.e., to provide *verbal protocols*, as discussed in Chapter 1) as he tried to remember each string of digits. After some of the trials, he also reported on what he had done to remember the digits. From those protocols and reports, Ericsson and colleagues concluded that there were two critical processes underlying S.F.'s skill: (1) he used his knowledge to *encode* or *process* groups of digits into *single units*, or *chunks*; and (2) he developed a method for *retrieving* the chunks from memory.

Encoding and Chunking

As all of us would, S.F. at first simply tried to rehearse the items, by repeating them to himself as he heard them. This produced little success: His digit span stayed the same. After about a week, however, S.F. began to develop the skill that led to his increase in performance. He was a distance runner, and some of the groups of digits reminded him of running times. For example, the group 3492 was processed or *encoded* as "3 minutes and 49.2 seconds, near world-record mile time" (Chase & Ericsson, 1981, p. 150). Running times were used to encode about 60% of the strings. The remainder was encoded as ages (893—"eighty-nine point three, very old man") and dates (1944—"near the end of World War II"). Thus, the first step in S.F.'s development was his realization that he could use his familiarity with numbers to encode groups of digits as *chunks*, and thereby increase his recall. This is a clear example of top-down and active processing: S.F.'s knowledge allowed him to detect patterns in the digit strings, and those patterns helped him increase his memory. Using his encoding scheme, S.F. was able to greatly surpass the ordinary person's level of performance. Where you or I would recall a total of six or seven digits, S.F. would recall 3 or 4 times as many, since for each single digit of ours, he could recall a chunk of three or four numbers.

It should be noted, however, that S.F.'s chunking skill is no different than what we all can accomplish, although perhaps on a smaller scale, if the circumstances are right. Please read aloud the following string of letters *once*, and, without looking at it again, try to repeat it.

FL YDI GRU NPE NR OT

This string of letters is too long for most people to repeat without error after a single reading, but encoding and recall can be greatly improved if the string is constructed so that it matches our knowledge. Try to repeat the following string after reading it aloud once, while not looking at it.

FLY   DIG   RUN   PEN   ROT

Even though the letters are exactly the same in both strings, recall is usually much greater for the second, because those letters form words. We can encode the 15 letters as five units or chunks, which greatly reduces the memory load. Once it is organized into words, the letter string may become more meaningful, in the same way that strings of numbers became meaningful to S.F.

Ericsson and his colleagues (1980) did not merely rely on S.F.'s protocols and verbal reports of his strategy to determine how and why his memory improved over the course of the study. Based on S.F.'s reported strategy, the researchers constructed strings that could not easily be analyzed as running times, ages, or dates. On such strings, S.F.'s performance deteriorated. In contrast, when strings were constructed that fit his encoding scheme well, his performance improved. In addition, on one occasion the experimenters gave S.F. strings of *letters* to recall. Since letter strings could not be analyzed as running times, dates, or ages, S.F.'s performance dropped greatly. This result indicates that S.F.'s memory was not being strengthened in general terms. Rather, he had developed a specific skill, which capitalized on his existing knowledge to more efficiently process and retrieve information. In sum, Ericsson et al. (1980; Chase & Ericsson, 1981) used behavioral data as well as S.F.'s verbal reports to support their analysis of his performance. This is an example of how cognitive scientists study hidden processes.

Retrieval

When S.F. tried to recall more than three or four chunks (when his digit span reached approximately 18 items), he began to confuse the order of the chunks. It then became necessary for him to construct a method to determine which chunk was to be recalled first, second, and so forth. In other words, S.F. had to develop a *retrieval scheme*: a method for bringing back to consciousness information previously encoded into memory. In order to facilitate retrieval, S.F. began to organize the chunks, by putting them into groups. This organization produced what is called a *hierarchy*, in which there are groups of units, each of which is made up of other items.

An example of how S.F. might have organized an 18-digit string is shown in Figure 2.1a. In this hypothetical example, S.F. organized the string into three groups: a group made up of two chunks of 4 digits each; a second group of two 4-item chunks; followed by any remaining digits. As he encoded the first four digits, say, into a chunk, perhaps as a running time, he also encoded it as the *first item* in the *first group*. The second four digits might be encoded as a date, and would be encoded as the *second* chunk in the first group. The third chunk of digits was encoded as the first item in the second group, and the fourth as the second item in the second group. The remaining digits were encoded as the last items. S.F. gradually increased his span by making his organization more and more complex; his final organizational scheme for recall of 80 items might look like that shown in Figure 2.1b, with multiple chunks grouped together in several larger groups in a large hierarchy.

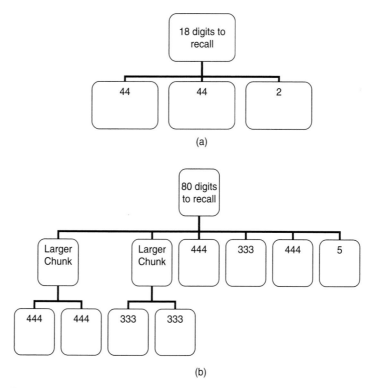

Figure 2.1 S.F.'s hierarchical organization scheme. (a) Initial organizational scheme: Each number indicates how many individual items are in a given chunk. (b) Later scheme, illustrating hierarchical strategy.

At recall, S.F. used the hierarchy to produce a set of *retrieval cues*, that is, pieces of information that could be used to retrieve the encoded chunks. S.F. began by searching for the group that had been encoded as the first chunk in the first group, then the second chunk from that group, then the third; then the first chunk from the second group, and so on. S.F.'s speech patterns during recall provided additional evidence for the hierarchical organization of the number string. When he was recalling the digits within a chunk, he spoke at his normal speed, about three digits per second; between chunks, he paused for a few seconds—presumably to retrieve the next chunk—before resuming his recall. Further evidence that S.F.'s encoding and retrieval scheme was the critical component of his memory development comes from a learning study carried out by Chase and Ericsson (1981). They taught S.F.'s scheme to another undergraduate runner, D.D. By learning S.F's strategies, D.D. (who also started with only an average digit span) was able to increase his digit span to 100 items, higher than S.F. Thus, the technique of encoding numbers into meaningful chunks, and then organizing the chunks to maintain the sequence of numbers during recall, was useful to people beyond S.F.

We have now examined the components of S.F.'s remarkable memory performance. As noted earlier, we will use the concepts developed from our discussion of S.F.—encoding, retrieval, and the role of knowledge in storing and retrieving information from memory—as the basis for our discussion of memory research in the remainder of this chapter and the next two. We begin that discussion by examining a pioneering theory or *model* that used information-processing concepts derived from the computer metaphor as the basis for understanding broad aspects of human cognition: Atkinson and Shiffrin's (1968) multi-store model of memory.

THE MULTI-STORE MODEL OF MEMORY

As noted in Chapter 1, James (1890) made a distinction between primary (short-term) and secondary (long-term) memory, and it certainly seems to many of us that there is a difference between recalling information that is stored only on a short-term basis versus recalling information that has been stored longer. By way of demonstration: Read the following words aloud, then turn away from the book and repeat them in the same order. Here are the words:

CLOUD, HAND, PENCIL

Presumably, this posed no challenge, since you had just read the words. Now, what was the name of your fifth-grade teacher, or the name of the kid who was the class troublemaker in fifth grade? Answering those questions requires retrieving information that was acquired long ago. Perhaps your fifth-grade teacher's name came to mind easily, but remembering the name of your classmate required more effort—you thought about fifth grade, then recalled some incident from that year, and then ran through a mental list of other classmates before you recalled the desired name. Unlike the case of recalling words that one has just read, retrieving some information from deep in the past has a very different feeling: One has to work at the remembering, and perhaps use retrieval cues to access the information fully.

Those different types of memory experiences led James (1890) to consider the possibility that there are more ways than one to store information in memory. That belief formed the basis for the multi-store model of memory, proposed by Atkinson and Shiffrin (1968, 1971). This theory proposes that there are three separate memory structures or stores (hence the name)—sensory store, short-term store (STS), and long-term store (LTS). Those memory structures are assumed to be permanent and unchangeable, like the hardware of a computer, and each has distinct properties concerning its *capacity* (how much information it can hold), *duration* (how long information is held in the store before being passed on), and *code* (the form of the information held in the store). The Atkinson and Shiffrin model, depicted in Figure 2.2, is also a prototypical information processing theory: The process of memory is decomposed into component stores and subprocesses; information comes into the system and is changed in code as it passes through the system. In addition to the structural features, the system also consists of *control processes*, which are flexible strategies that people use to deal with the tasks that they face. It is here where people's knowledge plays an active role in remembering information.

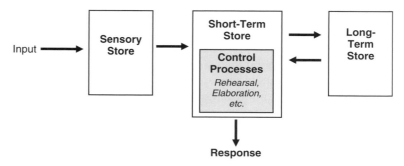

Figure 2.2   Atkinson and Shiffrin (1968) multi-store model of memory.

Sensory Store

Have you ever had the experience of asking someone to repeat what they just said, only to say "never mind" a second later, because you have understood their sentence? This phenomenon is due to one form of *sensory* memory, called *echoic memory*. Someone says something that you do not initially pay attention to, but it briefly remains (like an echo), so that you can process the speech once you turn your attention toward it. The *sensory stores* are structures that very briefly preserve information from each of the senses (Cowan, 2008). A similar occurrence happens in vision—a stimulus can be held momentarily, awaiting attention.

Capacity and Duration

Sperling (1960) conducted an early experiment demonstrating the existence of a visual sensory store, or what Neisser (1967) called *iconic memory* (an *icon* is an image). Sperling did not set out to study iconic memory; he was originally planning to study the *span of attention*, which is the number of items one can attend to at one instant in time. Early in the development of psychology, researchers found that if one very quickly presents a large array of items to a person, such as that in Figure 2.3, most people will typically report four to five items from it. That number is the span of attention, and it was taken to mean that people can attend to only a few items out of all the stimuli available in the world at any time. Sperling found the same result: His participants recalled four to five items from arrays such as that in Figure 2.3. The participants also told him, however, that they knew that there were many more items in the array than those they had reported: Those nonreported items "faded away" as they reported the other items.

Figure 2.3   Example of Sperling (1960) display.

The necessity of reporting the items made it impossible to accurately measure the span of attention.

Sperling was thus faced with the problem of how might one capture that other information before it was gone. He solved his problem by changing his design to a *partial report* technique. Participants viewed the matrix of letters, and, shortly after it disappeared, were randomly cued with a *tone*. A high-pitched tone meant that they were to report the top row, a medium tone cued the middle row, and a low tone cued the bottom row. Sperling used the participant's report from the cued row to deduce how much information was available from the whole array. Imagine that a subject has viewed a 4 × 3 array, as in Figure 2.3. She is randomly cued to report the middle row, and is able to report three of the four letters. Since the cue was random, Sperling assumed that the person would have been able to report just as many of the letters from either of the other two rows, had they been cued. This would tell us that she had stored 75% of the entire array in iconic memory.

Furthermore, Sperling was able to test how long the icon lasts: The tone cue can be delayed, by 100 milliseconds (equal to 1/10th of a second), say, or 300 milliseconds, or 1000 milliseconds (1 second), or whatever delay the experimenter wishes to use, to determine the duration of iconic memory. In Figure 2.4, the dotted line represents the full-report average, whereas the solid line represents the scores based on partial report (number of items recalled from a single row × the number of rows) at each delay. Look at the graph and see if you can determine the last interval at which partial report performance is superior to full-report performance. This will tell you the duration of iconic memory.

Does it appear from Figure 2.4 that the length of visual sensory memory is about 300 milliseconds (about 1/3 of a second)? This is the conclusion that Sperling drew, because after about 300 milliseconds (.30 on the graph), the partial-report memory for the items in the matrix drops to the 4.3 items in the full-report condition. Other experiments (e.g., Eriksen & Collins, 1967; Phillips, 1974) have also confirmed that iconic memory lasts about 1/3 of a second.

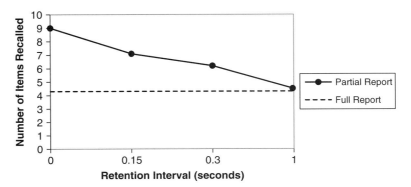

Figure 2.4   Duration of iconic store: Sperling (1960) results for nine-item matrices. Up to 0.3 seconds (300 milliseconds), the partial report performance is better than whole report performance, indicating that some information remains in the iconic store.

Iconic Memory and the Brain

Psychologists have attempted to determine where in the nervous system the iconic store might be located. Imagine a participant in the Sperling experiment who sees an array of letters on the screen. At first, the receptors in the retina (at the back of the eye) respond to the visual stimulus, and then pass their message on to the ganglion cells (which exit the eye as the optic nerve; see Figure 2.5a). Visual information is relayed

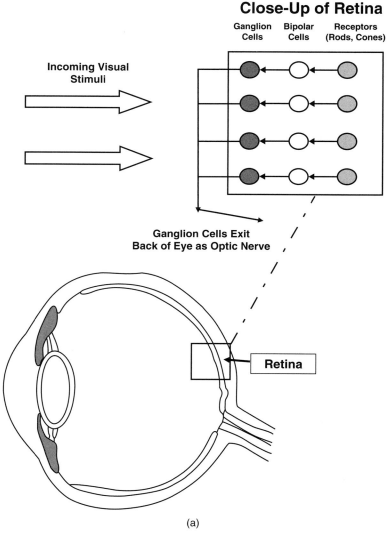

Figure 2.5 (a) Close-up of the receptors and neural cells in the retina. The receptors in the retina (at the back of the eye) respond to the visual stimulus, and then pass their message forward to the bipolar and then ganglion cells. The axons of the ganglion cells exit the eye as the optic nerve. (b) Superior temporal sulcus.

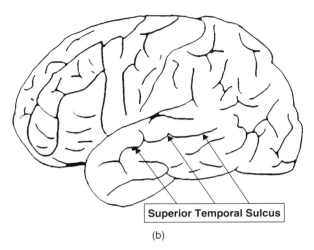

(b)

Figure 2.5   (*Continued*)

from the retina to the visual cortex through the lateral geniculate nucleus (LGN) of the thalamus, which performs most of the initial processing of visual information. The primary visual cortex then sends some of the information to the parietal lobe (which processes motion and spatial information) and to the temporal lobe (which is responsible for color and object recognition). Where, then, might the icon in sensory memory occur? It cannot be in the neurons in the retina of the eye (Levick & Sacks, 1970), nor in cells in the primary visual cortex (Duysens, Orban, Cremieux, & Maes, 1985), because activation in those areas does not continue long enough to account for maintenance of an icon.

Keysers, Xiao, Földiák, and Perrett (2005) measured neuronal activity in macaque monkeys when there was a gap between images in a slideshow. The primates saw rapid presentation of up to 720 images, with varying gaps between consecutive stimuli. Keysers et al. detected neural activation in the superior temporal sulcus (part of the temporal lobe; see Figure 2.5b) during gaps between consecutive images in the slide show, for gaps up to 93 milliseconds. They concluded that this region is responsible for iconic memory because neurons in this region might be "holding" the icon (see also Kovács, Vogels, & Orban, 1995; Rolls & Tovée, 1994). Since the temporal lobes are known to be responsible for our ability to recognize objects presented visually (Ungerleider & Mishkin, 1982; see also Chapter 5), it may be that having an "icon" represented here, even briefly, facilitates our ability to recognize objects that are seen only briefly or in rapidly changing scenes.

Other Sensory Stores

Brief sensory stores may exist for all of our senses, such as when your hand still seems to feel something slimy even after you've dropped a worm. However, the only other sensory store that has been studied extensively is auditory sensory memory, or *echoic memory*. Darwin, Turvey, and Crowder (1972) used presentation of stimuli through headphones to determine the capacity and duration of echoic memory (see also Moray, Bates, & Barnett, 1965). Three streams of auditory stimuli were presented simultaneously, one on the right (e.g., M–5–R), one on the left (e.g., 2–T–F), and the third stereophonically from both headphones, which gives the illusion that the sound is coming from the midline (e.g., X–4–S). Participants then received a visual cue, signaling which stream they should report: left, right, or center. Partial reports with auditory stimuli were superior to whole reports at delays up to 4 seconds. Darwin et al. concluded that the echoic store can hold information usefully for 2 seconds. Echoic memory, like iconic memory, has a limited capacity; maximum capacity in the Darwin study was approximately five items (roughly the length of an average sentence).

Code of Sensory Store

The code of the information in each store is the same as that in which the material was presented. If stimuli are presented visually, sensory memory is a visual image (or icon). If stimuli are presented auditorily, sensory memory is maintained as a sound-oriented code (or echo), and so forth for all other types of sensory memory.

Sensory Stores: Conclusions

Research studies have supported the claims of the participants in Sperling's experiment: The first stage in processing seems to be the initial retention of information in sensory form for a brief period of time. This function is served by the sensory stores, which preserve a relatively detailed record of stimuli for attention and further processing. The next step in processing is the transfer of information from the sensory stores to the short-term store (STS). We now turn to a consideration of the characteristics and functions of the STS.

SHORT-TERM STORE

Atkinson and Shiffrin (1968, 1971) conceived of the short-term store as a temporary and limited-capacity buffer. Its purpose was to hold information on a short-term basis so that it might be processed further (and perhaps make its way into the long-term store). One could say that STS served as a *working memory* (WM), in which information was processed during cognitive operations. For example, deciding how much of a tip to leave in a restaurant depends on our ability to carry out a mental calculation, which occurs in working memory. Although Atkinson and Shiffrin noted that STS as working memory plays a wide role in basically all cognitive processes, they emphasized the role that STS played in transferring information to LTS. Thus, after describing the characteristics of STS, we will discuss research that has examined its function in the long-term storage of information, through rehearsal of various sorts. More recently, Baddeley and his colleagues (e.g., Baddeley, 1990, 2007; Baddeley & Hitch, 1974) have looked at the broader functioning of STS as WM, and have studied its role in a range of tasks broader than processing information for long-term storage. We also review research on the structure and functioning of STS as WM.

Capacity of STS

Recall the digit-span test that you performed in Box 2.1. The digit span is a good indicator of the capacity of short-term store (i.e., how much information we can hold in mind on a short-term basis). If you are a typical college student, chances are that your digit span was between five and nine numbers. After reviewing many articles on short-term memory, Miller (1956) claimed he "had been persecuted by an integer" (p. 81) as the number *seven* kept popping up as the average amount of information one can hold temporarily, with a range of plus or minus two. In other words, the STS has a capacity of 7 ±2 (equal to a range of five to nine items); Miller (1956) dubbed this "The Magical Number Seven." He also claimed that "[t]he persistence with which this number plagues me is more than a random accident" (p. 81); in other words, there are structural constraints on the storage capacity of STS.

However, what is meant by 7 ±2 items? In the digit-span test, each number is processed individually (as "5," "8," not as "58"), so each digit counts as one item. If you try to recall the list "Fast...Train...Red...Apple...Little...Dog...Yellow...Curtain," you would expect one of two things to happen. You might exhaust your short-term store because there are eight words, but you might fill it only halfway, because there are four easily assembled phrases (fast train, red apple, etc.). Being able to *chunk* either verbal (Simon, 1974) or visual information (de Groot, 1965) into meaningful units reduces the number of items to be held in STS. Furthermore, the type of information itself affects the capacity of the short-term store, with more familiar and more meaningful information (e.g., digits, letters, words) permitting greater STS spans than less familiar material (e.g., nonsense syllables such as *gix* or *pah*, or random shapes; Wickens, 1984).

If you look back at the multi-store model (Figure 2.2), you will see a two-way arrow between the short-term and long-term stores. This is because Atkinson and Shiffrin (1968, 1971) recognized that what we already know: Information stored in our LTS plays a top-down role in maintaining information in the STS. Our examination of S.F.'s memory strategies provided a graphic example of how the top-down use of one's knowledge (in his case, of running times, dates, and ages) can serve to help in remembering new information in the form of chunks.

But how big can a chunk be before it no longer functions as a single item? One word? Two words? Phrases? Sentences? Paragraphs? The chunks that S.F created tended to be made up of three to four digits (e.g. "3492—3 minutes 49.2 seconds—a near world-record mile time"), and he never used a chunk longer than five items (Ericsson et al., 1980). Herbert Simon (1974)—a later Nobel Prize winner—tested his own memory span using lists of one-syllable, two-syllable, and three-syllable words, two-word phrases, and eight-word phrases/sentences. His span was within Miller's (1956) 7±2 for words up to three-syllables in length. However, it dropped to four items for two-word phrases, and to three chunks for eight-word sentences. Once the chunks reached too large a size, the capacity of STS did not remain in the five-to-nine range predicted by Miller. Thus, size matters when one attempts to remember chunks of information on a short-term basis.

The idea of a fixed-capacity short-term store was adapted by Atkinson and Shiffrin (1968, 1971) from the notion of a fixed-capacity buffer memory in a computer. The finding that the capacity of STS varies depending on the type of information being processed raises a question concerning how literally one should take the analogy between the buffers in a computer and human short-term store. Because the short-term store is subject to influence from long-term memories, it may be a more flexible system than a computer's short-term buffer (see Cowan, 2001, for a discussion of whether the capacity of the short-term store should be four, rather than 7 ±2).

Duration of Storage in the STS

Let us now consider the question of how long information can be maintained within STS. This seems like an easy question to answer, but, as we shall see, storage in short-term store does not necessarily have a specific time limit in the way that sensory memory does. J. Brown (1958) and Peterson and Peterson (1959) independently developed a technique now referred to as the Brown–Peterson task to measure the duration of storage in STS. You can carry out a reduced version of their experiment by following the instructions in Box 2.2.

BOX 2.2 DEMONSTRATION OF BROWN–PETERSON TASK

This task is most easily carried out with a partner. You will need a pencil, paper, and a watch with a second hand. Read each set of three letters (known as a trigram), then read the number next to it and immediately start counting backwards aloud by threes from that number (e.g., if the number is 412, start counting, "409, 406, 403 . . ." You (or your partner) will have to time the duration listed (e.g., 3 seconds, or 12 seconds, etc.).

Trigram	Number	Duration
BFX	592	12 seconds
PDL	129	3 seconds
YMC	766	9 seconds
WRZ	900	18 seconds
JPT	432	0 seconds
HRQ	619	6 seconds
NFG	864	15 seconds

Scoring: What was the longest duration at which you could accurately remember the three letters after counting backwards? This procedure was used by J. Brown (1958) and Peterson and Peterson (1959) as an indicator of the duration of STS.

The demonstration experiment in Box 2.2 presented eight trials testing short-term retention of information. During each *retention interval* (the interval during which you had to remember or *retain* the item), there was a *distractor task* (counting backwards), designed to distract you from rehearsing the three letters, known as the *trigram*. This makes the situation comparable to the use of memory in real life, where events may serve as distractors that result in our attending to information other than that which we have to remember. For example, you notice the number for a take-out pizzeria on the sign on top of one of its delivery cars. As you rustle in your backpack for pencil and paper, a friend sees you and stops to chat. A minute later, the delivery car and friend are both gone, as is your memory of the pizzeria's phone number. The phone number is comparable to the trigram you tried to remember in Box 2.2, and the friend's conversation is analogous to the distractor task.

The original experiment of Peterson and Peterson (1959) used trigrams and retention intervals of 0–18 seconds. In contrast to our demonstration, participants in their experiment did not know the retention interval on each trial; they counted backward until signaled to recall the material. Participants were exposed to 48 trials (instead of the seven trials used in our demonstration), and the experimenters averaged people's recall of the trigrams for each retention interval. The results of the Peterson and Peterson study are presented in Figure 2.6, and they show large amounts of forgetting over very short retention intervals. After a delay of as little as 12 seconds, recall fell to approximately 10%.

What brought about that forgetting? Based on the results in Figure 2.6, one might conclude that information in STS only lasts up to 12–18 seconds before it *decays* or fades away. However, this issue is more complicated than it seems. The retention interval in the Brown–Peterson task is filled with counting backward, and longer retention intervals mean more counting. Perhaps the counting backward resulted in *interference* with recall of the trigram. This would be *retroactive interference*, since the counting is working *backwards in time*, or retroactively, to interfere with the trigram that was stored earlier.

Waugh and Norman (1965) attempted to examine the roles of time versus retroactive interference in producing forgetting from STS, and they concluded that interference was much more important. They asked people to listen to strings of up to 16 digits at either a fast (4 digits per second) or slow (1 digit per second) pace. The last digit in

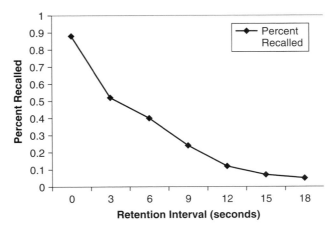

Figure 2.6 Percentage of trigrams recalled as a function of retention interval. Recall is good with short intervals but little is recalled after 9 seconds.
From Peterson and Peterson, 1959.

Fast (4 digits/second) rate:

5 1 9 6 / 3 5 1 4 / 7 3 9 <u>4</u>

Slow (1 digit/second) rate:

5 / 1 / 9 / 6 / 3 / 5 / 1 / **4** / 7 / 3 / 9 / 4

With *4* as probe, the correct answer is 7.

Figure 2.7 Example of a Waugh and Norman (1965) digit string: Participants listened to a string of digits at either a fast (4 digits/second) or slow (1 digit/second) rate. The last digit served as the probe, and they were to think back to when the probe had occurred earlier in the list and report the number after it.

each list, which had appeared once earlier in the list, served as a *probe* (see Figure 2.7). When the probe occurred, participants had to think back to the first time that number had appeared in the list, and then report the number *after* the probe. Thus, as depicted in Figure 2.7, if the probe is 4, people should report the number 7, because it followed 4 the first time that the 4 had occurred in the list. Across multiple trials, the probe appeared randomly and equally often in positions 3, 5, 7, 9, 10, 11, 12, or 14. If the probe number had first appeared in position 14, there would have been only one potentially interfering item between the probe and the first time that number had appeared; if in position 3, there would have been 11 such items.

If loss of information from STS is due to decay, those in the slow-paced group should have a more difficult time with this task, because the longer time between the digits permits more time for decay. If, on the other hand, STS forgetting is due to interference, the fast and slow groups should not differ significantly, but performance should decline with more items intervening between the probe and that number's first appearance in the list (e.g., when the probe occurs in position 2 versus position 14). As is evident in Figure 2.8, the number of intervening items was the main factor that affected people's memories. These results support the conclusion that loss of information from the short-term store is mainly due to retroactive interference, not decay (see also Reitman, 1971).

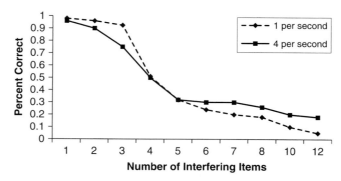

Figure 2.8 Forgetting as a function of decay versus interfering items.
Adapted from Waugh and Norman, 1965.

There is also another possible kind of interference that might cause forgetting in STS. In the studies that we have examined so far, the participants were exposed to multiple trials during the experiment (e.g., 48 trials in the Peterson & Peterson study). It is possible that trigrams from earlier trials might interfere with performance on a later trial. For example, when you tried to recall the letters from the fourth trial in our demonstration, perhaps interference from the letters from the trigrams from the first three trials produced forgetting on trial four. This type of interference would be *proactive interference*, since items from the earlier trials are working *forward in time*, or proactively, to interfere with later items.

In order to test that possibility, Keppel and Underwood (1962) carried out an experiment similar to the original study by Peterson and Peterson (1959), but performed an additional analysis of the data, in which they examined performance for everyone on the *first* trial alone, then the *second*, the *third*, and so on. Keppel and Underwood found that there was good performance on the first trial of the experiment, even for people who had a retention interval of 18 seconds, but performance got worse as more trials were given, especially after longer retention intervals. This is an example of forgetting brought about by proactive interference. That is, performance on Trial 5, say, is worse than on Trial 4 because the items from Trials 1–4 interfere with Trial 5.

However, proactive interference is not the whole story; it interacts with retention interval to affect memory. We can see from Figure 2.9a that, on Trial 1, with no previous items to interfere proactively, retention was roughly equivalent (.95) in the 3-second delay and the 18-second delay condition (Experiments 2 and 3). By Trial 3, information in the 3-second interval dropped to approximately .80, whereas memory for the trigrams in the 18-second condition had dropped to about .60 (as seen in Figure 2.9a). By trial 6, the discrepancy was even greater; the 3-second condition was over 80% accurate whereas the 18-second condition was averaging 40%. Thus, long retention intervals (e.g., 18 seconds) were more affected by proactive interference than short intervals (3 seconds; Keppel and Underwood, 1962, Experiments 1, 2, 3). The worst memory loss for the trigrams appeared to be due to the combination of proactive interference (from the cumulative effect of trials) *and* retroactive interference (within each trial, more counting backwards during longer retention intervals caused more forgetting of the trigram; see Figure 2.9a).

Research on proactive interference in STS has also found that the more similar the interfering material is to the to-be-remembered material, the greater the interference. Loess (1967, Conditions 3 and 4; see also Wickens, Born, & Allen, 1963) asked subjects to remember three words from a given category, such as bird names (e.g., *robin, canary, ostrich*). After a 9-second delay with a distractor task, people recalled the words. Performance on the first trial was very high. When participants again received bird names on the second and third trials, performance dropped, which is another example of proactive interference. On the fourth trial, the participants were given words from a different category (e.g., country names: *Ireland, Mexico, China*), and memory performance improved to first-trial levels. There was a release from proactive interference, because the second category (e.g., country names) was dissimilar to bird names (see Figure 2.9b).

Nilsson and Bäckman (1991) found release from proactive interference when a shift occurred in the category of the words (e.g., *furniture* to *flowers*); or in aspects of the

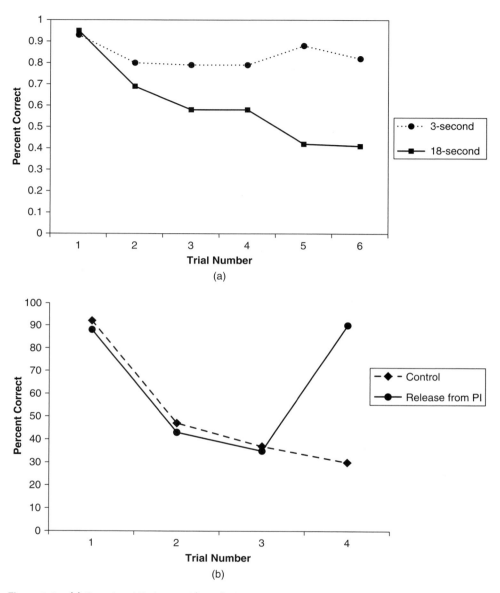

Figure 2.9 (a) Keppel and Underwood (1962) trial-by-trial results: The proportion of trigrams recalled after a 3-second versus an 18-second delay per trial was recorded. As can be seen, there is no difference between the 3- and 18-second delay trigrams on the first trial. However, proactive interference starts to affect trigrams in the 18-second delay items, as performance in this condition declines with increasing number of trials. (b) Release from proactive interference: Change of category of materials on trial 4 (Release from PI group) causes recall performance to improve.

items described by the words, such as their weight (e.g., heavy items such as *piano* to light items, such as *feather*); color (e.g., red items such as *apple* to yellow items such as *sun*); or size (e.g., small items such as *button* to big items such as *elephant*). Not all changes in items cause release from proactive interference, however: release was not found when people learned nouns and then switched to adjectives (Wickens, Clark, Hill, & Wittlinger, 1968). Thus, some characteristics, such as aspects of word meaning, are more likely to cause interference than other word characteristics (such as grammatical class), and shifts in meaning are more likely to lead to a release from proactive interference.

In conclusion, we started this section with the question of how long material is held in STS. We have concluded, however, that duration is less important than interference in determining whether information is lost from STS. Therefore, if there were no items available to interfere proactively or retroactively with items one attended to, one might be able to recall those items after a relatively long period of time (e.g., significantly longer than 15 seconds).

Code of STS

When we try to retain material on a short-term basis—a phone number or a person's name—it often seems subjectively as if we are internally rehearsing or talking to ourselves. Results from a number of psychological studies also indicated that encoding information in our short-term store is carried out by translating the material into a verbal code, regardless of the modality through which the information entered the system (visual or verbal). The earliest evidence for verbal encoding in short-term store came from studies that presented strings of letters, such as $U\,W\,X\,V\,L$, as the to-be-recalled materials (Conrad, 1964). When people made a recall mistake, the incorrectly recalled letter often *sounded* like the correct letter, rather than looking like it. If V was one of the letters to be recalled, for example, a person might incorrectly recall B or T, rather than W or Y (which physically resemble V). This was true even though the letters had been presented visually. It was as if the visual information had been translated into a verbal format for processing and storage (see also Conrad & Hull, 1964). Thus, Atkinson and Shiffrin (1968) considered the code of STS to be acoustic or auditory in nature.

However, the view that STS is purely acoustic may be too simple. Solso and Short (1979) demonstrated that several different sorts of codes can be used in STS. They asked subjects to view a colored stimulus (e.g., a string of *red Xs*) followed by a second stimulus, and to judge whether the two stimuli matched or not. The second stimulus was related to the first in one of several ways: (1) visually (a string of Xs of the same or different color as the first stimulus; see Table 2.1); (2) by color name (same or different color name; e.g., the word *red* versus *black*); or (3) semantically (a word associated to the color of the stimulus; e.g., *blood* [associated with red] versus *lime* [not associated]). Solso and Short also varied the *interstimulus interval* (or ISI)—the delay between the two stimuli. Subjects had to report whether the second stimulus corresponded to (or in some way was the same as) the first string of XXXXs. Consider a sample set of trials (see Table 2.1): If a red string of XXXX$_{[red]}$ served as stimulus 1, then XXXX$_{[red]}$ (in red) would match visually; the word RED would match in color name (and thus match

Table 2.1 Experimental Conditions in Solso and Short (1979)
The participants' task was to determine if one of the second-stimulus pairings matched the first stimulus in one of three conditions: A visual match, color-name match, or semantic match. (Words in brackets depict the color in which the stimulus appeared.)

	First Stimulus	Second Stimulus MATCH	Second Stimulus Non-MATCH
Visual Match	XXXX [red]	XXXX [red]	XXXX [green]
Color-Name Match	XXXX [red]	RED	BLACK
Semantic Match	XXXX [red]	BLOOD	LIME

acoustically); and BLOOD would match semantically. If the assumptions of the multistore model are correct, then as soon as people see the red string of XXXX$_{[red]}$, they should immediately think the word "red," and the color name condition should thus show the fastest response times for ISIs of up to 12–20 seconds (when one is still clearly using STS).

Solso and Short found evidence for *all three* codes in STS—visual, acoustic, and semantic. At very short ISIs (0 milliseconds), response times were fastest for visual matches (XXXX$_{[red]}$ to XXXX$_{[red]}$). At 500-millisecond ISIs, people responded very quickly in the color-color name condition, indicating that they had accessed the color word (e.g., "Red") within half a second after seeing the red XXXXs. At longer ISIs (1500 milliseconds), subjects were also quick to match associated or semantically related concepts (e.g., BLOOD; see Figure 2.10). These results indicate that visually presented information goes into STS in visual form, then an acoustic code is activated,

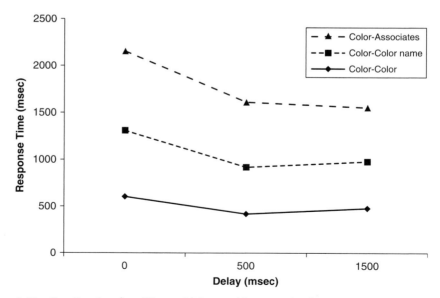

Figure 2.10 Reaction time (in milliseconds) for matching two stimuli.
From Solso and Short, 1979.

and, finally, semantically associated ideas are activated a second or two later. However, all of those various sorts of activations are taking place during the time span when information is assumed to be in STS. Thus, multiple codes may be operating within short-term store, even if a verbal code is dominant.

STS: Conclusions

The multi-store model proposed that the short-term store had a limited capacity for information, held it for a limited duration, and maintained that information in a largely acoustic code (much like talking to oneself). Contrary to those proposals, research has revealed that interference, rather than the passage of time, is a major factor in loss of information from STS, and that multiple codes may operate in STS.

As noted earlier, one important function of STS is the transfer of information to LTS, (i.e., to a more permanent form of storage). We now turn to a consideration of research examining the role of STS in the storage of information.

SHORT-TERM TO LONG-TERM STORES: THE CONTROL PROCESSES

Look back at Figure 2.2, and consider the two-way arrows going from STS to LTS. The short-term store is the main processing unit of the system, where cognitive activities, known as *control processes*, are carried out. Atkinson and Shiffrin (1971) assumed that control processes were under our conscious control and were used to maintain information in short-term store and to help transfer information to LTS. Hence, the two-way arrows indicate that: (1) control processes are based in LTS, but are carried out in STS; and (2) information processed in STS is transferred to LTS. As noted earlier, Atkinson and Shiffrin emphasized the role of STS in the transfer of information to LTS, and we will examine that issue here. We will then turn to a consideration of the broader functioning of STS as a working memory in which cognitive activities are carried out. Please carry out the demonstration in Box 2.3 before continuing.

Rehearsal is one particularly important control process that can be applied to information in STS, resulting in its being copied to LTS. Have you looked at a clock, noted the time, and then found yourself looking again a minute later? Merely attending to a stimulus, such as looking at the clock, does not mean that the information will be remembered. The first noting of the time was not done in a manner that resulted in the information being transferred to LTS. Perhaps, as you tried to remember the list of words in Box 2.3, you mentally repeated the words to yourself. Some readers may have used other control processes, perhaps imaging each word and constructing a picture out of those images (*imagery*), or organizing the words into meaningful groups (*organization*). Still others may have tried to string the words together into a story, which illustrates *elaboration*, in which one encodes material by expanding on it, and giving the stimuli extra meaning. Control processes can also include development of *retrieval cues*, such as remembering the first letters of words to help you recall them.

BOX 2.3 MEMORY FOR A WORD LIST

You will need a paper and pencil. Study the following list of words (take approximately two seconds to study each word), and then try to write them from memory (in any order you wish) on the paper:

People
Diamond
Cotton
Season
Round
Interest
Flag
Army
Crown
Garage
Paper
Chief
Seat
River

We have already seen that S.F., studied by Ericsson et al. (1980), used encoding operations that enabled him to chunk strings of numbers into a single item (such as a world-record running time for a mile). This clearly involves the control processes of elaboration and organization—S.F. went beyond the stimuli to endow random strings of digits with meaning. He also organized the material hierarchically and developed cues that he could use to retrieve the chunks of digits from that hierarchy. S.F. thus used several control processes to improve his digit span (Ericsson et al., 1980).

The Serial Position Curve

The demonstration in Box 2.3 is called *free* recall, because you are free to recall the words in any order. Free-recall performance is usually presented as a graph, such as that shown in Figure 2.11, where recall is plotted as a function of the position of the word in the presented series of words. Thus, Figure 2.11 is referred to as the *serial position curve* of free recall; it contains a number of important parts. The first words in the list are recalled well, which is called the *primacy effect* (since *primacy* means first). The words at the end of the list are also recalled well, which is the *recency effect* (those words are the ones presented most recently). Finally, the words in the middle of the list are recalled relatively poorly. Look again at the words you recalled from the memory demonstration in Box 2.3: If you are like most people, the words you remembered will come mainly from the beginning and end of the list (with perhaps a few from the middle).

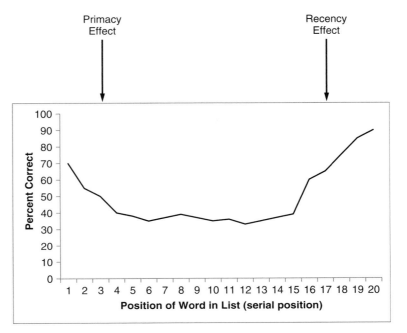

Figure 2.11 Serial position curve of free recall, with primacy and recency portions of the recall curve marked.

The serial position curve of free recall can be explained easily on the basis of Atkinson and Shiffrin's (1968, 1971) multi-store model of memory. Assume that the person attends to the list words as they are presented, and tries to rehearse as many of them as possible. Problems arise as more words are presented, because short-term storage capacity soon becomes filled. A decision must be made: Either one can keep rehearsing the first few words at the expense of incoming words, or one can rehearse the incoming words at the expense of the earlier words. For example, after the fifth word has been presented, one could continue to rehearse the first four (*people-diamond-cotton-season*) and ignore *round*. Alternately, one could add *round* to the rehearsal group, and drop off an earlier item (e.g., *diamond-cotton-season-round*).

Rundus and Atkinson (1970; Rundus, 1971) asked participants to rehearse out loud while they were studying a list for free recall, and then simply counted the number of times each word on the list was rehearsed by each person. The words from the beginning of the list were both rehearsed most often and recalled best. (See Figure 2.12.) The words in the middle of the list were not rehearsed much, and recall for them was poor. The words at the end of the list, however, were hardly rehearsed, but were recalled well. They were also typically recalled first. What this result shows is that different factors seem to account for the primacy versus recency effects: Recall of the first words is good because of many rehearsals, but enhanced recall for the words at the end of the list is due to the fact that they are still available in STS.

What do you think would happen if we delayed recall of the entire list for a while, say by having the participant carry out some distractor task (e.g., simple math

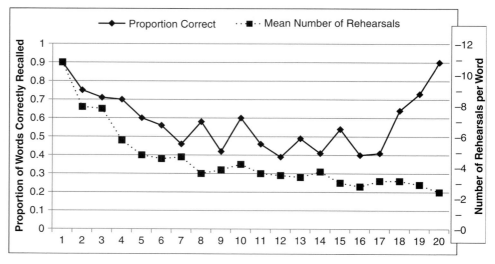

Figure 2.12 Relation of rehearsal to the serial position curve in free recall, based on Rundus and Atkinson (1970). Number of rehearsals each word (right axis), as well as recall performance (left axis) is shown.

problems) between studying the list and recalling it? Given what you have just read, which component of the serial position curve—the primacy or recency effect—should remain? Which one should disappear? The words at the beginning of the list should still be recallable, since they were extensively rehearsed and information about them was put into LTS. The words from the end of the list, however, should not fare well. Since they have not been rehearsed, they should be lost from STS as the participant attends to the distractor. Such a study was carried out by Glanzer and Cunitz (1966). They asked participants to listen to a 15-word list, and then to count backwards for 10 or 30 seconds before recalling the words. As can be seen in Figure 2.13, the 30-second interval completely wiped out the recency effect, without significantly changing the rest of the curve. Thus, the recency effect is fragile, since it can be wiped out by other activities (also see Craik & Lockhart, 1972).

Development of the Control Processes

As adults, we know that if we want to remember a large amount of information, such as a chapter that is to be covered on an exam, we will have to actively process the material, through rehearsal, elaboration, organization, or some other strategy. Young children, on the other hand, often exhibit a *production deficiency* in the use of memory strategies: They do not spontaneously produce or use strategies that would help their memory performance (Flavell, 1970). Children are somewhat ignorant of their own cognitive processes, and tend to overestimate their own abilities (Kreutzer, Leonard, & Flavell, 1975). Thus, one difference between adults and children is in what psychologists call *metamemory*—our knowledge of the functioning of our own memory processes, including the possible role of strategies or control processes in remembering. One

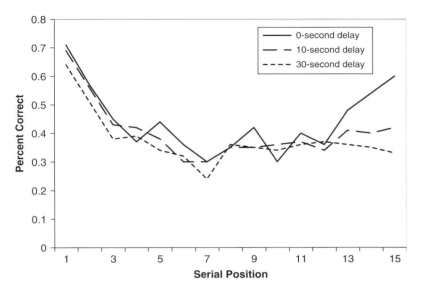

Figure 2.13 Glanzer and Cunitz (1966) results. Serial position curves for free recall after differing amounts of distractor activity. The recency effect is eliminated by having participants count backward for 10 or 30 seconds before recall.

can study the development of metamemory by examining children's versus adults' use of control processes during memory tasks, and their awareness of the need for such strategies.

In developmental studies of recall of word lists, even third-graders show a recency effect, but only a moderate primacy effect (Ornstein, Naus, & Liberty, 1975), as seen in Figure 2.14. Young children can keep information in STS, but don't use control processes effectively to achieve a strong primacy effect (see also Tam, Jarrold, Baddeley, & Sabatos-DeVito, 2010). As children get older, the primacy effect becomes more pronounced, because they both realize that it is important to engage in memory strategies and begin to use such strategies more efficiently. In one memory study, 85% of fifth-graders (ages 10–11) used rehearsal, but only 10% of kindergartners did so (Flavell, Beach, & Chinsky, 1966; see also DeMarie, Miller, Ferron, & Cunningham, 2004; Justice, Baker-Ward, Gupta, & Jannings, 1997; Schneider & Sodian, 1997). Older children begin to consistently use more effective strategies such as organization by age 10–11 (Moely, Olson, Hawles, & Flavell, 1969), and elaboration and imagery by adolescence (Pressley & Levin, 1977).

Schneider and Pressley (1997) found a moderately high correlation between the development of metamemory and enhanced use of memory strategies, indicating that older children are more likely to understand their own memory processes and what skills are needed to retain information (Kreutzer et al., 1975; Lyon & Flavell, 1993; Schneider & Bjorklund, 1998). They also are more likely to use control processes in an efficient way. The combination of these factors helps account for the enhanced primacy effects found among older children (Ornstein et al., 1975).

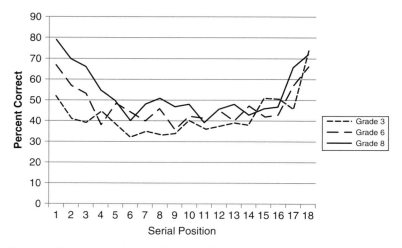

Figure 2.14 Ornstein et al. (1975) results: Serial position curve as a function of grade level. All children show a recency effect; younger children do not show a strong primacy effect, indicating that they are not extensively using rehearsal or other memory strategies.

Control Processes: Conclusions

In the multi-store model, the control processes such as rehearsal, organization, use of retrieval schemes, and so on were seen as strategies for keeping information alive in STS, and helping to transfer it to LTS. Rundus and Atkinson (1970) found that the amount of rehearsal used on to-be-remembered items was directly related to better retention of initial items in a list—the primacy effect—but not to better retention of the final items in a list—the recency effect. There are also clear developmental trends in the use of control processes.

NEUROPSYCHOLOGY OF THE MULTI-STORE MODEL

In addition to behavioral studies indicating a distinction between the short-term and long-term stores, neurological evidence also supported this dichotomy. The prefrontal cortex most often has been linked to short-term maintenance of information (Funahashi, Bruce, & Goldman-Rakic, 1989), while the temporal lobes have been assumed to store information on a long-term basis. The temporal lobes in particular have been shown to store semantic information—in the medial temporal lobe (Scoville & Milner, 1957)—and visual object memory representations in the inferior temporal lobe (Gross, 1972). For example, Talmi, Grady, Goshen-Gottstein, and Moscovitch (2005) measured brain activity via fMRI while participants learned a list of 12 words, and then were probed for words that had occurred at the beginning (items 1 or 2) or end (items 11 or 12) of the list. Recall that the primacy effect in a serial position curve is assumed to be due to better processing of those items, which helps transfer them to the LTS, whereas recency effects are thought to be due to items being maintained in the STS. Talmi et al. found medial temporal lobe activation when early-occurring items were probed (indicating involvement of longer-term memories), and right inferior parietal lobe activation for late probes.

However, a sharp distinction between the STS and LTS has been challenged on neurological grounds (Nee, Berman, Moore, & Jonides, 2008). First, damage to the medial temporal lobe, which should disrupt long-term memories, has also been found to impair short-term storage (Ranganath & Blumenfeld, 2005). The MTL may be engaged in short-term tasks mainly when the stimuli presented are unfamiliar. Other studies have found that damage to frontal cortex areas does not necessarily disrupt performance requiring only short-term maintenance of information (D'Esposito & Postle, 1999). In addition, Cabeza, Dolcos, Graham, and Nyberg (2002) found left-hemisphere lateral frontal cortex activation for retrieval of information from both the STS and LTS. The anterior frontal lobes were engaged during the long-term retrieval task, but not the short-term task. The collective results indicate that both the prefrontal cortex and the medial and inferior temporal lobes can be activated during either short-term or long-term memory tasks, depending on the type of encoding or retrieval activity the person is asked to perform.

EVOLUTION OF THE MULTI-STORE MODEL: STS TO WM

The multi-store model generated a great deal of research examining the postulated sensory, short-term, and long-term memory components and their functions. One criticism raised about the multi-store model concerned the functions attributed to STS. As noted, Atkinson and Shiffrin (1968) focused most on the role of STS as a gateway to LTS. Other researchers, most notably Baddeley and Hitch (e.g., 1974; Baddeley, 1986, 2007) explored further the possibility that STS, as a working memory (WM) or mental work space, played a role in virtually all cognitive tasks. The model of WM developed by Baddeley and Hitch now dominates how psychologists think about the processing of information on a short-term basis.

Baddeley and Hitch (1974, 1994; Baddeley, 1986, 2007) proposed that the moment-to-moment information-processing activities of humans are more complex than those assumed to be carried out in STS in the multi-store model. They suggested that a better way to conceive of STS was as a work space for whatever cognitive activities one is currently carrying out: trying to comprehend a billboard from a brief glance; considering a conversation from 2 weeks ago retrieved from LTS; or mentally calculating your annual salary from 1 week's pay. Thus, the information one deals with can be incoming (the billboard), retrieved from LTS (the conversation), or some combination of incoming and past information (mental calculations). Baddeley and Hitch also argued for a multicomponent or modular WM system, which carried out not only verbal processing of information, but also visual processing. One can get a feeling for the functioning of WM by carrying out the demonstration in Box 2.4. Please do so before reading further.

BOX 2.4 WORKING-MEMORY DEMONSTRATION

Perform the following calculation in your head, and speak your thoughts aloud as you do it (assuming that you are alone or with friends, and will not make a fool of yourself in doing so):

How much is 52 − 24?

One way to carry out the calculation in Box 2.4 is to think, "52 minus 20 is 32; 32 minus 4 is 28." That is, one could first break the calculation down into two parts dealing with the tens and ones columns, then carry out the first part of the calculation by using your knowledge of subtraction (52 − 20 = 32). If you keep track of the result of that calculation, and then use it as the basis for the second part of the calculation (32 − 4 = 28), it will yield the correct answer. Using this process might seem as if you were *talking* yourself through the problem. Another solution strategy may be to *visually image* 52 − 24 vertically, as if you were visualizing a blackboard. Then, your attention can focus on the ones column, where you realize that you will have to borrow from the 5 in 52 to complete the 2 − 4 calculation. Having borrowed so that you now calculate 12 − 4 = 8, you will then need to shift your attention back to the tens column (where you are left with 4 − 2), culminating in *viewing* the correct answer as 28. Employing either technique requires: (a) using the incoming information from the problem, (b) retrieving knowledge about subtraction from long-term memory store, and then (c) carrying out the calculations to arrive at the correct answer. Both strategies and the cognitive requirements to carry out the subtraction task can be explained by Baddeley and Hitch's (1974, 1994) WM model.

Components of Working Memory

Figure 2.15a depicts Baddeley and Hitch's (1974, 1994) original conception of working memory, as a limited capacity system "allowing the temporary storage and manipulation of information necessary for such complex tasks as comprehension, learning, and reasoning" (Baddeley, 2000, p. 418). WM consisted of three modules. First was the *central executive*, a system that determined what tasks would be carried out at various times. This central executive had at its disposal at two *slave systems*—the *phonological loop* and *visuo-spatial sketchpad*—that could process information or keep it active for later use or retrieval. The phonological loop is verbal in nature, and carries out rehearsal and other verbal strategies, whereas the visuo-spatial sketchpad keeps information active in a more pictorial and spatial form. This latter system marked a departure from earlier models of memory, such as Atkinson and Shiffrin's multi-store model, where, as we have seen, an emphasis was placed on verbal coding of information. A third slave system, the *episodic buffer*, has more recently been added to the model (Baddeley, 2000, 2007; see Figure 2.15b). This system holds recent events as integrated memory traces (memory for *episodes*) on a short-term basis.

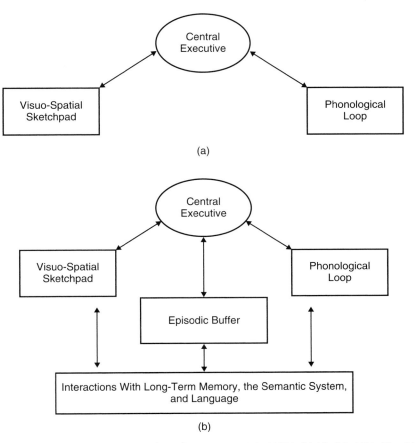

Figure 2.15   (a) Baddeley and Hitch's (1974) original model of WM. (b) Modified Working Memory model (Baddeley, 1986), with added Episodic Buffer.

Central Executive

The central executive is called upon when decisions have to be made concerning information, such as whether two words mean the same thing (e.g., *massive* and *large*). It also determines whether a task requires the phonological loop or the visuo-spatial sketchpad; oversees the allocation of attention during processing (as when one focuses on the ones versus the tens columns in a mathematical calculation); and initiates any decision-making processes that are required in carrying out a task. The central executive also must keep track of information that results from various steps in carrying out tasks (such as the result of the ones-column subtraction in the exercise just discussed).

Phonological Loop

The phonological loop both stores auditory information (such as sounds or words) and refreshes those words or sounds through rehearsal, in order to prevent their loss

(Baddeley, Lewis, & Vallar, 1984). Both the limited capacity of the phonological loop and its articulatory or speech-based code have been supported by a number of key findings. Baddeley, Thomson, and Buchanan (1975, Experiment 1) found that short-term recall of one-syllable words (e.g., *chair*) was better than recall of five-syllable words (e.g., *organization*). Presumably, one-syllable words take less time to rehearse than do five-syllable words, so more of them can be rehearsed in a limited period of time, resulting in a greater short-term recall for those words.

While the phonological loop has obvious utility in memory, Baddeley and Hitch (1994) have proposed that its original function may have been linked to language learning. Several researchers have found that the size of a person's verbal WM is related to acquisition of a second language, but not to memorizing random word pairs in a person's already-learned native language (Papagno, Valentine, & Baddeley, 1991; Service, 1992). That is, people with longer verbal-memory spans learn a second language more quickly (see also Andrade & Baddeley, 2011).

Visuo-Spatial Sketchpad

As noted, Baddeley and Hitch (1974, 1994) made an important contribution to the discussion of WM when they proposed that visual information is processed in WM through use of the visuo-spatial sketchpad. There is both psychological and neuropsychological evidence for the dissociation of the visuo-spatial sketchpad from verbal processing in WM. For example, some patients with right-hemisphere brain damage have normal auditory memory, but are impaired at a memory task requiring them to keep track of spatial location (de Renzi & Nichelli, 1975).

Also, if information can be retained in a visual form in the visuo-spatial sketchpad in WM, then visual similarity of stimuli should cause interference in the same way that acoustic similarity causes interference in verbal WM (Baddeley, 1966b). Logie, Della Sala, Wynn, and Baddeley (2000, Experiment 1) asked people to try to remember either visually similar rhyming words (e.g., *fly, cry, dry*) or visually dissimilar rhyming words (e.g., *guy, sigh, lie*). People remembered slightly more visually dissimilar words, indicating that they had retained the visual representations of the words as well as the words' verbal codes. The resemblance of the visually similar words to each other made those words harder to recall (see also Hue & Ericsson, 1988; Yik, 1978). The evidence supports the assumption that people do use visuo-spatial codes to maintain information on a short-term basis.

Episodic Buffer

The episodic buffer (Baddeley, 2000; Baddeley, Allen, & Hitch, 2010) brings together phonological, visual, spatial, and other relevant information into a single, but temporary, memory trace (see Figure 2.15b). This slave system is also controlled by the central executive, and helps explain how information from long-term store can be imported into WM, such as when S.F used his knowledge of running times and historical facts to improve his memory span (Ericsson et al., 1980). This component of WM also allows us to remember information we learned at a specific time (e.g., the particular words that you heard in a memory experiment 1 hour earlier).

Selective Interference From Simultaneous Tasks

Support for the idea that WM has several components came from studies in which participants were asked to carry out multiple tasks at once (*concurrent* tasks; for review see Baddeley, 1986). In the Atkinson-Shiffrin multi-store model, which has only a single short-term system, there should be interference between tasks whenever people try to carry out more than one task at a time and the tasks overwhelm the limited capacity of STS. However, in the WM model, interference between tasks should depend on the types of tasks that are being carried out, and whether they use the same or different slave systems. Hitch and Baddeley (1976) showed that interference between concurrent tasks occurs only under certain circumstances. They asked subjects to carry out a spatial reasoning task (Task 1) while simultaneously rehearsing a set of letters for later recall (Task 2). In the reasoning task, a sentence was presented that described a pair of letters. Then a letter pair was presented, and the participant had to say *true* if the sentence correctly described the pair, or *false* if it did not. Here is an example of an experimental trial:

In the pair, the B follows the A.   **B   A**

(The correct answer is "false," because B does not follow A.)

While people were performing this logical-reasoning task, they could also remember up to six random letters without slowing their responses to the logic task. Since six letters is within normal memory span, this suggested that the processing mechanisms needed to carry out the spatial reasoning task were independent of the mechanisms needed to rehearse the letters. The letter-rehearsal task presumably requires phonological processing and rehearsal (the phonological loop); the reasoning task is a spatial one, presumably requiring use of the visuo-spatial sketchpad. If those two systems are separate, people should be able to use both at the same time, with little or no interference between them, which is what Hitch and Baddeley (1976) found.

Selective Interference Within the Phonological Loop or Visuo-Spatial Sketchpad

People can accomplish two tasks simultaneously if different slave systems are operating. But what if two tasks use the same slave system—for instance, they either both use the phonological loop or both use the visuo-spatial sketchpad? Performance on the joint tasks should be worse than (a) either task on its own, or (b) two tasks using separate working memory processes. We could occupy the phonological loop by having the person say "tah, tah, tah" over and over, while at the same time asking her to try to remember a list of words in order. Assuming that the person attempts to remember the words by rehearsing them through internal speech, then repeating "tah, tah, tah," should occupy the phonological loop and make rehearsal difficult, resulting in a reduced memory span for the words. Baddeley et al. (1975, Experiments 7 and 8) found that participants had poorer memory for words when they counted from 1 to 8 repeatedly while trying to maintain the words (see also Baddeley & Salame, 1986; Salame & Baddeley, 1982, 1989, 1990).

Other experiments have also found interference effects when people carry out two tasks that simultaneously use the same slave system. For example, Quinn and

McConnell (1996; also see McConnell & Quinn, 2000) determined that looking at a flickering computer screen (a visual distractor task) interrupted memory for words when people attempted to use visual imagery to remember the words (which would occupy the visuo-spatial sketchpad), but not when they tried to remember the words using rote rehearsal (which would occupy the phonological loop). Thus, attempting to perform two tasks that engage the same slave system (verbal-verbal or visual-visual) leads to the most interference and has a negative impact on memory for the to-be-remembered items.

Conclusion: Working Memory

The conception of WM as a workspace has largely replaced the multi-store model's notion of a short-term store. Baddeley and Hitch's (1974, 1994) theory proposed that a central executive directs attention during memory tasks, and that information is maintained either via a phonological loop (for verbally-oriented material) or a visuo-spatial sketchpad (for visually oriented material). A more recent addition to the model of working memory has been the episodic buffer (Baddeley, 2000; Baddeley et al., 2010), which pulls together phonological and visual information about a stimulus into a single memory trace. As we have seen, there is evidence for the independence of the two main slave systems in Baddeley and Hitch's model, based on findings that phonological tasks most interfere with verbal rehearsal of to-be-remembered material, and visual-spatial tasks most interfere with visuo-spatial sketchpad processing.

BRAIN SYSTEMS IN WORKING MEMORY

Attempts have been made to localize in the brain each of the postulated subsystems of Baddeley and Hitch's (1974, 1994) WM system—the phonological loop, visuo-spatial sketchpad, and central executive. One common experimental technique that has been used to study working-memory functioning in monkeys and humans is a *delayed match-to-sample* test. A *sample* stimulus, such as a picture, shape, or colored light, is presented. The sample (say, a red square) is then removed, a delay period follows, and then two (or more) test stimuli appear (e.g., a red square and a blue triangle). The monkey or human is to choose the test stimulus that matches the original sample (and the monkeys are rewarded for doing so). In order to carry out this task, the *memory trace* (i.e., the record in memory) of the sample must be retained, presumably by WM. The hippocampus has been found to be active during the delay, and this activation is assumed to both maintain a brief memory of the sample until a response is needed (Ranganath & D'Esposito, 2001), and potentially help encode information about the sample into LTS (Schon, Hasselmo, Lopresti, Tricarico, & Stern, 2004).

Central Executive Processes
The prefrontal cortex, an area located at the very front of the brain (see Figure 2.16a1), has also been implicated in WM tasks, particularly in activities associated with the central executive functions outlined earlier, such as making decisions. Brain-imaging techniques have shown the prefrontal cortex to be active, for example, while a person is

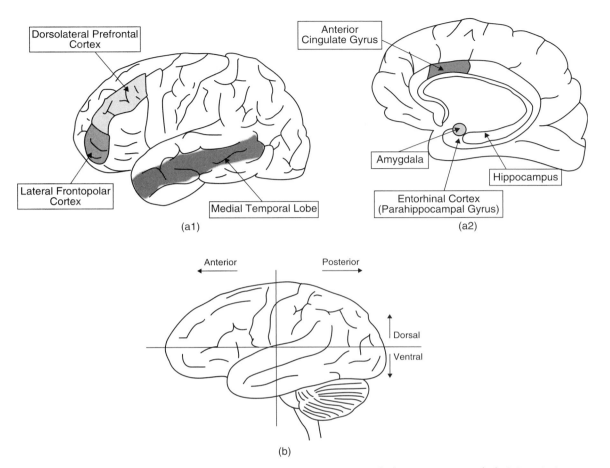

Figure 2.16 (a) Brain areas relevant to memory. (a1) Cortical areas. (a2) Subcortical areas. (b) Dorsal/ventral and anterior/posterior orientations.

planning moves in a problem solving task (Owen, Doyon, Petrides, & Evans, 1995), or allocating attention as he or she switches back and forth between two tasks (D'Esposito, Detre, Alsop, Shin, Atlas, & Grossman, 1995). Smith and Jonides (1999) determined that the dorsolateral prefrontal cortex (DLPFC) and cingulate gyrus were active during both selective attention to stimuli and management of attentional switches between tasks (as when people engage in multiple tasks or operations at once). Petrides (2000) found that particular regions of the dorsolateral prefrontal cortex may be specialized for particular aspects of WM; for example, the mid-DLPFC is responsible for executive monitoring of working memory, as when one item in an array is selected at the expense of other stimuli.

Parts of the parietal lobe may also participate in executive functioning, such as regulating attention, and uniting various parts of an experience into a single episodic whole. For example, damage to the right fronto-parietal lobe has been found to interfere with the ability to hold two pieces of information simultaneously in WM (Lazar, Festa, Geller, Romano, & Marshall, 2007; see also Campo et al., 2008).

There are also subcortical areas related to encoding memory traces (see Figure 2.16a2), which we discuss later in the chapter.

Phonological Loop and Visuo-Spatial Sketchpad

Analysis of brain activity during tasks that require working memory has also provided evidence concerning the possible locations of the phonological loop and visuo-spatial sketchpad. This is usually studied by ascertaining brain activation differences in the encoding and maintenance of verbal versus visual working memory. In a series of studies on working memory, Smith, Jonides, and their coworkers (summarized in Smith & Jonides, 1997) asked people to participate in three different working-memory tasks—verbal, visual, and spatial—while their brain activity was measured via PET scans. The verbal task required that the participant keep in mind an array of letters for 3,000 milliseconds (3 seconds), until a target letter was presented (see Figure 2.17a). The person's task was to say if the target matched any of the letters in the original array. If the letter array appeared in capital letters, the target letter would appear in lower case (and vice versa) so that the participants could not simply match the letters based on

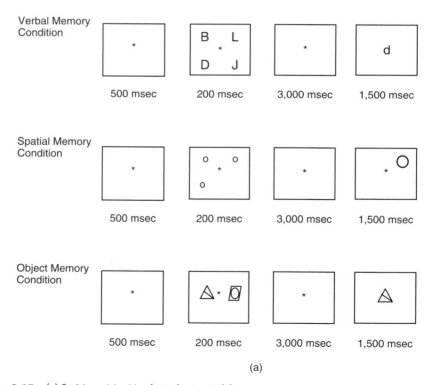

(a)

Figure 2.17 (a) Smith and Jonides (1997) stimuli. (b) Brain areas activated per task
Adapted from Smith and Jonides, 1997, Figures 1 and 2.

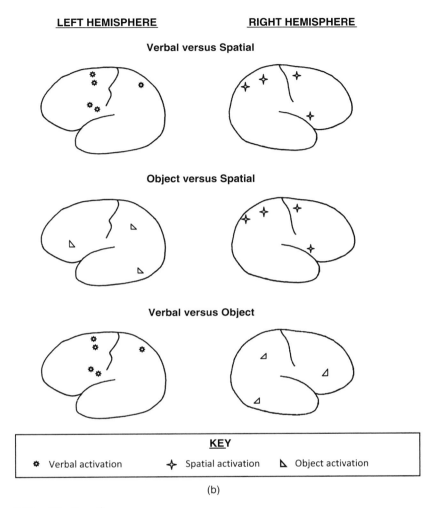

Figure 2.17   (*Continued*)

physical appearance (Awh et al., 1996). The visual working-memory task required that novel geometric shapes be kept in mind (Smith & Jonides, 1995). The spatial working-memory task presented three dots and required that the person keep track of their locations (Jonides et al., 1993). The verbal task should require use of the phonological loop, while the spatial and visual shape tasks should require the visuo-spatial sketchpad.

As shown in Figure 2.17b, each task activated a selective set of areas in the cortex, indicating that different areas in the brain may serve as working memory for different types of materials. The verbal-letter task activated an area in the left frontal regions around Broca's area (mentioned in Chapter 1), which is known to be connected to speech production. Activity was also seen in the left parietal region, which had previously been shown to play a role in verbal short-term memory tasks (Shallice, 1988). The spatial task, on the other hand, mainly activated two areas toward the back of the brain—sections of the occipital and parietal lobes. The anterior (front, see Figure 2.16b) portion of the right occipital cortex was activated, which other studies have shown is related to production of visual imagery (e.g., Kosslyn et al., 1993; Kosslyn, Thompson, Kim, & Alpert, 1995; these studies will be discussed further in Chapter 7). The second area was in the posterior (rear) section of the right parietal lobe, which has previously been shown to process motion and visual-spatial information (Ungerleider & Mishkin, 1982) and is implicated in spatial memory (McCarthy & Warrington, 1990).

The visual-shape memory task activated both the inferior temporal cortex—responsible for object recognition (Mishkin, Ungerleider, & Macko, 1983; Ungerleider & Mishkin, 1982), and areas connected to speech, such as the premotor cortex and posterior parietal region (which had also been active during the verbal tasks). This suggests that viewing and remembering objects involves both visual object recognition and maintaining a verbal description of each novel shape (Smith & Jonides, 1997).

The role of the parietal cortex in visual working memory has been confirmed by other studies (e.g., Todd & Marois, 2004). Particular areas of the parietal lobe, working in conjunction with prefrontal cortex and object recognition areas, accomplish the attentional, maintenance, and decision-making processes in WM. Pessoa, Gutierrez, Bandettini, and Ungerleider (2002) determined that sustained activity in the intraparietal cortex and frontal eye field (in the prefrontal cortex) best predicted correct performance in a visual memory task (see Figure 2.18). Based on a number of neuroimaging studies, Xu and Chun (2006) have identified specific roles for three areas in visual WM: They concluded that the inferior intraparietal sulcus (IPS) maintains spatial information about stimuli and directs visual attention, the superior IPS maintains

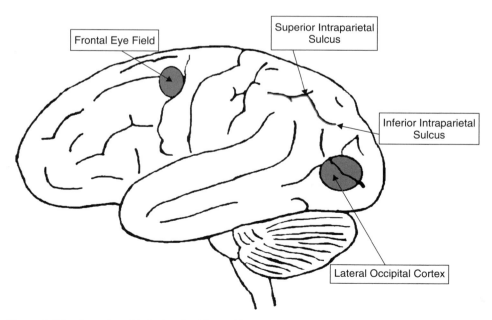

Figure 2.18 Areas found to be involved in working memory.

both visual and spatial information about to-be-remembered items, and both areas coordinate with object information maintained in the lateral occipital cortex (Kourtzi & Kanwisher, 2000). The superior IPS may also determine the capacity of visual working memory, as its activity level is correlated with the number of items to be held in the visual store (Todd & Marois, 2004, 2005).

Some types of visual information, such as familiar shapes, can be simultaneously coded visually and verbally, and this may affect their neurological processing. Rothmayr et al. (2007) gave people verbal-only or visual-only instructions during a visual matching task. While undergoing an fMRI, participants viewed one visual stimulus followed by another 2 or 8 seconds later. They were told to decide whether the two stimuli were at the same orientation [e.g., / /] or different orientations [e.g., / \ ]. The verbal instructions emphasized verbal encoding of the material (e.g., as "right-leaning" or "left-leaning"); nonverbal encoding only emphasized the visual-spatial aspect of the stimuli. Visual (nonverbal instructions) WM tasks engaged the right dorsolateral prefrontal cortex, especially at long delays, whereas the verbal WM instructions led to greater activity of the left hemisphere, including areas connected to speech centers.

Left-hemisphere lateralization of verbal/numeric stimuli has been confirmed by a number of studies, as detailed in Cabeza and Nyberg's (2000) analysis of 60 working-memory studies employing PET and fMRI scans. Both prefrontal cortex and superior parietal cortex in the left hemisphere subserve working memory for verbal materials. Frontal lobe activation, especially around Broca's area, is thought to be due to maintenance of verbal information employing the phonological loop (Awh et al., 1996; Becker, MacAndrew, & Fiez, 1999; Davachi, Maril, and Wagner, 2001; Paulesu, Frith, and Frackowiak, 1993), whereas the left superior parietal cortex may serve a storage function in verbal working memory (Awh et al., 1996; Paulesu et al., 1993).

While there is substantial evidence for differential neural processing of verbal and visual information in working memory, there are also brain regions that are active in both kinds of tasks (Cabeza & Nyberg, 2000). You may have noticed that multiple types of memory components—central executive processes, phonological processing of verbal material, and visual-spatial processing—all stimulate the parietal cortex. D'Esposito et al. (1998) suggested that activation of the parietal region in both visual and verbal tasks means that its function may be general maintenance of information and/or preparation of a motor response, regardless of the type of material to be remembered.

Working memory thus appears to be dependent on a distributed network of areas in the prefrontal, parietal, and temporal regions of the brain. When stimuli are strictly controlled, there is support for both psychological and neurological dissociation of processing of verbal, visual, and spatial information, and attention-direction/decision-making within memory tasks, corresponding to Baddeley's (2007) phonological loop, visuo-spatial sketchpad, and central executive processor.

FROM WORKING MEMORY TO LONG-TERM STORE

Much of the function of short-term processing is to encode information into long-term store. LTS serves as the depository of our experiences and skills, as well as other sorts of information, retained on a longer-term (and perhaps permanent) basis. We will first review the analysis of LTS as proposed in the original conception of Atkinson and Shiffrin (1968, 1971), and will then examine more-recent analyses of the structure and functioning of LTS. Given the variety of types of information in LTS, it, too, may have its own organization. We will consider whether long-term memory might be modular, according to the type of material that we encode and store.

LONG-TERM STORE

Before we begin the discussion, please read and try to memorize exactly the following sentence:

Along Broadway, the lights shown brightly, but Sara couldn't help but think how easy it would be for misfits and robbers to blend into the shadows and startle theater-goers.

Atkinson and Shiffrin (1968, 1971) envisaged LTS as the final structure of memory, with a capacity, duration, and code different from both the sensory and short-term stores.

Capacity

Unlike the limited capacity of the sensory stores and STS, the capacity of LTS was assumed by Atkinson and Shiffrin (1968) to be limitless. As far as we know, no one has ever used up all of their long-term memory capacity (think of the man who memorized 67,890 digits of *pi*).

Duration

The multi-store model also assumes that some information can, in principle, be remembered permanently (Shiffrin & Atkinson, 1969). Thus, the duration of LTS is indefinite. The potential for some memories to be retained for a lifetime will be addressed in more depth in Chapter 4.

Code

Without looking, try to recall the sentence about Sara that was provided at the beginning of this section, as exactly as you can. Now look back at the sentence. Did you recall the sentence verbatim? Most people easily remember the gist of the sentence, but are not able to recall it perfectly. This is because the code of LTS is typically *semantic*, or meaning-based (rather than based on exact form, like sensory store). Recall that Baddeley (1966b) found that words that sounded alike were most likely to be confused in a short-term memory task (consistent with the idea that STS has an acoustic code). When Baddeley (1966a) tested long-term memory for lists of words, however, lists constructed of semantically similar words (e.g., *great, large, broad, wide, high* , etc.) were more poorly recalled than lists of unrelated or acoustically related words (e.g., *pit, few*, *bar*, *hot*). Thus, in LTS, semantically related words interfered with each other, supporting the assumption that the code of LTS is meaning-based.

As with Atkinson and Shiffrin's (1968, 1971) assumptions about the phonological code of STS, the assumption that LTS is exclusively semantic is, however, too simple. As we will see in Chapter 4, although meaningful aspects of material are often best remembered, we can under certain circumstances maintain details and also what seems to be irrelevant information. Another complexity concerning LTS that modern research has uncovered is that long-term memory may be organized into separate systems, each of which maintains a different kind of information.

LONG–TERM MEMORY SYSTEMS: SEMANTIC, EPISODIC, AND PROCEDURAL KNOWLEDGE

What is your earliest memory? Your first day of kindergarten? Getting a new puppy or kitten? Moving to a new house? Do you still remember historical facts about Christopher Columbus from an early grade (e.g., that the names of his ships were the *Nina*, the *Pinta*, and the *Santa Maria*)? When was the last time you roller-skated? Are you confident you could still skate well, even if it has been years since you were last on roller skates? These examples point out the different kinds of memories that we acquire and retain—experiences, facts, and skills. As depicted in Figure 2.19, Tulving (1983, 2002) proposed a functional modularity of memory systems, dividing memories into *declarative* and *nondeclarative* memories.

Declarative memories are memories that can be *declared*—that is, memories that can be both assessed through verbal queries and reported verbally. The declarative-memory system consists of two components. The first is *semantic memory*, which involves our knowledge of facts (e.g., the names of Christopher Columbus's ships; who painted the *Mona Lisa*), of word meanings (e.g., what *lacuna* means), and of

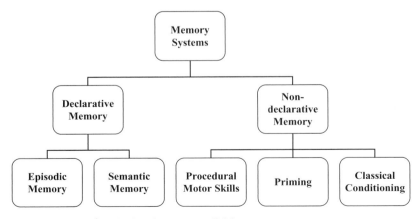

Figure 2.19   Declarative/nondeclarative memory division.

category information (e.g., birds have wings and lay eggs). *Episodic memory*, the second component of the declarative-memory system, retains autobiographical incidents from our past; that is, things that we remember as having happened to ourselves (Wheeler, Stuss, & Tulving, 1997)—for example, our first day of kindergarten or walking into a new house for the first time.

Nondeclarative memory is comprised of information that cannot easily be conveyed verbally. It consists of *procedural knowledge*—our memories for how to perform some motor action or skill, such as knowing how to skate or ride a bike—as well as more subtle memories that we do not usually access consciously (e.g., classically conditioned memories, among others). It is interesting to note that one can exhibit procedural knowledge without having any recollection for the episodes in which it was acquired. I can roller-skate, but I do not remember when I learned to do so. Procedural knowledge is described as knowing *how*, whereas semantic and episodic knowledge are described as knowing *that*. You know *how* to ride a bike. You know *that* $4 \times 5 = 20$ (semantic knowledge), and *that* you ate breakfast this morning (episodic knowledge).

Episodic Versus Semantic Memory

When we remember a specific episode, we can sometimes have the feeling of reliving the event. In contrast, we can typically report a fact or the meaning of a word without any recollection of the specific time and place in which the information was first acquired. Thus, it seems as if the two types of memories are cognitively distinct, as Tulving proposed. The question of whether episodic and semantic memories are stored in one system, or if there is a modular system for each, is one that psychologists have grappled with since Tulving's original proposal. Wilson and Baddeley (1988), for example, have argued that semantic memories are, of necessity, built up out of episodic memories. General facts (*birds have wings*) are simply accumulated from multiple personal episodes (e.g., of seeing a lot of individual birds with wings), and are stored in the same memory system as those episodes. That view assumes that long-term memory is one single system, rather than two modules.

According to Wilson and Baddeley (1988), any tendency to remember facts better than episodic memories may simply be due to differential repetition of those two types of information: We are typically exposed to definitions and semantic facts numerous times, whereas specific episodes of our lives take place only once, and would be forgotten more easily. Here is a simplified example of how the transition from episodic to semantic memory might come about. To remember the names of Christopher Columbus's ships, perhaps you had an episode in which your second-grade teacher told you the story of Christopher Columbus discovering the new world, and the names of the ships were part of the story. Another episode in which the same set of ship names was presented occurred in third grade, say, when you learned the rhyme, "In 1492, Columbus sailed the ocean blue." That same information about the ships might also have been presented in an episode when you read a book in preparation for a history test the following year, and so forth. Thus, the semantic knowledge was built up from numerous instances in which the same facts—the names of Columbus's ships—were encoded in different circumstances. If your grandchildren ask you someday when and where you learned the names of Columbus's ships, chances are you will remember the *Nina*, *Pinta*, and *Santa Maria* without being able to recall the associated episodes, because the names have been rehearsed several times more than any one of the episodes.

This tendency to remember information without remembering when and where we learned it is, of course, a quite common experience. It is called *source amnesia* by psychologists, since the *source of the information* has been forgotten, but not the information itself (Cooper, 1966; Evans & Thorn, 1966; Schacter, Harbluk, & McLachlan, 1984). As we shall see, research largely supports Tulving's (1983, 2002) distinction within declarative memory for semantic versus episodic memories, though the two systems have overlapping brain areas.

MODULAR STORAGE SYSTEMS: EVIDENCE FROM AMNESIA

Because our memory systems typically function so efficiently, much of the research on the possible existence of modular memory systems comes from amnesic patients (*amnesia* comes from the Greek for *a-*, meaning *without*, and *mnemonikos*, memory). Amnesics show: (1) a definite dissociation between procedural and declarative memories (Corkin, 1968; Milner, 1962); (2) a difference in the ability to remember semantic versus episodic memories (e.g., Cavaco, Anderson, Allen, Castro-Caldas, & Damasio, 2004; Cohen, Eichenbaum, Deacedo, & Corkin, 1985; de Renzi, Liotti, & Nichelli, 1987; Reinvang, Nielsen, Gjerstad, & Bakke, 2000; van der Linden, Brédart, Depoorter, & Coyette, 1996); and (3) a distinction between short- and long-term memory stores (Scoville & Milner, 1957), which supports the original stores proposed by the multi-store model. By linking amnesic patients' memory deficits to their specific areas of brain damage, researchers can determine what brain areas are implicated in encoding versus retrieval of various types of memory.

Causes of Amnesia

Although amnesia can sometimes be psychologically induced, we will be concerned mainly with cases where it is caused by some type of brain damage. Many types of physical trauma can bring about amnesia. In one case, a fencer suffered brain damage when his opponent's sword accidentally entered his right nostril and pierced his brain (Teuber, Milner, & Vaughan, 1968). Amnesia can also be brought about by illness, such as *encephalitis* (De Renzi et al., 1987), which is an infection of the brain; or *meningitis*, an inflammation of the membrane that covers the brain (Aggleton et al., 2005; Wilson & Baddeley, 1988). Other documented amnesia cases have been caused by strokes (Cowan, Beschin, & Della Sala, 2004), surgery (Scoville & Milner, 1957), and auto accidents (Maravita, Spadoni, Mazzucchi, & Parma, 1995). In these cases, the trauma is relatively sudden. Amnesia can also develop slowly, such as in Korsakoff's Syndrome, a *syndrome*, or set of symptoms, named for Sergei Korsakoff, the Russian physician who first described it (Gazzaniga, Ivry, & Mangun, 1998). Korsakoff's syndrome is the result of excessive alcohol consumption over many years. Drinking and metabolizing alcohol depletes a number of vitamins, including thiamine (vitamin B_1; Leo & Lieber, 1989). The hippocampus, in particular, is one brain structure that is very sensitive to long-term thiamine deficiencies, which can result in anterograde amnesia. Other parts of the brain are likewise damaged by nutritional deficiencies, and Korsakoff's patients suffer a multitude of amnesic and cognitive deficits, including dementia.

Types of Amnesia

There are two major types of amnesia. Consider a person's life on a timeline from birth until death (see Figure 2.20), and assume that some trauma befalls a person in the middle of the timeline—a stroke, or a car accident. If the person cannot learn new information from that point onward—their amnesia extends forward in time from the trauma—it is known as *anterograde* amnesia (*antero* is Latin for *forward*). However, if the person loses information from before the trauma, this is known as *retrograde* amnesia (*retro* means backwards, or in the past). Soap opera cases where a character forgets his wife and children after a bump on the head illustrate retrograde amnesia. In retrograde amnesia, memory for the more recent past is usually more impaired than memory for a person's childhood or distant past. Most patients suffer from both retrograde and anterograde amnesia, although there may be large differences in the severity of the two types of memory deficits within a single patient.

A patient known as H.M. is one of the most well-studied amnesia cases (Scoville & Milner, 1957). H.M. died in 2005 at age 82. He suffered epileptic seizures from childhood, possibly due to a bicycle accident before age 10 (Scoville, 1968). By the time he was a young adult, those seizures were so frequent and severe that he could not function normally. No drug or therapy was effective in reducing the seizures; as a last resort, in 1953 the interior of the central portions of H.M.'s temporal lobes on both sides were removed, including the entorhinal and perirhinal cortex, as well as much of the limbic system—the hippocampus and amygdala (Corkin, 1984; refer back to Figure 2.16a2). The operation reduced the frequency and severity of the seizures, but it also had unexpected drastic side effects. Following the operation, H.M. suffered a profound anterograde amnesia, with some mild retrograde amnesia. For example, he was not able to learn the names of the people treating him after the surgery, nor those of most politicians or artists who became famous after his surgery (Gabrieli, Cohen, & Corkin, 1988; Marslen-Wilson & Teuber, 1975). H.M. was unable to

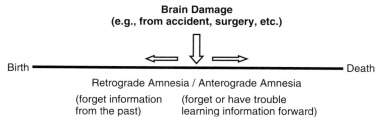

Figure 2.20 Hypothetical birth-to-death timeline, and depiction of which memories are affected in retrograde and anterograde amnesia.

learn new vocabulary such as computer terminology that arose after his brain damage (Gabrieli et al., 1988; Postle & Corkin, 1998), and he often read the same magazines over and over again. Late in his life, he still thought of himself as around 30 years old, was surprised by his reflection in the mirror, and exhibited fresh grief every time he was reinformed about the death of his mother (www.brainconnection.com). Thus, both semantic and episodic memory were impaired in H.M.

Declarative Versus Nondeclarative Memory

The distinction between declarative and nondeclarative memory is well supported in amnesia. Amnesic patients such as H.M. are readily able to learn new skills, that is, they can acquire procedural memories (as we have seen, a type of nondeclarative memory), even when they are unable to remember other types of information, including the fact that they have learned those skills. Cavaco et al. (2004), for example, were able to train amnesic patients on five new procedural tasks, such as weaving and tracing geometric figures with a stylus, even though the amnesics did not retain declarative memories for the tasks. Amnesic patients can also be taught basics of computer use and word processing (Glisky & Schacter, 1987; Glisky, Schacter, & Tulving, 1986), and can acquire other motor skills (e.g., Gabrieli, Corkin, Mickel, & Growdon, 1993; Milner, 1962; Wilson et al., 1996).

Neuropsychology of Procedural Knowledge

Two structures appear to be important in procedural memory: the cerebellum (at the rear of the brain), which is involved in learning new motor skills; and the basal ganglia (see Figure 2.21), which are subcortical structures that have been implicated in motor

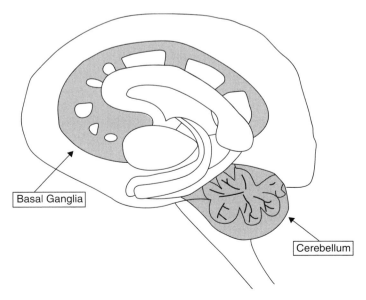

Figure 2.21 Cerebellum and basal ganglia.

movement. Damage to the basal ganglia produces the slow motor movements and awkward gait of Parkinson's patients (Maschke, Gomez, Tuite, & Konczak, 2003). The ability to learn motor tasks, such as weaving, is largely dependent on the basal ganglia, which are intact in most amnesia patients. Lesions of the cerebellum are correlated with impairment in mirror-tracing tasks, in which the person must learn to trace figures that can only be seen in a mirror, which requires that some movements be reversed (Sanes, Dimitrov, & Hallett, 1990). One hypothesis is that the basal ganglia are more responsible for repetitive motor actions (e.g., weaving), but new visual motor mappings (e.g., mirror tracing) are dependent on the cerebellum (Willingham, Koroshetz, & Peterson, 1996). In sum, the brain areas responsible for procedural memories differ depending on the kind of task being tested—whether visual-motor or purely motor.

Semantic Versus Episodic Memory Within Declarative Memory

The independence of nondeclarative memories (such as procedural knowledge) from declarative memories is well accepted. However, there is more controversy surrounding the distinction within declarative memory between semantic and episodic memory. Amnesic patients have provided much of the empirical support for Tulving's (1983, 2002) distinction between semantic (or factual) knowledge and episodic knowledge. As we have discussed, an alternative view is that episodic and semantic memory are not modular systems (Wilson & Baddeley, 1988).

In Chapter 1, we introduced you to the concept of *double dissociation* in neuropsychology: If one patient shows intact skill A, but impaired skill B, and another has the converse set of skills (impaired A, but intact B), researchers assume that the two skills are functionally (and perhaps neurologically) modular. There is evidence from amnesic patients of a double dissociation between semantic and episodic memory. However, psychological and neuropsychological data suggest that the two memory systems do share *some* processes and brain structures. In addition, the amnesic literature supports a distinction within episodic memory between recall of personal episodes versus autobiographical semantic information—remembering the details of one's wedding day versus remembering that one is married (van der Linden et al., 1996).

De Renzi et al. (1987) examined a 44-year-old woman, L.P., who demonstrated memory loss after suffering brain damage from encephalitis. A CT scan (see Chapter 1) showed damage to her left posterior temporal lobe, and she evinced a profound semantic impairment that permeated her daily life and her speech. For example, she could not complete grocery shopping easily because she could not recognize ingredients for favorite recipes (such as minestrone soup) unless she took pictures of items to the store to match to cans, boxes, and vegetables. L.P. also showed anterograde amnesia for semantic information, as well as profound anterograde and retrograde amnesia for world and public events, and geographical and historical information (including the identity of figures such as Stalin, Hitler, and Khaddafi).

However, L.P.'s ability to learn and remember episodic events was remarkably intact. Although she did not remember her psychologist from visit to visit, when reminded of the psychologist's identity, L.P. could recall, in detail, previous conversations with the woman and what had taken place in prior sessions. She could also talk about family events that had been ongoing since her encephalitis, and was able to provide extensive details on her high school years, her marriage, births of her children, and both distant and recent summer holidays. As noted, L.P. did not remember public events, such as the 1986 Chernobyl nuclear disaster, but she did remember personal consequences of such events (e.g., she recalled being warned not to eat vegetables out of her garden because nuclear fallout had made them unsafe). This patient thus exhibited severe anterograde and retrograde impairment of semantic knowledge, but had intact autobiographical memory for both past and ongoing personal episodes.

Conversely, H.M.—the patient already extensively discussed—maintained a profound amnesia for episodic information from the time of his surgery until his death, although he did acquire some knowledge of famous people and events after 1953, the date of his operation. When Kensinger and Corkin (2000) presented H.M. with pictures of famous politicians, musicians, and other celebrities who became known after 1960, H.M. spontaneously identified only two—John F. Kennedy, Jr., and Ronald Reagan (and in the case of Reagan, we cannot rule out that H.M. may have known about Reagan during his Hollywood days prior to 1960). However, when prompted with phonemic cues (either the person's initials, or first name and the initial of the last name), he fully named 18 of 36 (50%). He was also able to provide at least partial information about the person's profession or why they were famous, but he was deficient at remembering temporal information (such as the decade in which the person had been famous).

The collective data thus suggest that semantic and episodic knowledge are largely functionally and neurologically distinct (de Renzi et al., 1987; van der Linden et al., 2000). However, some evidence suggests an additional division may be made within autobiographical memory, which includes both personal episodes and personal semantic information. Some patients have been found to show more pronounced impairment of one than the other (Tulving, Schacter, McLachlan, & Moscovitch, 1988; van der Linden et al., 1996). For instance, van der Linden et al. (1996) examined a patient, A.C., who could remember personal semantic information (e.g., prior addresses where he had lived, names of teachers, where he was married) but not personal episodic incidents (e.g., a particular wedding he had attended, his first day of work at a new job). A.C.'s proficiency in recalling personal semantic information was matched by his ability to learn new semantic information of a less personal sort (e.g., identities of politicians and celebrities who had become famous after his brain damage had occurred). This provides partial support for Wilson and Baddeley's (1988) contention that semantic information can be built up out of repetitive episodic information; personal information to which one is more frequently exposed (e.g., the name of the teacher one had for a whole school year) may be stored and retrieved differently than single personal episodes.

EXPLICIT VERSUS IMPLICIT MEMORY

There is a further basis for distinguishing how memories are stored in and retrieved from LTS. Let us say you meet an amnesic patient and introduce yourself. You leave the room for 10 minutes, and then return only to find that the patient has forgotten your name or, indeed, ever having met you before. This is common with anterograde amnesics such as H.M. (Milner, Corkin, & Teuber, 1968). However, indirect tests often reveal that such patients have stored information about their experiences, although they cannot consciously retrieve it. The Swiss physician Édouarde Claparède (1873–1940) routinely saw a woman suffering from amnesia, who could remember nothing about Claparède from one visit to the next. One day Claparède hid a pin in his hand, so that when the patient reached out to shake his hand, she was slightly hurt. The next time Claparède saw the patient, she did not extend her hand, but could not explain why she refused to shake his hand. The woman did not have an *explicit* recollection of Claparède or the incident with the pin, although the painful experience with the pin appeared to have affected her behavior (Claparède, 1911/1951, described in LeDoux, 1996). One can say that her memory for the incident is implicit or *hidden*, in the sense that she cannot recall it consciously. A memory that can be consciously remembered is called an *explicit* memory.

There may also be a distinction between explicit remembering of the factual versus the episodic nature of the patient's memory for Claparède's pin: When Claparède asked the woman why she would not shake his hand, she responded that sometimes people have pins hidden in their hands. Thus, she may have been able to recall the semantic aspect of the experience, but not the details of the episode, including the information that Claparède himself had hidden the pin. (Another possibility is that she remembered the episode but was afraid to tell the doctor, because she would be accusing him of a misdeed.)

All the memory research we have discussed so far has examined explicit memories: people study material and then are tested for their memory. If a memory is implicit or hidden, however, even if a person's performance on explicit tests is poor, he or she may demonstrate retention for some aspects of the experience, if we test in the right way. Researchers' use of procedures designed to measure implicit memory can show that people are affected by information that they do not consciously (or explicitly) remember. Those tests are designed to demonstrate that previous exposure to a stimulus alters later perception, memory, decision making, or behavior.

Methods for Testing Implicit Memory

Word Stem Completion

After asking a person to learn a list of words, he is then provided two- or three-letter stems and asked to say the first word that pops into mind. Imagine that one of the words in the original list was *attach*, but an amnesic was not able to recall it. However, when presented with the word stem, AT-, the amnesic may say, "attach," indicating that he retained information about the word (Graf, Squire, & Mandler, 1984). Given that there are many other words that begin with AT—*attack*, *atlas*, *attic*, *atom*—and that many of those alternatives are more frequent than *attach*, it is reasonable to conclude that the amnesic did remember the word *attach* from the original memory list (but could not retrieve the word explicitly).

Priming

One other type of implicit memory is *priming* (Gold & Squire, 2006; Hamann, Squire, & Schacter, 1995; Schacter, Church, & Treadwell, 1994), in which presentation of a stimulus (e.g., the word *table*) primes people—or makes them ready—to respond to it at a later time. That is, people respond faster to a word when it is re-presented (in the same way that reading over your class notes right before an exam may prime you to retrieve the correct answers on the exam itself). Priming also occurs for words related semantically to the priming word. That is, reading *table* primes you (or makes it easier) to read *chair*.

Classical Conditioning

Classical conditioning is another form of implicit memory. This was illustrated by Claparède's patient, who implicitly learned to associate shaking hands with Dr. Claparède with the pain from a pinprick (and thus avoided shaking his hand). An innocuous way to bring about classical conditioning is to have a tone precede a puff of air to the eyes. At first people (and animals) blink just from the puff of air; over time they learn the association with the tone and blink to the tone alone. Some, but not all, amnesic patients show classical conditioning of an eye-blink response (Corkin, 2002; Daum & Ackerman, 1994; Gabrieli, Fleischman, Keane, Reminger, & Morrell, 1995; Woodruff-Pak, 1993). This may be because some forms of conditioning require a functioning hippocampal system (Clark, Manns, & Squire, 2002).

Differences Between Explicit and Implicit Memory

A provocative set of findings showing the distinction between explicit and implicit memory was presented by Graf, Squire, and Mandler (1984, Experiments 1–3; also Graf and Schacter, 1985). A group of amnesic patients, consisting of Korsakoff's patients and patients undergoing electro-convulsive therapy (ECT), as well as non-amnesic control subjects (alcoholics and psychiatric in-patients), underwent a series of explicit and implicit memory tasks. In each task, participants were presented with a list of words and then tested on their memory for the words under free-recall, recognition, or word-completion conditions. On the free-recall test (Experiment 1), the amnesics recalled significantly fewer words than did the controls, as seen in Figure 2.22. Experiment 2 used a recognition task to see if merely having to detect the correct answer out of several options would improve the amnesics' explicit memory performance. Each word from the list (e.g., MARKET) was paired with two physically similar distractor words (e.g., MARY, MARBLE), and the participants were asked to choose which one had been on the learning list. On this explicit memory task the amnesics also performed better than chance level, but had poorer memory than the control subjects. This indicates that the amnesic patients were able to learn and remember some of the study words, but had trouble accessing them in the free-recall test. This is a common memory problem, as we will see in Chapters 3 and 4.

Graf et al. (1984, Experiment 3) then administered an implicit memory test: Subjects were presented with three-letter word stems, and asked to respond to each stem with *the first word that came to mind*. The experimenters did not mention that the stems could be completed with list words. The normal controls and the amnesic participants produced words from the original list as responses to the word stems at the same rate, and at a higher level than a control group who had not seen the words on the original

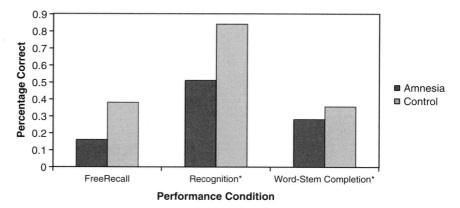

Figure 2.22   Graf, Squire, and Mandler (1984) results: Free recall data from Experiment 1; recognition data and word-stem completion data from Experiment 2. Performance of amnesic individuals is worse than that of controls on explicit tasks (free recall and recognition), but is not worse on the implicit task (word-stem completion).

*Chance performance on the recognition task was 50%. Both the recognition and word-stem completion data are taken from the immediate test in Experiment 2.

list. Thus, the amnesics had encoded and stored information about the word lists in memory, but this information was mainly accessible through implicit tests.

Gabrieli et al. (1995) studied a man, M.S., who provides the second half of a double dissociation between explicit and implicit memory. After surgery to relieve epilepsy, which severed part of his visual cortex in the occipital lobe, M.S. showed normal explicit memory, but was impaired at word priming. Thus, the systems that serve explicit and implicit memory processes are functionally and neurologically distinct, and neuroimaging data has confirmed this dissociation in normal patients without brain damage (see Knowlton & Forde, 2008, for a review of the research).

Amnesia and Models of Memory: Summary

Amnesic patients have been a rich source of information for testing Tulving's (1983) hypothesis that nondeclarative and declarative memories are functionally and anatomically distinct, and also that semantic and episodic memories may constitute largely separate memory systems. Double dissociations among neuropsychological patients for semantic and episodic memory, and for explicit and implicit memory processes, confirm the functional independence of different memory systems (consistent with the concept of modularity).

CONCLUSION: LONG-TERM MEMORY SYSTEMS

Cases of amnesia have provided much of the foundation for exploring distinctions between declarative and procedural (nondeclarative) memories, and for assessing Tulving's (1983, 2002) division of declarative memory into semantic and episodic memories.

Amnesic patients are often able to learn new skills without the accompanying knowledge of when and where they learned them. Nondeclarative memories, such as procedural knowledge, utilize lower-level brain areas, such as the cerebellum and basal ganglia. We have all experienced differential recall for facts versus personal episodes of our lives. Even within our autobiographical past, we can remember personal facts ("I am a student") without vividly remembering the details of personal episodes (the first day of college). Although there may be some merit to Wilson and Baddeley's (1988) contention that semantic facts are often better remembered because of repetition, whereas episodes in our lives only happen once, double dissociations between amnesic patients with episodic versus semantic amnesia support Tulving's claims for the relative independence of the two sub-types of declarative memory. Even "normal" (i.e., nonamnesic) people show some source amnesia—the ability to remember facts or new information, without being able to remember when and where they learned the facts. Neuropsychological evidence also suggests that episodic and semantic memories are encoded and retrieved using some of the same brain structures, such as the hippocampus. However, episodic memories are more dependent on the prefrontal cortex, and semantic knowledge appears to be more heavily distributed throughout the brain.

We have now examined the structural components of memory. In Chapter 3, we turn to a discussion of how information gets encoded into, and retrieved from, our long-term memory. Before completing your reading of this chapter, however, it will be useful for you to work through the review questions in the next section.

REVIEW QUESTIONS

Here is a set of review questions to help you organize and remember the material in this chapter. To maximize your retention of the material, try to answer each question from memory before reviewing the section of the chapter in which the material is covered. That attempt at recall, even if the recall is not correct, will increase your memory for the material after you review it.

1. What are two general functions of memory?

2. What were the components of S.F.'s remarkable memory ability?

3. What are the functions of the sensory stores in the multi-store model? How is information stored in the sensory stores?

4. How does capacity of STS vary, depending on the type of material being studied?

5. What factor(s) are important in bringing about forgetting from STS?

6. What changes have occurred in psychologists' beliefs about how information is coded in STS?

7. What kinds of processing play a role in storing information in LTS?

8. How is the serial position curve (e.g., primacy effect, recency effect, etc.) explained by the multi-store model of memory?

9. How does the capacity to store information in LTS develop during childhood?

10. What are differences between the concepts of STS and WM?

11. What are the components of WM? Why are some components called slave systems?

12. What major brain components seem to be important in the various components of WM?

13. What are the basic functional components of long-term memory?

14. What are two views concerning the relationship between episodic and semantic knowledge?

15. How do amnesic syndromes support the distinction between declarative and non-declarative knowledge?

16. How do amnesic syndromes support the distinction between explicit versus implicit memories?

17. What brain areas are associated with semantic versus episodic memory?

CHAPTER 3

MEMORY II: ENCODING AND RETRIEVAL

In Chapter 2, we examined models of memory, focusing on short-term storage (in the short-term store or working memory), and on the ways in which long-term store might be organized into procedural, semantic, and episodic memories. That discussion emphasized the overall structure or organization of memory, whereas this chapter emphasizes the *processes* involved in memory: How does information get into the system to begin with? How do we find it when we need it? This chapter examines encoding and retrieval—the processes underlying how information is put into memory and its later access, respectively. We are already familiar with those processes from the discussion earlier of the development of S.F.'s memory. We will now consider broader aspects of encoding and retrieval. As we have done so far, we will take a historical perspective in this chapter, so we will be able to see why modern-day cognitive psychologists are interested in certain issues.

OUTLINE OF CHAPTER 3

This chapter begins with an examination of two ways psychologists have thought about memory, from the pioneering work of Ebbinghaus (1885/1964) and the study of *rote learning*, to more modern views, based on the work of Bartlett (1932), that emphasize the active or top-down storage of information. We then turn to encoding and retrieval processes, their interdependence, and how each is influenced by top-down processing. Finally, we further examine the phenomenon of metamemory, already mentioned in Chapter 2 in the discussion of control processes in the multi-store model. People can make accurate judgments as to how well they will be able to remember various types of information; one consequence is that we realize that optimum memory performance often requires using strategies—referred to as *mnemonic devices*—to remember new information. We will discuss the usefulness of mnemonic devices in remembering.

TWO CONCEPTIONS OF MEMORY PROCESSES: BOTTOM-UP VERSUS TOP-DOWN

During the 20th century, as psychology developed and changed from behaviorist to cognitive in orientation, there was a shift in the way psychologists thought about memory. When researchers in the behaviorist tradition discussed memory, they were careful to avoid any explanations that might incorporate consciousness or related phenomena, taking what could be called a *passive* or *bottom-up* view of memory. As noted in Chapter 1, much research on memory in the first half of the 20th century developed out of the pioneering work of Ebbinghaus (1885/1964). Ebbinghaus's method centered on rote repetition of the material to be remembered, which fit very well with most psychologists' desires to move away from the study of consciousness. It was assumed that information is encoded into memory through repetition. One does nothing strategic to store the information; it is simply stamped in after multiple exposures, much like the lyrics to a song on the radio that is played over and over again.

Bottom-up processing is also referred to as *data-driven*, because the incoming information (or data) proceeds through the system in a relatively automatic fashion and drives the process. Related to a data-driven theory of memory is a specific conception of the *memory trace* (James, 1890/1950, Ch. 11; Martin & Deutscher, 1966)—the record left behind in memory—which we have discussed in Chapter 2. Following from the notion of bottom-up processing is the idea that the memory trace is an exact copy of information as it is taken in by the cognitive system (though perhaps condensed). The system does nothing to the information; it just records it. Upon retrieval, the same information is reactivated, in the exact form in which it was stored. Theoretically, this suggests that memories should remain relatively accurate. They should also be discrete or separate from each other—a memory for an event might fade or become less accessible over time, but separate memories should remain discrete, and not be easily combined.

Many cognitive scientists, as we already know, place more emphasis on the active, or top-down, role of the person in remembering. A classic example of studying memory as an active process was Ericsson, Chase, and Faloon's (1980) analysis of S.F.'s performance. The experimenters' focus was on S.F.'s role in processing the material so that he would be able to remember it later. S.F. deliberately chunked numbers into units that would be meaningful to him (e.g., "my best mile time"). In this perspective, people are assumed to *construct* their memories, aided by the use of memory strategies and knowledge. The top-down view was influenced by Bartlett's (1932) writings concerning the role of the person's knowledge in processing and remembering events. In this constructivist view, the person's thought processes and knowledge play a crucial role both in storing and retrieving information. We begin our discussion of memory processes by tracing the historical development of this changing conception of memory, from bottom-up to top-down.

REMEMBERING AS A BOTTOM–UP PROCESS: EBBINGHAUS'S STUDY OF ROTE REHEARSAL AND MEMORY

The Stream of Consciousness

We experience a succession of thoughts, which follow one another in regular patterns. Thoughts of home are followed by thoughts of one's parents, or of childhood friends; thoughts of school are followed by thoughts of tests to be prepared for. This sequence of thoughts makes up the stream of consciousness. Ebbinghaus (1885/1964) began his investigation of memory because he was trying to understand how our stream of consciousness is constructed. One explanation for the connections among thoughts was based on the notion that the connections among our ideas mirror the structure of events in the external world. Aristotle (384–322 B.C.), for example, believed that one reason that ideas followed each other in thought was because the events corresponding to those ideas had followed each other in our experience. If a police siren becomes associated with a traffic ticket, you may think *ticket* and feel nervous each time you hear a police siren (and perhaps even a fire engine siren). This notion, that *contiguity* of events in the world (being close together in space and time) results in ideas being linked or associated in the mind, became central to discussions of memory in philosophy and psychology. The emphasis on contiguity as the basis for association among ideas was carried into more modern times by the associationistic philosophers, most especially the British empiricists, such as Locke (1690) and the elder and younger Mills (John Mill, 1829; and John Stuart Mill, 1843).

The formation of associations did not receive its first systematic experimental analysis until Ebbinghaus's (1885/1964) research. Ebbinghaus was interested in studying how the mind acquires a chain of *new* associations, which required that he have available sequences of units with no associations among them. He therefore invented stimuli without associations, meaningless *c*onsonant-*v*owel-*c*onsonant strings (called CVCs), such as BEV, REZ, and ZOR, that he could memorize, free from the influences of experience. CVCs are also sometimes called *trigrams* (which means *three letters*), or *nonsense syllables*. Ebbinghaus studied lists of CVCs using *rote rehearsal*: He read the items aloud, without thinking more deeply about them. He paced his reading to the ticking of a watch, to further limit his study of the items to simple repetition, and to control the time and number of rehearsals per trigram. Ebbinghaus constructed lists of up to 36 randomly selected CVCs to learn, and measured the time he needed until he could repeat the items in the order in which they were studied. You can get a feeling for Ebbinghaus's method by carrying out the demonstration in Box 3.1.

BOX 3.1 ROTE REPETITION DEMONSTRATION

Recite each of the following trigrams (aloud, if possible) until you can remember the list perfectly. Time yourself on how long it takes, or count how many repetitions of the list are necessary before you attain perfect performance:

ROP

YIM

SEK

LUF

DAJ

If you followed the instructions in Box 3.1, and only processed the trigrams by simply repeating them several times, without attempting to take advantage of any meaning they might possess, then you engaged in truly rote rehearsal. This should make clear what is meant by a bottom-up process.

Studies of Incidental Rote Rehearsal

Although Ebbinghaus (1885/1964) consciously tried to carry out only rote rehearsal, he realized that he was not a fully objective subject, since he had designed the experiment and the materials, and had formulated the hypotheses. Researchers who followed Ebbinghaus tried to test naïve participants—people not familiar with theories of memory, and who had not designed the stimulus materials. Several studies tried further to ensure that participants were carrying out rote rehearsal by using what is called an *incidental encoding* design (e.g., Hasher, Zacks, Rose, & Sanft, 1987; Hyde & Jenkins, 1969, 1973). Please carry out the demonstration in Box 3.2 before continuing.

BOX 3.2 INCIDENTAL ENCODING DEMONSTRATION

Below is a list of words. Each word is followed by an instruction. If the instruction is *pronounce*, please repeat the word five times quickly, and then rate how easy it is to pronounce it (1 = easy, 5 = hard). Write your rating in the space. If the instruction is *pleasant*, please rate the pleasantness of the word (1 = unpleasant, 5 = pleasant) and write your rating in the space after the word.

Word	Instruction	Rating
Map	pleasant	
Tribe	pronounce	
Defense	pleasant	
Sailor	pronounce	
Teeth	pronounce	
Bread	pronounce	
Minister	pleasant	
Passenger	pleasant	
Pupil	pronounce	
Giant	pleasant	

Now that you have finished rating the words, **without looking back at the list**, take a piece of paper and a pencil and write all the words that you can remember from the list.

Incidental Versus Intentional Encoding

Information can be encoded in at least two ways. First is through conscious rehearsal or study, as when S.F. coded a string of digits as a running time, or when you prepare for an exam by studying the assigned material. This is *intentional encoding*, because the person knows his or her memory will be tested, and intentionally tries to remember the material. Encoding of information can also occur without conscious intent to remember, however. You may witness a dramatic automobile accident and later be able to recount it to someone else without trying to remember it. This type of encoding is *incidental encoding*: Any storage comes about incidentally, as an unintended result of the processing of the experience.

In experimental studies of incidental encoding, participants who are not expecting a memory test are instructed to process material in various ways, presumably for some other purpose (e.g., under the guise of helping the experimenter choose words for another experiment). Participants might be asked to rate words on how pleasant they are, or how easy they are to pronounce, as in Box 3.2. These processing tasks are called *orienting tasks*, because the participant orients to the material in a particular way, which presumably controls the encoding operations. The participants are then given a surprise memory test, and one can compare different orienting tasks on their effectiveness in encoding information. If you are like most experimental participants, you recalled more of the words in Box 3.2 rated for pleasantness than those encoded through simple repetition.

Memory After Incidental Rote Rehearsal

Glenberg, Smith, and Green (1977) carried out a study examining incidental memory for words after rote repetition. On each trial, a *four-digit number* was presented for later recall, and then participants had to repeat *words* for 2, 6, or 18 seconds before recalling the number. The number of repetitions of each word was controlled by asking people to repeat the word every time a tone sounded, so that each word was repeated 3 to 27 times during the retention intervals. This design resulted in nine times more repetitions for the words in the 18- versus 2-second conditions. Participants were told that they should only try and remember the numbers; they were told that the purpose of repeating the words was to stop them from rehearsing the numbers. Thus, the participants thought that repeating the words served as a *distractor task*, since it presumably served to distract them from rehearsing the to-be-recalled number. Only people's memory for the numbers was tested in the initial part of the experiment.

After working through 63 trials of recalling numbers, the participants were then surprised with a request to recall the distractor words from all the trials. Recall was poor in all cases (around 10%), and the number of repetitions each word had received did not affect recall performance (Glenberg et al., 1977). However, in a second experiment, participants were given a recognition test, where 60 words from the experiment and 60 new words were presented, and they merely had to recognize which words had been distractor words in the first part of the experiment. Now, the more repetitions that a word had received, the more likely it was to be recognized. Thus, rote repetition helped people *recognize* words to which they had been exposed, although it had not helped them *recall* those words.

However, there are limits on the role that bottom-up processes play in memory. Logan and Etherton (1994, Experiment 1) examined incidental memory for pairs of words. Participants were asked to determine whether at least one of the words was a member of a category, say, *metals*. For example, if *Canada/Steel* was the pair, people in the metals condition should respond "Yes." The nontarget word (*Canada*) was always an unrelated word that could be ignored once the target was identified. Half of the target words were always paired with the same nontarget in the first 64 trials (e.g., in those *consistent* pairs, *Steel* always occurred with *Canada*); the remaining target words had varied pairings. The question of interest was whether the participants would remember the association of the words in the consistent pairs. That is, even though there was no reason to learn the consistent pairs, might that occur anyway, just because of the repeated pairings?

If both words per pair were always presented in the same color ink, so that the participants had to read both words in order to determine the presence of the target, then response times got faster over repeated trials. Participants also had slightly better memory for the words in the consistent pairs (Experiment 1). It thus seems that the people had learned something about the pairs. However, in subsequent experiments (e.g., Experiment 3), if the target word in each pair always appeared in a specific ink color (e.g., green) so that people only had to attend to the green words, participants did not learn the pairings, even when they were exposed to the consistent pairs 17 times over five sessions of the experiment (Experiment 3). When the participants could distinguish the target words by color, and thus did not have to attend at all to the nontarget words, they did not learn anything about the pairs. In conclusion, simple exposure resulted in some memory for information, but the best memory occurred only after multiple repetitions, and, not surprisingly, only if the participants paid some attention to both stimuli (Experiment 1).

Automatic Encoding of Information Into Memory

Research just reviewed indicates that some information can be encoded as the result of bottom-up processing, although that information is not very rich. In contrast, a series of studies by Hasher and Zacks (1979, 1984) demonstrated that detailed information about an event can sometimes be encoded in a bottom-up manner. Imagine that you ask your mother if you can borrow that great mystery novel she raved about last summer. You ask, "What was the name of that novel?" She responds, "I don't remember, but it's on the top shelf of the bookshelf, to the left." How could she not remember the name of the book (which seems more meaningful to recall), but know its location? Hasher and Zacks proposed that some kinds of information—such as the spatial location of an item—are processed without intention, in a bottom-up manner. In Hasher and Zacks's view, we all are endowed with the ability to encode *spatial* information, *frequency* information (how often something occurs), and *temporal* information (the order in time in which events occur).

As one demonstration of this sort of encoding capacity, Hasher and Zacks (1979) presented students with a long list of words, with each word occurring one, two, three, or four times. The repetitions of a given word were randomly interspersed throughout the list. Half the subjects (the informed group) knew that they would be tested on their memory for the *frequency* with which the words had occurred. The uninformed group was only told that their memory would be tested (not specifically about the frequency test), and so it is likely that they engaged in only incidental encoding of frequency information. Nonetheless, when asked to report the number of times each word had been presented, the uninformed participants—although they were surprised about the frequency-recall test, and in some cases complained that it was unfair since they had not been warned about it—performed as well as the informed participants.

In support of automatic processing of spatial information, Zechmeister and McKillip (1971) found that people asked to memorize a paragraph could subsequently remember *where* on a page a sentence had occurred (even though they had no reason to think that spatial location would be tested). However, as in the Logan and Etherton (1994) study discussed in the last section, Naveh-Benjamin (1988) reported that processing of spatial information is further facilitated by paying attention to the location of objects in an array.

BOTTOM-UP PROCESSING AND MEMORY: CONCLUSIONS

Rote repetition can result in some information being retained, although it is not a particularly effective method of encoding information into memory. Bottom-up encoding is limited to certain kinds of information (such as spatial or frequency information), but will not apply to the vast majority of material that is important for us to remember. We now consider top-down encoding processes, and we will see that when individuals are able to apply their knowledge to information that they are trying to remember, the results are very different than when they use rote rehearsal.

REMEMBERING AS A TOP-DOWN PROCESS: THE BARTLETT TRADITION

Recall S.F.'s remarkable memory span, introduced in Chapter 2, which was based on his ability to organize incoming digits in accordance with his knowledge of history and running times. That is an excellent example of memory as a top-down process. Bartlett (e.g., 1932) was one of the first researchers to advocate the importance of knowledge to cognition. In Bartlett's view, as introduced in Chapter 1, the crucial aspect of human cognition was the use of knowledge to first interpret and then remember one's experiences. From this perspective, restricting a person's ability to meaningfully process information made the results uninteresting, so Bartlett rejected Ebbinghaus's use of CVCs, and used narratives in his research. An important pioneering experiment of Bartlett (1932) is presented in Box 3.3. Please carry out that demonstration before reading further.

Knowledge and Reconstruction in Memory

Bartlett (1932) proposed that knowledge, which he called *schemata* (the plural of *schema*), played a role both in the encoding of events and in our remembering them. The first step involved the interpretation of the event, which he called an *effort after meaning*. The individual attempts to make sense out of what is occurring, by relating the event to what he or she knows. This could be called *constructing* the event, since the meaning is not given in the event itself, but arises from the person's interpretation of it. The belief that our knowledge heavily influences what we remember is the opposite of the idea that the memory trace is an exact copy of an event or piece of information. A top-down perspective argues that knowledge affects the information that is stored during encoding. The presented material interacts with what we already know, and what is stored is a combination of the two. At retrieval, the situation is reversed, as the person uses aspects of the original stimulus as well as his or her knowledge to *reconstruct* the event. (Since the initial processing and encoding of the event is a *construction*, then remembering the event is a *re*construction.) Thus, according to Bartlett, retrieval is not a case of activating the original memory verbatim, but of activating multiple sources—information from the original experience plus background (schema) information—and then imposing an interpretation on that material that is consistent with our existing knowledge structures.

BOX 3.3 BARTLETT'S (1932) *WAR OF THE GHOSTS*

One night two young men from Egulac went down to the river to hunt seals, and while they were there it became foggy and calm. Then they heard war cries, and they thought, "Maybe this is a war party." They escaped to the shore, and hid behind a log. Now canoes came up, and they heard the noise of paddles, and saw one canoe coming up to them. There were five men in the canoe, and they said, "What do you think? We wish to take you along. We are going up the river to make war on the people."

One of the young men said, "I have no arrows." "Arrows are in the canoe," they said. "I will not go along. I might be killed. My relatives do not know where I have gone. But you," he said, turning to the other, "may go with them." So one of the young men went, but the other returned home.

And the warriors went up the river to a town on the other side of Kalama. The people came down to the water, and they began to fight, and many were killed. But presently the young man heard one of the warriors say, "Quick, let us go home: That Indian has been hit." Now he thought, "Oh, they are ghosts." He did not feel sick, but they said he had been shot.

So the canoes went back to Egulac and the young man went ashore to his house, and made a fire. And he told everybody and said, "Behold I accompanied the ghosts, and we went to fight. Many of our fellows were killed, and many of those who attacked us were killed. They said I was hit, and I did not feel sick."

He told it all, and then he became quiet. When the sun rose he fell down. Something black came out of his mouth. His face became contorted. The people jumped up and cried.

He was dead.

Now try to recall as many ideas from the story as you can.

"The War of the Ghosts," presented in Box 3.3, is a folktale adapted by Bartlett for research in memory. The passage was interesting to him because it does not make complete sense to an educated Western reader: The incidents do not follow in a logical manner, and the descriptions of several events are not clear. Bartlett was drawn to somewhat unusual materials, which did not easily match his subjects' knowledge. He proposed that people use schemata to fill in any gaps in their understanding and memory for an event or narrative. In such a case, constructing the event initially and reconstructing it at recall will result in distortions. The individual will fill gaps with information not in the event, to help the material make more sense. Bartlett (1932) did, indeed, find inaccuracies in people's memory for the *War of the Ghosts*. Several major types of distortions occurred. First, participants *rationalized* the hard-to-understand parts of the story, to make them more comprehensible. For example, it is not clear in the story how one of the two young men is in a position to tell the other that he may go to fight, since nothing explicit is said about their relationship. This often led to *sharpening errors*—the tendency to elaborate some details. Some of the participants "recalled" that the two young men were brothers, which would allow one (the older brother) to give permission to the other one to go and fight. Similar distortions occurred concerning the ending of the story, where the "something black" coming out of the young man's mouth was recalled as being blood (Bartlett, 1932). Another common error Bartlett termed *flattening errors*—inability to remember unfamiliar details of the story, especially if they did not fit with the schema that the person had imposed on the story.

Bartlett found increasing rationalization and memory distortion with subsequent retestings of people's memory for *The War of the Ghosts*. This effect has been confirmed by Bergman and Roediger (1999). Schema effects have also been found for memory in other domains. Castel, McCabe, Roediger, and Heitman (2007) asked undergraduates with a deep interest in American football to memorize a list of animal names which happened to correspond to the names of professional football teams (e.g., *lions*, *broncos*, *dolphins*, etc.). Those interested in football were more likely both to remember more animal names, and to incorrectly "remember" names of animals that corresponded to football teams but had not appeared on the list (e.g., *eagles*, *panthers*). Football fans' knowledge of team names—their "professional football teams" schema—influenced both the ability to remember the word list and the tendency toward *intrusions* of similar words not on the list.

Many studies have found that imposing a schematic-based organization on material facilitates memory (e.g., Yussen, Mathews, Huang, & Evans, 1988); that schema-consistent details of material are better retained than schema-inconsistent details (e.g., Ainsworth & Baumann, 1995; Bower, Black, & Turner, 1979; Bransford & Johnson, 1972, 1973); and that when individuals produce memory distortions, they will do so in schema-consistent ways (e.g., Frawley, 2008). There is thus ample evidence to support a schematic view of memory (see Brewer, 2000b, and Ost & Costall, 2002, for reviews of Bartlett's position).

Schematization of Visual Memory

Intraub and her colleagues have demonstrated that people often schematize visual objects and scenes that they have been asked to remember. Intraub and Richardson (1989; Experiment 1) presented people with photos of objects (e.g., a lamp, a bicycle, a slice of pizza) in which at least one or two edges of the objects had been cropped, resulting in close-up versions of each picture. Participants were then given the name of an object and asked to draw its picture. Ninety-five percent of the drawings included details that had not been in the original photo, but would probably have been present had the edges not been cropped (e.g., the pointed tip of a pizza slice, that had not been visible in the original). Once again, evidence suggests that people often "forget" specific details of to-be-remembered visual information, and commit errors by filling in details about cropped objects based on their knowledge. Schematic effects in picture memory, such as "remembering" cropped parts of close-up objects, are found in children as young as 6–7 years of age (Seamon, Schlegel, Hiester, Landau, & Blumenthal, 2002; see also Pezdek et al., 1988).

Scripts as Further Evidence for Schematization of Memory

One specific type of schema, which contains information about routine events, is known as a *script* (Schank & Abelson, 1977). Scripts are organized knowledge structures about typical actions, and the order of such actions. For example, if you awake with a very sore throat and fever, you will use your script for a doctor's visit to organize your day. You know that patients must first call for an appointment, then go to the doctor's office, check in at reception, and then wait for a nurse to call you to an examining room, and so forth. Other examples of scripts might involve eating at a fast-food restaurant and going to the movies.

Bower, Black, and Turner (1979) had participants read several paragraphs recounting people carrying out "scripted" activities (e.g., a patient going to the doctor, going swimming, shopping for a coat), and then tested their memories for the details of each paragraph. The components of the scripts were carried out either in standard order (as in the visit to the doctor's office presented above), or in a nonstandard order (e.g., the doctor sees you before anyone else does). Participants recalled about 50% of scripted actions presented in standard order, but only 18% in nonstandard order. Furthermore, participants often filled in missing script details; when the doctor's office paragraph omitted mention of the patient having his temperature taken, subjects often "remembered" that step. This last result is consistent with Bartlett's (1932) finding that people use schematic knowledge to fill in or alter details of events.

Brain Processes in Script Memory

The correct order of actions within a script is important information; one would not want to tip a waiter, for example, before a meal had even been ordered. Zanini (2008) asked patients with frontal lobe damage and normal controls to describe the steps involved in scripted actions, such as going to the cinema or catching a train at the train station. The frontal-lobe patients remembered as many of the actions in each script as did normal subjects, but were significantly impaired at recalling the correct sequence of steps. Thus, script information can be intact, but the frontal lobes are responsible for the planning or sequential nature of scripts.

Remembering Details

The studies just reviewed provide evidence for Bartlett's assumption that memory for an experience becomes generalized and often loses specific details, and that we construct events and reconstruct memories as incoming information gets blended together with schematic knowledge. It thus becomes difficult to tell where a given part of a memory comes from. This does not, however, mean that all details are lost from memory (for review, see Alba & Hasher, 1983). Bartlett (1923, 1932) acknowledged that memory could entail both *innovation*, in the sense of constructing a memory that best makes sense to us in light of our experiences, and *conservation* of details.

Hintzman, Block, and Inskeep (1972), for example, found that participants in a memory experiment remembered whether words that had been visually presented had appeared in upper- or lowercase letters, and whether spoken words had been said by a male or a female voice. Other studies using realistic materials have also supported the finding that details of an event are often encoded and available for recall. In one set of studies (Bates, Kintsch, Fletcher, & Giuliani, 1980; Bates, Masling, & Kintsch, 1978) college students were unexpectedly tested for recognition for dialogue from a soap opera they had watched. The students recognized such changes as substituting proper nouns for pronouns, or roles (e.g., "doctor") for proper names, which suggests that they maintained memory for specific details of dialogue that one might expect would be lost after the meaning is processed. Vogt and Magnussen (2007b) found that people remembered seemingly insignificant details of pictures for over a week.

Thus, Bartlett seems to have been correct in his belief that people search after meaning and that their interpretation of an event influences greatly how well they will be able to remember it. However, we should keep in mind that people can also store much detail about their experiences, even as they interpret them in a top-down manner.

CONSTRUCTION IN MEMORY: CONCLUSIONS

Research has revealed that memory is subject to top-down processes, but sometimes can be both accurate and detailed. A number of researchers have proposed that the information encoded in response to some message depends on the specific goals that the person has in relation to the text (Alba & Hasher, 1983; Murphy & Shapiro, 1994). Sometimes it may be important to attend to the precise wording of the message. If you ask someone to do something for you, it becomes very important to know if he said, "I might be able do it" or "I will be able to do it." In such a case, one may remember exactly what was said. At another time, one might simply be acquiring some general information about some event, such as the day of an exam, in which case it is not necessary to remember the precise words, and one probably will not. Murphy and Shapiro call this a *pragmatic* view of memory, which means that whatever processing is carried out depends on what information is needed.

Expertise and Memory

Additional evidence for the importance of top-down processing in memory comes from studies of the memory performance of experts in their area of expertise. There is much informal evidence that experts can have prodigious memories. For example, expert bridge players can recount games in detail, long after they have been played. A pioneering study of the role of expertise in memory was conducted by de Groot (1965/1978), who examined chess masters' memory performance as part of a study of chess-playing ability. De Groot presented chess masters with a chessboard with 25–30 pieces set up in a position taken from the middle of a master-level game. The board was presented for only 5 seconds, then covered, and the participant was given an empty board and a set of chess pieces. The task was to put the pieces on the board as they had been in the original stimulus. The masters could replace almost all the pieces correctly after the 5-second exposure, whereas chess novices replaced only about 40% of the pieces correctly.

This excellent memory performance was not due to the chess masters simply having extraordinary memory abilities in general. When chess masters and experts viewed 25–30 pieces *randomly* placed on the board, their memory performance was no better than that of beginning chess players—both remembered only around four pieces (Chase & Simon, 1973). Thus, the masters' excellent performance in the real-chess game trials was due to their knowledge of chess. Masters study chess manuals and play games for thousands of hours, and this knowledge is used to analyze any chess game that they are exposed to, as well as to remember what they have seen.

Chase and Simon (1973) also recorded eye movements of chess players during the learning or encoding part of the experiment, to determine how the masters processed the chessboards that they were studying. The knowledgeable participants scanned groups of pieces that made sense in the context of the game (an example of Bartlett's [1932] effort after meaning), while people ignorant of chess simply looked at pieces that were close together, or that were of the same type, such as pawns. At recall, the experts tended to replace groups of pieces as a unit, one after the other (with pauses in between groups of pieces). This indicated that the same organizing principles were being used to scan the board (to encode the position) and to retrieve the memory of chess piece formation.

Expertise effects on memory and other processes have been found in many domains. Halpern and Wai (2007) compared Scrabble experts (people who play in competitions and are in the middle to top Scrabble division rankings) to novices on a number of skills that might be enhanced by playing Scrabble. Although Scrabble players reported that, when they study words for Scrabble, they do not pay attention to their meaning, experts nonetheless had higher vocabulary scores than novices. That result might be due to incidental encoding of meaning, if the experts were accurate in reporting that they did not try to learn meanings but merely studied the spelling of words. Experts also were faster in responding in a *lexical-decision task* (Experiment 2), where they had to identify whether strings of letters presented on a computer screen were words or not (*lexical* means "word"). Optimizing one's game points on a Scrabble board also requires visuo-spatial skills, as expert players must often plan their next moves while their opponent is playing (and thus they are seeing the board upside down). Expert Scrabble players had higher scores on a shape-memory test and were faster on a paper-folding test (Experiment 2). Thus, specific components of experts' skill facilitate their memory for information related to their domain of expertise, and make them faster at cognitive processing.

In the domain of music, Kalakoski (2007) found that expert musicians were better at recalling note sequences that had been presented visually. Visual artists have also been found to remember more details in pictures than artistically untrained novices (Vogt and Magnussen, 2007a). At least some of the explanation for that result is due to enhanced encoding by the artists, as they fixated on more details of the pictures (but also spent less time processing each detail in order to remember the information, perhaps because their expertise facilitated encoding).

Expertise and Memory: Summary

Research has supported the notion that memory is greatly enhanced if a person has expertise in the area that is being tested. The expert is able during encoding to apply knowledge to the information that helps to organize it and which facilitates its later retrieval. It should be noted that one does not have to have an exceptionally high level of expertise in order to use it to assist memory. We all have hobbies or interests that make us "experts" in those areas. If tested on new information within such a domain, we will perform like de Groot's (1965) chess experts. For example, Voss, Vesonder, and Spilich (1980) determined that people with a deep interest in baseball remembered more details from a description of a baseball game. Thus, memory is very much influenced by our expertise, with information from domains that we know and understand well remembered better than that from unfamiliar domains.

BOTTOM-UP AND TOP-DOWN PROCESSING: COORDINATED, NOT MUTUALLY EXCLUSIVE

Analysis of S.F.'s remarkable memory skills in Chapter 2, coupled with research summarized so far in this chapter, including research on expertise in memory, provides support for Bartlett's (1932) emphasis on the role of top-down processing in memory. Bartlett's position contrasts with the bottom-up orientation taken by Ebbinghaus, who concentrated on the initial acquisition of *new* associations, which were not meaningful and could not be linked to any knowledge. Although we have contrasted these two ways of analyzing memory, it must be emphasized that the bottom-up versus top-down views of memory are not mutually exclusive. Whether a processing strategy counts as bottom-up or top-down is best characterized along a continuum, rather than on strict either/or criteria. The continuum reflects the influence of a person's knowledge on the processing of new material. When a person does not have knowledge within a domain (such as chess or Scrabble), new information must be acquired in bottom-up fashion. As the person's knowledge base in that area becomes more complex and organized, top-down processing can occur. Thus, rather than talking about top-down *versus* bottom-up encoding, we should talk about the interactive role of both types of processing in memory. This view is summarized in Table 3.1.

BETTER VERSUS WORSE TYPES OF ENCODING?

Levels of Processing

The type of encoding in which a person engages—whether top-down, knowledge-based encoding or bottom-up rote rehearsal—can result in large differences in memory performance. These sorts of results might cause one to raise a question: Are there better or worse ways to encode information? Imagine a friend says to you: "You are studying memory in cognitive psychology, right? I have a biology quiz next week, what is the best

Table 3.1 Summary of Differences Between Top-Down and Bottom-Up Processing in Memory

Phenomenon to Be Explained	Bottom-Up View	Top-Down View
Rehearsal (How is information put into memory?)	Rote repetition	Encoding based on meaning— thinking in response to event
Associations (How are connections established among ideas?)	Contiguity of events in the world leads to association of ideas corresponding to events	Can also be based on construction by the thinker—links between ideas can be constructed by thinker
Memory trace (What is in memory?)	Idea corresponding to external event	Information corresponding to external event plus information from cognitive activities in response to event
Recall (How is information remembered?)	Stimulus activates relevant idea through association	Encoding is retrieved, based on combination of retrieval cues and encoded information. Memory report is then made, based on these two types of information

way to prepare?" This question has been studied extensively by cognitive psychologists, and the results may be somewhat surprising. Please carry out the demonstration in Box 3.4 before going further.

BOX 3.4 LEVELS OF PROCESSING DEMONSTRATION

Each word below is followed by one of three instructions. *Syllables* means you are to estimate, without counting, the number of syllables in the word. Write it in the space after the word. *E/G?* means that you are to determine whether or not the word contains an E or G. If so, write Yes in the space; if not, write No. *Pleasant* means that you are to rate the pleasantness of the word on a scale of 1 to 7, with 1 being unpleasant and 7 being extremely pleasant. Write your rating in the space next to the word.

Word	Instruction	Rating
Bottle	Pleasant	_____
Flour	E/G?	_____
Cattle	Syllables	_____
Tongue	E/G?	_____
Capital	Syllables	_____
Hospital	Pleasant	_____
Contract	Pleasant	_____
Furniture	E/G?	_____
Bell	Syllables	_____

Now take a blank piece of paper and a pencil and, *without looking at the above*, write the words from memory.

Levels of Processing

In an early discussion of the relationship between encoding and memory, Craik and Lockhart (1972) proposed that memory for information was dependent on the type of processing (that is, the type of encoding) that the information received. They postulated that information is processed through a series of stages, or *levels of processing*, as shown in Figure 3.1. One can process an experience—say, a word presented in an experiment—to any level, from *shallow* to *deep*. Shallow processing deals with the surface characteristics of the item, such as its sound (male versus female voice) or visual appearance (lower- or uppercase letters). Intermediate levels of processing include the particular letters that make up a word (orthographic information), the sounds that make up its verbal representation (phonological processing), and its part of speech: noun, verb, and so on (syntactic information). Finally, deep processing deals with its meaning or semantic characteristics, including its relations to other items. In processing a word, one would first identify the shallow characteristics, then identify the word, which would lead to the meaning and to other information associated with the word.

In Craik and Lockhart's view, processing an item serves to encode the item into memory; there are no separate short- and long-term stores. Furthermore, the level of processing is the only determinant of the "strength" of the memory: Deeper processing produces stronger memories. An individual's *intention* to remember an item is irrelevant; all that matters is the depth of the encoding. If people can be induced to process an item deeply (i.e., semantically), then they will remember that item well, whether they want to or not. Some advertisers, for example, try to get viewers to deeply process the information about the product in an advertisement (such as when a toothpaste manufacturer presents graphics showing how their toothpaste permeates the enamel to strengthen teeth). Conversely, if one wanted to remember an item, but only processed the item at a shallow level, then one might not be able to remember it later, even though one had intended to do so.

Craik and Lockhart (1972) discussed two types of rehearsal: *maintenance* and *elaborative*. Maintenance rehearsal maintains the item at the same level of processing, as

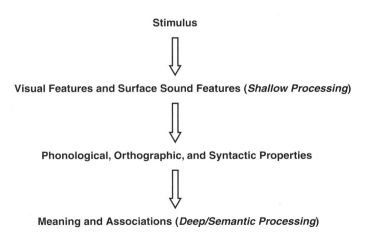

Figure 3.1 Levels of processing theory: Stages.

when one repeats a word over and over by rote. This type of rehearsal, by itself, produces no additional storage of information, since the item is simply being maintained at one level of processing. Elaborative rehearsal, in contrast, entails moving to a deeper level of processing, and linking the incoming information to more meaningful concepts. This improves a person's memory for the information, because, according to the levels-of-processing view, deeper processing is the only way to strengthen memory.

Early research support for the levels-of-processing theory came from a number of studies carried out by Jenkins and his coworkers (e.g., Hyde & Jenkins, 1969, 1973; Till & Jenkins, 1973; Walsh & Jenkins, 1973), in which memory for words was examined after incidental encoding. Walsh and Jenkins asked experimental participants to listen to a list of 24 recorded words while engaged in various orienting tasks, some shallow (i.e., counting syllables; checking whether the words contained an *e* or *g*) and some deep (i.e., rating the pleasantness of the words). Half the people were engaged in a single orienting task for all the words (e.g., checking all words for the letters *e* or *g*); the other people were engaged in two orienting tasks for each of the words. A final set of control participants were told to simply remember the words and were informed that a memory test would follow. This control condition was included to test the hypothesis that intention to recall would not affect performance and that the level of processing would be all-important.

The results are summarized in Figure 3.2. The deep (semantic) task consistently produced higher levels of recall than the shallow tasks, which supported the levels-of-processing analysis. Also, when more than one orienting task was given to the same participants, recall depended most on the deeper task. As can be seen in Figure 3.2, when the shallow tasks and the pleasantness task were carried out by the same individuals within a single list, recall was higher than when the shallow tasks were carried out alone. Finally, the deeper pleasantness orienting task produced recall equal to that in the intentional condition. The main factor that affected level of recall was the type of orienting task.

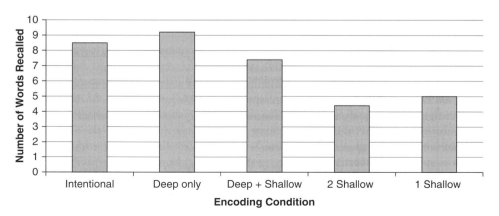

Figure 3.2 Results of Walsh and Jenkins (1973): Number of words recalled (out of 24) as a function of processing condition.

Use of elaborative or "deep" study techniques is related to classifications of giftedness in school. Thornton, Haskell, and Libby (2006) found that gifted/talented high-school students reported greater reliance on deep levels of processing than did nongifted but college-bound students. This result indicates that there is a correlation between high intelligence and more meaningful or elaborative processing (though whether more intelligent people selectively use deeper processing or whether deeper processing is the cause of their intelligence is not clear from those results).

What Happens in Deep Versus Shallow Processing?

The levels-of-processing view assumes that different levels of processing result in different kinds of information being encoded into memory (shallow versus deep), and that deeper processing results in stronger memories. Other investigators have tried to determine more precisely what happens during different types of processing that makes semantic processing more advantageous for remembering information.

Distinctiveness

Research has shown that level of processing also influences incidental memory for visual materials. Bower and Karlin (1974) asked participants to process pictures of faces in one of two ways. Some participants judged whether the face was male or female—a relatively shallow level of processing. Other participants judged the perceived honesty of the person, which presumably requires deeper processing. No mention was made of a memory test following the processing task. All participants were then given a surprise recognition test for the faces they had just processed. Honesty judgments produced better memory performance than male/female judgments, supporting the idea that deeper processing produces better memory for visual materials.

However, Intraub and Nicklos (1985) found the opposite: Pictures were better remembered under *shallow* encoding conditions. Participants viewed 80 color pictures of indoor and outdoor scenes taken from magazines. Subjects did not know there would be a memory test, but were asked either a shallow or deep processing question before each picture. The shallow questions focused on physical attributes of the pictures: *Is this angular? Is it vertical? Cluttered? Sparse?* The deep orienting questions asked about semantic attributes of the object or scene: *Is it animate? Inanimate? Edible? Indoors?* Recall was better for pictures that had been encoded under physical versus semantic orienting questions at a rate of 52% to 38%.

Why do the results of Bower and Karlin (1974) differ from those of Intraub and Nicklos (1985)? Intraub and Nicklos argued that pictures may be automatically processed at a semantic level, no matter what the encoding condition. (When was the last time you looked at a scene and did not recognize the objects in the picture?) If all pictures are being processed at the semantic level, physical orienting questions may further direct subjects' attention to details that create a more distinctive memory than what would be produced by semantic processing alone. This leads to the possibility that deeper processing simply causes more *detailed* processing, which then leads to a distinctive memory which is easier to retrieve.

This interpretation is supported by research by Winograd (1981). He asked people to encode pictures of faces, either under deep processing instructions (judging whether the person was honest) or shallow processing instructions (judging whether the person had large eyes). Some of the faces were chosen because they had a distinctive physical feature (e.g., large eyes), and some of the shallow orienting questions asked participants to scan the face in order to find that feature, thereby ensuring that the distinctive feature had been encoded. Recognition memory for that face after detailed shallow processing was just as good as after encoding the face based on honesty judgments. Thus, deeper processing may facilitate better memory by ensuring that any distinctive features of a stimulus (words or pictures) are encoded. To judge that a person is honest or likable (deep processing tasks), one may have to scan the details of the face more carefully than when judging whether the person is male or female (shallow processing task). These results support the view that deep processing, at least of faces or scenes (Intraub & Nicklos, 1985), does not result in some new type of information being encoded; it simply makes it highly likely that whatever distinctive features are available will be scanned and encoded.

In ordinary circumstances, then, different strategies may be required for optimal memory of words versus pictures, with words best remembered under semantic conditions, and pictures best processed under physical orienting conditions. Thus, optimizing memory is not as simple as recommending deep or semantic processing for all materials in all situations.

SUMMARY

The results of research reviewed in this section have shown that deeper levels of encoding may have positive effects on memory performance because they ensure that participants attend to distinctive aspects of the to-be-remembered material and they result in participants encoding the specific item in relation to other information, consistent with elaboration. Carrying out these encoding activities facilitates memory performance.

IS DEEPER ENCODING ALWAYS BETTER?

Test-Appropriate Encoding

Most professors and students would agree with the basic premise of the levels of processing theory: Information is better remembered if you understand it and process it at a deep or meaningful level. However, memory can sometimes be good after shallow processing. Recall that Intraub and Nicklos (1985) found that memory for pictures was better after *shallow* processing. We also know that mere repetition of trigrams or words (Ebbinghaus, 1885/1964; Glenberg et al., 1977), or word pairs (Logan & Etherton, 1994), can result in information about them being retained in memory. These results raise a further question: If shallow processing sometimes allows information to be retained in memory, then why have experiments typically shown that performance is poor after most shallow processing tasks (e.g., Walsh & Jenkins, 1973; see Figure 3.2)?

The answer may reside in the kind of test used to assess memory. Walsh and Jenkins (1973), as we have discussed, tested memory using a recall test. Perhaps good recall performance requires that one encode the items in a particular way (that is, through semantic processing), since words are typically accessed through their meanings on those tests. In other words, deep processing might be effective because it matches the demands that the later recall test will put on memory—one is asked to retrieve words based on meaning. This analysis raises the possibility that there might be information in memory after a shallow task, but testing for recall is not the best way to find out. If, however, one used a memory test specially designed to measure shallow information, memory performance might be good after shallow processing.

This prediction has been supported in a series of studies by Bransford and colleagues (e.g., Bransford, Franks, Morris, & Stein, 1979; Morris, Bransford, & Franks, 1977), who proposed that any memory test involves what can be called *transfer* of information. In the typical memory study, participants first process material, and then are tested on their memory. In effect, the researcher is testing to see if the information from the processing task transfers to the memory task. Morris et al. (1977) used the term *transfer-appropriate processing* to refer to the necessity that the encoding operations must be appropriate to the upcoming memory test, or must enable maximum transfer from encoding to test. We will use the phrase *test-appropriate encoding*, since it more directly captures the notion that the processing carried out during encoding must fit the test. In this analysis, no particular type of encoding is inherently "better" than any other. The most important factor in determining memory performance is whether the memory test taps into how that information was encoded.

Morris, Bransford, and Franks (1977) tested whether matching encoding and test conditions leads to optimum memory performance (see Table 3.2). All participants encoded words incidentally (without expectation of a memory test). The deep-processing group judged whether the target word fit into a sentence frame, such as: "The ____ had a silver engine" TRAIN (the answer is *yes*). The shallow-processing group made judgments concerning the sound of the words: "rhymes with legal" EAGLE (the answer is *yes*). There were also two types of recognition tests used. The standard test contained words from the list (e.g., TRAIN, EAGLE), as well as new words (e.g., SHIRT, SPARROW), and the participants indicated which words had

Table 3.2   Morris, Bransford, and Franks (1977). (a) Design summary. (b) Results of Experiment 1

(a)

Incidental Encoding Task: Does the capitalized word fit in the sentence?
Deep Processing: The _____ had a silver engine. **TRAIN** (yes)
Shallow Processing: _____ rhymes with legal. **EAGLE** (yes)

(b)

		Memory Test (Proportion correct)	
		Standard Test	Rhyming Test
Study Condition	Deep (Semantic)	.844	.333
	Shallow (Rhyming)	.633	.489

been on the list. This test would be expected to test for deep information in memory. In order to test for shallow information, Morris and coworkers designed a *rhyming recognition test*. This test did not contain any of the original list words. Rather, it was made up of some words that rhymed with the words from the original list, as well as nonrhyming control words. The participants indicated whether each word on the test list rhymed with any word from original list. Thus, if the original list word had been EAGLE, the recognition test might contain REGAL.

The results of the study, shown in Table 3.2b, support the test-appropriate-encoding view (see also Fisher and Craik, 1977; Hunt and Elliott, 1980; Jacoby, 1975). On the standard recognition test, as we would expect, semantic processing produced better performance than shallow processing (which supports the levels-of-processing theory). On the rhyming recognition test, however, the results were reversed: The shallow rhyming-encoding task resulted in better recognition than the deep encoding task. This means that memory is not necessarily better after a semantic or deep encoding task: If the test taps *shallow* processing, then performance will be better after shallow processing. The important issue is whether or not a memory test matches the encoded information (for similar results, see also Stein, 1978).

These results have an important implication for theories of memory: There may be no universally best type of encoding. Whether or not the memory of a given experience can be tapped by a test depends on how the test matches the information that was processed at encoding. Thus, if a friend asks you the best way to study for a biology quiz, the first thing to do is ask a question in return: "What sort of a test will it be?" Because most memory tests involve recall or recognition, deep processing is usually most effective at creating a memory that transfers to those types of tests. However, if your friend's biology professor is interested in determining whether or not the students have paid attention to the kinds of diagrams in the text, then shallow processing might be better (Intraub & Nicklos, 1985).

ENCODING PROCESSES IN MEMORY: CONCLUSIONS

The scientific study of memory was initiated by Ebbinghaus (1885/1964), and the discussion in this chapter began with his study of the acquisition of new associations through the mechanism of rote rehearsal. This work and that of those who followed demonstrated that information can be acquired through rote rehearsal, but acquisition is slow. We then looked at memory as a top-down process, a view that can be traced back to Bartlett (1932). There is support for Bartlett's schematic view of memory processing, which assumes that information about the general meaning of events is left behind in memory, at the expense of details. There is also, however, ample evidence that specific details of events can be retained (see Alba & Hasher, 1983).

We also considered the level-of-processing theory's (Craik & Lockhart, 1972) proposal that there might be better or worse ways of encoding information in memory. That analysis led to the conclusion that memory performance, in part, depends on the relationship between how information was originally encoded and how memory is tested, which is the focus of research on test-appropriate encoding (Morris et al., 1977). There is evidence that information of many different sorts can be encoded into memory, but in order for it to be remembered, the test must match the encoding (see Kolers & Roediger, 1984, for a review).

Now that we have examined the role of encoding in memory, we must go beyond it. Turning again to S.F.'s remarkable memory span, encoding was only the first step: Once material has been encoded into memory, remembering it depends on being able to retrieve it at a later time. There must be information available at the time of remembering that can serve to bring the needed material back to consciousness—so that it can be given in response to a test question, say. We now examine retrieval processes, and the discussion will parallel that of encoding in several ways, as we will examine bottom-up versus top-down aspects of retrieval. In addition, considerable research suggests that maximum memory performance depends on the coordination between encoding and retrieval: Memory performance is best when the retrieval conditions match those at encoding.

Retrieval as a Bottom–Up Versus Top–Down Process

The basic function of retrieval is to make available for use information that has been stored in memory but is not currently being contemplated. Please carry out the demonstration in Box 3.5 before reading further.

BOX 3.5 PERSPECTIVE TAKING IN EPISODIC MEMORY RETRIEVAL (FROM NIGRO AND NEISSER, 1983)

1. Think of a time when you were involved in an accident or near-accident in your car. Try to remember the emotional response you had to the event. Did you remember the event as something happening to you, or did you remember the event as if you were an outside observer?

2. Recall the last time you exercised, such as running outside or working out in the gym. Try to recall as much detail as you can from the event. Did you remember the event as something happening to you, or did you remember the event as if you were an outside observer?

3. Try to recall the last time you spoke in public, in a class or meeting, and so on. Try to remember the event from the perspective of an observer, rather than from your perspective as the person who experienced the event.

Computer Memory Versus Human Memory: Bottom–Up Versus Top–Down Retrieval

As with encoding, retrieval can be carried out as either a bottom-up or a top-down process. The term *retrieval* is one of many that cognitive psychologists adopted from computer science (see Chapter 1). In a computer memory, retrieval is typically a passive process—when we retrieve a file that we have stored in our computer's memory, the act of retrieval does not change the contents of the file. Accessing information from human memory might work similarly: Retrieval might simply bring back the verbatim record of an earlier experience, like storing a book in the library and reclaiming it later. Much of our ability to function in daily life is due to bottom-up retrieval; for example, you recognize your roommate's face even if you meet her outside your apartment, because visual features of her face automatically trigger recognition.

Retrieval in human memory does not always work in this way, however: Human retrieval is also top-down, and is influenced by our expectations and knowledge. We have all had an occasion where we passed someone on the street who looked familiar, but whom we did not recognize out of context. What could be called the *retrieval environment* (e.g., the context in which retrieval occurs; Schacter, 1996) affects if, and how, information is remembered. We already know that encoding processes can affect the information that is stored in response to an event and thereby affect what is remembered; sometimes the act of retrieving information alters what is remembered, too.

Field Effects in Remembering and Consciousness

One bit of evidence for the top-down nature of retrieval comes from the phenomenon of *perspective-taking* in memory. In some cases, we remember an experience as if we were *reliving* it. This type of memory is called a *field* memory; we feel as if we are immersed again in the original stimulus conditions or the *stimulus field*. Sometimes, however, we remember a personal experience from the perspective of an outside observer, that is, as an *observer memory*. The fact that you can recall your own experiences from someone else's perspective indicates that the memory is being constructed by you at retrieval (since the experience probably was originally stored from your own perspective). In addition, those specific features of a memory that are retrieved depend on our goals or perspectives at the time of retrieval.

Nigro and Neisser (1983) carried out a laboratory investigation of perspective taking in memory (see Box 3.5). They asked participants to remember particular events from their lives, such as being in an accident or near-accident, or a time when they went running. Participants were first asked to classify the way they had remembered the event—either as a field memory or that of an outside observer. The researchers asked the participants to recall the objective aspects of the experience, and then the emotional content of the event. Observer memories tended to be reported when the person was asked about the objective circumstances surrounding the experience—people would recount their memories as if they had been watching the events. When participants were asked about the emotional content of the experience, however, field memories were more frequent. Thus, the memory being retrieved is not an unchangeable record: We can construct a memory as we need it.

Markus (1986) carried out an investigation of people's long-term memory for their own attitudes, which demonstrated another way in which the retrieval environment can play a role in determining what is remembered. In 1973, Markus had asked participants to rate their feelings concerning a number of social issues, such as attitudes toward minorities and the question of equality of women. Nine years later, those same people were asked to indicate their *then-current attitudes* on the same issues, and also to try to recall what their *original attitudes* from 1973 had been. Participants often misrecollected their original attitudes as being more like their later attitudes than they actually were. Thus, their current political perspective influenced recall of their original attitudes.

Memory for concrete experiences shows a similar effect. Eich, Reeves, Jaeger, and Graff-Radford (1985) asked chronic headache sufferers to keep a diary, in which they made hourly ratings on a 10-point scale of the intensity of their headache pain. At the end of a week, the individuals came to the headache clinic for a treatment session. They were asked to rate their present pain, and to recall the minimum, maximum, and average levels of pain during the past week. Individuals who were experiencing high levels of pain during the memory test *over*estimated their recollected pain for the past week, whereas individuals experiencing low pain did the opposite.

PARALLELS BETWEEN ENCODING AND RETRIEVAL

Similar processes thus appear to operate during encoding and retrieval (see Figure 3.3). At encoding, an individual thinks about the experience as it unfolds: He or she interprets and encodes it. The person's interpretation, plus information directly from the

Encoding

Stimulus Event

Encoding (interpreted stimulus event)

Memory Trace (information from experience + encoded interpretation)

Retrieval

Retrieval Environment (specific request[s] + information in environment)

Retrieval Cue (interpreted retrieval environment)

Retrieved Memory Trace

Remembered Event (interpreted trace)

Figure 3.3   Relationship between encoding and retrieval.

event itself, serves as the basis for the trace that is stored in memory. Upon remembering, similarly, the person retrieves a trace, using any available retrieval cues from the environment and/or the stimulus itself. The kind of retrieval cue provided may determine which aspects of a memory get activated (as in field effects). What is remembered can also be altered by how one remembers. A specific request, for example, can trigger a person to recall how he felt when he was in a near-accident while driving. Background attitudes and information (such as thinking that other people often drive irresponsibly) may influence the person's recollection of the near-accident. He may overestimate how fast the other car was going when it almost collided with him. In this way, remembering becomes a reconstruction, as Bartlett (1932) hypothesized.

For the rest of this chapter, we focus on how people use or construct retrieval cues to activate memories. Chapter 4, which deals with forgetting and the accuracy of memories, continues the discussion of how memories can be altered by preexisting attitudes, post-event information, and misleading retrieval cues.

RETRIEVAL PROCESSES IN MEMORY

Psychologists have extensively investigated retrieval processes in the laboratory, and have found that providing retrieval cues can help activate material that is otherwise not easily accessed.

Positive Effects of Retrieval Cues

Tulving and Pearlstone (1966) carried out a classic demonstration that retrieval cues can facilitate remembering, using lists made up of words taken from up to 12 different taxonomic categories (e.g., *minerals, fruits, names of rivers*) with up to four words in each category (Figure 3.4). The category structure of the list made it likely that the participants would use the categories to encode the words. However, the large number

A long list of words in a variety of categories is presented for study; participants are told that memory for items, not category names, will be tested.

> Fruit: banana, pear, grapefruit, grape
> Transportation: car, boat, wagon, sled
> Body parts: neck, foot, back, elbow
> Metals: brass, iron, gold, tin
> Etc.

(a) Recall is tested; since the list is long, some items are forgotten.

(b) Category names are then presented as cues to see how many forgotten items people can recall. Examples of category-based retrieval cues:

> *Any methods of transportation?*
> *Any fruits?*
> *Any minerals?*

Figure 3.4 Design of studies showing that retrieval cues facilitate memory.

of unrelated categories also made it likely that some categories would not be recalled. This allowed the researchers to examine the possible role of retrieval cues.

Tulving and Pearlstone (1966) found that, at recall, items in the same category tended to be produced together, which is called *category-based clustering*. This is to be expected if the participants were using the categorical organization of the material as the basis for recall. However, as expected, participants usually forgot some categories. When given the names of those forgotten categories, participants were able to use them as retrieval cues to recall many words that they had originally seemed to have forgotten. Furthermore, they usually recalled those words together, in a cluster. This experiment illustrated an important distinction between words that were *available* in memory (words that had been encoded and stored) versus words that were *accessible* (words that had been encoded and stored and could also be retrieved). Available information is not always accessible, and one way to make information accessible is to provide appropriate retrieval cues.

Subjective Organization of Random Material

In the Tulving and Pearlstone (1966) study just reviewed, the participants were familiar with the structure of the list (Figure 3.4), since we all know such categories as *minerals*, *fruits*, and *names of rivers*. However, what happens when there is no obvious organization in the material, such as with the list of random words shown in Box 3.6? People process such random material by finding some sort of *subjective organization* in it, and they then use that organization as a set of retrieval cues.

BOX 3.6 FREE–RECALL LIST OF RANDOM WORDS

Please study the following list of words:

Root

Bone

Palace

Hospital

Liberty

Cousin

Artist

Shell

Map

Factory

Pattern

Bottle

Thread

Close your book and try to recall as many as you can.

In an early investigation of subjective organization, Tulving (1962) gave participants a list of randomly selected words to study for free recall (as in Box 3.6). The list was presented several times, in a different random order each time, with the participants recalling as much as they could after each presentation, in any order. Tulving found that once a person had recalled more than one word together (e.g., *jungle* then *office*), they tended to recall those words sequentially over all the trials (even though the words were presented in a different random order from one trial to the next). Thus, once a participant had formed subjective groups of unrelated words, they functioned like categories during retrieval.

BRAIN SYSTEMS IN ENCODING AND RETRIEVAL

Investigators in cognitive neuroscience have begun to specify brain areas involved in the encoding and retrieval of information from memory. The complexity of the researchers' task is immediately evident: People can encode information under a variety of processing instructions; the stimuli can be words, numbers, pictures, random shapes, events from one's own life; the words or pictures can be from one category (e.g., tools) or another (e.g., famous people). Participants in a memory study may be asked to recall information or engage in a continuous-recognition test, a forced choice-recognition test, or some other technique (see Table 3.3 for a description of various types of memory tests). Thus, trying to isolate the area of the cortex devoted to memory is unlikely to be successful. However, the use of fMRI has resulted in fascinating research on a number of fronts. Several principles have emerged from this research. First, memory processes involve many brain structures. The hippocampus and parts of the cortex participate in both encoding and retrieval, including the prefrontal cortex and the temporal and parietal lobes. Secondly, the specific brain areas that are most active during encoding or retrieval of information may depend on whether one carries out shallow or elaborative encoding of the material (e.g., Nyberg, McIntosh, et al., 1996).

Consolidation: Storage of Information

Consolidation is the process whereby a memory trace for an experience is laid down in the brain. Hebb (1949) proposed that consolidation was accomplished through changes occurring in neurons and in synaptic connections between neurons. Activity of the hippocampus appears to be necessary both to maintain information on a short-term basis and to permanently store or consolidate information in memory. As we have seen with amnesia patients, damage to the hippocampus from strokes, surgery, or prolonged alcoholism (as in Korsakoff's syndrome) often results in anterograde amnesia, in which patients are unable to encode and store new information (Rempel-Clower, Zola-Morgan, Squire, & Amaral, 1996). Thus, the hippocampus appears to be integrally involved in initial encoding processes, and its role in learning has been confirmed with experimental primate studies (Zola-Morgan & Squire, 1986).

However, the hippocampus is important for laying down new memories only for a limited time after presentation of new material (Clark, Broadbent, Zola, & Squire, 2002; Zola-Morgan & Squire, 1990). Hebb's (1949) early and still-influential theory of memory consolidation proposed that neural circuits will *reverberate*—keep on firing—even for several days after one's exposure to a piece of information has ended (Bliss & Gardner-Medwin, 1973). If those reverberating neural circuits are interrupted, the neurological process of long-term storage, which neuroscientists call *long-term potentiation* (*potentiation* means *to strengthen*), may not be complete, and recent memories may be lost. Patients who learn a word list shortly before undergoing electroconvulsive shock therapy (ECT) are unable to remember the word list (Squire, Shimamura, & Graf, 1985), presumably because the ECT interferes with neural circuitry. It is probable that neural circuits between the hippocampus and medial temporal cortex are responsible for the consolidation of long-term memories (Remondes & Schuman, 2004; Squire & Alvarez, 1995). See Figure 3.5.

Table 3.3   Types of Memory Tests: (a) Recall; (b) Recognition; (c) Implicit Memory

(a)

Recall Test	Description	Example
Free Recall	Information is presented, and then people are asked to spontaneously retrieve the information.	A person hears the words *broccoli, yam, onion, eggplant, carrot*. She is then asked to report all the words she can remember.
Cued Recall	Information is presented (e.g., a list), and then people are given a hint to help them retrieve the information (e.g., the first letter of each word).	A person hears the word pairs: *bread-shoe, lamp-grass, stamp-fork*. He is then given the first word in each pair and asked to remember the word that went with it (e.g., *bread-_____, lamp-_____, stamp-_____*).

(b)

Recognition Test	Description	Example
Forced-Choice	After learning a stimulus set (e.g., list of words), one correct answer (the *target*) is paired with at least one wrong answer that had not been in the original stimulus set (the *foil* or *foils*).	Multiple-choice exams are forced-choice recognition tests. One target (correct answer) may occur along with one or several foils. A person hears the words *broccoli, yam, onion, eggplant, carrot*. She is then asked which of these were on the list she just heard: *zucchini or carrot? broccoli or cauliflower?*
Absolute Judgment	After learning a stimulus set, such as a list of words or sentences, a person is presented with each stimulus one at a time, interspersed with foils, and asked whether that item had been in the original list or not (yes/no judgments).	A person hears the words *broccoli, yam, onion, eggplant, carrot*. He is then asked to decide whether each of a string of words was in the original list or not (correct answers in parentheses after each): *broccoli?* (yes), *zucchini?* (no), *yam?* (yes), *onion?* (yes), *cauliflower?* (no)
Continuous (or Running) Recognition	Participants in a memory study may begin to listen to a string of words, and have to respond "yes" when a word had already appeared in a list or "no" if a word appears for the first time.	Here is a string of words and the correct memory response after each word: *sky* (no; after all, the first word in a list could not have already appeared in the list); *wind* (no), *sky* (yes), *snow* (no), *clouds* (no), *sky* (yes), *stars* (no) . . .

(continued)

Table 3.3 (*continued*)

(c)

Implicit Memory Test	Description	Example
Relearning	Information is learned, then forgotten. The "old" information is then relearned and compared to the number of trials it originally took to learn the information (or to newly learn an equivalent list of words/paragraph/etc.). The amount of *savings* is calculated by comparing the relative percentage of trials needed to relearn a set versus the number of rehearsals needed to learn the set initially. Relearning is a very sensitive implicit measure of knowledge that we have retained from an earlier experience.	Hermann Ebbinghaus learned a set of nonsense syllables. After he had forgotten the set, he restudied the list, and was able to compute his *savings*—the relative percentage of trials needed to relearn a set versus the number of rehearsals needed to learn the set initially. For example, if it took him 12 trials to relearn a group of syllables, and it taken him 24 trials to learn the set originally, his savings would be 12/24, or 50%.
Word Stem Completion	After being presented with a set of words to learn, participants are then given two or three letters and asked to respond with the first word that pops into their mind. This test is often used with amnesic patients to see if they remembered words from a list, even if they have trouble spontaneously recalling the lists.	An amnesic hears a list of words that includes the word "attach." He does not recall that word in a subsequent memory test, but when he sees the cue "AT..." in the word stem completion task, he blurts out "attach."
Priming	Early-learned information influences the likelihood of retrieving later-learned information (at an unconscious level).	Cave (1997) asked people to name 130 pictures of common objects. Six to 48 weeks later, they named 200 pictures, half of which had been presented the first session. Average naming times to the "old" pictures was 50 msec faster than to new pictures, with the biggest discrepancies between old and new pictures seen at the shortest delays (e.g., 6 weeks).
Guilty Knowledge	Differences in galvanic skin response (GSR) are used to distinguish earlier-learned information that people remember at an unconscious level from either new information or information that the person has forgotten. (It is called a "guilty knowledge" test because the GSR is one technique used in lie-detector tests.)	For example, Newcombe and Fox (1994) took pictures of preschoolers when the children were 4 or 5. Five years later, when the children were 10, they recognized only 21% of their preschool classmates. However, the 10-year-olds showed an increase in GSR for pictures of their former preschool classmates, even if they had not recognized that particular classmate in the recognition test.
Classical Conditioning	A stimulus that typically causes a response (e.g., a puff of air to the eye leads to an eyeblink response) is paired with a neutral stimulus (e.g., a tone). With learning, the neutral stimulus alone causes the response.	Claparède's amnesic patient refusing to shake the doctor's hand after he had injured her with a pin in his hand on the previous visit.

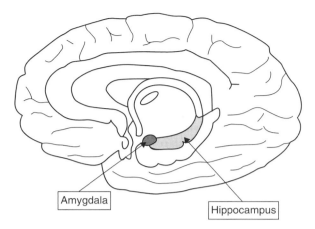

Figure 3.5   Brain diagram. Subcortical areas related to encoding: hippocampus and amygdala.

Not only is the hippocampus activated during encoding of new memories, it also plays a role in retrieval. Suzuki, Johnson, and Rugg (2011) asked people to engage in a continuous-recognition task while undergoing fMRI. Participants were presented with blocks of photographs of common objects surrounded by either a gray, blue, or orange frame. Two responses were permitted: Participants could identify a photograph as being "new" or "old." A *new* response was to be given for: (a) items presented for the first time (new items), and (b) repeated items in a blue or orange frame whose frame differed from its original color (nontargets). *Old* responses were required for repeated pictures in a gray frame (regardless of original frame color) or repeated pictures that appeared in the same blue or orange frame as the earlier presentation. Thus, participants had to keep in mind both the picture itself and its frame. Correct recollection of both nontargets and targets was associated with greater hippocampal activity in high- (but not low-) performing subjects. Thus, retrieval of items correctly remembered led to reactivation of the hippocampus. This study illustrates that hippocampal areas are involved in both encoding and retrieval processes.

Cortical Areas

An interesting paradigm for testing brain areas involved in encoding is to carry out fMRI imaging while people are exposed to stimuli (e.g., words or pictures), and then to determine differences in activation for the items that people remember versus those they don't on a memory test. Over 100 studies have used this *subsequent memory* (SM) procedure (Uncapher & Wagner, 2009). Kim (2011) conducted a meta-analysis of these studies and found that five areas were engaged during successful encoding: (1) the left inferior frontal cortex, (2) bilateral fusiform cortex, (3) bilateral hippocampus, (4) bilateral premotor cortex, and (5) bilateral posterior parietal cortex. The inferior frontal cortex and bilateral fusiform cortex are assumed to process the content of what one is trying to remember (Kirchhoff, Wagner, Maril, & Stern, 2000). The hippocampi, along with the medial temporal lobes atop them, store the information

(Diana, Yonelinas, & Ranganath, 2007; Squire, Stark, & Clark, 2004). The premotor cortex and posterior parietal cortex control visual attention during encoding (Corbetta, Kincade, & Shulman, 2002; Corbetta, Patel, & Shulman, 2008). Kim (2011) also found differences in activation for words versus pictures: Activation in the left inferior parietal cortex was greatest for processing words, while picture encoding activated the fusiform cortex.

The medial temporal lobes (MTL) lie atop the hippocampus and have multiple connections to it; the MTL has been implicated in storing long-term memories. Patients with extensive damage to both the hippocampus and MTL often suffer extensive anterograde or retrograde amnesia (Bayley, Hopkins, & Squire, 2006; Bright et al., 2006; Squire & Bayley, 2007; Zola-Morgan, Squire & Amaral, 1986), or both anterograde and retrograde amnesia (Di Gennaro et al., 2006; Gilboa et al., 2006).

Studies have also found that the prefrontal cortex (PFC) plays an important role in executive processes that operate during both encoding and retrieval of information (see Figure 3.6). For example, the prefrontal cortex monitors information in working memory (Petrides, Alivisatos, Meyer, & Evans, 1993), and may underlie the use of memory strategies (Bor & Owen, 2007).

Damage to the frontal cortex often results in people not spontaneously making use of memory strategies, such as spontaneously organizing material into chunks when they rehearse word lists for a later memory test (Gershberg & Shimamura, 1995; Hirst & Volpe, 1988). It is not that the patients cannot use such strategies, however; if the patients are instructed to group related items into chunks, memory is improved.

The prefrontal cortex has also been implicated in elaborative encoding of material. Nyberg, Cabeza, and Tulving (1996) used PET scans to study brain activation while participants encoded information at a shallow or deep level. Shallow encoding required the participant to decide if the word contained the letter *a*; deep encoding involved deciding whether or not the word referred to an animate or inanimate object. Deep encoding produced greater activation in the left prefrontal cortex, which is consistent with claims that the prefrontal cortex is involved in strategic encoding of information

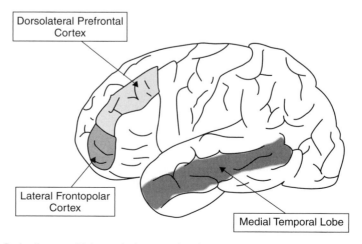

Figure 3.6   Brain diagram: Main cortical areas related to memory.

(such as takes place in elaborative rehearsal). Similar results were obtained by Gabrieli et al. (1996) using fMRI.

In addition, multiple studies have found greater activation of the PFC during correct recognition of old items in memory tasks, relative to items correctly rejected as not having been seen before (see Fletcher & Henson, 2001, for a review). Further analysis shows that the PFC's role in recognition may be linked to executive processes, rather than activation of a memory, *per se*. Activity in specific regions, such as the right dorsolateral prefrontal cortex, may reflect decision-making processes in memory, such as when a person must determine whether a stimulus had been seen before (Hayama & Rugg, 2009; Henson, Shallice, & Dolan, 1999; Rugg, Henson, & Robb, 2003).

Rugg, Allan, and Birch (2000) determined that retrieval areas differ depending on the type of encoding. They presented participants with blocks of words that were to be encoded via either deep (sentence generation) or shallow processing (judgment about whether the first and last letter of the word were in alphabetical order). ERP was stronger in the *left parietal cortex* for correctly remembered items that had been studied under deep encoding instructions (see also Henson, Hornberger, & Rugg, 2005; Rugg & Allan, 2000). However, items that were remembered after shallow encoding led to stronger ERPs in the *central and frontal areas* (especially on the right), although the peak in ERP to shallow items took longer to occur. Because time to respond to these items was also longer, the researchers hypothesized that the stronger ERPs may have been due to greater cognitive effort to retrieve the shallowly encoded words.

These studies provide examples of the rich network of brain systems involved in encoding and retrieval processes. Although some parts of the cortex and hippocampus may be important in different aspects of memory (e.g., encoding versus retrieval), and in processing different kinds of stimuli (e.g., words versus visual stimuli) or memories (facts versus episodic memories), it is clear that there are numerous brain regions that interact, with the exact circuitry depending on the specific memory task being carried out. Encoding is largely carried out by neural circuits traversing the hippocampus/cingulate gyrus, temporal, and prefrontal areas, with greater prefrontal-cortex activation in semantic or elaborative encoding. Retrieval is carried out by networks of neurons, in the hippocampus, medial temporal lobe, prefrontal cortex, and parietal areas.

MAXIMIZING REMEMBERING: COORDINATION OF ENCODING AND RETRIEVAL

In our discussion so far, we have treated encoding and retrieval separately, as if they were two independent processes. However, we have already seen some evidence that remembering depends on the close coordination of encoding and retrieval. Research on test-appropriate encoding has demonstrated that memory performance is best when the memory test is designed to tap into the specific type of encoding—deep or shallow—that the material received (e.g., Bransford, Franks, Morris, & Stein, 1979; Morris, Bransford, & Franks, 1977). This finding is only one of many experimental results that indicate that maximal memory performance comes about when encoding and retrieval are coordinated. This coordination can occur in several ways. First, there can be coordination between the *retrieval environment*—the physical situation in which one is trying to remember something—and the encoding environment—the situation in which one first encountered the material. Second, there can be coordination between the person's psychological and physical state at encoding and retrieval. Finally, there can be coordination between the specific methods used to encode and retrieve material.

Coordination Between Encoding and Retrieval Environments: Physical Context

Every college student knows the adage that it is best to take an exam in the same room in which lectures were held, but how true is this advice? Within the psychological memory literature, the term *context* is used to refer to the physical setting in which material is learned. McGeoch (1931) proposed many years ago that maximal recall would occur when there was a match between the environment in which material was studied and that in which it was tested. The possible importance of a match between encoding and retrieval contexts has been investigated in several studies. Material is presented in one of two contexts, say, in a laboratory room versus in a student lounge. The participants' memory for the material is then tested in either the same or different context. When the study and test occur in the same context, the contexts are said to be *congruent*; different contexts for study and test are *incongruent*.

In a now-classic study, Godden and Baddeley (1975) asked scuba divers to put on scuba diving equipment and then listen to a tape of 36 words. Half of the subjects listened while on dry land; the other half listened while underwater. After several minutes' delay, the researchers asked the participants to recall the words, either in the same environment in which they had studied the words (if studied on dry land, recalled on dry land; if studied underwater, recalled underwater), *or* in the different environment. Thus, the study/recall contexts were either congruent or incongruent. Table 3.4 shows the results in each of the four conditions. Congruent context resulted in a substantial increase in recall performance. Martin and Aggleton (1993) replicated the Godden and Baddeley results. It has also been found that it is not necessary that the actual physical context be the same for recall to be maximized. In one study, *imagining* the original context resulted in recall as high as that of participants who were tested in the original room (Smith, 1979).

There is a very important practical aspect of the Godden and Baddeley (1975) study. Scuba divers must be able to recall safety procedures in order to deal with

Table 3.4   Godden and Baddeley (1975) Results*

		Retrieval Condition	
		DRY	WET
Study Condition	DRY	**13.5**	8.6
	WET	8.4	**11.4**

*Congruent conditions in **bold**

emergencies that occur underwater. How can we maximize the probability that a diver will remember the safety instructions when an emergency arises underwater? By having divers be taught safety procedures while underwater.

However, there are limits to the usefulness of context as a retrieval cue. In another condition of their experiment, Godden and Baddeley (1975) tested participants' memory with a forced-choice recognition test. Pairs of words were presented, one word from the experimental list and one new word, and the individual was asked which word had been on the study list. There was no difference in recognition performance between the congruent and incongruent context conditions. Thus, recall is more sensitive to context effects than is recognition.

At about this point in discussions of the role of context in memory, students begin to wonder about studying for examinations. If you want to minimize the forgetting of the material you have studied for an exam, should you study for the exam in the room in which you will take the test? A study by Saufley, Otaka, and Bavaresco (1985) examined the role of the classroom environment in performance on examinations. Results based on a total of 21 exams over 3 years indicated no differences in performance between students who stayed in the lecture room for the exam versus those who took the exam in a different room. Contrary to the findings from laboratory studies, changing the context made no difference on performance.

Saufley et al. (1985) mention several possible reasons why they might have failed to find any effects of context on exam performance. First, some of the exam questions were multiple-choice, which are recognition questions. As we have just seen, Godden and Baddeley (1975) found that context is less important when recognition tests are used. Second, in most classes, some material is presented only in the book. That material would be studied outside of *any* classroom, so all groups would be equal on that material. In addition, much studying of lecture material also takes place outside the lecture room, so all groups would have learned some material outside the lecture room (and thus would not have been as susceptible to context effects). Finally, context effects may be less salient in delayed testing. Most context effects have been found almost immediately after learning the information (e.g., Godden & Baddeley, 1975). Based on the Saufley et al. (1985) study, then, students probably do not have to worry about sneaking into lecture halls late at night to study class material, nor should they panic if the exam is scheduled for a different room than the standard classroom.

Coordinating the Physiological or Psychological States at Encoding and Retrieval: Psychological Context

A person's psychological state can play a role in memory similar to that of the physical context. The term *state-dependent memory* refers to the finding that memory for information may depend on the internal state of the person doing the remembering. Memory will be best if a person is in the same physiological or psychological state at study and test (we will use *psychological context* to refer to physiological and psychological changes). Kelemen and Creeley (2003) presented participants with 40 noun pairs to study after the people had drunk a sweet drink containing caffeine or no caffeine (placebo). A day later, the participants again drank a sweet drink and were given a cued recall test, where they were provided with the first word in each noun pair and asked to retrieve the second. People in the congruent physiological state (caffeine/caffeine or placebo/placebo) remembered about 33% more of the target words than did those in incongruent physiological states.

However, it should be noted that other experiments have not found state-dependent memory effects using alcohol or caffeine (e.g., Lowe, 1988; Mitchell & Redman, 1992); and some have found state-dependent memory only after delayed (but not immediate) recall (Warburton, 1995). Thus, the evidence is not clear-cut as to the strength of state-dependency in memory. The varied results might be because those state-dependency studies involve application of drugs or substances that may decrease the overall efficiency of encoding processes.

Some emotional states, such as fear, cause internal physiological states (e.g., arousal), which may also play a role in state-dependent memory. Lang, Craske, Brown, and Ghaneian (2001) had people who reported being spider- or snake-phobic view a list of 16 emotionally neutral probe nouns and generate an autobiographical event in response to each word (e.g., *leaf* might spur a memory of raking leaves in childhood). Participants generated memories either while relaxed (listening to classical music) or in a fear state (next to a caged spider or snake; the insect or snake was moved close to the person until he or she indicated feeling fear). Several days later, half the subjects in the each condition were asked to recall their memories and the probe words while in a fear state, half while in a relaxation state. This procedure yielded four groups of congruent versus incongruent encoding/retrieval conditions: fear/fear, fear/relax, relax/fear, relax/relax. The fear/fear group recalled the most words, followed by the relax/relax group, and both congruent groups recalled more than the incongruent groups. Thus, being in a similar state of arousal at encoding and retrieval facilitated memory.

Coordinating Encoding and Retrieval Operations: Cognitive Context

The research discussed earlier examining test-appropriate processing (e.g., Bransford, Franks, Morris, & Stein, 1979; Morris, Bransford, & Franks, 1977), demonstrated that memory after "shallow" processing could be enhanced if the memory test was designed to detect that type of information. Those results demonstrated the necessity of coordinating *cognitive context*—the cognitive operations that the person carries out—at encoding and retrieval. As a further example of this idea, Tulving and Thomson (1971, 1973) have shown that maximal memory performance occurs when the cognitive operations at encoding and retrieval are congruent. In one study (Tulving & Thomson, 1973; see Table 3.5A), they presented people with 24 word pairs, in which one word was weakly or strongly associated with the other word (e.g., *plant-BUG* [weak association] versus *insect-BUG* [strong association]; *sun-DAY* [weak] versus *night-DAY* [strong]). People were told to pay attention to the word in capital letters for a later memory test, but to note the other word as a cue that might be helpful. During the cued recall test, participants were provided a list of 24 cues; half were the same cue they had seen during the encoding phase (e.g., if they had seen *plant-BUG*, the cue would be *plant-*) and half were different associative cues (e.g., if they had seen *plant-BUG*, the cue would be *insect-BUG*).

Table 3.5   Tulving and Thomson (1973) Design and Results

A. Participant studies information within one verbal context. Stimulus words to be remembered are in CAPITALS (participants did not have to respond to the other word in the pair, but were told the other word may be useful as a memory cue):

    i. Verbal Context$_1$ (weak associations): <u>plant</u> BUG; <u>coffee</u> HOT; <u>hungry</u> FAST

    ii. Verbal Context$_2$ (strong associations): <u>insect</u> BUG; <u>sun</u> HOT; <u>run</u> FAST

B. Memory is tested in the same (constant) or different (changed) verbal environment. In other words, people study material in one environment and are tested either in that environment or in the other environment. This results in four conditions in the experiment, as shown below.

		Retrieval Condition	
		<u>1</u> Insect?	<u>2</u> Plant?
Study (Encoding) Context	(1) *insect* BUG (strong)	Constant (strong) **84%**	Changed (weak) 38%
	(2) *plant* BUG (weak)	Changed (strong) 58%	Constant (weak) **65%**

Same encoding/retrieval cues depicted in **bold**. Recall is better when the verbal context stays the same for study and test (encoding and retrieval). Recall is better in constant conditions.

As shown in Table 3.5B, people recalled more words in response to the same cues as they did to different cues. This finding is particularly interesting in light of the fact that in some cases the cue at retrieval was strongly related to the target word (e.g., *night* as a cue for *DAY*). If you ask 100 people to give you the first word they think of in response to *night*, many will respond with *day*. However, if *DAY* had originally been studied in the context *sun-DAY*, then *night* is *not* effective in cuing its recall. This indicates that the whole context in which the word was studied originally, not just the word itself, is what must be retrieved for recall to occur. Tulving and Thomson used the term *encoding specificity* to refer to the idea that encoding and retrieval operations must match for memory performance to be maximal. From our perspective, that label leaves out the retrieval half of the situation: A better term might be *encoding-retrieval coordination*.

In a further demonstration of the importance of coordination of encoding and retrieval, Fisher and Craik (1977) used a procedure similar to that of Tulving and Thomson (1973), but with rhyming orienting questions and retrieval cues. A person might see the orienting question, *Does [————] rhyme with pail?* followed by a card with two words: *sleet* and *HAIL*. Participants were told to answer the question about the capitalized word. During the memory test, subjects prompted with the same orienting cue (e.g., *rhymes with pail*) recalled 24% of the words; those prompted with different rhyme-orienting cues (e.g., *rhymes with rail*) recalled only 18%. Even though the cues (*rhymes with pail*; *rhymes with rail*) pointed to HAIL, changing the specifics of the cue affected recall. Thus, the more similarity between encoding and retrieval, the better people's memory.

Coordination of Encoding and Retrieval: Conclusion

We have seen several demonstrations that aspects of the study environment (e.g., physical context, internal states, and cognitive operations) can serve as useful retrieval cues when someone tries to remember information. The type of memory test used also determines whether context effects will be found. People tested on recall benefit more from being in the same external or internal context than do people tested on recognition.

RETRIEVAL PROCESSES: SUMMARY AND CONCLUSIONS

Two themes emerge from research on retrieval processes. First, some information may be inaccessible without hints, as illustrated by positive effects of retrieval cues on activating stored memories. Secondly, one cannot discuss retrieval independently of encoding. The ways in which we encode information are integrally tied to how we use and access that information later. Even seemingly nonessential information, such as the physical setting, or our inner mental or emotional states, may subtly influence how much we are able to recall or recognize. When there are no overt retrieval cues, people will often impose a subjective organization on the material that helps them to remember. Retrieval, like encoding, can be a top-down process: Sometimes the remembered event can be altered, based on one's perspective or the retrieval cues that trigger activation of a memory.

RETRIEVAL AND META–MEMORY: OUR KNOWLEDGE OF WHAT WE KNOW

Our discussion of encoding and retrieval has emphasized the top-down nature of both of those processes. To maximize the chances of remembering some information, people should use what they know about the material they are dealing with and the context in which they find themselves. This perspective leads to the more general question of how well we can understand and monitor our own memory processes. This topic was briefly discussed in Chapter 2, in the context of examining control processes in the multi-store model of memory. Our knowledge about the functioning of our own memory is known as *metamemory,* and it is part of the more general area of *metacognition,* our knowledge about the functioning of our own cognitive processes (Dunlosky & Metcalfe, 2009; Flavell, 1976; Metcalfe, 2009). Metamemory judgments may be related to retrieval processes. Please carry out the demonstration in Box 3.7 before reading further.

BOX 3.7 FEELING-OF-KNOWING DEMONSTRATION

Answer each of the following questions. If you *cannot* answer the question, indicate how confident you are that you would be able to *recognize* the answer if it were given, using a scale where 1 is very confident and 5 is not confident.

1. What is the minimum age allowed by law for a U.S. president?

    a. Answer: _____ If no answer, confidence: _____

2. What is the capital city of Peru?

    a. Answer: _____ If no answer, confidence: _____

3. What is the name of the longest river in the world?

    a. Answer: _____ If no answer, confidence: _____

4. In the Bible, who had the coat of many colors?

    a. Answer: _____ If no answer, confidence: _____

5. In what novel is the character Captain Ahab found?

    a. Answer: _____ If no answer, confidence: _____

6. Who was the first man to step on the moon?

    a. Answer: _____ If no answer, confidence: _____

Below are several possible answers for each of the above questions in multiple choice form. Make your choice and then check your answers at the bottom.

1. a. 25   b. 40   c. 30   d. 35

2. a. Lima   b. Callco   c. Bogotá   d. Trujillo

3. a. Amazon   b. Mississippi   c. Nile   d. Yangtze

4. a. Jacob   b. Joseph   c. Abraham   d. Peter

5. a. *Mutiny on the Bounty*   b. *Two Years Before the Mast*   c. *Lord Jim*   d. *Moby Dick*

6. a. Edwin Aldrin   b. Neil Armstrong   c. Frank Borman   d. John Glenn

Answers: 1. d; 2. a; 3. a; 4. b; 5. d; 6. b

Feeling of Knowing and Retrieval

In studies of metamemory, researchers have asked people questions that tap general knowledge of various sorts, and interest has focused on the questions that the person cannot answer (for review, see Dunlosky & Metcalfe, 2009). As in Box 3.7, the person provides a judgment of his or her *feeling of knowing* concerning the answer to some question that the person has been unable to retrieve. This is done by, for example, rating their confidence concerning whether they would be able to recognize the answer if it were shown to them. Feeling-of-knowing judgments are reasonably accurate as predictors of later memory performance: Unknown answers with higher feelings-of-knowing are recognized more accurately than those with lower ones.

One possible explanation of accurate feeling-of-knowing judgments assumes that they are based on partial information that is retrieved by the question (Koriat, 1993). If a person can think of *something* in response to a question, such as a first letter of the answer, then the person will tend to believe that he or she could recognize the correct answer. One prediction from this retrieval view is that it is the *amount* of partial information that is retrieved, not whether or not it is *correct*, that determines the strength of the feeling-of-knowing judgment. Koriat tested this analysis by giving participants several strings of random letters to study. The participant tried to recall the strings, and, after each recall attempt, gave a feeling-of-knowing judgment, rating how confident he or she was that the string had been recalled correctly. Feelings of knowing increased when more letters were retrieved, whether the letters were the correct ones or not. Thus, the feeling of knowing may be a judgment made as a result of partial retrieval success.

Another possibility, which does not contradict Koriat's partial-retrieval hypothesis, is that feeling-of-knowing judgments are based on a subject's familiarity with the question material (Metcalfe & Finn, 2008; Reder & Ritter, 1992; Schunn, Reder, Nhouyvanisvong, Richards, & Stroffolino, 1997; Schwartz, 2008). People are more tempted to think that they could retrieve the answer to a question they have heard before (whether or not they have partial information available to them).

Developmental Changes in Accuracy of Metamemory Judgments

When children are asked to make feeling-of-knowing judgments, they are reasonably accurate (Cultice, Somerville, & Wellman, 1983), although accuracy may increase with age (Wellman, 1977; Zabrucky & Ratner, 1986). However, children's performance is worse when they are asked to predict how well they will be able to carry out some memory task. Yussen and Levy (1975) asked 5-year-old preschoolers, 9-year-old third-graders, and college students to estimate how well they would perform on a memory-span test with pictures as the stimuli. The college students were accurate in their predictions, while the preschoolers were very inaccurate, predicting that their performance would be three times better than it actually was. By the third grade, predictions were much closer to actual performance. One may need extensive experience using memory before one can make accurate predictions about how well one will do when one has to use it.

Retrieval Processes in Metamemory: Conclusions

The ability to give accurate feeling-of-knowing judgments seems to be based in large part on retrieval processes. People may respond on the basis of partial retrieval of information relevant to the answer (Koriat, 1993), or on the familiarity of the question domain (Reder & Ritter, 1992; Schunn et al., 1997). This leads to another important question related to metamemory: What can you do if you know that you do not remember new information as well as you would like? Your metamemory is developed enough so you know that you might benefit from extra strategies. Collectively, strategies used to improve memory for new material are known as *mnemonic* devices or *mnemonics*. In the last section of the chapter, we review some mnemonic devices that have been studied by psychologists.

PRACTICAL ASPECTS OF MEMORY: INCREASING MEMORY PERFORMANCE WITH MNEMONIC DEVICES

An advertisement comes on TV in the middle of your favorite program, offering you the chance to improve your memory dramatically—to remember the names of people whom you meet once; learn your biology vocabulary in half the time. How can one do that? Chances are that memory improvement courses use some form of what we call *mnemonics* (from the Greek, *mnemonikos*, for memory). Mnemonic devices are comprised of both visually oriented and verbally oriented strategies, and many of them will sound like fancy versions of the control processes discussed in Chapter 2, as well as the encoding and retrieval processes discussed in this chapter. Mnemonic devices often capitalize on encoding new information (such as people's names or biology terminology) in a way that facilitates later retrieval of that information, and many of them use top-down processing by encouraging you to link new information to your existing knowledge.

Visual Imagery Mnemonics

The memory-improvement programs that promise to help you remember people's names, learn a second language, or remember anatomy terms most likely use an imagery technique called the *keyword method*. Over 10 years ago I heard an advertisement for a memory program to learn Spanish. It provided the example of *lo siento*, which means "I'm sorry." To remember this phrase, the advertisement suggested using an image that was linked both phonologically and semantically to the words. One could picture oneself doing something wrong, and then being so contrite that one bowed, "so *low* that I can *see into your toe*." This information would cue both how to say *lo siento*, and its meaning. In other words, the English words would serve as the *key* to learning the new Spanish vocabulary. Apparently this method was effective, because I remember the phrase and meaning to this day (although it may have helped that I heard the advertisement about the time I was lecturing on memory to my cognitive psychology class, and thus had tremendous motivation to remember it as an example of the keyword method).

Research has shown that the keyword method is very effective for remembering many sorts of information: names of composers (Brigham & Brigham, 1998), foreign language vocabulary (Carney & Levin, 1998a; Wang, Thomas, & Ouellette, 1992), medical and scientific terminology (King-Sears, Mercer, & Sindelar, 1992; Trout-Ervin, 1990), psychological terminology (Carney & Levin, 1998b), and even the names of unfamiliar animals (Carney & Levin, 2001). However, the keyword technique tends

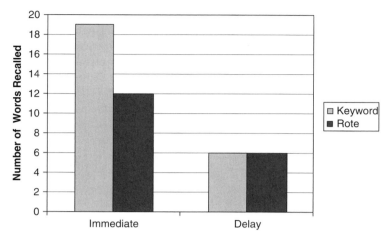

Figure 3.7   Results of Wang, Thomas, and Oullette (1992): Number of words recalled under keyword technique versus rote rehearsal, in immediate and delayed test conditions.

to be most effective immediately after learning the keywords: It is no better than rote rehearsal after a delay of even 1 week (Carney & Levin, 1998a; Wang et al., 1992; see Figure 3.7), and sometimes is *worse* than rote rehearsal after a delay (Thomas & Wang, 1996). Thus, as with bizarre imagery (see Box 3.8), experimental factors, such as how keywords are learned, the length of time between a learning and testing situation, and the quality of the keywords themselves, determine the usefulness of the keyword method in promoting memory (Carney & Levin, 1998a; Thomas & Wang, 1996).

BOX 3.8 BIZARRE IMAGERY

Imagine that three people are asked to remember word triplets such as *dog-bicycle-street*. One is told to image the three objects side-by-side, another is given the sentence, "The dog chases the bicycle down the street" to image, and the third is given the sentence, "The dog rides the bicycle down the street," to image. Which one will remember the word triplet best—the one who images the more commonplace scenario (dog chasing a bicycle), or the one who images the bizarre scenario (dog riding a bicycle)?

Most people's intuition is that bizarre imagery leads to better memory because it creates a more interesting image, which is then easier to retrieve. However, the empirical findings indicate that intuition is not always correct. Wollen, Weber, and Lowry (1972), in a classic imagery study, found that interactive imagery facilitated learning word pairs, but bizarreness did not have any advantage over common, interacting images. McDaniel and Einstein (1986) and McDaniel, Einstein, DeLosh, May, and Brady (1995) determined that using a few bizarre images in the middle of commonplace images did lead to better memory for words in the bizarre sentences. Why? Research results point to a retrieval advantage of bizarreness, if and when bizarreness effects are found (McDaniel, Dornburg, & Guynn, 2005). Because strange images (such as a dog riding a bike) are unlike anything we have ever seen before, they are more distinctive and easier to retrieve. When bizarre images are used to remember some sentences in a list, they then stand out from the more commonplace sentences in the list.

One technique used by orators in ancient Greece to remember the content of their speeches, in the order needed, was the *method of loci* (for *location*). Greek houses were arranged with interlinking rooms, often around a central courtyard (like the arrangement of rooms in the board game *Clue*). Greek orators would form an image of the first point they wanted to make and "place it" in the entrance room, then mentally "walk" into the next room and "place" an image representing the second idea of their speech, and so on. When it came time to deliver the oration, the orator "walked" through each room in imagination, retrieved the image from that room and used it to cue the next part of the speech. This mnemonic is effective: Ross and Lawrence (1968) found that college students could remember 38/40 words after one exposure, in order, by imaging the words on the sides of campus buildings!

How does the method of loci (and many of the other visual-imagery techniques) work to facilitate encoding and retrieval? First, as we have seen from the discussion in Chapter 1 of Paivio's pioneering research (e.g., Paivio, 1971, 2006; see also Chapter 7), imagery itself is often advantageous in memory. Secondly, use of the method of loci requires that people link new information (the ideas in a speech, a list of words) to well-known information—the layout of one's house, campus locations, and so on. We already know how effective it is to use familiar knowledge as a base for encoding and retrieving memories. In addition, the layout of one's house provides a ready-made set of retrieval cues, congruent with those used at encoding.

Another mnemonic, the *peg-word method*, requires that a person first learn the following rhyme: "One is a bun, two is a shoe, three is a tree, four is a door, five is a hive, six is sticks, seven is heaven, eight is a gate, nine is a line, ten is a hen." One then memorizes a series of items by imagining each of them interacting with the object named by the appropriate rhyming word. For instance, suppose you had a list of tasks to carry out on a given day, including: (1) dentist appointment, (2) post office, (3) call your father, and so on. You could imagine your dentist inside a hamburger *bun*, the post office perched on giant *shoes*, and your father with a cell phone up in a *tree*. In this way, you would link your task list to the already-learned rhyme via imagery, and you could recall your list of tasks in order, using the rhyme as a set of ready-made retrieval cues. The peg-word method has also been used to help patients with memory impairments recall simple lists of things that they must do or remember each day, such as their errand or shopping lists (Patten, 1972).

Verbal Mnemonics

Much of the material we want to learn is verbal (vocabulary words, words in a memory test, etc.). One strategy for remembering sets of words is *narrative chaining*—stringing a series of words together into a story, or long sentence. Your professor in class asks you to remember "attic, pajamas, train, . . ." You can convert this to "Jessica went up to the attic in her pajamas and found an old toy train, . . ." You have taken each word, chained the next one to it in a meaningful way, and thus encoded each set of words as linked in memory. Upon retrieval, each word should help to recover the next: *attic* will help retrieve *pajamas*, and so on. In this way, you can string together a random set of words into a meaningful story to facilitate memory.

A second verbal strategy is to use the first letter of each in a string of words to construct an *acronym*. Did you learn the planets in order by memorizing some version of the sentence *My very energetic mother just served us nine pizzas*? The first letter of each word points to one of the planets in our solar system, in order (Mercury, Venus, Earth, Mars, Jupiter, Saturn, Uranus, Neptune, Pluto; of course the acronym will have to be modified now that Pluto is no longer a planet). Some acronyms become so popular that their original meaning is lost—how many people recall what IBM originally stood for?

Mnemonics: Conclusions

As we have seen, there is evidence that mnemonic devices can be effective in facilitating memory, although there may be limitations to their effectiveness. Also, their assistance does not come without cost: In order to use a mnemonic device, you have to do some work. You may have to learn a new technique, such as a keyword technique or the peg-word rhyme. In general, one must carry out top-down processing, using imagery or a verbal scheme to organize the material and develop a set of retrieval cues. In general terms, we can see that the aspects of encoding, retrieval, and their coordination, discussed in this chapter, are relevant to understanding why mnemonic devices are effective.

ENCODING AND RETRIEVAL IN MEMORY: CONCLUSIONS

Both bottom-up and top-down processes are evident in encoding and retrieval. As Ebbinghaus (1885/1964) demonstrated, material can be learned through rote repetition, though the availability of knowledge helps us organize, and better remember, incoming information. The role of expertise in memory illustrates the important role that knowledge plays in both encoding and retrieval of information. In addition, much evidence demonstrates the interdependence of encoding and retrieval. Aspects of a learning situation, such as the instructions under which material was learned, as well as environmental factors (context) and psychological factors (the mood of a person) can become encoded along with facts or events themselves. When reinstated at time of retrieval, these seemingly extraneous factors nonetheless provide effective retrieval cues and facilitate memory. Research on metamemory indicates that we are moderately effective in knowing what we can and cannot remember; we may know that we have memories stored that are not immediately accessible by recall. Finally, research indicates that memory for a wide variety of visual and verbal material can be improved through the use of mnemonic devices, although the results may be more short-lived than permanent.

REVIEW QUESTIONS

Here is a set of review questions to help you organize and remember the material in this chapter. To maximize your retention of the material, try to answer each question from memory before reviewing the section of the chapter in which the material is covered.

That attempt at recall, even if the recall is not correct, will increase your memory for the material after you review it.

1. What is the difference between bottom-up and top-down memory processing?

2. What is the difference between *intentional* and *incidental* encoding?

3. What effects does bottom-up processing have on storage of information?

4. What was Bartlett's "effort after meaning"? What sorts of results provided support for Bartlett's view of memory as an active process, based on schematization?

5. What evidence is there that, contrary to Bartlett's view, details about events are sometimes stored?

6. How does research on expertise in memory provide evidence for the importance of top-down processes?

7. What is the relationship between bottom-up and top-down processes in memory?

8. What evidence supports the levels-of-processing view?

9. Is deep processing always better than shallow processing?

10. How do field effects support the top-down nature of retrieval?

11. What parallels are there between encoding and retrieval?

12. Describe research results demonstrating positive effects of retrieval cues on memory for categorically organized and random lists of words.

13. What role does the hippocampus play in storage of information?

14. What areas in the cortex are important in encoding and/or retrieval?

15. What evidence supports the encoding-specificity principle (the need for coordination of encoding and retrieval)? Should you worry about taking an exam in a room different from your normal classroom?

16. What factors influence metamemory (e.g., feeling-of-knowing) judgments?

17. What are the effects of mnemonic devices on memory?

CHAPTER 4

MEMORY III: ERRORS OF OMISSION (FORGETTING) AND COMMISSION (FALSE MEMORY)

We all have occasions when memory fails us—a trip to the store is delayed while we search for our keys (only to find them in the lock, where we left them when we came in earlier). We heard of one gentleman who reported his car stolen, only to find it 2 weeks later, its windshield covered with parking tickets, where he had left it. People always complain about their poor memories, and we all know that forgetting is something to be avoided or counteracted. Books that present methods for improving memory have been best sellers (e.g., Foer, 2011). On the other hand, many of us know people in their 80s or 90s who can provide detailed recollections of events from their childhoods. How can they retain information for decades, when we often forget what we did minutes ago?

Even worse than forgetting, perhaps, is when we misremember something: Think how embarrassing it would be to be at a new job and to call your boss by the wrong name. More dramatic examples of misremembering can be found in court cases in which key witnesses misidentify an innocent person, who sits in prison for many years. In fact, it is estimated that 75% of overturned criminal cases are due to faulty eyewitness testimony (www.innocenceproject.org).

Memory researchers (e.g., Kimball & Bjork, 2002) categorize two main ways in which our memories can go awry: errors of *omission*, when details or information are missing or forgotten; and errors of *commission*, when our memories contain extra but incorrect details, so they are not reflective of reality (Koriat, Goldsmith, & Pansky, 2000). Forgetting a person's name completely would constitute an error of omission; calling someone *Rebecca* instead of *Rachel* would be an error of commission. In this chapter, we will address both kinds of memory errors: *forgetting*—when we lose details of events or materials; and *false memories*—when our memories are modified from the original.

OUTLINE OF CHAPTER 4

This chapter first examines research on forgetting, focusing on the question of how long our memories last. Researchers have devised methods to enable them to test memory for experiences from many years past, even experiences from very early in life. We also examine the question of whether some types of information are better remembered than others. After we have reviewed the basic phenomena concerning forgetting, we will examine how forgetting might be brought about, centering on the question of whether forgetting occurs because information fades from memory or because memories interfere with each other, which produces forgetting. Research supports the conclusion that much forgetting is the result of interference from information in memory. We reexamine research presented in Chapter 3, indicating that forgetting can result from a mismatch between the conditions at encoding and retrieval. We also consider possible positive functions that forgetting might serve. The second half of the chapter addresses the question of how memory distortions, or false memories, might occur. This research has direct implications for eyewitness testimony in court cases, and other arenas in which accurate memories are important in everyday life.

LABORATORY STUDIES OF MEMORY AND FORGETTING

In a pioneering study, Shepard (1967, Experiment 1) had participants study a deck of 540 index cards, with one randomly selected word printed on each; half the words were high frequency (e.g., *office*), the other half were very-low-frequency (e.g., *ferule*). Participants studied the words at their own pace, which took on average about an hour. Memory for the words was tested immediately after the list was read. Shepard used forced-choice recognition to test memory: pairs of words were presented, one from the list (the *target*) and one new word (the *foil*), and the participant was asked to choose the target word. Results from Shepard's Experiment 1 are presented in Table 4.1. Overall word recognition performance was very good. In a second experiment, Shepard asked participants to study a set of 612 randomly chosen sentences, and two additional participants studied a longer list comprising 1,224 sentences. Again performance on the forced-choice recognition test was very good, almost 90%, even for the long-sentence list (see Experiment 2 in Table 4.1).

Table 4.1   Recognition Memory Studies for Large Amounts of Material of Differing Types: Shepard's (1967) Results and Standing's (1973) Picture-Recognition Results

Type of Material	Time of Test	Number of Items in Study List	% Correct
Shepard (1967)			
Experiment 1: Words	Immediately after list	540	88
Experiment 2: Sentences	Immediately after list	612	89
	Immediately after list	1224	88
Experiment 3: Pictures	Immediately after list	612	97
	2 hours		100
	3 days		92
	7 days		87
	120 days		58
Standing (1973)			
Pictures		10,000	73

In the final experiment of Shepard's study, participants studied 612 pictures taken from a variety of sources, including advertisements in magazines. In this experiment Shepard tested the participants twice, using different test pictures each time, in order to measure forgetting. Participants were tested immediately after studying the pictures, and after delays from 2 hours to 120 days (2880 hours; see Experiment 3 in Table 4.1). Visual recognition performance was excellent—basically 100% on the immediate test and after 2 hours (see Table 4.1). Even 120 days later, people's accuracy was 58%, which is still significantly above chance performance (50% on a two-choice recognition test).

Shepard's (1967) study also produced two further interesting findings. When one looks in detail at the results of Experiment 1 in Table 4.2, one sees that low-frequency words are better remembered in a recognition test. While we are more likely to *recall* high frequency words (Watkins & Watkins, 1977), because they are easier to access spontaneously, rarer words may be easier to identify in a *recognition* task because we simply need to identify the correct word out of two (or more) options. This combination of results—high-frequency words recalled better, low-frequency words recognized better—is referred to as the *word frequency effect*. A comparison of the results of Shepard's Experiments 2 and 3 in Table 4.1 also reveals that memory for pictures was superior to memory for words, a phenomenon known as the *picture superiority effect*. Look at Table 4.1 and compare the level of recognition for pictures after 7 days (Experiment 3) to the recognition for words immediately after being exposed to them (Experiment 1). The rates are similar (around 87%), indicating that participants recognized picture stimuli after 1 week at a rate equivalent to an almost-immediate test of words. One possible explanation for the difference in performance on pictures versus words is the distinctiveness of pictures versus words—English words are made up of the same 26 letters in various combinations, whereas there are almost unlimited varieties of configurations of visual stimuli. Pictures also permit depiction of detail, meaning that they may encourage more elaborate encoding, *and* provide more retrieval cues. Pictures may also have a memory advantage because of our evolutionary history. We humans would have seen and remembered scenes long before words were even invented. Thus, we have a great proportion of our brains devoted to visual processing and visual memory; this may make memory for visual stimuli superior to memory for verbal stimuli.

Shepard's (1967) research demonstrating relatively little forgetting of large amounts of material was extended by Standing (1973). In one study, Standing presented much longer stimulus lists to his participants: 10,000 pictures, at 5 seconds per picture (it took several sessions, spaced over 5 consecutive days, to present all the items). He then

Table 4.2   Shepard (1967) Results, Experiment 1: Word Recognition as a Function of Frequency of Target and Foil

	High Frequency FOIL	Low Frequency FOIL
High Frequency TARGET	82.1%	86.7%
Low Frequency TARGET	93%	92%

Table 4.3 Standing (1973) Results

Type of Material (200 items)	Recognition (%)	Recall (%)
Normal pictures	94	26
Words (visual)	83	12
Words (auditory)	86	19
CVCs (visual)	62	6

tested recognition performance 1 to 2 days later, so that the average retention interval, including study time, was approximately 4 to 5 days. Standing's results, shown in Table 4.1, are consistent with Shepard's evidence of good recognition memory. In conclusion, these findings demonstrate that on recognition tests people can remember vast amounts of information. In another study, Standing (1973) compared recognition performance with that on recall tests for different kinds of materials (Table 4.3). He presented people with lists of 200 items—either pictures, words presented visually, words presented auditorily, or nonsense syllables—and then gave the participants 40 minutes to recall as much as they could (for pictures, they recalled by writing a description of the picture). Following the recall test, a forced-choice recognition test was given. As one might expect, the ability to recall 200 items, even immediately after studying them, was not very high (6–26%). Recall performance was particularly poor for the nonsense syllables. Recognition results matched Shepard's, with recognition best for pictures (the picture-superiority effect again), but still good for words. Recognition of consonant-vowel-consonant visuals (CVCs) yielded the worst performance (although better than chance—62% versus a chance performance of 50%).

The Question of Ecological Validity

We have now looked at several laboratory studies that have demonstrated high levels of memory for different types of materials. Some researchers, such as Neisser (1976), have criticized almost all laboratory studies of memory as lacking *ecological validity*. The term *ecology* is used to refer to the natural environment, so a study that is ecologically valid is one that is relevant to our natural environment (i.e., the real world). Therefore, in saying that laboratory studies of memory are not ecologically valid, one is saying that those studies are not a valid representation of how we use memory in real life. In most laboratory investigations of memory, the information is not relevant to the participants; sometimes, as we know, the materials are actually designed to be meaningless (e.g., CVCs). In addition, memory experiments usually do not require that the participants hold material in memory for a very long time (although several of the studies just reviewed have used intervals of days or months). In the ordinary course of our lives, we sometimes retain information for years. It is therefore important to study people's memories for real-life experiences, even though it may be difficult to conduct such studies. One basic problem is *subject attrition* (or drop out)—an experimenter must keep track of the participants over long periods of time, and there is a risk that participants may not be willing or able to complete the study. There is another advantage to controlled laboratory experiments: They filter out potentially confounding variables by carefully manipulating the main variables to be studied (e.g., words versus pictures) and controlling or eliminating others. However, a needed complement is found in studies of memory and forgetting for real-life events in a variety of contexts, to which we now turn.

REMEMBERING AND FORGETTING OVER LONG PERIODS OF TIME

Studies of Autobiographical Memory

In order to examine retention of real-life experiences over several years, Linton (1975, 1986) studied her own memory for incidents in her life. Every day, for 6 years, she recorded at least two memorable events. She wrote a description of the event on one side of an index card, and on the other recorded the date and other information. Linton subsequently tested herself by randomly selecting two cards, first judging which of the two items had occurred earlier, and then trying to remember the exact dates of the two events. In addition, she tested some events up to four times over the course of the study. Linton's performance on items tested once is shown in Figure 4.1. Considering only the items tested once, performance was excellent for the first 2 years, good for the next 1 1/2 years or so, and then dropped relatively quickly, to 70% forgetting at 4 1/2 years. Testing an item more than once resulted in large increases in performance. At 4 1/2 years, only 33% of those items were forgotten. Thus, repeated exposure to a piece of information functioned as a kind of rehearsal, which seems to be as important in remembering autobiographical events as it is in laboratory experiments.

Overall, Linton's results indicated that memory for autobiographical information can be surprisingly good (although it must be noted that she wrote down *memorable* events, which would be expected to facilitate memory). There were, however, some mild memory distortions in Linton's memories. Sometimes when she tried to remember when an event occurred (e.g., dinner with a friend), she would confuse it with other events of the same sort, which indicated to her that similar events were beginning to blend together into more general memories. One could say that some

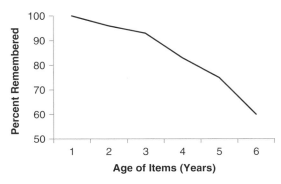

Figure 4.1   Linton's (1986) memory results: Performance on items tested once as a function of "age of items" (retention interval).

of Linton's forgetting occurred because her memory was becoming *schematic* (see Chapter 3)—details were lost or altered, though the gist remained.

Similar conclusions came from a study by Barclay and Wellman (1986), in which student participants used a diary to record memorable events, the context in which each occurred, and their reaction to it. Barclay and Wellman tested recognition memory for the events at intervals up to 2 1/2 years. The correct item was the diary description of the event. Some of the incorrect items, or foils, were slight rewritings of the original event. If a person had reported going to lunch at a new restaurant, a foil might be that the waiter had asked them if they wanted coffee. For other foils, the original item was rewritten so that the meaning changed (e.g., a positive evaluation of the restaurant was made negative). Still other foils were items from other students' diaries.

People were able to recognize events for up to a year, with an average of 90% correct recognition. Over time, there was a tendency to falsely recognize foils that were plausible substitutions for the original memory. Even after two years, though, participants usually could distinguish their own diary entries from those of others. Those results led Barclay and Wellman (1986) to conclude that our memories are accurate in general terms, but that they may lose details and become schematized, like other types of memories (see also Brewer, 1986, 2000a).

A number of researchers have maintained that, even though constructive memory does occur (i.e., people may report information that was not part of the original event; see discussion of Bartlett's (1932) research in Chapter 1), autobiographical memory for events can nonetheless be quite accurate (Brewin, Andrews, & Gotlib, 1993). Brewer (1988) had undergraduates record events from their lives in response to a beeper that went off randomly, about every 2 hours. The students' memories were tested on a randomly selected sample of the events over a period of just over 3 1/2 years. They were provided with a cue (e.g., "having lunch with a friend") and asked to recall as many details as possible. The students responded correctly to over 60% of the autobiographical episodes. Only 1.5% of the errors were constructive (Brewer, 1986), in which people reported details that were grossly discrepant from their original reports.

The collective results of Linton (1975; 1986), Barclay and Wellman (1986), and Brewer (1996) demonstrate that autobiographical events can be maintained over long periods of time, though specific details may be forgotten. Memory is enhanced for items that have been thought about, that is, rehearsed or tested, during the retention interval. Long-term forgetting may in some cases involve loss of detail, as memories of specific episodes begin to blend into more general memories. Brewer, however, maintained that memory is only partially reconstructive, because people are good at reporting details of events from their personal past (even if some details are lost with time).

REMEMBERING AND FORGETTING OVER VERY LONG PERIODS OF TIME: BAHRICK'S ANALYSIS OF PERMASTORE

While studies of autobiographical memory spanning intervals of several years are impressive, Bahrick and his coworkers have carried out an ingenious series of studies that assessed people's memory and forgetting for material that had been learned up to 50 years earlier. In order to examine forgetting after really long periods of time, without being derailed by such problems as participants or researchers dying before the study was completed, Bahrick and his coworkers (e.g., Bahrick, 1984; Bahrick, Bahrick, & Wittlinger, 1975) reversed things. Rather than giving young people material to remember, and then trying to retest them years later, Bahrick and coworkers started at the end, with the test for forgetting. They tested adults of various ages for recall of material that had been learned many years earlier. As one example, in a now-classic study, Bahrick, Bahrick, and Wittlinger (1975) tested more than 400 people, aged 17–74, on their memories of their high-school classmates. The participants were tested on recognition for classmates' names and faces, their recall for names, and their ability to match names and faces. The information was obtained from high-school yearbooks. Bahrick et al. also asked the participants how much they had interacted with their former classmates in the years since high school: whether they had attended class reunions, if they lived in the same neighborhood with people they grew up with, and so on. This information enabled the investigators to take into consideration the amount of contact that might have occurred in the intervening years.

The results are shown in Figure 4.2a. Recall of names was good shortly after graduation (70–80%), but declined steadily over time. Performance was consistently good on the recognition tests, however. Recognition for faces did not fall below 80% for more than 35 years. Face recognition was superior to name recognition, but even name recognition did not decline significantly for 15 years after graduation. Throughout the 47-plus-year retention interval, recognition memory for names and faces was always significantly above chance. There seems to be very little forgetting of this information, even after relatively long periods of time.

The study of very long-term recall of information from one's life was carried further by Bahrick (1984), who tested memory for Spanish, which individuals had learned in high school or college. Based on class records, people who had taken Spanish were contacted and asked to participate in the study. The time since study of Spanish for those individuals varied from a few months to almost 50 years. If a person agreed to participate in the study, he or she was sent various tests of Spanish. Participants were also sent a questionnaire that assessed how much use they had made of Spanish since studying it, which allowed Bahrick to screen out those who had used Spanish significantly. The results of this study are shown in Figure 4.2b, and again two important points are seen. There was better performance on recognition versus recall tests, and there was also significant forgetting, but most of it came during the first 6 years after learning. All the curves are essentially flat, from 6 years out to almost 50 years.

How could people remember information, some of which they had not deliberately encoded, for almost half a century? Bahrick et al. (1975) proposed that recognition performance for both high school classmates and Spanish that one had learned earlier was so good was because the information resided in a *permastore*, in which it was not subject to forgetting. Bahrick et al. attributed very long-term retention to two factors: *over-learning*—as an example, people had been exposed to classmates' names and faces multiple times (perhaps hundreds or thousands of times) over the course of high school; and *distributed practice*—learning was spread out or *distributed* over time.

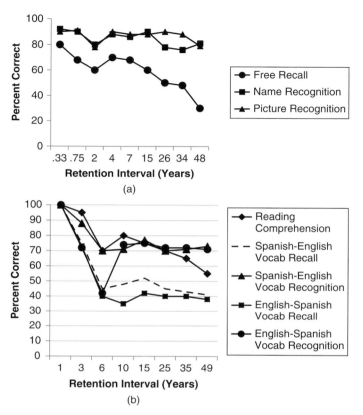

Figure 4.2 (a) Bahrick, Bahrick, and Wittlinger (1975) results: Memory for high-school classmates. (b) Bahrick (1984): Memory for Spanish.

One's high-school classmates are, by and large, constant over one's high-school career, and thus contact with classmates extends over several years. This would result in large amounts of exposure to information about high school classmates over an extended period of time.

Similarly, in examining retention of Spanish, one is looking at information that was studied relatively intensively over several years in school, and perhaps earlier as well, which undoubtedly contributed to its good retention. Bahrick (1984) also found that people who achieved higher grades in their Spanish courses forgot less over the intervening intervals, supporting the idea that better initial learning provides resistance against forgetting.

Very Long-Term Memory for Cognitive Psychology

In an experiment that is directly relevant to students reading this book, Conway, Cohen, and Stanhope (1991) examined people's long-term memory for cognitive psychology. Participants had completed a standardized university course from 3 months

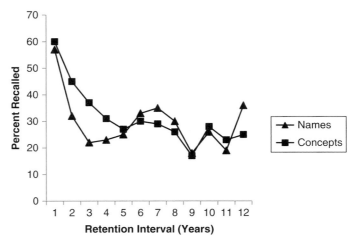

Figure 4.3   Recall results from Conway, Cohen, and Stanhope (1991): Memory for cognitive psychology information.

to 10$^1/_2$ years earlier. Conway et al. used several memory measures: recognition of proper names (e.g., Baddeley) and concepts (e.g., *working memory*); cued-recall of researchers' names and concepts; true/false questions for specific and general facts about theories and experimental findings; and a forced-choice recognition test to determine subjects' memory about research methods. The sharpest decline in memory took place within the first 3 or so years after learning (see Figure 4.3). However, recognition memory for researchers, terminology, and experimental facts remained above chance (50%) for the entire retention interval. General information was maintained longer than specific facts and names, which is consistent with previous research on how memory becomes more general over time. Also, comparable to the results from Bahrick and Phelps's (1987) study of retention of Spanish, Conway et al. found that students who had received higher grades in the cognitive psychology course forgot less over time, again indicating that, not surprisingly, learning information thoroughly to begin with reduces the rate of forgetting.

In conclusion, numerous studies have supported the conclusion that many types of information may be retained for long periods of time. Autobiographical material as well as other types of information may not be lost even after many years.

METHOD OF STUDY AND FORGETTING: DISTRIBUTED VERSUS MASSED PRACTICE

Studies of very long-term memory (e.g., Bahrick, 1984; Bahrick et al., 1975) have indicated that distributing one's exposure to material (such as classmates' faces) over long periods of time may lead to relatively little forgetting. However, those studies did not (and could not) control the way in which the material was encoded, since the events that people were being tested on had taken place naturally, and up to 50 years before. Laboratory studies, which are able to systematically control how people encode new material, confirm what we have already discussed—*distributed practice*, in which studying is spread over hours, days, weeks, or even years—is far superior to *massed practice*, where studying occurs for the same amount of time but in a single session or in a series of closely spaced sessions. The tendency to remember information better after distributed practice is also called the *spacing effect* (Peterson, Wampler, Kirkpatrick, & Saltzman, 1963). The spacing effect has been found with skill learning (Lorge, 1930), learning of word pairs (Keppel, 1964, 1967), remembering names and faces (Bahrick, Bahrick, & Wittlinger, 1975), and remembering how to solve mathematics problems (Rohrer & Taylor, 2006).

A particularly thorough examination of the role of distributed practice in long-term retention was carried out by Bahrick, Bahrick, Bahrick, and Bahrick (1993), in a study that had the advantages of both real-life memory studies and highly controlled experimental studies. The four authors—four family members—served as the participants, and each chose a foreign language studied previously (French for three; German for one). Each researcher compiled a set of 300 words they no longer remembered, divided into six blocks of 50 words each. Each block of words was studied for either 13 or 26 sessions, and those sessions were scheduled either every 14 days, every 28 days, or every 56 days, yielding six combinations of delays and numbers of sessions. As one example, one set of words was studied for 13 sessions, with the sessions scheduled every 14 days. Studying those words required a total of 170 days. At the other extreme, one set of words was studied for 26 sessions, with sessions every 56 days, requiring a total of almost 4 years (!) to complete the sessions.

The Bahricks then tested themselves at retention intervals of 1, 2, 3, or 5 years after last having seen the test words. The test first involved recall of the English translation of each foreign word, followed by a multiple-choice test for the words that had not been recalled. As can be seen in Figure 4.4, the benefits of distributed practice were well demonstrated: The best-remembered words were those that had been studied every 56 days. In fact, memory for the words that had been studied for 13 sessions under 56-day spacing was equivalent to that for words studied for 26 sessions every 14 days. Thus, only *half* as much studying was needed to learn foreign vocabulary words if learning sessions were spaced out over longer periods of time. (What does this suggest about how and when you might start studying for your next cognitive psychology exam?)

Virtually every experiment that has tested memory for material learned under distributed versus massed practice has found an advantage for distributed practice. Optimum spacing depends on the length of time that the material must be retained; a recent review and analysis of more than 317 experiments determined that greater spacing between study sessions led to longer retention intervals for the material (Cepeda, Pashler, Vul, Wixted, and Rohrer, 2006). If you want to remember material over several years, the study sessions should be spaced further apart than for material you need to remember for several weeks.

But *why* does distributed practice facilitate memory and slow down forgetting? Different explanations have focused on encoding versus retrieval. One possibility is *encoding variability* (Estes, 1955; Glenberg, 1979; Johnston & Uhl, 1976). Spreading out study time means that a person will study the material at several different times

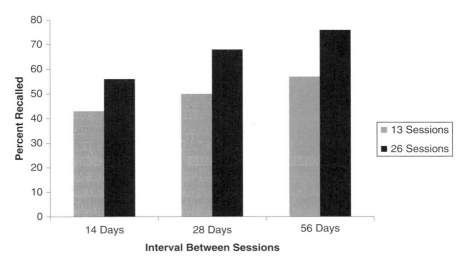

Figure 4.4   Results from Bahrick, Bahrick, Bahrick, and Bahrick (1993): Recall as a function of interval between study sessions and total number of study sessions (recall performance summarized over all recall tests).

and perhaps in several different places. At each of those times, contextual cues will be stored with information about the item, increasing the likelihood that some of those stored cues will match those present when the person is tested. Put another way, those multiple cues facilitate memory by providing a more varied set of possible retrieval cues. Under this scenario, distributed practice provides a retrieval advantage when one attempts to recall or use the information.

A second explanation, *attenuation of attention* (Hintzman, 1974, 1976), proposes that the advantage of distributed study sessions rests mainly with encoding processes. As people undergo massed presentation of the same item, the attention paid to each repetition decreases (or *attenuates*). Thus, the amount of processing decreases when presentations are close together. As an example, if you watch a movie one night, and your roommate watches the same movie the next, you probably won't pay much attention the second night (though you would pay more attention if your second exposure to the movie was months later). There is experimental evidence that people do spend less time processing material repeated in massed-practice trials (Shaughnessy, Zimmerman, & Underwood, 1972); however, it is likely that the attenuation effect cannot fully explain the robustness of the spacing effect (see Hintzman, Summers, Eki, & Moore, 1975).

A related neuropsychological hypothesis, which has empirical support as well, also asserts that encoding is enhanced by distributed practice. As discussed in Chapter 3, Hebb (1949) proposed that neural circuits process information by *reverberating*, or continuing to respond, even after the person has stopped paying attention to the material. Reverberation leads to *consolidation*, or strengthening of the memory trace, as the result of changes in the neurons and neural connections. Those physiological changes, called *long-term potentiation* (see Chapter 3), are responsible for storing material on a long-term basis. If information is stored (i.e., during the first study session), and then restudied later, the same neural circuits will be reinforced more than if only one study session is used. That is, if there are two study sessions, there will be two opportunities for reverberation; one long study session provides only one opportunity. Thus, at a neural level, information that receives distributed practice will have an advantage over information processed closer in time.

VERY LONG-TERM RETENTION OF INFORMATION: CONCLUSIONS

A number of studies have found relatively little forgetting over very long periods of time, in some cases extending over 50 years. Overlearning and distributed practice are important factors that influence retention on a very long-term basis, whether that material is semantic knowledge (foreign-language vocabulary), factual knowledge (cognitive psychology), or autobiographical knowledge (high-school classmates). How well the material was learned in the first place predicts long-term forgetting (Bahrick, 1984; Bahrick et al., 1975; Conway et al., 1991). Bahrick's concept of a permastore has empirical support, as tests of very long-term memory show the steepest decline during the first few years after a person has learned the material, and then a leveling out of forgetting.

Although in some cases information can be retained over many years, it is still true that some forgetting does occur over that time, and it is also true that we often forget material that we once knew, such as who won the Super Bowl 2 years ago. Thus two questions remain from this review: When information is forgotten, how and why does that forgetting occur? We now turn to those questions.

THEORIES OF FORGETTING

Researchers have considered two major possibilities, outlined in Table 4.4, for the mechanism whereby forgetting occurs. First, information might *decay*, or *fade from memory* as time passes (Table 4.4, Column A); the inability to recall something would then be due to its no longer being present in memory. An alternative to decay is that we retain much more information than we can access, and forgetting is attributable to *retrieval difficulties*, that is, an inability to retrieve information (not because it has disappeared; Table 4.4 Column B). As discussed in Chapter 3, an *encoding-retrieval mismatch* often causes memory performance to suffer. Changes in context—physical, psychological, and cognitive (e.g., Godden & Baddeley, 1975; Keleman & Creeley, 2003; Tulving & Thomson, 1971)—can all produce forgetting. Another explanation for retrieval problems is *interference*, which assumes that other information in memory, especially information similar to that which you are trying to remember, makes remembering particular items difficult. We already discussed some aspects of interference in Chapter 2, where it was considered as a source of short-term forgetting.

Table 4.4   Summary of Theories of Forgetting

| Question About Forgetting | Theory | | |
| | | B. Retrieval Difficulty | |
	A. Decay	Encoding-Retrieval Mismatch	Interference
Is there a change over time in the information in memory?	Yes	No	No
What is the source of forgetting?	Time	Retrieval cue does not match encoded information.	Cue overload—Multiple similar items related to single retrieval cue.
What is the role of other information in memory in bringing about forgetting?	Irrelevant	Irrelevant	Interference from similar items is the cause of forgetting.

Interference might occur because too many events or pieces of information become associated with the same retrieval cue. As an example, you might be asked: "What are all the things you have received as birthday gifts since childhood?" You might be able to recall only a few of them, because there are too many memories—all those gifts over all those years—competing for activation. Forgetting in this situation has occurred because of *cue overload* (Roediger & Guynn, 1996): Many items are associated with the cue "birthday gifts." The degree of interference would be based on the number of memories similar to a target piece of information (G. Brown, Neath, & Chater, 2007). Thus, cue overload is closely related to issues concerning retrieval discussed in Chapter 3. (For another possibility concerning how interference might work, see Wixted, 2004, 2005.)

The notions of encoding-retrieval mismatch and cue overload both assume that the problem is accessing information that is in memory. There are, however, differences between the two views (see Table 4.4, Column B). According to cue overload, forgetting comes about because similar items get activated and interfere with retrieval of a memory. In situations with no similar interfering items, there should be no forgetting. You might easily remember the details of your high-school graduation, for example, because it only happened once, but fail to remember the details of each individual day at high school, because there were over 1,000 of them. On the other hand, the encoding-retrieval mismatch view predicts that forgetting could occur even if no similar items were available to interfere with the target. If the person's internal and external contexts changed enough between encoding the target and trying to remember it, then the cue(s) used at retrieval might be different enough from the encoding that no retrieval would occur. Thus, the mismatch theory would predict that the best recall for your high school graduation would be when you were sitting in the same auditorium (and preferably in the same state of excitement, dressed in your graduation outfit).

As we work through these various explanations of forgetting, it should also be kept in mind that forgetting could be brought about in multiple ways: decay, encoding-retrieval mismatch, and interference might all contribute to forgetting. Support for one view does not mean that the other views must be wrong.

MEASURING DECAY IN MEMORY: HOW COULD WE TELL IF MEMORY TRACES WEAKEN AS TIME PASSES?

As events recede into the past, we usually remember less about them (see Table 4.4 and Figures 4.1 and 4.2). Most of us thus assume that memories *decay* (i.e., fade or weaken) over time. As an analogy, a man wearing strong cologne visits your house, and people entering for several hours thereafter can smell his presence. With time the odor fades, and after a while it is as if the person had never been there. Perhaps something similar happens with memories. However, decay as an explanation for forgetting is very difficult to test. Imagine that a researcher wants to test the hypothesis that memory traces decay with time. The researcher: (1) has people study some material, such as a list of words, until they learn it; (2) lets time pass, say several days (that is, introduces a retention interval); and (3) tests the people's memories. If they have forgotten some of the material, then one might be tempted to conclude that memory decays over time. There is, however, as McGeoch (1931) noted many years ago, one crucial difficulty with this proposed study: A retention interval is not made up of *empty time*, but is composed of *events*. Those events—the study participants go to their jobs or attend classes, see a movie, read a novel, socialize with friends—could potentially disrupt memory for the material in either of two ways.

First, the events occurring after the people had learned the words could interfere with remembering the material, which would be an example of *retroactive* interference. The participants would have been exposed to a lot of words—at their job or school, while socializing, and in other situations—that might interfere with retrieval of the words on the list. If so, then forgetting would not be due to decay. Second, the participants' internal states could change between study and test, or they might be tested in a different location. If so, a mismatch might occur between the retrieval and encoding environments, and again, any forgetting that occurred might not be due to decay. In addition, the information about words that a person already has stored in memory, or previous memory tests in which he had participated, might interfere *proactively*, which again would be forgetting that is not due to decay.

In principle, the only way to test the decay hypothesis directly would be by inducing a state of suspended animation in the participants, such as occurs in science fiction. The impossibility of directly testing decay as a factor in forgetting means that we can only indirectly draw conclusions about decay: We must first see if the events occurring in a time interval and/or changes in the retrieval environment are important in bringing about forgetting before we can draw conclusions about time itself causing forgetting. Therefore, we now turn to an examination of interference in forgetting, which will also provide us with evidence about the role of decay in memory.

INTERFERENCE THEORY

Retroactive Interference Theory

The idea that interference can bring about forgetting has a long history, and some researchers claim that all forgetting is the result of interference rather than decay

(G. Brown et al., 2007). The theoretical importance of interference in memory was first proposed by McGeoch in the 1930s. McGeoch (1931) critiqued the then-prevalent concept of *disuse* as an explanation of forgetting: the idea that forgetting came about because a memory was not "used," or recalled, as time passed. This idea is the same as the notion of decay. McGeoch pointed out that in no other scientific explanation was *time*, by itself, used as an explanatory concept. For example, if we ask a chemist why unpainted iron rusts when left exposed to the elements, we would not be told that it rusts because of the passage of time. Rather, we would be told about oxidation, and how unpainted metal is subject to it, and how oxidation changes the appearance of metal, and so forth. We would be given an explanation that involves a series of events, and the outcome of this series of events is the rust that we asked about. McGeoch proposed that psychological explanations of forgetting also must say more than it simply happens over time. We must provide a series of events or processes that bring about forgetting as their result. McGeoch proposed that forgetting occurred because of events that took place after the initial learning experience, which interfered retroactively with the old learning, and made its retrieval more difficult.

Let us assume that an English-speaking individual decides to learn Spanish. She begins by studying English-Spanish word pairs (e.g., *man:hombre*; *arm:brazo*), so that when each English word is presented later, she can recall the Spanish word. This is Stage 1 of her language learning (see Figure 4.5a). Now let us say that the woman decides to major in languages, so she starts to learn French, Stage 2 of her language learning. During Stage 2, she is exposed to the same English words and a French word for each: *man:homme* and *arm:bras*. The diagram in Figure 4.5b shows the situation

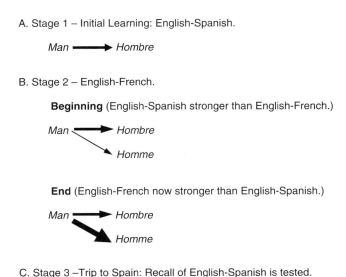

A. Stage 1 – Initial Learning: English-Spanish.

Man ⟶ Hombre

B. Stage 2 – English-French.

Beginning (English-Spanish stronger than English-French.)

Man ⟶ Hombre
⟶ Homme

End (English-French now stronger than English-Spanish.)

Man ⟶ Hombre
⟶ Homme

C. Stage 3 –Trip to Spain: Recall of English-Spanish is tested.

Man: ? in Spanish

Person cannot produce Spanish, because of the strength of English-French.

Figure 4.5   McGeoch's (1931) three stages of retroactive interference.

at the beginning of Stage 2: The English-Spanish connection is much stronger than English-French, and therefore the Spanish word may mistakenly be given in French class when "man" and "arm" are presented. However, the English-French connection will be strengthened as *man:homme* and *arm:bras* are studied in Stage 2. Finally, presentation of the English words will result in the individual's producing their French equivalents (Stage 2 – End in Figure 4.5b).

Now let us say that the woman takes a trip to Spain (Stage 3 in Figure 4.5c). She is talking about a *man* and she needs to produce the Spanish word (*hombre*). However, she will be slower to retrieve the correct translation, because *man:homme* (the French) has become stronger than *man:hombre*, and dominates. This is *retroactive interference*, because the interfering material (the more-recent English-French connection) is working backward in time, or retroactively, to interfere with English-Spanish. McGeoch's (1931) analysis of forgetting due to retroactive interference assumed that interference was brought about through *response competition*: When an English word is presented, the Spanish and French words are in competition, and the one that is stronger at a given time will be retrieved first.

A more formal analysis of retroactive interference is shown in Line 1 in Table 4.5. The participant first learns a series of English-Spanish pairs (Time$_1$). A series of

Table 4.5   Retroactive Interference

A. Outline of Retroactive interference

1. Interference group: Learn **Spanish** (100%) / Learn French (100%) / [retention interval] / Recall **Spanish** (40%)

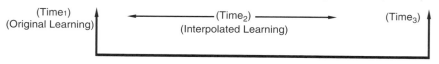

(Time$_1$)
(Original Learning) ⟵————— (Time$_2$) —————⟶ (Time$_3$)
(Interpolated Learning)

60% Forgetting—Due to retroactive interference from French?

2. Control group: Learn Spanish (100%) / Learn Japanese (100%) / [retention interval] / Recall Spanish (90%)

B. Summary of factors that affect retroactive interference

Factor	Effect on Retroactive Interference
Degree of learning of original material (Spanish)	More original learning, less interference
Degree of learning of interpolated material (French)	More interpolated learning, more interference
Temporal relation between original material (Spanish) and interpolated material (French; effects of retention interval)	Original and interpolated learning close in time, more interference
Recency of interpolated learning (French)	Interpolated material more recent, more interference
Similarity of original learning and interpolated material (Spanish-French vs. Spanish-Japanese)	More similarity, more interference

English-French pairs is then studied until they are recalled correctly (Time$_2$). We then present the English words alone, and ask the participant to produce the *Spanish* words (Time$_3$). Assume that we find that the person's recall of the English-Spanish vocabulary is now only 40%, meaning that 60% of the original English-Spanish pairs have been forgotten. What brought about that forgetting? Learning the English-French pairs may have resulted in the forgetting of the English-Spanish pairs due to retroactive interference. Alternately, however, forgetting of the English-Spanish vocabulary could have been brought about by the *time* it took to learn the English-French pairs (Time$_2$). We cannot separate those two possibilities—forgetting due to interference versus forgetting due to the passage of time—without testing a control group that receives no intervening information. As noted earlier, this is impossible, because even if a person is told to sit quietly between learning and testing, it is likely that they will be thinking of *something* during that time.

Researchers have taken several different paths in trying to find appropriate control conditions in experiments studying interference in memory. Jenkins and Dallenbach (1924) attempted to eliminate possible retroactive interference by giving people a list of nonsense syllables to learn either in the evening just before going to sleep or in the morning as they started their day. In this design, time passes for both groups, but very little new material is experienced by the participants who slept. That allows one to see if time alone produces forgetting. Participants were tested on their memory for the syllables 1, 2, 4, or 8 hours after studying them, and the Sleep group (who should have been subject to very little retroactive interference) did show a lower rate of forgetting than the Awake group. So empty time (if sleeping can be described in that way) produced less forgetting than did an awake interval of equal length, indicating that time alone was not an important factor in forgetting.

Experimenters have also used physiological interventions to prevent retroactive interference and thereby examine the effects of time alone on forgetting (Sangha et al., 2005). For example, it is well known that people do not learn as much under the influence of alcohol as they do sober. Bruce and Pihl (1997) asked a group of men to read sentences referring to themselves (e.g., "I feel great!") before consuming either alcohol or a placebo drink. When tested on their memory for the sentences a day later, the Alcohol group recalled more sentences. Drinking the alcohol after reading the sentences may have prevented retroactive interference, by changing the men's psychological state, and permitted better memory for the sentences themselves. Coenen and Van Luijtelaar (1997) found similar effects for word lists learned before taking benzodiazepines (such as Valium), which also inhibits new learning and thus may prevent retroactive interference for previously learned material.

A final method used to examine the role of time in forgetting is to take the opposite strategy, and show that if we fill a time interval with material very different from the material that was learned, then little or no forgetting occurs. Such a finding would indicate that the time interval itself was not critical in forgetting. Let us look again at the study outlined in Table 4.5. The group that learned English-Spanish vocabulary followed by English-French vocabulary showed 60% forgetting. Now let us say that we take a second group of people and have them first learn the English-Spanish pairs (see the Control group on Line 2 in Table 4.5), and then have them learn a set of very different pairs (e.g., English-Japanese pairs). They study those pairs for the same amount of time as the other group studied the English-French pairs (Time$_2$). We then test this control group for their retention of the English-Spanish vocabulary pairs (Time$_3$), and let us say (hypothetically) that they can remember 90% of them (i.e., there is 10% forgetting). Now we *can* infer that the English-French pairs interfered retroactively with recall of the Spanish vocabulary, since the 10% forgetting in the control group is less than the 60% forgetting in the retroactive-interference group. This result indicates that it is not the time interval, but the material in that interval, that produces most of the forgetting (through interference). In conclusion, although it may be difficult to test directly the idea that decay produces forgetting in memory, studies that have tried to indirectly test decay have indicated that time is much less important than retrieval difficulties as a cause of forgetting, and these retrieval problems are often due to interference.

Laboratory Studies of Retroactive Interference

Numerous laboratory studies have demonstrated retroactive interference in controlled conditions for word lists (Burns & Gold, 1999), spatial memories (Tlauka, Donaldson, & Wilson, 2008), and language learning (Isurin & McDonald, 2001), and there is no doubt that it can play a significant role in forgetting. The amount of retroactive interference that occurs in a given situation depends on several factors, which are summarized in Table 4.5. First, if the original learning (the English-Spanish pairs) is stronger than the second-stage (English-French) learning, then there will be less retroactive interference. The better you know Spanish, the less interference will occur from later learning French. In a more extreme example, taking a semester of Italian in high school or college will not make you forget your native language of English because you have already learned English so proficiently. However, people who move to a foreign country and are immersed in a second language with little chance to use their native language may find it harder to retrieve vocabulary from the first language (Ammerlaan, 1997; Isurin, 2000; Leopold, 1939; Olshtain & Barzilay, 1991). The second-stage learning is called *interpolated* learning, because it is interpolated, or comes between, the original learning and its recall.

In addition to the amount of original learning versus interpolated learning, retroactive interference also depends on the relationship in time between them. If the English-Spanish vocabulary and the English-French vocabulary are learned closely in time, say during the same semester, then retroactive interference will be greater than if they occur at widely spaced points in time. In a classic study, Müller and Pilzecker (1900) found that people had better memory for a list of words (List A) if they studied a second list (List B) 6 minutes later, versus another group who studied List B only 17 seconds later. This general finding has been replicated many times (see chapters in Cofer & Musgrave, 1961, 1963). The final important variable that affects retroactive interference is the similarity of original material and the interfering material (Wagner & Davachi, 2001). In the terms we have been using, if you have learned Spanish, then learning Russian will interfere less than will learning French, and learning Japanese will interfere still less.

In conclusion, retroactive interference can be a potent source of forgetting, as McGeoch (1931) proposed. Storing new material in memory may make old information less retrievable. The amount of retroactive interference depends on the relative strengths of the original and interfering material in memory, their relations in time, and their similarities, as outlined in Table 4.5.

Proactive Interference as a Source of Forgetting

When McGeoch (1931) proposed interference theory, he assumed that retroactive interference was the only type of interference. As we already know from Chapter 2, there are two kinds of interference that influence forgetting. The discovery of the second type of interference—*proactive interference*—came about as the result of a fascinating Sherlock-Holmes analysis by Underwood (1957). He was examining the results of a number of experimental studies that had tested individuals' recall of a list of words or CVCs. After each person had learned the list so that it could be recalled perfectly, they were sent home. When tested 24 hours later, an average of about 75% forgetting was found. This raised a puzzle in Underwood's mind. Surely those participants had not been exposed to any CVCs during the 24-hour retention interval. Therefore, McGeoch's retroactive-interference theory would predict that there should be little or no forgetting, yet large amounts of forgetting were found.

Underwood (1957) then reexamined the experimental studies, to see if he could find any reason for the large amount of forgetting over 24 hours. He found that the participants often had been exposed to many lists of the same sort of items over the course of the experiments. In some of the studies, the participants might be tested again and again over 2 or 3 weeks. They would come to the lab and study $list_1$ until they recalled it perfectly; come back the next day and be tested on $list_1$ and then study and learn $list_2$; come back the next day for a test on $list_2$ and learning of $list_3$; and so forth. Underwood then examined a larger group of studies, in which the participants had studied and recalled differing numbers of lists of different types of materials—words, CVCs, geometric forms—and he examined the forgetting of only the very last list. If you had participated in a study for a week—Monday to Friday—then Underwood would have looked at your performance on Thursday's list (tested on Friday), when you would have already studied and recalled three lists (Monday, Tuesday, and Wednesday).

Underwood's analysis of one set of those experimental results is presented in Figure 4.6, and the results are now striking in their consistency: The more lists studied previously, the greater the forgetting of the last list. This was forgetting due to *proactive* interference: Old material was operating proactively, or *forward in time*, to interfere with material learned more recently. Proactive interference was an important discovery, since, as Underwood noted, if you think about your whole life as a source of interfering material, it seems obvious that proactive interference is potentially much more important than retroactive interference. If you learn some new material as a college student, and forget it over 1 or 2 days, say, it seems more likely that some information from your earlier experiences interfered with it than material encountered over the short time since the material was learned.

The research design to demonstrate proactive interference is presented in Lines 1 and 2 of Table 4.6. The situation is similar to retroactive interference, except that one is interested in the forgetting of the material learned at $Time_2$ rather than

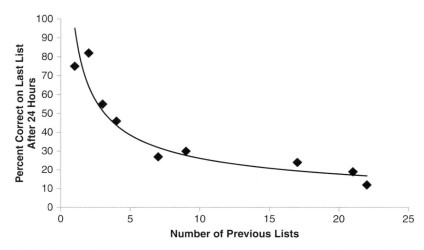

Figure 4.6 Underwood's Demonstration of Proactive Interference: Recall of paired words as a function of number of lists previously learned.
Adapted from Underwood, 1957, Figure 3.

Table 4.6   Proactive Interference

A. Outline of proactive interference

Interference group: Learn Spanish (100%) / Learn **French** (100%) / [retention interval] / Recall **French** (40%)
           (Time$_1$)   (Time$_2$)   (Time$_3$)

60% Forgetting—Due to Proactive Interference from Spanish?

Control group: Learn Japanese (100%) / Learn French (100%) / [retention interval] / Recall French (90%)

B. Summary of factors that affect proactive interference

Factor	*Effect on Proactive Interference*
Amount of old material (Spanish)	More old material, more interference
Temporal relation between old (Spanish) and new (French) material	Old and new material close in time, more interference
Recency of new material (French)	New material more recent, less interference
Similarity of old and new material (Spanish-French vs. Spanish-Japanese)	More similarity, more interference

Time$_1$. Otherwise the situations are the same, including the control condition. Factors influencing proactive interference are shown in Table 4.6.

Many studies have supported Underwood's (1957) conclusion concerning the importance of proactive interference in bringing about forgetting. Proactive interference depends most importantly on the amount of earlier information that is available to interfere with the newly learned material. With more prior information available, greater amounts of proactive interference are found (Underwood, 1957; Figure 4.6). Similar to effects found with retroactive interference, the degree of proactive interference depends on the similarity between the old information and the new: Similar material produces greater proactive interference. Finally, the relationship in time between the old and new material also plays a role in proactive interference. Immediately after the new material is learned, proactive interference is minimal—the new material will be recalled well. Proactive interference increases, however, as the new material fades into the past. For example, say you learn English-Spanish vocabulary in the fall semester and then you learn English-French vocabulary in the spring. If you have to use the French vocabulary very soon after learning it—say, you go to Paris over the summer—the Spanish will not interfere proactively with the recall of the French. However, if you wait a while before using the French, then the Spanish will come forward over time, and interfere with your French.

Interference Theory: Conclusions

We have reviewed evidence that supports the idea that interference plays an important role in forgetting. There are two different ways in which information in memory can interfere with remembering: retroactively and proactively. Evidence indicates that these types of interference operate by making it more difficult to retrieve the target information. In terms we have already used, interference comes about as a result of cue overload: When a cue is relevant to more than one piece of information in memory, it loses its efficiency, and forgetting can result. Also, the more similar the target and interfering material are, the more interference will occur.

MIGHT THERE BE POSITIVE FUNCTIONS OF FORGETTING?

Common sense (as well as the extensive discussion in Chapters 2 and 3) tells us that the basic function of memory is the retention of information. If so, then forgetting would seem to be its archenemy. However, perhaps surprisingly, possessing a perfect memory may not be as great as we think. The neuropsychologist Luria (1968) described the memory performance of a man called S, a professional mnemonist, who seemed never to forget anything. After only 3 minutes of study, he was able to recall perfectly a table of 50 numbers by column, by row, on a diagonal, or in any pattern requested. He claimed to be able to mentally "read off" the numbers from the table as he imagined it. S also could remember verbatim speeches he had heard and the smallest details of a room he had entered only once. Surely it would be wonderful to be like S.

From S's point of view, however, the situation was not optimum. The capacity to use images to remember information interfered with his ability to carry out many routine cognitive activities. S reported that images arose spontaneously in response to material he was reading, and associations among images led him off the topic and made comprehension very difficult. In addition, the occurrence of concrete images in response to abstract words (e.g., "eternity" produced an image of an ancient figure) made it particularly difficult for S to think in abstract terms. S's problems lead to another intriguing question: Might there be a purpose or benefit that arises from forgetting?

Intentional (or Directed) Forgetting

Sometimes we may want to forget information. For example, the embarrassing time we told a stale joke at a party, or the trauma of a favorite pet dying when we were children, might be things we would like to forget. S himself deliberately tried to forget information because his memories became so distracting. On one occasion, he wrote down his memories and then burned the paper, but to no avail (Luria, 1968). In memory experiments, this intentional forgetting is accomplished through *directed forgetting* (MacLeod, 1998). Directed forgetting is more effective with ordinary folks, who lack S's fantastic memory. Joslyn and Oakes (2005), for example, asked people to keep a personal diary for 2 weeks. The Directed Forgetting group was told to forget anything that happened to them during Week 1. When asked to recall events from their diary, they remembered fewer details from Week 1.

Intentional forgetting reduces interference in memory; people asked to forget a first list remember more of a second list of words (Kimball & Bjork, 2002). However, the intentionally forgotten information has not disappeared: People can often recognize material that they had not recalled because of forgetting instructions (Basden, Basden, & Gargano, 1993). Bjork and Bjork (1996, also Bjork, Bjork, & Anderson, 1998) proposed that *retrieval inhibition* underlies directed forgetting; the "forgotten" material remains in a person's memory, but is suppressed from being retrieved at the time of a memory test. This may happen at an implicit, unconscious level. Bjork and Bjork (2003) asked participants to review a list of names, and then to forget some of them. Simply being exposed to a person's name repeatedly can lead people to mistakenly think the person is famous. This is what happened in the Bjork and Bjork experiment: Participants were likely to make false "famous" judgments about the names that they were supposed to have forgotten, presumably because previous exposure to those names had not been entirely erased from memory.

Research on directed forgetting has implications for real life. In court cases, for example, jurors are sometimes told to disregard a statement by a witness that has been objected to by a lawyer. However, evidence suggests that such instructions are not always effective at preventing jurors from using the forbidden information to determine the guilt or innocence of defendants (Golding & Long, 1998; Steblay, Hosch, Culhane, & McWethy, 2006). Likewise, during job interviews, employers are forbidden by law to consider an applicant's religion, age, number of children, and so on unless directly relevant to the job. But if an applicant puts one of these pieces of information in his or her resumé, can employers truly ignore it? Oien and Goernert (2003) asked people to review job applicants in which forbidden information was made available for half of the applicants (e.g., "has a DUI—Driving Under the Influence of Alcohol/Drugs—conviction"). The researchers found that forbidden information was better remembered than job-relevant information. However, interviewers who were directed to forget forbidden information remembered more job-relevant information than those not directed to forget forbidden information (confirming the effects in Kimball & Bjork [2002] discussed earlier).

Thus, while directed forgetting appears to be effective during explicit memory tasks, the "forgotten" information may influence decisions during implicit memory tasks or judgments (Johnson, 1994). Intentional forgetting may reduce interference effects in memory, as the unintentionally-forgotten information is then better remembered (e.g., Oien & Goernert, 2003).

Brain Processes in Directed Forgetting

If forgetting sometimes serves a practical function, then we could consider intentional forgetting a useful memory strategy. Wylie, Foxe, and Taylor (2008) asked participants to view 108 words, each followed by a signal to either remember or forget it. Participants underwent fMRI during this procedure. Intentional forgetting trials led to greater activation in the hippocampus and superior frontal gyrus relative to unintentional forgetting. Compared to intentional remembering, intentional forgetting caused greater activity in the medial frontal gyrus, middle temporal gyrus, parahippocampal gyrus, and cingulate gyrus. In addition, Knox (2001) found that the dorsolateral prefrontal cortex is active during inhibition of information in a directed-forgetting task. Thus, similar brain areas in the prefrontal cortex are active during strategic processing of information that we want to remember and during intentional forgetting. In the case of directed forgetting, people must *suppress* memory retrieval by using the prefrontal cortex, which is responsible for inhibition of responses and other executive functions; intentional forgetting is thus an active strategic process.

A Possible Positive Function of Forgetting: Facilitating Adaptation

We have now reviewed research that has examined directed forgetting in the laboratory, and we have seen that sometimes forgetting can have a positive function, such as reducing interference in memory. With this information as background, it is interesting to consider in more general terms possible positive functions played by forgetting in cognitive processing. William James (1892, p. 300) remarked, "In the practical use of our intellect, forgetting is as important a function as remembering." There are a number of hypotheses that have been proposed concerning possible positive functions of forgetting. First is Freud's concept of repression (Rofé, 2008), the forgetting of material that is too painful to remember. Repression will be discussed later in the chapter, as part of the discussion of *recovered memories*. A second possible function of forgetting is less dramatic: It has been proposed that forgetting serves to reduce information overload and retroactive interference (Wixted, 2004, 2005). We have already seen that directed forgetting can reduce interference. It has also been suggested that forgetting may play a role in the development of abstract concepts. Recall S, Luria's (1968) memory expert, who had difficulties thinking abstractly because he kept producing concrete images in response to abstract words. In Chapter 3 and earlier in this chapter, we discussed the role of forgetting in the schematization of memory, or the development of abstract concepts.

A final possible function for forgetting is that it allows us to adapt most efficiently to our changing environments. That is, if the world has changed significantly since you learned some information, so the old learning is no longer relevant, then it may be most efficient to forget it. In that case, retroactive interference would allow new information to be easier to retrieve than older and now-outdated memories. A good example is computer technology: People with extensive experience with computers who only remembered how to use the original operating systems that they learned would not be in a strong position in today's world. On the other hand, if some aspect of the world has only changed a little, then old information will still be relevant (such as switching from an early version of a smart phone to an updated model). Under those circumstances, it should be more efficient to retain old and well-learned information. There is no question that this way of functioning is on the whole adaptive. What we recall in a situation will, all other things being equal, reflect our experiences in that situation. Thus, forgetting may result in our behavior matching the long-term regularities we have encountered in the environment (Anderson & Schooler, 1991).

RESEARCH ON FORGETTING: CONCLUSIONS

We have now reviewed studies that examined forgetting for many different types of materials, including CVCs, words, pictures, and autobiographical memories of various sorts. This research has used many different types of methods, including recognition and recall tests and physiological responses, to measure retention and forgetting over intervals ranging from several minutes to several decades. Forgetting seems to be related to the type of material being learned, as well as to the amount and distribution of the original learning experiences with the material. Information without meaning, which can only be processed in a bottom-up manner, is forgotten faster, which is why forgetting for CVCs has been found to be very rapid compared with that for pictures or words (e.g., Shepard, 1967; Standing, 1973). In addition, both *overlearning* and *distributed practice* (i.e., spreading learning experiences out over periods of time) decrease the rate of forgetting. The wider the distribution of learning episodes in time, the less forgetting that is found (Bahrick et al., 1993).

ACCURACY OF MEMORY FOR DRAMATIC EVENTS: THE QUESTION OF FLASHBULB MEMORIES

One of the reasons that researchers are interested in forgetting is because it would seem that all of our memories are subject to it. However, it has been proposed that there may be one kind of memory—memory for an unexpected, dramatic, and highly emotional event—that is not subject to forgetting. The study of those memories, called *flashbulb memories* by researchers, raises several interesting questions about possible limits to forgetting.

Do you remember what you were doing when you first heard about the theater shootings in Aurora, Colorado in July, 2012? Who told you about it? What was your first reaction? Which movie was the theater showing at the time? Do you know older people who claim that they remember exactly what they were doing when they heard the news of President John F. Kennedy's assassination, or the assassination of Martin Luther King, Jr.? We all have at least one or two dramatic memories that seem seared into our minds, which remain vivid and which we seem unable to forget. Often, those dramatic recollections are for shocking or surprising and highly emotional public events—the assassination of a president or a terrorist attack. But vivid emotionally charged memories can also occur for more personal events: Hearing about a relative's serious car crash or reading the acceptance letter from the college that was your top choice.

Researchers have studied memory for emotional experiences because of the possibility that those memories may be processed and stored in a manner different from that involved in storing nonemotional experiences. Freud, for example, proposed the concept of *repression* (Rofé, 2008), which is the mechanism whereby painful emotional memories are blocked from being retrieved or becoming conscious. He predicted that highly emotional memories should be harder to remember because of repression, but, if those memories could be retrieved, they would be very accurate. Repressed memories of childhood trauma, often involving sexual abuse, could have effects on behavior, however. For example, a repressed memory of early childhood trauma at the hands of a parent might express itself as excessive shyness toward adults. If those lost memories could be recovered during therapy, the person's psychological problems would be alleviated.

One difficulty with Freud's analysis of repression was that he provided no evidence that his patients had actually experienced trauma. Modern studies investigating the possibility of repression have examined people's memories for traumatic events, such as being kidnapped, where there is objective evidence concerning the details of the event. Those studies (summarized in Schacter, 1996) have found that widespread amnesia for traumatic events does not occur, which seems to go against the notion of repression. In fact, some theories have hypothesized that, contrary to the notion of repression, memories for highly emotional experiences may be immune to forgetting (R. Brown & Kulik, 1977). Others have proposed that emotionally tinged recollections are no more or less accurate than other memories, and are subject to the same reconstructive processes and to forgetting (McCloskey, Wible, & Cohen, 1988; Neisser, 1982). We will examine the evidence to determine whether memories for dramatic events are somehow different than more ordinary memories.

Flashbulb Memories

Accuracy of people's memories for shocking or dramatic experiences was studied in a pioneering investigation by R. Brown and Kulik (1977), who were struck by the fact that people reported having vivid recollections of dramatic events with "almost perceptual clarity" (p. 73) and "permanent registration" (p. 76). They coined the term "flashbulb" memories to capture the vividness of those recollections, much like a flashbulb captures a single moment in time in great detail. Based on a neurophysiological theory developed by Livingston (1967), R. Brown and Kulik proposed that the high emotionality of a dramatic event triggered a special memory mechanism that captured the event in great detail. Borrowing a term from Livingston, R. Brown and Kulik proposed that this detailed memory was the result of a *Now Print* mechanism, a special process that evolved to register the circumstances before, during, and after extraordinary experiences. Livingston had hypothesized that activation of such a system helped our ancient ancestors to better remember events that might promote their survival. Based on the *Now Print* theory, R. Brown and Kulik predicted that flashbulb memories should be immune to forgetting, remaining vivid over long periods of time.

R. Brown and Kulik (1977) questioned people about possible flashbulb memories for 10 significant and shocking events, nine public events (such as the assassinations of President John F. Kennedy and Martin Luther King, Jr.) and one personal event (such as the sudden death of a family member). They determined that the more emotionally significant the event, the more vivid the memory: The assassinations of Kennedy and King were better remembered than assassinations of less significant figures. A second factor playing a role in formation of a flashbulb memory was personal relevance; for example, African Americans had more vivid and detailed flashbulb memories for the assassination of Black civil rights leaders (Martin Luther King, Medgar Evers) than did Whites. Likewise, Kvavilashvili, Mirani, Schlagman, and Kornbrot (2003) found that British subjects had more vivid flashbulb memories of the events surrounding Princess Diana's death than did Italians.

Some kinds of information contained in flashbulb memories were found to be highly resistant to forgetting. People were most likely to report their location (where they were when they heard the news), the informant (who told them about the event), their ongoing activity (what they were doing when they heard the news), and the emotional reaction of others and themselves. R. Brown and Kulik's (1977) results appeared to provide support for the Now Print theory of flashbulb memories.

Other researchers (e.g., Neisser, 1982; Rubin & Kozin, 1984), however, raised questions about the need to postulate a special memory mechanism to encode dramatic or shocking events. Neisser, for example, suggested that people's subjective recollections of flashbulb memories might not be accurate, as it is difficult to retroactively verify where a person was and what they were doing 10 or 20 years earlier. This is true of R. Brown and Kulik's (1977) study, since they only tested their participants once—significantly after the events occurred. They had no way of knowing how accurate the memories were, and whether or not any forgetting had taken place. Neisser also proposed that so-called flashbulb memories do fade with time, as do other memories, and are likely to become schematized—that is, only general information is remembered. Furthermore, if the details of such events are recalled, they may be the result of people's exposure to extensive media coverage of public events, coupled with people's tendency to discuss those events for months afterwards. Neisser proposed that any findings of detailed memory for dramatic events might be due to this repeated exposure or rehearsal, rather a special memory mechanism, *per se.*

As an example of the less-than-perfect recollection of a surprising event, consider Neisser's own flashbulb memory for how he heard of the bombing of Pearl Harbor:

> For many years I have remembered how I heard the news of the Japanese attack on Pearl Harbor, which occurred the day before my thirteenth birthday. I recall sitting in the living room of our house—we only lived in that house for one year, but I remember it well—listening to a baseball game on the radio. The game was interrupted by an announcement of the attack, and I rushed upstairs to tell my mother. This memory has been so clear for so long that I never confronted its inherent absurdity until last year: No one broadcasts baseball games in December! (Neisser, 1982)

In this case, the event was a particularly significant one, and subjectively the memory was clear and accurate to Neisser. However, he later realized that the memory of listening to a baseball game on the radio must have been a reconstruction, where he added details to his actual memory of hearing about the attack on Pearl Harbor. How might this have happened? Thompson and Cowan (1986) attempted to trace the origin of Neisser's constructed memory, and found a plausible source: There had been a broadcast of a *football* game the *night before* the attack on Pearl Harbor, and the teams in that game had names that were identical to those of well-known baseball teams (*Yankees* and *Dodgers*). Thus, Neisser had combined his memory of listening to a football game on the radio with the events of Pearl Harbor the following day, and then substituted baseball for football, probably because of the similarity of the names of the football and baseball teams. On December 7, 1941, Neisser had probably been listening to a radio program, which was then interrupted for the announcement about the attack. Years later, he confused the December 6 football broadcast with the December 7 program. The core of the memory was basically accurate (e.g., hearing about the Pearl Harbor attack on the radio), but the final product was constructed, based on the synthesis of several different memories at the time of retrieval.

The analysis by Thompson and Cowan (1986) of Neisser's (1982) memory for Pearl Harbor is fascinating; however, one individual's account of one memory must be supplemented with studies examining flashbulb memories on a wider scale. McCloskey, Wible, and Cohen (1988) examined whether people formed flashbulb memories in response to the explosion of the space shuttle *Challenger*. They asked 45 people to detail their recollections of the explosion immediately after it occurred, and then were able to track down 27 of these people nine months later. In this way, they could directly compare each person's later memory with his or her earlier one, which had not been done in earlier studies.

As with previous research, McCloskey et al. (1988) found that people were most likely to remember their location, informant, and ongoing activity during flashbulb events, and 61% of the time, people gave the same answer in the immediate and 9-month test. However, 14% of the answers were either inconsistent from the first to the second test, or were reported as "don't remember." Nineteen percent of the answers were more general at 9 months than they had been immediately after the *Challenger* episode (for instance, if someone reported having coffee and a blueberry muffin when hearing about the *Challenger*, they later reported only having coffee). This supports Neisser's (1982) contention that memory becomes more schematized over time. In addition, over 6% of the answers became more specific over time. While that percentage is not very large, the fact that those responses occurred at all is important. How could memories become more detailed over time? McCloskey and colleagues hypothesized that participants might have reconstructed their memories, perhaps relying on a disaster schema to fill in details (e.g., if you didn't remember your actual reaction after a public tragedy, you might recollect that you felt shock and horror). McCloskey et al. (1988) concluded that, even on the relatively short-term basis of 9 months, flashbulb memories become less vivid and less accurate, in the same way that more ordinary memories do.

To explain why details of those flashbulb events might be better remembered than the details of events in ordinary life, McCloskey and his colleagues proposed that *distinctiveness* is the cause. We may have parked our car numerous times in the same parking lot at the mall and attended numerous college classes, but we have only experienced a few truly dramatic events in our lives: the Oklahoma City bombing of 1995, Princess Diana's death in 1997, the September 11, 2001, attacks on the World Trade Center, the 2012 theater shootings in Colorado. Thus, we can better retrieve details of those events because they stand out from the more mundane occurrences of our lives.

Studies of flashbulb memories have also found that personal information connected to a dramatic event, such as who told us about the event, where we were, what we were doing (episodic information) is remembered better than the facts of the event itself (semantic information; Bohannon, 1988; Nachson & Zelig, 2003; Pezdek, 2003; Smith, Bibi, & Sheard, 2003). That result also casts doubt on the *Now Print* theory: If information about a flashbulb memory is automatically encoded due to a special mechanism, semantic facts that are available as the event occurs should be as well-encoded as the autobiographical information, but they are not.

Brain Processes in Flashbulb Memories

Davidson, Cook, Glisky, Verfaellie, and Rapcsak (2005) studied two groups of patients whose memory deficits confirmed the psychological independence of the episodic and factual aspects of memories for dramatic—flashbulb-style—events. The medial temporal lobe is known to be implicated in fact memory (e.g., Schacter, Harbluk, & McLachlan, 1984), whereas the frontal cortex controls memory for the source of information (Janowsky, Shimamura, & Squire, 1989). Davidson et al. studied a group of participants with medial temporal lobe (MTL) damage and another comprised of patients with frontal lobe (FL) damage. When asked about the 9/11 World Trade Center attacks, both immediately afterwards and 6 months later, the MTL participants forgot more factual information about 9/11 than the FL patients or normal control participants. Both sets of patients lost information about who had told them about the disaster, but forgetting was more drastic for the FL patients (who nonetheless retained good event memory). These results illustrate that different mechanisms, and distinct brain areas, control memory for, and forgetting of, episodic and semantic details of flashbulb memories.

Flashbulb Memories: Conclusion

Evidence indicates that flashbulb memories are forgotten, just as all memories are (McCloskey, Wible, & Cohen, 1988). Encoding and retrieval for emotional memories seem to be similar to memory processes that operate during remembering of more ordinary kinds of memories, and emotional memories are forgotten in ways that are similar to those for nonemotional experiences. Thus, it may not be necessary to posit a special memory mechanism, as the Now Print theory assumes (R. Brown & Kulik, 1977; Livingston, 1967). In addition, active processes play a role in encoding and retrieval of emotional memories, which can sometimes result in constructed flashbulb memories of emotional situations, such as that reported by Neisser (1982).

MEMORY ERRORS OF COMMISSION: THE QUESTION OF FALSE MEMORIES

Our discussion thus far in this chapter has centered on the loss of information from memory, in the form of forgetting. Not all memory errors involve loss of information; however, sometimes our memories are *false*, either because we embellish an existing memory (as was seen in the flashbulb memory research), or we merge two distinct memories into one. An example of both phenomena—forgetting and merging two memories—occurring at the same time is Neisser's (1982) memory of hearing about Pearl Harbor while listening to a baseball game in December.

Fallout From False Memories

The possible occurrence of false memories has had important implications far beyond the laboratory. There have been a number of court cases in which an adult member of a family has accused a relative of abuse, carried out when the accuser was a child. In the Ramona case in California (detailed in Johnston, 1997), a woman seeking counseling for depression and bulimia became convinced that her father had sexually abused her as a child. The alleged events supposedly had been forgotten for many years, and came to light during treatment. She then publicly accused her father of abuse on the basis of her purportedly resurrected memories. After years of family heartache, the daughter recanted her story and the father successfully sued the daughter's therapist and psychiatrist. Those sorts of accusations have brought great strife into the families in question, with the accused person usually strenuously denying the accusation (also see Pendergrast, 1996; van Til, 1997).

Let us assume that the person bringing the accusation in such a case believes that the abuse occurred, based on a memory for the event. We are then left with two possibilities: (1) the accusation is correct and the accused individual is lying in denying the accusation; or (2) the accuser has a false memory about the alleged abuse. Could the memories reported in these cases be constructions, arising perhaps out of interaction with others, such as a therapist? The memories reported and then recanted by the woman in the Ramona case, for example, seemed to be based on a combination of therapist's suggestions and ideas from a book that the woman had read on sexual abuse (Johnston, 1997). The possibility that people can become convinced of false sexual abuse as a result of suggestions by therapists raises the question of whether similar suggestions might affect the reliability of witnesses' testimony in court cases, which also depends on memory, in this case people's memories for a crime.

Possible Sources of False Memories

False memories, or errors of commission, may have several sources. First, after experiencing an event (such as witnessing a burglary), information that we hear or read might alter or add details to our original memory. Trials often occur months or even years after the crime, and, during that time, witnesses may have been questioned multiple times by police officers, lawyers, and others. Repeated questioning by a police officer, or suggestions by a therapist, might convince a person of details that never happened. Defense attorneys are particularly interested in whether witnesses' memory reports could be affected by insinuations or leading questions (what we could call post-event misinformation) during interviews by police and prosecutors. Our memory for an event can also be combined with information already stored in memory to create a false memory. If we know that many burglars carry guns, we might incorporate this schematic knowledge into our memory of a burglary, and misremember that the burglar had a gun when he did not.

Stimulus Conditions in False Memories

In order to study false memories in the laboratory, it is necessary to be able to produce them reliably. One technique used within false memory research is presented in Box 4.1. Please carry out that demonstration before reading further.

BOX 4.1 ROEDIGER AND MCDERMOTT DEMO

Instructions. Study the following list of words, spending approximately 2–3 seconds on each word. After you have finished studying the list, continue with the instructions at the top of the next page.

sour

candy

sugar

bitter

good

taste

tooth

nice

honey

soda

chocolate

heart

cake

tart

pie

Instructions: For each of the following words, mark it "old" if it was on the list you just studied (do not look back at the list) or "new" if it was not on the list.

sour	old	new
steal	old	new
sugar	old	new
good	old	new
ice	old	new
citrus	old	new
open	old	new
nice	old	new
window	old	new
sweet	old	new

Check your answers against the correct words. Did you incorrectly mark as "old" any words that weren't on the original list?

Laboratory studies of false memories use stimulus materials designed to make it very likely that the person will think of some specific piece of information during encoding (Deese, 1959). Roediger and McDermott (1995) constructed word lists in which the words were all related to one *critical word* (in Box 4.1, the critical word is *sweet*). Participants heard a list of words, and then were tested for recall and recognition of those words. The critical word (e.g., *sweet*) was included in the recognition-test list as one of the incorrect responses. Many of the participants mistakenly remembered that *sweet* had been on the list, and they expressed strong confidence in this mistaken belief. Brainerd and Reyna (1998) proposed that false memories in this situation come about because the lists are structured so that there is a strong tendency for the participant to think of the meaning or gist of the list when it is presented. That is, in the list presented in Box 4.1, all the words are related to a common meaning, which then activates the critical (but incorrect) word.

Chances are that you, too, showed false memory during the demonstration in Box 4.1, since research shows it is difficult to prevent false memories from occurring in this situation. Gallo, Roberts, and Seamon (1997) tried to inoculate people against false recognition errors, by giving them detailed information about such errors and warning them that they should try to avoid them. The forewarned participants were better at avoiding false recognition than unwarned subjects (46% versus 81% false recognition, respectively), but they still falsely recognized the critical word almost half the time.

Brain Activity in False Recognition

A multitude of studies have found that false recognition causes widespread activation of the prefrontal cortex (e.g., Cabeza, Rao, Wagner, Mayer, & Schacter, 2001; Goldmann et al., 2003; Schacter, Buckner, Koutstaal, Dale, & Rosen, 1997) relative to correct recognition of memory items. In addition, areas linked to the type of specific stimuli used may also be activated. Schacter et al. (1997) asked people to engage in a memory test for auditorily presented words, while undergoing a PET scan. The PET scan results found that areas in the medial temporal lobe were active during both correct (e.g., *sugar*) and false recognition of words (e.g., *sweet*) for the list in Box 4.1. Temporal-parietal areas, including Wernicke's area, which store information about the sound of words, were also active during correct recognition of words that had been heard. These language-related areas were not active during false recognition, presumably because the participants had not actually heard the words; Brainerd and Reyna (1998) stated that a false recognition item may be recognized because it matches the semantic category of the list. There were, however, regions in the prefrontal and orbitofrontal cortex that were activated by false recognition items, but not during correct recognition. False recognition of abstract shapes, on the other hand, led to less activation in the visual cortex than did true memories (Slotnick & Schacter, 2004).

In a further examination of brain areas involved in false recognition, Garoff-Eaton, Slotnick, and Schacter (2006) used abstract geometric forms as stimuli, and then asked people to respond whether test shapes were the *same* as a training exemplar, *similar* to a training exemplar, or *new*. PET scan activity occurred in the prefrontal, medial-temporal, and parietal regions for both true recognition (same) and similar items, whereas false recognition items activated only language areas in the left hemisphere corresponding to Wernicke's area (as if people had matched the false stimuli to labels from actual stimuli). This result indicates that false items that are similar to actual training stimuli may be treated like the real items.

The type of material being falsely recognized may also determine which brain regions are activated. Garoff-Eaton, Kensinger, and Schacter (2007) carried out an fMRI study to examine the brain areas active during false recognition. Participants received word triplets that were either perceptually related to each other (*bell, sell, fell*) or conceptually related to each other (*silver, bronze, brass*). They rated each triplet's similarity and tried to remember the words for a subsequent memory test. During the recognition test, people saw either old perceptual (e.g., *bell*), old conceptual (e.g., *silver*), perceptual lures (e.g., *yell*), conceptual lures (e.g., *gold*), and unrelated new words (e.g., *cake*). Regions in the middle, medial, and inferior frontal lobe gyri were most active during false recognition of both conceptual and perceptual lures (refer back to Figure 2.16 for the brain areas associated with memory). However, false recognition of conceptual items caused the greatest activation in the prefrontal cortex in a multitude of areas, as well as the precentral gyrus and precuneus. Previous research has determined anterior left inferior frontal cortex involvement in conceptual/semantic processing (Poldrack et al., 1999; Poldrack & Wagner, 2004); Garoff-Eaton et al. (2007) confirmed this association but only for false recognition items.

Collectively, the research indicates (a) some overlap of neural networks involved both in correct and false recognition, (b) with additional brain areas that are connected to the specific kinds of stimuli used in an experiment; and (c) false recognition of both verbal and pictorial items causes activation of widespread areas in the prefrontal cortex.

Accuracy of Eyewitnesses

Elizabeth Loftus (e.g., Loftus, Doyle, & Dysert, 2008) has carried out a seminal research program on the accuracy of eyewitness testimony, demonstrating that post-event information can affect the accuracy of witnesses' testimony. This raises important questions for the legal system, which often relies heavily on eyewitness testimony during criminal trials. In a now-classic study, Loftus and Palmer (1974) showed participants a film clip depicting a traffic accident and requested that participants describe what they had just seen. Participants were then asked a series of more-specific questions about the accident, including one that asked, "How fast was the car going when it _____ the other car?" The blank contained one of the following verbs: *contacted, hit, bumped, collided*, or *smashed*. The verb affected people's estimates of speed: those who saw *contacted* estimated the speed as 31.8 miles per hour, whereas those who saw *smashed* had an estimate of 40.8 miles per hour, with the other verbs in between. In a second experiment, 32% those who had seen the verb *smashed* misreported having seen broken glass after the accident versus 14% of those who had seen *hit*. Thus, even though no specific misinformation was presented in the speed question, the nuances of the verb's connotation affected people's reports of the accident.

In a second set of experiments (Loftus, Miller, & Burns, 1978), participants viewed a series of slides that depicted an accident in which a car came to an intersection, paused at a sign, then turned right and hit a pedestrian who was crossing the street. The slide sequence was followed by a series of questions about the accident, and half the subjects received misinformation. For example, people in the Misinformation group who had seen the car stop at a *yield* sign were asked, "Did another car pass the car when it was stopped at the *stop* sign?" Those in the Consistent Information group were correctly asked about a *yield* sign. After 20 minutes of intervening activities not related to the experiment, the participants were tested on their recollection for the slide sequence. Two slides were presented, one with the car stopped at a stop sign and the other with a yield sign, and the participants were to choose which slide had been seen originally. Those who had been asked earlier about the incorrect stop sign were more likely to err and choose the stop sign as having been in the original sequence.

Thus, implanted misinformation (e.g., the stop sign) led to less-accurate memory performance. Furthermore, with a delay between the slides and the post-event misleading information, people were more likely to accept the misinformation (Loftus et al., 1978, Experiment 3). This result has implications for real-life eyewitness testimony, as people may not be questioned about a crime or accident scenario for days or weeks after the event. During this interval, they may have read newspaper accounts or heard other witnesses' testimony, which might have altered their memory for the event.

There are a number of different ways in which post-event misleading information could affect test performance in experiments on memory after misinformation. We will consider only two possibilities here (but see Table 4.7 for a more complete set of mechanisms whereby misinformation effects might occur). One possibility is that the incorrect piece of information might have actually replaced the original information in memory (Loftus & Loftus, 1980; Loftus, Miller, & Burns, 1978). This position has been referred to as *memory impairment* (Belli, 1989; Loftus & Hoffman, 1989; see also

Table 4.7   False Memories: Various Possibilities Concerning Information in Memory During Eyewitness Studies

Possible Condition	Status of Old Information	Status of Misleading Information	Basis for Test Response
Perfect memory	Present	Present	Original information correctly remembered
Memory impairment (Loftus, 1979; Loftus & Loftus, 1980)	Replaced or overwritten by misleading info	Present	Misleading info has replaced memory for original.
Misinformation acceptance (*Demand Characteristics*) (McCloskey & Zaragoza, 1985)	Present	Present	Misinformation answer—chosen by participant based on what researcher has portrayed as correct answer in the misinformation passage.
Misinformation interference (Belli, 1989)	Present	Present (more recent)	Misleading info is easier to retrieve.
Original information never encoded	Never encoded	Present	Only misinformation is available for retrieval.
Neither original nor misleading information is remembered	Never encoded	Never encoded	Guessing.

Loftus, Donders, Hoffman, & Schooler, 1989). A second possibility is that the participant actually remembers the correct answer (e.g., the *yield* sign), but when presented with misinformation (e.g., about the *stop* sign) incorrectly responds "yes" because he or she feels either that the experimenter wants that response or knows better than the participant herself. "Otherwise," the participant reasons, "why would the stop sign have been included in the sequence of questions?" This explanation for the participants' performance is known as *misinformation acceptance* (McCloskey & Zaragoza, 1985), and is thought to be based on *demand characteristics* (people's interpretations of what they think the researcher wants them to do). In this case, the suggested information has had no actual effect on memory for the original detail; both the initial (and accurate) detail and the post-event detail (the inaccurate misinformation) coexist in memory.

Lindsay (1990) carried out a memory-suggestibility study with one added piece of information, which allowed him to separate demand characteristics and memory effects. Participants saw a slide sequence, followed by a description of the sequence that included incorrect information (*stop* sign rather than *yield* sign). However, just before the test for memory of the slide sequence, some of the participants were told that any information they remembered from the post-slide description was *incorrect*, and should *not* be used to answer any of the questions. With this change in the design, the demand characteristics are now working *against* the misinformation. Therefore, if participants *do* answer any questions with information from the post-slide description, it must be because they think that information came from the slide sequence itself, and are thus making a memory-based error. Some of Lindsay's participants who were warned about the incorrect information still produced false recognitions, indicating that they believed that the suggested information had actually been presented in the slides. Other studies have produced similar results (Weingardt, Loftus, & Lindsay, 1995; Zaragoza & Lane, 1994).

Source Amnesia and Eyewitness Errors

The Lindsay (1990) study illustrates that an important factor affecting memory errors after misleading information may be *source amnesia*—we forget how we acquired some information. Research as well as anecdotal evidence support the role of source amnesia in incorrect eyewitness testimony. A number of years ago, cognitive psychologist Donald Thomson was questioned as a potential suspect in a rape; his description (race, facial appearance, hair color, height, etc.) closely matched the victim's memory of her assailant (Schacter, 1996). However, Thomson was totally innocent of the rape: He had been giving an interview on television just before the rape occurred. Thomson had spent many years studying memory, and was particularly interested in questions concerning accuracy of eyewitness identification. In fact, he had been discussing that very topic—eyewitness testimony—during his television appearance. Thomson had been talking about how to effectively remember faces, and had used his own face as an example. The victim's recollection of her attacker as someone who looked very much like Thomson was probably the result of her having watched his interview just before she was attacked. She recollected Thomson's appearance accurately, but she misremembered *where* she had seen him. Parts of two different events that occurred close together in time were fused into one remembered event. The fact that the television program was the source of the woman's memory for Thomson's face had been forgotten (source amnesia).

CONSTRUCTION OF LARGE-SCALE MEMORIES

Research on eyewitness suggestibility shows that one can produce false memories with post-event information, and studies of false recognition show that people can sometimes confuse their own responses with the stimulus material in an experiment (Roediger & McDermott, 1995; see Box 4.1). However, the effects in these studies are relatively small-scale—mistakenly recognizing a single critical word (e.g., *sweet*), or misremembering a traffic sign. If one is interested in the possibility of constructing false memories concerning abuse, for example, one would want to investigate suggestibility for memories of wider scope. Several studies have shown that it is possible to produce false memories that are much closer to the types of memories produced as evidence in court. This issue is particularly important when children serve as witnesses in court cases.

Large-Scale False Memories in Children

During the 1980s, the fragility of children's memories after suggestive questions from authority figures resulted in what seem to have been several serious miscarriages of justice in the United States, Canada, and New Zealand. One such case took place in Fells Acres, Massachusetts, in which three employees of a day care center—Violet Amirault, her daughter Cheryl, and son Gerald—were accused of widespread sexual abuse of the preschool children under their care. The case began after a 5-year-old boy reported that his pants had been pulled down and his penis touched by Gerald

Amirault. Although it was later determined that Amirault had merely changed the boy's clothes after he wet himself at naptime, parents removed their children from the day care center and urged authorities to act.

Many of the interviews with the children who had been at the center were conducted by a pediatric nurse. Transcripts of her interviews reveal suggestive questioning of the children (e.g., "Do you think that you could help me out the same way April did by telling me the story about what happened with the clown in the magic room?"), as well as pressure being applied if they reported that nothing happened, and reinforcement for revealing sexual details. All of the children's initial disclosures were devoid of any sexual content, but eventually they produced "recollections" of the Amiraults giving them magic drinks; taking them to secret rooms to rape them; abusing animals to intimidate the children; dressing up like a bad clown and throwing fire around the room; and perpetrating numerous acts of sexual abuse. During the ensuing court trials, many children who testified admitted practicing their testimony with parents or authorities because they had trouble remembering things. All three defendants were convicted solely on the basis of children's "eyewitness" testimony; there was no physical evidence uncovered during any examination of the children (including no injuries to a girl who reported that a 12-inch butcher knife had been inserted into her), nor did anyone find a secret room, a clown suit, or animal carcasses. Violet and Cheryl Amirault both spent 8 years in prison before being released on bail pending a second trial; Gerald Amirault spent 18 years behind bars before being paroled in 2004.

Ceci, Bruck, and colleagues (e.g., Bruck, Ceci, & Hembrooke, 1997; Ceci, Loftus, Leichtman, & Bruck, 1994; Principe & Ceci, 2002) have examined the susceptibility of children to memory errors. In one series of studies, Ceci et al. (1994) tested young children's ability to distinguish between events that had occurred and events that they had imagined. Children were interviewed for 10 consecutive weeks as to whether various events had ever happened to them, such as being involved in an accident that resulted in a trip to the hospital. Some of the events had occurred, while others had not. Each week the child was asked to think "real hard" about each event, including visualizing the episode, to determine whether or not it had occurred. After the 10 weeks of interviews, a new adult carried out a structured interview with the child, much like what might be carried out by the police or a lawyer in an investigation of some possible crime. The interviewer asked the child if each of the various stimulus events had occurred, and then asked follow-up questions to elicit more detail. The following is a young boy's recollection of a time when he was taken to the hospital because he got his finger caught in a mousetrap.

> My brother was trying to get Blowtorch [an action figure] from me, and I wouldn't let him take it from me, so he pushed me into the wood pile where the mousetrap was. And then my finger got caught in it. And then we went to the hospital, and my mommy, daddy, and Colin [the child's brother] drove me there, to the hospital in our van, because it was far away. And the doctor put a bandage on this finger [indicating]. (Ceci, 1995, p. 103)

The child, although only a preschooler, was able to recount the event in considerable detail. However, the child had never had his finger caught in a mousetrap, and he had never been to a hospital. The child's memory is the result of a questioner's repeatedly asking him try to think about whether he been taken to a hospital because he had once had problems with a mousetrap. At first, the child denied ever having gone to the hospital for that reason, but several weeks of thinking hard led the boy to construct a memory, which became more and more detailed as weeks passed (also see Steward et al., 1996). The children also became convinced about the truthfulness of their false memories, and their reports of the manufactured memories remained consistent over time. Bruck, Ceci, and Hembrooke (2002) also found that the fictional narratives contained more details than true ones.

The truthfulness of the false memories was also impressive to professionals. Leichtman and Ceci (1995) presented videotapes of children reporting true and false memories to professionals in child development and forensics who specialized in interviewing children. The professionals could not tell which memories were true and which were false. Ceci (1995) is of the opinion that the children seemed so truthful to the professionals because the children came to believe the narratives they had made up. In some cases the children argued that the events *must* have happened, because they remembered them so well!

The Fells Acres case, discussed earlier, is one instance of a wave of sex abuse hysteria regarding childcare facilities in the 1980s. Such cases, in conjunction with research by cognitive psychologists such as Ceci, Bruck, and their colleagues helped to spur important reforms concerning how therapists and attorneys question children. Such interviews are now standardized to avoid suggestive questions or reinforcing children for dramatic answers, and it is recommended that such interviews be videotaped. Caution is also urged in the use of anatomically correct dolls, based on findings that they are more likely to increase the reporting errors by children (Bruck, Ceci, Francoeur, & Barr, 1995; Gordon, Ornstein, Nida, Follmer, Crenshaw, & Albert, 1993). Thus, cognitive psychology research on false memory (e.g., Bruck, Ceci, & Hembrooke, 2002) has been used to make changes in clinical interviews and public policy. This may have the additional bonus of making children's testimony more believable, and thus result in a higher percentage of guilty offenders being convicted.

Large-Scale False Memories in Adults

One might be tempted to dismiss the results of Ceci et al. (1994) as applying only to young children, who probably are more susceptible to external influences than are adults. However, Loftus and Pickrell (1995) showed that large-scale false memories could also be implanted in adults. In one study, college students and their siblings were tested together, and were asked about events that the experimenters knew had never happened, based on the siblings' reports (e.g., being lost in a mall). During the experimental session, the siblings, assisting the experimenters, falsely indicated that certain events had occurred, and supplied some "recollections" about them. A significant proportion of the participants in the study, on hearing their siblings' reports of those events, also reported remembering them. Thus, adults also are vulnerable to false memories induced by interactions with others. However, Loftus and Pickrell found that the manufactured memories were never reported as being as vivid as real childhood memories (which differs from the children's data).

False Memories: The Question of Generalization

There seems to be little doubt that it is possible to produce false autobiographical memories in the laboratory (Ceci et al., 1994; Loftus, Miller, & Burns, 1978). From such results, one might be tempted to conclude that false memories are a very likely explanation for those cases in which an adult accuses another person of having abused them in childhood. We should be leery of taking seriously any such accusations, based as they often are on unsubstantiated "recovered memories." In fact, in 1995, an American Psychological Association (APA) report warned, "At this point it is impossible, without other corroborative evidence, to distinguish a true memory from a false one" (*Questions and Answers About Memories of Childhood Abuse*). Alan Gold, the president of the Criminal Lawyers Association in Canada has remarked, "Recovered memories are joining electroshock, lobotomies, and other psychological malpractice in the historical dustbin."[1]

However, some researchers have warned that we should be careful before we generalize from the laboratory results to court cases involving remembered abuse (DePrince, Allard, Oh, & Freyd, 2004). Pezdek and her colleagues (e.g., Pezdek, 2001; Pezdek & Lam, 2007; Pezdek & Roe, 1997), for example, have speculated that recovered memories of sexual abuse may often be true memories. Pezdek and Roe (1997) found that, while children were susceptible to subtle misinformation effects about memory, it was difficult to either implant or erase a memory altogether. They argue that because memories about sexual abuse are are emotionally charged and dramatic, it is difficult to fabricate or implant such memories entirely. Since most people have been to a mall numerous times, Loftus and Pickrell (1995) may have been able to convince their subjects that they had (falsely) once been lost in a mall. However, child abuse is a more emotionally charged and distinctive event, and not something that happens to most of us. Thus, it should be much harder to induce false memories of child abuse.

Pezdek, Finger, and Hodge (1997) attempted to induce false memories in college students, and varied the plausibility of the false event. Catholic and Jewish college students discussed three actual events from their childhood (as reported by each participant's mother) and two fictitious events, which were about the person's involvement in separate religious services at age 8. The false memory about a Catholic mass mentioned taking Communion, getting lost on the way back to one's seat, and then sitting down next to a stranger. The false memory about a Jewish ceremony suggested that the student had dropped the ceremonial bread at a Sabbath prayer service as a child. Pezdek et al. (1997) found that false memories were induced only when the description of the service matched the religion of the participant. Additionally, even those people reporting a false memory reported it in fewer words than true memories, and rated the false memories as lower in clarity. In Experiment 2, the same researchers were able to implant a false memory about being lost in a mall in several subjects, but no one became convinced that they had received an enema as a child.

---

[1] In Stephen Bindman, "Can Recovered Memories Be Trusted? Justice Minister Rejects Call for Inquiry," *The Ottawa Citizen*, May 4, 1998.

Pezdek et al. (1997) argued that the enema condition is analogous to sexual abuse memories, because both involve sensitive events that are relatively implausible in most people's lives. The researchers concluded that it is highly unlikely that people who report having been abused as children have been subject to false memories induced by others. However, in response to that conclusion, more recent research by Laney and Loftus (2008) has demonstrated that highly emotional memories—such as a memory of being in a hospital overnight or witnessing a physically violent fight between your parents—can be implanted in individuals. Thus, the acquisition of false memories may not be limited to events with little or no emotional content. That result supports the proposal made by Loftus and colleagues that false memories may influence our recollections in a wide variety of situations, including situations of high emotional content.

FALSE MEMORIES: CONCLUSIONS

False memories are relatively easy to create in the laboratory, even false memories of wide scale. However, it is easiest to induce wide-scale false memories when such episodes or suggestions are repeated (Ceci et al., 1994), and when the event is plausible within the context of a person's life (Loftus and Pickrell, 1995; Pezdek et al., 1997). In addition, research has also shown that witnesses' reports of an event can be influenced by interactions with others that take place after the event. Based on such results, some investigators believe that one must be very skeptical when an individual reports a recovered memory of childhood abuse (Loftus et al., 2008). However, other investigators are more cautious before dismissing all or even most recovered memories as being the result of constructions at retrieval (e.g., Pezdek et al., 1997). Thus, the veracity of recovered memories must be decided on a case-by-case basis. There is no doubt that this issue is of critical importance, and that cognitive research will play an important role in resolving the questions that remain.

FORGETTING: SUMMARY AND CONCLUSIONS

We began this chapter by asking how long memories can last; that is, can we store information permanently? Research has supported our observations concerning the long lives of some memories. If material is studied over relatively long periods of time (as over the years in high school or college), if it is processed in a top-down manner (as when one interacts with one's classmates of those years or when one learns and uses a foreign language), then there is evidence that there may be little forgetting of that material, even over decades. Second, we asked whether forgetting occurs because information is lost from memory, or whether information might be there but we cannot find it. Information may be forgotten if it is not used for long intervals, or if it was not well learned to begin with (Bahrick, 1984). However, forgetting is strongly influenced by interference from other material in memory, especially similar material that was stored around the same time—both before and after—as the material you are trying to remember. Third, we asked what sorts of information might be remembered best. Research indicates that emotional experiences are remembered well (e.g., flashbulb memories), including details surrounding their occurrence. This does not seem to be the result of a special mechanism dedicated to storing emotional experiences, however. Rather, people pay attention to such experiences, rehearse them in discussions with their friends, and encounter descriptions of them in the media.

It is important to re-emphasize, however, that research also indicates that our memories may be fallible. Details of scenes we witness can be altered based on our prior knowledge (e.g., we misremember seeing broken glass at the scene of a car accident because it matches our schema for accidents), or because later information misleads us into misremembering details. The good news is that our memories are generally accurate and, most of the time, are as detailed and accurate as we need them to be.

THE STUDY OF MEMORY: CONCLUSION

We began in Chapter 2 with a discussion of the development of research in memory and the movement away from a passive to an active view of memory processes. The thought processes carried out as some event occurs play a large role in determining what will be stored in memory concerning that event. In Chapter 3, we saw that active processes also play a role in retrieving information from memory: The retrieval environment is critical in determining the experience of remembering. Finally, the present chapter examined the factors that play a role in determining whether or not retrieval will be successful—that is, the factors that influence forgetting.

Once information is stored in memory, it plays a crucial role in many cognitive processes that are not at first glance memory processes. Examples are perceptual processing, selectively attending to information in the world, producing and comprehending sentences, logical reasoning, and solving problems. We now turn to these other areas. In the sections comprising the rest of the book, one of the guiding principles will be the role of knowledge—information stored in memory—in directing cognition.

REVIEW QUESTIONS

Before going on to the next chapter, here is a set of review questions to help you organize and remember the material in this chapter. To maximize your retention of the material, try to answer each question from memory before reviewing the section of the chapter in which the material is covered. That attempt at recall, even if the recall is not correct, will increase your memory for the material after you review it.

1. What are errors of *omission* versus *commission* in memory?

2. Briefly describe results of laboratory studies on memory for large amounts of material.

3. What does it mean to say that a laboratory study of memory lacks *ecological validity*?

4. What are the results of studies examining our memories of incidents from our lives?

5. Discuss evidence supporting the idea that sometimes information might be permanently stored.

6. What are the effects of massed versus distributed practice on memory and what might be the basis for those effects?

7. Discuss decay versus interference theories of forgetting. Outline some possibilities as to how interference might work in producing forgetting.

8. Why is it difficult to test the idea that decay is important in forgetting? Based on research examining decay versus interference, what is the most reasonable conclusion concerning the role of decay in forgetting?

9. Outline the differences between retroactive and proactive interference as sources of forgetting. How does one test for the effects of retroactive versus proactive interference in forgetting?

10. Briefly outline the development of Underwood's analysis concerning the importance of proactive interference in forgetting.

11. How have studies of directed forgetting pointed to potential usefulness of forgetting? What might be some positive functions of forgetting?

12. What are flashbulb memories? Does research on flashbulb memories support the idea that they are based on a different mechanism from that involved in storage and retrieval of more ordinary memories?

13. Why is the possibility of the formation of false memories of potential importance beyond psychology?

14. Based on research of Loftus and others, should we be concerned about the accuracy of eyewitness testimony?

15. What are two possible ways in which post-event information might affect memory performance?

16. What role might source amnesia play in errors in eyewitness testimony?

17. Discuss evidence that large-scale false memories can occur in children and adults.

18. Why do some researchers urge caution before we conclude that most adult reports of childhood abuse are based on false memories?

CHAPTER 5

VISUAL COGNITION: PATTERN RECOGNITION AND SPATIAL LOCALIZATION

Look around the room you are in. You will have no difficulty recognizing assorted objects: furniture, books, family photos, knickknacks. We also recognize objects through our other senses: You may hear voices and also words; you will recognize the aroma of coffee. All of those objects—visual, auditory, olfactory—count as *patterns*. *Pattern recognition* is a term that originated with computer science to describe how incoming raw data—a pattern—is matched to information in memory related to that stimulus. When we take in sensory input from the world, we need to match that input to a representation stored in memory in order to recognize it. We recognize someone calling our name, for example, because we have information in our memory about the sound of our name.

Chapters 5–7, the second section of the book, deal with the family of activities involved with perception, through which we take in and interpret information from the world. These activities include: (a) the already mentioned pattern recognition, the processes by which we identify words, objects, and faces (discussed in this chapter); (b) spatial localization, the ability to deal with objects, including ourselves, in space (also discussed in this chapter); (c) attention, our ability to process selectively some information in a world full of stimuli, and to multitask, by dividing attention among several activities at the same time (Chapter 6); and (d) mental imagery, experiences in which we reconstruct perceptual experiences from memory (Chapter 7).

Perceptual processes were at one time believed to be lower-level functioning, both because they are accomplished without our conscious control and because even animals can do such things as recognize patterns (e.g., Glezer, Leushina, Nevskaya, and Prazdnikova, 1973) and learn spatial layouts (e.g., Morris, 1984; Olton and Samuelson, 1976). Perceptual processes were contrasted with the higher mental processes, such as problem solving, logical thinking, and decision making, which are accomplished consciously, and are much less obvious in animals. There is, however, a basic problem with labeling perceptual processes as lower-level: The ability to recognize patterns and direct our attention involves very elaborate cognitive computations, which are heavily influenced by top-down processes that depend on one's knowledge and interpretation of situations. Thus, it is very difficult, if not impossible, to separate lower and higher forms of cognition.

We recognize visual and auditory patterns effortlessly, and that lack of effort may delude us into thinking that the processes underlying pattern recognition are simple. Some of the everyday cognitive skills that we take for granted have proved to be tremendously complex engineering problems; for example, when computer scientists have attempted to program computers to recognize faces, speech, or handwriting. Those difficulties indicate that we are simply unaware of the complexities involved in our abilities. Human infants readily recognize their mother's face (de Haan & Nelson, 1997) and voice (DeCaspar & Fifer, 1980); well-trained dogs recognize the difference between combinations of sounds in "sit" and "stay"; and rats easily navigate around a novel maze after only minimal experience (Tolman, 1932). What is the cognitive program that allows us to engage in pattern recognition, or that provides us with awareness of where things are located in our visual environment? This chapter is devoted to answering those questions.

OUTLINE OF CHAPTER 5

The chapter first examines evidence that supports a modular view of visual processing: a *what* system, which serves to recognize patterns (such as objects), and a *where/action* system that processes their spatial locations, and permits us to perform actions on those objects. We first discuss details of the what system, specifically how recognition of various types of visual patterns—faces, objects, words—is carried out. We then examine the where/action system and how we localize objects in space in order to interact with them. This is followed by an examination of the role of top-down processes in pattern recognition, and we will discuss how visual (or auditory) inputs from the world, in conjunction with our knowledge and expectations, function to produce our perceptual experiences. The chapter concludes with an analysis of whether pattern recognition can take place at an unconscious level.

VISUAL PROCESSING

When our eyes detect an object, light is picked up by receptor cells in our retinas. Information from receptor cells is passed to ganglion cells, the fibers of which comprise the optic nerve. The optic nerve exits the back of each eye, and half of the fibers from each eye cross over to the opposite hemisphere at the optic chiasm. This results in *contralateral* (opposite side) processing of each visual field (VF), as seen in Figure 5.1a. Information from the left VF goes to both eyes (as can be seen by the gray lines), but is largely processed in the right hemisphere. Information from the right VF (black lines) is largely processed in the left hemisphere. Foveal information (at the overlap of the two VFs) is bilaterally processed. The bulk of neurons from the optic nerve connect with other neurons in the lateral geniculate nucleus of the thalamus in the process of sending information to the *primary visual cortex* in the occipital lobes at the back of the brain. Two major pathways then emerge from the occipital cortex and head to the parietal and temporal lobes, as can be seen in Figure 5.1b.

In 1959, Hubel and Wiesel used microelectrodes to measure activity in single nerve cells in the primary visual cortex of cats, and determined that these cells acted as "feature detectors": They were sensitive to lines of a given angle in a particular part of the visual field. For example, one specific cell in the cortex might respond strongly to a

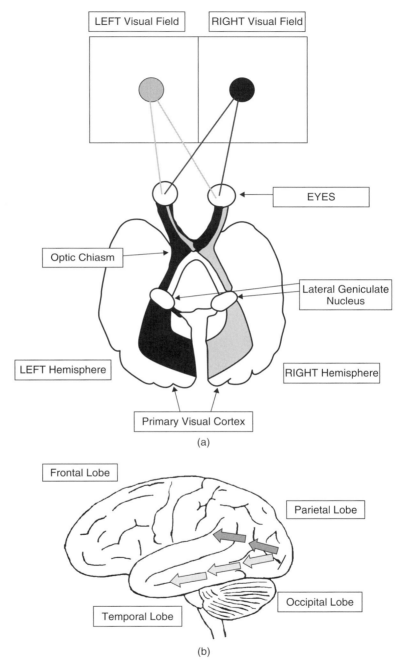

Figure 5.1 Visual processing in the brain. (a) Contralateral processing of visual fields: Information from each visual field goes into both eyes, but then is routed to the contralateral (opposite) hemisphere. (b) Lobes of the brain, with depiction of two major visual pathways.

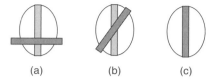

(a)   (b)   (c)

Figure 5.2 Receptive field of a single cell, from Hubel and Wiesel's (1959) research. (a) Little to no activation. (b) Moderate activation. (c) High activation.
The ovals depict the on-center receptive field of a cell, with inhibitory surround. The dark gray bar is a bar of light that falls within the receptive field of the cell. The degree of activation of the cell depends on the extent to which the stimulus bar falls on the receptive field, relative to the inhibitory surround.

line oriented at a specific angle. Change the angle of the stimulus, and that cell reduced its firing rate, but an adjacent cell *increased* its firing rate. The same thing happened if the researchers changed the line's spatial orientation within the visual field. Each such specific stimulus can be called a *feature*. Hubel and Wiesel termed these neurons *simple cells*, and also determined that each one was sensitive to whether a dark edge appeared on a white background, or a white edge on a black background. Examples of results from these studies are shown in Figure 5.2 (which repeats Figure 1.11).

Obviously, the brain must perform further processing on the incoming visual information (or we would never be able to perceive anything other than lines and edges). The simple cells transfer information to *complex* cells, which are also sensitive to lines of a given orientation, but are also sensitive to whether the lines are *moving* in one direction or another. The complex cells then send input to *hypercomplex* cells, which are responsive to more intricate stimuli, such as two lines at a right angle that form a corner.

Information is sent from the primary visual cortex to the association cortex, and the information is processed along several distinct but interacting pathways. This complex network, which involves significant parts of the occipital, temporal, and parietal cortices, is responsible for object recognition, color and depth perception, and recognition of spatial orientation.

BAYESIAN ACCOUNTS OF VISUAL PROCESSING

Visual perception can be defined as the ability to extract information about objects and scenes in the world, based on the pattern of light that enters the eyes. Vision researchers often point to *underdetermination* in this process (Marr, 1982): The pattern of reflected light itself is insufficient to support our interpretation of the world as composed of solid, three-dimensional objects. That is, the information in the light *underdetermines* our perceptual achievements. Objects maintain their color under different lighting conditions, and appear to maintain their shape even as their impact on our retina changes, as our eyes move or as the object itself moves. The perceptual system must make sense of objects and scenes which are often highly complex and uncertain—we view objects under dim lighting, when they are occluded or blocked by other objects, or when viewed in the midst of a complex array of objects (Kersten, Mamassian, & Yuille, 2004). Often, objects are recognized at rapid speeds, as when you recognize a cow or a tree in a field as you speed past in an express train.

One useful account of how we make sense of the visual world under such uncertainty comes from *Bayesian* accounts of visual perception. Bayesian statistics are based on conditional ("If..., then...") probabilities, and are used to calculate the likelihood of a given hypothesis based on the available evidence. As applied to vision, we use principles of Bayesian reasoning based on experiences to make *inferences* (hypotheses) about the world, typically in the face of incomplete or underdetermined data, as just discussed. As Scholl (2005) states, "Bayesian inference is a method of optimal reasoning under uncertainty, and specifies how to choose rationally from among a set of mutually exclusive hypotheses (H) based on a given pattern of data (D)" (p. 43). For any perceptual scenario, then, we mentally (and unconsciously) compute the *likelihood* of various possible interpretations, consistent with the incoming data and prior beliefs. For example, imagine looking at a box with an umbrella propped against it. If the umbrella occludes the straight line at the top of the box, we assume that the line of the box is continuous (even though we can only see part of the line on one side of the umbrella and part on the other). Why? Because continuity of lines is a fairly common visual phenomenon. Thus, hypotheses that have "worked" in the past will be more heavily weighted than those that have been unsuccessful.

The visual system abhors coincidences (Scholl, 2005), and thus automatically makes certain assumptions in order to optimize its interpretation. For instance, we readily interpret Figure 5.3a as an angle or an L, because it would be highly unlikely for two lines to end (or co-terminate) in exactly the same place unless they were somehow connected.

One important finding from studies of object perception has been that people use changes in luminance (brightness) and contrast to make inferences about segmentation of objects in natural scenes (Brady & Field, 2000; Frazor & Geisler, 2006; Geisler & Kersten, 2002; Laughlin, 1981; Ruderman, 1994; Tadmor & Tolhurst, 2000). A visual stimulus that contains luminance differences in two-dimensional objects leads us to perceive depth and tri-dimensionality in a shape (see Figure 5.3b), perhaps because that has been the most supported hypothesis in our analysis of real-world scenes in the past.

We also make use of assumptions about lighting that result in interpretations about whether surfaces are convex or concave. For example, Figure 5.3c depicts an egg carton in which, based on shading cues, we perceive the bottom end circles as being concave dents, but the others as convex bumps upward. This perception is based on the conditional assumptions that the light source is from overhead (Berbaum, Bever, & Chung, 1983; Rittenhouse, 1786), and that there is only one source of light (Scholl, 2005). In the Kanizsa triangle (see Figure 5.3d), we mentally "fill in" missing lines in a visual stimulus, similar to the umbrella example discussed above.

The importance of prior beliefs in Bayesian accounts of vision means that the visual cortex not only responds to bottom-up information from a visual scene, but uses processing constraints to make inferences about scenes based on the most likely interpretation of the data, even under conditions of uncertainty. These processing constraints may be completely learned, or (more likely) involve innate constraints on visual processing which can be modified based on experience (Scholl, 2005). In other words, the visual system can update constraints based on additional interaction with the environment.

For example, Rivers (1905) and Segall, Campbell, and Herskovits (1963, 1966) both found that people who do not live in heavily carpentered worlds (such as Papuans

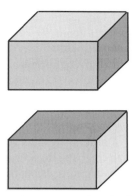

(a) When two lines co-terminate in the same place, we perceive a single shape.

(b) In the top cube, we perceive the light source as coming from above; in the bottom cube, we perceive the light source as coming from the right side.

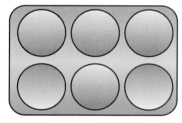

(c) The shading leads to the interpretation that the light source on the egg crate is coming from above the figure, leading to the assumption that most of the bumps are convex (raised), whereas the two on the ends in the bottom row appear to be concave.

(d) Although there are no actual lines indicating a triangle, we mentally fill in those lines based on the implied lines in the cut-out sections of the triangles.

Figure 5.3 Illustrations of how people use regularities in the visual world to interpret stimuli. (a) Co-termination of lines. (b) Cubes in which shading is used to convey depth. (c) Egg carton diagram (recreated from Scholl). (d) Kanizsa figure.

Adapted from Scholl, 2005.

from New Guinea) are less prone to the Müller-Lyer illusion (see Figure 5.4) than Westerners. Those of us in the Western world are exposed to environments where convex corners (such as when the corner of a building sticks out toward us as we approach it) and concave corners (as when we view the inside corner of a room in which we are standing) are prevalent in our living spaces (see Figure 5.4). This exposure allows us to develop the knowledge that helps us interpret novel scenes (and illusions) a particular way.

Neurological evidence supports an effect of top-down processing even in the early stages of visual processing. Lee (2002), for example, found that neurons in the primary visual cortex of the monkey brain respond to features that are traditionally considered features of higher-level vision. When presented with Kanizsa figures (Figure 5.3d), cells in the secondary visual cortex responded to its illusory contours 65 milliseconds after presentation, and then fed that information back to the primary visual cortex, which responded to the illusory contour at 100 milliseconds.

Bayesian accounts of visual perception have been particularly fruitful in explaining a number of perceptual phenomena and regularities in the way people interpret visual scenes under very diverse circumstances (see Geisler, 2008 and Scholl, 2005 for reviews). This is part of a greater trend in cognitive science to explain cognitive processes on the basis of statistical principles (e.g., Geisler, 2008; Steyvers, Griffiths, & Dennis, 2006; Tenenbaum, Griffiths, & Kemp, 2006; Yuille & Kersten, 2006).

(a)

Figure 5.4   The potential influence of environment on susceptibility to an illusion. (a) Photos of convex (top) and concave (bottom) corners. (b) Müller-Lyer illusion corresponding to convex (left) and concave (right) corners.

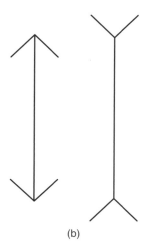

(b)

Figure 5.4 (*Continued*)

TWO MODULES IN THE VISUAL PROCESSING SYSTEM

In recent years, much evidence has been presented that supports the hypothesis that pattern recognition and spatial localization are carried out by different modules in the brain. Based on studies with monkeys, Ungerleider and Mishkin (1982) proposed that after initial visual processing, the visual stream splits into two main components (see Figure 5.5). The lower or *ventral* pathway, from the occipital to the temporal lobe of the brain, is concerned with identification of objects (the *what* module); the upper or *dorsal* pathway, from the occipital to the parietal lobe, processes information about spatial location (the *where* module). Additional research by Milner and Goodale (1995; Goodale & Milner, 2004), which we cover later in the chapter, suggests that the purpose of this dorsal system allows us to accurately orient our motor system *to act on* objects in the environment. Experimental studies of animals and neuropsychological studies of humans have demonstrated that two systems are functionally and neuroanatomically separate—a *what* and a *where/action* system.

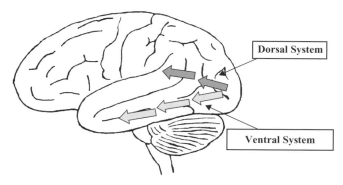

Figure 5.5 Dorsal and ventral systems.

WHAT VERSUS WHERE MODULES: LESION STUDIES IN ANIMALS

Ungerleider and Mishkin (1982) trained monkeys to find food in one of two closed containers presented to them, one on the left and one on the right. In one condition, each of the two containers was covered by a different distinctively patterned lid, say, stripes versus a checkerboard. The animal learned that food was always in the container covered by one specific lid (e.g., the striped one), no matter where it was located. This condition required a discrimination on the basis of the *pattern* on the lid. In the second condition, discrimination was based on *spatial location* or position; both lids were gray, and food only appeared in the container in a specific position (e.g., the righthand one). Monkeys learn either discrimination quickly when reinforced with a food treat.

The experimenters then produced lesions in the brains of the animals. Animals with bilateral damage in the temporal lobes (the ventral or *what* pathway) could not learn to make the pattern discrimination, but could learn the spatial-location discrimination. In contrast, monkeys with bilateral damage to the dorsal (*where*) pathway could not learn to discriminate on the basis of spatial location, but could learn the pattern discrimination. Thus, those lesions produced a double dissociation: The temporal lobe plays a role in identifying objects; the parietal lobe plays a role in processing spatial location.

Dissociation of What and Where/Action in Humans: Effects of Brain Damage

One cannot ethically produce lesions in the brains of humans to determine the type of behavioral deficits that result. The effects of lesions can however be studied in people who have suffered strokes, accidents, or illness. A pioneering report by Holmes (1918, cited in Kosslyn & Koenig, 1995) described patients who could not use vision to reach for objects in space, to estimate distance correctly, or to navigate correctly. Those patients could, however, recognize objects. Those deficits were due to damage to the occipital-parietal areas in both hemispheres (and mirror the problems found in animals with lesions in the parietal lobes). In contrast, a patient studied by Milner et al. (1991), who had damage to the occipital-temporal cortex, was impaired at recognizing objects, though she could successfully reach for them. These cases jointly illustrate a double dissociation in humans between the *what* and *where/action* systems (see also Landau, Hoffman, & Kurz, 2006; Levine, Warach, & Farah, 1985). However, those case studies also sparked revision of the interpretation of the actual function of the *where* system to include its role in operating on objects in the world.

Visual–System Deficits: Types of Visual Agnosias

Evidence for different symptoms resulting from selective damage to the dorsal and ventral systems comes from the study of *agnosias*, or deficiencies in visual processing (*agnosia* comes from Greek: *a*- "without" and *gnosia* "knowledge"). The term was originally introduced by Freud (1891). Agnosia occurs when a patient cannot process aspects of objects by sight, even though he or she is not blind. Lissauer (1890) initially specified two agnosic syndromes: *apperceptive agnosia* is a condition in which people seem to see objects in the world as fragmented rather than integrated wholes. *Associative*

Table 5.1   Neuropsychological Syndromes: Dorsal and Ventral Systems

	Type of Agnosia	CAN Perceive, Recognize, or Do	CANNOT Perceive, Recognize, or Do
Ventral System	Form Agnosia	Individual lines	Basic shapes
	Integrative Agnosia	Shapes; parts of objects	Full objects
Dorsal System	Transformational Agnosia	Objects in usual positions	Objects in unusual or rotated positions
	Object Ataxia and other Spatial Deficits	Object recognition	Reach correctly for an object in space

agnosia patients, on the other hand, perceive objects and whole scenes normally, but have trouble linking their visual percept with existing knowledge, and thus cannot recognize what they are seeing. Humphreys and Riddoch (1987; Riddoch, Humphreys, et al., 2008; also Farah, 1990) have argued that Lissauer's two-classification system is too simple. The term *agnosia* is applied to patients with widely divergent symptoms; the dorsal/ventral modularity in vision provides a way to analyze agnosias (see Table 5.1).

Ventral System Deficits

Form Agnosia

The most profound visual impairments are seen in form-agnosia patients, who have trouble discriminating or copying basic shapes (Benson & Greenberg, 1969; see Figure 5.6). These patients have usually suffered severe damage to the primary occipital cortex (Benson & Greenberg, 1969; Campion & Latto, 1985) or the lateral occipital complex in the ventral system (Milner et al., 1991). Their deficits are sometimes described as seeing through a peppery mask (Farah, 1990), as if they can perceive individual features but cannot combine them into simple shapes.

Integrative Agnosia

Patients with integrative agnosia can discriminate and draw shapes and can also copy objects and more elaborate scenes, such as St. Paul's Cathedral in London. One famous case, H.J.A., studied by Humphreys and Riddoch (1987; Riddoch, Humphreys, et al., 2008), could identify parts of objects (e.g., the long legs and neck of a flamingo, the pointy hat of a garden gnome), but not recognize the whole object (NOVA documentary, *The Stranger in the Mirror*). Such patients appear to be able to see basic two- and three-dimensional forms, but cannot integrate these forms into

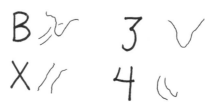

Figure 5.6   Simulated drawings of diagnostic drawings by agnosia patients.
Adapted from Farah, 1990.

whole-object percepts. Typical cases involve bilateral brain damage involving the inferior fusiform gyrus in the temporal lobes, and/or occipital-temporal cortex (Delvenne, Seron, Coyette, & Rossion, 2004; Riddoch, Humphreys, Gannon, Blott, & Jones, 1999; Shelton, Bowers, Duara, & Heilman, 1994).

Further understanding of integrative agnosia can be obtained by carrying out the demonstration in Box 5.1.

BOX 5.1 COPYING DEMONSTRATION: CIRCLE AND TWO DIAMONDS

Instructions: Copy the figures below, and pay attention to the order in which you draw lines.

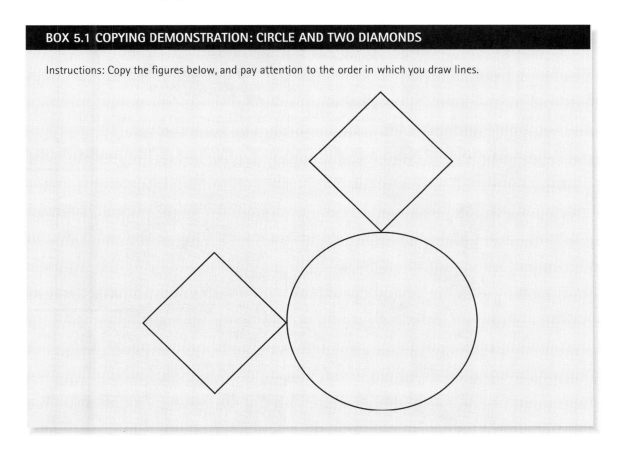

Most non–brain-damaged people analyze the stimulus in Box 5.1 as three shapes: two diamonds touching a circle, and they draw the stimulus one shape at a time. The patient C.K. (studied by Behrmann, Moscovitch, and Winocur, 1994) preserved the overall pattern relatively well, but the order in which C.K. drew the lines indicates that the stimulus features were not integrated into three distinct shapes (Figure 5.7).

Dorsal System Visual Deficits

Transformational Agnosia

In transformational agnosia, patients are unable to recognize objects from unusual angles, such as a teacup from above (Humphreys & Riddoch, 1987; see Figure 5.8

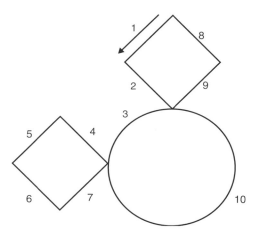

Figure 5.7   Replica of drawing of two diamonds and a circle by agnosia patient, C.K.: Order of drawing of lines is indicated by the numbers.
Adapted from Behrmann, Moscovitch, and Winocur, 1994.

Figure 5.8   Different views of common objects.

for some examples). This rare disorder is usually due to damage to the right posterior parietal lobe, which, under Ungerleider and Mishkin's (1982) theoretical framework, would be expected to interrupt knowledge of the spatial orientation of objects.

Spatial Deficits

Patients also have been reported with deficits in spatial processing, usually after damage to the occipital-parietal areas in both hemispheres. In one syndrome, called *object ataxia*, the patient cannot localize objects in space, although he or she can recognize the object by sight (*ataxia* comes from *a-*, without and *taxis*, order). The patients cannot reach accurately for objects, and are not able to locate an object that has been named by another person. They also navigate through the environment with difficulty. This syndrome was reported many years ago by Holmes (1918, in Kosslyn & Koenig, 1995, p. 121; see also Goodale & Milner, 2004; Milner & Goodale, 1995).

In conclusion, the pattern of agnosias just discussed can be understood in terms of the modularity of the visual system. Brain damage in the ventral path interferes with processing of object identity, while lesions in the dorsal path interfere with processing of spatial or location information concerning a stimulus, and/or being able to act on objects in space.

Brain Imaging Studies of Dorsal Versus Ventral Systems in Humans

Evidence for Ungerleider and Mishkin's (1982) separate modules in humans also comes from studies of brain imaging as people perform different types of tasks. In a *match-to-sample* paradigm used by Haxby et al. (1994), a face appeared at the top (the *sample*) and the subjects had to identify which of two lower faces depicted the same person (see Figure 5.9). All stimuli (the sample and two potential matches per trial) were depicted within a small box inside a larger box, so that researchers could use the same stimuli to test for spatial-location matching. In the spatial task, people were asked to decide which of two test objects was in the same *relative location* within the boundary box as the sample. As the tasks were carried out, PET scans and CBF (cerebral blood flow) measurements were used to measure brain activation. The face-identification task caused glucose uptake bilaterally in the fusiform gyrus and occipital-temporal regions (the ventral system), whereas the spatial task led to activation in occipital-parietal pathway (the dorsal stream). Thus, the areas of PET scan activity corresponded to locations of lesions in human patients with impairments.

Why Are There Two Modules?

Much evidence thus supports the separate functions of the dorsal and ventral system in our processing of the visual world. This research raises a question: when we look at an object, we simultaneously see both what it is and where it is located. Since both types of information are packaged together when we look at the object, why has our visual system developed separate modules to process each component? There is some

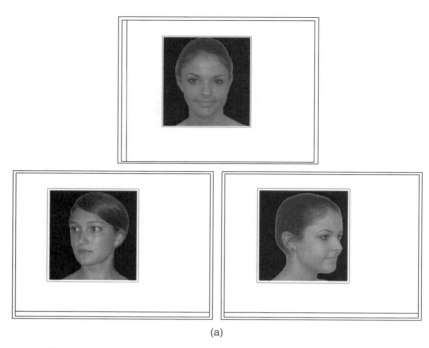

(a)

Figure 5.9 *What* and *where* tasks: In the face-matching task, participants were shown a target face and then asked to judge which of two test faces matched the target picture. In the location-matching task, people saw a target object in a given location within the larger box, and were then asked which of two test pictures appeared in the same relative location. (a) Face matching ("What" task). (b) Location matching ("Where" task). (c) Results of PET study of What versus Where, based on Haxby et al. (1994).
Stimuli adapted from Haxby et al., 1994.

evidence that it may be more efficient to have two dedicated modules, rather than one nonspecialized system that processes both what and where information. Rueckl, Cave, and Kosslyn (1989) attempted to model perceptual analysis of what and where information, using a parallel-distributed-processing network set up in one of two ways. In one condition, all the input units were connected to all the hidden units, which were in turn all connected to all the output units. This model had no modules (Figure 5.10a). In the second condition (Figure 5.10b), the network was divided into two modules, one of which processed the identity of the stimulus, and the other the location. The purpose of the study was to train the two networks to identify a set of objects and the locations in which they appeared.

In each condition, the model was presented with a stimulus in a specific location (as depicted in Figure 5.10b). The model produced an output classifying both the stimulus and its location, and feedback was given by the experimenter. Results showed that the model with what and where modules learned more quickly to process both pattern and location information. Thus, the modular system was more efficient than the integrated system. Perhaps that is why the system evolved that way in the human brain.

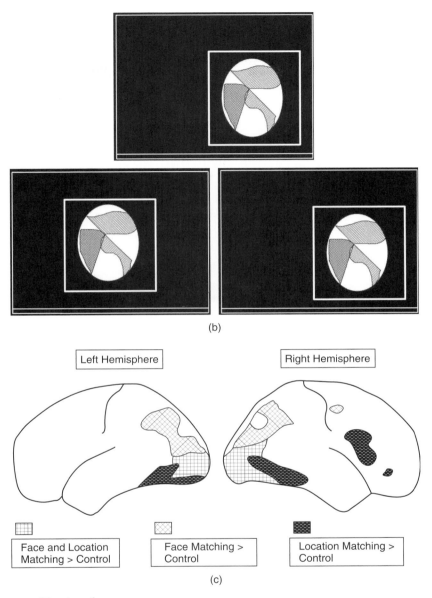

Left Hemisphere   Right Hemisphere

Face and Location
Matching > Control

Face Matching >
Control

Location Matching >
Control

(c)

Figure 5.9   *(Continued)*

WHAT VERSUS WHERE, OR PERCEPTION VERSUS ACTION?

As we have already mentioned, a more recent hypothesis about the bifurcation of the visual system into two systems has been proposed by Goodale and Milner (1992; Milner & Goodale, 2006, 2008). They, too, believe that the ventral system serves object recognition, but they propose that the dorsal system is a *visual action system*, in which

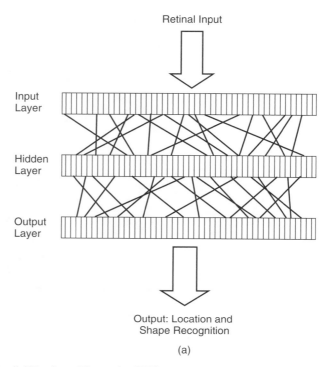

Figure 5.10   Parallel Distributed Processing (PDP) models of *what* and *where* Information. (a) Standard PDP model. (b) PDP model of *what* versus *where* dedicated modules (adapted from Kosslyn & Koenig, 1995).

visual input is used to determine how we reach for or grasp an object. The researchers studied a patient, D.F., who had damage to the occipital-temporal cortex. While she could not report the size or dimensions of objects presented to her visually, she nonetheless would accurately adjust her hand and finger positions to pick up different types of items (Milner et al., 1991). For instance, D.F. was asked to mail a pretend letter in a mailbox with a slot. Across trials, the orientation from the horizontal of the slot was varied at 30-degree increments (e.g., 0 degrees, 30, 60, . . . 180, 210, etc.). D.F. was almost as accurate as the control subjects (Goodale, Milner, Jakobson, & Carey, 1991). On the other hand, lesions to the dorsal system often lead to *optic apraxia*, in which patients cannot visually guide their hand toward an object, despite having overall intact visual and motor skills (Perenin & Vighetto, 1988). This double dissociation has provided support for the perception-action distinction.

Even people with normal sight show a distinction between the object-recognition and object-action systems: Most people are highly subject to the Müller-Lyer illusion (presented again in Figure 5.11). Van Doorn, van der Kamp, and Savelsbergh (2007) presented people who had normal vision with aluminum rods within either outward (Figure 5.11a) or inward facing (Figure 5.11b) Müller-Lyer configurations. Participants were asked to manually estimate the horizontal line in each figure with their fingers, and then to actually grasp the longitudinal length of each bar. As depicted in Figure 5.11c, people manually estimated outward-facing figures as being longer than

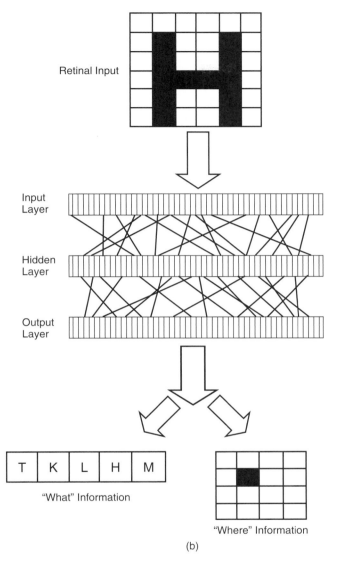

Retinal Input

Input Layer

Hidden Layer

Output Layer

| T | K | L | H | M |

"What" Information

"Where" Information

(b)

Figure 5.10 (*Continued*)

inward facing arrows, but they did not show the same illusion when asked to grasp the objects; the dorsal motor action system was less susceptible to the Müller-Lyer illusion. Furthermore, people were accurate in adjusting their finger or hand positions to pick up the rods end-to-end. Thus, even when their ventral system was tricked by the illusion, their dorsal visual-action system could accurately adjust motoric actions in accordance with the incoming visual information.

There are additional predictions that arise from Goodale and Milner's hypothesis concerning the action versus perceptual functions of the dorsal versus ventral streams. First, the two streams are assumed to operate independently, so it should be possible for

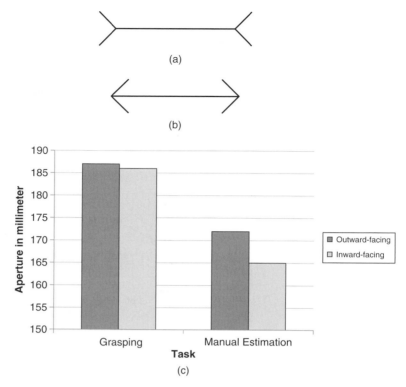

Figure 5.11 Müller-Lyer Illusion. (a) Outward-facing. (b) Inward-facing. (c) Discrepancy between outward- and inward-facing Müller-Lyer illusion in grasping versus manual estimation tasks, based on results of van Doorn, van der Kamp, and Savelsbergh (2007).

reaching actions to be accomplished without input from object recognition, and vice versa. Second, it is assumed that the ventral perception system is conscious, but that the dorsal action system does not necessarily operate consciously. Third, of necessity, the representation upon which the action system is based is *egocentric*, as it requires information about the visual world as it relates to one's own hand/finger positions; alternately, the perception system is *allocentric*, or object-based, as its function is to provide an objective account about the state of objects in the environment.

Research has upheld the general perception-action dissociation proposed by Goodale and Milner (1992; Milner & Goodale, 2006, 2008), though some of the specific claims of the theory, including a sharp neurological division between the two visual subsystems, have been challenged (see Cardoso-Leite & Gorea, 2010 for a review). For example, the independence of the two systems has been called into question following evidence that the dorsal stream responds to perceptual features such as shape (Konen & Kastner, 2008; Lehky & Sereno, 2007) and color (Claeys et al., 2004; Toth & Assad, 2002). In addition, in primate studies, cells located in the ventral stream have been found to be sensitive to motion, which is considered a dorsal stream feature (Gur & Snodderly, 2007). Evidence for interaction between the perception and action streams has also been found, which challenges the strictly modular conception of the two systems. Schenk and Milner (2006) asked patient D.F. to name the shape of an object (e.g., square versus rectangle) as she was reaching for it. Her performance without reaching was at chance, but catapulted to 80% accuracy as she was reaching, suggesting that the dorsal action system was able to provide information to the ventral object-recognition system (and thereby increase the accuracy of her verbal responses).

In conclusion, Goodale and Milner's (1992) refashioning of the original what/where dissociation as one of perception versus action has provided a useful framework for much research with both normal and brain-damaged patients, even if specific tenets of the theory have not been fully supported.

Two Visual Modules: Summary

Results from a number of different types of investigations—animal studies, neuropsychological patient studies, brain scanning experiments, and connectionist modeling—have coalesced to support the idea that processing in the visual system is carried out through the operation of two modules. The ventral *what* system (from the occipital to the temporal lobe) processes information concerning the identification of objects in the world, while the dorsal *where* system (from the occipital to the parietal lobe) processes the location of stimuli in space, and changes in locations (as during motion). More recent evidence from Milner and Goodale (1995, 2006, 2008; Goodale & Milner, 1992) suggests that the two systems are better characterized as object-perception (ventral) and object-action (dorsal) systems, rather than *what* and *where* systems. The coordinated findings from different areas of investigation are an impressive example of the contributions of multiple disciplines to our expanding knowledge of how cognition is carried out. The two proposed subsystems also have utility for categorizing sets of symptoms illustrated by agnosia patients with varying degrees of impairment.

SPATIAL NAVIGATION

While examining evidence for modular processing in the visual system, we have been concerned with relatively small-scale processing of information (e.g., identity and location of individual objects). However, there is evidence that humans and animals process large-scale information about the spatial layout of the environment they are in. There is evidence that people can construct cognitive maps to help them navigate through a space, in the same way that Tolman's (1948) rats did to find their way in a maze (see Chapter 1). People may maintain hundreds or thousands of such maps (Stankiewicz & Kalia, 2007), which can be looked upon as mental representations that are *functionally isomorphic* to—that is, have the same geometric layout as—a building, or a familiar neighborhood, or even a city. Those maps help people to plot a course to get to a desired location. Many other species can also construct spatial maps, such as when bees and ants leave their nests to find food, and then return efficiently (Gould, 1986; Menzel, Geiger, Müller, Joerges, & Chittka, 1998; Müller & Wehner, 1988).

Technology has provided the means to study spatial learning and navigation, using virtual-reality environments, in which viewers can walk through an area, seeing only a limited amount of space at a time. Newman et al. (2007) used a simulated 3-D environment of three small towns, and asked people to drive a virtual taxicab through each in order to pick up 25 passengers per town and deliver them to specified buildings (see Figure 5.12a for simulated maps of those towns). The participants earned virtual

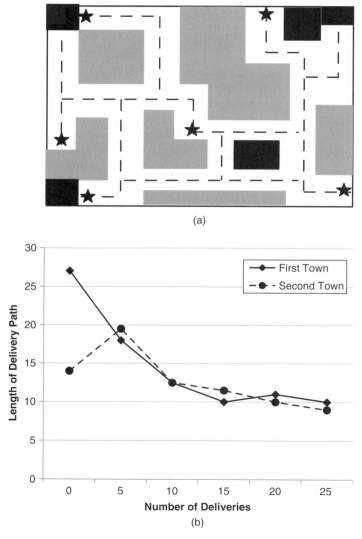

Figure 5.12 Spatial navigation experiment tasks. (a) Replica of stimuli from Newman et al. (2007). (b) Learning curve for first and second towns in Newman et al.'s (2007) spatial navigation experiment.

money for each passenger, and they earned more money for delivering passengers via the most efficient route. Time to deliver passengers decreased over the number of deliveries, indicating that the participants were developing a representation of the virtual space (see Figure 5.12b).

Further evidence for the development of spatial maps comes from a study by Bower and Rinck (2001), who asked people to memorize a diagram of a multiroom building and the contents of each room (e.g., blackboard, microscope, calendar). People then read a narrative, one word at a time, describing a person who was navigating the building searching for a lost item. The narratives described the person as starting in a Source room, moving through an implied Path room, and then winding up in a Location room. Some of the sentences mentioned an *object* in a *room*; e.g., "She remembered that she had been standing in front of the *chair in the storage room* earlier that day." Reading times for the object names (e.g., *chair*) were fastest when the object was in the Location room that the person in the narrative was in. Reading times increased with greater distance from that room, which indicated that people were answering the questions by "walking through" a mental model that included a spatial array of the rooms and their contents.

Brain Areas in Spatial Navigation

The hippocampus is responsible for learning a spatial map of an environment, and contains *place cells* that have been found to fire when a rat is in a particular place within a maze (O'Keefe & Dostrovsky, 1971), and when monkeys move to a specific location within a navigation task (Matsumura et al., 1999; Rolls, Robertson, & Georges-François, 1997). A similar function of the hippocampus has been found in humans. Stepankova, Fenton, Pastalkova, Kalina, and Bohbot (2004) studied patients with damage to the right hippocampus who were impaired at remembering the location of objects (but who remembered the objects themselves). In an fMRI study, both the hippocampus and parahippocampal area (the area surrounding the hippocampus) were activated during retrieval of spatial information during a taxi-driver game (Ekstrom & Bookheimer, 2007).

Spatial decision making (e.g., "What is the best path from point A to point B?" "Which way should I turn at this intersection?") and memory for the steps necessary to navigate within space are linked to the prefrontal cortex. Ciaramelli (2008) described a patient, L.G., with ventromedial prefrontal cortex damage who had difficulty navigating around his hometown. Unless he was reminded of his goal state periodically, the patient tended to go to popular places instead of navigating to his goal location. Ciaramelli suggested that the prefrontal cortex is responsible for maintaining the planned directional steps in spatial navigation.

We have now examined the modular structure of the visual system and have reviewed evidence supporting the existence of two modules for visual processing, one concerned with recognition of objects (the *what* system) and the other processing information concerning location of objects and how we act on them (the *where/action* system). We now turn to a more detailed examination of the processes involved in visual pattern recognition—the *what* system.

PATTERN RECOGNITION

Feature Analysis in Pattern Recognition

Please carry out the exercise in Box 5.2 before reading further.

BOX 5.2 JUDGMENTS OF LETTER SIMILARITY

Rate each pair on their similarity (on a 1–5 scale).

		Not at All Similar				Very Similar
B	Q	1	2	3	4	5
M	N	1	2	3	4	5
B	P	1	2	3	4	5
F	Q	1	2	3	4	5
E	F	1	2	3	4	5
C	Q	1	2	3	4	5
M	G	1	2	3	4	5

Humans not only recognize patterns as individual objects ("That is an A"; or, in another sensory modality, "That is the smell of a rose"), we also perceive patterns as being similar to each other to varying degrees. In Box 5.2, the bases for judgments of similarity are clear: Letters that are more alike in terms of their physical features usually are judged as being more similar. For example, B, P, and R share a number of features and are considered similar; likewise for O and Q. When attempting to identify patterns, people often confuse the correct or *target* pattern with one that is similar to it in terms of having overlapping features (Kinney, Marsetta, & Showman, 1966). For example, when people make a mistake in identifying R, they might say B or P, but it is unlikely that they will say M or U.

Perform the task in Box 5.3 before proceeding (you will need a watch with a second hand).

More evidence that supports feature analysis as an initial step in pattern recognition comes from interference studies, such as that presented in Box 5.3. Neisser (1963) asked people to scan a matrix of either angular letters, such as W, E, and L, or rounded letters, such as C, O, and G, to detect the number of Qs or Zs (the task in Box 5.3 only asked you to scan for Qs). People took longer to scan for Qs in the rounded-letter matrix, but longer to scan for Zs in the angular-letter matrix. The overlapping features of the target Q within the rounded-letter matrix interfered with the speed with which the Q could be recognized (the same was true for recognizing the Z in the angular-letter matrix).

BOX 5.3 SCAN FOR Q (ADAPTED FROM NEISSER, 1963)

Scan the first matrix as quickly as you can to see how many Qs you can find. Write down the number of Qs and how long (in seconds) it takes. Repeat the task with the second matrix.

DUQGRODBBC	HVMXEWFXHM
UCGRODUPCG	EWQMHXKVEH
DGURCGUBOR	EXWMVHHMFW
BDOCGUDRPD	QXEMWVHTMX
CGUROJPQJC	VSWEMHWXME
OCDURSPORD	MXVEWQFWVM
UOCGBDORBC	XVWMEHTQFK
RGGQOUDCJD	MWXVHEFHFW
GRDPOBCOQR	VMWHEXHFMH
GDOUCBRPUS	XVWMEHTNWE
GCURDODRJU	WXVEQHVMWF
DUCOBPRDQO	WMEXHVXFHQ
CGRDSUUURC	MXHVEWVEFH
UDRCOGRPUB	VEWMHXWTMF
GPQORUPDBU	QMVXWHEXMF
GOQUCDCJOG	HVWMEXVWEM
GDSUOCJBCO	EHVMWXTQXV
URDCGOQBBR	WVXMXEMFTH
GDOROCCDRG	XEMHWVNTHV
PDOCGUORPB	WXHMEVWMFQ
CGUROUJCPQ	EMWHVXTFNX
OCDURBDJBJ	HVEMXWVMXF
UOCGGDJPBC	WXVEMHVMWE
UOCQSDORBC	XMEWHVXFHW
RGQCOUDCJD	MSHVEWQEFH
SRUDPOBCOR	WVQMXEMXHT
QCDUGOJPOC	FXEHWVNTVH
CBOCRDUPBJ	HVEMXWVMXF
GUGCDQPUDO	WXVEMHVMWE
URDGJOPRJD	XMEWQVXFHW
BRUPDJUBPC	MVHXEWVEFH
GQUDUOBCOR	VEWMXHWTFM
DRJUCGRPUS	VMVEWHQWVM
JCURQORBUP	XVWMEHTHFK
PDOCGUORPB	WXQEMHVMWE

Neurophysiological Evidence for Feature Analysis

Neuroscience research has provided support for feature analysis as an early process in pattern recognition. As discussed earlier, Hubel and Wiesel's (1962, 1968) Nobel Prize–winning studies found that individual neurons in the primary visual cortex of cats were sensitive to lines at a given angle in a particular part of the visual field, and thus acted as feature detectors. Examples of results from these studies were shown in Figure 5.2.

TWO STAGES IN PATTERN RECOGNITION—FEATURE INTEGRATION THEORY

Our review of the visual system has revealed it is modular: Different features of stimuli—their form and color, for example—are processed in different (though often adjacent, and perhaps overlapping) areas of the cortex. Yet our experience is not one of perceiving color and form separately. When we see a yellow banana, we do not have one experience of its yellowness and another experience of its basic shape. In addition, we know that the identity of the banana is processed by a different system than its location (*what* versus *where* system). Here again, we do not experience the object and its location separately. Rather, we perceive all those pieces of information as one stimulus: We see a *yellow banana over there*. Thus, at some point in visual processing, information from the dorsal and ventral systems comes together to yield our perception of a single experience. Those various features of the banana have become bound together into a single percept. The question of how separate visual components are perceived as one object is called the *binding problem* in pattern recognition.

To explain the binding problem, Treisman (e.g., Treisman, 1993; Treisman & Gelade, 1980; Treisman & Gormican, 1988) has proposed that it is solved in two stages. The first stage involves *detection* of features (e.g., color, form) in the environment, and the second involves *integration* (or grouping or binding) of features into percepts of whole objects, based on attention (see Figure 5.13). We have already encountered the term *feature* in the discussion of feature analysis in pattern recognition, where it was used to denote a single component part of a stimulus. The term is used a bit differently in Treisman's feature integration theory. Treisman uses "feature" in conjunction with the term "dimension." Form, color, and motion, for example, are *dimensions* of stimuli (Treisman & Gormican, 1988). *Feature* is used to denote specific values on any dimension (e.g., red and blue are features on the color dimension; F and T are features on the dimension of form). In this way, "feature" is being used at a higher level than merely individual lines and edges (as the term was just used, for example, during the discussion of Hubel and Wiesel's research).

The detection process determines the presence of a given feature anywhere in the environment. This stage occurs automatically, and in parallel, throughout the visual field (that is, in all locations at once). This stage provides a map of the visual field, and permits detection of discontinuities of features. A discontinuity is a change from one feature to another, which can be of shape (e.g., a + in the midst of random lines), or color (e.g., a red stimulus in the midst of blue stimuli), or texture. Furthermore, this map contains both *what* and *where* information (Treisman & Gormican, 1988) (e.g., an X in a particular part of the visual field).

One type of psychological evidence to support the notion of automatic feature extraction comes from the way in which people break the world into separate regions. Please work through the examples presented in Box 5.4 before reading further.

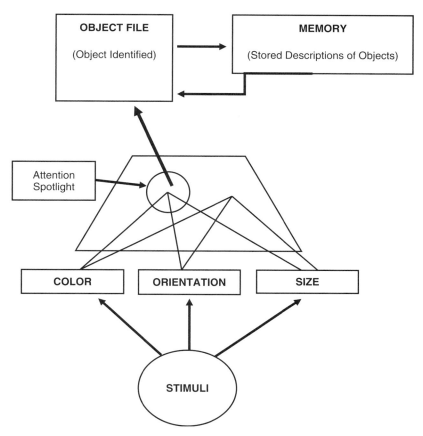

Figure 5.13   Simulation of preattentive and attention/binding phases of Treisman's theory of visual attention.

In Box 5.4A, the odd object in the array seems to *pop out* at you. There is no effort involved; Treisman proposed that an object should pop out of an array when it differs in terms of a single feature.

However, as noted earlier, objects are perceived as unified wholes, not as groups of separate features. In Treisman's model (see Figure 5.13), the psychological unity of an object is the result of *feature integration*, the second stage of pattern recognition, during which individual features are *synthesized* (or bound together) into perceptions of objects (Treisman & Gelade, 1980). The idea that integration of features into an object requires a second state of processing has interesting implications for our understanding of perception of objects (Posner & Raichle, 1994, p. 103). Stop your reading and look at some object in the room, and *without moving your eyes from that object*, try to get a feeling for the other objects in the room. Do it now. If you are like we are, you will feel that outside the point of fixation there are objects waiting to be looked at. However, if Treisman's theory is correct, then outside of the point of fixation there are no fully integrated objects in the visual field. Rather, there are only shapes, colors, plus other features, at specific locations, waiting to be assembled into coherent percepts of objects.

BOX 5.4 POP-OUT DEMONSTRATION TO ILLUSTRATE THE TWO STAGES OF VISUAL ATTENTION

A. Objects that differ in a single attribute from their surroundings pop out because they only engage preattentive phases, according to Treisman (1993; Treisman & Gelade, 1980). For example, in the top figure a different shape (e.g., letter) pops out; in the bottom figure, a different color pops out.

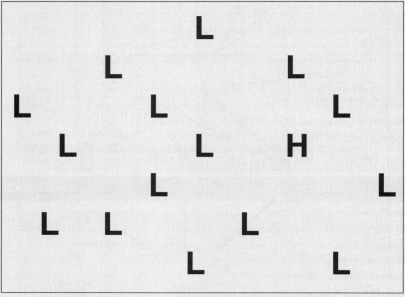

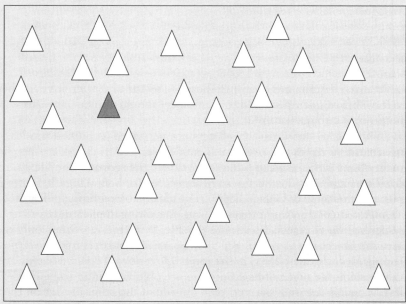

(a)

B. *Find the white diamond*. Objects that differ in multiple attributes from their surroundings take longer to detect because they require the integration phase.

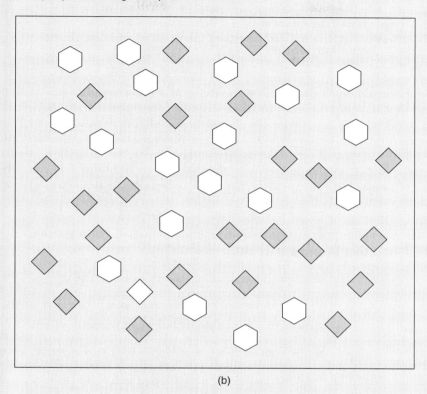

(b)

Illusory Conjunctions

If features are bound together in a separate stage of processing, as proposed in Treisman's model, then mistakes in binding might occasionally be made. There is the possibility that separate features could be integrated incorrectly, which might result in *illusory conjunctions of features* (that is, illusory groupings of features), resulting in illusory objects. For example, let us say that an array contains these stimuli: [red]A [green]Y [blue]G. The first stimulus contains the features *red* and *A*; the second contains the features *green* and *Y*; and so on. Identifying such stimuli under normal conditions is easy. Treisman hypothesized that feature-integration errors might occur, however, if processing the information were made difficult, such as under rapid presentation (Treisman & Gelade, 1980, Experiments 8 and 9), or if additional cognitive demands were imposed on the participant by the experiment, such as requiring a second processing task in addition to the letter-identification task. Under those conditions, features might be combined incorrectly, so that the person would see a red Y, or a blue A, or a green G.

As an example, Treisman and Schmidt (1982, Experiment 1) asked participants to scan an array of two black digits placed on either end of a row of three larger colored letters, such as the following.

5   [red]A   [green]Y   [blue]G   9

The people first had to identify the digits, and then report the location, color, and name of each letter. The array was presented for an average of 120 milliseconds (about one-eighth of a second). The additional cognitive demand produced by the number-identification task resulted in feature-integration errors, and the experimental participants reported illusory conjunctions one-third of the time. Thus, we have evidence that feature integration can be interfered with by cognitive demands, which supports Triesman's hypothesis that perceiving unified objects is a second, separate stage of processing.

Brain Areas Involved in Feature Integration

Brain damage can also interfere with the feature-binding process. Bernstein and Robertson (1998) studied a patient, R.M., with damage to the parietal lobes on both sides of the brain (see Figure 5.1). Those areas, which are part of the dorsal system according to Ungerleider and Mishkin's (1982) division, seem to play a role in integration of features into objects. R.M. makes many integration errors when processing visual objects, even with essentially unlimited viewing time. Even when only two objects are presented, and he was given 10 seconds to identify them, he reported illusory objects. Thus, one function of the dorsal system might be to integrate into a perceived object those features found at a given location in space.

BEYOND FEATURES: STRUCTURAL DESCRIPTIONS OF PATTERNS

Recognizing two-dimensional letters is a simpler process than recognizing objects in the world. First, there are many more parts of objects, and combinations of those parts, than there are letter features and combinations of those features. Secondly, objects can be viewed from various angles. We also recognize objects in a number of formats—in photos, line drawings, paintings, and in real life. Objects are also rarely viewed under the exact same conditions each time we encounter them. Even though you may view the same object (say, your car) multiple times, its appearance can be very different from one time to the next, because of changes in lighting (in the morning versus after dark) and differences in the angle from which you approach the car (from the side, head-on, diagonally). The ability to recognize objects despite large changes in appearance is not a trivially easy task; consider again the difficulty that transformational agnosics have in recognizing objects from unusual angles (Warrington & Taylor, 1973).

An even harder problem for our analysis comes from the fact that we can also recognize particular objects that we have never seen before, such as a new neighbor's dog or her new hybrid car. In these examples, interactions with dogs and automobiles have made it possible for us to recognize a new object as being of the *same kind* as those we already know.

Consideration of questions like those just outlined has led to the conclusion that feature analysis is but the first step in pattern recognition. There is evidence that the representations that serve in recognition of objects must go beyond sets of features, and must also include the relations among those features. Consider the following set of patterns:

b, p, d, q

Each of them contains the same features: (1) a straight line and (2) a loop. We recognize these patterns as four different letters, however, based on the spatial relationship between the curved loop and vertical line. Analysis of whether the loop is at the top or bottom, and to the left or the right of the line, produces what is called a *structural description* of the pattern (e.g., "the curved loop is attached at the bottom of the vertical line, to the right"). We now turn to an important theoretical approach that proposes that structural descriptions underlie our object-recognition abilities.

Recognizing Complex Objects: Recognition by Components

Marr's Theory

A pioneering analysis of object recognition using structural descriptions was proposed by Marr (1982; Marr & Nishihara, 1978), and then elaborated by Biederman (1987). In order to explain how people can recognize complex objects, such as people (see Figure 5.14a), researchers have hypothesized that we use structural descriptions made up of large-scale shapes (Biederman, 1987; Marr, 1982). People, for example, are made up of parts (a head, a trunk, arms, and legs), as shown in Figure 5.14a. Recognition of a person is based on activation of a set of interrelated cylinders (see Figure 5.14b); these cylinders serve as the *primitives*, or *building blocks*, for more complex objects. Each of the body parts can also be further analyzed into its component parts (Figure 5.14b shows how the hand can be analyzed).

Marr (1982; Marr & Nishihara, 1978) proposed a modular and computational approach to object recognition that has been used as the basis for understanding both human (Biederman, 1987) and computer-based (e.g., Bennamoun & Boashash, 1997) visual systems. In Marr's theory, the first stage of object recognition is edge extraction—we use information about light/dark contrasts in the visual field to process the features or lines that make up an object (see Figure 5.14c). This set of lines is then used to determine the areas of sharp concavity (where areas bend inward) and convexity (where areas bend outward), which are needed to segment the object into parts, notably cylinders. Once we determine the relationship of the parts to each other, we recognize the fish (in Figure 5.14c) by matching it to a structural description stored in our memory.

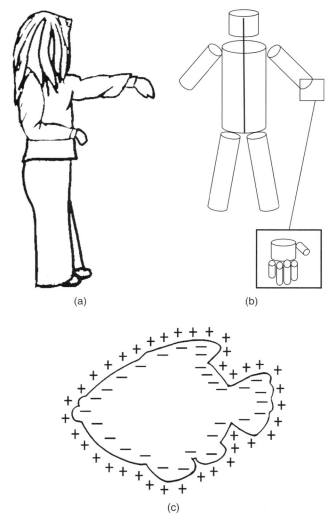

Figure 5.14 Components of objects. (a) Drawing of a realistic person. (b) Analysis of components of a person, based on Marr and Nishihara (1978). (c) Segmentation of an object (based on Figure 6 in Marr & Nishihara, 1978).

GEONS: COMPONENTS OF COMPLEX OBJECTS

The main psychological components of Marr's theory were taken up by Biederman, who both further developed the theory and conducted experiments to test it. Biederman (e.g., 1987, 1995) expanded the number of basic visual primitives to include not only cylinders, but also simple geometric forms, which he called *geons* (shorthand for *geometric ions*). As in Marr's (1982) theory, the geons are found by breaking the object

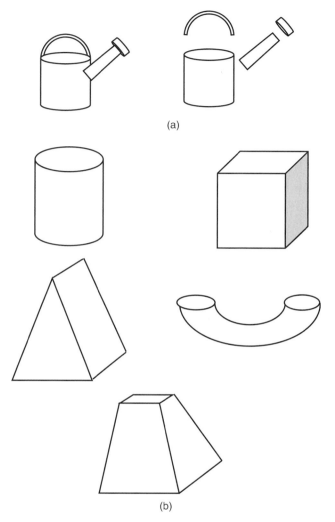

Figure 5.15 Recognition-by-components theory (Biederman, 1987). (a) Common object broken down into component parts (based on Biederman, 1987). (b) Examples of geons, from Biederman (1987). (c) Objects: Whole and with component parts evident (based on Biederman, 1987). (d) Examples of different combinations of same set of geons (based on Biederman, 1987).

into its parts at concavities, known as *vertices* (plural of *vertex*). Vertices indicate the intersection of two geons, and allow us to divide or *parse* an object into geons (see Figure 5.15a).

Examples of geons are shown in Figure 5.15b. Biederman assumes that, upon seeing an object, we determine the set of geons that compose it (Figure 5.15c), and those particular geons and their arrangement determines the classification of the object; a different arrangement of the same set of geons will result in different object being seen

(c)

Figure 5.15 (*Continued*)

(see Figure 5.15d). Biederman's theory is thus a *structural* theory: The arrangement of an object's components is important, not the components in isolation.

Evidence for Recognition by Components

Recognition of Objects Lacking Components

A number of studies by Biederman (1987, 1995) have provided evidence to support the recognition-by-components (or RBC) view of pattern recognition. First, object recognition is based on the *form* of an object (not its color or texture, etc.). Biederman and Ju (1988), for instance, found that people were as accurate and fast at identifying objects in line drawings as in color photographs, suggesting that edge information was sufficient for recognition. Secondly, objects vary in their complexity, and the number of geons of which they are composed. The RBC view predicts that recognition should depend on a minimum number of geons being activated per object. Biederman, Ju, and Clapper (1985, reported in Biederman, 1987) used line drawings of objects containing two, three, six, or nine components. The objects were presented either intact or with some of their geons deleted (see Figure 5.16a). People made more errors and took longer to recognize objects when a minimal number of components were shown (e.g., only three out of nine geons). However, in most conditions, rapid and

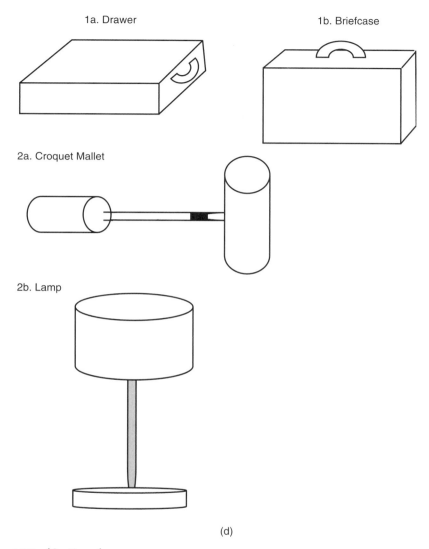

1a. Drawer

1b. Briefcase

2a. Croquet Mallet

2b. Lamp

(d)

Figure 5.15 (*Continued*)

accurate identification of objects occurred (over 90% accuracy) when only three or four geons were evident. This indicates that the visual system is adept at recognizing objects from just a few components.

Perception of Degraded Objects

In the recognition-by-components view, concavities are the points at which objects are parsed. If the contours or outline of an object are deleted at the vertices, it should be hard to parse the object into its component geons and to detect relations among them. The drawing of the object in Figure 5.16b illustrates what Biederman calls

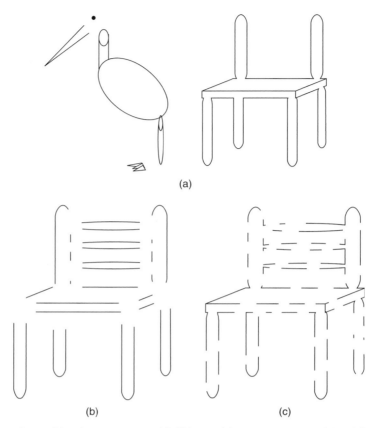

(a)

(b)   (c)

Figure 5.16 Recognition-by-components. (a) Objects with component parts deleted (based on Biederman, 1987). (b) Degraded object: Nonrecoverable. (c) Degraded object: Recoverable.

nonrecoverable degradation, because the removal of the concavities makes it impossible to recover the components of the object. *Recoverable* degradation is illustrated in Figure 5.16c—the outline is removed in the middle of a line segment and is easy to fill in mentally. Biederman (1987) found that people were much more accurate at identifying figures like that in Figure 5.16c than figures like that in 5.16b at fast presentation rates (e.g., 100 milliseconds). Recognition became extremely difficult when concavities were made nonrecoverable.

Questions About Recognition by Components

Although results from multiple studies provide support for the recognition-by-components view, other research has raised the possibility that global shape of visual stimuli (e.g., the overall shape of an object) is more important than are geons for object recognition. After all, we can identify objects based on their silhouettes, or mere outlines (see Figure 5.17a), which suggests that sometimes the overall shape of an object is more important for its identification than parsing its component parts.

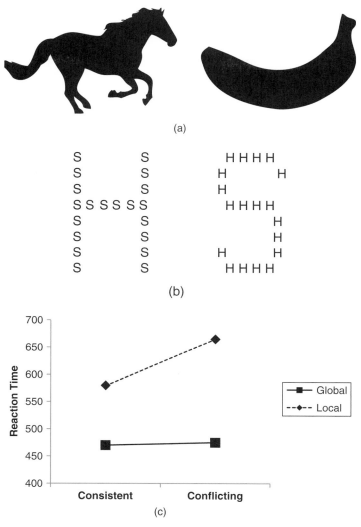

Figure 5.17 Object recognition by shape or global features. (a) Silhouettes of familiar objects. (b) Navon (1977) stimuli. (c) Navon results, Experiment 3. (d) Adaptations of stimuli, based on Cave and Kosslyn (1993): Notice that the natural, disconnected stimulus is broken into geons, whereas the unnatural, disconnected is not. (e) Reaction times per condition, based on Cave and Kosslyn (1993) results.

Navon (1977, Experiment 3) explored whether global processing of a stimulus (e.g., its overall outline) is an earlier or more dominant stage in object identification than processing of local features (e.g., its component parts). He used figures, as shown in Figure 5.17b, which were made up of parts that were themselves recognizable letters or shapes (now called *Navon* figures). Participants were shown target stimuli in which larger letters were composed of a consistent smaller letter (e.g., a global H composed

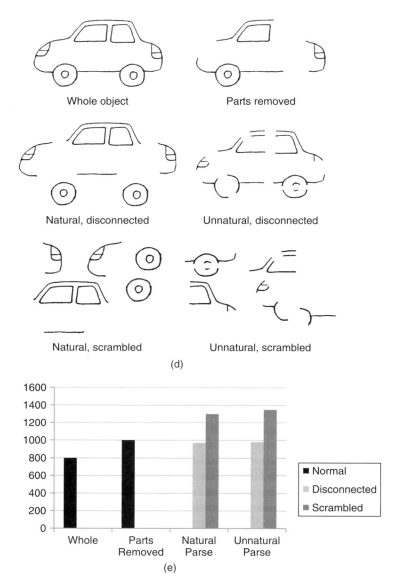

Figure 5.17 (*Continued*)

of many small H's), or in which the stimuli were conflicting (the global letter H was composed of small S's). They were then asked to identify either the global (larger) stimulus or the local (small) ones. The global shape was recognized more quickly than the components, even when composed of conflicting parts (see Figure 5.17c). This seems to refute the hypothesis that analysis of an input into its component parts is the first step in recognition of complex objects. In addition, when the overall letter shape was different than the component letters, the conflict slowed down the identification of the smaller components (e.g., it took longer to say "S" when the small S's appeared within a large H form, see Figure 5.17c). However, as we just saw, the reverse did not occur: The conflict between the overall shape and the component letters did not slow down identification of the overall shape. This result indicates that the overall shape is determined first. Thus, some researchers (e.g., Hayward, 1998) have argued that any theory of object recognition must account for how people recognize objects by the outline or global shape of an object.

Cave and Kosslyn (1993) carried out a study of recognition of degraded objects, similar to Biederman (1987). Cave and Kosslyn divided pictures of 48 objects (e.g., eyeglasses, wagon) either into parts corresponding to geons that were in a natural but disconnected array, into parts that appeared scrambled, or into arbitrarily made unnatural cuts (which did not maintain geon parts), and examined how easily participants could recognize the objects (see Figure 5.17d). The objects broken into natural geon parts were not recognized significantly faster or more accurately than the objects broken into unnatural parts, but both were identified faster than objects divided into geons in a scrambled state. Cave and Kosslyn concluded that the most important factor influencing object recognition was the overall shape of an object, rather than activation of parts as Biederman (1987) claimed. The scrambled condition, in which the overall shape *was* disrupted, led to higher error rates and slower response times (see Figure 5.17e).

The results of the Navon (1977) and Cave and Kosslyn (1993) studies indicate that although we *can* analyze objects into their component parts as predicted by Marr (1982) and Biederman (1987, 1995), such an analysis may not be the only method through which we recognize objects. We may sometimes use the overall shape of an object to determine its identity.

RECOGNITION OF COMPLEX OBJECTS: SUMMARY

Research on object recognition has been influenced by the notion that recognition of complex objects depends on analysis of those objects into components, and organization of those components into structural descriptions of the object. Biederman's (1987, 1995) recognition-by-components view claims that complex objects are first analyzed into basic geometrical forms, which serve as the basis for recognition of the whole object. Research has also indicated that the overall shape may override recognition of individual parts (Navon, 1977).

MODULARITY IN VISUAL PATTERN RECOGNITION: ARE FACES SPECIAL?

The discussion so far has assumed that all patterns—cars, trees, people, birds—undergo the same series of steps as pattern recognition is carried out. Feature analysis is followed by creation of a structural description, and the structural description is then matched with information in memory. Some researchers have proposed, however, that there are modular systems within the visual pattern-recognition system: The human brain has evolved separate modules to deal with recognition of faces versus objects, based on their relative importance to survival and adaptation (e.g., Caramazza & Shelton, 1998). Farah (1992) extended this reasoning further, and proposed that psychological and neuropsychological evidence supports the existence of three major visual pattern-recognition systems—for faces, objects, and words.

Visual deficits caused by brain damage from strokes and other agents fall into three categories: *alexia*—the inability to read words (*without words* in Greek); visual *agnosia*—the inability to recognize objects by sight (*without knowledge* in Greek; we are already familiar with some agnosias from earlier discussion); and *prosopagnosia*—the inability to recognize faces (*prospon* means *face* in Greek; e.g., Humphreys & Riddoch, 1987). Some patients are selectively impaired, with problems in recognition of only words or objects or faces, which suggests modularity in the visual recognition system. It is easy to see how face and object recognition are evolutionarily important: Distinguishing friends from foes, and safe-to-eat foods from poisonous ones, would have promoted survival. Since written language is a more recent development in the history of humans, it may have developed through different mechanisms.

A second proposal by Farah (1992) is that the three types of visual pattern recognition are accomplished by two different cognitive strategies. In *decompositional* processing, stimuli are first decomposed into their component parts, features, and geons, as we have discussed extensively; in *holistic* processing, the relations of the parts to each other is most important in recognition. Face identification is accomplished holistically; every person we meet has two eyes, a nose, and a mouth, and the exact configuration of those features is important in triggering activation of a specific facial representation stored in memory (e.g., of our mother). On the other hand, evidence from research on reading suggests that words are initially recognized based on their component letters. Object recognition, Farah's third system, shares both a decompositional strategy with words and a holistic strategy with faces.

Based on Farah's (1992) analysis, there are predictable patterns of visual pattern-recognition deficits in neuropsychology patients. Consider patients who are impaired in two out of the three systems. Such impairments should occur in recognition of either faces+objects (based on damage to the holistic-processing module) or objects+words (based on damage to the decompositional module). There should never be a patient demonstrating loss of recognition of faces+words with intact object recognition because recognition of objects depends on the face and word systems that have been lost. Farah's review of 99 cases in the neuropsychology literature supported that hypothesis (see Figure 5.18a). In order to demonstrate experimentally that faces and objects are processed differently, Tanaka and Farah (1993) presented normal individuals with pictures of faces or objects (such as houses; see Figure 5.18b). When asked whether an isolated part from each picture had been part of the original (e.g., a nose from the face, or a door from the house), people were much less accurate at judging face parts. Farah concluded that, since faces are processed more holistically, parts of faces are not processed or remembered well in isolation. Other psychological and neuropsychological evidence, to which we now turn, provides additional support for the hypothesis that face recognition is a modular part of the pattern recognition

Impaired: FACES Spared: objects, words	27
Impaired: FACES, OBJECTS Spared: words	15
Impaired: FACES, OBJECTS, WORDS	22
Impaired: OBJECTS, WORDS Spared: faces	16
Impaired: OBJECTS Spared: faces, words	1?
Impaired: WORDS, FACES Spared: objects	1?
(Selective impairment of words not included in study)	

(a)

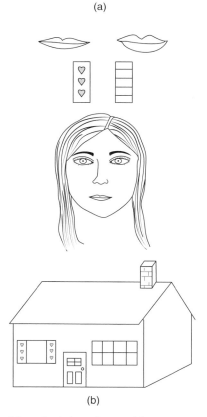

(b)

Figure 5.18   Data and stimuli from Farah (1992) study. (a) Neuropsychology data: Number of research cases per set of symptoms. (b) Adaptations of face and house stimuli from Tanaka and Farah (1993).

system, and that this domain-specificity is innate (Biederman & Kalocsai, 1997; Ellis, 1986; Zhao, Chellappa, Rosenfeld, & Phillips, 2003).

Psychological Evidence for Modularity of Face Recognition

Several studies have demonstrated that, sometimes within hours after birth and definitely by 2 months of age, infants show a preference for looking at faces over other stimuli (Fantz, 1961; Johnson & Morton, 1991). Developmental research confirms the importance of facial configurations in recognition of faces: Newborns discriminate between simplified faces with all the features in a correct configuration versus faces with scrambled features (Easterbrook, Kivilesky, Muir, & LaPlante, 1999), and they show a preference for looking at correctly configured faces by 1 month of age (Johnson, Dziurawiec, Ellis, & Morton, 1991). Further evidence for a developmental emphasis on facial configurations was illustrated by Cohen and Cashon (2001). The researchers presented 7-month-old infants with a picture of a female face until they stopped paying attention (i.e., they became bored). The technique is known as *habituation*; the person habituates, or becomes accustomed to, the continually presented stimulus. When a second face was presented—either the same female, a scrambled version of that female, or a different female face—the infants continued to indicate boredom only in response to the same upright face, but not to the scrambled face. Cohen and Cashon argued that if the children only treated faces as sets of features, they should also have stopped paying attention to the scrambled face of the first female, since it contained all the same features, but they did not. This illustrates that, well before their first birthday, infants are sensitive to relational aspects of faces.

Faces also tend to have privileged access in memory, as they are remembered better than names or other types of information (e.g., Bahrick, Bahrick, & Wittlinger, 1975). In addition, both innateness and modularity claims are substantiated by double dissociations of prosopagnosia and object agnosia. Some patients show impairments in object, but not facial recognition (Moscovitch, Winocur, & Behrmann, 1997), and others present cases of prosopagnosia without non-face, object-recognition problems (Duchaine, Yovel, Butterworth, & Nakayama, 2006; Henke, Schweinberger, Grigo, Klos, & Sommer, 1998; Riddoch, Johnston, Bracewell, Boutsen, & Humphreys, 2008; for a different view, see Gauthier, Behrmann, & Tarr, 1999).

Furthermore, face- and object-recognition systems are differentially affected by experimentally manipulated visual conditions. Face recognition, but not object recognition, is negatively affected by contrast reversal, in which the white and dark areas of a picture are seen in reverse (similar to what one sees in a photographic negative; Galper, 1970; Hill & Bruce, 1996; Johnston, Hill, & Carman, 1992; Nederhouser, Yue, Mangini, & Biederman, 2007). We have also seen that most objects are easily identified by their form, even when color and surface information are missing (Biederman & Ju, 1988). However, pigmentation or skin tone of faces (which is dramatically altered by contrast reversal) is almost as important as shape in recognition of familiar faces (Russell, Sinha, Biederman, & Nederhouser, 2006).

Configural Processing of Faces

As we saw earlier, Tanaka and Farah (1993) have shown that faces are processed more holistically than are objects. A number of researchers (e.g., Young, Hellawell, & Hay, 1987) have suggested that configural information is essential for identifying faces. Relational features, such as the distance between mouth and nose, play a significant role in face recognition (Diamond & Carey, 1986; Leder & Bruce, 2000), and elongating the face area by raising the eyes impairs identification of famous faces (Cooper & Wojan, 1996). Also, reconfiguring the spatial relations of the eyes relative to the nose and mouth resulted in longer identification times and more errors in recognition of familiar faces (Cooper & Wojan, 2000; see Figure 5.19).

In an interview with the New York Times (Svoboda, 2007), Pawan Sinha reported he has found that only 12 relational features (e.g., two eyes side by side, eyes above mouth, etc.) are needed for a stimulus to be characterized as a face. This may explain why adults see faces in the most unlikely places—a likeness of Mother Teresa in a famous cinnamon bun in Nashville, the face of Fidel Castro or Jesus in potato chips and cloud formations, and the man in the moon (also see Sinha, Balas, Ostrovsky, & Russell,

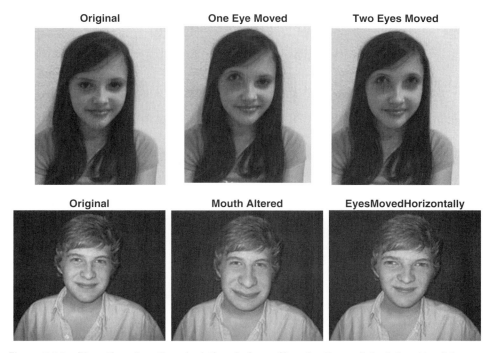

Figure 5.19   Disruption of configural relations in faces: Changing the spatial relationship of the eyes to the rest of the facial features led to the longest recognition times (stimuli based on Cooper & Wojan, 2000).

2006a, b). Individual features facilitate face identification mainly when those features are distinctive to the person, such as Groucho Marx's bushy eyebrows (Valentine & Bruce, 1986).

Although we readily recognize non-face objects when upside-down, inversion has more negative consequences for face recognition (Yin, 1969; see Figure 5.20), largely because turning a face upside-down disrupts configural information. The Thatcher Illusion (see Figure 5.21)—so-called because it first became famous with an inverted, manipulated picture of Margaret Thatcher—by Thompson (1980), is possible because inversion causes the focus to be on local features. Separately, the eyes and mouth are normal (after all, they are right-side-up), and the nose appears normal, simply upside-down. Figure 5.21, however, illustrates that even minor violations of features that interrupt the normal configuration of a face (e.g., curve of the mouth, distance between ends of lips and nose) are only detectable when the face is right-side-up (which is how we would normally view faces).

First Face: Presented During Study Phase   Second Picture: Test Phase

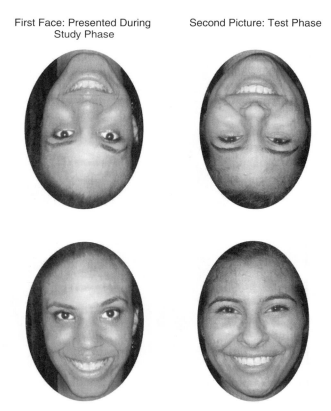

Figure 5.20 Importance of configuration in face perception: Yin (1969) found that face recognition was more affected by an upside-down orientation than recognition of other objects. This is because upside-down faces interrupt facial configuration.

Figure 5.21   Adaptation of Thatcher illusion from Thompson (1980). (a) Upside-down pictures emphasize processing of individual features, with less emphasis on exact configuration of facial features. (b) Right-side-up faces are processed with greater attention to the exact configuration of features, so violations are more easily detected.

In conclusion, psychological evidence supports a distinction between face and non-face object perception, with face identification more negatively affected by contrast reversal and disruption of configural information (as when a stimulus is turned upside-down). Although identification of both faces and non-face objects requires access to the structural relations among parts, the holistic nature of face processing makes it more dependent on small alterations in relations among features.

Neuropsychology of Face Recognition

Grandmother Cells

One intriguing finding pointing to the modularity of recognition of faces has been the discovery that cells in the medial temporal lobe (MTL) respond selectively to faces of specific individuals. The assumption is that after basic visual processing has been carried out in the primary visual cortex, neurons further along in the processing stream become increasingly specialized for specific configurations of features. Although pejoratively called "grandmother cells" by Lettvin (see Rose, 1996), who thought it absurd that specific objects could be recognized by specific small-scale structures in the nervous system, there is recent evidence that individual neurons may indeed be dedicated to particular individual faces (e.g., that of your grandmother). While testing epilepsy patients about to undergo surgery, Quiroga, Reddy, Kreiman, Koch, and Fried (2005) found individual cells in the medial temporal lobe that were selectively responsive to pictures of specific people from a variety of angles (e.g., responsive to photos of Jennifer Aniston, but not to photos of Halle Berry or Julia Roberts). (The cells have not been relabeled "Jennifer Aniston cells.")

However, the authors issued several cautions about assuming that each MTL neural cell stores visual information about a specific person (Quiroga et al., 2005). First, some

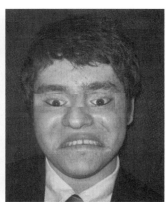

Figure 5.21   (*Continued*)

cells responded to associated individuals, such as *Friends* costars Jennifer Aniston and Lisa Kudrow. Second, statistical analysis led to the prediction that only 2 million of the over 1 billion MTL neurons might be dedicated to specific faces (Quiroga, et al., 2005). Third, since some cells responded not only to photographs of an individual but also to the name of the person, the MTL neurons may correspond to more abstract memory representations (Connor, 2005), and thus may be better characterized as "person identity nodes" (Bruce & Young, 1986).

The Fusiform Face Area: Neuropsychological Modularity or Expertise?

It has long been known that a small, pea-sized region of the fusiform gyrus (medial and inferior temporal lobe) is active as we view faces. This particular area is often referred to as the *fusiform face area*, or FFA (Kanwisher, McDermott, & Chun, 1997; Sergent, Ohta, & MacDonald, 1992), and its functioning seems to support the existence of a face-processing module. However, there are two competing explanations for why the FFA is active during face processing. The *domain-specificity* theory, proposed by Kanwisher and colleagues (Grill-Spector, Knouf, & Kanwisher, 2004; Kanwisher et al., 1997) assumes that face recognition is a specific type of pattern recognition (much like Farah's [1992] proposal discussed earlier), and that, given the importance of face recognition in our survival, the FFA has evolved to discriminate and remember faces.

In contrast, the *expertise* theory, advocated by Gauthier and her collaborators (Gauthier, Tarr, Anderson, Skudlarski, & Gore, 1999; Gauthier, Skudlarski, Gore, & Anderson, 2000), proposes that the FFA is active in all situations in which people must use detailed visual knowledge to distinguish one individual item from another (such as birdwatchers, car specialists, sheep herders, or art experts). The expertise view assumes that face recognition is not modular, but is simply one example of the development of expertise in visual processing. All people become expert in recognizing faces, which allows them to make exact within-category distinctions (not merely recognizing that something is a face, but that is a given individual's face). This skill is assumed to be analogous to when an experienced birdwatcher (but not a novice) can distinguish a tree swallow from a barn swallow. Likewise, you may have known identical twins that you could not initially tell apart until you got to know them better (and thus became expert in identifying them).

There is impressive neuropsychological evidence for the domain-specificity view. The fusiform face area has been found to be selectively active when viewing faces when experimenters use PET scans (Haxby, Grady, Ungerleider, & Horwitz, 1991; Sergent & Signoret, 1992), fMRI (Kanwisher et al., 1997; Puce, Allison, Asgari, Gore, & McCarthy, 1996), and even during single cell recording (Ojemann, Ojemann, & Lettich, 1992). The same area is active also when people view faces (O'Craven & Kanwisher, 2000). Neurological modularity for face recognition, and the hypothesis about its evolutionary origins, has been confirmed in monkeys, where an area of the anterior (front) inferior fusiform gyrus is known to be face-specific (Baylis, Rolls, & Leonard, 1987; Harries & Perrett, 1991). Tsao, Freiwald, Knutsen, Mandeville, and Tootell, (2003; also see Tsao, Friewald, Tootell, & Livingstone, 2006) found that two macaque monkeys showed fMRI activity in cells in the inferior temporal gyrus (in an area known as the *monkey middle face patch*), when viewing faces of monkeys and humans, but not monkeys' bodies or hands, or tools or fruits. Recent research has also implicated the human anterior inferior temporal lobe in face recognition (Kriegeskorte, Formisano, Sorber, & Goebel, 2007), which would make the anatomical area in humans analogous to face processing areas in monkeys.

There is, however, also neuropsychological evidence in favor of the expertise view. Support for the expertise theory has come from studies showing that the fusiform gyrus is most active when people discriminate not only faces, but also types of cars and birds (Gauthier et al., 2000; Xu, 2005). Such results have led Gauthier et al. (1999) to propose that the FFA is activated anytime that visual discrimination among individual stimuli requires expertise.

Recent research may help resolve the discrepancy between the domain-specific and expertise views. Several studies have found that the FFA is, indeed, face-specific, and that a nearby area known as the *lateral occipital complex* (LOC) mediates perceptual expertise effects (Yue, Tjan, & Biederman, 2006). Thus, face recognition may be accomplished by a very particular region of the brain, the FFA, but this skill is neuropsychologically (and perhaps psychologically) adjacent to the parts of the brain that mediate expertise in visual perception. Further support for a double dissociation between face identification and visual expertise has been reported by Sergent and Signoret (1992). They studied a prosopagnosic patient, R.M., who was severely impaired at identifying faces, but, as a car expert, maintained the ability to visually discriminate between different types of cars. On the other hand, two farmers who suffered brain damage, M.X. and Mr. W, were unable to recognize their individual cows, though they retained an ability to recognize individual human faces (Assal, Favre, & Anderes, 1984; Bruyer et al., 1983).

Modularity in Visual Pattern Recognition: Summary

Face recognition appears to show at least some characteristics of modularity (Kanwisher, 2006), based on both psychological and neuropsychological evidence. It involves more holistic processing than do other objects, and is an expert system, in that we use subtle relations among interior characteristics—the eyes, nose, and mouth—to determine individual identity. External characteristics, such as hair and face shape, are used when identifying unfamiliar people. Pigment and textural cues are more important in face recognition than in object recognition. Case studies with brain-damaged patients also support a dissociation between recognizing objects and recognizing faces (Farah, 1992). Although it is worth being a little skeptical about the concept of grandmother cells, some neurons in the FFA appear to be dedicated to face recognition in both humans and monkeys.

THE TOP-DOWN NATURE OF PERCEPTION: THE PERCEIVER'S CONTRIBUTION

As we detailed in our earlier discussion of Bayesian explanations of visual processing, many aspects of pattern recognition involve top-down processing, in which the perceiver's knowledge or expectations play a role in interpreting the incoming stimulus. The top-down nature of perception is illustrated when: (a) the context in which an object occurs plays a role in recognition, or (b) when the individual's knowledge is used to anticipate the stimuli that will occur in the environment. As a Bayesian perspective on perception predicts, stimuli that are probable in a given situation can be perceived more quickly and easily than those that are not.

Context in Pattern Recognition

Examples of top-down processing in pattern recognition can be seen in Figure 5.22. Both displays contain one stimulus—a configuration of lines—presented in two contexts. That configuration is perceived in different ways—as an **H** or an **A** (Figure 5.22a), or as a number or a letter (Figure 5.22b)—depending on the context. Thus, pattern recognition must involve more than simply extracting features from a stimulus and matching these features against information in memory. Rather, the context in which a stimulus occurs, combined with our knowledge (e.g., about words or numbers), leads to top-down processing.

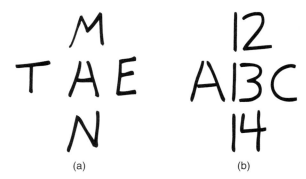

(a)   (b)

Figure 5.22   Ambiguous stimuli.

The Word–Superiority Effect in Letter Recognition

We have seen that there is both psychological and neuropsychological evidence that feature analysis is the first stage in letter recognition; there is also evidence that letters are recognized before whole words. Johnston and McClelland (1980), for example, found that identification of words presented very briefly was disrupted more by a post-stimulus mask of letters than by a mask of letter fragments, suggesting that letter recognition is one of the early stages of word recognition. Patients with *alexia*, an inability to read words, nonetheless maintain the ability to identify individual letters. When alexics do read, it is done laboriously—letter by letter (Kinsbourne & Warrington, 1962). Additionally, children who are beginning to read take longer to identify long words than short words in a lexical decision task (Acha & Perea, 2008), suggesting an influence of individual letter recognition.

By adulthood, though, bottom-up and top-down processes interact to accomplish letter and word recognition. One robust experimental finding that illustrates top-down processing in letter recognition is the *word-superiority effect*. This refers to the discovery, originally reported over 100 years ago (see Rayner & Pollatsek, 1989), that letters are recognized better when presented in words than when presented in isolation. Modern interest in this area was stimulated by a study by Reicher (1969). Participants saw briefly presented letter displays (presentation rates were about 50 milliseconds) of three types. In the Word condition, the letters made up a word (see Figure 5.23a); in the Non-word condition, the letters were scrambled to make a non-word. In the Letter condition, only an individual letter was presented. Immediately after the stimulus, a *mask* (a pattern of random lines) was presented, followed by a two-letter recognition test. The participant had to pick which letter—the target or the foil—had just been presented in the tested location in the display. For example, if the stimulus was WORD, and the target letter was the D in the fourth position, a choice of D or K appeared. As seen in this example, the foil was chosen so that it, too, formed a legitimate word within the word display (K added to WOR- forms WORK). This prevented participants from simply guessing the letter that made a complete word.

Participants were more accurate in identifying a letter when it was presented in a word than when it was presented alone. This finding, while perhaps surprising at first glance, has been replicated by many different investigators (Rayner & Pollatsek, 1989; Wheeler, 1970). Figure 5.23c depicts a connectionist model of pattern recognition developed by McClelland and Rumelhart (1981) to explain a number of letter- and word-recognition phenomena (including the word-superiority effect). The one-way arrows depict how information from a visual stimulus is processed in a bottom-up fashion; the two-way arrows depict how word recognition can facilitate letter recognition in a top-down fashion. If a person sees the word WORD, the multiple features of each letter are activated in parallel; e.g., the features \ / \ / are activated, which then triggers activation for the W. Recognition of the letter W in the first position results in activation that then spreads to words that start with W (e.g., WORD, WHALE, WOK, etc.). However, since only WORD also receives simultaneous input from the letters O, R, and D, it will be recognized before any of those competing words.

How, then, is the word-superiority effect brought about in this spreading activation model? Notice the arrows from the Word- to the Letter-level nodes in Figure 5.23c. These indicate that once a word is activated, that activation spreads downward, to

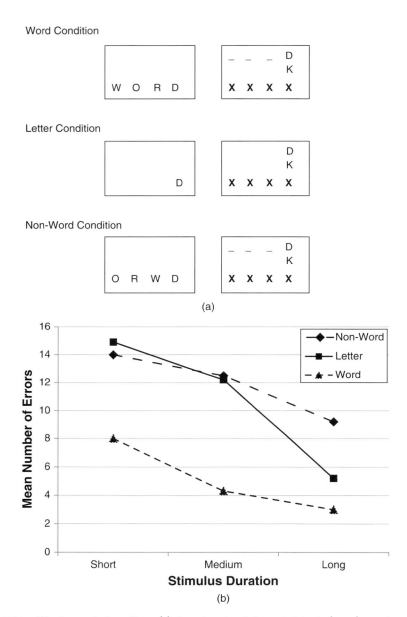

Figure 5.23 Word superiority effect. (a) Sample stimuli from Reicher's (1969) word superiority experiment. (b) Results of Reicher's (1969) word superiority experiment: Average number of errors in individual letter recognition, per condition and stimulus duration (single stimulus, no-cue presentation data only). (c) McClelland and Rumelhart (1981) model.

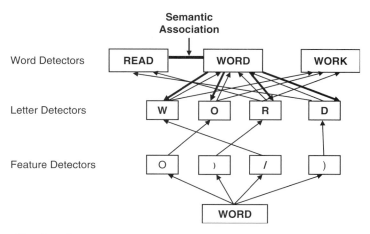

Figure 5.23 (*Continued*)

further activate the individual letters that make up that word. Therefore, the letter D in Reicher's Letter-display condition receives activation only from the incoming stimulus, but the letter D in the Word condition receives bottom-up activation from the incoming stimulus *and* top-down activation. Thus, a letter presented in a word is recognized more quickly and/or accurately. The connectionist model also predicts that missing information might be filled in because of top-down processing. For example, if we read a misspelled word, say, *cogitive*, enough information might be present to activate the word *cognitive*, which means that our system will provide enough activation to its component letters to trick us into thinking the word is correctly spelled. This is sometimes referred to as *proofreader's error*. In the days before spell-check in word processing programs, writers looking for typos were advised to read their work backwards, to avoid expectation effects as to what word should come next (and thereby minimize top-down processing).

Context Effects in Picture Recognition

Similar top-down effects in picture recognition have been demonstrated by Biederman, Glass, and Stacy (1973). Participants first briefly saw a picture of a target object (e.g., a flower pot). A picture was then briefly presented (e.g., a street scene), which appeared either coherent or scrambled (see Figure 5.24), and the person was asked to identify whether the target was in the scene. The scrambled picture was constructed by taking the coherent picture, cutting it into parts, and randomly rearranging them. The target object had appeared in the same location in both conditions. People were faster to respond to target objects in coherent than scrambled pictures, illustrating that recognizing a scene as a whole can play a role in the recognition of the individual objects that made it up.

Context in Speech Recognition: Phonemic Restoration

An intriguing example of the influence of contextual information in pattern recognition was reported by Warren and Warren (1970; see also Warren and Sherman, 1974),

(a)

(b)

Figure 5.24   Examples of organized versus unorganized pictures, based on Biederman, Glass, and Stacy (1973). (a) Organized picture. (b) Unorganized picture.

investigating speech perception, that is, auditory pattern recognition. The basic stimulus material was a set of four sentences, which were identical except for the last word. Here is an example of a stimulus set.

It was seen that the ***wh***eel was on the axle.

It was seen that the ***h***eel was on the shoe.

It was seen that the ***p***eel was on the orange.

It was seen that the ***m***eal was on the table.

One of the sounds on the tape (written in ***this*** font) was removed by cutting the tape, and was replaced by a cough. If you listened to any of the tapes at only that point, you would hear nothing except that cough. That made all the tapes identical up to the last word of the sentence.

In the experiment, each participant heard only one of the four sentences, and was asked to report what was heard. Nothing was said about a cough having replaced one of the sounds in the sentence. All participants reported hearing the word that fit the sentence context: *wheel* on the *axle*; *heel* on the *shoe*; and so forth. Furthermore, no one reported that they heard a cough rather than a sound at the critical point. Everyone reported that they heard complete words: The people *restored* the missing phoneme to the tape. Some reported that they heard a cough on the tape, as well as the missing phoneme (the linguistic sound).

In a second go-round, the participants were told that one of the sounds on the tape had been removed. They were asked to listen again to the sentence and to report the missing sound. They were not able to do so. Putting the distorted piece of tape into an appropriate context made it impossible for fluent speakers to hear what was actually on the tape (including detection of the missing phoneme). There is one further striking aspect of those sentences: The context that influenced phonemic restoration occurred at the *end* of the sentence, after the critical segment of the tape had been presented. That is, *axle*—the last word—is what changes the cough into ***wh***eel, and so forth. If the last word in the sentence is influencing how the person hears an earlier word, it must mean that listeners do not process each of the sounds immediately as they come in. Full word recognition must lag behind the stimulus, so that the critical point of the sentence has not yet been processed completely when the last word comes in. Only in this way could a word at the end of a sentence influence perception of an earlier word.

Context in Pattern Recognition: Summary

People make extensive use of context in recognizing visual and auditory stimuli. Recognition of a given stimulus depends on the other stimuli that appear with it at any time. For this to happen, a person's knowledge must play a role in the processing of incoming information, and influence the organization of the stimulus material.

Expectancies in Pattern Recognition

In the examples discussed in the last section, the context in which a stimulus appears influences recognition of both its parts (e.g., letters, phonemes) and interpretation of the whole stimulus (e.g., whether one reads MHN or MAN). However, what a perceiver *expects* to see can also play a role in pattern recognition. Consider these words:

1. area 2. decoy 3. justice 4. curfew 5. statement 6. hybrid 7. country 8. apology

All are easily recognized English words, but some are much more frequent in the language (the odd-numbered words), and therefore are more familiar to us. When the words appear on the printed page, they are all easy to read, but if each word is seen very quickly on a computer screen in an experiment (e.g., for only 1/50 of a second—about 20 milliseconds), then recognition becomes more challenging. One robust finding in such studies is a *word-frequency effect* in recognition (e.g., Chalmers, Humphreys, & Dennis, 1997). Under rapid presentation, words that are frequent in the language are easier to identify than infrequent words (Forster & Chambers, 1973; Fredrikson & Kroll, 1976). We seem to tabulate information about the frequency of different events (or words) as we encounter them; this knowledge then influences the speed with which we process events.

Specific Expectancies: Priming in Pattern Recognition

The word-frequency effect demonstrates that our general knowledge, independently of any specific situation, plays a role in how efficiently we process stimuli. More specific expectancies about stimuli in a specific situation can also play a role in identifying stimuli in that situation. An important form of this top-down influence occurs when processing one stimulus makes it easier to process certain other stimuli. This is called *priming*, because the first stimulus *primes* the processing of a second stimulus, leading to faster recognition of certain stimuli. Priming has already been mentioned in the discussion of implicit memory in Chapters 2 and 4. The design of an experiment to study priming in pattern recognition is very simple: A *priming* stimulus is presented, followed by a *target* stimulus that the person must identify (Figure 5.25a). The priming stimulus can be related to the target in any of several ways, either in the relationship between the two stimuli (e.g., they may look alike, or may be semantically related), and also in the format of the two stimuli (e.g., word-to-word, picture-to-word, picture-to-picture, or word-to-picture). The question of interest is whether presentation of the prime facilitates processing of the target. Priming occurs when the target is processed more efficiently in the priming condition than in a nonprimed control condition.

The basic priming design can be varied in a large number of ways, depending on the specific research question the investigator is interested in studying. The priming and target stimuli are usually words, as shown in the first line of Figure 5.25a, but one or both might be pictures (see Figure 5.25a and b; Irwin & Lupker, 1983). Researchers have demonstrated that presentation of a word (e.g., *dog*) results in faster identification of a related word (e.g., *leash*) or of a picture that it names (i.e., a picture of a dog). Similarly, researchers have found that a picture (e.g., of a dog) can prime the identification of a related picture (e.g., a leash) or a related word (e.g., *leash*). Pictures and words may also prime recognition of fragmented pictures (Kennedy, Rodrigue, & Raz, 2007), as well as objects from the same semantic category (Lupker, 1988; Figure 5.24c). Sets of dots have been shown to prime recognition of corresponding

Word Prime

Condition	Prime	Target
Priming	"dog"	"leash"
Control	"table"	"leash"

Picture Prime

Condition	Prime	Target
Priming	Picture of dog	"leash"
Control	Picture of table	"leash"

Example (arrows indicate priming)

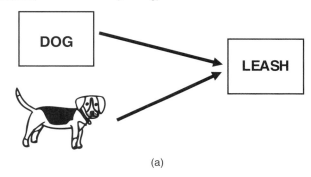

(a)

Word Prime

Condition	Prime	Target
Priming	"dog"	Picture of leash
Control	"table"	Picture of leash

Picture Prime

Condition	Prime	Target
Priming	Picture of dog	Picture of leash
Control	Picture of table	Picture of leash

Example (arrows indicate priming)

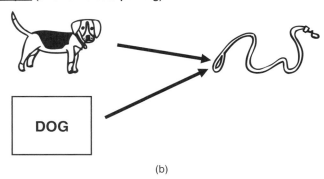

(b)

Figure 5.25   Priming designs. (a) Prime and target words. (b) Prime and target pictures. (c) Fragmented pictures. (d) Varying responses to target.

Word Prime

Condition	Prime	Target
Priming	"dog"	Fragmented picture of leash
Control	"table"	Fragmented picture of leash

Example **(arrow indicates priming)**

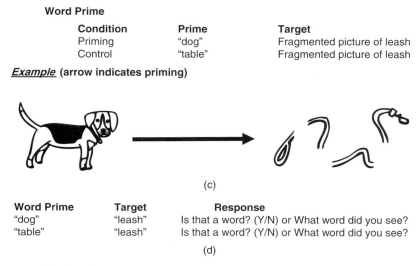

(c)

Word Prime   **Target**   **Response**

Word Prime	Target	Response
"dog"	"leash"	Is that a word? (Y/N) or What word did you see?
"table"	"leash"	Is that a word? (Y/N) or What word did you see?

(d)

Figure 5.25 *(Continued)*

digits; for example, presentation of five dots primes the numeral 5 (Herrera & Macizo, 2008). Priming can also be used with auditory word recognition (Ellis, 1982) and with musical tones (Hutchins & Palmer, 2008).

The strongest priming effects are found when there is a considerable degree of physical similarity between the prime and the target. For example, the largest amount of priming is found with *repetition priming*, when the same word or picture is presented as the prime and the target. (Forster & Davis, 1984; Wiggs & Martin, 1998). The degree of priming depends on the amount of exact physical overlap between the prime and target. If a word is presented initially in capital letters, then there will be more priming if it is repeated in capital letters than if the second presentation is in lowercase letters. Similarly, *black* facilitates recognition of *block*, due to physical overlap, although not as strongly as in repetition priming. Priming can also be found, however, when the relationship between the prime and target is *semantic*, that is, based only on meaning, in which case there is no physical similarity at all between the prime and target. For example, presentation of *nurse* primes processing of *doctor* (Meyer & Schvaneveldt, 1971). In addition, as previously mentioned, presentation of a word can prime later recognition of a picture that the word names, and vice versa, which is also priming based on meaning. In conclusion, priming can occur on the basis of either physical similarity or relatedness of meaning between prime and target, although physical factors may be stronger.

How can priming effects be understood in a spreading-activation model, such as that proposed by McClelland and Rumelhart (1981; see Figure 5.23c)? In repetition priming, when a word node is activated (e.g., for *doctor*), it may take some time for the activation to fade away. If the same word (*doctor*) is presented again within a short enough period of time, the second presentation will benefit from the remaining activation from the first presentation, allowing the threshold of recognition to be reached more quickly on its second appearance). To explain semantic priming, it is necessary to assume that activation of one word (one semantic node) spreads activation to semantically related nodes. That spread of activation would facilitate processing of related words.

Brain States in Priming

One brain mechanism that has been proposed to explain repetition priming is that presentation of the prime results in activation of pathways or areas in the processing system, and the target stimulus activates parts of the same pathways. Thus, priming may be brought about because the neural processing systems themselves are changed by exposure to a stimulus, making later processing more efficient. Measurement of brain states using various brain-imaging techniques, such as PET and fMRI, confirms that repetition priming is brought about through activity in the areas that process the stimulus initially, but typically it results in *decreased* activation of the pathways relative to the first presentation of a word or a face (see Henson, 2003, for a review). This is known as *repetition suppression*, as the neural response is not as strong on the second presentation of a word since not as much processing is required for recognition. Semantic priming, on the other hand, may enhance neural activity; Raposo, Moss, Stamatakis, and Tyler (2006) found stronger neural activity in frontal and temporal regions to the second word in a primed pair (e.g., when *string* was processed after it had followed *cord*).

Knowledge and Expectancies in Pattern Recognition: Summary

We have now reviewed several different types of evidence concerning the top-down nature of pattern recognition. Stimuli that are predictable within a specific context (either through repetition or semantic priming) are more easily recognized in that context. It is evident that a person's knowledge (e.g., about word frequencies, etc.) plays an important role in the pattern recognition process, and can often be used to speed processing of incoming information.

The examples of context effects, the word superiority effect, and the phoneme restoration effect have been informative in illustrating the role of top-down processes in pattern recognition. However, a more significant illustration of the role that top-down processes play in cognitive activities comes from research in reading—a complex skill that most adults carry out with little or no effort. Please carry out the demonstration in Box 5.5 before reading further.

BOX 5.5 DEMONSTRATION OF EYE MOVEMENTS DURING READING

Ask a friend to read a book. Watch his or her eye movements, and count the number of fixations (i.e., times the eyes stop) per line. Calculate, approximately, how many words are being taken in with each fixation by dividing the average number of words per line (count them) by the average number of fixations per line.

TOP-DOWN PROCESSES IN READING

When one reads a line of text, one has the feeling that one's eyes are sweeping smoothly across the page, and that the whole line is clearly in focus all the while. However, research has shown that both of these intuitions are incorrect (Rayner, 1998). When one reads a line of print, the eyes move in a series of *jumps*, called *saccades*, each of which takes about 50 milliseconds (1/20 second) to carry out; it is difficult to take in information during each saccade. When reading a typical line of text, each saccade covers about 7–9 characters. Between saccades, the eye remains stationary, in a *fixation*, which lasts about 250 milliseconds (1/4 second); this is when word recognition is accomplished. Jumping 7–9 characters between fixations means that one's eyes do not fixate on every word as one reads a line of text (as many words contain from 1–6 letters). Furthermore, research has shown that one can only see clearly a few spaces to the right (Rayner, 1998). Our eyes sometimes jump farther than that, so we sometimes must be reading beyond where we can fixate.

When readers jump over a word when reading, they are most likely to skip a word that is of high frequency in the language and very predictable in the text (Rayner, 1998). Also, if a frequent and predictable word *is* fixated upon, the fixation typically will be of short duration. This means that the reader uses knowledge about the language and expectations about what is likely to come next to fill in information between fixations. One can then move one's eyes beyond the words to which one is attending, and if the material in the next fixation matches one's expectation, one has the conscious experience of having seen the words that one jumped over. Although controlled experimental studies show that readers often have not clearly seen those skipped words, the subjective experience is of having read all the words. One could say that *we are meeting the world halfway* when reading, in the sense that our knowledge and expectations allow us to fill in information that is not available in detail from bottom-up processing.

Speed Reading?

We are all familiar with advertisements for speed-reading courses that promise to increase greatly one's speed of reading without loss of comprehension. Those courses claim that they will be able to teach you to use more information in each fixation, and thereby allow you to take in much more at once. But how well do they work? Just and Carpenter (1987, Chapter 14) tested reading skill in people who had taken speed-reading courses. Just and Carpenter recorded the eye movements that the readers made while reading passages, so they could tell which words readers had fixated on directly. Participants were tested for comprehension, and some of the questions asked for details about a specific word in the text, such as a person's name. On such questions, the researchers found that speed readers were able to produce the answer only when they had directly fixated on that word during reading. When the target word was in the periphery, readers were no better than guessing at answering questions about it. This suggests that their peripheral span had not been increased by their having studied speed reading. Speed-reading courses thus do not change the basic perceptual capacities of the reader, which remain relatively limited.

Reading as a Top-Down Process

This brief discussion of reading has served to point out the broader implications of top-down processing: Our knowledge plays a dynamic role in our acquiring information from the world. We use what we know about events in the world (in this case, knowledge of how the words in the language are likely to be presented on a page when discussing a particular topic) in order to predict what will occur over time in order to construct a representation of the events in the world. This perspective on information processing has broad implications, which are briefly outlined in the next section.

Pattern Recognition as a Cycle

A number of years ago, Neisser (1976) outlined a model of pattern recognition in which information processing was viewed as a process that cycles between bottom-up information and top-down processing, as outlined in Figure 5.26. The cycle is made up of two parts: (1) sampling information from the world and (2) using that bottom-up information in a top-down manner, to generate expectations about what will occur at the next moment in time. For example, during reading, an individual takes in visual information about the stimuli on a page, recognizes the words, and then generates expectations about which words are likely to follow as well as the probable sentence structure. Those expectations are the result of the individual's knowledge about the content of the passage and the structure of the language. So, in reading a sentence about baseball, one might expect that the verb is more likely to be *hit* or *throw* than *kick* or *eat*. These expectations facilitate word recognition and guide the person's saccadic eye movements during reading. This illustrates how pattern recognition (such as occurs during reading) is a combination of expectancies generated by top-down knowledge and the bottom-up input, whether in visual or auditory processing. This perspective is relevant to all of our interactions with the world—the phonemic-restoration effect is evidence for the cyclical nature of auditory perception.

Top-down information can also guide attentional processes (as we will see in Chapter 6). For example, if we come into another person's living room, we expect to see certain things such as a couch, a lamp, and knickknacks, based on our knowledge of living rooms. We may miss other things that are not typical of the living rooms that we know. A popular parlor game in England is *Hide the Thimble*, in which a thimble

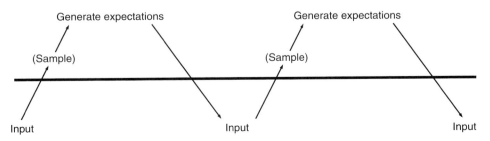

Figure 5.26 Neisser's pattern-recognition cycle.

is hidden in plain view within a room, and people are apt to miss its presence. The perceptual cycle of pattern recognition, then, interfaces between incoming perceptual stimuli and our hypotheses based on our prior knowledge and *schemas* that direct what we process. As just noted, this perspective will also be important in the discussion of attention in Chapter 6.

UNCONSCIOUS PRIMING: PATTERN RECOGNITION WITHOUT AWARENESS

The discussion so far has addressed pattern recognition as a conscious process. However, it is possible that pattern recognition can occur unconsciously. You may have heard the story about the attempt to use subliminal stimulation to sell soda in a movie theater, where "Drink Coke" was allegedly flashed on the screen during the movie, so quickly that no one was able to consciously read it. That day, so the story goes, the concession stand quickly sold out of Coke. This story is taken as evidence for unconscious processes in pattern recognition: Theatergoers were primed to drink Coke by the manipulation. If true, this is also evidence that we can be manipulated in ways that are out of our control, and that subliminal messages are able to control our behavior better than above-threshold messages can. There is a wide-ranging concern about the possibility that people's choices in a marketing context can be influenced by subliminal manipulations. Subliminal advertising has been banned in Australia, Britain, and the United States (Karremans, Stroebe, & Claus, 2006).

Though the "Drink Coke" story is known far and wide, it turned out not to be based on fact (Weir, 1984). It was a story made up by an advertising executive to drum up business for his firm. Although the original demonstration of subliminal advertising turned out to be a hoax, laboratory studies have demonstrated that pattern recognition without conscious awareness can come about under some circumstances.

Unconscious Priming

In the priming studies reviewed earlier (e.g., Forster & Davis, 1984; Irwin & Lupker, 1983; Meyer & Schvaneveldt, 1971), the words and pictures that served as primes were consciously experienced. Other experimental studies, however, examined priming when words were shown for too brief a time to be available for conscious analysis. Most people report that they are not able to recognize words or pictures presented faster than a certain threshold (e.g., around 50 milliseconds). However, even though those quickly presented words might not be recognized, they can still affect the recognition of related words, indicating that priming must be the result of unconscious processing of the initial word/stimulus. Even though the prime was not consciously recognized, it influenced processing of words that followed it.

Bar and Biederman (1998) found similar effects of unconscious processing with pictures. They presented people with drawings of common objects, and each drawing was presented in one of nine different locations on the screen. The drawings were presented very quickly (an average of 47 milliseconds), followed by a mask (a set of random lines), which interrupted iconic memory and prevented further processing of the drawing. A set of 28 pictures was presented twice, at the same fast rate, in a different random order each time. The presentation of the drawings was so brief that, during the first pass through the list, the participants could only name 13.5% of the pictures. During the second presentation of the set of pictures, some of the pictures were identical to the first presentation, while other pictures were changed: (1) only in location; (2) by depicting a drawing of a different item that was a member of the same class as the original (e.g., a desk lamp versus a table lamp), presented at either the same location as the original or a different one (see Figure 5.27). The remaining test pictures were control pictures, which had not been presented earlier.

When the exact same picture reappeared in the same location, people were able to name it with 34.5% accuracy. This is evidence for unconscious repetition priming, because recognition of a picture the second time was higher than the original 13.5% identification rate. However, when the location of the repeated picture was changed, performance was not as high (25.5% recognition). In addition, no priming was evident when the two pictures depicted different visual objects (e.g., from desk lamp to a table lamp). This result indicates that the priming found in this study was at the *visual* level (i.e., the repeated object had to be identical for priming to occur).

Drink Iced Tea

The studies of unconscious priming just reviewed have demonstrated that unconscious priming can occur, but they are several steps removed from the original "Drink Coke" report, since the participants in the laboratory studies simply read words or

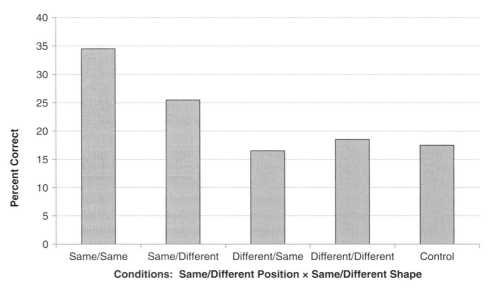

Figure 5.27   Results from Bar and Biederman's (1998) subliminal priming experiment: Percent correct naming on control and priming trials, as a function of position × shape.

identified pictures; they did not choose products. Thus, based on those studies, banning subliminal advertising seems to have been a bit of an overreaction. However, a recent study that looked directly at the "Drink Coke" scenario under controlled laboratory conditions did support the hypothesis that subliminal advertising can be effective, although only under a specific set of circumstances. Karremans et al. (2006) exposed participants to 25 presentations of the name of a brand of iced tea, presented so briefly (23 milliseconds) that people never reported seeing it. After the presentation, participants were asked to participate in a study of consumer behavior. As part of that study, the participants were asked to indicate which of two beverages they would prefer to drink if they were offered them at that point. People expressed a preference for the unconsciously primed brand, but only if they were thirsty. Nonthirsty participants showed no preference. Thus, there does seem to be a possibility that we can be manipulated outside of our awareness, but that manipulation must coincide with our motivational state at that time. Priming us to drink a specific beverage is ineffective if we are not thirsty.

The Breadth of Unconscious Priming

In recent years, the study of unconscious influences on our behavior has grown greatly, and there is now evidence that unconscious processes can have broad effects, far beyond the "drink iced tea" effect just discussed. As one example, Zhong and DeVoe (2010) presented fast-food logos (McDonald's, Wendy's, Burger King, etc.), so quickly that they could not be seen, in the context of a list of words to be read. The logos were presented in the corners of the computer screen and the participants were instructed to ignore the flashes in the corners (since the logos were presented too quickly to be seen, all that the participants saw were flashes). A control group read the same words without being exposed subliminally to the fast-food logos, but they saw actual flashes (with no marketing logos) in the corners of the screen. Both groups then took part in a second activity, which included reading a set of instructions. The group primed with the fast-food logos read the instructions faster than the control group did, which Zhong and DeVoe interpreted as evidence that the experimental group had been made impatient by the subliminal stimuli. This is an effect that goes beyond facilitation in reading a word or biasing the choice of a beverage in a thirsty person. In this study, the researchers seem to have induced a psychological state with their subliminal stimulation.

A related question currently being explored by cognitive researchers is the influence of emotion on both conscious and unconscious processing. For example, Li, Paller, and Zinbarg (2008) found that highly anxious individuals showed greater unconscious priming of threat-related words (e.g., *ridicule, sinister, murder*). Thus, people with certain personality traits or psychological histories may be influenced by events or signals that other people do not even process.

Unconscious Cognition: Conclusions

It thus appears that unconscious recognition of words or other stimuli can take place (see Westen, 1998, for review). Furthermore, there is also evidence that more broad aspects of responding can be affected by unconscious stimuli. This research area is undergoing rapid growth, as researchers broaden the search for situations affected by unconscious processes (see, e.g., Zhong, Dijksterhuis & Galinsky, 2008). Unconscious processing is a domain where the interests of clinical psychologists, psychiatrists, and social psychologists converge with of the interests of cognitive psychologists.

PERCEPTUAL PROCESSES: SUMMARY AND CONCLUSIONS

This chapter has investigated processes involved in the recognition of words, faces, and objects, as well as their localization in space. We have seen that, after initial visual processing, there are two diverging visual brain systems: one that deals with localization of objects in space (and relevant actions we make regarding those objects), and the other with pattern recognition. Furthermore, the three main kinds of patterns that we encounter in the world appear to be subserved by different psychological strategies and modular recognition systems. Identification of words, objects, and faces are subject to both bottom-up and top-down processes. As a bottom-up process, pattern recognition begins with extraction of information or features from the stimulus array. These features are then combined to provide information related to a specific object. Top-down processes—that is, the person's knowledge and expectancies—also play a role in pattern recognition. Pattern recognition does not require conscious awareness; information can be extracted from words and objects that we are not aware of having perceived.

REVIEW QUESTIONS

Here is a set of questions to use as organizing material for review of the chapter. As with the other chapters you have encountered so far, it will be most helpful if you try to answer each question from memory before you review the answer.

1. Trace the path of visual information as it travels from the eye to the visual areas in the brain. Where does it go from the primary visual cortex?

2. What types of feature-detector cells were discovered by Hubel and Wiesel?

3. What are the locations of the *what* and *where* modules in the human visual system? How did Milner and Goodale (1995) change the conceptualization of the *where* systems?

4. Briefly summarize evidence from humans and animals in support of two visual modules.

5. What is agnosia? How do dorsal-system versus ventral-system agnosias differ?

6. Why might there be two modules in the visual system?

7. What does it mean to say that a mental representation is functionally isomorphic to a neighborhood?

8. What brain systems are involved in spatial navigation?

9. How are judgments of physical similarity between letters related to theories of letter recognition?

10. Outline some basic problems faced by researchers studying object recognition.

11. Outline Marr's theory of object recognition and Biederman's elaboration of that view.

12. Why can we call the recognition-by-components theory of pattern recognition a theory based on structural descriptions?

13. Briefly summarize evidence in support of the recognition-by-components theory. What evidence raises questions for the theory?

14. Briefly summarize evidence that there is more than one way to recognize objects.

15. What types of pattern-recognition modules have been postulated in the human visual system? What sorts of processing strategies are used by each type, as proposed by Farah (1992)?

16. Briefly describe evidence for and against the idea that face recognition is carried out by a dedicated module.

17. What nervous-system areas play a role in face recognition?

18. Briefly summarize top-down factors in pattern recognition.

19. What brain areas are involved in top-down aspects of pattern recognition?

20. Describe Neisser's pattern-recognition cycle.

21. How are eye movements during reading evidence for top-down processing within reading?

22. What evidence supports the idea that pattern recognition can be carried out unconsciously?

CHAPTER 6

ATTENTION

You have probably heard a parent admonish a child by saying, "Pay attention!! Focus!" That is one common way we think of attention, as *selective attention*, the ability to focus on or select one stimulus in the environment and block out competing stimuli. In a different vein, a teacher might respond to multiple students who are asking questions all at once with, "I can't pay attention to five of you at one time!" In this case, the teacher is unable to attend to, or divide attention among, multiple sources. *Divided attention* is a second common way in which we think about attention: How efficiently can we divide our cognitive resources (multitask) in order to accomplish several things at the same time? Both selective and divided attention fall under what are called the *executive processes* (Rabbitt, 1997), by which we plan and carry out the cognitive and motor processes through which we deal with the world.

At some times, selection or division of attention is involuntary. It would be difficult not to notice or pay attention to a loud noise outside our door, even if we are immersed in the whodunit chapter of a gripping mystery novel. In such cases, we can say that our attention is *captured* by the intense outside event, as we *orient* toward the noise. Attention can also be captured by the psychological significance of a stimulus rather than its intensity, as when someone quietly says our name in the next room, causing us to shift our attention away from the TV. We can engage in selective attention voluntarily, based on our goals, as when we focus on the songs in our iPod in order to block out background conversations. We can also divide our attention or multitask voluntarily, as when we carry on a conversation as we drive. How we direct our attention to stimuli, and then selectively allocate resources to one or more pieces of information, will be one focus of this chapter.

There are also situations in which we fail to attend to a change in the environment. For example, while watching *Inception*, we might admire the character Ariadne's earrings, but fail to recognize that those earrings disappear when the scene cuts away from her and then cuts back. In this case our attention has failed: We were blind to the change in the status of the earrings and did not notice an error in the editing of the film. Researchers have studied myriad aspects of attention within our cognitive functioning, and in this chapter we will address more subtle uses—and failures—of attention, as well as the more common phenomena of selective and divided attention.

OUTLINE OF CHAPTER 6

The analysis of attention will be an extension of our discussion of perceptual processing, especially the idea of the active, top-down nature of functioning. Our discussion begins with a brief presentation of the history of research in psychology on attention, in order to place modern work in historical perspective. Many of the topics studied by modern researchers were also of interest to early psychologists. We then turn to a consideration of relatively simple situations, and discuss research that has examined the factors involved in involuntarily and voluntarily attending to a single stimulus. We then consider more complex situations, in which the task is closer to what occurs in the real world. Here the individual must selectively attend to one stream of information while ignoring others, but must also be ready to shift attention, in order to process potentially important new stimuli. The final section of the chapter examines people's ability to selectively process information, and sometimes to divide our attention between two tasks simultaneously.

THE STUDY OF ATTENTION IN EARLY PSYCHOLOGY

The first psychologists emphasized the importance of attention in cognition, particularly the close relationship between perception and attention. Wundt (see Chapter 1) discussed the relation between the large number of stimuli that comprise the field of consciousness at any given time and the particular stimuli attended to within that field. He concluded that focusing attention on a particular element of the environment resulted in other elements becoming less clear, and fading into the background. In this view, attending is an active process, since attention to something involves a reduction in the intensity of our interaction with the rest of the world. Titchener, one of Wundt's earliest students (see Chapter 1), proposed the *Law of Prior Entry*, which states that a stimulus that is being attended to will enter conscious awareness prior to an un-attended stimulus. Assume that a person has been signaled to expect a specific stimulus at a specific location (e.g., in the top right-hand corner of a computer screen). According to the law of prior entry, if both the expected object and another object in a different location are flashed on the screen at the same time, the person will become aware of the one that he has been instructed to expect before he becomes conscious of the other. Modern research has also supported this prediction. In a related vein, Külpe (1901) proposed that when one is thinking about something, the content of one's thought will determine what one will attend to next. For example, if I am thinking about my hunger, I may become more aware of the smell of nearby food. A person's current focus will, in a top-down fashion, play a role in determining what to focus on next. As we will see later in this chapter, modern research supports Külpe's proposal (e.g., Huang & Pashler, 2007).

James (1890) also extensively discussed attention, although he did not approach it from the introspectionist perspective that Wundt and Titchener had adopted. James attempted to provide a detailed description of the *phenomenology* of consciousness, including when we attend to something. In a well-known passage, already seen in Chapter 1, James described attention as "the taking possession of the mind, in clear and vivid form, of one out of what seems several simultaneously possible objects or trains of thought. . . . It implies withdrawal from some thing in order to deal effectively with others" (1890, pp. 403–404). Once again, attention is seen as an active process, since the individual is *selecting* one thing at the expense of something else. James also drew a contrast between involuntary attention, as when attention is captured by a loud noise, and more voluntary cases, in which we attend to something because it is related to our current goals, such as being drawn to the smell of cooking food when we are hungry.

Pillsbury (1908, 1911) who, like James, was a philosopher as well as a psychologist, raised hypotheses about the physiological processes underlying attention, although at the time very little of a concrete nature was known about the relation between brain structures and psychological processes. Pillsbury assumed that two sorts of processes were involved in attention: *reinforcement* (also called *facilitation* or *enhancement*) and *inhibition*. In reinforcement, attention directed toward a stimulus results in an increase in neural activity related to it. At the same time, inhibition results in a decrease in neural activity to stimuli not being attended to. Pillsbury's prediction that facilitation and inhibition of attention should correspond to enhanced or decreased neural activity in relevant parts of the brain does have empirical support.

Early Conceptions of Attention: Summary

There are several ideas that are seen consistently in the thinking of these early researchers:

1. A distinction was made between involuntary versus voluntary attention. Involuntary attention is largely bottom-up, or stimulus-driven, in that one's attention is captured by a stimulus. Voluntary attention is attending to some event that is related to one's current concerns.

2. The process of selection of one item for attention involves the enhancement of the clarity of that item, and leads to the inhibition of other items.

3. A link was proposed between attentional processes and underlying physiological mechanisms. These questions and ideas have also been relevant to more recent investigations, and they will serve to organize the discussion in this chapter.

INVOLUNTARY ATTENTION: OVERT ORIENTING TO STIMULI

The simplest form of attention occurs involuntarily, as when an ongoing activity (such as reading a textbook) is suddenly interrupted by the sound of loud voices in the next room. In this case, selection has been made between two stimuli, the words on the page and the sound of the people talking, but it is involuntary—your attention shifts without your realizing it. The tendency for stimuli to capture our attention because of their intensity is a good example of bottom-up processes acting within attention. When attention is involuntarily switched in response to a novel stimulus, there occurs a set of reactions, collectively called the *orienting response* (Sokolov, 1975). The orienting response may include behavioral changes, such as looking in the direction of a new stimulus. There may also be various bodily changes (e.g., breathing slows down; heart rate also slows), as the organism prepares to deal with the new stimulus. Some components of the orienting response are *overt*, that is, they can be seen or measured by an observer (e.g., turning one's head).

One robust research finding is that our attentional system is geared toward novelty; our attention is captured most easily when a new stimulus is presented (Burtt, 1931; Sokolov, 1975). It has long been known that even infants show a preference for novelty (Caron & Caron, 1968; Fagan, 1970; Fantz, 1964; Welch, 1974). When a stimulus is repeated a number of times, with no significant consequences, it loses the ability to produce an orienting response: The orienting response is *extinguished*, through a process known as *habituation*. The occurrence of habituation indicates that the organism keeps a record, perhaps in working memory (WM), of what happens where and when, and thereby becomes capable of implicitly predicting what might happen next. When a novel or unpredictable item occurs, our attention is enhanced. Habituation makes it possible to ignore stimuli that have had no significant consequences, and to better attend to new items. One prediction from this analysis is that the orienting response should be reinstituted if the regularly occurring event does *not* occur. Siddle and Packer (1987) presented two stimuli together repeatedly, with Stimulus A preceding Stimulus B 15 times. On the 16th trial, Stimulus A was not followed by Stimulus B, and people showed an increase in responsiveness. That is, the nonappearance of a previously predictable event was unexpected, and resulted in a greater orienting response.

In sum, involuntary switching of attention to a novel stimulus may come about because that stimulus does not match the organism's expectations or model of the world. This means that the organism must be capable of storing information about past events and using this information to monitor, or keep track of, what is happening now. An event that does not match one's model of the world can produce an orienting response. Thus, the capturing of attention by an unexpected stimulus has top-down aspects, since it depends, at least in part, on our expectancies about what events occur when.

COVERT ORIENTING OF ATTENTION

Many of the components of the orienting response are *overt*, including eye movements and turning of the head toward a novel stimulus. We are also able to orient *covertly*, however, without any visible behavioral signs. We all have had the experience of being involved in a boring conversation and listening to a more interesting one nearby, while still nodding occasionally, as if you are listening to your companion. Covert orienting can be voluntary or involuntary. On the one hand, if someone says your name in another conversation, it may involuntarily capture your attention, but you might not give any outward sign that your attention has wandered. On the other hand, when you are engaged in a boring conversation, you may actively try to listen to other conversations, without giving your conversation partner any indication that you are not hanging on his or her every word.

There can be both costs and benefits to directing attention covertly. Posner, Nissen, and Ogden (1978) instructed participants to maintain focus on a fixation point, while target stimuli were presented to the right or left of that point. The participant was told to signal upon seeing the target. On some trials, the target was presented without any advance warning; those were *neutral* trials. On the other trials, there was a signal that pointed to the location in which the target might appear (such as the arrow in

Time 1: Cue is presented.

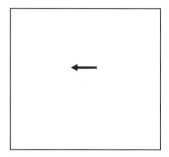

**Time 2: Time to respond to a stimulusis measured for
(a) location signaled by the cue versus (b) different location.**

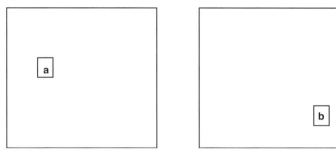

Figure 6.1   Design for studying covert orienting.
Adapted from Posner et al., 1978.

Figure 6.1). The signal accurately predicted the location of the target 80% of the time (Figure 6.1, Time 2, a); the other 20% of the time, the target appeared at the location *opposite* to that signaled (Figure 6.1, Time 2, b). Thus, overall, the signal was generally reliable, but it was not perfect.

Benefits and Costs of Attention

The times to respond to the target in the different conditions in the Posner et al. (1978) study are shown in Figure 6.2. The participants were more efficient at attending to the correctly signaled target, compared to the neutral condition, even when they did not move their eyes. There is thus a *benefit* to attending in advance to the location of an input (which is demonstrated by the difference between the neutral and valid cue trials). In addition to faster processing of the stimulus, orienting also allows the person to respond to weak stimuli that they would otherwise not detect. This is evidence of the *enhancement* of an item that is attended to, which, as we saw earlier, was noted by Pillsbury (1908).

Ghatan, Hsieh, Petersson, Stone-Elander, and Ingvar (1998) used PET scans to measure cortical activity while participants engaged in an arithmetic task. Participants

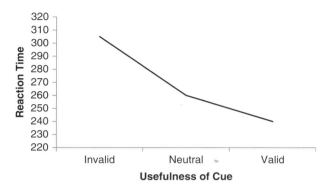

Figure 6.2 Benefits and costs from valid and invalid cues in covert orienting.
Adapted from Posner et al., 1978, Figure 1.

mentally counted backwards from a given number by sevens, either with no distraction task, or when listening to irrelevant speech (a list of words). During the irrelevant-speech trials, participants showed an *increase* in activation in the left parietal cortex, which is known to be responsible for arithmetical processing, but a *decrease* in neural activity in the auditory cortex. This suggests that people were able to inhibit the irrelevant word list—both physiologically and psychologically—and to enhance processing of the arithmetic task. In conclusion, there are many benefits resulting from selectively orienting our attention.

Attention also has its costs, however, which is demonstrated by the difference in processing time between the invalid and neutral trials in Figure 6.2. On invalid trials, the person took longer to process the target than if there had been no signal at all, because the cue had misdirected their attention. This misdirection then required a shift of attention to the new location, which takes a measurable amount of time. In conclusion, performance is influenced positively and negatively by advance warning, depending on a cue's accuracy, which is evidence for the role of top-down strategies in attention.

Inhibition of Return

Just as the study of overt orienting has indicated that the attentional system is designed to respond to novelty, covert orienting also demonstrates a sensitivity to novelty. This is shown by the phenomenon of *inhibition of return*. Consider the following sequence of events: An experimental participant fixates on the center of the array, and a target is presented, say, at the right-hand location. Without making an eye movement, the person responds to the target by pressing the space bar on a computer keyboard—call this the *initial* location. A new target is then presented, either at the location just responded to (*same* condition), or the other one (*different*). If the second target occurs in the same position 100–300 milliseconds later, the response to the second target is enhanced, or made faster (McAuliffe & Pratt, 2005). However, if the second target appears in the old location and is delayed by 500–3,000 milliseconds, responses to that target are slowed or inhibited (Posner & Cohen, 1984; Pratt & Abrams, 1995; Pratt &

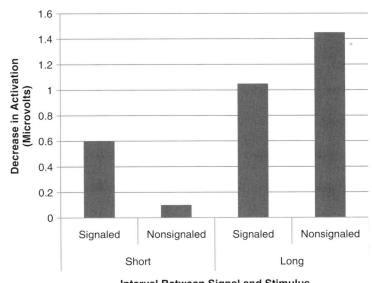

Interval Between Signal and Stimulus

Figure 6.3 Amount of decrease in activation to attended stimulus as a function of short/long interval, based on results of Hopfinger and Mangun (1998).
Adapted from Hopfinger and Mangun, 1998.

McCauliffe, 2002). Thus, return to the initial location is inhibited. Inhibition of return seems to maximize the chances of attending to new stimuli within the environment (sometimes at the expense of stimuli that occur at recently-attended-to locations).

In addition, measurement of brain electrical activity indicates that the electrical response to the target stimulus is strongest if it follows the signal after only a short interval (34–234 milliseconds). At longer intervals (566–766 milliseconds), the response to the target is *less* strong than when no signal has been presented (Hopfinger & Mangun, 1998; see Figure 6.3). This is evidence that the neural response to the target is actually being modified as time passes.

BRAIN SYSTEMS AND ORIENTING

There are two systems involved in transmitting information from the eye to the brain, as outlined in Figure 6.4 and Table 6.1. One visual subsystem—the *geniculo-striate* system—transmits information through the lateral geniculate nucleus in the thalamus (*geniculo-*) to the visual cortex (*striate* cortex; the visual cortex under the microscope looks striped or *striated* when it is stained). This neural pathway serves the occipital-temporal object recognition system (the *what* system) and the occipital-parietal pathway that processes spatial awareness (the *where/action* system). The *tecto-pulvinar* subsystem goes through the superior colliculi in the lower brain. This system seems to play a role in controlling orientation to visual stimuli, including guiding eye movements (Sparks, 1986). On the one hand, hamsters with lesions in the tecto-pulvinar

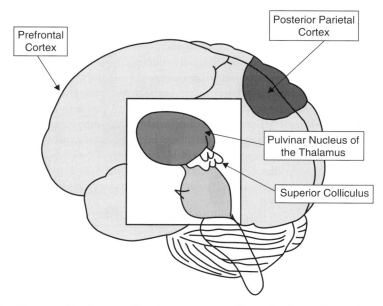

Figure 6.4 Diagram of brain areas: Visual systems controlling orienting and attentional processes. The white rectangle represents a transparent window through the cortex into subcortical areas in the center of the brain.

Table 6.1 Brain Areas Involved in Different Types of Attention

Brain Area	Functions
Superior Colliculus	Orient to stimuli.
Pulvinar Nucleus of Thalamus	Enhance stimulus that has been selected for attention so it is given priority in subsequent processing and responses.
Parietal Lobe	Visual and spatial attention; helps disengage attention from one stimulus (in order to attend to another stimulus).
Prefrontal Cortex	Executive functions of attention: selective and divided attention, inhibition of nonattended stimuli.

system were able to learn to respond to visual patterns, but did not orient when their whiskers were stimulated. On the other hand, animals with lesions in the geniculo-striate system were not able to learn visual discriminations based on the appearance of objects in the visual field (VF), but they oriented normally to stimulation of their whiskers (Schneider, 1969). We thus have a double dissociation, and the two pathways seem to serve different functions—one for processing visual patterns and their spatial positions, the other for directing orienting at a basic level.

In addition, orienting toward an expected event involves the prefrontal cortex. For example, in an fMRI study, Small et al. (2003) found greater prefrontal activation when participants received a spatial cue to orient toward a stimulus. Degree of brain activity in this region was highest for participants who showed the most benefit from the cue (based on the behavioral response-time data). As we will see later in the chapter, the prefrontal cortex is also implicated in selectively attending to stimuli and blocking out other competing stimuli (such as when you study while your roommate listens to the radio).

Blindsight

Given the separation of the tecto-pulvinar and cortical systems, one might expect that patients with occipital-cortex damage would still be able to orient to stimuli as evidenced by overt eye movements or an inhibition of responding to a stimulus in another area. Humans with certain types of brain damage to half of the primary visual cortex are blind in the opposite half of the VF. However, such patients can be affected by visual stimuli presented to their blind field, even though they report that nothing has been presented. Weiskrantz (1986) proposed the term *blindsight* to refer to responsiveness to stimuli that are not consciously perceived. One task presented to blindsight patients is to ask them to report a visual stimulus in their good VF, which they can do, and measure how long it takes them to respond. On some trials, the target stimulus is preceded by a distractor stimulus in the blind field, which the person does not report seeing. Presentation of the distractor stimulus does, however, increase the time to respond to the target in the good field, which means that the person did orient to the stimulus in their blind VF without realizing it. As just noted, blindsight might occur because the system that directs visual orienting is dissociable from the system that controls object recognition (Rafal, Smith, Krantz, Cohen, & Brennan, 1990). In this way, one could fail to recognize an object while still being able to orient to its location.

Overt and Covert Orienting: Conclusions

There are several ways in which a stimulus can receive attention. The orienting response is an involuntary response that prepares the organism to deal more extensively with an unexpected stimulus. The response occurs because the stimulus does not match the person's expectations as to what will occur in the environment. The orienting response involuntarily interferes with current processing. Attention can also be switched voluntarily to a stimulus, as the result of signaling the person in advance where a stimulus will appear, which can result in either overt or covert orienting. The occurrence of orienting in anticipation of a stimulus makes it easier to process a stimulus that appears at the location to which the person has oriented.

ATTENTION AND INHIBITION: NEGATIVE PRIMING

As noted earlier, the earliest psychologists (e.g., Pillsbury, 1908) believed that attending to one object resulted in inhibition of responses to other possible objects; that is, enhancing one stimulus through attention was assumed to have negative consequences for other stimuli not being processed at that time. That expectation has been supported

	Control Trial	Experimental Trial
Prime Display	B M	B T
Correct Response	"B"	"B"
Test Display	C T	C T*
Correct Response	"T"	"T"

In the experimental trial, the T had first appeared as the item to be ignored in the prime display.

Figure 6.5 Design of studies of negative priming: In each trial, participants are told to name aloud the letter in bold font, and ignore the letter in normal font.
Adapted from May et al., 1995, Figure 1.

by recent studies of *negative priming*, which demonstrate that ignoring a stimulus makes it harder to respond to that stimulus at a later time. The design of studies of negative priming is shown in Figure 6.5. One presents a series of pairs of stimuli—letters in this example—and the participant's task is to read one of the letters and ignore the other. The target letter in each pair is signaled in some way, say, by color. The crucial feature of the design is that in some pairs, a previously incorrect item (the *foil*; e.g., the T in the experimental trial in Figure 6.5) becomes the correct one in a subsequent test trial. Studies have shown that the seemingly simple act of ignoring one letter in a pair has a negative effect on later positive responses to that letter (May, Kane, & Hasher, 1995). There seems to be some sort of inhibition occurring when we choose not to respond to a stimulus, and this inhibition has effects that last at least for a short amount of time.

Studies have found that when the test trial follows the experimental trial by a very short time period (e.g., 20–50 milliseconds), no negative priming occurs (Lowe, 1985; Neill & Westberry, 1987). Thus, inhibition appears to take a small amount of time to build up. However, when the test trial follows by more than 50 milliseconds, inhibition occurs (May et al., 1995). The function of negative priming may be to keep the letter to be ignored from interfering with subsequent processing. In other words, once a person has made a choice between two stimuli, inhibitory processes function to keep the rejected item from capturing attention.

Inhibition and Working Memory

Hasher and Zacks (1988, 1994) and their colleagues (e.g., Kane, May, Hasher, Rahhal, & Stoltzfus, 1997) have theorized that, in general, negative priming functions to keep extraneous thoughts from interfering with our ongoing activities. Please carry out the short exercise in Box 6.1 before reading further.

BOX 6.1 WORKING MEMORY DEMONSTRATION TASK

Please read the following passage. You will then be asked to answer questions about it.

Findley woke up as the sun streamed in his window. He called his dog, Scamp, who leapt onto his bed and licked his face. Findley was anxious to get onto his bicycle, which he had recently received for his birthday. It was a red 10-speed bike, and really fast, although he hadn't fully worked out how to use the gears properly. His new best friend was a neighbor, Gwynneth, who liked to explore as much as Findley. They planned to take a picnic lunch to the woods that day, and to see how many toads, small fish, and crayfish they could find in the shallow creek that ran through the trees. Occasionally, they even spotted a turtle basking on a rock in the creek. Findley longed to have a turtle as a pet, although his mother had warned him not to bring home any more creatures. She still had not recovered from the snake he had brought home the summer before, even though it had been just an ordinary garter snake.

After Findley had thrown on some shorts and a green T-shirt, he raced downstairs. His mother had already packed some peanut butter and jelly sandwiches and apples for a picnic lunch. "Don't forget to fill your thermos with water," she said, "you can't drink creek water. And lock up your bike to a tree when you go into the woods."

"I will," said Findley, "I don't want my new bike stolen." A knock on the door made Scamp start barking, alerting Findley and his mother that Gwynneth had arrived. She entered excitedly and opened her backpack to show the entire box of chocolate chip cookies that she had brought for the picnic lunch, and a jar to bring home some creek water. Gwynneth's mother was a chemist and she had promised to let the friends look at the tiny animals in the creek water under her microscope.

"Let's get going!" said Gwynneth. Findley shoveled the last of his cereal quickly into his mouth. After tying his shoes, the kids exited the house, leaving Findley's mother to think a whirlwind had just passed through the kitchen. Scamp followed them, barking excitedly.

"Okay, you can come," said Findley, "but don't scare the frogs and turtles." The two friends saddled their bicycles and rode off to a string of adventures, Scamp trailing behind them.

Please answer the following questions based on your memory of the story, without looking back at it:

1. What were the names of the two friends? The dog?
2. What did the boy receive for his birthday?
3. What types of creatures are they likely to see in the creek?
4. How do the friends get to the woods?
5. What profession is the girl's mother in?
6. What had the boy brought home from a previous trip to the woods?

In the activity in Box 6.1, one has to carry out certain mental operations. As we saw in Chapter 2, such cognitive work is carried out in WM, part of the processing system that deals with information relevant to our current activities (e.g., Baddeley, 1990; Richardson et al., 1996). In order for processing to be efficient, it is necessary that the contents of WM be limited to information relevant to the task; that which is irrelevant to the goal must be kept out. As an example, when reading the information in Box 6.1, it is important to attend only to the characters and events mentioned in the story, and inhibit thinking about other boys or girls, or errands to accomplish today, in order to stay on task.

Zacks and Hasher (1994; also Hasher, Stoltzfus, Zacks, & Rypma, 1991; Hasher & Zacks, 1988) have also proposed that WM difficulties that some individuals experience may be the result of a deficiency in inhibiting extraneous thoughts. For example, normal elderly individuals often have problems with comprehension of written and spoken verbal materials. One possible reason for those problems may be that the elderly are unable to inhibit irrelevant thoughts from becoming activated, and these unwanted thoughts enter WM, where they can interfere with online comprehension of the task at hand. Research using the negative priming design has shown that elderly adults perform especially poorly, which can be taken as evidence for difficulties in inhibiting irrelevant thoughts (Zacks & Hasher, 1994).

The Stroop Task

Another task that has been used to study the role of inhibition in attention is presented in Box 6.2. Please work through Box 6.2 before reading further.

BOX 6.2 STROOP TASK

Instructions: Measure the time it takes you, in seconds, to state aloud the **number of figures** (either X's or written numerals) in each column.

Neutral (A)	Interference (B)	Facilitory (C)
X X X X	5 5	4 4 4 4
X X	7 7 7 7 7	1
X X X X X	2 2 2	5 5 5 5 5
X X X X	8 8 8 8	2 2
X	4	3 3 3
X X X	9 9 9 9	4 4 4 4
X X X X X	3	2 2
X X	6 6 6 6	5 5 5 5 5
X X X X	2 2 2 2 2	1
X	7 7	4 4 4 4

The task in Box 6.2 Columns A–C is a modification of the Stroop task, named after the psychologist who first investigated it (Stroop, 1935). The interference condition (Box 6.2 Column B) typically takes longer than a neutral condition (Column A) or a facilitory condition (Column C), because it sets in competition two responses to the same stimulus. In order to identify the number of digits in the interference condition, we must inhibit a stronger response (reading the numeral of which the set is composed). Furthermore, the task is designed so that the incorrect response and the correct one are members of the same category, numbers. The Stroop test is thus a marvelous example of difficulties that arise when strong responses must be inhibited to carry out a task.

Attentional Blink

We have so far looked primarily at *spatial* aspects of attention; that is, the studies reviewed have been concerned with what happens when attention is directed toward *locations* in the world. Attention can also be distributed over *time*, rather than space (e.g., Broadbent & Broadbent, 1987; Raymond, Shapiro, & Arnell 1992; Shapiro, Driver, Ward, & Sorensen, 1997). To examine temporal aspects of attention, a series of visual items—a string of letters, say—is rapidly presented in the same location in a procedure called rapid serial visual presentation (RSVP). The person's task is to respond whenever a designated target (e.g., a letter appearing in **bold** font) appears within the series. For example, imagine the following string was seen by a person, with a gap of about 100 milliseconds between letters:

A, X, F, **T**, Z, **M**, C, Q

Identifying a target interferes with detecting a second target that follows it within 500 milliseconds (Broadbent & Broadbent, 1987; Shapiro et al., 1997). In the example just presented, if the experimental participant detects the T, she is likely to miss detection of the M that appears 200 milliseconds later. It is as if the person has blinked when the target is seen, and therefore he or she misses several stimuli. However, since the person's eyes have not actually closed, it is only an *attentional blink* (Raymond et al., 1992).

One hypothesis as to the origin of the attentional blink is that it is due to the cognitive system's tendency to fully process one target before going on to process following items. If this hypothesis is true, then anything that makes it harder to fully process a target should increase the attentional blink to stimuli that follow it. Seiffert and Di Lollo (1997) found that masking the target, by presenting other visual information in close proximity to it, did increase the attentional blink. These results indicate that the distribution of attention over time is similar to the distribution of attention over space. We have seen that when we attend to information in one location in the world, that attention negatively affects our ability to process information at other locations. Similarly, attending to information at one point in time affects processing information that occurs shortly thereafter.

Repetition Blindness

Another deficit in processing sequential stimuli is seen when the *same* stimulus is presented twice in close succession in a string of items (Kanwisher, Yin, & Wojciulik, 1999), as in the following sequence:

A, **X**, F, **X**, Z, M, C, Q

If the repeated letter is presented within about 250 milliseconds after the first occurrence, people show poor performance at reporting the second appearance. If the repetitions are separated by 500 milliseconds, then both items are reported. Since people seem to become blind to the repetition within a short time of a stimulus, this phenomenon is called *repetition blindness* (Kanwisher, 1987; the phenomenon also occurs in audition, where it is known as repetition deafness; Miller & MacKay, 1994). Repetition blindness may be another example of the processing system's being designed to respond most efficiently to novelty. When processing has been carried out to deal with a stimulus, processing of that same stimulus is inhibited for a very short period of time, leaving attentional capacity available for the processing of new stimuli.

Attention and Inhibition: Conclusions

Research from a number of different experimental situations supports the role of inhibitory processes in attention. As the first psychologists believed, it seems that positively responding to a given stimulus requires that processing of any other stimuli be inhibited. This inhibition may serve to keep the person's attention on task. Once the task-relevant stimuli have been identified, extraneous stimuli are ignored in an active manner. Furthermore, as we have already seen, the attentional system is geared toward novelty, as we are inhibited from responding to a stimulus that has already been processed.

NEUROPSYCHOLOGICAL SYNDROMES: DISRUPTION OF VISUAL ATTENTION

The attentional blink, inhibition of response, and negative priming are examples of processing difficulties that may be brought about by overloading attention (i.e., giving a person too much to do within a short period of time). More dramatic attentional difficulties can be seen in syndromes caused by brain damage.

Hemispatial Neglect Syndrome

Patients who suffer extensive damage in the parietal lobe often exhibit a deficit known as *hemispatial* (for *half-space*) *neglect*, in which they ignore or neglect visual information in the side of the VF opposite the lesion (Harvey, Milner, & Roberts, 1995; Robertson & Halligan, 1999). That is, if the patient suffers damage in the right parietal lobe, neglect is seen in the left half of the VF, and vice versa (though RH damage is most likely to lead to the symptoms; Gainotti, Messirli, & Tissot, 1972; Stone, Halligan, & Greewood, 1993). These patients only describe objects that they see in the *contralateral* VF (the VF on the side opposite to the side of the location of the lesion). When they draw an object such as a flower, they only draw the portion appearing in the half of space opposite the location of their lesion (see examples in Figure 6.6). Some patients also shave only the right side of their face and fail to eat food on the left side of a plate (Mesulam, 1985).

Why, you might ask, is hemispatial neglect not a visual problem? Perhaps these patients only *see* one half of the VF. A clever experiment was designed by Marshall and Halligan (1988) to test that possibility. They flashed a hemispatial neglect patient

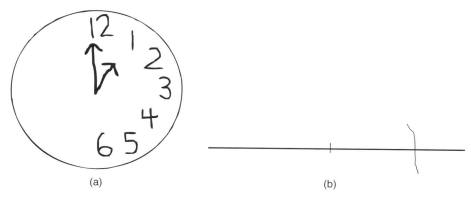

Figure 6.6 Replication of drawings by patients with hemispatial neglect. (a) Clock face. (b) Bisected line task: Patients are asked to draw a line in the middle of the line. Since they attend to only half of the line (typically the right half), their bisection is drawn in the middle of the attended half.
From Heilman and Valenstein, 1979; replica of standard hemispatial neglect patient responses.

two pictures of houses. One depicted a normal house, and the other depicted burning flames coming out of the left side of the house (on the side that the patient normally ignored). Although the neglect patient reported that both houses appeared to be the same, she claimed to prefer the nonburning house (but could not explain why). In this way, Marshall and Halligan were able to illustrate that those suffering from neglect can visually process the left half of space, but do not consciously attend to stimuli in that hemifield. Other studies have confirmed that neglect patients can visually process information in the ignored VF without conscious awareness. For instance, when words are flashed to their ignored VF, hemispatial neglect patients cannot report seeing these words but are faster to respond to semantically related words in the intact VF, thus exhibiting semantic priming (McGlinchey-Berroth, Milberg, Verfaellie, Alexander, & Kilduff, 1993).

Posner and his colleagues (e.g., Posner & Petersen, 1990; Posner & Raichle, 1994) have proposed that neglect patients' parietal lesions have interfered with patients' ability to *disengage attention*. The two visual fields compete, and stimuli in the VF on the same side as the lesion (the *ipsilateral* VF) are given attentional preference, leading to neglect of objects that appear in the contralateral VF. The patient, having oriented toward a stimulus in the ipsilateral VF, cannot shift attention to the con-tralateral VF, and thus exhibits "sticky attention" to one half of space. Evidence for the disengage-attention-deficit hypothesis came from a study by Pavese, Coslett, Saffran, and Buxbaum (2002), who tested the ability of a hemispatial-neglect patient to identify pictures flashed to both sides of the VF. When two pictures were flashed simultane-ously, they were typically only able to identify one picture—the one in the ipsilateral VF. However, when the pictures alternated every 500 milliseconds (Experiment 2), this allowed enough time for the patients to "unstick" their attention, and both pictures were often correctly identified.

In summary, damage to the dorsal visual system often results in attentional deficits in which patients are less apt to orient to stimuli in a particular region of space, as shown in hemispatial neglect.

Dorsal Simultagnosia

Another neuropsychological syndrome that affects visual attention is dorsal *simult-agnosia*. This syndrome is seen in people who have suffered bilateral damage to the occipital-parietal lobe pathways, and as a result can only attend to one object at a time. If presented with the array depicted in Figure 6.7, those with dorsal simultagnosia tend to latch on to one object in the mix, at the expense of perceiving the other objects. Thus, their attention appears to stick to objects, rather than a particular region of space.

Summary: Spatial– Versus Object–Based Views of Visual Attention

Dorsal simultagnosia and hemispatial neglect syndromes are relevant to a debate about whether visual attention is captured by regions of space, as if our attention is like a spotlight (Treisman, 1993; Treisman & Gelade, 1980), or whether visual attention is captured by objects. Hemispatial neglect, inhibition of return, and studies we discussed earlier in which attention was facilitated by spatial cuing (e.g., Posner et al., 1978) seem to support the conclusion that visual attention is based on spatial location (though see Behrmann & Tipper, 1999, for a more complex attentional view of hemispatial neglect). However, dorsal simultagnosia, negative priming, and repetition blindness suggest that visual attention can be deployed to objects. Research indicates that both space-based and object-based theories of attention have support (Egly, Driver, & Rafal, 1994; Soto & Blanco, 2004).

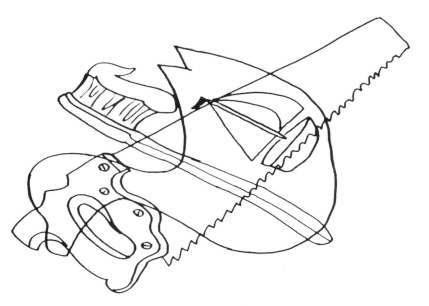

Figure 6.7 Stimuli used to diagnose dorsal simultagnosia.

CHANGE BLINDNESS

A disruption of visual attention from which we all suffer may be illustrated during your usual Friday night tradition of watching a movie on TV. You settle into a comfortable chair with popcorn and soda, and insert the DVD for the film *The Wizard of Oz*. Two hours later, you call your friend to extol the virtues of this classic film. Your friend says, "Do you realize that people have counted over 300 errors in that film? [See the list at www.moviemistakes.com/film1418] Didn't you find the mistakes distracting? I mean, when the Scarecrow and Dorothy are fighting with the trees, right after the shot in which the Scarecrow gets hit with apples, Dorothy is wearing black shoes instead of her ruby slippers from the shot just before!" You stay up late watching the movie again, but only manage to detect four scene changes (nowhere near the hundreds that your friend mentioned).

Failure to detect these sorts of errors—while viewing a movie or in real life—is known as *change blindness*, and is surprisingly common. Popular movies such as *Titanic*, *The Matrix*, and *Jurassic Park* often contain well over 20 continuity errors during scene changes (www.moviemistakes.com). Researchers first became interested in change blindness in the 1990s (e.g., Grimes, 1996), when it was found that people often failed to register even large scale changes in photos (such as two people exchanging heads).

Theories of change blindness tend to fall into two camps. The first believes that it is due to a deficiency in noticing objects to begin with, while the second believes that we notice many aspects of a visual array but fail to detect a difference between two scenes unless directed to compare the two scenes. The *representational failure* hypothesis (Levin, Simons, Angelone, & Chabris, 2002; O'Regan & Noë, 2001b; Rensink, 2000, 2002; O'Regan, & Clark, 1997) proposes that target items are either not initially represented in a person's visual array (Rensink et al., 1997) or not retained from one view to the next (Simons & Levin, 1997). For example, when the first shot of Dorothy and the Scarecrow in *The Wizard of Oz* shows her in ruby slippers, you may have only paid attention to the magical trees and not to what Dorothy was wearing on her feet. Thus, failure to attend to and represent the ruby slippers assured that you would not remember them, even on a short-term basis. In this explanation, change blindness is due to inattentional blindness (Mack & Rock, 1998; Mack, Pappas, Silverman, & Gay, 2002), and its resulting impoverished WM representation.

The second explanation for attentional blindness, the *Comparison Failure* view (Angelone, Levin, & Simons, 2003; Hollingworth, 2003; Silverman & Mack, 2006), proposes that people do represent the richness of visual scenes, but fail to compare the scenes for differences (Simons, Chabris, Schnur, & Levin, 2002). In other words, you *did* register Dorothy's ruby slippers in the first shot, and did detect her black shoes in the subsequent scene, but you did not compare the two representations for differences. This theory predicts that people might overcome change blindness when specifically asked if there was a scene change (because both the before and after representations are intact).

Rensink et al. (1997), who were the first to use the term "change blindness," tested those two explanations by using a flicker technique, whereby a picture flashes on and off, and is alternated with a nearly identical picture. During the flickers, a change in an object of either central or marginal interest to the picture is instituted (e.g., if a clown was depicted in front of a building, the clown would be a central object; the building would be of marginal interest). The experimenters varied the types of changes instituted in the materials: an object change (e.g., a wine bottle on a table disappeared), a color change of an object (e.g., from blue to red), or a location change (the railing behind a couple having lunch moved downward several inches). On average, it took twice as many flickers for people to notice marginal changes relative to central changes; location changes of central items were noticed somewhat faster than object or color changes (a tendency to notice location changes more than object changes was confirmed by Simons, 1996; Simons et al., 2002). The researchers concluded that lack of attentional focus to the altered item must have been the reason for change blindness, since people often did not notice an object to begin with.

Yet there is also evidence that sometimes people do retain both the initial representation *and* the scene change representation, but fail to compare the two working memory scenes unless directed to do so. The *comparison failure* hypothesis was tested experimentally by Simons et al. (2002). An experimental confederate, holding (or not holding) a basketball, asked for directions from an unsuspecting pedestrian on a college campus. Shortly after the discussion with the pedestrian began, a group of people—more confederates of the experimenter—walked behind and between the first confederate and the pedestrian, and one member of the crowd removed (or added) the basketball. Fewer than 25% of the pedestrians spontaneously noticed the change. However, an additional 50% reported the basketball change when asked about it, and were even able to state the unusual color of the red and white basketball (Experiment 2). Simons et al. concluded that the high rate of change detection after a hint meant that the pedestrian subjects must have stored an initial prechange representation in WM, but those who detected the change only after the hint had failed to spontaneously compare the initial visual representation (with the basketball in the removal condition) to the more current visual scene (without the basketball). The remaining 25% of subjects, who never reported the change of the basketball, may not have encoded the basketball to begin with, supporting the representational failure view.

Top-Down Influences and Memory in Change Blindness

Top-down processing may influence our propensity toward change blindness. There is evidence that change blindness is subject to factors known to influence memory, such as a tendency to schematize the details of pictures, with schema-relevant details either added or deleted (Intraub, Bender, & Mangels, 1992; Intraub, Gottesman, & Bills, 1998; Pezdek et al. 1988). We may abstract what we need from a visual scene, and in so doing, fail to attend to or remember details for later use (Levin & Simons, 1997; Simons and Levin, 1997). Hollingworth and Henderson (2000) used a flicker technique similar to that of Rensink et al. (1997). Objects were added, deleted, or changed to a mirror (reverse) orientation within the base picture. Changes in objects that were semantically inconsistent with a scene (e.g., a fire hydrant in a living room changing color) were noticed more quickly than were changes in consistent objects (e.g., a chair in a living room changing color). This may be because objects inconsistent with a scene are given attentional priority and receive longer fixation times (Brockmole and Henderson, 2008).

Change Blindness: Conclusion

There is evidence that some instances of change blindness are due to representational deficiencies resulting from a failure to attend to details within a visual scene. In other cases, in support of the comparison failure view, people do represent objects and their properties in working memory, but fail to notice visual changes until explicitly told to compare an "old" with a new visual representation. In addition, top-down processing may contribute to our inability to detect alterations between scenes in movies or other stimuli. Our tendency to assume that objects will remain stable from one visual scene to another may be adaptive, as it reduces the amount of information that we must process from minute to minute. The study of change blindness thus illustrates the coordination of attention, pattern recognition, and memory processes. We will see further evidence for the coordination of those processes in the next section, when we examine selective and divided attention. Before moving on to the next section, please carry out the demonstration in Box 6.3.

BOX 6.3 VISUAL SHADOWING DEMONSTRATION

Try to read the following passage while ignoring all the italicized words. If you read an italicized word, you have made a mistake.

This task can be difficult if you do not attend carefully to the material you are to read. That is why you are getting some practice before the hard task begins. Now *room butler* the *eight nine ten* hard *race* part *upon* begins. *where what who* The *narrow and wide* material *game* you *deal* are *coin collectors* to *above* read *skin* must *plane* not *fruit* be too *doubt* difficult *hare* or *shell turtle beach* too *left and right* easy. *birthday gift* With *bury* a *corn chowder* little *peace and love* practice, *all the world is a stage* most *funny* people *flag* report *hero* that *cotton polyester wool* they *bless* are *average* able *chief* to *history* read *place to develop skills* the *doubt fruit* material *sports* in large *a penny saved* print *fishtank* without *fool* the *moral* other *instead* words *table* interfering. *upper* We *worth* do *yourself and others* similar *single double triple* things *idea* all *instant* the *fruit* time *purchase* when *urge* we *left* read *shell* ordinary *very* text, *hundred years equals a century* since *doubt* we *now read italicized words* have little *into* trouble *before during and after* following *now* the *begin* words *to* in *read understand remember* the *on* line other we words are *fruit* reading, *left* while *contain* ignoring *shell abalone* all *crime* the *wine* other *have* words *doubt* in *profit* the *regular* passage. So *fold* we *narrow* are *never promised you a rose garden* always *left* attending *save* to *percent* some *can't see the forest for the trees* material *intend* while *crown king queen throne* we *entirely* are *shell* ignoring *effort* other *another country* material. *pine needles* That *during* ability *doubt uncertainty worry* will *upper* be *jump* the *diamond emerald and sapphire* topic *deed* of *judge and jury* discussion *left* in *profit* this *jump rope* chapter.

EXECUTIVE FUNCTIONS OF ATTENTION: SELECTIVE AND DIVIDED ATTENTION

Much of the research we have covered thus far has focused on visual attention, and attention at its simplest level: The individual is presented with a stimulus or stimuli, and the experimenter measures how quickly a target can be processed or whether a change in stimuli can be detected (as in change blindness). In our ordinary activities, however, things are much more complicated, and attention can also involve hearing or other modalities. For instance, we are often bombarded with multiple stimuli at the same time. This means that we have to selectively attend to one stimulus, blocking out potentially distracting information. There are also situations in which we try to divide our attention among several streams of information, such as when we try to carry on a cell-phone conversation as we walk or drive. Selective and divided attention fall under the *executive functions* of attention, because both can be influenced by our goals and our decisions about how to allocate cognitive resources.

Selective Attention

Techniques for Studying Selective Attention

The laboratory task most frequently used to study selective attention is a *dichotic* listening (*two-eared* listening) task. There are two *sources*, or *channels*, of information that are usually presented through earphones, one message to each ear, as shown in Figure 6.8. In selective attention tests, the message in one channel (the *primary* message) is to be attended to, and the second (the *secondary* message) is to be ignored. One way to assess whether a person is attending to the correct message is to have the participant verbally *shadow* the primary message; that is, *repeat that message aloud* as soon as it is heard. If the participant can shadow without mistakes, it indicates that he or she has been able to attend to the primary message while ignoring the secondary message.

In a classic experiment, Cherry (1953) found that people were able to shadow accurately one of two messages, but that they tended to shadow in a monotone, with a slight delay between what they heard in the attended message and what they said aloud. Furthermore, the participants were very effective at blocking out the unattended message: They did not remember what had been said in that channel, and did not even detect when the same voice switched from speaking English to speaking German.

Researchers can also ask participants to shadow only a particular word or set of words (in one or both channels). For example, a person might be told only to detect

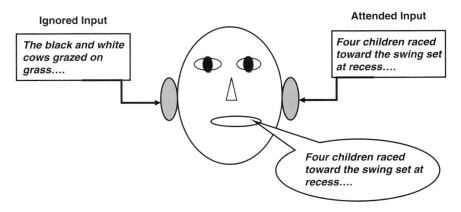

Figure 6.8 Auditory shadowing task.

and say aloud target words in the attended message, (e.g., words that denote items of furniture). This technique has also been studied using visual material. In this case, two streams of visual information are presented at once. In Box 6.3, the normal font, which you were told to read, constituted the attended message; the smaller italicized words (which you were to ignore) made up the unattended message. The results from visual shadowing tasks parallel those found for auditory stimuli. For example, most people are able to read the primary material in Box 6.3 without being significantly distracted by the material they have been asked to ignore. In one interesting variation on the visual-shadowing design, Neisser and Becklen (1975) superimposed two videos on top of each other—one of people passing around a basketball, the other of two pairs of hands playing a game in which they take turns trying to slap each other—so the two streams of information occupied the same physical space (the same screen). The experimenters found that participants were able to follow one stream of information and report information from it, such as the number of slaps in the hand-slap game. Furthermore, they were not distracted by the information in the unattended message, even when an odd event happened (e.g., the players in the basketball game stopped to shake hands). In conclusion, people are very good at selectively attending to one of several streams of information, whether in an auditory or a visual modality.

Factors That Affect Selective Attention

Selective attention is influenced both by bottom-up factors (e.g., loudness) and by top-down processes, such as our goals and expectations. In order to try to understand how selective attention is accomplished, one can vary the relationship between the primary and secondary channels, and measure how well people perform. If people make errors, that is, if people have more trouble shadowing under some conditions than others, it provides information as to how they are carrying out the task. Experimental studies have isolated a number of different factors that affect how easily people can selectively attend to material in a dichotic listening task.

Physical Characteristics

If the primary and secondary messages are presented in different locations, such as left versus right ears, people have less difficulty in shadowing than if both messages are presented in the same physical location (e.g., on the same audiotape played to both ears; Cherry, 1953). If each message is made distinctive physically, say by presenting each in a different person's voice, the task is easier than if the same voice presents both messages.

Semantic Information

The meaning of the messages also affects ease of shadowing. If the two messages are similar in meaning, then participants may have problems keeping them separate, and may unknowingly begin to shadow the secondary message. Treisman (1960) asked participants to shadow a message in one ear, say the right, while ignoring a secondary message in the other ear. The messages presented to each ear were hybrid sentences, composed of coupling the first half of Sentence 1 and the second half of Sentence 2 in the attended channel (and vice versa in the unattended channel). Thus, complete sense could not be made of either message. The following depicts the words that were actually presented to each ear; the backslash (/) indicates where the two sentences have been combined in each ear. The capital letters indicate what a person actually said.

Primary (Attended) Channel :

SITTING ON A MAHOGANY/ three POSSIBILITIES . . .

Secondary (Unattended) Channel :

. . . let us look at these/ TABLE with her head . . .

As can be seen in the example, most of the participants were unable to stop themselves from switching ears to follow the "sitting on a mahogany table . . ." sentence into the unattended channel for at least a word or two. Thus, selection of what to attend to next depended at least in part on what they expected to hear, based on the meaning of the first half of the sentence in the primary channel. This finding indicates that top-down expectancies play a role in selectively attending to a message.

In conclusion, people are very capable in selectively attending to, or processing, one out of multiple streams of information. Both physical characteristics and meaning can be used to select information to be processed and to exclude irrelevant information.

Dividing Attention

We now turn to situations in which we *want* to attend to two or more streams of information simultaneously. There are plenty of occasions that require us to accomplish two things in a limited period of time, and multitasking may seem like an efficient method. But how good are we at multitasking? One example of dividing attention is the *cocktail-party phenomenon*. We have all had situations where we are locked into a boring conversation, say at a cocktail party, and our attention is suddenly caught by the mention of our name in another conversation. We must have been somewhat able to divide our attention here, or we would never have become aware of our name. In laboratory settings, using the dichotic listening task, evidence for divided attention is seen in a person's ability to extract information from both messages (if instructed to do so), or from the secondary message while efficiently shadowing the primary message. Researchers can determine what information, if any, is gleaned from the secondary message by simply asking participants what they remember about the secondary message after the task is completed. One can also obtain evidence online concerning the processing of the secondary message, for example, by asking the participant to respond to a specific target word in either channel (sometimes while shadowing what is heard in the primary message). The participant's responding to the target in the secondary channel—while still processing the primary channel efficiently—is evidence that he or she was able to divide attention while carrying out the task.

Memory for the Secondary Message

If participants are asked about the material in the secondary message after the shadowing task is over, they typically can report very little about it (Cherry, 1953). However, some of the same factors that affect selective attention also affect whether a person can detect or remember information from the secondary channel.

Physical Characteristics

Gross physical changes in the secondary message are typically reported; for example, if a verbal message in the secondary channel changes into a steady tone, or if a man's voice changes to a woman's voice, participants will report having heard the change in the secondary message (Cherry, 1953). Thus, physical changes in the secondary message are relatively easily picked up, and often lead participants to make errors in shadowing the primary message at that point (Kahneman, 1973). The physical change in the secondary message may have caused the participant to orient involuntarily to that message (Broadbent, 1958), which disrupted shadowing.

Semantic Information

Meaningful information in the secondary channel, on the other hand, is usually not reported after the shadowing task is over (if at all). Cherry (1953) found that a change in the language of the secondary message in the middle of the task, say, from English to German and then back to English, was not detected by experimental participants. A similar negative conclusion about the participants' ability to process information from the unattended channel came from an early study by Moray (1959). A short list of words was presented repeatedly in the secondary channel (up to 35 times) while the participant was shadowing the other channel. The participant was told nothing about the repeated words in the secondary channel. After the shadowing was completed, the participant was given a recognition test for the material in the secondary channel. Participants did not recognize the multiply-repeated words from the secondary channel at a level higher than control words that had not been heard at all.

It thus seems that participants are able to remember almost nothing about the meaning of secondary message in selective attention tasks, although they do detect changes in the physical characteristics (similar to your not having remembered the italicized words when you participated in the demonstration in Box 6.3). However, it is possible that people did indeed *detect* meaningful information from the unattended channel at the time, but, by the end of the audiotape, they no longer *remembered* what was heard in the secondary message, because it had not been maintained in working memory. To test this possibility, one can ask the participant to shadow the primary message and also to try to respond in real time to some aspect of the secondary message, such as a pre-designated target word. In such a situation, memory does not play a role: If the person were not able to report the target from the secondary message under these conditions, it would indicate a limitation in the ability to *attend* to more than one stream at once.

Treisman and Geffen (1967) asked experimental participants to shadow a message in one ear while simultaneously tapping the table any time they heard a target word (e.g., "baseball") in *either* channel. People detected 87% of the target words in the channel that they were shadowing, but only 8% of targets in the unattended message. Thus, in this study, the problem in reporting content of the secondary message was not due to memory lapses; rather, the information largely seems not to have been processed in the first place, though some of the target words in the unattended message were attended to (also see Moray, 1959). There is, however, evidence that sometimes people are able to divide attention and process the meaning of information in the secondary message when it is relevant to them. Moray (1959; see also Wood & Cowan, 1995) instructed participants to shadow a primary message; every once in a while, a prompt was inserted into the secondary message preceded by the participant's own name: "John, now start to shadow *this* message." Under those circumstances, a significant number of the participants (about 33%) did respond to the instruction in the secondary message. In another demonstration of processing meaning in the secondary message (Treisman, 1964), fluent French–English bilinguals were tested with specially constructed stimuli: The secondary message was a *translation* of the primary message, in the bilinguals' second language. The bilinguals were eventually able to recognize that the two messages were identical in meaning. Thus, they were able to process the meaning of the secondary message.

In conclusion, early studies showed that participants who shadowed one message could detect physical changes in the unattended message, but were not able to engage in much semantic processing of the secondary message. However, some aspects of the secondary message did increase the likelihood of processing that message: if it was meaningfully related to the attended message, or preceded by the person's name. On the whole, those results indicate that people are not very good at dividing attention across more than one task. This negative conclusion leads us to an important question: the question of the possibility of multitasking in our busy modern lives.

DIVIDING ATTENTION IN REAL LIFE: HOW WELL DO WE MULTITASK?

Many of us take pride in our ability to multitask: We text-message as we walk; we talk on the cell phone as we do everything; we listen to music while we work or study. Many of us believe that we can multitask with no negative effect on performance on any of the tasks. However, there is reason to doubt this optimism: Research has shown that people have great difficulty multitasking. Ophir, Nass, and Wagner (2009) interviewed people about the degree to which they multitasked by engaging in activities such as sending text messages, talking on cell phones, surfing the web, playing computer games, and so on, while engaging in other tasks. Perhaps surprisingly, people who reported high levels of multitasking—habitual multitaskers—were *less* able to carry out a controlled laboratory task in which they had to multitask. They had more difficulty switching back and forth between two relatively simple tasks to filter out and ignore potentially distracting environmental stimuli.

These results do not tell us if the habitual multitaskers were poor at task-switching and focusing attention *because* of their history of multitasking, or if people who initially have problems focusing on one stream of information tend to multitask a lot. However, the result does show that high levels of multitasking are associated with attentional difficulties. This difficulty in shifting of attention shown by habitual multitaskers may have dangerous consequences when people engage in a very common—and potentially very dangerous—multitasking activity in contemporary life: talking on the cell phone while driving.

Cell-Phone Conversations While Driving

Research suggests that a driver has 4 or 5 times the risk of an auto accident while talking on a cell phone, a level of impairment equivalent to having imbibed several alcoholic drinks (Redelmeier & Tibshirani, 1997; Strayer, Drews, & Crouch, 2006). Several studies of real-life driving practices have shown a link between cell-phone use and unsafe driving. A study by the Virginia Tech Transportation Institute and the National Highway Traffic Safety Administration (April, 2006) tracked 241 drivers of 100 vehicles for over 1 year by installing a video camera and sensor in each car. There were 82 accidents, 761 near-crashes, and 8,295 critical traffic events that could have resulted in an accident. Eighty percent of crashes, and over half of near-accidents, followed driver distraction, with the most common distraction being cell-phone use (second was drowsiness).

A majority of U.S. states, and Australia and many countries in Europe, Asia, Africa, and North America, have either passed or are considering laws that limit cell-phone use while driving (the website www.ghsa.org/html/stateinfo/laws/cellphone_laws.html keeps an updated list). However, most U.S. states do permit cell-phone conversations while driving if one uses a hands-free device, despite the fact that evidence shows that handheld and hands-free cell-phone conversations are equally disruptive to driving (Strayer & Johnston, 2001). According to research from multiple sources, not only is a cell phone ban necessary, but laws should not make exceptions for hands-free devices: The problem with cell phones is not that they occupy our hands, it is that they occupy our *minds*.

Recent research has used realistic driving simulators to examine the effects of cell-phone conversations on driving; the "driver" is seated in front of the dashboard and steering wheel of a car, with pedals on the floor, and a realistic display of a view of the road is projected in front of the driver. Findings from these studies indicate that talking on a cell phone has a wide range of negative effects on driving (Cooper & Strayer, 2008; Strayer & Johnston, 2001). First, the most basic-level components of driving are interfered with. As one example, drivers talking on a cell phone are more likely to drift out of their lane than are drivers not on a cell phone. Second, drivers talking on a cell phone respond more sluggishly to significant events during driving: They are slower to hit the brake when a car in front of them slows down (Cooper & Strayer, 2008), for traffic signals (Strayer & Johnston, 2001, and when objects appear in the road (Insurance Company of British Columbia, 2001). Finally, drivers on the cell phone also make decision errors in very high-level planning aspects of driving. Drews, Pasupathi, and Strayer (2008) found that half of the drivers on cell phones who were instructed to leave the highway at the next rest stop missed the exit, and were more likely to initiate risky left turns while on a cell phone (Insurance Corporation of British Columbia, 2001).

Sometimes people raise the question whether in-car conversations with passengers, or listening to books on tape, have the same negative effects on driving as cell-phone conversations (Drews et al., 2008). Critically, in-car conversations are more likely to be adjusted to deal with the changing conditions on the road, while cell-phone conversations are harder to adjust, since one participant in the conversation cannot see what is happening on the road. Also, both members of an in-car conversation can pay attention to driving, so the passenger can actually assist the driver in carrying out the task of driving. For example, in the Drews et al. (2008) study, passengers would sometimes remind the driver to exit at a rest stop.

There is also evidence that the interference effects of cell-phone use on driving do not decrease with practice. Cooper and Strayer (2008) selected people for a study of multitasking based on their reports of how frequently they used the cell phone while driving. High users reported that they talked on the cell phone while driving more than 40% of the time; low cell-phone users talked on the cell phone while driving approximately 5% of the time. These two groups of drivers were given four sessions of practice in a realistic driving simulator, in which they "drove" both on highways and in a city. They were then transferred to a new scenario, to see if the effects of practice, if any, would go beyond the specific scenarios that they had seen.

The results of the study indicated that the self-reported highly experienced cell-phone users were no better than the low-experienced users in multitasking: Both groups performed worse when talking on the cell phone. In addition, there was little improvement in performance in either group across the practice sessions (see Figure 6.9). Finally, in the final transfer session, multitasking performance was at the levels as the initial session. The lack of improvement even after significant practice indicates that it is difficult to learn to coordinate driving and talking on a cell phone. Although one might say that four sessions of practice is not enough to produce real improvement in multitasking, it should be noted that the high-use group consisted of participants who were selected based on their real-life frequent cell-phone use, and their driving when talking on the cell phone was as disrupted as the low-use group. So the longer-term real-world usage by one of the groups seems not to have done much in the way of positive effects either.

In sum, these studies confirm that dividing one's attention has cognitive costs, which may be due to neurological costs. Shomstein and Yantis (2004) found that as people listened to a cell-phone conversation, there was less fMRI activity in the visual cortex. In a simulated driving task, parietal lobe activation was measured after presentation of a brake light to which people were to respond. People talking on a cell phone showed a 50% reduction in parietal lobe activation, indicating less attention was paid to the visual stimulus (Strayer & Drews, 2007). Thus, cell-phone use may cause a kind of *inattentional blindness* that can have a deleterious effect on driving.

Cell Phones and Walking

Cell-phone use not only interferes with driving, it interferes also with walking. Hyman, Boss, Wise, McKenzie, and Caggiano (2009) studied the behavior of randomly selected people walking across an open plaza on a college campus. People talking on a cell walked more slowly, and were less likely to acknowledge the presence of others. They were also less likely to detect the presence of an individual in a clown costume, riding a unicycle off to the side of the path, than were pedestrians not talking on a cell phone.

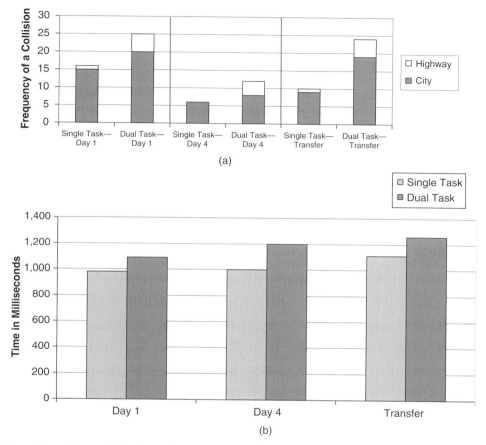

Figure 6.9   Effects of divided attention while driving. (a) Probability of a collision, based on results from Cooper and Strayer (2008). (b) Mean time to apply brakes in response to traffic signals (in milliseconds), based on results from Cooper and Strayer (2008). Different levels of cell-phone use are combined.

Even when asked directly if they had seen a clown, only 25% of the cell-phone users said yes, while over 50% of the other people did. After several pedestrian deaths, New York state legislators considered a bill to ban the use of iPods, BlackBerrys, and MP3 players in New York City (http://www.wnbc.com/news/10948106/detail.html). This is further evidence that cell-phone use interferes with processing of visual information from the world—the inattentional blindness we referred to earlier.

Multitasking: Summary

Research of several sorts indicates that attentional factors are of critical importance in safe driving, and that any nondriving activity that occupies the attention of a driver can result in unsafe conditions. However, the attention usurped by cell phones appears to be greater than that of other activities, such as talking with a passenger. Repeated demonstrations that there is no difference in the level of driving impairment between handheld and hands-free phones confirms the idea that general attentional processes are to blame for increased errors in this commonplace divided-attention task.

Selective and Divided Attention: Conclusions

Much evidence indicates that people are able to attend selectively to one stream of information in the face of potentially distracting stimuli. However, there are circumstances in which attention may be captured involuntarily by the stream that is to be ignored. If the message in the attended channel switches to the previously ignored channel, the participant will follow it for a few words into the new channel. One's expectancies—top-down processes—thus influence selectivity in attention. Similarly, when one's name appears in the secondary message, or if the same message is presented in both channels, participants can become aware of that, even if the same messages are only translations of each other. On the other hand, when one is attempting consciously to respond to target words in the nonattended message, most (though not all) targets will be missed, indicating that it is difficult to divide attention voluntarily. Evidence from recent studies on multitasking supports this pessimistic conclusion: People have difficulty in carrying out two tasks in an error-free manner, and reported experience with multitasking does not predict superior multitasking performance. In addition, there is evidence that one of the multitasking activities that is most frequently attempted—driving while talking on the cell phone—results in decrements in driving performance on many levels, ranging from staying in one's lane to remembering one's exit from the highway.

With the results from studies of selective and divided attention as a background, we can now examine theories that psychologists have proposed to explain people's ability to selectively attend to information in the environment, and their difficulties in extracting information from the nonattended message or, in more general terms, difficulties in multitasking.

STRUCTURAL MODELS OF ATTENTION: EARLY VERSUS LATE SELECTION

During World War II, Broadbent (1958) was one of a number of British psychologists who worked in the war effort. One of the areas of study to which psychologists were assigned was the investigation of phenomena concerned with attention. Particular interest centered on the factors influencing performance of radar operators, who had to spend long hours observing screens in order to detect flights of enemy aircraft approaching Britain on bombing raids. Questions arose concerning how long those operators could be expected to function efficiently, and what working conditions would maximize the likelihood of an observer's not missing a blip on the screen. Those issues led to the study of attention and vigilance, and, after the war, Broadbent and a number of other psychologists in Britain continued the work (Broadbent, 1958; Cherry, 1953), which led to modern interest in attention as an important area of study. The same issues have been raised in connection with air traffic controllers, who must pay attention to both visual and auditory stimuli simultaneously, as well as make decisions, and maintain information in working memory for both the flight paths of multiple planes and decisions already made (Xing & Bailey, 2005).

Broadbent's Filter Model of Attention

Based on the results of research by Cherry (1953) and himself (Broadbent, 1958), Broadbent developed the *Filter model* of human information processing presented in Figure 6.10. He proposed that human information processing was limited and that at any given time we can process only one channel or set of stimuli. Broadbent assumed that, to prevent overload, there must be some structure in the nervous system that serves as an attentional filter (see Figure 6.10), to block all stimuli except the one that is to be processed. This filter can be set to allow only a very specific type of stimulus to pass through, based on its sensory characteristics. For example, if you are carrying out a conversation in a crowded room, you are able to attend to that conversation because your filter can be set to pass through the stimulus that is spoken in a specific voice (that of the person with whom you are speaking) and that comes from a specific location (from in front of you). All irrelevant stimuli will be blocked by the filter, and only the relevant conversation will be meaningfully attended to and processed further.

This model is called an *early selection* model, because selection of the relevant stream of information occurs early in the processing sequence, before meaningful processing has taken place. Thus, sensory characteristics of an unattended message may be noticed, but it will not be processed semantically unless attention is switched to it (at the expense of processing the primary message).

There were a number of reasons for Broadbent's assumption that selection of one message occurred early in the process. First, if all stimuli in all channels were always processed for meaning, the chances of making mistakes during processing would increase dramatically. Second, as we know, experimental results found that while shadowing a message from one ear, little or no meaningful information could be reported from the ignored channel (Cherry, 1953). Individuals could detect when the voice in the unattended channel switched its sensory characteristics, as from a man's to a woman's voice, or speech to a tone (Cherry, 1953), but little else.

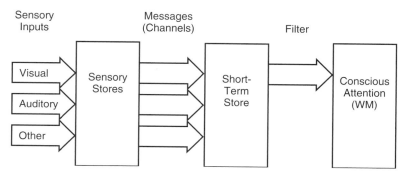

Figure 6.10 Bottleneck theory of attention, Broadbent's filter model: Only one message can get through for full processing and conscious awareness.

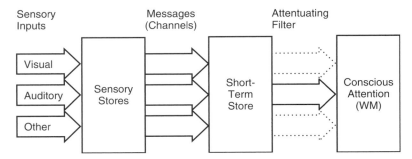

Figure 6.11   Bottleneck theory of attention, Treisman's attenuator model (a modification of Broadbent): Unattended messages (indicated with dotted arrows) are weakened, not blocked by the filter.

However, Broadbent's model does not easily account for findings that some information in the ignored channel is processed for meaning. For example, how are people able to detect their name in the unattended ear (Moray, 1959), if only one message can get through at a time? Also, recall that Treisman (1960) found that people's attention would "follow" a message when it switched ears. Those results indicated that meaning of the unattended message was being processed from the ignored channel. As a response to these and other findings, Treisman (1969) proposed the *Attenuator model* of attention (Figure 6.11). It shared several components of Broadbent's (1958) filter theory: Sensory characteristics of messages are processed before the attentional bottleneck, and a filter interferes with a second or unattended message being processed for meaning. However, Treisman hypothesized that the filter merely weakened (attenuated), rather than completely blocked, unattended stimuli. This left open the possibility that an occasional exceptional stimulus in the nonattended channel might be strong enough to reach consciousness or intrude into one's speech stream during a shadowing task.

Treisman (1969) proposed that all stimuli, including words, had different thresholds for recognition. Some stimuli have permanently low thresholds (e.g., alarm words like "Fire!" or one's own name; Howarth & Ellis, 1961), which means that they are always relatively easy to process. Other stimuli would have temporarily lowered thresholds (i.e., they temporarily become easy to process) because they were related to information in the primary message. This explains the semantic intrusions that occurred in Treisman's 1960 study (e.g., the "MAHOGANY/TABLE" finding), and her finding that bilingual participants often noticed that the unattended message was the same passage in their second language (Treisman, 1964). Thus, although Treisman agreed with Broadbent's model's emphasis on early attentional selection, her model was more flexible, in allowing that some stimuli from an unattended source might get through for processing.

Late Selection Theories

A second general type of structural theory of attention assumed that selection took place late in the processing sequence, after *all* inputs were processed for meaning

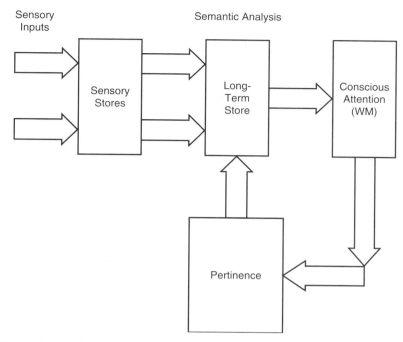

Figure 6.12 Bottleneck theory of attention, Norman's (1968) pertinence model: A late selection model.

(Deutsch & Deutsch, 1963; Norman, 1968). An outline of a late-selection model of attention, known as the *Pertinence Model* (Norman, 1968), is presented in Figure 6.12. Both channels are processed by the sensory systems, and then are analyzed semantically. Following that analysis, only one stream is selected to reach WM. This view, like those of Broadbent and Treisman, proposes that there is a bottleneck in the system, but the bottleneck is located after meaningful processing of multiple channels. Determination of which specific stream of information makes it to working memory is based on the *pertinence* or *relevance* of the various channels of information to one's goals or on-going activities. Thus, information that is related to the information now being processed, such as a string of words that will continue a sentence that one is listening to, will capture attention.

A late-selection model could explain a number of the findings from experiments on selective and divided attention, such as how people sometimes made the mistake of following the shadowed message into the wrong ear (Treisman, 1960). Since both messages were being analyzed for meaning, the continuation of the meaning of the shadowed message into the wrong ear would cause the individual to follow it. This view could also explain how a fluent bilingual could realize that the secondary message was a translation of the first (Treisman, 1964). If the meaning of both messages were being processed, then the semantic identity of the two messages (albeit in two different languages) would be easy for the participant to discover. Similarly, responding to one's name in the secondary message was explained by assuming that the meaning of the message was processed, and that one's name, once processed, caught one's attention because of its importance.

However, some experimental results did not fit the late-selection view. Consider again the participant's responding to his or her name. The late selection view proposes that the meaning of the name is processed, and that sets off the attentional response to the name. As we saw earlier, though, Moray (1959) found that the participant's name was an effective stimulus for only about one-third of the participants. However, if the meanings of all stimuli are processed before selection, it becomes hard to understand how one's name could be missed by two-thirds of the participants. Similarly, the finding that participants could detect a target word 87% of the time in the attended channel, but only 8% of the time in the secondary message (Treisman & Geffen, 1967) raises problems for late-selection views.

Structural Models of Attention: Conclusions

Based on the discussion so far in this chapter, it is clear that selective attention is both bottom-up—because attention is heavily influenced by the physical characteristics of a message—and top-down, because personal goals and expectations can play a role in selecting information for further processing. Both early- and late-selection models of attention are based on the idea that there is a bottleneck in the processing system through which multiple streams of information cannot pass. Both of these types of models have problems with the finding that one's name can capture attention, although the problems are of different sorts. Early-selection models, such as Broadbent's (1958) Filter model, would have trouble explaining how one's name can be an effective stimulus, since they assume that the secondary channel is not processed for meaning. Treisman's (1969) Attenuator model, an elaboration of Broadbent's view, can better explain how one can sometimes detect one's own name in a secondary message, or how semantic intrusions from the unattended channel can be shadowed without the person realizing it.

Late-selection models (e.g., Norman, 1968), in contrast, can explain why one's name can capture attention. On the one hand, if we are processing all channels for meaning, as the Pertinence model proposes, then our name should be processed 100% of the time, and its meaning can then capture the person's attention. However, late-selection models have problems with the fact that one's name is effective in capturing attention for only one-third of people (Moray, 1959), or that a target word is detected infrequently in the unattended channel (Treisman & Geffen, 1967).

SELECTIVE ATTENTION AND THE PERCEPTUAL CYCLE

Given these questions that can be raised about structural models of attention, let us try to examine the important research findings on attention from a different point of view. We have proposed that attention and pattern recognition are closely related phenomena, and some of the discussion in this chapter has pointed that out. As further evidence of the close relation between those areas, the perceptual cycle discussed in Chapter 5 (Neisser, 1976) and presented again in Figure 6.13, provides a useful way

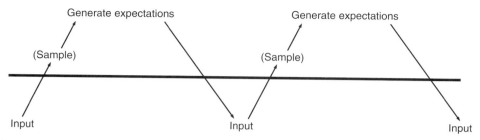

Figure 6.13 Perceptual cycle.

to begin to organize the findings from studies of attention. The expectations that were important in pattern recognition also play a role in selecting information for further processing, that is, in attending to one stream of information and ignoring others.

Let us apply the perceptual cycle to the behavior of a person shadowing some verbal message and ignoring a competing message. The person is generating expectations as to what will occur next, based on what he or she has shadowed so far. Those expectations would presumably include the information that a certain voice, coming from a specific location, is speaking words related to a particular topic. It seems reasonable to assume that the stimulus processed at the next moment in time will be that which best matches the person's expectancies. As noted during the discussion of early research on attention, this view was first articulated by Külpe (1901) over 100 years ago (see also Norman, 1968). In this analysis, selective attention is related to *priming*, as discussed in Chapter 5: Processing the primary message at any point in time can be looked upon as priming the person to process related stimuli presented later in time. In this way of looking at perception and attention, the same top-down processes—knowledge and expectations—that allow one to efficiently process individual stimuli in the environment also allow one to selectively attend to relevant stimuli from the multiple streams impinging on us at any point in time. That is, object perception and selective attention are inextricably linked, and use the same top-down processes.

There is experimental evidence to support this analysis of the role of top-down processes in selective attention. Huang and Pashler (2007) carried out an experiment in which individuals had to keep a single stimulus in WM for a later memory test. For example, they might see the *prime shape* shown in Figure 6.14 and would have to retain it for a later test (the *test shape* in Figure 6.14). During the retention interval, three other *background shapes* were presented, first alone, and then with digits written on them (*background shapes + 3 digits*). The person had to choose whichever one of those digits he or she wished to report. The background shapes played no role in this task, and could be ignored by the participants. On some of the trials one of the background shapes was related to the shape being held in WM (see Figure 6.14). Although the participants were completely free to choose any of the three digits to report, they tended to choose the digit superimposed on the shape that was being held in WM. The shape in WM—being held in memory for another purpose—directed or primed the participants' attention selectively to one of the number-shapes. Similar results have been reported by other researchers (e.g., Downing, 2000; Pashler & Shiu, 1999; Stolz, 1996, 1999).

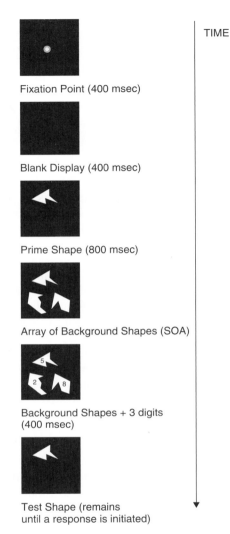

TIME

Fixation Point (400 msec)

Blank Display (400 msec)

Prime Shape (800 msec)

Array of Background Shapes (SOA)

Background Shapes + 3 digits
(400 msec)

Test Shape (remains
until a response is initiated)

Figure 6.14 Adaptation of Huang and Pashler (2007) stimuli.

If we assume that attention is related to expectancies, we can begin to understand how people are able to selectively attend in the first place by simply affixing their attention to the most relevant information for that task. We can also understand why they will sometimes mistakenly follow a message when it switches from one ear to the other (as in the "MAHOGANY/TABLE" example). However, the attentional system also has to have flexibility, so that sometimes our attention can be captured by something that we were *not* expecting (such as when we orient to a novel stimulus), and so that we can make a conscious decision to divide our attention between two tasks. One such flexible model, which views attention as a system with a certain amount of capacity that we decide how to allocate, is presented next.

ATTENTION AND CAPACITY

Kahneman (1973) proposed an explanation for the results on divided attention that was built on the notion of *limited processing capacity*: The idea that organisms are limited in the amount of cognitive activity that they can carry out at any one time (see also Pashler & Johnston, 1998). If a task (or a set of tasks being carried out simultaneously) demands more capacity than we have available, then it cannot be carried out without mistakes. This view is presented graphically in Figure 6.15.

Let us consider the typical shadowing experiment from this perspective. Most of the time, shadowing the primary channel is itself a difficult task, and therefore little or no information can be processed from the secondary message: there is not enough capacity available. However, two circumstances will make it possible for attention to

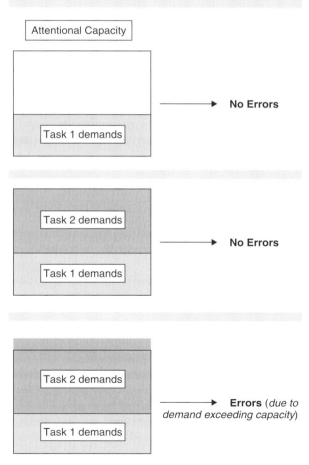

Figure 6.15   Representation of task performance as a function of cognitive capacity and task demands: Errors do not occur until task demands exceed attentional capacity.

be divided between the two messages: (1) if the primary task momentarily becomes easy, and/or (2) if the information in the secondary message is particularly easy to process. For example, your name is a stimulus that you have heard thousands of times, which makes it particularly easy to detect. Second, it is highly significant to you and would be likely to produce an orienting response even in the unattended channel.

The idea of attentional capacity as a pool of resources can help us understand some of the important results from studies of selective and divided attention. When carrying out any task, two interrelated factors determine how well we can carry out that task and how easily we can divide our attention and respond to information outside the primary task. First, the difficulty of the primary task and the available capacity determines whether or not one will be able to carry out the primary task without error. In addition, the moment-to-moment available capacity, combined with the difficulty of the secondary task, determine whether or not we will be able to extract any information from the world beyond the primary task.

Practice and Capacity: The Question of Automaticity

The notion of limited processing capacity is based on the idea that, at any given time, a person has a limited pool of resources available to carry out cognition. The size of this pool is not fixed, however; it is subject to moment-to-moment changes. For example, more resources are available when one studies while alert versus tired. In addition, as we have just discussed, different tasks demand different amounts of processing capacity. There may be short-term changes in the difficulty of a given task, as when a book we are reading begins to address a topic that is more difficult to understand than what it had been dealing with. If we do not have spare capacity available, we may lose the thread of the discussion. There can also be longer-term changes in task difficulty: The more practice we have carrying out some task, the less capacity it requires. When you first learn a new skill, such as driving a car, the task may be close to impossible to carry out without making at least one driving error. A new driver may be able to steer the car smoothly until he has to turn on the windshield wipers, and then starts to veer off the road. Each separate driving component must be consciously attended to, and thus constitutes an *effortful* task.

With time and practice, however, things become easier and more *automatic*, so that the various elements of driving are integrated into one action, which can be carried out smoothly. Another way to describe the situation is to say that driving now requires significantly less attentional capacity. However, even a highly practiced task like driving may still make some demands on capacity: If traffic becomes very congested, for example, even an experienced driver may briefly stop conversing with a passenger, to pay more attention to driving. As we have seen, even the highly practiced task of walking may not be completely automatic, since it too can be disrupted by a cell-phone conversation (Hyman et al., 2009).

Researchers have studied the development of automatic processing in the laboratory, using tasks such as that in Figure 6.16, first used by Shiffrin and Schneider (1977; Schneider & Shiffrin, 1977). On each trial, a set of target stimuli was presented to the

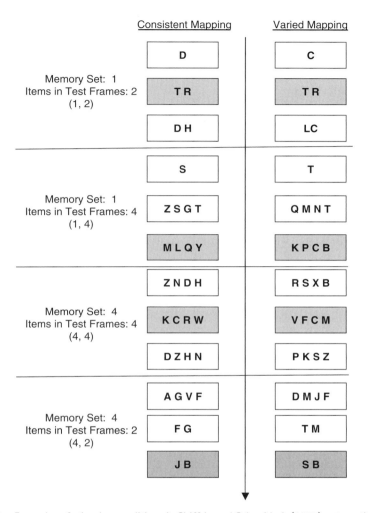

Figure 6.16   Examples of stimulus conditions in Shiffrin and Schneider's (1977) automatic processing task: Positive frame sets that contain at least one target are indicated in white boxes. Negative frames in which no targets occur are indicated in grey boxes. In the Consistent condition, each letter can only be a target *or* a distractor through all trials. In the Varied Mapping condition, a letter that was a distractor in one trial could be a target on another trial (and vice versa).

participant (e.g., five letters designated as targets), followed by one, two, or four comparison stimuli. The participant's task was to determine as quickly as possible if any of the targets were in the comparison display. The comparison display was made up of some combination of target/s and *distractors*. On any given trial, there might be one or more targets in the comparison set, or there might not be any. In one condition—the *varied mapping* condition—the targets changed from trial to trial, so that a given letter could be a target on one trial and a distractor on the next. Shiffrin and Schneider varied the number of stimuli in the target and the display sets, and found that the time to

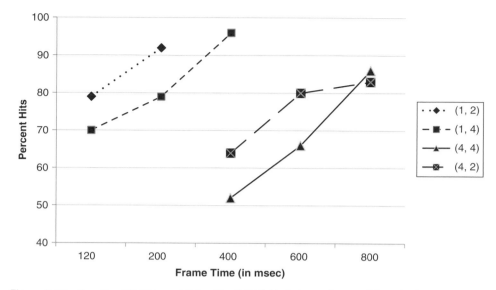

Figure 6.17   Results of Shiffrin and Schneider (1977): Varied mapping conditions. In the key, the first number in each set of parentheses indicates the memory set on a set of trials; the second number indicates the number of items in the test frames.

respond correctly depended on the number of stimuli in each: The more targets a person had to detect, and the more items in the display set, the longer it took to make the judgment (see Figure 6.17). Those results indicate that the display was being examined one letter at time in order to determine if there were any targets in it.

However, in a *consistent mapping* condition, the target set and the distractors stayed the same for many sessions on the task. If Q were a target on the first trial, then it was always a target. In the constant mapping condition, after a large number of trials, the amount of time to determine whether a target was in the display became more equal, even when the display set was made larger (see Figure 6.18). With extensive practice in the constant-mapping condition, participants became capable of processing multiple target stimuli as quickly as single stimuli, indicating that the task had become more automatic, and required much less capacity.

Another task used to study the development of automatic processing is shown in Figure 6.19. The task is very simple: the participant determines the *numerosity* of each array, i.e., how many items are in it. Green (1997) presented people with arrays of stimuli that contained 8, 9, or 10 items. The people were tested with several hundred arrays in the course of several hours in the experiment. The measure of interest was how long it took the participant to determine the number of items in each array.

Early in training, the time to determine the number of items in any array depended on how many items there were, which indicated that the participants were counting the array. However, with increasing amounts of practice, the amount of time needed to determine the number of items in a given array began to equalize for the different numbers of items, so that more items in an array did not make the task take longer. This indicated that the participants were no longer processing the array one item at a time.

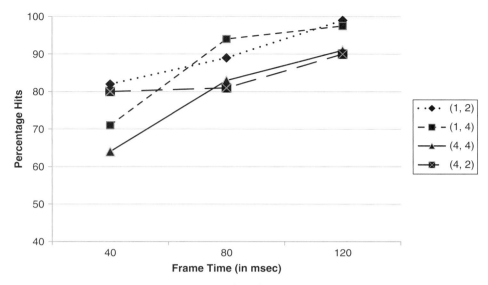

Figure 6.18 Results of Shiffrin and Schneider (1977): Consistent mapping conditions. In the key, the first number in each set of parentheses indicates the memory set on a set of trials; the second number indicates the number of items in the test frames.

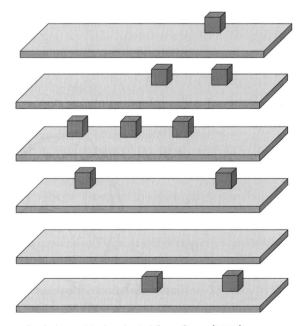

Figure 6.19 Numerosity-judgment task, adapted from Green (1997).

Rather, they had become capable of processing the whole array at once, so that more items did not take longer to process. The results of Green (1997; see also Lassaline & Logan, 1993) thus support the conclusion that with extensive practice individuals can become automatic in processing tasks that initially required that they attend to individual items.

Explaining the Development of Automatic Processing

We have now reviewed several studies in which major changes in performance have been brought about by extensive practice (e.g., Green, 1997; Shiffrin & Schneider, 1977). The changes in processing in those studies raise the question of how people become able to process items automatically. One way to explain the changes in processing is to assume that as a task becomes well-practiced, it requires less cognitive capacity to carry out. This would result in faster response times. Another possibility, however, is that the development of skill in a task may be the result of information stored about the task. As one has extensive practice with a task, one may become able to use information from the task as the basis for responding.

Automaticity and Memory

Logan and his co-workers (e.g., Lassaline & Logan, 1993; Logan, 1988, 2002) have proposed that automatic processing occurs because of relatively specific information about the task that is stored in memory as we practice. Let us analyze the numerosity-judgment task shown in Figure 6.19. When a participant begins the task, he or she knows basically nothing about the specifics, such as the items that will be presented and how they will be arranged. On the early trials, a person would have to use a *counting rule* or *algorithm*, which allows a person to perform the task well. However, in addition to counting each array when it is presented, we are also encoding information about what each array looks like and how many items it contains. Each time an array is presented, a new memory is formed. When any array is repeated in the sequence, there are now two ways to determine how many items it contains: One can use the counting algorithm, or one can remember the specific array, and then simply recall the number of items it contains, without counting them. Logan (1988, 1992) assumed that carrying out the counting algorithm takes an approximately constant amount of time per item in the array. In contrast, the amount of time to retrieve from memory specific information about a given array varies for each of the traces in memory related to that array. Sooner or later, one of the memory traces from that array will result in faster retrieval of the answer than will the counting rule, and from then on the person will respond on the basis of memory. At that point, responding will no longer depend on the number of items in the array.

Memory Versus Capacity

We now have two different explanations of the development of automatic processing. The capacity view argues that practice results in the task becoming less demanding. From this perspective, the specific information in the task does not matter; what is important is that a person receives enough practice through repeated trials to reduce the amount of attention needed to perform the task. It does not matter if the *items* are the same or different from trial to trial; what matters is whether or not the *task* is the same. According to the memory view, on the other hand, the items do matter: If one changes the items from trial to trial, then automatic processing should not develop. One way to test these two views is to determine if information about specific items is important in carrying out the task. First, train participants until they take the same time to respond to arrays of different sizes that are repeated randomly. In other words, train the participants until they are processing each familiar array automatically. At that point, change the specific items in each array (e.g., from dots to letters) while keeping the numerosity and shape of each array the same.

According to the capacity view of automatic processing, changing the items in the array should not have a major effect on performance. Since the basic task is the same, then the extensive practice that the person has had should be relevant to the new version of the task. According to the memory view, however, changing the specific items in the arrays should have a large effect on the ability of participants to carry out the task. If we modify the task so that the new items no longer match memory, then the ability to carry out the task automatically should disappear. Results from a study by Green (1997), using this design, supported the memory view. Changing the specific items interfered with the ability to carry out the task: participants' performance went back to what it was when they started, with the number of items in the array determining how long it took to report how numerous they were. This indicates that very specific information from memory is being used in this task, rather than the task itself has become easier or automated. It should be noted, however, that, although Green's (1997) experiment did not support the reduced-capacity view, it is possible other tasks may indeed show automation.

Practice and Automatic Processing: Conclusions

When people have large amounts of practice on a task, it changes the way the task is carried out. Processing which was effortful—filled with errors, and requiring all of our capacity—becomes automatic—without errors, and requiring little or no capacity. In explaining these changes in performance with practice, two different sorts of explanations have been proposed. One view is that, with practice, a task comes to demand less capacity; an alternative explanation is that task-relevant information in memory allows the task to be carried out more efficiently. Research designed to test these two views has found that changing the specific items on the task interferes with performance, which indicates that memory processes may be the basis for development of automatic processing.

ARE THERE NO LIMITS TO OUR CAPACITY? A CENTRAL BOTTLENECK

The results of Shiffrin and Schneider (1977) and Green (1997) that we have just discussed indicate that, with extensive practice, people can learn to process multiple stimuli as quickly as single stimuli. This result could lead one to the hypothesis that with enough practice people might become capable of doing anything. That is, with enough practice we might become able to carry out multiple complex tasks as easily as we carry out a single simple task. However, the situations used by Shiffrin and Schneider and by Green were relatively simple; in many situations (such as driving) we must do more than simply detect the presence of one of more targets or the numerosity of an array of items. We usually have responses to carry out, in addition to detecting the presence of relevant stimuli. A classic study by Spelke, Hirst, and Neisser (1976) investigated whether people could learn to carry out two relatively complex tasks at the same time as efficiently as they could carry out either one by itself. They asked participants to shadow a verbal message while simultaneously writing a second dictated message. At the beginning of training, the dictated material consisted of single words, to keep the difficulty to a minimum. As the participants became better able to do both tasks (shadowing and taking single-word dictation), the experimenters made the dictated materials longer. The dictation stimuli changed to strings of words, then progressed to short sentences, and then to groups of related sentences. At several points during the training, the participants were extensively tested for performance on the tasks, both separately and simultaneously.

At the beginning of training, the participants could not write even single words without it totally interfering with shadowing, and they missed many of the dictated words because of the demands of shadowing. With several months of practice, performance began to improve, and the two participants became capable of taking dictation of simple sentences, and understanding those sentences, while shadowing without error. In addition, they were better able to integrate the meanings of several dictated sentences in order to derive inferences that followed from them. Thus, tasks that had seemed impossible to carry out simultaneously did, with extensive practice, become possible. However, before we conclude that, with enough practice we could learn to effectively coordinate *any* multiple tasks, it should be emphasized that neither of the Spelke et al. (1976) participants got beyond three-word sentences in dictation, even with several months of practice at the next level. So it appears there are limits on attentional capacity, even though it is possible to improve simultaneous performance on two tasks with extensive practice. At the very least, the results of Hirst et al. lead one to believe that it would take years of practice before people could carry out two complex tasks at the same time without error. Research by Pashler, Johnston, Ruthruff, and their colleagues (e.g., Levy, Pashler, & Boer, 2006; Pashler, Johnston, & Ruthruff, 2001; Ruthruff, Johnston, & Van Selst, 2001; Van Selst, Ruthruff, & Johnston, 1999) provides additional evidence that there may be limits to attentional capacity that are essentially impossible to overcome.

Selective and Divided Attention: Summary and Conclusions

The analysis of selective attention in the last several sections has examined a number of related phenomena, beginning with involuntary or passive shifting of attention in selective attention tasks using dichotic listening. Shifts of attention, as to an unattended or secondary message, can be seen when there are physical changes in the secondary message, and when information appears that is directly relevant to us (e.g., our name) or relevant to information in the attended or primary message. Thus, both bottom-up and top-down processes are at play. Attempts to multitask, or to divide our attention, typically result in more errors being made on one or both tasks, because two tasks may exceed our attentional capacity (as shown in the driving and cell phone research). Well-learned skills may become more automated over time, thus leading to better performance and reduced attentional capacity. However, there is some evidence that tasks that become more efficient with practice (e.g., numerosity judgments) may simply be due to having stored prior trials in memory, rather than improving at the task *per se*. Once again, we see the importance of information from memory in the active interaction of a person with the world.

SUMMARY: ATTENTIONAL PROCESSES

Part of the difficulty in studying attention is that there are so many different aspects to attention, from merely orienting to a stimulus that we see, such as a moving car that catches our attention, to deciding how to allocate our resources in order to multitask. Furthermore, there are both overt behavioral responses that can be used to study attention (as when we turn our heads to attend to the source of a loud noise), and covert attentional processes, in which an orienting response is accomplished without any overt signs. Some ways to allocate attention are under our conscious control; others are more automatic.

Attention also appears to be sensitive to novelty, such as when we start to ignore a repetitive stimulus (e.g., the hum of a fan) and then pay more attention to a new noise (e.g., our roommate calling out as she enters the room). Yet, attentional processes are also responsive to familiarity, such as when you catch a continuity error in a film after repeated viewings, or when participants in a dichotic listening experiment detect their name in a supposedly unattended channel. Both bottom-up processes and top-down influences play a role in attention: We may automatically orient to loud noises or changes in the physical characteristics of a message (e.g., a male voice that changes to female) indicating the role of bottom-up effects. Yet, it is easier to detect a friend's face in a crowd than a stranger's, and attention to the details of tasks do improve with both practice (e.g., shadowing a message while taking dictation) and memory (e.g., judging the numerosity of items in previously-seen displays), which illustrates effects from top-down processing.

In other words, attention is a complex phenomenon that plays an integral part of many other cognitive processes: pattern recognition, memory, reasoning, creativity, and so on. The factors seen to influence attentional processes may depend heavily on what aspect of attention one is studying, and the experimental techniques being used.

REVIEW QUESTIONS

Here is a set of questions to use as organizing material for your review of the chapter. As with the other chapters you have encountered so far, it will be most helpful if you try to answer each question from memory before you review the answer.

1. What is the difference between divided attention and selective attention?

2. What basic ideas were raised by early psychologists in discussions of attention?

3. What factors determine whether a stimulus will draw attention to itself?

4. What are costs and benefits of directing covert orientation toward a particular part of the world?

5. How does inhibition of return develop over time?

6. What brain systems are involved in orienting?

7. How do the results from studies examining negative priming demonstrate the importance of inhibition in attention?

8. What role does WM play in inhibition in attention?

9. How does research using the Stroop task demonstrate the importance of inhibition in attention?

10. Compare the *attentional blink* with *repetition blindness*.

11. How do the neuropsychological syndromes of hemispatial-neglect and dorsal simultagnosia shed light on visual attention?

12. What are two explanations for *change blindness*, and what findings support each of those explanations?

13. What evidence from auditory and spatial tasks indicates that people are good at selectively attending to one stream of information?

14. What characteristics—physical and semantic—affect ease of shadowing in studies of selectivity of attention?

15. Summarize experimental evidence concerning whether people can divide attention during shadowing.

16. Are habitual multitaskers good at multitasking?

17. Summarize experimental research relevant to the question of whether talking on hands-free cell phones while driving should be outlawed.

18. Outline differences between early- versus late-selection models of attention.

19. Applying Neisser's cyclical model of pattern recognition to attention, how does one explain the role of top-down factors in selectivity of attention?

20. How does the cyclical model of attention have to be expanded in order to deal with results concerning people's ability to notice their names in the unattended channel?

21. Outline two views—*capacity* versus *memory*—concerning how automatic processing develops.

22. Based on experimental results, can capacity limitations be eliminated with practice?

CHAPTER 7

IMAGERY

This chapter addresses the phenomenon of *mental imagery*, a particular kind of conscious experience that feels as if we are experiencing a perceptual object or sound, but without the object or sound being there. The study of mental imagery has undergone great changes in the 50 or so years since the beginnings of the cognitive revolution. As we saw in the discussion in Chapter 1, the early psychologists were interested in the study of imagery, but that subject matter was rejected by the behaviorists, leading to imagery being ignored by most researchers for the first half of the 20th century. With the development of cognitive science, however, there came a surge in the study of imagery. This chapter traces the development of that stream of research, and we trace the path of imagery as a subject matter that could be addressed through the methods of cognitive science.

The question-answering exercises in Box 7.1 provide examples of situations in which people usually report that they experience imagery.

BOX 7.1 IMAGERY EXERCISES

A. What is darker green in color, a frozen pea or a Christmas tree?

B. Does the tip of a horse's tail come below its knees? (The knees are the bend of the rear legs.)

C. John is smarter than Jim; Bill is not smarter than Jim. Who is smartest?

D. If a lowercase N is rotated 90 degrees clockwise, is the resulting form a letter? What about 180 degrees clockwise?

When you attempted to answer the questions in Box 7.1, did you have the sense of mentally picturing a pea and a Christmas tree? In other words, did you imagine a pea and a Christmas tree while answering the question? Did you imagine a horse? We all experience imagery on a regular basis, and images can affect our behavior. For instance, picture a hot cinnamon bun, fresh out of the oven. Does it make your mouth water? Or have you ever thought you heard your phone ringing, and run to answer it, only to find that it was an illusion? All those experiences involve *mental imagery*, a particular kind of conscious experience, that feels as if we are perceiving an object or sound, but without the object or sound actually existing in our environment. For example, I can imagine the Beatles singing "Can't Buy Me Love," in which case I have an experience that *seems* like hearing; that is an example of auditory imagery. Similarly, I can imagine the smell of freshly cut garlic (olfactory, or smell, imagery), the taste of pea soup (gustatory, or taste, imagery), the sight of a basketball player leaping through the air (visual imagery), and the feel of the cold ocean water covering my feet at the seashore (tactile, or haptic, imagery). While those examples of imagery are based on memories of particular experiences that I have had, I can also imagine things I have never experienced, such as my mother playing tennis, or a pink elephant. In each case, whether the image is recalled or created, it seems to retain some of the properties of a perceptual experience: A visual image of an evergreen tree retains the tree's familiar shape, color, and a sense of depth (assuming one does not image a photograph of the tree); our auditory image has the same melody as the original tune we heard.

One critically important aspect of imagery from the perspective of cognitive science is that imagery seems to be an inherently subjective phenomenon: Our images occur inside us, making it difficult to accurately ascertain what another person is imaging. That subjectivity would seem to make it impossible to study imagery using the objective methods of science. However, one of the truly revolutionary aspects of modern cognitive science is that researchers have developed methods that have made the study of imagery a legitimate topic for scientific investigation. Thus, in addition to its inherent interest, the research to be discussed in this chapter is also important because it is a case study in how one can apply scientific methods to the analysis of cognitive phenomena that seem to be inherently subjective. That development is what makes the study of imagery so fascinating, and it is what we hope to convey in this chapter.

OUTLINE OF CHAPTER 7

As we work through the examination of imagery in this chapter, we will see support for the organizing themes of this book. Continuing our functional analysis of cognition, we begin by examining the possible roles that imagery might serve in cognitive processing. What might be the usefulness of our ability to re-create or reexperience perceptual experiences? We then turn to a discussion of the study of imagery from a historical perspective, as we will trace how modern research has evolved out of ideas and studies from the past. We review early research on imagery, and examine why the study of imagery was abandoned by mainstream psychology during the first half of the 20th century. However, during those years, methodological and theoretical advances led to a greater willingness by researchers to reexamine the possible role of imagery in cognition, beginning with its role in memory. Thus, in the late 1950s and early 1960s, several pioneering researchers carried out studies on imagery that utilized quantifiable and rigorous methods for measuring how imagery processes were carried out.

Cognitive scientists also began to study possible parallels between perception and imagery, and that renewed interest in imagery research continues strongly today. The idea that imagery is closely related to perception provides evidence for the integration of cognitive processes, although we will also see that there are critical differences between imagery and perception. We also review modern theories of imagery, which attempt to explain how images are created and processed. Overall, we will see further evidence that cognition is knowledge-based, and in favor of the important role of memory and top-down processing in imagery. Finally, the renewed interest in imagery has brought with it a controversy concerning the question of whether imagery can serve as a medium of thought (e.g., Kosslyn, Thompson, & Ganis, 2006; Pylyshyn, 2003, 2007), and we review that controversy.

FUNCTIONS OF IMAGERY

What purposes might be served by the ability to recreate one's previous perceptual experiences (such as remembering your fifth-grade teacher's face), or to create new ones (e.g., imagining your dog or cat wearing a hat)? Kosslyn, Seger, Pani, and Hillger (1990) had people keep diaries in which they recorded experiences of imagery in their ordinary activities. The participants reported that imagery accompanied four different sorts of activities: (1) accessing information in memory; (2) reasoning; (3) learning new skills; and (4) comprehending verbal messages. For example, one participant reported imaging his house as he was describing it to a friend; another reported mentally rehearsing how to ask a boss for a raise. While images were reported in all sense modalities, most reported images were visual. Let us examine in more depth the ways in which mental imagery influences cognitive processing.

Imagery in Memory

Imagery can be invoked for several purposes. First, a person might have a stored representation of a perceptual object or event that can be retrieved from memory in order to answer a question (this may be especially useful in recalling information that is difficult to recall verbally). Two examples were questions A and B in Box 7.1, where you were asked about the color of peas versus Christmas trees, and the height of the horse's tail. The original information was received through the senses, and it seems to most people that answering those questions is based on recall of visual information. People report that they *see* the color of the pea, and then *compare* it to that of the Christmas tree. The experience is reported to be much like what would happen if the objects were actually in front of them, and available to be examined. There is also much evidence that studying nonperceptual information using imagery can help people to remember that information (such as words).

As we saw in Chapter 3, one method for memorizing words or pairs of words is through *mnemonics*, which comes from the Greek word meaning "to remember." Many mnemonic methods depend on imagery, and results of numerous studies (e.g., Bower, 1970; Carney & Levin, 1998a, 1998b; Patten, 1972; Wang, Thomas, & Ouellette, 1992) have shown that memory is much better for material that has been encoded using imagery, compared to when verbal techniques are used (e.g., rehearsing the items verbally).

Imagery in Reasoning

Imagery also seems to be an important component in many different sorts of reasoning processes. Question C in Box 7.1 presented one type of reasoning task that many people claim to carry out using imagery. This task tests the ability to make a *transitive inference*, which is drawing a conclusion about how objects are ordered along some dimension. The information in the problem does not directly lay out the answer; the person must *deduce* the answer, or reason it out, from the information presented in the problem. The simple transitive inference task in Box 7.1 involves putting people along a dimension of smartness. People report that when they solve such a problem, they imagine a line, and put the people in their respective places on it (Hummel & Holyoak, 2001). They then use that information to see the answer to the question.

Thinking about perceptual or spatial information also involves imagery. As in Question D, one can imagine objects or events in the world (e.g., the capital letter N), and one can imagine the outcomes of operations, such as rotation, on these events (e.g., where the N is rotated to see a Z). One can also imagine complex scenes, such as the layout of the rooms in your house or apartment. You can "walk" through your dwelling in your imagination, and "see" the various objects in their places in order to answer questions about the relative locations of the various objects (Kosslyn, Thompson, & Ganis, 2006). People also appear to construct mental maps based on a verbal description of a building or town. For example, Denis (2008) found that people who heard a verbal description of a spatial layout used an image to make distance judgments (also see Péruch, Chabanne, Nesa, Thinus-Blanc, & Denis, 2006a, b).

Learning and Comprehension

There is evidence that practicing some activity using imagery can improve performance (Kosslyn & Koenig, 1995). For example, using one's imagination to practice correct form while shooting a basketball may help one improve one's shot. Others have found that mental practice playing an instrument improves performance in both adults (Pascual-Leone, 2003) and children (Humphreys, 1986).

Imagery has also been used in therapy sessions to help overcome phobias and anxiety (e.g., Kim, 2008; Lazarus & Abramovitz, 2004). For example, patients with post-traumatic stress disorder (PTSD) often suffer from nightmares in which they relive a trauma. While awake, they are trained to image better endings to the traumatic dreams, and told to rehearse the images every day until the nightmare declines (Krakow, 2004; Krakow et al., 2000; Moore & Krakow, 2007).

Study of Imagery: A Brief History

Asking people to report on the functions of imagery may seem like a straightforward way to answer the question of how we use imagery. However, the history of research on imagery has been filled with controversy. As was introduced in Chapter 1, in the early years of psychology, there was a dispute first over whether all thought was conducted with mental imagery (Humphrey, 1951; Mandler & Mandler, 1964) and then over whether imagery could even be the subject of scientific study because of the subjective nature of images (Watson, 1913). More recently, as cognitive scientists have adopted new scientific techniques that allow us to study imagery more objectively, there has been additional controversy over whether information can actually be stored in a picture format, and then retrieved as an image which must be reperceived (Pylyshyn, 1973, 1981, 2003, 2007). One could say that we have gone in recent years from the *mystery* of imagery to the *problem* of imagery as a form of mental representation. Methodological and technological advances have helped cognitive scientists to begin to solve the problem of how imagery works and to consider the functions that it might serve.

Early Research in Imagery: The Method of Self-Report

Galton (1883) is usually credited with being the first investigator to attempt to study imagery. He asked a number of individuals to recall their breakfast table, and to describe their experience. Some people reported vivid imagery of breakfast, while others denied experiencing any imagery at all. Although Galton's *findings* might strike one as interesting, and perhaps of potential importance for understanding cognition, his subjective *method* was looked upon as raising problems for the study of imagery. Simply asking people to report their subjective experiences, as we have already seen in Chapter 1, raises problems of verification: How could Galton determine whether a person's report was accurate? The fact that a person *feels confident* that he or she experienced an image in response to a question about breakfast does not mean that that feeling is *accurate*. This problem of building a science on unverifiable results plagued the study of imagery until new methods were developed, some 75+ years after Galton.

The introspectionist psychologists such as Wundt and Titchener (see Chapter 1) were also interested in mental imagery. Their methods were different than Galton's, because they were interested in analyzing consciousness into its basic elements through the method of introspection. As with Galton's research, the introspectionists found differences among participants in their reports concerning imagery: People differed in whether they reported that all, some, or none of their thinking was conducted with imagery. Those differences became the basis for what is known as the *imageless thought* controversy: a disagreement over whether or not thought could occur without imagery of any kind (Humphrey, 1951; Mandler & Mandler, 1964; Thomas, 2008). It should also be noted that even though introspection was based on reports of trained observers, it was still based on people's subjective reports, which is the same problem that plagued Galton.

Behaviorism's Questions About Subjective Reports

As we saw in Chapter 1, Watson (1919), one of the earliest behaviorists, raised questions about collecting subjective reports as a scientific method. Watson reminded psychologists that in no other science was there a reliance on unverifiable reports as data.

> "Prove to me," [the behaviorist] says, "that you have auditory images, visual images, or any other kind of disembodied processes. So far I have only your unverified and unsupported word that you have them." Science must have objective evidence to base its theories upon. (p. 248)

Watson proposed that psychology pattern its methods after those in other sciences, such as physics and chemistry, where the only results of interest were those that all observers could measure for themselves. Because one's inner thoughts (including images) cannot be directly observed by an experimenter, they have no place in science. For 50 years following Watson's critique, researchers generally ignored imagery as a phenomenon of study. The modern resurgence in research on imagery began with the examination of imagery's role in facilitating memory. Thus, in order to trace the development of the study of imagery in modern cognitive psychology, it is necessary to examine briefly what had happened to the study of memory over the first half of the 20th century.

Research in Memory: CVCs to Verbal Mediators

As we know, Ebbinghaus (1885/1964) invented the CVC (consonant-vowel-consonant string, or nonsense syllable; see Chapters 1 and 3) to study memory without the burden of using words that already had meaningful associations. However, researchers who followed after Ebbinghaus soon discovered that CVCs themselves were not completely without associations; and the meaning provided by those associations could affect how CVCs were learned and recalled. In an early study of memory for CVCs, Müller (1911; cited in Woodworth & Schlossberg, 1954) examined situations in which CVCs were memorized easily, based on what he called "spontaneous associations." Sometimes a CVC would suggest a familiar word, which made memory better. For example, if you were a participant in a memory study and received the trigram XIT, it would be easy to remember if you remembered it as "eXcITe." Also, participants' knowledge was used sometimes to construct links among the to-be-recalled items, and in other ways to relate the material to what was already known (e.g., if XIT was followed by MOV, you might be tempted to remember "eXcITing MOVie"). The discovery of spontaneous associations during the memorization of CVCs led to the question of how to measure the meaningfulness of those meaningless units.

Measuring Meaningfulness

In an early attempt to measure the meaningfulness of CVCs, Glaze (1928) asked participants to report whether a given syllable conveyed any meaning, and found large differences in meaningfulness. Consider TAK versus XOL: TAK, which suggests a word, seems obviously more meaningful than XOL. Glaze also tried to memorize CVCs of low meaningfulness (examples are KYH, QUJ, and XIW), and found it very difficult. Meaningfulness of a set of CVCs can also be measured by asking participants to produce words as associations to each of them (Noble, 1961); CVCs that produce more responses are more meaningful. For example, JOK would probably produce more associations (joke, joker, jock, etc.) than XUD. Both measures of meaningfulness—subjective ratings and number of associative responses to a trigram—turned out to be highly correlated, so researchers used one or the other.

Numerous studies showed that stimuli high in meaningfulness (such words as *country*, *window*, *building*, *street*, and *garden*) are easier to recall than low-meaningful stimuli (such words as *reply*, *journal*, *promise*, *matter*, and *question*; Paivio, 1971, Ch. 8). It was hypothesized that the reason for the memory advantage of high meaningfulness words is that they have a richer network of *associations* that can serve as retrieval links to the to-be-recalled words. Those associations that fill in connections among stimuli are called *mediators*, since they serve to *go between*, or *mediate between*, the items. (See Paivio, 1971, Chapter 8, for discussion.) A demonstration of the usefulness of verbal mediators in memory is presented in Box 7.2; please carry out that demonstration before reading further.

BOX 7.2 BOWER AND CLARK (1969) SERIAL-RECALL DEMONSTRATION

Have a paper and pencil ready. Study the following list of words so that you can recall the words in order, **by making up a story to link one word to the next**. After you have made up the story, write the list in order from memory.

telephone

brush

tree

woman

lamp

bottle

plant

shoe

paper

clock

Verbal Mediators in Memory

A study by Bower and Clark (1969; presented in Box 7.2) provided strong evidence for the positive role of verbal mediation in serial recall for lists of nouns. One group of participants was told simply to learn each list so that they would be able to recall the words in order of presentation. A second group was instructed to make up a story to link the nouns in each list, in a technique known as *narrative chaining*. A total of 12 different lists was presented, with the participants in both groups learning each list perfectly before the next list was presented. After the twelfth list, the participants were asked to recall words from all the lists, and those who had used stories to encode the lists recalled 6 to 7 times as many words, as shown in Figure 7.1.

Studying verbal mediation led researchers to the examination of more-complex processes involved in encoding, storing, and retrieving information in memory. The ultimate result of investigators' interest in meaningfulness of CVCs was the conclusion that internal representations could influence our memory, even for material that was designed to be meaningless (such as trigrams). Semantic associations were then

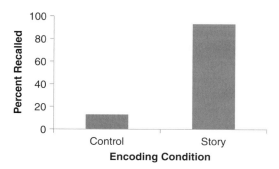

Figure 7.1   Results of Bower and Clark (1969) study of constructing stories as an encoding strategy.

found to affect memory for all sorts of verbal materials, including organized lists of words, paragraphs, and stories (e.g., Bower & Clark, 1969; for review see Paivio, 1971, 1991).

Imagery Makes a Comeback: Dual–Coding Theory

In addition to meaningfulness, *concreteness* was found to influence memory for words (e.g., Paivio, 1971). People can rate the concreteness of words, where *highly concrete* words refer to tangible objects in the world (e.g., *table*, *car*), while *low concrete* (or *abstract*) words refer to nonphysical things, like *truth* and *faith*. Studies of memory for different types of words showed that high-concrete words were much easier to recall than low-concrete ones (Paivio, 1963, 1965; Yarmey & O'Neill, 1969a, 1969b). In Box 7.3, you will rate words on two dimensions, employing a technique used by researchers to measure both concreteness and a related dimension—imageability.

The work of Paivio in the 1960s led to the realization that not only verbal associations, but also visual images could serve as mediators and influence memory processes (see Paivio, 1971, 1991, 2006 for summaries). Paivio reasoned that the concreteness ratings of words were actually indirect indicators of how easy it was to image a word's meaning. The possible importance of imagery in memory had been noted by the ancient Greeks and Romans (Luria, 1968; Yates, 1966—recall our discussion of the *method of loci* from Chapter 3), but Paivio's work provided a technique by which the imageability of words could be measured (see Box 7.3). He proposed that the imagery value of a stimulus could be measured in the same way as meaningfulness and concreteness were measured. Paivio, Yuille, and Madigan (1968) provided people with a long list of nouns and asked them to try to produce an image of the referent and rate how easy it was to do that using a 1–7 scale, with 1 indicating "not easy to image" and 7 "highly imageable." Those imageability ratings were then used by researchers to construct lists of high- and low-imageability words that could be used to study memory. In Paivio's view, those ratings allowed researchers to establish an objective basis for the study of imagery (also see Cortese & Fugett, 2004). Perhaps more importantly, Paivio also proposed a theory—*dual coding theory*—that attempted to explain how imagery might function in learning and memory.

BOX 7.3 RATING CONCRETENESS AND IMAGERY

Rate each word below on the following scales.

Concreteness: A *concrete* word refers to something in the environment, like *car*.

Abstractness: An *abstract* word refers to something that is not in the physical world, such as *conscience*.

Rate the concreteness of each word in the list below, using this scale. Put the rating in the "Concreteness" column for each word.

Concrete   *Abstract*
  1   2   3   4   5   6   7

Imagery: Rate how easy it is to image the reference of the word, using this scale. Put the rating in the "Ease of Imagery" column for each word.

Easy to image   *Difficult*
  1   2   3   4   5   6   7

Word	Concreteness	Ease of Imagery
Table	____	____
Emotion	____	____
Certainty	____	____
Pencil	____	____
Soul	____	____
Agreement	____	____
Finger	____	____
Personality	____	____
Brain	____	____
Lamp	____	____
Furniture	____	____
Lawyer	____	____
Book	____	____

Dual Coding Theory

Paivio (1963, 1965, 1971) proposed that highly concrete words, such as *squirrel*, were easier to recall because such words could be encoded in two ways: through verbal associations and through imagery. Abstract words such as *freedom*, on the other hand, did not produce images easily, so they were typically encoded using only verbal associations. This meant that there were two possible encodings in memory for concrete words, versus only one for abstract words. All other things being equal (e.g., equal frequency of the words), memory should be better for concrete words, because such words benefitted from *dual coding*.

Paivio (1971) raised the possibility that many results from earlier memory experiments might have been due to the participants' uncontrolled use of imagery. For example, when Bower and Clark (1969; see Box 7.2) asked participants to construct stories by stringing together a list of words, the story group might have recalled many more words because of the use of imagery rather than the verbalized stories per se. Participants might have been forming visual images of the scenes they were describing, and that those *images* might have facilitated recall, not the stories themselves. This suggestion required a reanalysis of many classic memory studies, to consider the possibility that nonverbal imagery might have been used during encoding.

Evidence for Imagery in Cognition

Paivio and other researchers then began to produce evidence for the use of imagery in cognition in two separate areas: (1) the use of imagery to facilitate memory, and (2) the use of pictorial representations to make judgments about objects. Both lines of research paved the way for enhanced study of the role that visual images play in cognition (as we shall see in the second half of this chapter).

Imagery in Memory

A number of different methods were used to demonstrate the uses of nonverbal imagery in memory, several of which closely parallel those used to study verbal mediation. First, people often report having used imagery after having studied and recalled material in a memory experiment, and those reports are most common when participants have been asked to learn concrete words or material (Paivio, 1971, 1991). We already saw in Chapter 3 that memory performance can be greatly enhanced by instructing participants to use mnemonic techniques that rely on the use of imagery (e.g., Ross & Lawrence, 1968; Wollen, Weber, & Lowry, 1972). Wallace, Turner, and Perkins (1957) gave participants pairs of concrete nouns to learn, such as *hat-lion* and *ham-whiskey*, and instructed them to form a mental picture connecting the two members of each pair. Different groups of participants studied from 25 to 700 word pairs. Participants studied the pairs only once, at their own speed. Memory for each pair was tested by presenting the left-hand word as a cue and asking for recall of the other word in the pair. Cued recall performance was consistently excellent, with perfect recall for up to 300 pairs, and 95% performance for 700 pairs. This study is impressive evidence for the effectiveness of instructions to use imagery, and it supports the dual-coding prediction that high-imageability stimuli are easier to remember. Research indicates that mnemonic methods using imagery are very effective in facilitating memory for various sorts of materials.

Imagery in Other Cognitive Functioning

Other research by Paivio, not focused specifically on memory, also suggested that thinking can take place in two modalities—visual and verbal. As one example, Paivio (1975) presented people with pairs of stimuli (names or pictures of animals and physical objects) and asked them to make judgments about which item in the pair was larger in real life. Each pair of stimuli consisted of either two words (e.g., SCREW

ELEPHANT) or two pictures (e.g., pictures of a screw and an elephant). In addition, the sizes of the presented stimuli were either congruent with their relative sizes in real life (e.g., the word ELEPHANT appeared in a larger font than SCREW, or the picture of the elephant appeared larger than the screw; refer to Figure 7.2a), or incongruent with their actual relative sizes (e.g., the picture of the screw was depicted as larger than the picture of the elephant, and the font for SCREW was larger than the font for ELEPHANT). As can be seen in Figure 7.2b, judgments based on incongruent pictures led to longer response times (RTs) than congruent pictures, but size congruency had no effect on response times when words were presented.

Paivio (1975) hypothesized that, in order to make judgments about the relative sizes of objects, people retrieved an image of each object that was visually and spatially analogous to that object's depictions in real life. In the Incongruent-Picture condition,

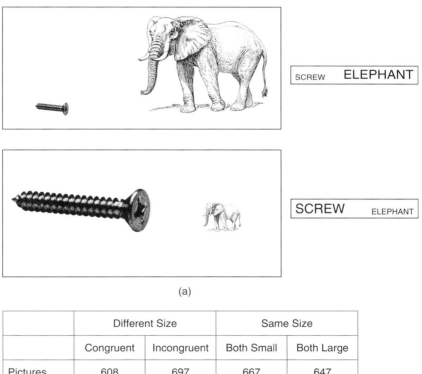

(a)

	Different Size		Same Size	
	Congruent	Incongruent	Both Small	Both Large
Pictures	608	697	667	647
Words	803	800	855	842

(b)

Figure 7.2 (a) Examples of congruent (top row) and incongruent (bottom row) physical-size and memory-size relations for picture and word pairs used in Paivio's (1975) experiment. (b) Paivio's results (reaction time in milliseconds).
Adapted from Paivio, 1975, Table 3.

since the picture before them was *in*consistent with their imagistic representation of relative size, this led to interference between the pictures and people's images, resulting in longer RT. However, in the word conditions, people had to access a pictorial code independently of the font of the words, and since they then imaged the objects depicted by those words, the size of the font itself had no significant impact on RT. Thus, Paivio argued that people were generating visual images, and using these visual codes to answer questions concerning the relative sizes of objects. However, when asked (in a separate experiment) to make judgments about which of two words was easier to *pronounce*, size congruency or incongruency had no effect in either the picture or word condition, because *pronounceability* is a verbal characteristic.

In sum, Paivio's experiments supported a distinction between verbal and visual codes, and showed how each code can be made more or less important by task requirements. Imagistic representations are important when deciding on relative size; verbal codes are needed to answer questions about ease of pronounceability.

Imagery and the Dual Coding Hypothesis: Conclusions

Results of numerous research studies on memory are consistent with Paivio's dual-coding hypothesis in suggesting that participants often form images while studying materials (Paivio, 1971). Dual coding theory is still influential in the area of imagery and memory (Binder, 2007; Campos & Alonso-Quecuty, 2006; Kanske & Kotz, 2007; Kuo & Hooper, 2004) and other areas, such as language comprehension (Duthie, Nippold, Billow, & Mansfield, 2008). Most importantly, it appears that both verbal and visual codes can be used in reasoning and judgment tasks. When visual judgments are required, information is recalled in a visual form; when verbal judgments are needed, a verbal code is used (Paivio, 1975). Although the theory is not without its critics (e.g., Marschark & Hunt, 1989; for review see Paivio, 1991, 2006), Paivio's research is also important for its historical significance; that is, for the influence his ideas had on the broader development of cognitive psychology.

Imagery Ratings and the Problem of Subjective Reports

Although Paivio's research endeavors yielded impressive results as to the role of images in memory, imageability ratings are still subjective, because they ask how easy it is for a person to image a word's meaning. Subsequent experimenters, such as Shepard (e.g., Shepard, 1978; Shepard & Metzler, 1971) and Kosslyn (e.g., Kosslyn, 1973, 1975, 1976; Kosslyn, Ball, & Reiser, 1978), developed new methods of studying imagery that provided more-objective behavioral evidence in support of the occurrence of imagery.

SHEPARD'S STUDIES OF MENTAL IMAGERY

Concurrent with Paivio's (1971) work on the role of imagery in memory, Shepard and his coworkers (e.g., Cooper & Shepard, 1973; Shepard & Metzler, 1971) were carrying out studies that supported the claim that imagery was important in other cognitive processes. A series of studies examined *mental rotation* skills. Before reading further, please carry out the task in Box 7.4, which is based on an experiment by Shepard and Metzler (1971).

BOX 7.4 DEMONSTRATION OF SHEPARD'S ROTATION STUDY

For each pair of items, determine whether the two items are identical or not.

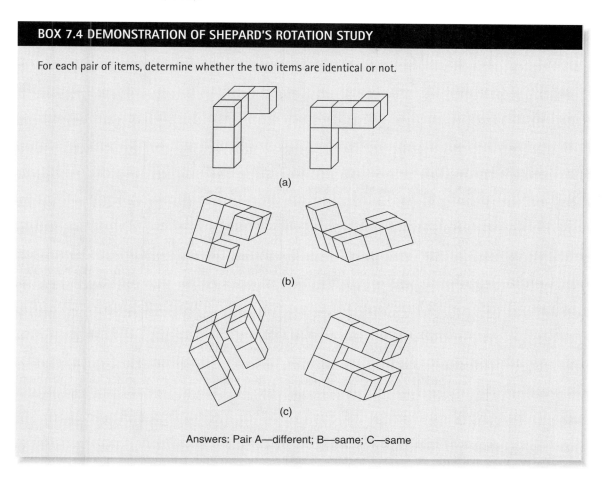

(a)

(b)

(c)

Answers: Pair A—different; B—same; C—same

Mental Rotation

Participants in the Shepard and Metzler (1971) study were presented with pairs of visual stimuli of various sorts, and asked to determine whether the two stimuli in each pair were identical or different. The results, shown in Figure 7.3, indicated that, the larger the angle of rotation between the stimuli, the longer was the response time. To explain that relation between angle of rotation and response time, Shepard and Metzler (1971) proposed that the stimuli had to be brought into alignment before a judgment could be made. That is, one of the stimuli had to be *mentally rotated*, until the two stimuli appeared to be lined up, and then the two stimuli were judged to be *same* or *different*. The relation between the angle of rotation and response time was explained by assuming that the internal or mental rotation was carried out at a constant rate of speed. A

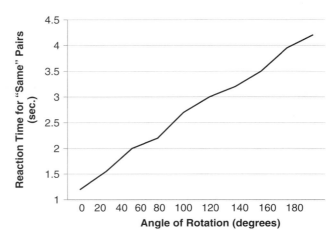

Figure 7.3 Shepard and Metzler's (1971) rotation study results.

larger angle would therefore require more rotation time before the two stimuli could be brought into correspondence to make the same/different judgment. This explanation assumed that a basic process in the comparison task was a *mental action* that entailed rotating one of the stimuli to see if it matched the other. If we examine the results in Figure 7.3 carefully, it appears to take people, on average, 3 seconds longer to answer the question when the stimuli were separated by 180 degrees of rotation versus when the difference was 0 degrees. This means that imagined rotation was carried out at a speed of about 60 degrees per second (Shepard and Metzler, 1971). Thus, researchers could measure the speed with which a person could carry out an act in the imagination.

Similar results were obtained using other types of stimuli. For example, Cooper and Shepard (1973) presented people with a single letter or number, and had them judge whether the stimulus was printed normally or backward (see Figure 7.4 for letter stimuli). The stimuli were presented at various angles relative to vertical position, and the RT to make a judgment about each stimulus was measured. Response times were a function of the angle at which the stimulus was presented. As the stimulus was rotated away from vertical, RT increased, with the maximum RT occurring when the stimulus was presented at an angle of 180 degrees (i.e., upside down). One explanation for this finding is that, in order to determine whether the stimulus is normal or backwards, the person has to compare it with his or her mental representation of a normal stimulus, say the letter Q. That normal representation is vertical, since that is the orientation in which letters and numbers are typically encountered. The greater the degree of rotation away from vertical, the longer a person needs to mentally rotate the test stimulus to Q vertical position, so it can be compared with the representation that the person has in memory.

Projecting Images into the World

The mental-rotation studies provided quantitative evidence that people were carrying out mental operations on information that involved visual-spatial manipulation. Other

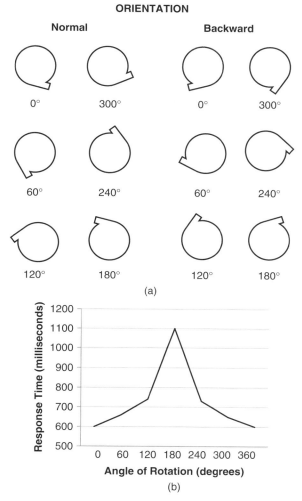

Figure 7.4   Cooper and Shepard (1973) study of judgments concerning rotated letters. (a) Examples of letter stimuli. (b) Cooper and Shepard (1973) results.

studies examined people's processing of the visual and spatial properties of mental images. Podgorny and Shepard (1978) devised a method whereby it became possible for people to "project" their images into the world, so they could be used in tasks in the way that perceptual objects can be. The participants were shown a blank grid, and they were asked to either (a) *watch* as a block letter was actually printed on the grid (perceptual condition), as in Figure 7.5a, or (b) *imagine* a block letter projected onto the grid (imagined condition), as in Figure 7.5b. They were then asked whether an actual dot projected onto the grid fell on a square that was part of the letter. In both the perceptual and imagined conditions, the amount of time to respond to the dot was

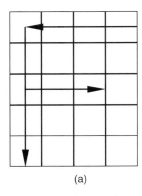 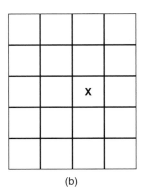

(a) (b)

Figure 7.5 Podgorny and Shepard (1978) study of judgments concerning images versus perceptual stimuli. (a) Block letter *printed* or *imagined*. (b) Stimulus presented. (c) Participant responds: Is the "X" on a square covered by the letter? (Answer is "Yes.")

a function of the position of the dot relative to the letter: RT was fastest when the dot fell *within* the figure. Also, when a dot fell in an empty cell, the farther away that cell was from the letter, the faster participants were to respond "no," and this too occurred in both the perceptual and imagined conditions. Thus, participants in the imagined condition seemed to be using a pictorial code to make judgments about dot placement, which was parallel to the code that they used for judgments in the perceptual condition.

Conclusions

The research of Shepard and his coworkers on mental rotation and projection provided evidence that images played a role in human cognition that was analogous to that played by perception. That is, images seem to maintain some of the visual properties of the scenes or objects that they represent. In addition, images play a role in thought similar to that played by objects in perception. Shepard's work also provided objective evidence for the existence of internal images and their function in cognition.

STUDYING AND MEASURING IMAGERY

The pioneering work of Paivio (1971, 2006) and Shepard (Cooper & Shepard, 1973; Podgorny & Shepard, 1978; Shepard & Metzler, 1971) stimulated other researchers to investigate further the structure and functioning of images. Research carried out by Stephen Kosslyn and his colleagues (e.g., Kosslyn, 1973, 1975, 1976; Kosslyn, Ball, & Reiser, 1978) provided much evidence concerning the characteristics of images and their usefulness in various sorts of cognitive tasks. Kosslyn was the first researcher to provide a detailed theory of how images might be generated and used by people, and has also extensively investigated the role of brain systems in imagery (e.g., Kosslyn, Behrmann, & Jeannerod, 1995; Kosslyn, Maljkovic, Hamilton, Horwitz, & Thompson, 1995).

IMAGERY AND PERCEPTION: THE ANALOGUE VIEW

One of the most important developments to arise out of the modern work on imagery was an emphasis on the idea that imagery and perception were closely related activities, and that *images* served a causal function in *mental processing* similar to that served by *objects* in *perceptual processing*. The main difference between imagery and perception is that in perception, the processing system is activated by an external stimulus in the world. In imagery, the activation comes from a mental representation of an object or scene that we have stored in memory. However, the central components of processing are assumed to be similar in imagery and perception. The idea that imagery and perception are closely related is not a new one; it can be traced back at least to Aristotle (*De Anima*, 350 B.C.).

Kosslyn (1980) developed a comprehensive theory in which he proposed that the images we generate are analogous to pictures in the way that they depict visual and spatial information. When we take in visual information, it is stored so that the visual characteristics (color, shape, etc.) and spatial relations among the parts are easily retrieved. This is not to say that an exact duplicate of a visual stimulus or scene is stored; details can be lost or some spatial information misrepresented (Kosslyn & Chabris, 1993). The image representation is thus more like a *quasi-picture* (Kosslyn, 1980; Tye, 1991), in that an image *functions* as if it has visual and spatial characteristics. That is, an image of your mother seems to represent her as being three-dimensional (rather than a 2-D drawing), even though the image itself is not three-dimensional. Given its seeming tri-dimensionality, you can mentally rotate the image of your mother, so that, when she is viewed from the side, it is analogous to having a person in front of you turned to the side. We will refer to Kosslyn's theory and others related to it as the *Quasi-Picture* view of imagery.

Furthermore, Kosslyn's (1980) theory proposes that processing of both images and objects or scenes is carried out by the same sensory, attentional, and working-memory (WM) systems. Although most of the research has examined visual imagery, the same equivalence applies in other domains. Thus, if one were imagining someone singing a song, the auditory processing system would be active; imagining the smell of coffee would involve the olfactory system; and so on. The ability to create images comes about because people store information about appearances of stimulus events, which can be used to generate images. This view proposed that images are *analogues* of perceptual experiences: *They are constructed out of similar information and are processed using similar parts of the cognitive system*.

In order to explain how humans generate and manipulate images, Kosslyn (1980) used the analogy of how a computer generates an image on the screen of its monitor. In the memory of the computer, there is a graphics program of some sort. This program takes information from the computer's memory and uses it as the basis for carrying out operations that result in lines and colors being projected on the screen, which results in our seeing a graphic of some sort. There is no picture, per se, in the computer's memory; rather, there is information that can be used by the appropriate program to generate a picture. For example, there could be instructions for how to construct an image from its elemental parts. Once this graphic is generated, it is now an object that can be scanned by an observer, say, to determine if there is a right angle in it. Kosslyn assumed that humans also possess something like an internal "monitor screen," on which an image is "projected." We can then "examine" the image, and answer questions about it, which can sometimes result in our discovering something new about the object in question, such as whether a horse's tail is below its rear knees (see Box 7.1). Laeng and Teodorescu (2002) determined that people's eye movements when examining an image are similar to their eye movements when examining the same object in vision. This supports the hypothesis that the cognitive processes used to mentally examine images are analogous to the processes that function when vision is used to examine a physical object.

If there is such an internal screen, then, in Kosslyn's view, the images we create should be subject to limitations of that screen. For example, the internal screen must have a definite size, which should put a limit to how big an image can be, as well as a limit to how much detail can be projected in an image. This analysis of images is summarized in Figure 7.6. Based on our encounters with the world, we have perceptually based information stored in memory. To generate an image, we retrieve information from long-term memory (LTM) about what something looks like and transfer that information to visual working memory. The information in the visual working memory can then be operated on further—for example, through scanning or rotational

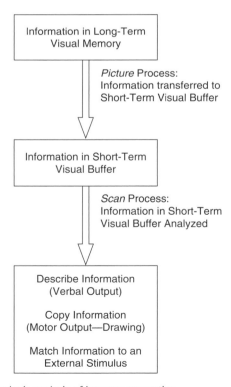

Figure 7.6 Sketch of Kosslyn's analysis of imagery generation.

processes. Kosslyn hypothesized that we could zoom in on details of the image and determine if it contains a specific part, such as whether a German Shepherd has pointed ears (Kosslyn, 2003). As a further example, I can ask you if someone we saw yesterday was wearing a hat, which can be answered using this process. You are also able to use the information in visual working memory to answer questions about an object or scene, to describe what you experienced, and to draw it. Kosslyn and co-workers designed many experiments that tested various aspects of this proposed mechanism of image formation and processing.

Finke (1989), a former student of Kosslyn, synopsized five principles illustrating how visual images and percepts are *functionally* analogous. First, Finke proposed that images are *perceptually* equivalent to pictures. As we examine an image we have generated, it seems to have shape, size, and physical characteristics in the same way that a picture of an object or scene, or the object or scene itself, would contain those physical characteristics. In an early study by Perky (1910), people were asked to imagine an object, such as a leaf, in the middle of a blank screen. Perky then projected a faint patch of color (e.g., green) in the appropriate shape onto that screen. All of her subjects thought that the projection was actually part of their image, and several added details that they described, such as the veins of the leaf. Similarly, Farah (1985) found that people could more easily detect a faint letter (e.g., an H) projected on a screen if they had already been imaging that same letter.

A second principle (Finke, 1989) is that images have *spatial* equivalence to pictures or objects. If one images a map of the United States, then California will be depicted to the west (or left) of Nevada, and Pennsylvania will be to the north of (or above) Maryland, in the same spatial relations that these states have to each other on an actual map. Spatial equivalence should also mean that if people scan across an image, scanning times will take longer for longer distances (in the same way as they take longer to rotate images based on the degree of rotation). How do we know that North Carolina is below Maryland in our mental map? In some cases, we may have been trying to memorize the capitals of each state, but did not deliberately pay attention to the spatial relationships of the states. However, as a result of having stored a picture-like representation of the United States, you engaged in *implicit—unintentional—spatial encoding* of the general location of each of the states. This implicit encoding of spatial information is another of Finke's (1989) principles. Thus, you can recover spatial information even if you did not deliberately attend to all the specific spatial relations at the time of encoding. (In Chapter 3, we discussed a similar view, presented by Hasher and Zacks (1979), concerning automatic encoding of spatial and other sorts of information into memory.)

A fourth principle (Finke, 1989) is that images have *transformational* equivalence to percepts; we mentally manipulate, rotate, and scan images in the same fashion as we do pictures, objects, or scenes. As we saw from some of the rotation experiments carried out by Shepard and his coworkers (Cooper & Shepard, 1973; Shepard & Metzler, 1971), people can rotate images in a way similar to how they would manipulate an actual object in front of them, with longer RT linked to longer rotation angles.

When one encodes and retrieves pictorial information, the resulting image will have *structural* equivalence to the actual object or scene—the fifth of Finke's (1989) principles. That is, the integrity of the shape and details of an object will be maintained (e.g., a German Shepherd will have pointed ears), and the spatial relations of the object parts will mirror the object itself (e.g., the head of the German Shepherd will be above the body, and the tail at the end opposite the head).

More recently, researchers have also presented evidence for neurological similarity of imaging and seeing, as brain-imaging studies have confirmed that both processes activate overlapping cortical areas (e.g., Ganis, Thompson, & Kosslyn, 2004; Goldenberg, Steiner, Podreka, & Deecke, 1992; Kosslyn et al., 1993; Kosslyn, Thompson, & Alpert, 1997; Kosslyn, Thompson, Sukel, & Alpert, 2005).

Kosslyn and his coworkers have presented much evidence to support the theory outlined in Figure 7.6.

Image Scanning: Distance and Size

In one set of experiments, participants were asked to memorize a map of an island (Kosslyn, Ball, & Reiser, 1978), shown in Figure 7.7a, which contained various landmarks on it, such as a boat on a beach, a tree, a house, and a windmill. The people studied the map until they could draw the locations of the various objects on a blank map within a quarter-inch of their correct locations. Participants were asked to remember the map, and to focus on one landmark in the image. They were then asked whether a second landmark was on the map (on half of the trials, the second item was present). If the object was there, they were to imagine a dot moving from the first to the second item, and they were to respond when the dot reached the second landmark. Of interest were the scanning times as they related to the map distance between the pairs of objects. As seen in Figure 7.7b, the time to scan the image was linearly related to the distance between the objects on the map, presumably because visualizing the dot moving across the image involves movement across distance at a constant rate of speed, in the same way it would take us more time in vision to scan a long distance than a short one. Those results were taken as evidence that the relative spatial distance among objects in an actual picture or scene are represented in images.

Kosslyn (1975, Experiment 5) also examined the influence of the size at which an image was imagined on how easy it was to imagine the object in the first place and, once the object had been imagined, to answer questions about its parts. Again, the logic of the study is based on the computer image–generation metaphor: if an object is imagined large, then it should contain more detail than the same object imagined small, just as when we see something large versus small. Analogously, when an object is close to us and occupies more of our visual field, we see more details than when the object is perceived as smaller and farther away. Because closer (and larger) images should contain more detail, it should take longer to generate them, but less time to answer questions about *specific features* of that large object, because the details are already present in the image.

For example, imaging a pinecone up close allows us to notice the characteristic segments that make up the cone. If the pinecone is imaged small, however, as if far away, the individual segments are not readily accessible. To answer questions about specific details of small images, one should have to mentally "zoom in" to make those details visible. Kosslyn (1975) controlled the size of people's imagined objects by having the participant imagine each object within the boundaries of a square, such as those

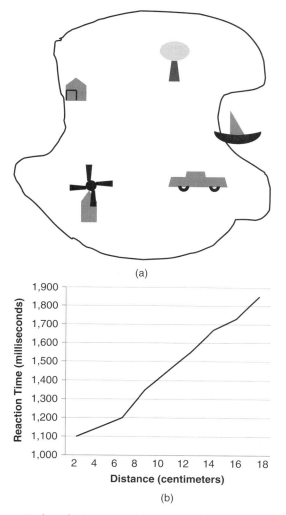

(a)

(b)

Figure 7.7 Kosslyn et al.'s (1978) island task. (a) Stimulus. (b) Time to scan between all pairs of locations on the imaged map.

shown in Figure 7.8a. Participants had been given familiarization with squares of four sizes. On each trial, the experimenter named an object, such as a *rabbit*, and told the participant which square it was to be imagined in. Participants signaled when they felt that they had imagined the object as requested, which provided a measure of how long it took for image generation. They were then asked a question about some part of the object ("Does it have a nose?").

Several results are of interest. First, it took longer to generate images of the *large* objects, as shown in Figure 7.8b, which supports the idea that time is required to add more details when imagining an object in large format. However, it took participants

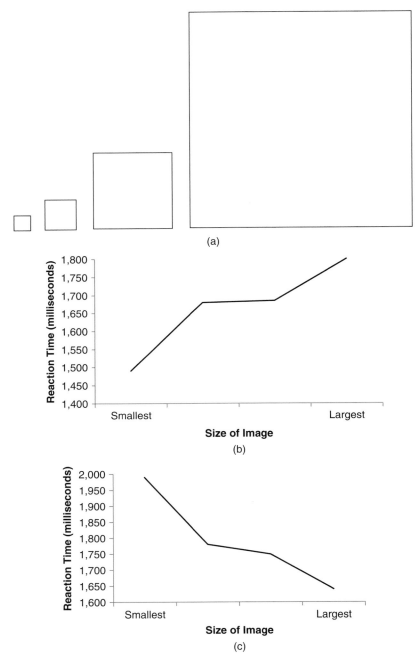

Figure 7.8 Kosslyn's (1975, Experiment 5) study examining generation of images at different sizes. (a) Rectangles for imaging. Starting with the leftmost square, each square is one-sixth of the area of the square to its right. In the experiment, each side of the largest square measured 14 cm. (b) Time to generate images, based on size. (c) Time to evaluate properties of images of different sizes.

longer to answer questions about the parts of *smaller* objects, as shown in Figure 7.8c, consistent with additional time needed to zoom in and to both generate and examine the details of the smaller images.

The characteristics of imagined objects also influence how easy they are to remember. Kosslyn and Alper (1977) tested recall of imagined objects. Participants were given high-imageability word pairs (e.g., *radio-mug*), and told to either image each item at normal relative size or to image the second object as very tiny. They were then administered a surprise cued recall test for the word pairs, in which one of the two words in a pair was randomly presented and people had to recall the second. Kosslyn and Alper found worse average recall for word pairs that had contained objects imagined at small sizes, than for word pairs in which each object in the pair had been imagined at its correct size. These results can be explained by assuming that when an object was imaged as tiny, it was more difficult to identify, which led to worse memory for the word pair. It is similar to looking at a photograph in which there is a very small object. Just as one would not be able to see what that item was in enough detail to encode or remember it, one would have trouble seeing a very small object in an image.

Measuring Generation of Images

Kosslyn, Cave, Provost, and von Gierke (1988) have also measured the steps involved in creation of an image. Kosslyn and colleagues used information about the way that people write letters to make predictions about how they would construct images of those letters. Before reading further, please take a pencil and write an uppercase *C*, in block letter form, in Figure 7.9a, paying attention to the order in which you draw the lines. Write the *C* now.

Most people write the letter by first drawing the top horizontal line, from right to left; followed by the vertical line, from top to bottom; and then the horizontal line on the bottom, from left to right; as shown in Figure 7.9b. Kosslyn and his colleagues assumed that people would construct the image in parts by mentally constructing it in the same way that they would write it. If so, then certain components of the letter should become available in imagination before others. In order to measure when the parts of an image were available in imagination, participants in the study first examined block letters printed on grids, as shown in Figure 7.9c. After they became familiar with the letters, participants were asked to image a given letter as it had appeared on the grid. After 500 milliseconds—presumably before they had time to generate the complete image—two X's were then flashed on the grid in two of the squares, and participants were asked to determine whether or not the X's were in squares covered by the imagined letter. In the Imagery condition, response times were longer when the second probe appeared on a later-drawn square. For example, participants were fastest when the first X was in one of the squares covered by the top horizontal line of the *C*, and the second X covered a square within the vertical line (rather than within the later-drawn bottom horizontal line). This indicates that people were mentally generating the image part-by-part, in the same way they would draw the letters, and their responses to later-drawn positions were slowed because they had not yet completed the image-generation process.

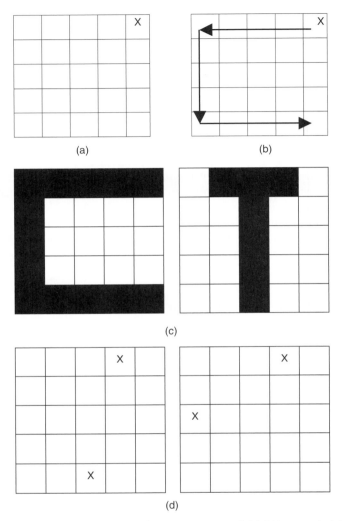

Figure 7.9   Externalization of images from (Kosslyn et al., 1988). (a) Write a capital C in this matrix, starting with the cell marked with the X. (b) A typical writing pattern. (c) Stimulus letters studied by participants. (d) Results: Left-hand panel produces slower response times for imagined C, because it takes longer to generate the last segment of the image (on the bottom). (e) Stimuli similar to those used by Kosslyn et al., 1983, Figure 5. (f) Results of Kosslyn et al., 1983, Experiment 3; adapted from Figure 6.

In a further study of image generation, Kosslyn, Reiser, Farah, and Fliegel (1983) first presented people with descriptions of abstract geometric figures. The descriptions varied in whether they contained few or many elemental parts. For example, in Figure 7.9e, the left-hand figure would be described in the *Few Parts* condition as being composed of two rectangles; in the *Many Parts* condition, the description

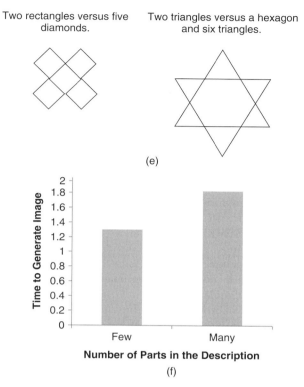

Two rectangles versus five diamonds.

Two triangles versus a hexagon and six triangles.

(e)

(f)

Figure 7.9 (*Continued*)

provided was five diamonds. The right-hand figure would be described as "two over-lapping triangles" versus "a hexagon surrounded by six triangles." All participants were then shown the same figure, and asked to generate an image of it. Although the figure was physically identical in both conditions, participants in the *Many Parts* condition took longer to generate the image, presumably because they generated the images piecemeal, based on the number of parts in their description for each figure (see Figure 7.9f). Furthermore, when asked to judge whether the overall figure was symmetrical (either in the vertical, horizontal, or diagonal direction), people also took longer to make those judgments when their descriptions had contained many parts.

Thus, these simple demonstrations provide evidence that images are generated in parts, and suggest that the order in which the parts are generated corresponds to how we might draw the same figures if asked to generate them. The simplicity of these studies is impressive; without fancy equipment (no multimillion-dollar brain-recording apparatus, for example), and with nothing more than a way to measure reaction time (e.g., a timer), one can provide evidence concerning "mental processes" that were points of dispute for 100 years.

Modality–Specific Interference

The Visual Buffer

Recall that one theoretical assumption of the Quasi-Picture view is that perception and imagery share a common mental screen and similar visual processes. If this is the case, then imagery and perception might interfere with each other, because our single visual system might not be able to carry out two tasks at once using the same mechanisms. In contrast, a task involving auditory perception should be *less* disruptive of visual imagery, since auditory perception involves a different modality than visual perception and visual imagery. Thus, one would expect to find *modality-specific interference* between imagining and perceiving: Tasks using the same processing modality will interfere with each other more than tasks using different modalities. That is, if one is imagining some *visual* experience, then that should make it harder to *see* things; similarly, imagining an auditory experience should make it harder to hear sounds.

Consider the hypothetical experiment shown in Figure 7.10a. Participants are asked to generate either visual or auditory imagery. For visual imagery, one could be asked to imagine a dollar bill; for auditory imagery, imagine a person singing the "Star-Spangled Banner." At the same time, the participants are asked to detect either visual or auditory signals. For visual detection, the participant watches a computer screen, and responds whenever a dot is flashed. For auditory detection, they are asked to respond to tones. There are thus four conditions in the experiment, as shown in Figure 7.10a: visual imagery task with either a visual or auditory response, and an auditory imagery task with either a visual or auditory response. Predicted patterns of response are also shown.

Signal for Detection	Image Generation	
	Visual	*Auditory*
Visual	Poor	Good
Auditory	Good	Poor

(a)

Signal for Detection	Image Generation	
	Visual	*Auditory*
Visual	1.70	2.23
Auditory	2.13	1.78

(b)

Figure 7.10 Hypothetical modality-specific interference (similar to Segal & Fusella, 1970) (a) Outline of modality-specific interference study. (b) Results from Segal and Fusella (1970, Experiment II): Accuracy in detecting the signal (higher scores indicate better performance). Modality-specific interference can be seen (compare with predictions in Figure 7.10a).

The results of a similar study, carried out by Segal and Fusella (1970; see also Brooks, 1968) are shown in Figure 7.10b. One can see that imagery interfered with perceptual processing, but only in the specific modality in which the imagery was carried out. Visual imagery interfered with detection of visual signals, and auditory imagery interfered with detection of auditory signals.

If the visual-processing system is involved both in seeing and in generating images, then an effect opposite to that reported by Segal and Fusella (1970) should also be found: Engaging in visual processes should disrupt our ability to generate images. Logie (1986) asked participants in a memory experiment to encode words either by using visual imagery or rote repetition. At the same time, they looked at a computer screen, on which was projected either a series of line drawings or a series of words corresponding to the names of those drawings. Participants were instructed to look at the screen, but to ignore anything that appeared there. Presentation of line drawings, even though they were to be ignored, interfered more with memory for words encoded under imagery instructions, while presentation of the names of the drawings had no such effect. Thus, instructions to use imagery to encode words requires the utilization of the visual system. If the system is simultaneously occupied by presentation of drawings, people may have difficulty forming images, resulting in poorer memory for the material to be encoded using imagery. This finding provides further evidence that similar cognitive mechanisms are being used for construction and examination of images and actual perception of visual pictures or scenes.

BRAIN MECHANISMS IN PERCEPTION AND IMAGERY

We have reviewed much evidence for *psychological* overlap of imagery and perception. A further assumption of the analogue view of imagery is that there should be overlapping brain areas involved in both perception and imagery. Neuropsychological evidence for the role of brain mechanisms in imagery has come from two main research endeavors: (1) measurement of activity in different brain areas as participants follow instructions that ask for visual versus other types of processing, and (2) examination of the influence of brain damage on processing of both perception and imagery.

Brain Activity During Imagery and Perception

Farah, Weisberg, Monheit, and Peronnet (1989) presented a series of words to participants, who were asked to either read each word or read it and form a visual image of its meaning. Increased electrical activity was found in the occipital and occipital-temporal region of the cortex when people generated images (see Figure 7.11). As we know from the discussion in Chapter 5, those regions play an important role in visual processing of objects. Activation was also greater in the left than the right hemispheric visual areas, illustrating a hemispheric laterality for image generation. Goldenberg, Steiner, Podreka, and Deecke (1992) found similar results when people answered yes/no (or two-choice) sentences involving visual imagery (e.g., *the green of fir trees is darker than that of grass*) versus sentences that did not (e.g., *the blending of an acid and a base yields*

Figure 7.11 Cortical activity in generating images in response to words. Darker areas indicate more activity.
Adapted from Farah et al., 1989.

salt and water). When participants reported using visual imagery to verify statements, there was increased blood flow in the left inferior occipital region.

Petersen, Fiez, and Raichle (unpublished manuscript, cited in Posner & Raichle, 1994/1997) presented letters either verbally or written in uppercase, and asked participants to determine whether or not a given word would contain *ascending letters* if it were to be printed in lower-case letters (ascending letters are those that go above the central line on which the word is printed; examples are *d* and *t*, but not *a*). PET scans were used to record brain activity as people viewed and made judgments about the letters, and the results are shown in Figure 7.12. In both the verbal and uppercase conditions there was activity in the parietal lobes, with additional temporal activity when the word was presented in visual form. Petersen et al. concluded that the visual imagery was carried out in the parietal area, while *translating* the upper-case form of the visually presented word into lowercase form activated the temporal region.

Kosslyn et al. (1993) used the same technique as Podgorny and Shepard (1978; see Figure 7.5) to examine brain systems involved in projection of images. Participants either saw a letter projected on a grid, or imagined it appearing in that grid, and then reported whether or not an X projected on the grid was in a square also occupied by the letter (see Figure 7.13). In the original Podgorny and Shepard study, the time to

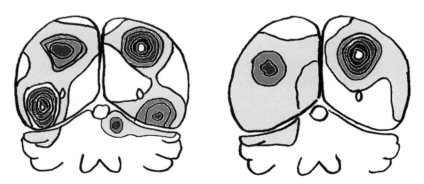

Figure 7.12 Petersen, Fiez, and Raichle (unpublished) study of imagery: Areas active in generating images. Darker areas indicate more activity.

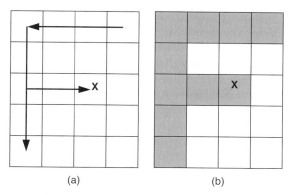

Figure 7.13   Kosslyn et al. (1993) imagery-versus-perceptual-judgment task. (a) Imagery task: Person imagines a letter and determines whether stimulus (X) falls on the letter. (b) Perception task: Person sees a letter and determines whether stimulus falls on the letter. Control task: Person sees only the X.

respond was shorter when the X was farther away from the letter in both the perceptual and imagery conditions. Using PET-scan measurement, Kosslyn et al. found similar patterns of activation in the parietal and temporal lobes, which supports the claim that similar brain systems are involved in imagery and perception.

Furthermore, parallels between imagery and perception are not limited to the visual modality. Lambert, Sampaio, Scheiber, and Mauss (2001) asked blindfolded (but normally sighted) participants and blind participants to explore *haptically*—that is, through touch—20 objects that were easy to identify. The experimenters then read aloud the labels of those 20 items and instructed people to form a haptic mental image for each, as they underwent an fMRI scan. Both blind and sighted participants showed activation in the somatosensory cortex (the area responsible for perceiving stimuli by touch).

Auditory Imagery

We have all had an occasion when we can't get a song out of our head. Sometimes we don't even like that particular song, but it has been played on the radio so often that we start humming along to our auditory "image." Or, we hear on the radio a song playing that we have on an iPod playlist, and as the song ends on the radio, we immediately start "hearing" the tune that normally comes next in our playlist. The ability to recall the melody of a song, or a familiar person's voice as if they are talking to us, is a common phenomenon. In recent years, psychologists have carried out an increasing number of experiments investigating auditory imagery. As in vision, scientists have found psychological and neuropsychological parallels between actual hearing and auditory imagery.

Kraemer, Macrae, Green, and Kelley (2005) asked people to rate their personal familiarity with songs with lyrics (e.g., "Satisfaction" by the Rolling Stones) and instrumental songs (e.g., theme songs from popular movies). For each participant, a soundtrack was developed which contained both familiar and unfamiliar songs, with lyrics versus instrumentals. Two to 5 seconds were deleted from each song to see if people would fill in the melody and/or lyrics from familiar ones. Using fMRI, the researchers measured brain activity in the primary auditory and auditory association cortex during these musical gaps (see Figure 7.14a). There was greater brain activation in the left auditory cortex during gaps of familiar songs (see Figure 7.14b), both for songs with and without lyrics. These neuropsychological findings corresponded to participants' report that they "heard" the missing lyrics and/or melodies during the gaps of familiar songs (but not of unfamiliar songs).

Halpern and Zatorre (1999) found PET-scan activation in auditory association areas (in the right superior temporal cortex) that are active during both actual perception of music and imagery of familiar instrumental music. Purely instrumental music tends to result in greater right-hemisphere activation (Halpern, Zatorre, Bouffard & Johnson, 2004), whereas songs with lyrics are associated with bilateral activation, because of involvement of left-hemisphere speech areas (Zatorre, Halpern, Perry, Meyer, & Evans, 1996). Stimulation of these same areas by a researcher can result in imagery for music or sounds; in a classic study by Penfield, a patient about to undergo brain surgery was electrically stimulated in areas of the temporal lobe, which caused the patient to "hear" familiar songs (Penfield & Perot, 1963). Likewise, Wu, Mai, Chan, Zheng, and Luo (2006) found activation in parts of the brain linked to auditory processing as people imagined animal sounds.

Those experimental results are confirmed by subjective reports that people engage in auditory images which mimic actual hearing: For example, musicians claim to be able to "hear" their instrument when they mentally practice (Zatorre & Halpern, 2005), and the time for musicians to image a familiar piece of music is about the same amount of time necessary to play that piece (Langheim, Callicott, Mattay, Duyn, and Weinberger, 2002). When people know how to play music, not only does activation increase in their auditory cortex: They may also be using haptic imagery to mentally "play" the piece. Haueisen and Knösche (2001) found that, while professional pianists listened to a familiar piece of music, there was activation in areas of the motor cortex that corresponded to fingers used to play a given note.

Brain Damage Effects on Imagery and Perception

Studies have shown that damage to specific areas of the brain can disrupt both visual processing and visual imagery. Although there is neuropsychological evidence for parallel deficits in visual perception and imagery (e.g., Brown, 1966; Farah, Soso, & Dasheiff, 1992; Symonds & Mackenzie, 1957), other cases indicate some neurological independence of visual recognition and imagery abilities. Farah (1984) surveyed 100 years of clinical literature to find case studies of brain-damaged patients who showed deficits in generating visual images. Eight such patients had been reported historically, and most had bilateral or left-hemisphere damage in the posterior or parietal-occipital region of the brain. Those eight patients had no problems recognizing objects that were presented to them, which indicates that they had visual information *available* in memory. However, they could not answer questions from memory about objects that

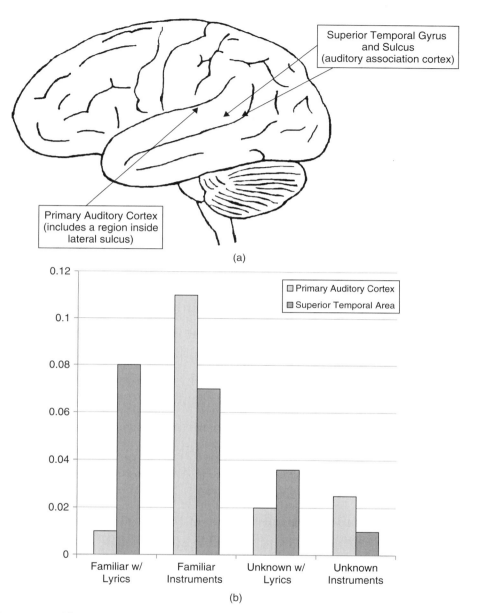

Figure 7.14 (a) Brain areas active during silent gaps in songs: The primary auditory cortex and auditory association area, largely in superior temporal sulcus (STS), shown in left hemisphere. (b) Signal changes in the primary auditory cortex (PAC) and superior temporal suclus (STS) as a function of familiarity versus unfamiliarity of songs, with and without lyrics.

Adapted from Kraemer et al., 2005, Figure 1.

depend on the ability to *access* visual information, such as whether or not Abraham Lincoln had a beard. Farah suggested that these patients retained visual information about objects, but were unable to *generate* images in order to answer questions about what objects looked like.

Dorsal and Ventral Streams of Mental Imagery

We saw in Chapter 5 that a number of studies have converged on the conclusion that there are at least two visual processing systems, one dealing with the identification of objects (the *ventral* system), and the second dealing with how we orient to and act on objects in space (the *dorsal* system). The two visual systems also seem to play separate roles in representing objects in imagery. Levine, Warach, and Farah (1985) documented a double dissociation between generating images and remembering the spatial location of objects in imagery. One patient, with occipital-temporal damage, exhibited both object-recognition and image-generation problems. He was unable to describe or draw objects, animals, or faces from memory; for example, he could not decide whether George Washington had a beard (which may be dependent on the ability to imagine Washington's face). However, he was able to remember the locations of objects, such as pointing to where a city should be placed on a map.

The opposite set of symptoms was shown by a second patient, with occipital-parietal damage. This patient was able to give detailed descriptions of the visual characteristics of objects from memory, but had great difficulty remembering the locations of familiar things (he routinely got lost trying to navigate in his own house). Thus, this double dissociation of brain damage and related behavioral deficits supports the claim that there are two separable systems within visual imagery: One that processes visual object information, the other that processes spatial information. It is important in the context of this chapter to note that Levine et al.'s (1985) patients also showed deficits in imagery that were parallel to their perceptual problems. The first patient had deficits in both object recognition and image generation, but not spatial location. The other patient had problems with spatial imagery, but not with image generation. These patients also had patterns of brain damage that corresponded to the different brain sub-systems processing *what* versus *where/action* information.

Neglect in Imagery and Perception

Researchers have discussed other neuropsychology patients who also show analogous deficits in vision and imagery. In Chapter 6, we discussed the syndrome of hemi-field neglect (e.g., Robertson & Halligan, 1999). This syndrome typically results from damage to the parietal lobe (usually the right hemisphere), and leads to the patient ignoring the contralateral visual field (usually the left half of space). Results from patients with neglect also support the claim that perception and imagery use overlapping brain structures (e.g., see Sacks, *The Man Who Mistook His Wife for a Hat*, 1985). Bisiach and Luzzati (1978) discussed patients who showed neglect in imagery that was parallel to their deficits in perception. Patients with right parietal lesions were asked to imagine the buildings in a plaza with which they had been familiar before suffering the lesion. When requested to imagine the plaza from one end, they neglected to report the buildings on the left side of the plaza, which is analogous to what they would have reported had they been observing the plaza. The patients were then asked to imagine the plaza from other end, and now they reported the buildings they had just left out, and neglected the buildings that they had just reported (also see Sacks, 1985).

Dissociations Between Perception and Imagery

Although the results discussed in the last few sections have been supportive of the idea that similar brain systems are used in imagery and perception, not all neuropsychology patients show parallel deficits in visual perception and imagery. In Chapter 5, we discussed the case of C.K., who suffered from integrative agnosia as the result of a head injury received in an automobile accident (Behrmann, Moscovitch, & Winocur, 1994). He was unable to recognize line drawings of objects or faces, or to integrate parts of visual objects; for example, when given two diamonds and a circle to draw, he drew the overall shape of the objects, but the pattern of lines he drew indicated that he did not break the overall pattern into three objects, as most of us would (see Box 5.1 and Figure 5.7).

Despite his debilitating agnosia, C.K. was able to carry out a variety of tasks that seem to be based on visual imagery, and he did not show a problem integrating the parts of an image into a whole. For example, C.K. was able to answer imagery-based questions, such as, "What letter do you get when you take the letter L, flip it from top to bottom and add a horizontal line in the middle?" (The answer is *F*.) Thus, he was able to carry out imagery tasks that require organizing parts into a whole object and transforming the overall image through rotation processes. C.K. also performed well on tasks requiring image generation, e.g., drawing items from memory (e.g., a guitar; see Figure 7.15), answering questions about the relative sizes of two objects (*Which is larger?*), and verification of high-imagery sentences (*The letter W is formed by three lines*; the answer is false). H.J.A. (first described in Chapter 5), who was an integrative agnosic studied by Riddoch, Humphreys, Blott, Hardy, and Smith (2003), also retained some image-generation abilities, such as being able to draw objects from memory, including visual details in his definitions of words (such as recalling that a goat was "a four-legged domesticated animal . . . with an extended head and neck . . . "; from Humphreys & Riddoch, 1987), and accurately answering questions that typically require imagery. Other researchers have also described patients who showed a dissociation between imagery and perceptual abilities (Cocchini, Bartolo, & Nichelli, 2006; Farah, Hammond, Levine, & Calvanio, 1988; Jankowiak, Kinsbourne, Shalev, & Bachman, 1992; Servos & Goodale, 1995).

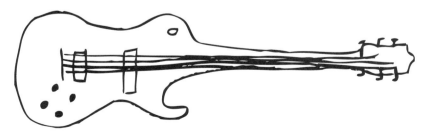

Figure 7.15   Guitar drawing.
Adapted from Zatorre and Halpern, 2005.

Collectively, the neuropsychology evidence suggests strong but not complete parallels between brain areas used in imagery versus perceptual tasks. There is clearly overlap in processing of objects and space between perception and imagery, both psychologically and neurologically. It is clear from several double dissociations, though, that imagery and object/spatial recognition do not share all processing components, and that some operations may be specific to either imagery or perception. Depending on the extent and the locus of brain damage, parallel deficits in imagery and perception will occur, whereas less extensive injuries or damage to a different brain area may affect only one of the processes.

Images as Analogous to Perception: Summary and Conclusions

We have just reviewed a large amount of evidence (e.g., Farah et al., 1988; Kosslyn et al., 1983; Segal & Fusella, 1970; Shepard & Metzler, 1971) that supports the conclusion that many of the processes involved in generating and processing images are psychologically and neurologically related to perceptual processes, such as those used in object recognition. Imagery and perception both rely on visual-spatial information, and that information is processed and manipulated in similar ways. Studies of modality-specific interference (e.g., Segal & Fusella, 1970) have shown that forming and manipulating images can interfere with perceptual processing, indicating that there is an overlap of processing systems. Likewise, studies of brain structure and function have shown that similar (but not always identical) brain areas are active in perception and in the construction of images; and brain damage can have similar effects on perception and imagery. There are still component processes and parts of the brain that may be specific to imagery or perception, but the two functions operate in similar ways. Furthermore, the functional and neurological overlap of imagery and perception is not limited to the visual realm; activation of similar brain areas has also been found in auditory imagery (e.g., Kraemer et al., 2005; Wu et al., 2006) and tactile imagery (Lambert et al., 2001).

A FURTHER DEBATE: IMAGERY VERSUS PROPOSITIONS AS THE MEDIUM OF THOUGHT

Although there seems to be ample evidence that images can be generated and manipulated during various cognitive tasks, the area of imagery is still not without controversy. Although most investigators became convinced that the *occurrence* of imagery could be studied scientifically, questions were raised concerning how to interpret the results of those experiments. As we have seen, some investigators (e.g., Finke, 1989; Kosslyn, 1980; Kosslyn et al., 2006) concluded that imagery serves as an internal analogue of perception, and that images are functionally equivalent to pictures. This perspective, as noted, has been called the quasi-picture view of imagery. One of the principal critics of the quasi-picture view was Pylyshyn (1973, 1981, 2003, 2007). He argued that all information in long-term memory, even information about what things look like, is stored in a *propositional code*, a code that is more like a verbal description than a picture of an object (see also Anderson, 1983; Anderson & Bower, 1973). Pylyshyn (1973, 1981) argued that it was a mistake to assume that imagery could be the medium (or "stuff") of thought. Rather, he proposed what is called a *descriptional* (or *propositional*) *view*, which argues that information about objects, object parts, and spatial relationships is stored in a representation that does not contain sensory-specific information, but is similar to an abstract sentence—a *proposition* or description of the information. Our experiences have a perceptual component, but those "perceptual" experiences are not the thinking itself, nor are they similar to the underlying representations of knowledge that we use to answer questions (such as whether a German Shepherd's ears are pointed). Our experiences of imagery simply *accompany* thinking, they are not the thinking itself.

According to Pylyshyn, when we are asked a question, such as the shape of a German Shepherd's ears, we activate a propositional-knowledge structure that contains descriptive information about the structure and shape of the dog's ears. It is that proposition which enables us to answer the question, and which *may* also cause us to generate an image. However, any image that is experienced during cognitive tasks is an *epiphenomenon*: a secondary phenomenon that accompanies some process—in this case, thinking about visual-spatial information—but which is not a causal part of that process. A generated image itself does not serve as the basis for our ability to answer questions about visual information, e.g., about a German Shepherd's ears. Rather, both the image and the ability to make a visual or spatial judgment are based on abstract propositions that may include descriptions of visual information. In Pylyshyn's view, just because imagery is experienced when we think about some problem does not mean that the image itself is part of the thought processes by which we solve the problem. An analogy using computer processing would be a case where (if we provided the correct commands), we could retrieve and print a computer file even if the computer monitor is not turned on. Displaying information on the monitor is epiphenomenal to the computer's ability to carry out the *retrieve* and *print* commands; these functions can take place even if the monitor is turned off.

Evidence in Support of the Propositional View of Imagery

The Abstract Nature of Concepts

When we think, it seems as if our experiences are in words or images. If you read the words, "cinnamon bun," you probably have no difficulty forming an image; conversely, if you have an image of a beach with turquoise water and palm trees, you can easily describe it in words. Thus, we can readily translate from the verbal to the visual modality, and vice versa. This ability to communicate between visual and verbal systems indicates, according to Pylyshyn (1973, 1981, 2003), that there must be a *third* system, in which that translation is carried out. If so, then this system must not be speech or imagery; it must be more abstract than either, so that it can communicate between them. Therefore, argued Pylyshyn, if this system of abstract concepts must exist to provide the medium of communication between words and images, it could also serve directly as the medium in which we think. Pylyshyn argued, based on efficiency, that there is reason to believe that the cognitive system is designed so that thinking is carried out in a medium that is neither speech- nor imagery-based, but is more abstract and in propositional form.

Experimental evidence that, in Pylyshyn's view, argued against imagery as the medium of thought, and in favor of a system of more abstract concepts, was based on the results of studies that examined verbal versus imagery mediation in memory (Pylyshyn, 1981). In these studies, participants were given lists of pairs of words to study, and were instructed to use verbal mediators for some pairs, and imagery for others. Memory for the pairs was then tested, and one additional question was asked: The participants were asked for each pair if they had studied it using language or imagery. Results indicated that participants often became confused as to whether they had used language or imagery to study a given pair. In Pylyshyn's view, the reason people could not remember which mediation system they had used was because they had used neither verbal mediation nor visual imagery: *both* types of mediation had actually occurred in the abstract propositional code, which was neither verbal nor visual imagery. Hence, there is a more abstract code in which we actually carry out our thinking.

Images and Percepts

The idea that images are similar to objects is based on the proposal that both can be examined in order to obtain new information from them. This analysis leads one to think that images contain information waiting to be processed, like a familiar painting that might still hold new things for us to see. However, there is evidence that images are not simply passive pieces of information, waiting to be processed as we wish, nor are they fully analogous to pictures (Pylyshyn, 1981, 2003). We can see this in the following simple demonstration. Imagine a tiger, not moving, in any pose you like, not too far away. Most people report that they can do this with little problem. Now, with your image in mind, answer the following question: *How many stripes does your tiger have?* Most people report that they cannot answer that question; if a *picture* of a tiger were in front of you, it would be an easy task to count the stripes, so why are you not able to count them in your *image* of a tiger? Pylyshyn argued that this *indeterminacy*—the inexactness—of images (Tye, 1991) illustrates that an image of a tiger is not like a picture of a tiger. A picture of a tiger must have a specific number of stripes, but an image does not; an image of a tiger can have the property of being *striped*, but an exact number of stripes might not be specified. So, an image is not made up of specific pieces of information, like a percept. Rather, an image is constructed out of concepts that may or may not provide specific information.

The Already-Organized Nature of Images

A further difference between images and pictures discussed by Pylyshyn is that our interpretation of images is bound by the original interpretation or label supplied for an object or scene. Relative to pictures, from which new information can be garnered, images are less flexible and are not subject to reinterpretation. For example, perform the first task in Figure 7.16 before reading further.

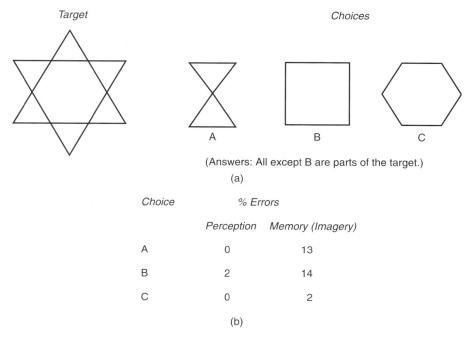

Figure 7.16   Hidden-figures task. (a) Which of the choices (A–C) is contained in the target figure?
(b) Hidden-figures test done from memory: Results from Reed and Johnsen (1975).
From Reed & Johnsen 1975, Figure 1.

The task in Figure 7.16a is called the *hidden-figures* task, and has been studied for many years (e.g., Reed, 1974; Reed & Johnsen, 1975). Pylyshyn noted that when we *look* at an actual object, we can *reorganize* our perception, and reinterpret it as needed. This ability is demonstrated by the fact that we can carry out the hidden-figures task; when the figure is right in front of us, we can detect the hourglasses, diamond, and parallelogram. If images are like percepts, then we should be able to reorganize and reinterpret our images as well. However, several studies appeared to show that images cannot be reorganized in the way that percepts can. In one study, Reed and Johnsen (1975) presented the hidden figures task with one change in procedure from the task in Figure 7.16a. The task was done from memory. Instead of having the original stimulus present when the choice stimuli were presented, the person had to *imagine* the original stimulus, and then try to determine if any of the choice stimuli were contained in it. Reed and Johnsen found that people were more accurate at detecting hidden figures from perception—when the initial figure remained in front of them—than from imagery. Also, in the imagery condition, they made more errors, and were slower to respond to some hidden figures than others (see Figure 7.16b for error rates). For example, they were more accurate and faster to detect that the hexagon had been a component of the Star of David than other shapes, such as the "hourglass" had been a component. In one further experiment, in order to ensure that the person had an accurate memory for the original stimulus, Reed and Johnsen (Experiment 3) asked participants to draw it from memory when the part-detection task was over. All participants were able to do so, indicating that they had accurately imagined the stimulus when carrying out the hidden-figures task.

In Pylyshyn's propositional view, the explanation for the difficulty in carrying out the hidden-figures task using imagery is that images cannot be reorganized in the way that perceptions sometimes can be, because they are based on a propositional representation. Since information about the original figures is not stored in a picture form, an image is an already-organized object. For example, when one imagines the Star of David, one might imagine it as two overlapping triangles. At a conceptual level, one should easily be able to analyze the Star of David into two triangles, but other "parts" should not be evident (because they are not explicitly contained within your proposition describing the Star of David shape). Adherents to a propositional view point out that the Reed and Johnsen (1975) data indicate a disanalogy between perceiving and imaging a figure.

Chambers and Reisberg (1985) presented other data on the difficulty of reinterpreting images by using the duck-rabbit figure shown in Figure 7.17. This stimulus is reversible: We can interpret it in two different ways—as either a duck or a rabbit, and accordingly, its appendages as either a duckbill or rabbit ears. Chambers and Reisberg introduced the figure as either a rabbit or a duck, and asked people to study it for 5 seconds. After a brief introduction to another ambiguous figure, participants were asked to image the original duck-rabbit stimulus, and to report if they could see an alternative interpretation to the way in which they had originally processed it. People were not able to reinterpret the figure when it was only available in imagery. When they had *drawn* the figure, however, all were now able to see the second interpretation. Chambers and Reisberg (1985) thus concluded that images are not functionally analogous to pictures, because reinterpretation is rare or nonexistent with images, even though it can be accomplished with an actual picture. This dissociation raises questions about the perceptual nature of images.

Propositions Rather Than Images: Conclusions

Several different sorts of evidence have been presented to support the view that thinking is carried out in propositions rather than images, despite our subjective

Figure 7.17 Duck-rabbit reversible figure.

experiences of thinking and answering questions about objects using mental pictures. Images do not possess the same specificity as perceptual experiences (e.g., number of stripes on the tiger) and they also do not possess the flexibility of perceptual experiences (reorganization in hidden-figures test). These characteristics of images make it unlikely, according to the propositional view, that images are a medium of thought.

ANALOGUE RESPONSES TO THE PROPOSITIONAL CRITIQUE

Researchers who supported the analogue view have responded in various ways to the criticisms raised by Pylyshyn (1973, 1981) and others (Chambers & Reisberg, 1985).

Processing Images Versus Pictures

Consider again the difficulty in counting the stripes on an image of a tiger. In his analysis of the indeterminacy argument, Pylyshyn (1973, 1981, 2003) seemed to assume that the parts of an image must be available continuously, as are the parts of a physical object or a picture. However, images are complex psychological phenomena, and are not necessarily generated holistically, which might make the stripe-counting task difficult. As an example, perhaps images must be constantly refreshed, and while you are concentrating on one part of an image as complex as a tiger, other parts will tend to fade. This might make it very difficult (if not impossible) to count the stripes. In this analysis, the inability to count the stripes on one's image of a tiger is because the specific counting task requires that the image in question be more stable than images can be. This is not a critical problem for the analogue view, since it assumes that images can be generated in parts, need to be refreshed in working memory, and can be indeterminate with regard to details.

Weber (cited in Posner & Raichle, 1994/1997, p. 89) carried out a study in which people's ability to process perceptual information was directly compared to their ability to deal with the same information from imagery. The task involved having people examine strings of lowercase letters, and to judge whether or not each letter in the string had an ascending feature (part that extends above the mid-line of the letter, like *l* or *k*), a descending feature (part that extends below the baseline, like *j* or *g*), or neither (*a* or *c*). The letter strings varied in length, and the participant had to scan the strings either forward or backward. Weber found that with strings up to three letters in length, participants were just as fast and accurate scanning images as they were scanning actual strings projected in front of them, for both the forward and backward scanning conditions. With longer strings of letters (4 or more), on the other hand, participants were at a disadvantage when the task was done from imagery. Thus, although it is not impossible to carry out this scanning task from imagery, imagery does impose an additional burden on the both attentional processes (as when images have to be constantly refreshed), and on working memory. Thus, difficulties in carrying out some task using imagery do not mean that imagery and perceptual operations are basically different; rather, imagery may bring with it additional processing burdens.

Reorganizing and Reinterpreting Images

The other major criticism of the analogue view concerns people's inability to reorganize images in the way that they can reorganize perceptions, which indicates a dis-analogy between imaging and visual perception. The relevant data came from negative results from studies of Reed and Johnsen (1975) and Chambers and Reisberg (1985), among others (see Figures 7.16a and b and 7.17). However, as students learn in courses on experimental design, one must be very careful in interpreting negative results. A person's inability to carry out some task could be the result of either of two reasons:

1. The person is indeed not able to carry out the skill in question (which is how supporters of the propositional view interpreted the negative results from the studies of reinterpretation of imagery).

2. The person may be able to carry out the skill at some level above zero, but the task used to test the skill is so difficult or has such strict time limitations that one sees no trace of the skill.

This second interpretation of the negative results raises the possibility that there might have been what psychologists call a *floor effect* in the experiments, meaning that the tasks were so difficult that performance was on the floor (i.e., very poor), and so one could not get any information about what the people might have been able to do.

For example, if a talented high-school baseball player were asked to try and hit a ball thrown by one of the best pitchers in the major leagues, chances are the young hitter would be unable to even contact the ball. An observer might then conclude that the high school player was totally unable to hit a baseball, when really the task we had asked him to perform was much too difficult for someone at his level. Similarly, in order to conclude that people *cannot* reorganize images, one has to make sure that the task used is not so difficult that performance is "on the floor." Recall that in the Chambers and Reisberg (1985) study, none of the subjects were able to reinterpret the duck-rabbit figure from imagery. This is an example of a floor effect, perhaps because of the short 5-second exposure. Please perform the tasks presented in Box 7.5 before continuing.

BOX 7.5 FINKE ET AL. (1989) IMAGERY REORGANIZATION TASK

1. Imagine the letter K. Place a square next to it on the left side. Put a circle inside of the square. Now rotate the figure 90 degrees to the left. What do you have?

2. Imagine a capital letter D. Rotate the figure 90 degrees to the left. Now place a capital letter J on the bottom, with the top of the J touching the bottom of the rotated D. What figure do you have?

Answers:

1. A TV with antenna

2. An umbrella

Finke, Pinker, and Farah (1989) used simple familiar stimuli (e.g., shapes, letters, and numbers) and asked people to manipulate (e.g., rotate) and combine them into simple, schematic shapes. About 70% of the time, participants were able to find an alternate interpretation based on the visual-spatial properties of their images (such as when a rotated K on top of a square formed a picture of a television). This makes it fairly easy to reinterpret the images, as you presumably did when carrying out the tasks in Box 7.5. The ability to reorganize images is evident as one suddenly realizes that the composite image is a different object than the component items with which one started, and that the reinterpretation is based on visual-spatial characteristics (rather than the descriptions of the component items). Squares and K's become televisions; combinations of letters become umbrellas, and so on.

Mast and Kosslyn (2002) used a more complex figure (see Figure 7.18), which is ambiguous in that it portrays an old woman if perceived one way, but a young woman if rotated upside down (and vice versa). However, unlike the 5-second exposure to the ambiguous duck-rabbit figure used by Chambers and Reisberg (1985), they allowed experimental participants a longer time to encode the old/young woman figure. By guiding people through a mental rotation process, Mast and Kosslyn found that almost half of their subjects were able to discover the alternate interpretation during the imagery phase of the experiment. Those most successful in reinterpretation were people who had proved adept at mental imagery transformations in an earlier independent task. The results of Mast and Kosslyn provided further evidence for analogous characteristics of images and perceptual objects, especially among those people who were efficient at image transformation. Although there is still disagreement in this area, it seems reasonable to conclude that reinterpretation of images can be accomplished in many circumstances, and is more flexible than early studies indicated.

Figure 7.18   Ambiguous old/young woman figure similar to that used by Mast and Kosslyn (2002).

THE STUDY OF IMAGERY: CONCLUSIONS AND IMPLICATIONS

We have seen that the modern-day study of imagery is an area in which differences of opinion are common. However, the areas of disagreement have changed; early in the development of psychology, the main issue of contention was whether subjective experiences such as imagery could even be part of a scientific psychology. Modern developments seem to have put that question to rest, but now there has arisen the question of the role played by imagery in cognitive functioning. Some researchers have proposed that imagery plays a functional role in cognition; we generate images from information stored in long-term memory that we can then rotate, scan, and use to answer questions about objects or scenes. In contrast, other researchers have proposed that all information is stored in abstract representations known as propositions, and that we may think that we generate images in response to questions, but the imagery plays no role in processing.

At present, the empirical evidence seems to support the notion that images are functional components of some sorts of processing, and that the imagery system shares many parallels to perceptual processes. As Finke (1989) outlined, considerable evidence supports the view that: (a) visual images are *perceptually* equivalent to pictures, in that it seems to us as if images share many visual characteristics with actual objects or pictures; (b and c) visual images have *spatial* and *structural* equivalence to pictures or objects, in that spatial relations and configurations of the parts of objects mirror those relations in actual objects or scenes; (d) many of those visual-spatial properties were encoded *implicitly*, which allows us to reexamine and reinterpret images to find properties we had not attended to during the initial encoding; and (e) visual images have *transformational* equivalence to percepts because we appear to mentally manipulate, rotate, and scan images in the same fashion as we do pictures, objects, or scenes. Recent research on auditory images suggests that analogous properties may exist between auditory images and sounds: that those images maintain pitch, melody, and timbre qualities of the original song, instrument, or animal sound (Halpern & Zatorre, 1999; Kraemer et al., 2005; Wu et al., 2006).

The research reviewed in this chapter is important for several reasons. First, it provides a fascinating story concerning how cognitive scientists were able to bring under scientific investigation an area that had previously been thought to be inaccessible to scientific methods. Research on imagery shows us that mental events can be studied using scientific methods comparable to the methods used in other sciences to examine processes that are hidden from ordinary methods of observation. Second, research has provided information concerning how imagery functions in various activities. Finally, research on imagery has provided strong evidence of the interrelations among the various cognitive processes. We have seen that imagery and perception are closely related, and that both are related to memory.

REVIEW QUESTIONS

Here is a set of questions that will serve in organizing the material in the chapter as you review it.

1. In general as well as more specific terms, outline possible functions of imagery in cognitive functioning.

2. What were the results of the early research on imagery by Galton and the introspectionists?

3. What criticisms did the behaviorists raise concerning psychologists' study of imagery?

4. What is *meaningfulness* of a CVC? How is it measured? How is it related to verbal mediation in memory?

5. In Paivio's dual coding theory, how does imagery function in memory?

6. What early evidence was brought forth in support of the dual coding theory?

7. Summarize the results of studies of mental rotation carried out by Shepard and his coworkers. How were those results interpreted by researchers interested in mental imagery?

8. Summarize Kosslyn's *quasi-picture* view of mental imagery. In this view, how do people generate and manipulate images?

9. What are Finke's principles concerning the relations between images and percepts?

10. Summarize results of studies by Kosslyn and coworkers on scanning and generation of images.

11. What is *modality-specific interference* in imagery and perception? How does that phenomenon support the quasi-pictorial view of mental imagery?

12. What results from studies of brain activity during imagery and perception support the overlap between imagery and perception?

13. Summarize studies of auditory imagery that support the idea that auditory imagery and auditory perception involve overlapping operations and brain areas.

14. What results from studies of brain damage support the overlap between visual imagery and visual perception?

15. What results from studies of brain activity and brain damage do **not** support the idea of an overlap between imagery and perception?

16. Summarize Pylyshyn's propositional view of imagery and his analysis of the relationship between imagery and thinking.

17. Summarize Pylyshyn's arguments against the quasi-pictorial view of imagery.

18. How do results from studies investigating the hidden-figures task and studies examining reversible figures seem to raise problems for the quasi-picture view of imagery?

19. How did researchers who support the quasi-pictorial theory respond to the findings that images could not be reorganized like pictures can?

20. What is one possible reason for the different results from different studies of reorganization of images?

CHAPTER 8

CONCEPTS AND CATEGORIES

A father and his young son are walking through the woods on a summer's day. They come upon a small furry animal with a fluffy tail, black with a white stripe down its back. The child joyously shouts, "Skunk!" and runs toward the animal. The father quickly scoops the child into his arms, and heads in the other direction. Later in the day, the father recounts the incident to the child's mother, and tells her, "He knows the *word* 'skunk,' but I guess he doesn't have the *concept* 'skunk' yet."

A biology class takes a field trip to a local cave. While trekking through the mud, one student sees movement and bends down to pick up a 6-inch grayish amphibian. She turns to a classmate and asks, "Is this a berry cave salamander or a Tennessee cave salamander?" The classmate says, "I don't know; let's ask Professor Collins—he's the expert."

Two 3-year-old children are playing. Carol constantly takes toys away from Susan, with a loud, "That's mine!" Carol's mother takes each toy and gives it back to Susan, each time telling Carol to share with her friend. Finally, after several more incidents, Carol's mother takes her home, thinking to herself, "She has no concept of sharing."

Our basketball team is playing an important game. One player constantly keeps the ball in his possession, shoots whenever he can, and never passes to a teammate, even when another player has a much easier shot. The coach takes the player out of the game, and asks angrily, "Don't you understand the concept of teamwork?"

The comment made by the little boy's father, the question raised by the biology student, the complaint raised by Carol's mother, and the question asked by the coach all address issues concerning what it means when someone has—or does not have—a concept. For more than two millennia, students of human behavior, philosophers, psychologists, computer scientists, and neuroscientists, have spent much time and effort analyzing the structure and functioning of concepts. Those efforts will be the focus of this chapter.

OUTLINE OF CHAPTER 8

The discussion in this chapter will begin with a consideration of some general aspects of conceptual functioning, and then center on four issues:

1. What information is used in the process of categorizing some new experience as an example of some concept (e.g., "That is a dog over there.")? We review several different theories of how the categorization process is carried out.

2. How are all the concepts we possess represented in our memories? That is the question of the structure of semantic memory.

3. How do we use our conceptual knowledge in thinking about objects? For example, when you categorize a never-before-seen object as a DOG, how do you then apply your knowledge to this object, and conclude, for example, that it probably does not get along with cats? (In this chapter, we will use ALL CAPS to refer to the names of concepts or categories.)

4. Finally, we consider the question of how concepts might be represented in the brain.

Before continuing Chapter 8, please perform the exercises in Box 8.1. You will need a pencil and piece of paper.

BOX 8.1 EXAMINATION OF CONCEPTUAL ABILITIES

(1) Please take a few seconds to list several members of each of the following categories: grandmother, bird, furniture, bachelor, even number, island.

(2) For each of the categories in (1), list the features or attributes that an object must contain in order to be included in the category. For example, what features must someone possess in order to be a grandmother? What about an island?

(3) For the items you listed as members of the categories furniture and bird, rate each on a 1–7 scale as to whether it is a very good (7) or not good (1) member of the category.

(4) Let's say you read about previously unknown kind of dog that has just been discovered in the desert in Mongolia. Do you think this animal has eyes? How about a brain? About how long do you think it lives? Do you think it could get epilepsy?

CONCEPTS AND CATEGORIES

Concepts and categories are closely related, yet critically different: A concept is a mental representation, made up of one's knowledge about a type of object (e.g., *DOGS*) or an idea (e.g., *SHARING*). Categories, on the other hand, are the actual divisions that we use in dividing up the world. The category *DOG*, for example, consists of those objects in the world that we consider to be representatives of the concept DOG. The concept is inside us, while the category is often out there.

Some Functions of Concepts

To say that a person has a concept, such as the concept DOG, is a shorthand way of saying that the person knows a number of different things. First, a person who possesses the concept DOG may have perceptual knowledge about what dogs look like—and perhaps sound like—so that he can identify an individual dog as belonging to the category DOG. Categories are not only based on visible perceptual characteristics; someone with an accurate concept of DOG knows that a Chihuahua, West Highland

DOG Category

Perceptual Similarity

Figure 8.1 Variability within versus across categories: A Russian red fox, Chihuahua, West Highland White Terrier, and Boxer.

White Terrier, and a Boxer, although very different in appearance from each other, nonetheless share many internal characteristics. There are resemblances in color and ear and nose shape between a Chihuahua and a Russian red fox (see Figure 8.1), but we place the dogs and the fox in separate categories. We also infer that all the dogs might like to play a game of "fetch," but the fox does not.

Secondly, in order to fully possess the concept DOG, one must have additional knowledge about what dogs typically *do*: Some dogs are used to protect or rescue people, others to pull sleds, and others to provide companionship to people. This is known as *functional* information. One can also possess scientific information about dogs that is not necessarily based on direct personal experience, for example, that dogs bear live young and have similar internal organs to humans (lungs, heart, intestines).

Concepts and Inferential Reasoning

When we categorize a new object or experience (such as a dog we have never encountered before) as a member of a familiar category (e.g., DOG) it enables us to respond to that new experience as if it, too, were familiar. For example, if you see an animal walking toward you that you categorize as a dog, you may approach and pet it; however if you decide that it is a skunk, you will probably avoid it. In other words, possessing concepts allows us to *infer* or reason about novel instances of a category. This reasoning can take place at any category level. For example, your concept DOG includes the knowledge that dogs are MAMMALS, which means you can infer (if you didn't know it before) that dogs will probably bear live young rather than lay eggs. Another illustration of inferential reasoning can be seen in an incident reported by a student. She had returned home for spring break and had been happy to see her family's dog. However, the next day the animal began to suffer seizures, in which the dog's whole body shuddered violently for long periods of time. The animal's physical actions reminded the student of the description of human epilepsy she had learned about in one of her courses, though she had no direct knowledge of whether dogs could suffer from that disease. She did know, however, that dogs are mammals, and thus have brains and nervous systems. She then inferred that the dog was suffering from epilepsy. Although the student had no direct experience with a dog's nervous system, she could apply some of her knowledge about mammals' nervous-system functioning to the animal she was observing, to reason about the dog's illness. The diagnosis was confirmed by the veterinarian.

Concepts and Language

Some concepts rely heavily on language, but language and concepts can be independent. Discussing concepts, of necessity, requires words, such as "triangle," "professor," or "animal." For some abstract concepts, language seems necessary for a full understanding. For example, how could we fully understand or convey the concepts JUSTICE or SHARING without using words to define those ideas? In addition, adults use words to help children define and delineate categories: The child who broadly applies "doggie" to all four-legged furry creatures, but then is told that a donkey is "not a doggie," will learn better how to distinguish dogs from nondogs. However, language is not required for all concepts: Infants (Quinn, 1987; Roberts & Horowitz, 1986) and animals such as dogs (Tapp et al., 2004) and pigeons (Nakamura, Wright, Katz, Bodily, & Sturz, 2009) show evidence of concept learning, even though they do not have language abilities.

Levels of Concepts and Categories

Concepts vary in their specificity, and some are sub-categories of others. For instance, the concept FURNITURE includes CHAIR, TABLE, LAMP, and so on. But

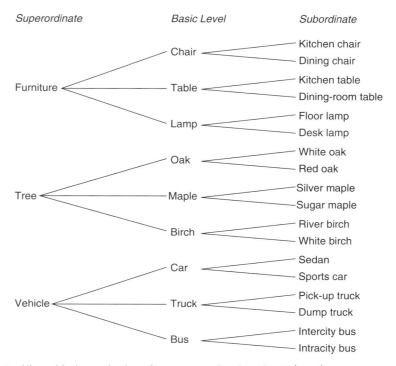

Figure 8.2 Hierarchical organization of some categories; from Rosch (1978).

CHAIRs themselves come in many forms (e.g., KITCHEN CHAIR, and DINING CHAIR). Those concepts can be depicted in a hierarchy, with lower levels (CHAIR, TABLE) nested in higher-level categories (FURNITURE), as seen in Figure 8.2. Many other categories, such as VEHICLE and TREE, can also be portrayed as hierarchies. For example, TREE contains the subcategories OAK, MAPLE, BIRCH (see Figure 8.2). Underneath that, there are different types of OAKs—WHITE OAK, RED OAK, and so on.

When depicted hierarchically, the most general concept (FURNITURE) is known as the *superordinate level*. The more commonly used level (CHAIR, TABLE, LAMP) is known as the *basic level*, and the subcategories under basic-level concepts are the *subordinate level* (e.g., KITCHEN CHAIR, DINING CHAIR).

Types of Concepts

Researchers often distinguish among types of concepts, each of which may function differently and be processed differently by humans. *Nominal concepts*, such as EVEN NUMBER, BACHELOR, or SQUARE, are based on definitions set by humans. *Nominal* means *name*, so those concepts are based on the names we use. *Natural-kind concepts* consist of objects found in the natural world: ANIMAL, PLANT, or GEOLOGICAL FORMATION (e.g., ISLAND, MOUNTAIN). *Artifactual concepts* consist of objects that are human-made ("artifacts"), including FURNITURE, VEHICLE, and ART-WORK.

With this background concerning the structure and organization of concepts and categories, we now turn to the first of the questions to be addressed in this chapter: What information is used as the basis for categorizing objects?

CATEGORIZATION BASED ON RULES: THE CLASSICAL VIEW OF CONCEPTS

Some concepts are precisely defined, and explicit *rules* tell us whether or not an object is a member of the category specified by the concept. An example is the concept GRANDMOTHER: To be a grandmother, you must be a mother (that is, you must be a woman who has had a child), and your child must have had a child. Similarly, EVEN NUMBER is precisely defined: Divide a number by 2; if there is no remainder, then it is an even number. These concepts have been created by humans; they are nominal concepts. GRANDMOTHER is part of the system of human kinship terms; and EVEN NUMBER is part of the system of arithmetic. In the case of nominal concepts, the basis for categorization is that an object possesses those *necessary and jointly sufficient features* that define the category. The components listed in the rule are *necessary* for inclusion in the category, and any object or item that contains all of those features must be in the category (the *jointly sufficient* aspect of the definition). So the necessary and jointly sufficient features of GRANDMOTHER are: (1) is a mother; (2) her child has a child. We could also call those features the *defining features* of GRANDMOTHER. Because it has a long history in philosophy and psychology, the view that concepts have precise definitions based on defining features has come to be called the *classical* view.

We are already familiar with the concept of *features* from the discussion of pattern recognition in Chapter 5, where it referred to the basic perceptual components (e.g., colors, lines, curves, angles) used to analyze visual objects into parts as the first stage of the recognition process. When talking about concepts and category membership, the use of the term *feature* is a bit different: The basic components are *semantic features*, which are *basic units of meaning* that combine to produce the meanings of words and concepts. So, for example, the meaning of MOTHER includes the semantic features *woman* and *has child*.

STUDIES OF THE FORMATION OF CLASSICAL OR RULE-DEFINED CONCEPTS

Bruner, Goodnow, and Austin (1956) carried out a pioneering experimental investigation of what has come to be called *concept formation*. They created artificial categories of shapes, in order to examine how individuals learned a new set of rule-based categories. The experimenters could manipulate the complexity of the rule and see how

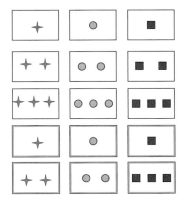

Figure 8.3   Sample of Bruner et al. (1956) stimuli.

that affected learning. The researchers designed a set of stimuli (see Figure 8.3) that differed along four *dimensions*, with three *features* within each dimension: (1) *shape* (square, circle, cross), (2) *color* (black, gray, white), (3) *number of figures* (1–3), and (4) *number of borders* (1–3). So, for example, one could have an object with the features *3 black squares* and *3 borders*. This method allowed the experimenters to construct a relatively large set of stimuli: 3 shapes × 3 colors × 3 different numbers of figures × 3 different numbers of borders = 81 different stimuli (Figure 8.3).

The participant was given one card to begin, say, one with two borders and three black squares, and was told that it was a member of the "correct" category, based on a rule chosen by the experimenter. The participant's task was to discover the rule. He or she had to pick out other cards from the set in Figure 8.3, one at a time, and the experimenter would say whether or not each was also a member of the category. Bruner et al. (1956) used various types of rules to define the category. An example rule might be: Correct cards must contain *three black figures*. In this case, the category was defined by the specific values or features on two of the dimensions (*three figures* + *black*). This sort of a rule is called a *conjunctive* rule, because it is based on the *conjunction* or grouping of features. Another rule might be that correct cards contained *either* two borders *or* three gray figures. Rules which are *either-or* are known as *disjunctive* rules (disjunction means *either* x *or* y).

Bruner et al. (1956) proposed that the miniature stimulus world that they had designed was a microcosm of the real world. In the real world, the number of stimuli is larger and they differ along more dimensions, but the basic processes of categorization were assumed to be similar. Examples of real-world concepts defined by conjunctive rules are BACHELOR (*male* and *not married*); and ISLAND (*piece of land* and *surrounded by water*). Also, in order to serve as a *senator of one of the states of the United States*, one must have been a *citizen of the United States for at least 9 years* and a *resident of the state in which one is running* and *at least 30 years of age* and *not have committed any crimes*. Using their stimulus set, Bruner and coworkers found that conjunctive rules were learned more easily than disjunctive rules (see also Nosofsky, Gluck, Palmeri, McKinley, & Glauthier, 1994).

In conclusion, the classical view of concepts assumed that concepts are defined by rules that specify defining features. In order to use categories, we must learn the rule or set of features that defines the concept underlying each of them.

Similarity–Based Concepts: Family Resemblance Theory

There is no doubt that some of our concepts are specified by precise rules, as the classical view assumes: An even number is a number divisible by two with no remainder; it is as simple as that. However, can the classical view explain all concepts? A number of years ago, Wittgenstein (1953) proposed that many concepts used by humans were not precisely defined, contrary to what the classical view assumed. As an example, Wittgenstein took a common concept that even children know—the concept GAME—and asked if there was any precise definition for it. Before reading further, please carry out the exercise in Box 8.2.

BOX 8.2 DEFINING AND SPECIFYING CONCEPTS

a. Make a list of five things that you consider to be GAMEs.

b. List some common features of games (such as "uses dice," "played on a field," etc.). Then try to specify a set of features from your list that can be used to define all activities that count as GAMEs.

Wittgenstein (1953) examined many examples of games, and could not find any necessary and jointly sufficient features; that is, features that were common to all games but not present in nongames. One might start with the notion of competition, but do all games involve competition? What about games you play alone, such as solitaire? Winning or losing is involved in solitaire, but not competition. Perhaps winning or losing is crucial to something being a game. But what if you play golf by yourself? No winning or losing is involved, but you are playing a game. What about "recreational," then? But do all games involve recreation? When professionals play baseball, it is not recreation, but they are still playing a game. One might say that all games involve enjoyment, but you can play a game even if you hate it—for exercise or money, among other reasons. Let's say that we discover that the only trait common to *all* games is "has rules." While we could argue that it constitutes a *necessary* feature (something must have rules for it to be counted as a game), it is certainly not a *sufficient* feature. Otherwise, all things that have rules would have to count as games. However, while registering for classes, paying taxes, driving, and obtaining vaccinations to meet school entrance requirements are certainly activities that have rules, we don't consider any of them GAMEs. Thus, that feature "has rules" alone cannot be used to delineate games from nongames. Those failed attempts at precise definition of GAMEs led Wittgenstein to propose that GAME and many other categories are not based on a precise definition, or necessary and jointly sufficient features. Nonetheless, we easily understand the concept and are able to use the word *game*.

Concepts and Family Resemblances

As an alternative to the classical idea that concepts involve defining features, Wittgenstein (1953) proposed that games make up a *family* of activities. The members of the category are related to each other in several different ways, similar to the way that members of a family look alike in different ways. There is no specific set of features that all the members of the family possess. Rather, the family resemblance of any single person to others is based on varying degrees of similarity to multiple other members of the category. We can see this pattern of varied similarity among the members of the concept GAME. Some (but not all) games involve use of a ball and a field, with teams working together in competition with another team, and the winner determined by the highest score. Examples are basketball, baseball, and football. Other games also involve keeping score and competition, but individuals participate, rather than teams (e.g., *Scrabble*, singles tennis). Still other games involve playing cards (e.g., poker), others use a game board (e.g., *Monopoly*), and others use music (e.g., musical chairs). Finally, some games can be carried out alone without any competition, such as solitaire. Thus, the set of games involves a large number of interconnected relationships. Two types of concepts already mentioned appear to have the same looseness of structure as GAMEs: (1) natural kinds, such as BIRD, TREE, and LIVING THING; and (2) artifacts, such as TOOL, VEHICLE, and FURNITURE (GAME is an artifact concept).

Family-Resemblance Theory: Prototypes and the Structure of Concepts

Rosch and coworkers (e.g., Rosch, 1973, 1975, 1978; Rosch & Mervis, 1975; Rosch, Mervis, Gray, Johnson, & Boyes-Braem, 1976) extended Wittgenstein's notion that many concepts are not specified by rules. Rosch (1973, 1975) proposed that family-resemblance concepts have a *graded structure*: Some members are more central than others. Family-resemblance concepts are organized around a *prototype*, a member that is central to the concept. The prototype is the best representative of that concept, because it possesses many of the typical features of the concept. Consider the concept BIRD. Prototypical members of this concept are a certain size and shape, have feathers, fly, build nests in trees, lay eggs in the nest, and sing. Those sorts of features, which set the class of birds apart from most other small animals, are *characteristic* of birds. Based on this analysis, a robin, canary or bluebird would be prototypical, while an ostrich or penguin would not be. Items that have minimal overlap with other items in the category (e.g., ostriches and penguins) are called *peripheral members.*

Because the structure of family-resemblance concepts is based on the degree of similarity among items, rather than necessary and jointly sufficient features, there should be no sharp boundaries around any given category. This means that some peripheral members of one concept might be similar to peripheral members of another. For example, a CUCUMBER is a FRUIT, though people may be tempted to consider it a VEGETABLE because it is not sweet, is often found in vegetable salads, and so on. Lakoff (1972, 1982; also Kay, 1979) noted that we often use *linguistic hedges* (or qualifying phrases) to indicate the peripheral status of some category members, such as when we say, "*Technically*, a cucumber is a fruit, but *loosely speaking*, it is a vegetable."

Evidence for Graded Conceptual Structure

A graded structure and lack of precise boundaries can be seen in many concepts, such as VEHICLE. Rosch (1975) used VEHICLE (along with a large number of other categories) in a study in which participants were asked to rate the extent to which basic-level examples (e.g., truck, sled, train) represented their idea or image of the superordinate category (VEHICLEs). The results were clear: *car* and *truck* received high ratings as VEHICLEs; *wagon* and *canoe* received intermediate ratings; and *skates*, *wheelbarrow*, and *elevator* received relatively low ratings. Further examples of concepts with graded structure include BIRDs, FRUITs, VEGETABLEs, CLOTHING, and TOOLs. Rosch (1975) asked experimental participants to use a 1–7 scale to indicate the extent to which basic-level exemplars (e.g., truck, sled, train) represented each of six superordinate categories. Rankings from Rosch's study are shown in Table 8.1. Items were rated on a scale of 1–7, based on how well they represented the idea of the superordinate category. Ratings of 1 indicated a very god example; ratings of 7 indicated a poor example.

Based on results like these, it has come to be accepted by many researchers that many concepts are structured in a family-resemblance fashion. Thus, humans appear to use at least two sorts of concepts: (1) *classical* or *rule-defined* concepts, and (2) *family-resemblance* concepts, which are not precisely defined by rules of membership, and have a graded structure.

Evidence for a Prototype-Based Structure of Concepts

Several sorts of evidence supported the idea that real-world categories are structured around prototypes: (1) people's ratings of the typicality of category members and (2) people's spontaneous production of category members. We will consider these in turn.

Ratings of Prototypicality and Possession of Characteristic Features

As we just discussed, Rosch (1975) asked a group of people to rate category members on typicality (i.e., what bird represents best their idea or image of a bird). She found that robins, sparrows, canaries, and blackbirds were deemed the most typical birds, whereas penguins, turkeys, and peacocks were rated as least typical. Thus, people are aware that some members of the category are more *bird-like* than others. Furthermore, there is a high positive correlation between the number of characteristic features possessed by an

Table 8.1 Ratings of Prototypicality for Items in Various Categories (Rosch, 1975)

Furniture		Fruit		Vehicle		Sport	
Item	Rating	Item	Rating	Item	Rating	Item	Rating
Chair	1.04	Orange	1.07	Automobile	1.02	Football	1.03
Ottoman	2.43	Watermelon	2.39	Bicycle	2.51	Auto Racing	2.78
Rug	5.00	Cranberry	3.22	Tank	3.84	Pool	3.82
Vase	6.23	Olive	6.21	Elevator	5.90	Chess	5.07

Table 8.2 Rosch and Mervis (1975) Results: Numbers of
Overlapping Features as a Function of Prototypicality

Category	Most Typical	Least Typical
Furniture	13	2
Fruit	16	0
Vehicle	36	2
Weapon	9	0
Vegetable	3	0
Clothing	21	0

object and the typicality rating for the object. Rosch and Mervis (1975) asked people to list the attributes of objects within one of six superordinate categories. For example, in the category BIRD, the *robin* possesses the characteristics *has feathers, flies, sings, is brown, has two legs, eats worms, and builds nests in trees*; *bluebirds* have very similar features (except that they are blue and eat bugs). *Penguins* have feathers, two legs, and lay eggs, but have few of the other characteristics listed for *robins* or *bluebirds*.

When Rosch and Mervis tallied the number of characteristics shared by the five most-typical items per category versus those shared by the five least-typical items, they found tremendous overlap among the five typical members (see Table 8.2), but very few shared traits among the five least-typical items of each category. These results support the idea that characteristic features of a concept are most heavily clustered around the prototypical item or items.

Accessibility of Category Members

If people are asked to list members of a given category (e.g., BIRD), prototypical items are more likely to be generated than are peripheral members (Battig and Montague, 1969; Storms, De Boeck, & Ruts, 2000), illustrating that prototypical members of a category are most accessible for recall. Prototypical members also tend to be the first examples of a category that we learn; children typically learn *robin* before *penguin* and *ostrich*. When researchers ask people to respond to *category verification sentences*, such as: *True or False—A carrot is a vegetable*, prototypical members are verified fastest (Smith, Shoben, & Rips, 1974). These results support the idea that all members of a category are not equal: Prototypical members are more likely to play a role in the structure of a category.

Family Resemblance, Concepts, and Categories: Conclusions

There is much evidence available that humans possess more than one kind of concept. Some concepts are defined by rules, and membership is based on possession of defining features. Other concepts, however, are not precisely defined, but are structured based on family resemblance, with overlapping features clustered around prototypes (Rosch & Mervis, 1975). These concepts do not have clear boundaries, as some members may share characteristics with members of two similar categories, and category membership is not always clear.

EXEMPLARS AS THE BASIS FOR CATEGORIZATION

Although the classical and family-resemblance views of concepts and categories are very different, they do have one idea in common: Concepts are based on a generalized mental representation that serves to *summarize* the information involved in the concept. In the classical view, that representation is the rule, or the set of necessary and jointly sufficient features, that defines the category. In the family-resemblance view, it is the *prototype*, the specific object that best represents that category in virtue of having the most characteristic features of the category (Rosch, 1975, 1978). However, an alternative view—the *exemplar view*—has been proposed that assumes that there is no single mental representation of a concept; rather, all one has in memory are the *specific items*, or *exemplars* (examples) of the concept that one has encountered in one's dealings with the world (e.g., Hintzman, 1986, 1988; Medin & Schaffer, 1978; Nosofsky & Zaki, 1998).

We can restate the exemplar view in terms familiar from earlier chapters: Concepts are based on *episodes* in memory. New items are put into a category (e.g., VEHICLE) because of their similarity to one or more already-stored exemplars. Then, memory for the exemplars is maintained, even after a more abstract representation of the category (e.g., a rule, or a prototype) has been developed. For example, Brooks, Norman, and Allen (1991) presented medical residents with slides of dermatological conditions that typified one of 16 common skin lesions. During the training phase, they were shown 30 slides, labeled with the diagnosis, and asked to briefly justify that diagnosis, given the features of the skin sample. The testing phase consisted of 60 test slides, some of which were the old slides (from the training series) plus others—new slides—that varied in terms of high or low similarity to the original training slides. As can be seen in Figure 8.4, participants were more correct for old exemplars than for new ones (even new ones that were perceptually similar to the training slides). Similar results were found when participants were tested after a 2-week delay. Other experiments using different types of stimuli (e.g., Allen & Brooks, 1991; Erickson & Kruschke, 1998;

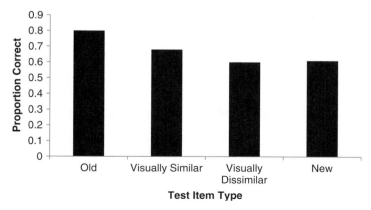

Figure 8.4 Memory for specific instances when learning concepts: Brooks, Norman, and Allen (1991) results.

Ross & Spalding, 1994) have also found that, after learning a category, people are most efficient at categorizing new objects that are similar to previously seen (i.e., training) exemplars.

Similarity and Frequency of Exemplars in Rule-Defined Categories

After people learn categories, they do not categorize all new test stimuli with equal efficiency. People are better at categorizing test stimuli that are similar to stored exemplars than those that are not, even when there is a rule available for them to use (Allen & Brooks, 1991; Brooks, 1978). This leads to the conclusion that memory for specific exemplars is important within categorization (Nosofsky & Palmeri, 1997). Erickson and Kruschke (1998) asked experimental participants to study a set of categories whose membership had been defined by a rule, similar to the items in Figure 8.5 (e.g., all LARGE OBJECTS in Category 1; all SMALL OBJECTS in Category 2). During the learning trials, some specific exemplars were presented more frequently than others. Since the categories were rule-based, using the rule was all that was actually needed to determine if an object was a member of Category 1 or Category 2. However, Erickson and Kruschke found that exemplars presented more frequently during learning were categorized more accurately than less frequent ones. Thus, even in concepts defined by rules, people remember the specific exemplars, and use that information to categorize objects that are presented.

A Question for the Exemplar View: Amnesics Learning Categories

The exemplar view assumes that specific episodes in memory serve as the basis for learning a concept. According to this view, learning concepts should pose a problem for amnesic patients, who we have seen often have difficulties with their episodic memory. However, several studies carried out by Knowlton and Squire (1993, Squire & Knowlton, 1995; summarized in Knowlton, 1997) have found that amnesic patients can learn to categorize stimuli accurately, at levels equivalent to normals' performance. However, amnesics perform significantly worse than normals on recognition for the specific items that were presented during training. To explain this dissociation between concept formation and memory for exemplars, Knowlton and Squire proposed that

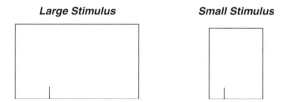

Figure 8.5 Erickson and Kruschke (1998) concept-learning stimuli. The rule governing the stimuli is: Large stimuli are in Category 1; small stimuli are in Category 2. The large-small split occurs at the mid-point of the horizontal scale. The vertical line varied from stimulus to stimulus, but it could be ignored.

learning concepts depends on *implicit memory*, while recognition for the specific exemplars depends on *explicit memory* for episodes. Since amnesia involves a loss of explicit memory, typically with retained implicit memory (see discussion in Chapter 2), Knowlton and Squire (1993) concluded that concept learning could take place independently of storage of the specific items. This conclusion raises problems for the exemplar view, which predicts that categorization should be related to recognition of individual items, though Nosofsky and Zaki (1998) have argued that there may be separate memory systems that underlie category formation and episodic memory for exemplars, allowing amnesics to maintain categorical processes despite their poor memory. One further interesting aspect of the Knowlton and Squire research (1993, Squire & Knowlton, 1995; see also Knowlton, 1997) is that they have attempted to explain the relationships among various cognitive systems, such as those of explicit memory, implicit memory, and categorization.

Models of Concepts and Categorization: Conclusions

We have examined three views of how concepts are structured and formed: (1) the classical view—based on defining features and rules; (2) the prototype view—based on an informative central member; and (3) the exemplar view—based on episodic information about specific members of the category. Formation of concepts seems to be a situation in which more than one process can be used, depending on the type of concepts involved. Some concepts are precisely defined, and thus rules can be used as the basis for category membership. Other concepts are loosely structured, with no precise boundaries, so they cannot be represented by rules. Even when an abstract representation, such as a set of necessary and jointly sufficient features, or a prototype, is used, there is also evidence that, in some situations, categorization may be based on memory for the individual exemplars of the category. In conclusion, any overarching theory of concepts and categorization must be complex enough—and flexible enough—to deal with the multiple ways in which concepts can be formed and category membership determined.

KNOWLEDGE- AND GOAL-BASED VIEWS OF CONCEPTS

Although the family resemblance and exemplar theories have different underlying assumptions about how categories are structured, they are similar in that they both assume that objects in the category are related to each other in terms of *similarity* (Ross & Spalding, 1994). In the family-resemblance view, category judgments are made on the basis of similarity to the prototype. The exemplar view proposes that an object is placed in some category because of its similarity to one or more exemplars of the concept. This *similarity-based* view of concepts and categories assumes that the similarity is in the world to start with, and that people often rely on *surface similarity*—that is, perceptual characteristics of the objects—as the basis for categorization. This is a *bottom-up* view of concepts and category formation, since it assumes that similarities and differences among objects are obvious, because of the way in which the world is structured and the way in which our perceptual systems are built.

Questions have been raised, however, about the notion that category membership is based purely on similarities between objects (Medin & Ortony, 1989). Sometimes other factors can override surface similarity in determining category membership.

Limitations to Similarity

As one example of how surface similarity can sometimes be less important than other factors, we can examine a study by Rips (1989). Rips presented college students with a circle three inches in diameter, and asked them whether it was more *similar* to a quarter or a pizza. The students judged it to be more similar to the quarter, presumably because pizzas are typically larger. Rips then asked the same people if it was more likely that the pictured circular object *was* a quarter or a pizza. In this case, the answer was that it was more likely to be a pizza, presumably because the size of quarters is fixed. Thus, the fact that the item was judged more similar to a quarter did not affect how it was categorized (see also Hahn & Chater, 1997; Tienson, 1988).

Theory-Based Concepts and Categorization: Psychological Essentialism

Other theorists have also proposed that categories are based on deeper knowledge than mere surface similarity (e.g., Medin, Goldstone, & Gentner, 1993). Consider the concept BIRD—one could say that birds are similar because they have feathers and wings. However, one could also ask: *Why* are those characteristics correlated in the world? There are no feathered animals that do not have wings—is that simply a random accident? Of course not; birds have wings and feathers because most of them *fly*. Furthermore, small male birds usually sing. Here, too, there is an underlying logic; singing serves in the process of reproduction: attracting mates and warning rival males to stay out of one's territory. The various characteristics possessed by the members of a category fit together if one understands the life of the animal in question. In addition, we know that some underlying cause (e.g., having bird genes) is the basis for those traits. Another way of putting this is to say that people have an implicit *folk theory* (that is, theory held by the "folk," or laypeople), which postulates that many objects have an underlying essence that dictates many characteristic features of those objects, and determines their category membership.

Several researchers (e.g., Gelman, 2004; Medin & Ortony, 1989; Shtulman, 2006) have posited that people believe that many categories have some essential components that explain how and why deep and surface features coalesce. This view is called *psychological essentialism.* Laypeople may not fully understand the essence of a category (e.g., DNA in animals), but it serves as the foundation for their reasoning about the structure of categories (Gelman, 2004; Medin, & Ortony, 1989). Thus, without necessarily understanding the exact genetic differences or the mechanism of genetic transmission, we know that birds and dogs differ in their DNA, and that their respective genes dictate their bone structure, whether they have feathers or fur, and behavioral characteristics (e.g., whether they chirp or bark). We thus behave as if there is an essence to some concepts. It is sometimes said that, rightly or wrongly, laypeople have "theories" that contain causal explanations about the origins and functions of a

Figure 8.6 Flamingo, bat, blackbird.
Adapted from Figure 1 from Gelman and Markman, 1986.

concept's features, and how and why many features are correlated (Murphy & Medin, 1985, in Cimpian, Gelman, & Brandone, 2010). For example, people surmise that feathers and wings are highly correlated because their function is to assist in flying, and that both features are predicated upon having a particular DNA which helps define the category's essence.

Psychological essentialism has several key components. First, the theory predicts that people will appeal to the "essential nature" of a concept when making category decisions, and the extent to which an object possesses this essential nature will determine its category membership. This means that essentialist categories should show all-or-none membership (Diesendruck & Gelman, 1999; Kalish, 2002). Secondly, if organisms or objects have an essential nature, then they should maintain certain traits even if placed in a different environment. Gelman and Wellman (1991) told preschoolers about a baby kangaroo who went to live with goats. The children agreed that the kangaroo would nonetheless still hop and have a pouch, rather than adopt the traits of goats (also see Johnson & Solomon, 1997; Springer, 1996; Waxman, Medin, & Ross, 2007).

Thirdly, psychological essentialism predicts that underlying essences should outweigh surface similarity when people make category judgments or engage in concept-based inferences, and that category membership will be used to infer nonobservable or internal traits. Gelman and Markman (1986; see also Gelman & Markman, 1987) presented 4-year-olds and college students with 20 trios of pictures. Each trio was composed of two initial pictures (e.g., a flamingo and a bat) and a third or *target* picture (e.g., a blackbird). The target shared category membership with one of the initial pictures (the *bird*), but was drawn to resemble the other item (the bat; see Figure 8.6). Adults and children were told a fact about each of the two initial pictures. For example, the flamingo was said to feed its babies mashed-up food, while the bat fed its babies milk. Both adults and children overwhelmingly inferred that the target item shared characteristics with the same-category item, even though the target more-closely resembled the out-of-category item (e.g., the blackbird was thought to feed its baby mashed-up food, like the flamingo).

Can Essentialist and Family Resemblance Representations Coexist?

As just noted, the essentialist view proposes that at least some concepts should produce all-or-none category membership. In contrast, the family-resemblance view, with its assumption that all concepts are structured based on similarity to a prototype, asserts that there are not firm category boundaries. Could people use essentialist information to make category decisions, and still exhibit graded structure effects? Two experiments have shown that this is, indeed, the case for many concepts.

Armstrong, Gleitman, and Gleitman (1983) examined whether the finding that many concepts have family-resemblance structures actually contradicted the essentialist view. Armstrong et al. attempted to determine whether they could distinguish rule-based categories from family-resemblance–style categories on the basis of typicality judgments. They compiled lists of members of rule-based categories (e.g., *geometric figure*, *odd numbers*) versus family-resemblance categories (e.g., *sports*, *vehicles*), and then asked people to rate the items on a 1–7 scale (the same one used by Rosch, 1975), as to how good they were as members of the category. Even for well-defined categories, people indicated that some examples of each category were better than others. So far, the results seem to provide strong support for graded structure.

However, in a second study, Armstrong et al. (1983) asked people whether it made sense to rate items in well-defined concepts (e.g., *odd numbers*) for degree of membership. Most people thought that such judgments did not make sense. Moreover, a significant number of people claimed the same thing about family-resemblance categories (e.g., *fruit*, *sports*, *vehicle*; see Table 8.3). The researchers concluded that, although experimental studies may present evidence that many concepts and their associated categories have a graded structure, people actually believe that some concepts have an all-or-none membership (which conflicts with the basic tenets of the family resemblance view). Armstrong et al. proposed a dual theory, in which people know the core criteria for a concept (e.g., GRANDMOTHER = *mother of a parent*), but still think that certain grandmothers may be more grandmotherly than others. In conclusion, research findings of graded category structure may not contradict the essentialist view, and it is possible that people may represent both the essential and the typicality of concepts simultaneously.

Malt (1994) used the essentialist concept WATER to explore how people represent items within that category (water is an essentialist concept because most people know its composition is H_2O). She first asked experimental participants to estimate the percentage of H_2O in each example of a list of WATER and NONWATER items. Essentialism might predict that there should be some cutoff above which all waters fall, and below which all nonwaters fall, but this was not the case (see Table 8.4A). For example, sewer water was judged to be composed of 67% H_2O, whereas the NONWATERS tea, saliva, and urine all had higher average H_2O estimates. In a second experiment, Malt asked people to rate the typicality of 43 WATERS, using a similar 1 to 7 scale as Rosch (1975), and found evidence for a graded structure (see Table 8.4B). Drinking water received the highest rating (6.5), and radiator water the lowest (2.7). This suggests that people may hold essentialist views about concepts such as water (after all, even schoolchildren can recite the chemical makeup of water as H_2O), but, as in the Armstrong et al. (1983) study, still adopt a graded-structure view of particular examples of that category.

Malt (1994) concluded that people's representation of WATER was structured to include information about how frequently people use different kinds of waters, and whether they come from a natural or home-based source.

Table 8.3 Assessment of "Family Resemblances": List of Stimuli and Ratings. (a) Protoypicality ratings for various categories, both "family resemblance" and well-defined categories. (b) Percent of subjects who said "No" when asked if ratings made sense.

(a)

Prototype Categories		Well-Defined Categories	
Exemplar	Rating	Exemplar	Rating
Fruit		**Even Number**	
Apple	1.3	4	1.1
Strawberry	2.1	8	1.5
Plum	2.5	10	1.7
Pineapple	2.7	18	2.6
Fig	5.2	34	3.4
Olive	6.4	106	3.9
Sport		**Odd Number**	
Football	1.4	3	1.6
Hockey	1.8	7	1.9
Gymnastics	2.8	23	2.4
Wrestling	3.1	57	2.6
Archery	4.8	501	3.5
Weight-Lifting	5.1	447	3.7
Vegetable		**Female**	
Carrot	1.5	Mother	1.7
Celery	2.6	Housewife	2.4
Asparagus	2.7	Princess	3.0
Onion	3.6	Waitress	3.2
Pickle	4.8	Policewoman	3.9
Parsley	5.0	Comedienne	4.5
Vehicle		**Plane Geometry Figure**	
Car	1.0	Square	1.3
Boat	3.3	Triangle	1.5
Scooter	4.5	Rectangle	1.9
Tricycle	4.7	Circle	2.1
Horse	5.2	Trapezoid	3.1
Skis	5.6	Ellipse	3.4

(b)

Percent of subjects who said "NO"	
Prototype Categories	
Fruit	43
Sport	71
Vegetable	33
Vehicle	24
Well-Defined Categories	
Even number	100
Odd number	100
Female	86
Plane geometry figure	100

From Armstrong et al. (1983, Tables 1 and 5).

Table 8.4 Analysis of "Water" as a Concept. (a) Percentage of estimated H_2O in WATER and NONWATER categories, from Malt (1994). (b) Typicality ratings of various WATERs (1–7 scale; 7 = most typical)

(a)

Water Example	Judged % Water
Pure Water	98.1
Rain Water	90.9
Ocean Water	78.7
Sewer Water	67.0
Nonwater Example	
Tea	91.0
Saliva	89.3
Urine	79.1
Cider	65.1
Soy Sauce	64.0
Lighter Fluid	42.3

(b)

Example	Rating
Drinking Water	6.5
Ocean Water	5.8
River Water	5.6
Well Water	4.6
Sewer Water	3.8
Radiator Water	2.7

Conclusion

There is ample evidence that people function as if they believe that many concepts have an underlying essence that both overrides surface similarity and explains correlations of features among exemplars within a category. The Armstrong et al. (1983) and Malt (1994) experiments illustrated that people can hold multiple representations of concepts, depending on the type of question that is posed to them, the context in which an exemplar appears, or how we use an entity in our daily lives.

DEVELOPMENT OF CONCEPTS AND CATEGORIZATION

Psychological essentialism proposes that categorization is based on hidden essences, which means that the conceptual basis for categorizing might sometimes be subtle and based on knowledge rather than perceptual features. We have also seen that essentialism may coexist with family-resemblance representations for some concepts (such as ODD NUMBER and WATER; Armstrong et al., 1983; Malt, 1994). Keil

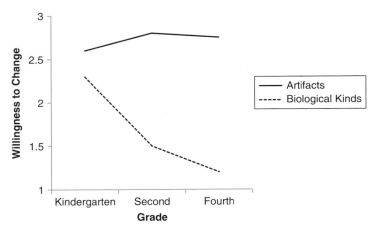

Figure 8.7 Results of Keil (1992, Chapter 9, Figure 9.2): Higher scores (up to 3) indicated more willingness to change category membership after superficial changes, and thus less adherence to essentialism. Graph indicates that all children were willing to change categorization for artifacts, but only younger children were willing to change category membership for biological kinds.

and Batterman (1984; see also Keil, 1989) have proposed that children's concepts go through a developmental shift, in which early concepts tend to be based on the surface features of objects, and then become more heavily influenced by adult definitions and more essentialist information. In one study of natural-kind categories, Keil (1983) showed children a picture of a raccoon, and told them that a doctor shaved some of its fur, dyed part of the remaining fur black, and painted a white stripe down its back. Then they surgically added a "smelly sac." When they were done, the animal looked like . . . and a picture of a skunk was produced. The identity of the original item was confirmed by telling participants that the *raccoon-now-resembling-a-skunk* nonetheless had raccoon parents and produced raccoon babies. Children were asked whether the creature was now a skunk or a raccoon (and to provide an explanation).

As can be seen in Figure 8.7, for biological entities, kindergartners were most likely to accept a change based on the physical characteristic features: If it now looked like a skunk, it must now be a skunk. The older children, on the other hand, appealed to the animal's origins, as well as the deeper and internal features of the animal when making their classification; they resisted surface changes. In contrast, if a coffeepot (an artifact) had its handle sawed off, a flat base attached, a stick inserted, and was then filled with birdseed, children at all ages were willing to say that it was now functioning as a birdfeeder. As psychological essentialism predicts, people are most likely to adhere to essentialist traits for biological categories (Rhodes & Gelman, 2009), and to deny that superficial changes alter an animal's (or person's) identity.

The Development of Essences

For other nonbiological categories, especially nominal categories, there may also be a developmental shift from characteristic to *essential* features. Keil and Batterman (1984)

Table 8.5   Examples of Keil and Batterman's Descriptions of Concepts, Containing Characteristic Versus Defining Features

This smelly, mean old man with a gun in his pocket came to your house one day and took your color television set because your parents didn't want it anymore and told him that he could have it. Could he be a robber?	This very friendly and cheerful woman came up to you and gave you a hug, but then she disconnected your toilet bowl and took it away without permission and never returned it. Could she be a robber?
Suppose a waitress handed you something shaped like this (experimenter handed subject a piece of paper folded in half) that had written inside it the restaurant's history—when it was built, the names of the waitresses and cooks, and so on, but it didn't say anything about food inside. Could that be a menu?	If there was this seashell sitting on a table in a restaurant, and on it was listed all the meals and foods that the restaurant served, could that be a menu?
There is this ugly building in the slums with bars on every window and rats who live in the corners. The men who live there are so poor they can only eat bread and water. They are allowed to leave the building whenever they want to. Could that be a jail?	There is this beautiful castle with horses and a swimming pool, and really delicious food. The people who live there can use all of these great things, but they are never allowed to leave unless they get special permission. They can only stay in the castle if they've done something wrong. Could that be a jail?

provided children (in kindergarten, second grade, and fourth grade; overall age range, 5 1/2–10) with descriptions of types of people or objects, and asked them whether or not the person/object could be a member of a given category. Each description was presented in two forms, as shown in Table 8.5. In one form, the defining features were not present, but characteristic or stereotypical features were. For example, a man fitting the surface description of a robber (gun in his pocket, etc.) arrives to take way an appliance that he has permission to take. In the second case, defining features were present, but surface features were not. In this case, a pleasant-looking woman arrives and without permission takes something away.

The children were asked whether each description fit the concept in question (e.g., robber) and asked to explain their decision. Younger children's category judgments were more influenced by surface features. Thus, an unkempt-looking person was accepted as a robber, although he had permission to take an object. Older children (e.g., fourth graders) made category judgments based on the defining features of concepts (e.g., a robber had to steal something without permission). These results support the idea that young children rely on what is most obvious about the objects and situations that they find themselves in, and only later use defining features that adults use.

There is thus support for many of the predictions of psychological essentialism (see also Bloom & Gelman, 2008; Rhodes & Gelman, 2009; Taylor, Rhodes, & Gelman, 2009). However, there is also evidence that reliance on surface similarity may be strong in children, and that there is a developmental shift to essentialism (Keil, 1992). Also, as we saw earlier, both types of categorization strategies may coexist in adults (Armstrong et al., 1983; Malt, 1994).

STRUCTURES OF CONCEPTS AND CATEGORIES: SUMMARY AND CONCLUSIONS

Research on the structure of concepts has seen a movement away from and then back toward the idea that at least some concepts are precisely defined. Wittgenstein's analysis of concept members as coalescing due to family resemblance was supported by much psychological research, particularly that of Rosch (e.g., 1975; Rosch & Mervis, 1975). In more recent years, however, the notion of essentialism represents a movement back toward the classical idea that there is something like defining features as the basis for our understanding and use of concepts (even if people do not fully know the exact nature of an essence).

RELATIONS AMONG CONCEPTS: THE STRUCTURE OF KNOWLEDGE

We now know a bit about the structure of individual concepts, and how they are used to carve up the world into categories. This background leads to the question of how our knowledge is organized. That is, how are our concepts related to each other, and how is information about a category retrieved from memory? Cognitive scientists have for many years been developing models of *semantic memory*: Our knowledge of concepts and their interrelations. There are two closely related aspects of our semantic knowledge: (1) how it is *structured* and (2) how it is *used* in thinking and reasoning. We examine the structure of knowledge in this section, and we discuss the use of concepts in thinking in the last section of the chapter.

Hierarchical Models of Semantic Memory

Collins and Quillian (1969) developed the first modern model of semantic memory (see Figure 8.8). The model assumes that each concept that we know is represented by a location, or *node*, in memory. This is comparable to specific locations in a computer's memory. In addition, concepts are related to each other through *connections*, or *links*.

There were two important aspects of this model. First, the hierarchical structure of knowledge was represented directly in the connections among the concepts. So, for example, the person who possesses the knowledge diagrammed in Figure 8.8 knows that CANARY is a type of BIRD and that BIRD is a type of ANIMAL because those specific links connect the concepts in question. Based on this knowledge structure, you can answer the question "Is a canary a bird?" in the affirmative by simply searching memory until the relevant node is found. You use the information in semantic memory by "moving" along the links, and at each point you activate new pieces of information, which can be used to answer questions, or make categorical inferences. Second, it was also assumed that any piece of information is stored at that place in the system where it can be used most efficiently. For example, the feature "can fly" is relevant to almost all birds, so it is stored with the concept BIRD, rather than with each specific bird.

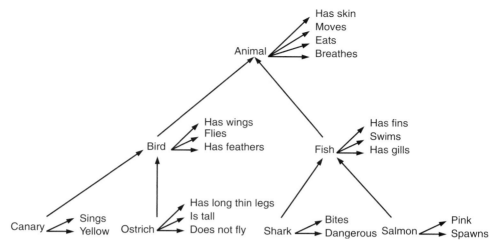

Figure 8.8   Collins and Quillian network model of a portion of semantic memory.

Imagine that you have just learned that the dodo, a bird previously thought extinct, has been discovered living in some remote area of the world. If you were asked about whether that bird could fly, you would answer by going through a reasoning process. You first check what you know about the *dodo*, but your DODO concept says nothing about flying, since you just learned that there was such a bird. You then check its category concept, BIRD, and there you find "can fly," so you would conclude that this bird probably flies.

Measuring Hierarchical Organization in Semantic Memory

If Collins and Quillian (1969) are correct that semantic memory is organized hierarchically, then one should be able to demonstrate that organization through experimental methods. One method involves determining how long people take to respond "true" or "false" in category-verification tasks, in which sentences are posed in "*An X is a Y*" form, such as (A) *A canary is a bird*; (B) *A canary is an animal*; (C) *An apple is an animal*. (A) and (B) are both true; however, according to the model in Figure 8.8, the relevant pieces of information are stored at different "semantic distances" from CANARY in the network. The information that a canary is a BIRD is one link away; on the other hand, the information that a canary is an ANIMAL is at least two links distant. Thus, people should be quicker at agreeing that canaries are birds than that canaries are animals, although both sentences are equally true. Collins and Quillian's results supported the hypothesis that semantic distance in the model would predict reaction times.

Questions About Hierarchically Organized Networks

The results just discussed provide support for the idea that we search memory by moving along the links in a hierarchical structure from one concept to another. However, there are several pieces of evidence that raise questions for this idea. In an early test of hierarchical models of semantic memory, Conrad (1972) asked people to determine the truth of sentences like the following:

1. A shark can move.

2. A fish can move.

3. An animal can move.

According to the hierarchical model, the information *can move* should be attached to the ANIMAL node, since virtually all animals can move. This analysis predicts that people should be fastest in verifying the truth of Sentence 3, since that sentence matches the way the network is organized. In order to verify Sentence 2, the person would have to spend additional time moving from FISH to ANIMAL. Similarly, Sentence 1 should take longer still, since the relevant information is two levels away. Contrary to those predictions, however, Sentence 1 produced the *fastest* responses, not the slowest. Such a result raises questions about whether semantic memory is organized in the manner postulated by the network model outlined in Figure 8.8 (see also Rips, Shoben, & Smith, 1973).

A second result that goes against the strict hierarchical model of semantic memory comes from a sentence-verification task using category members that varied in their prototypicality, such as these:

1. A canary is a bird.

2. An eagle is a bird.

3. A penguin is a bird.

4. An ostrich is a bird.

The sentences varied only in the typicality of the example as a member of the category in the question: Canaries and eagles are more prototypical birds than are penguins and ostriches. As far as the hierarchical model is concerned, all these sentences are interpreted in the same way (see Figure 8.8), since in each case the distance is the same. However, numerous experiments (e.g., Armstrong, Gleitman, & Gleitman, 1983; Rips et al., 1973), have found that more-typical items (e.g., canary and eagle) are responded to more quickly than are the less-typical ones (e.g., penguin and ostrich). This result cannot be explained by the model in Figure 8.8, since it predicts that category verification times are based on the number of links that connect any two concepts. Additionally, dominant *properties* of concepts (e.g., *A robin has feathers*) result in shorter response times than nondominant properties (e.g., *A robin is warm-blooded*; Ashcraft, 1978), even when those properties are stored at the same level.

Spreading Activation Model

Because of problems with a strict hierarchical model, a later version of a semantic network by Collins and Loftus (1975) removed the hierarchical structure of concepts in favor of an associative network, in which there are simply connections among related

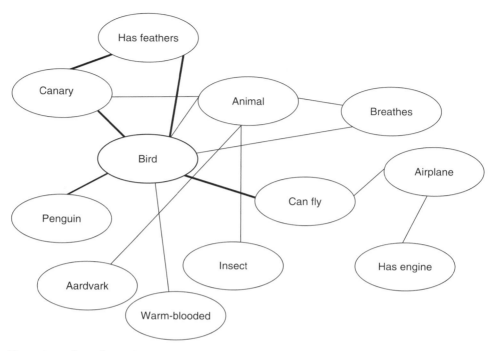

Figure 8.9 Spreading activation model of concepts. Diagram is simplified: All connections are not in place.

concepts and features. The connections among nodes allow activation to spread from one concept to a related one, and connections can vary in their associative strength, which translates into activation spreading at different speeds. Such a model can explain how more typical members of a category (e.g., canary, eagle) are verified as birds more quickly: The strength of the connection between CANARY and BIRD is stronger than the association between PENGUIN and BIRD (see the thickness of the lines in Figure 8.9). The same logic applies to individual features; highly salient features of a concept (such as "has feathers" for BIRD) will have stronger connections than less dominant or salient traits (e.g., "is warm-blooded").

Further evidence to support different associative strengths among concepts, and between concepts and related features, comes from studies of semantic priming (which we already encountered in Chapters 2, 3, and 5). If you read a word, say, *doctor*, recognizing that word would activate the node corresponding to the concept DOCTOR in semantic memory. When the node is activated, activation spreads along the links from that node to related conceptual nodes (e.g., NURSE, HOSPITAL, PROFESSION), and to property-related nodes (e.g., INTELLIGENT, CONFIDENT). In addition, the activation could spread even further: if HOSPITAL is activated, it could in turn spread activation to BUILDING, GERMS, and so on. Thus, activating a given concept can affect the level of activation of other concepts, and the degree of this activation depends on the strength of the connections among concepts or properties in the network.

Semantic priming was examined in a series of lexical-decision studies by Meyer and Schvaneveldt (1971). Pairs of stimuli were presented, and participants had to decide if both were words. Sometimes the pairs of stimuli were words, and sometimes they were not. When the stimuli were both words, Meyer and Schvaneveldt varied the relation between them. In *priming* pairs, the words were closely related (*bread – butter*), while control word pairs were not related (*nurse – butter*). The results of the study supported the notions of spreading activation and the network model. People were faster in responding *yes* to prime pairs compared to unprimed pairs. Thus, a closely related word primed or facilitated the processing of the second word.

Anderson's Analysis of Semantic Memory

These results leave us in a bit of a difficulty. On the one hand, there is no doubt that human knowledge is hierarchically organized. We know that canaries, robins, peacocks, chickens, turkeys, penguins, and ostriches are BIRDs, and that BIRDs are ANIMALs. On the other hand, it seems that we sometimes use this information less in a hierarchical than in an *associative* way. We have used and heard the word *bird* much more frequently in the context of *canary* and *robin* than in the context of *chicken* or *ostrich*. Those experiences with concepts can affect how efficiently we deal with them, and psychological models of semantic memory must take this into account.

One prevalent network model used to represent knowledge is that of Anderson (e.g., 1976, 1983, 2010; Anderson & Bower, 1973), who has developed a series of large-scale models of human cognition called the *Adaptive Control of Thought*, or *ACT*. An updated version of the original model, called ACT* (pronounced "Act-Star") proposes three memory structures—for declarative, procedural, and working memory (WM), though only the declarative memory portion of the theory is relevant to our discussion of concepts and semantic organization in this chapter.

Let us say that in a conversation you learn the following facts.

1. The dodo, a bird, was discovered in Australia.

2. The dodo does not fly.

3. The dodo eats flowers.

Assume that you were not familiar with the dodo before this conversation; a new node is then added to semantic memory to represent the DODO. Based on the new facts you have learned from the conversation, the new DODO node gets connected to several already existing nodes: BIRD and AUSTRALIA, among others. Then the new information, concerning the dodo's lack of flying and its eating habits, is also entered into semantic memory, by establishing the appropriate connections. Anderson's analysis of how this new information would be represented in semantic memory is shown in Figure 8.10.

Three types of learning can occur in ACT*: *generalization* (such as when we learn that robins, canaries, and ostriches are all BIRDs), *discrimination* (such as when a child learns to distinguish golden retrievers from Irish setters, and reptiles from amphibians),

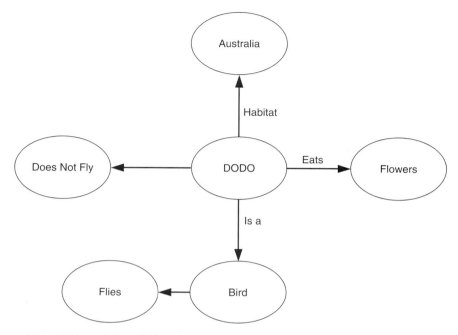

Figure 8.10 Anderson's formulation of semantic memory; a portion of a network.

and *strengthening* (connections among concepts and features are fortified with repeated use).

Anderson's model is more similar to the associative network of Collins and Loftus (1975) than it is to the hierarchical model of Collins and Quillian (1969; see Figures 8.8 and 8.9). The mechanism through which information is accessed in Anderson's model is, as with Collins and Loftus (1975), *spreading activation*. Anderson assumes that a concept in memory is activated by hearing or reading a word, or by seeing an object in the environment. Activation spreads outward along the links in memory, and the speed and amount of activation along each link depends on how many links *fan out* from a given node. The more links fanning from a node, the more weakly and slowly activation spreads. For example, let us say that one person learns only Sentence 1 above about the Dodo, while another person learns Sentences 1–3. If both these people are then given the following question: "True or false? A dodo is a bird," the person who learned all three sentences will be slower to respond because of the three-link fan. This is called the *fan effect* in sentence verification (Anderson, 1974). Anderson also assumes that the efficiency with which activation spreads depends on how often a link has been used in the past: More use results in faster spreading activation. The frequency with which we encounter and activate information can thus alter the network, leading to more frequent items being activated more quickly and easily.

Because of their associative nature, both Collins and Loftus's (1975) and Anderson's (1983, 2010) models can deal with some of the results that raise problems for the hierarchical model of Collins and Quillian (1969). For example, the fact that the property-verification sentence "Sharks can move" is verified more quickly than "Animals can move" can be explained because the latter proposition has probably been encountered very infrequently, and so would be slower to be verified. Similarly, the fact that sentences containing typical category members ("A canary is a bird") are verified more quickly than sentences containing atypical members ("An ostrich is a bird") is explained by noting that the proposition with the typical member is encountered more frequently.

Semantic Memory Developed From Associative Contexts

We have now considered two analyses of semantic memory that assume that hierarchical organization is represented in semantic memory, either directly, through links between concepts (Collins & Quillian, 1969), or indirectly, in terms of individual memory locations that contain the relevant information (Anderson, 1983, 2010; Collins & Loftus, 1975). In a more recent development with fascinating possibilities, models of semantic memory have been proposed that assume that any structure to human conceptual knowledge is simply built out of word associations, rather than knowledge of meaning, per se (e.g., Burgess & Lund, 1997; Burgess, Livesay, & Lund, 1998; Kwantes, 2005; Landauer & Dumais, 1997; Landauer, McNamara, Dennis, & Kintsch, 2007; Lund & Burgess, 1996; Stone, Dennis, & Kwantes, 2011). In contrast to the hierarchical model of Collins and Quillian (1969) or semantic associative models, such as Anderson's (1976, 1983, 2010), which assume that semantic memory is structured through some sort of links between meaningfully related concepts, the *Hyperspace Analogue to Language (HAL)* model of Lund and Burgess (1996; Burgess & Lund, 1997) and the *Latent Semantic Analysis* model of Landauer and Dumais (1997) propose that all verbal input is analyzed in an extremely simple way: The memory system keeps track of only the frequency with which words appear close to each other in speech or writing, i.e., the *global co-occurrences* of words. No other information is used to provide structure in memory.

The model developed by Burgess and Lund and their coworkers used as input a set of over 300,000,000 words, obtained from discussion groups on the Internet, as illustrated in Table 8.6. The model works with a *window of processing* set at 10, because this value corresponds reasonably closely to people's working memory for words in sentences (in Table 8.6, the window is only 5, for ease of presentation). The italicized words in the sentence mark the window of processing, which conducts its first analysis using the first word and then moves across the sentence. In the example in Table 8.6, the row marked *raced* gives the scores for the words in the sentence in relation to *raced*. *Horse* gets a score of 5 because it is next to *raced* in the 5-word window. *The* gets a score of 4, because there was one word between it and *raced*, and so forth. High numbers tell us that a given word appeared closely before or after that word in the sample.

Ultimately, what is calculated is the *global co-occurrence*: a measure of the relationships among the words that were used in the language sample, plus measurements on whether words appear in similar contexts or not. For example, in English *road* and *street* have a high relationship number, not because they often appear together in the same utterance, but because they have a high similarity in terms of the 10-word windows in

Table 8.6 Burgess's Analysis of a Language Input

A. Sample sentence: *The horse raced past the barn fell.*

B. Matrix for sample sentence, adapted from Burgess and Lund (1997; Table 1). Produced by applying a five-word co-occurrence window to the sentence.

	Barn	Fell	Horse	Past	Raced	The
Barn			2	4	3	5
Fell	5		1	3	2	4
Horse						5
Past			4		5	3
Raced			5			4
The			3	5	4	2

Note: Values in matrix rows represent values for words that preceded the word (row label), while columns represent values for words following the word (column label). The numbers represent the distance between the two words. So the *barn/fell* cell contains a 5 because, with the five-word window, those words were next to each other (similarly for *raced/horse*). Cells containing zeroes have been left empty for visual clarity. The column for *fell* is empty because no words followed that word in the sample sentence.

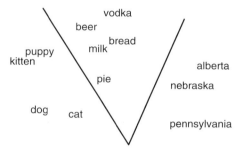

Figure 8.11 Burgess and Lund (1997) Figure 2: Patterns of word relationships.

which they occur. That is, *road* and *street* tend to appear in similar contexts and thus become conceptually linked (Burgess & Lund, 1997).

Researchers can use those context-similarity measures to investigate how people might build up semantic memory from scratch. Based on which words tend to co-occur in sentences, or in similar contexts, the model builds a conceptual organization from the bottom-up, including the development of subclasses of words. For example, *kitten* is closer to *puppy* than it is to *cat*, while *cat* and *dog* are close to each other (see Figure 8.11). These results indicate that one can develop conceptual categories without microanalyzing the words' meanings into features; all one has to do is keep track of the co-occurrence of the words which label concepts. One conclusion that can be drawn from this research on semantic memory is that structure in behavior does not mean that that structure is explicitly represented in our knowledge.

Organization of Semantic Memory: Conclusions

Cognitive scientists have proposed several different sorts of models of semantic memory. On the one hand are network models that assume that a hierarchical organization is directly represented in semantic memory (e.g., Collins and Quillian, 1969). On the other hand, there are diverse models that posit that organization in semantic memory is bottom-up, and based on: (1) associations among categories and the features of exemplars within those categories (Collins & Loftus, 1975), or (2) among categories, features, and other types of related information (e.g., Anderson, 1983, 2010). Although these models differ in many ways, they all assume that there is basic organizational structure in semantic memory, built on meaningful features that connect concepts. In contrast, the view developed by Burgess and others (Burgess & Lund, 1997; Burgess et al., 1998; see also Landauer & Dumais, 1997, Landauer et al., 2007) proposes that the relation between any two concepts is defined by similarities of contexts in which the concepts appear. Those similarities provide an associative basis for linking concepts, and thus semantic memory is constructed out of context-based associations among words, rather than meanings or features per se.

GOAL- AND USE-BASED INFLUENCES ON CONCEPTS, CATEGORIZATION, AND INFERENCES

The analyses of semantic memory that we have considered so far can be looked upon as snapshots of the organization of semantic memory at a given point in time, but our concepts can change over time. We often acquire knowledge about objects indirectly, through education, which also plays a role in the way we categorize and organize objects in the world (Markman & Ross, 2003; Murphy & Ross, 2007). For example, even a child who lives in a city with little access to wildlife could learn the difference between reptiles and amphibians during science class. In other cases, our conceptual knowledge is altered as a result of interactions with people, animals, and objects in the world. Such change is evident in studies of experts' conceptual systems. Experts' interactions with objects and the knowledge that arises out of those interactions change the way they classify and make inferences about objects.

Medin, Lynch, Coley, and Atran (1997) examined the influence of expertise on categorization of, and reasoning about, trees. Participants were three groups of experts, who had worked with trees for an average of 16 years. The first group consisted of taxonomists, who were primarily engaged in research and teaching. The second group, landscape workers, focused on use of trees for design and esthetic purposes. Finally, a group of maintenance workers dealt with planting and caring for trees for a municipality. The participants were asked to sort 48 names of tree species (e.g., *oak, maple, birch, elm, spruce*) into groups that "go together by nature" and explain their justifications.

Medin et al. found that the groups of experts differed in how they classified the trees. Taxonomists, not surprisingly, classified the trees mainly using scientific classifications typically found in a biology textbook. The two other groups had their own classification system, unique to their goals and needs. For example, one of the landscapers' groupings included trees that were desirable to plant along city streets, while another included small ornamental trees. Thus, the landscapers typically grouped the trees based on how they used them in their work. The maintenance workers grouped some trees on the basis of properties such as fruit-bearing or nut-bearing, which mirrors surface characteristics of the trees more than scientific taxonomy; for example, all nut-bearing trees are not classified together scientifically.

In a second study, Medin and his coworkers (1997) explored expertise differences in inferential reasoning about concepts. The three expert groups were asked questions that required that they reason about trees to see if they would use their own functional categories in reasoning. Here is an example of the questions presented to the experts:

> Say we discovered a new disease that infected [tree X]. If this disease could also infect other trees, is it more likely that the new disease would infect [tree A] or [tree B]?

The slots in the question were filled with names of trees. The trees given as possible answers in each question were chosen so that one of the alternatives came from the same *scientific category* as tree X, while the other came from the same category in the *expert's own functional classification*. The landscapers' reasoning was more likely to conform to scientific taxonomy, but the maintenance workers were more likely to adhere to their functional categories from the sorting task. Thus, the categories that one develops through extensive immersion in a domain may determine the ways in which one reasons about items within that domain. Categorization is thus a dynamic process.

USING CONCEPTS TO THINK ABOUT THE WORLD: THE IMPORTANCE OF THE BASIC LEVEL

Human concepts provide a rich basis for analysis of the world. That is, we all know many things about people, animals, birds, bees, cabbages, and kings. Indeed, our concepts are so rich that the question arises as to how we typically use them in our dealings with the world. For example, a glance out of a window might yield a perception of a robin sitting in an oak tree. This activates knowledge (perhaps implicitly) that the oak tree is not only a type of TREE, but also a PLANT, a LIVING THING, a PHYSICAL OBJECT, and so forth. If we are well-versed in trees, that OAK might be recognized more specifically as a PIN OAK or WHITE OAK or a NORTHERN RED OAK. A given object therefore can fit into any of a number of categories at varying levels of specificity (once again, see Figure 8.2). Since we have all these potentially useful categories at our fingertips, the question arises as to which level is the entry-level category at which we typically categorize items, and whether the level we use varies based on our goals and level of expertise within a domain.

Usefulness of the Basic Level

Many years ago, R. Brown (1958) proposed that we tend to use an intermediate category level—the *basic level*—when we communicate with each other (refer back to Figure 8.2). Brown noted that parents talking to children typically provide short, frequent names for things: *dog* and *cat*, rather than *collie* and *Siamese*. The parents' labeling tells the child what should be noted about an object, and how the child should expect to interact with it. If more specific information is needed, then a more specific label will be applied, but most of the time this intermediate level will be perfectly adequate. Multiple studies have confirmed that people across cultures and languages tend to categorize things at the intermediate or basic level (Atran, 1998, Atran & Medin, 2008; Atran, Medin, & Ross, 2002; Berlin, 1978; Lopez, Atran, Coley, Medin, & Smith, 1997).

Research Support for Usefulness of Basic-Level Categories

In order to demonstrate that basic-level categories are most useful in dividing up the objects in the world, Rosch and coworkers (Rosch, Mervis, Gray, Johnson, & Boyes-Braem, 1976; see also Markman & Wisniewski, 1997) asked participants to list attributes of objects that were at different levels of the hierarchy in Figure 8.2. For example, different groups of people were asked to describe the attributes of *vehicles* (superordinate); *cars* (basic level); or *sports cars* (subordinate). At the superordinate level, people were able to list very few attributes that fit all the members; for instance, there are very few things that we can say about all *vehicles*: They are simply things used for transportation. Not all vehicles have wheels (e.g., raft, sled), not all are powered by engines (e.g., bicycles), and so forth. At the basic level, on the other hand, one finds a large number of features that all or at least most of the members have in common. *Cars*, for example, typically have *wheels*, an *engine*, *doors*, *seats*, *windows*, *mirrors*, and so forth. At the subordinate level, people add few additional features from those they noted at the basic level. Knowing that something is a *sports car* provides very little in additional feature information, since we already know that it is a *car*. The most informative level seems to be the basic level.

The basic-level category also appears to be the most general level in terms of similarity in *shape* among the members of the category (Rosch et al., 1976). *Furniture* and *animals* (superordinate categories) do not bring common shapes to mind as easily as do *chair* and *cat* (basic-level categories). Once again, the subordinate level adds very little shape information; *kitchen chair* versus *dining chair* adds little in the way of new details of shape.

Coherence Versus Differences

Rosch et al. (1976) also proposed that the basic level may be most useful in our interactions with the world because this is where you find the most *coherence* within a category, but the most *differentiation* across categories. Coherence means that items within the category tend to be similar to each other, so that they *cohere*, or go together, and one can therefore make useful generalizations within the category. For example, within each of the *superordinate* categories in Figure 8.2 (e.g., ANIMALS), there is very little overlap among the items. For example, a *manta ray* and a *dog* are both animals, but differ widely in appearance, behavior, physiology, and so on. If you learned that something was true of a specific dog (for example, that it had diabetes), you might not be willing to conclude from that that manta rays can get diabetes as well. Thus, the superordinate category is too wide-ranging to be useful.

Subordinate-level categories, on the other hand, may provide more specificity than we need. If you learn that a German Shepherd has diabetes, for example, it would seem reasonable to generalize that fact to collies and Dobermans. However, if the subordinate category (i.e., German Shepherd) were used as the basis for thinking, then you would not as easily generalize that piece of information from the Shepherd to collies. According to Rosch, then, the basic level is most useful to us for making categorical inferences. This was supported by Sloman (1993), who found that people ranked arguments such as (a) in the following list, which mentions a trait at the basic level, more convincing than (b), which requires an inference from the superordinate level:

(a) All BIRDS require trace amounts of magnesium for reproduction.
Therefore, all sparrows require trace amounts of magnesium for reproduction.

(b) All ANIMALS require trace amounts of magnesium for reproduction.
Therefore, all sparrows require trace amounts of magnesium for reproduction.

CONCEPTS AND THINKING: BUILDING REPRESENTATIONS IN WORKING MEMORY

There is an assumption underlying much of the discussion of concepts presented so far in this chapter: It is assumed that there is a *constancy* in the concept that serves as the basis for our using it. The concept is the mental representation that is used to decide what objects are members of the category, to make inferences about those members, to communicate about them to other people, and so forth. Presumably, none of this activity could take place unless there was available some stable mental representation of a concept. However, Barsalou (1989) has presented evidence that not all concepts are fully stable mental entities (see also Smith & Samuelson, 1997). In a series of studies, Barsalou and coworkers (summarized in Barsalou, 1989; see also Barsalou 2005a, b, 2009) have looked at the similarities across different people's descriptions of concepts, and also stabilities within a single person's concepts over time. In both cases, some degree of *instability* was found. This research raises some important questions about just what concepts are, and how they function in thinking.

Barsalou and his colleagues (e.g., Barsalou & Sewell, 1984; Barsalou, Sewell, & Ballato, 1986) provided groups of people (e.g., undergraduates versus their professors) with a given category name (e.g., BIRD), followed by a list of exemplars from the category (e.g., robin, swan, chicken, ostrich etc.), and asked them to rate the typicality of each exemplar on a 1–8 scale (with 1 as "most typical"). However, instead of using averaged group ratings of concepts, as Rosch did (1975; see Box 8.1 and Table 8.2), Barsalou compared ratings from different groups (e.g., Barsalou & Sewell, 1984), or from the same individuals across times (Barsalou et al., 1986, in Barsalou, 1987, 1989). Table 8.7a shows variation in typicality ratings for the same people over a short period of time (Barsalou, et al., 1986, as cited in Barsalou, 1987). When asked to list the properties of familiar categories (e.g., fruits, birds, perfume), individuals also vary in the

Table 8.7 Barsalou's (1989) studies of group differences in typicality ratings. (a) Within-subject reliability of typicality ratings (from Barsalou, Sewell, & Ballato, 1986, cited in Barsalou, 1987). (b) Average typicality ratings for various exemplars: Undergraduates were asked to judge the typicality of exemplars (with 1 indicating the highest typicality), from either an international perspective, or from the point-of-view of different social categories within American society, and from their own perspective-"Self" (from Barsalou & Sewell, 1984, Experiments 1a, 1b, and 1c)

(a)

Delay:	One Hour Later	One Day Later	One Week Later
In-subject reliability	.92	.87	.80

(b)

Type of Category	Exemplar	International Point of View			Domestic Point of View			Self
		American	Chinese	African	Hippie	Businessman	Housewife	
FRUIT	Apple	1.7	4.4	4.6	3.9	1.4	1.8	2.6
	Banana	3.6	4.6	2.0	3.5	3.0	3.2	3.8
	Watermelon	4.8	6.5	4.1	4.2	4.8	5.1	4.6
	Mango	7.2	2.6	3.1	3.5	7.2	7.2	7.5
HOBBIES	Collecting stamps	5.1	4.2	6.5	4.8	4.6	5.8	5.1
	Photography	4.6	3.0	6.2	3.7	3.5	3.7	3.2
	Playing the piano	4.8	4.7	5.7	5.5	5.3	2.9	4.2
	Fishing	2.8	4.2	2.0	3.1	3.0	6.9	4.2

traits they list across multiple sessions over a several-week period (Gaillard, Urdapilleta, Houix, & Manetta, 2011). Differences can also be found in typicality judgments when people take different perspectives, e.g., from people of other nationalities or from different social categories (See Table 8.7b.)

Ad Hoc Concepts and Categories

In addition, sometimes we form categories as we need them, rather than relying on constant category representations from memory (Barsalou, 1982, 1983, 1987, 1991). As an example, in what ways are *old photographs, pets, jewelry, old letters*, and *cash* similar? There are few attributes that can be used to group them. However, if you were told that someone's house was on fire, then the grouping makes sense: Photographs, pets, jewelry, old letters, and cash might be things that she took out of the burning building because they all have sentimental and/or economic value, and are vulnerable to fire. In such ad hoc concepts (i.e., *impromptu* or *improvised* concepts; Barsalou, 1983), there is no obvious thread of similarity connecting the various members of the category. The broader context, the specific situation, and the goals of the person combine to stimulate the development of a new category that is not dependent on some stable concept in long-term memory.

The Role of Context in Categorization

People's judgments of category membership, and what counts as a typical item within a category, also vary greatly with context. A study by Labov (1973) examined artifactual

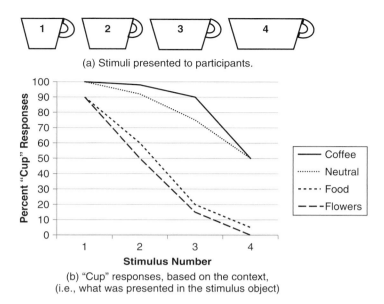

(a) Stimuli presented to participants.

(b) "Cup" responses, based on the context,
(i.e., what was presented in the stimulus object)

Figure 8.12 Labov cup/bowl study: Demonstration of fuzzy boundaries for some concepts and the role of context in setting concept boundaries.

concepts such as CUP and BOWL, and whether context influences category decisions. The stimuli presented to the participants are shown in Figure 8.12a. All the stimuli have basically the same shape, and have handles; the difference among them is the ratio of the height to the width, which ranges from 1:1 for the left-most stimulus, to approximately 1:4 for the right-most item. Labov first asked a group of people whether each of the four stimuli was a cup or bowl. As the width increased relative to the height, the probability of calling the object a cup gradually decreased (see "neutral" Figure 8.12b). That gradual decrease indicates that there was no clear boundary between the two categories. Labov also varied the context that the objects were presented in, by asking participants to imagine that the object held coffee, flowers, or mashed potatoes. When it was said to hold solid food, Stimulus 4 was now likely to be called a bowl. Thus, the boundary between those categories shifted, depending on the context in which a given object was found (see Figure 8.12b).

In another study, Barsalou and Sewell (1984) determined that in the context of discussing office workers taking a break, *coffee* was listed as a typical BEVERAGE, but in the context of school children taking a break, it was not. Once again, a difference in context results in a different representation being used to stand for the concept. A person's goals can also influence category groupings; health-conscious people were more likely to rate a granola bar and yogurt as similar to each other than a granola bar and candy bar that looked alike (Ratneshwar, Barsalou, Pechmann, & Moore, 2001).

In other studies, people were asked to produce properties that were relevant to a given category, and there was a great degree of instability in feature information (Baraslou, Spindler, Sewell, Ballato, & Gendel, 1987, in Barsalou, 1989; see Table 8.7.) When comparing different people's property lists, it was found that only about one-third of the properties were listed in common. In this task also, people did not agree with themselves when they were tested twice on the same concepts; they listed only about half the properties in common on their two attempts. When category membership was tested, similar results were found: People often disagree with each other concerning which specific objects they would put in a category. Even more impressively, there was little consistency when the same person made typicality judgments for the same exemplars twice over several weeks (Barsalou et al., 1986). That is, people do not necessarily agree with *themselves* over time on the structure of common concepts. If typicality ratings of category exemplars, and the accessibility of features connected with those exemplars, changes over time, then the *structure* of those concepts must be flexible.

Thus, there is a large degree of fluidity in how concepts are represented in the same person from one time to the next, and from one person to the next, based either on individual differences overall, or goal-oriented differences. Barsalou (1993) takes such results to indicate that when we think about a concept at different times, we probably will not represent it in the same way each time. That is, when we think about a concept, we construct a representation in working memory that is used to stand for or think about the concept *at that time*. As Smith (1998; Smith & Conrey, 2007) proposed, perhaps mental representations are dynamic *states*, not static *things*. Individual concepts could thus be understood as having multiple activation patterns (Clark, 1993), which are related to situational contexts and goals of a person at a given time. According to Barsalou (1993) and Smith (1998), this means that different information can be used to represent the same concept in working memory when we think about it in different contexts. Therefore, there may be no single representation that is always used to stand for a given concept.

The representation that is constructed in working memory at a given time depends on the information in long-term memory that is *accessible* at that time, that is, the information about the concept that can be retrieved. In Barsalou's (1987; Barsalou & Medin, 1986) analysis, there are three kinds of information available about each concept. First there is *context-independent information*, which is information that will be retrieved each time we encounter the concept. For example, if you hear *frog*, you might think *green* and *hops*. Each of us possesses context-independent information about each concept, but the specific information may be somewhat different for each of us.

Second, there is *context-dependent information*, which is information that you know about the concept, but which is only retrieved because of the context. So, for example, thinking about a frog in a French restaurant might make you think of *edible*, in addition to *green* and *hops*. We all know that frog legs are eaten, but we might not think about that spontaneously. A third type of information Barsalou calls *context-dependent-recent*, which means that you will think about it because of a recent experience with the concept. So, for example, if you recently saw a commercial on television in which a frog was using its tongue to catch insects, you might think *eats flies* on hearing *frog*. After some time passes, *eats flies* will no longer be thought about if *frog* is encountered. Thus, different sorts of information will be retrieved on each encounter with a concept—context-independent information will be retrieved every time, but the other two sorts of information will change—so our representation of the concept will change over time.

Concepts as Flexible Representations: Conclusions

Barsalou (1989; Ratneshwar et al., 2001; see also Smith, 1998; Smith & Conrey, 2007) has theorized that a concept is a flexible or dynamic product of our moment-to-moment cognitive activities. It is constructed in working memory, based on retrieval processes, our goals at a given moment, and contextual factors. If this view is correct, it means that cognitive scientists must alter their views of concepts and of thinking. *To think about X* will not mean to activate some static representation in memory that stands for the concept X. Rather, *to think about X* will mean to retrieve various pieces of information from memory that are related to X, and to use that information to construct a temporary representation that can serve our needs at that time. Categorizing and using concepts becomes, in this view, a very flexible and active process.

NEUROCOGNITIVE STUDIES OF CONCEPTS

Additional information concerning the structure and functioning of concepts has come from neurocognitive studies.

Dissociation Between Living Versus Nonliving Things

Potentially important information relating to neural structures underlying concepts has come from the study of patients with *semantic amnesia* who have a selective deficit in recognizing, naming, and/or providing definitions for *living* versus *nonliving* objects (Basso, Capitani, & Laiacona, 1988; de Renzi & Lucchelli, 1994; Hillis & Caramazza, 1991; Joubert et al., 2008; Laiacona, Capitani, & Barbarotto, 1997; Sartori & Job, 1988; Sartori, Job, Miozzo, Zago, & Marchiori, 1993; Warrington & Shallice, 1984; other patients, with anomia, visual agnosia, and progressive semantic dementia also exhibit problems in dealing with living vs. nonliving things). The most common pattern is when patients can identify and name pictures of objects such as *chairs*, *scissors*, and *pencils* with about 90% accuracy; when *dogs*, *fish*, and *birds* are presented, naming accuracy drops significantly. In addition, patients have been found who exhibit the opposite deficit: Their performance is better in recognizing living things than nonliving (Hillis & Caramazza, 1991; Moss & Tyler, 2000; Sacchett & Humphreys, 1992; Warrington & McCarthy, 1983, 1987, 1994). There is thus evidence for a double dissociation between recognition of living versus nonliving things. It should be noted that the double dissociation found in category-specific deficits does not mean that a patient shows 100% accuracy in identification of nonliving items and 0% in living items (and vice versa for a second patient); rather, there is a significant discrepancy between identification of living/nonliving items, as shown in Table 8.8.

These results can be explained by assuming that there is a basic functional separation between living versus nonliving objects in our conceptual system. One possibility is that information concerning living versus nonliving entities might be stored in separate parts of the brain, which would allow one to lose the ability to recognize one class of objects while retaining the ability to recognize the other. Caramazza and Shelton (1998) proposed that modular representation of living and nonliving things in anatomically distinct areas of the brain may have evolved because of relative differences in their

Table 8.8   Hillis and Caramazza (1991) Data

Patient	% Correct Naming of Pictures		
	All Animals	Nonanimals	
J.J.	80	12	
	All Animals	Vegetables	Other
P.S.	39	25	92

Table 8.9   Kolinksy et al. (2002): Recognition Task Data, to Illustrate Living/Nonliving Distinction

Biological	% Correct
Insects	13
Vegetables	20
Birds	22
Fish/mollusks	33
Reptiles	40
Fruits	46
Mammals	48

Artifact	% Correct
Musical instruments	72
Toys	72
Furniture	79
Buildings/parts	86
Vehicles/parts	89
Clothes/jewelry	91
Tools/weapons	100

survival value. Throughout human existence, the ability to distinguish different types of fruits as poisonous or edible; species of animals as dangerous or not; and so on, would have been important. Since many nonliving things that we encounter are human-made artifacts (furniture, vehicles, tools), and are more recent in human history, the brain represents these categories in a different area. Thus, damage to the medial and temporal lobe will tend to selectively impair identification of living things (Gainotti, Silveri, Daniele, & Giustolisi, 1995; Pietrini et al., 1988); damage to the fronto-parietal areas will lead to greater impairment of knowledge about nonliving things (Gainotti et al., 1995). For example, Kolinsky et al. (2002) found a sharp distinction in their patient E.R. between accurate identification for living/biological items versus artifacts, even when they controlled the stimuli for familiarity (see Table 8.9).

The assumption of functionally and anatomically separable representation of living (people, animals) and nonliving category items (tools), was supported by the results of a study by Damasio, Grabowski, Tranel, Hichwa, and Damasio (1996), who examined a large number of patients who, as a result of brain lesions, had an impairment in word retrieval. For example, someone might respond to a picture of a skunk by saying, "Oh,

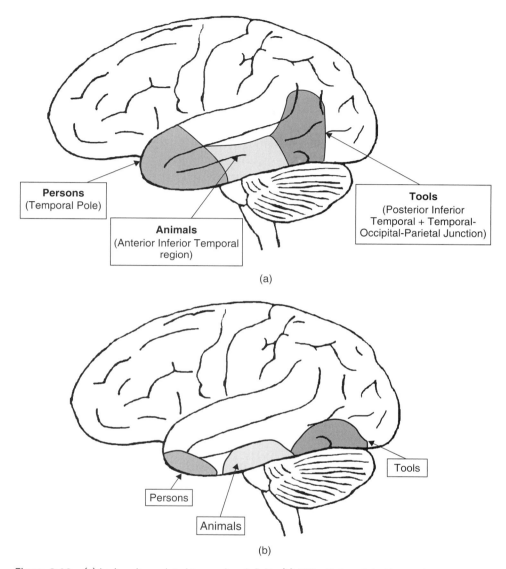

Figure 8.13 (a) Lesion sites related to naming deficits. (b) PET activity related to naming.
Based on Damasio et al., 1996; adapted from Gazzaniga, Ivry, & Mangun (1998), Figures 8.2 and 8.3, pp. 293–294.

that animal makes a terrible smell if you get too close to it; it is black and white . . . " but be unable to name it as a "skunk." The locations of the lesions of 29 patients with naming deficits are shown in Figure 8.13a, where it can be seen that the deficits for living and nonliving items were associated with lesions in different areas in the left temporal lobe. Difficulty naming animals was most prevalent in people with lesions in the left front (anterior) inferior temporal cortex and the posterior region of the temporal pole (the anterior, or front-most portion of the temporal lobe). Naming impairments for tools mainly occurred in patients with posterior inferior temporal lobe damage.

Those results were confirmed by PET scans which recorded brain activity in normal individuals while they named pictures of people, animals, and tools (Damasio et al., 1996). Activation sites are shown in Figure 8.13b, and there is similarity between the areas activated when these participants named animals or tools and the locus of brain damage in the patients who had problems naming those respective categories. In summary, many studies support the general contention that organization of semantic memory in the brain is along category lines, with living/nonliving perhaps serving as a major organizational axis. Like Damasio et al. (1996), Moore and Price (1999) found that nonliving things—vehicles and tools—were associated with greater activity in the left posterior temporal cortex. They also confirmed greater PET activity in the left anterior temporal lobe during object naming and object/name matching tasks of fruits and animals, but also found greater activity in the right posterior temporal cortex, which may be due to greater reliance on perceptual information for recognizing and discriminating living things. Right temporal cortical activation may reflect greater weighting of perceptual information for recognizing and discriminating living things. Moore and Price proposed that deficits for living things may be more prevalent because their identification is susceptible to damage to either the left or right hemisphere (whereas nonliving items are only associated with damage to the left; see also Devlin et al., 2002).

However, there are several pieces of evidence that do not support the hypothesis that concepts related to living versus nonliving things are represented in separate brain areas. First, although studies have shown a double dissociation between recognition for living versus nonliving things, it is somewhat rarer to find a patient with the loss of the ability to recognize nonliving things, while being able to recognize living things (Laiacona, Capitani, & Caramazza, 2003). There may be something about recognition of living things that is more difficult. Second, some patients who are impaired at recognition of living objects also have difficulty recognizing specific types of nonliving things, such as musical instruments (see Kolinksy et al. data in Table 8.9). Warrington and McCarthy (1987; also McCarthy & Warrington, 1988) have argued that the underlying mechanism for patients' deficits is because of a sensory-functional distinction. Living things are often classified in terms of visual appearance (or other sensory aspects, such as whether they bark or purr), while nonliving things are classified on the basis of their function, that is, how we use them. For example, a *leopard* is distinguished from other animals by its spotted appearance, while a *desk* is classified by how we use it (Warrington & McCarthy, 1983; Warrington & Shallice, 1984). This hypothesis assumes that the *living/nonliving* distinction is in actuality based on the analysis of objects in terms of visual versus functional characteristics. In addition, because the class of living things contains more objects with similar perceptual features (e.g., many animals have four legs, ears, and a tail), this might make discrimination among those objects particularly difficult. Nonliving things, in contrast can look very different from each other, which might make recognition of individual exemplars easier, and less subject to confusion from other similar items. If this hypothesis is correct, it means that the fact that patients might lose the ability to recognize living versus nonliving things does not mean that that distinction is represented in semantic memory.

Gaffan and Heywood (1993) tried to simulate effects of brain lesions in healthy individuals, to examine further the question of whether how the concepts living versus nonliving are represented separately in semantic memory. They presented healthy participants with pictures of familiar living versus nonliving objects to recognize. In order to make the task difficult, so that the performance of these participants would better resemble that of agnosic or semantic-amnesia patients, the pictures were presented very quickly (20 milliseconds each). Most interestingly, the *pseudo-agnosia* induced in the experimental participants was worse for recognition of living things compared to nonliving, which replicated the findings for patients. Thus, it may simply be more difficult to recognize and discriminate living things under typical experimental conditions. However, this cannot explain the flip side of the coin—that some patients are more impaired for nonliving than living category items (e.g., Moss & Tyler, 2000).

Farah and McClelland (1991) tabulated the frequencies of visual versus functional features in dictionary definitions of living and nonliving things. They found a 7:1 ratio of visual to functional features for living things, and a more nearly equivalent ratio of 1.4:1 for nonliving things. This supports the greater importance of visual features within categories of living objects (but does not fully support the contention that functional traits are more vital for representing nonliving items).

These various results indicate that the basic difference between of the categories of living versus nonliving things may be in the types of features by which they are identified and analyzed, rather than being based on broad category distinctions. Farah and McClelland (1991) tested this hypothesis by constructing a parallel-distributed-processing model of semantic memory, shown in Figure 8.14a. They used the same proportions of visual versus functional characteristics to represent living versus non-living items as had been found in the dictionary definitions. After the network was trained on a variety of exemplars, it was able to respond to a picture of each object by producing the name, and vice versa. In order to simulate patients with semantic impairments, "lesions" were then created, by randomly removing some of the connections between the input systems (name, picture) and either the visual or functional units within semantic memory. As can be seen in Figure 8.14b, damage to the visual units produced large deficits in identification of living things, with much less interference for nonliving items. Conversely, damage to the functional units produced the opposite effect. These results thus support Warrington and McCarthy's (1987; McCarthy & Warrington, 1988) sensory/functional theory as the basis for category-specific impairments.

Cree and McRae (2003) used a more complicated multidimensional model to see which types of objects were clustered together. They analyzed the results from feature-norming studies for 541 concepts, in which people are asked to list the features deemed most important for objects and entities (e.g., animals). They coded the traits based on feature type (e.g., whether an external, functional, or locational feature) and where that information is processed in the brain (e.g., for the concept MOOSE, "has antlers" counts as a visual-form distinction, "lives in the wilderness" is encyclopedic knowledge, and "is an animal" counted as a superordinate, taxonomic feature). Analysis of overlapping features among items led to development of a hierarchical clustering among various living and nonliving categories (example of clustering within the animals/creatures only is shown in Figure 8.15). In the larger cluster analysis,

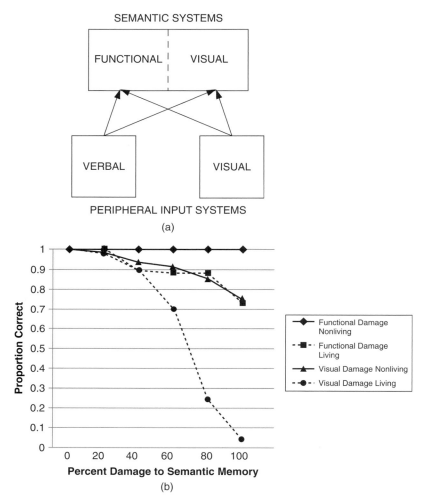

Figure 8.14 Analysis of the living/nonliving difference: Farah and McClelland's (1991) PDP model. (a) PDP model (adapted from Farah & McClelland, 1991, Figure 1). (b) Performance of the PDP model after different degrees of damage to functional versus visual semantic memory.

animals/creatures could be clearly distinguished from nonliving objects, because of greater reliance of external/perceptual features and actions they can perform, but less reliance on functional or internal information than for nonliving items. On the other hand, fruits/vegetables (normally counted with the living items in neuropsychological studies) clustered with nonliving objects because both functional (e.g., "eaten") and internal features ("has seeds") were listed for both. Musical instruments did not get grouped with other nonliving things until late in the hierarchical clustering because of the relative importance of external features (similar to animals, which may help explain some of the neuropsychological data in which patients are impaired at both living things and musical instruments; Sartori & Job, 1988; Warrington & McCarthy, 1984).

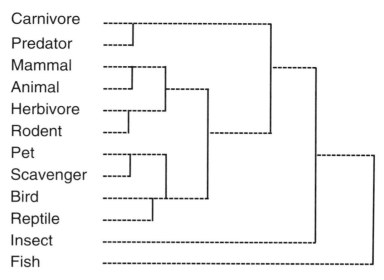

Figure 8.15 Example of a hierarchical cluster analysis of concepts.
Adapted from Cree and McRae (2003, Figure 4).

The Cree and McRae (2003) analysis explains some of the neuropsychological trends in category-specific impairments based on distribution of types of knowledge features (similar to the basis for the sensory/functional distinction proposed by Warrington and McCarthy (1983), but using a wider array of features). Their model thus provides a more complicated multidimensional approach by which to analyze and explain the patient data.

Summary of Neuropsychological Findings

Our discussion of the neuropsychological mechanisms underlying representations of concepts has centered on the finding that patients sometimes show deficits in dealing with living versus nonliving objects. In examining this finding, we began with the idea that the distinction between living and nonliving things is directly represented in the brain. However, further consideration of research results led to a very different idea: that the living versus nonliving deficit is a secondary result of a more primary difficulty, an inability to deal with visual versus functional characteristics of objects. This analysis is important for several reasons. First it alerts us to the possibility that concepts are not necessarily organized so that separate classes are represented in different parts of the brain. This conclusion is also consistent with the model of semantic memory proposed by Burgess (1998; Lund & Burgess, 1996, 1997; see also Landauer et al., 2007), which assumes that organization in semantic memory depends only on the similarities between the contexts in which items appear, analogous to assuming that taxonomic category structure is secondary to aspects developing out of our interactions with the objects. It is also consistent with Barsalou's analysis of the flexible nature of the representations that we construct to think about concepts. Second, the Farah and McClelland (1991) study is a striking example of how one can coordinate results from neurocognitive studies with those from more traditional cognitive psychology and computer models of cognition in order to test hypotheses. Cree and McRae (2003) have developed a multidimensional model that best characterizes the complexity of the patient data, based on which cluster (and at which level) their impairment occurs (see also Humphreys & Forde, 2001).

CONCEPTS AND CATEGORIES: CONCLUSIONS

This chapter has presented an analysis of the structure and content of individual concepts, as explained by several key theories that focus on the role of features—whether in the classical view's emphasis on defining features, or the role of overlapping features in creating a family resemblance among category items. More recent views, however, have emphasized that people may represent some concepts, especially those dealing with natural kinds, as having an essence that delineates category membership. Research shows that children may begin their understanding of concepts based on family resemblance principles, and then shift to a belief in essences, and that both types of concept representations may co-exist even in adulthood. Further evidence has pointed to the crucial roles that expertise, one's goals, the context, and one's interaction with objects play in conceptual knowledge. Thinking about a concept may thus depend on constructing a temporary representation in working memory, based on the kind of information that is accessible at a given moment in time.

Models of semantic memory have varied from early hierarchical structures (Collins & Quillian, 1969) to networks of associated concepts and features (Collins & Loftus, 1975) or propositions (Anderson, 1983, 2010). More recent ideas emphasize the possibility that there may be little in the way of formal semantic structure among concepts, and that semantic knowledge is built up out of co-occurrences of words in everyday language (Burgess, Livesay, & Lund, 1998; Burgess & Lund, 1997; Landauer & Dumais, 1997; Landauer et al., 2007; Lund & Burgess, 1996). Lastly, we have seen that brain damage sometimes results in category-specific impairments, in which patients systematically lose knowledge about some categories while maintaining information about others. Such deficits may be due either to differential representation of living versus nonliving items in distinct regions of the brain, based on evolutionary constraints, or due to differential distributions of types of features (e.g., perceptual versus functional) within categories.

REVIEW QUESTIONS

Here is a set of questions to help organize your review and study of this chapter.

1. What is the difference between a *concept* and a *category*?

2. What functions do concepts serve?

 3. Describe the hierarchical structure of some concepts.

 4. Describe the structure of "classical" concepts and summarize research studying development of that type of concept.

 5. Summarize the *family resemblance* theory of concepts.

 6. Describe evidence for graded structure and prototype-based structure in some human concepts.

 7. Summarize the *exemplar* view of concepts and summarize some evidence to support that view.

 8. Describe data from amnesics learning concepts that raise problems for the exemplar view.

 9. Discuss problems with the notion that category membership is based on similarities between objects.

10. Describe the key components of psychological essentialism and summarize research supporting that view.

11. Describe the study by Keil and Batterman (1984) and summarize the results and their relevance for our understanding of the development of concepts.

12. Describe hierarchically organized models of semantic memory and discuss research results supporting and contradicting those models.

13. How does the phenomenon of semantic priming support spreading-activation models of semantic memory?

14. Describe Anderson's model of semantic memory.

15. Describe how the HAL program of Burgess and Lund can develop conceptual knowledge without knowledge of meaning.

16. Describe research examining the role of expertise in conceptual functioning.

17. Summarize the importance of the *basic level* in conceptual functioning.

18. Describe evidence that concepts are not stable entities.

19. Describe evidence that concepts are constructed in working memory as we need them.

20. What were the results of Labov's (1973) study of the role of context in categorization?

21. According to Barsalou, what factors determine the structure of the representation of a concept that will be constructed in WM at a given time?

22. What is the potential importance of the results from patients with *semantic amnesia* with a selective deficit in naming *living* versus *nonliving* things?

23. What is an alternative way of explaining the results from patients concerning the naming problems with *living* versus *nonliving* things?

CHAPTER 9

LANGUAGE I: SOUNDS, WORDS, AND MEANINGS

Language may be the behavior that is most uniquely human. Most everything else that we do has reasonably close correspondence with behaviors in other species. Animals engage in complex social behavior; they are able to learn based on observation and imitation of others; they are able to remember various types of information, such as the location of key food areas or the identification of familiar individuals; they can solve problems; and more. Many animals also communicate with members of their species in various ways—through production of sounds, visual displays, and pheromones—but no species other than humans is able to use the complex, highly structured, open system that is language (Hauser, Chomsky, & Fitch, 2002; Pinker, 1994). There have been several attempts to teach highly intelligent animals, such as chimpanzees and gorillas, to use specially designed visually based languages (since their vocal apparatus is not geared toward spoken speech), but the consensus is that what they are able to acquire is not nearly up to the skill level of an average 3-year-old child (Pinker, 1994). Humans therefore may be unique in the animal kingdom as a species with language. That possibility alone would make language worthy of study.

However, language is also central to our social and intellectual lives. We use language not only to communicate with other people, but to help us solve problems, remember information (e.g., through verbal rehearsal), and engage in creative activities (e.g., writing a short story). Language also serves as a mode of thought; our thinking can involve something like talking to oneself. It is also closely related to our system of concepts (see Chapter 8), because some concepts may depend on the possession of language. For example, could there be concepts such as *bachelor* or *obligation* without the human ability to convey complex ideas with language? In sum, language plays a central role in many of our cognitive activities.

OUTLINE OF CHAPTER 9

This chapter and the next review what we know about humans' remarkable language abilities, and how the capacity to speak and understand language is related to other cognitive processes. Chapter 9 begins with an overview of the functions of language and the different levels of analysis in linguistic study. We then address language's role as a social communication system. Having set the broad stage, we turn to the different levels of analysis in linguistic study, beginning with the lowest-level component of language: the sound system. This includes *prosody*, the study of the role of intonation, pitch, and stress or emphasis patterns in language; and *phonology*, the analysis of the basic units of sound in language. Our analysis then moves to the structure of *words*, the building blocks of language, where sound and meaning come together. The study of the basic units of meaning that make up those words is called *morphology*. We will consider how words are stored in our *mental lexicon*—our mental dictionary—based on studies of how people use and process words, including occasions when they have difficulty retrieving words, as in tip-of-the-tongue (TOT) states. The discussion will also examine how children learn the meanings of words, an area in which many important theoretical questions have been raised.

Lastly, recent advances in brain-imaging techniques and in the study of neuropsychological syndromes have provided evidence concerning how language is processed in the brain. In several places we discuss the role of brain processes in understanding word meaning, and in assembling the phonological representation necessary to produce words. The chapter concludes with a discussion of the role of brain processes in understanding meanings of words. Combining words into sentences adds still more complexity to the phenomenon of language, and will be examined in Chapter 10.

LANGUAGE AS COMMUNICATION

In order to get a feeling for the multifaceted complexity of language, we now turn to an overview of language as a communicative device. This will provide us with an introduction to the various levels of processing involved in using language, and how they function together. Figure 9.1 presents an outline of the processes that might occur

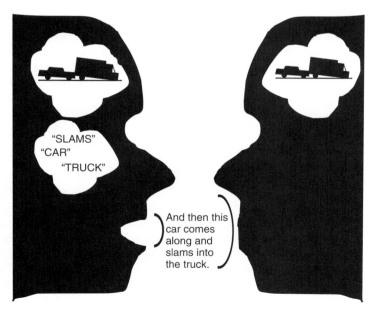

Figure 9.1 Outline of the communicative act: Speaker has in mind a scene of a car hitting a truck, and communicates it to a listener.

during a typical act of communication, where one person has some information that he or she wishes to transmit to another (e.g., a speaker attempting to convey a perceptually based memory of some experience to a listener).

COMPONENTS OF COMMUNICATION

Language is studied in one of two ways—through the *production* of words and sentences (whether verbally or in writing), or through *comprehension*. In order to set the process of communication in motion, the speaker must be able to put into words the information to be transmitted (see Figure 9.1). This skill depends on at least three kinds of knowledge. First, the speaker must have a vocabulary that allows him or her to put the idea into the right words. Our knowledge about words and their meanings is called the *lexicon* or *mental lexicon* (*lexis* means *word* in Greek). A fluent speaker also must know how to use the syntactic structure of a language to put words together into sentences, and to add the small *grammatical* or *function* words (such as *a* and *the*), so that a specific meaning can be transmitted accurately. Simply knowing the words *a*, *dog*, *man*, and *bites* does not allow you to communicate the difference between *A dog bites a man* and *A man bites a dog* (Pinker, 1994). Those words have to be put together in the correct way to communicate the difference between those two situations. When the message has been formulated, the final stage in language production is its transmission to the listener, usually by means of sounds.

In language comprehension, the process works in reverse. The listener must first process words from the sound stream, and determine the organization of a sentence. From the analyzed sentence, the listener then constructs a meaning, which, if the speaker was effective, will correspond to the idea that the speaker set out to communicate (see Figure 9.1).

Although language production and comprehension have often been used as separate measures of linguistic competence, there is considerable evidence for interaction between the two subsystems (Pickering & Garrod, 2004, 2007). For example, during comprehension, there is evidence that people engage the *production* system, by predicting which words will be said next (DeLong, Urbach, & Kutas, 2005; Lau, Stroud, Plesch, & Phillips, 2006), and, in so doing, engage their tongue and brain areas responsible for speech production (Fadiga, Craighero, Buccino, & Rizzolatti, 2002; Watkins & Paus, 2004; Watkins, Strafella, & Paus, 2003). Conversely, people use the words and syntactic structures they have just comprehended to influence their actual language production (Bock, 1986; Branigan, Pickering, MacLean, & Stewart, 2006). Thus, the distinction between production and comprehension is functionally useful to conduct research, but not necessarily reflective of what is happening cognitively.

LEVELS OF LINGUISTIC ANALYSIS

Table 9.1 depicts the various levels of linguistic analysis. As we have already discussed, language serves a *social*, communicative function. *Pragmatics* is the study of the rules of social discourse: how the broader context—including the intent of the speaker and

Table 9.1 Levels of Analysis in Language

Social Function	Cognitive Rule System		
Pragmatics	Meaning (Semantics)	Syntax (Grammar)	Sound
	Individual Word Meanings	Structure of Sentences	Prosody: Intonation, Pitch, Stress
	Sentence Meaning	Morphology: Structure of Words	Phonology: Sounds of Language Phonetics: Production of Phonemes

the linguistic knowledge of the speaker and listener—affects the interpretation of a linguistic message. Language also has many complex *cognitive* aspects to it, encompassing semantic, grammatical, and sound-related functions. *Semantics*, the study of *meaning*, examines the relationships between language, ideas, and events in the environment. In this chapter we will be concerned with the meanings of individual words; Chapter 10 examines how people process the meanings of sentences. *Syntax*, the study of the *grammatical organization of sentences*, is the study of how speakers of a language combine individual words into legal sentences that follow the rules or constraints of a language. Related to comprehension, the study of syntax involves analyzing how listeners use information from an utterance to determine its grammatical structure, as an early step in specifying the meaning that a speaker was trying to communicate. Syntax also involves *morphology*, the study of the structure of words (e.g., adding tenses).

Finally, we come to the sound system of a language, the actual string of sounds the speaker uses to convey the message. One component of the sound system is *prosody*, the study of the role of intonation, pitch, and stress in communication. Prosody plays an important role in communication. For example, we can change the meaning of an utterance—from a statement to a question, for example—by changing the intonation pattern (such as speaking the last word at a higher pitch). The sound system also involves the study of the individual sounds that make up a language, which linguists call *phonemes*, as well as how those sounds are combined to form words. The study of phonemes themselves is called *phonology;* while the study of the physical means through which the phonemes are articulated with the mouth and vocal cords is known as *phonetics.*

Having now examined the levels of linguistic analysis, and their relationship to each other, we examine the theoretical debates—both historical and current—that guide much of the research and interpretation of language studies.

LANGUAGE AND THE COGNITIVE REVOLUTION

Language, and how it develops, has fascinated people for centuries. For example, Psamtik, an Egyptian king, mandated that two children be isolated and raised by deaf-mute caretakers to see what language they spoke spontaneously, as that would be the root language. (He was chagrined when their first word appeared to be *bekos*—Phyrigian for bread, rather than an Egyptian word). As we noted in Chapter 1, a prominent impetus for the cognitive revolution was Chomsky's (1959) critique of Skinner's behavioristically based views on language, with Chomsky arguing that language in humans was a built-in behavior, part of our genetic structure, while Skinner proposed that language development came about through conditioning. However, nowadays most researchers are not directly concerned with the question of whether language learning is purely a function of nurture versus nature (Bates, 1997). Most researchers now acknowledge that humans have an innate ability to learn language. A more useful research question is *how* that skill is developed as a result of their exposure to language (Bates, 1997; Croft & Cruse, 2004).

Currently, the two dominant theories of language are a rule-based/computational one, based on Chomsky's theory and largely popularized by Pinker (1994, 1999), and an emergent perspective, advocated by a wide array of researchers. The rule-based/computational theory argues that environmental input triggers innate mechanisms for acquiring the rules of grammar for the language one grows up with. Furthermore, the rules for language learning and mechanisms by which we acquire speech are modular and language-specific. These computational rules then permit the *generativity* of language, and allow us to construct an infinite number of novel sentences. Under the emergent position, the mechanism for language learning is based on general, nonmodular, cognitive-based learning mechanisms, such as association, or induction of statistical principles, which also underlie many other cognitive skills. Thus, people detect *patterns* in language that influence speech production, rather than learning or activating rule-based computational subsystems. The two theoretical perspectives also differ in the importance that they place upon social modeling and social cues in language development. The rule-based perspective emphasizes that hearing other people speak merely activates existing syntactic structures that are innate; thus, they point to the *poverty of the input*—children's language abilities are often more complex than the speech they hear, because innate language knowledge fills in what is missing to allow them to achieve grammatical competence. Alternatively, within the emergent camp, advocates of the *social-pragmatic view* (Akhtar & Tomasello, 1996; Hollich, Hirsh-Pasek, Tucker, & Golinkoff, 2000; Nelson, 1988; Tomasello, 2006; Tomasello & Akhtar, 1995; Tomasello, Strosberg, & Akhtar, 1996) emphasize that children build up a vocabulary and grammatical knowledge based on the social and contextual cues surrounding linguistic input and use; there is not any innate linguistic framework to guide their language acquisition. Thus, critical areas in which the two theoretical perspectives differ include: (a) whether language is rule- or pattern-based; (b) whether language is a modular skill or is tied to the general cognitive system; (c) the extent to which language is influenced by an innate language module or constructed out of use; and (d) the relative importance of social cues and pragmatic knowledge in language acquisition. These issues will frame our discussion in this chapter and the next.

Having introduced the levels of linguistic analysis and their relationship to each other, as well as the main theoretical perspectives in the study of language, we can now examine in detail the psychological processes involved in speech production and comprehension. Whenever relevant, we will assess whether the available data better support a computational or emergent perspective.

PRAGMATIC ASPECTS OF COMMUNICATION

Language use involves more than words or sentences in isolation. As participants work their way through a conversation, for example, they acquire *common ground*—information that has been activated as the conversation proceeds and which serves as background to what they say (Stalnaker, 2002). This information comes in part from general knowledge and beliefs—*presuppositions*—from their shared cultural background, as well as information accumulated through their ongoing personal interaction. Common ground guides both what they say and how they interpret one another's speech.

Return to the situation in Figure 9.1. If both the speaker and hearer knew that the car in question had hit that same truck before, one might say, "*That* car hit *that* truck again." If neither knew about the history of the car and truck, one would be more likely to say that *a* car hit *a* truck. In the short-term, people assume that once a new topic has been introduced in conversation, the other person will remember that information. In the example in Figure 9.1, the speaker says that a car hit *the truck*, because he or she has already introduced the truck into the conversation. More generally, if one *conversant*—a participant in a conversation—says something like "The guy then said . . . ," she is assuming that the listener will have information in memory about the identity of "the guy" from earlier in the conversation, whereas someone who newly joins the conversation will not have that common ground and therefore will not be able to understand "the guy." Thus, we say things differently, depending on our common knowledge.

Grice (1975) proposed that participants in a conversation work under a set of pragmatic rules, or *conversational maxims*, which serve to keep communication on course and save effort on the part of speaker and listener (see Table 9.2). They ensure that the speaker does not say what he or she believes to be false, or go into detail that is either unnecessary to the thrust of the conversation or is already known by the listener. The listener is provided with sufficient information so that he or she does not have to keep struggling to determine the message that the speaker is transmitting. We all know people whose conversation violates one or more of these maxims, such as the person who gives a lengthy and detailed response to your casual query, "How are you doing?"

We now turn to an analysis of more detailed aspects of the linguistic message, beginning with the sounds that a speaker produces, focusing first on *prosody* and then on *phonology* and *phonetics*.

Table 9.2   Grice's Conversational Maxims

Maxim	Purpose
Relevance	Speakers' contributions should relate clearly to the purpose of the exchange.
Quality	Speakers should be truthful. They should not say what they think is false, or make statements for which they have no evidence.
Quantity	Do not say more than is necessary, but say everything that is necessary.
Manner	Speakers' contributions should be perspicuous: clear, orderly, and brief, avoiding obscurity and ambiguity.

Prosody in Speech

When we listen to language, we typically are cognizant mainly of *what* the other person is saying, but *how* they are saying is just as important. For instance, imagine playing quarterback for your intramural football team and throwing an interception that loses the game. A friend of yours says, "Well, that was a brilliant pass." Did she mean it? The words, by themselves, sound positive, but given that your pass was anything but brilliant, chances are your friend used sarcasm, which was reflected in her tone of voice. She probably accented "that" and "brilliant" differently than if she had meant the words sincerely. Likewise, if your professor announces that, "Term papers are due *tomorrow*," with the last word strongly emphasized, you might conclude that he will not accept late papers. Thus, the meanings of words or sentences can be affected by the intonation they receive (Norrick, 2009). Prosody includes the rhythm, intonation, and emotional tone of speech, as well as when stress is applied to certain words. There is one area of language in which prosody is particularly important: infant- and child-directed speech, where we exaggerate prosody to facilitate infants' attention to language. Neuropsychological evidence suggests that prosody is mainly controlled by areas in the right hemisphere, as a complement to speech areas in the left that process traditional elements of speech production and comprehension.

Infant- and Child-Directed Speech

Most adults speak differently to infants than they do to older children or other adults—with higher pitch, wider variation in intonation, and more-precise enunciation of individual phonemes. This particular type of speech—called *motherese* or *parentese*, or more technically, *infant-directed speech*—is nearly universal in human communities (Fernald, 1992). Infants prefer to listen to motherese compared with ordinary speech, (Fernald, 1985), which may largely be due to the elevated pitch (Fernald & Kuhl, 1987). Infant-directed speech may facilitate perception of the phonemes of a language (Kuhl et al., 1997). Sensitivity to prosody precedes word comprehension in infants. Fernald (1993) presented 9- and 18-month-olds with an attractive toy. The infants heard messages such as "No, don't touch," or "Yes, good boy/girl," using either a consistent or inconsistent intonation. For example, in the *inconsistent-negative condition*, "No, don't touch" would be said in a lilting, happy tone. The 9-month-olds responded only to the intonation, touching the toy when the voice was happy, no matter what was said. The older infants, on the other hand, modulated their behavior based on the sentence *content*, and often showed consternation when the voice told them "Don't touch" with positive intonation. Thus, infants' primary response to speech may be based on the intonation; only later is the meaning of an utterance of equal importance.

The question then arises as to whether intonation and prosody are controlled by the same speech centers in the brain as word and sentence production and comprehension.

Brain and Intonation

Prosodic components of language, most particularly intonation and the cadence or rhythm of speech, are represented in specific areas in the right hemisphere of the brain. Ross, Edmondson, Siebert, and Homan (1988) administered a *Wada test* (named after neurologist J. A. Wada) to five patients. This test involves injecting sodium amobarbital into one of the two carotid arteries, which temporarily incapacitates the ipso-lateral (same-side) hemisphere of the brain. In the Ross et al. study, the participants were asked to repeat a sentence using either a neutral, happy, sad, angry, surprised, or bored intonation. Participants were unable to speak the sentence at all after a left-hemisphere Wada test. In contrast, after a right-hemisphere Wada test, they could reproduce the words in correct order, but they lost the ability to adjust the emotional tone in their speech. Ross et al. (1988) concluded that, in most right-handed people, prosodic and affective elements of language are added to speech by the right hemisphere. Shapiro and Danly (1985) found that neuropsychology patients with damage to a right hemisphere area analogous to Broca's area (see Figure 9.2), tended to read paragraphs in a flattened emotional tone.

People also seem to vary their intonation patterns based on their regional accent; some dialects tend to have more of a musical rhythm, with a lilt at the ends of sentences (e.g., Irish and Scottish accents). Thus we could assume that accent might also be controlled by the right hemisphere. One unusual condition caused by brain injury is *foreign-accent syndrome*, in which people who have suffered some type of brain trauma or stroke appear to speak with a different accent. For instance, after a stroke, a native speaker of British English might sound like a *Noo Yawkah*. There have been several famous cases, such as that of a Norwegian woman who was struck by shrapnel in World War II and began speaking with a German accent (Monrad-Krohn, 1947), or the British woman whose severe migraine left her with a Chinese accent (*The Sunday Times*, April 20, 2010).

Both prosody and pronunciation of phonemes are often affected in foreign-accent syndrome (Haley, Roth, Helm-Estabrooks, & Thiessen, 2010). Albert, Haley, and Helm-Estabrooks (in preparation, cited in Haley et al., 2010) surveyed 30 cases of

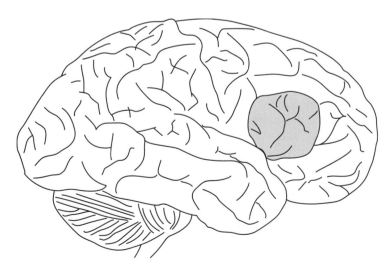

Figure 9.2 Grey area depicts right inferior frontal gyrus, used in processing/recognizing emotional tone and prosodic information, which corresponds to the right-hemisphere analogue to Broca's area.

foreign-accent syndrome for which neurological information was available, and determined that the most common lesion was in the left frontal lobe, in the white matter. Akhlaghi, Jahangiri, Azarpazhooh, Elyasi, and Ghale (2011) confirmed the left hemisphere (LH) correlation. What were the differences between foreign-accent syndrome and the patients just described who lost all prosody due to right hemisphere (RH) damage? While some have considered it an impairment of prosody (Blumstein & Kurowski, 2006), others have said that foreign-accent syndrome is due either to a side effect of aphasia (Ardila, Rosselli, & Ardila, 1987) or to *apraxia*—motor impairments in articulating phonemes (Coelho & Robb, 2001; Moen, 2000). For example, if a person has trouble pronouncing the *r* sound at the end of words after a stroke, it may sound as if the person had acquired a Boston accent. Most cases of foreign accent syndrome do, indeed, arise after periods of nonfluent (Broca's) aphasia, muteness, or apraxia. This would mean that foreign accent syndrome is a problem with speech production at the phonological/phonetic/motor level, rather than an intonation problem. Thus, it would be expected to result from LH damage.

PHONOLOGY

Another element of the linguistic sound system is the specific phonemes that are used in speech. Pronounce the following string of letters: *bnench*. English speakers agree that *bnench* is not an English word and also that it does not sound like it could be a legitimate English word. In order to understand why English speakers reject *bnench* as a possible English word, we must consider the phonemes that are used to construct words in English.

The human vocal apparatus is capable from birth of producing a very large number of sounds, ranging from coos to giggles to screeches, and our auditory system is capable of responding to all these sounds and many others. Each language uses a subset of those sounds, called *phonemes*, to construct words. English uses about 44 phonemes (http://www.dyslexia-speld.com/LinkClick.aspx?fileticket=Kh7hycbitgA%3D&tabid =92&mid=500&language=en); other languages use from around a dozen to well over 100 in Taa (or "!Xo'o"), a language spoken in Botswana and Namibia (DoBeS project on Taa language, http://www.mpi.nl/DOBES/projects/taa/). One can get a general idea of the phonemes of English by considering the letters of the alphabet. Most consonant letters correspond to single phonemes (e.g., *f, z, d*). Each of the vowel letters represents several different phonemes, depending on how each is pronounced in a specific context. For example, *a* can be pronounced "ay," as in *cake*, or "ah" as in *hard*; *e* can be pronounced "ee" or "eh"; and so forth. Some phonemes are made up of combinations of letters; *sh* and *ch* are single phonemes in English. (We will designate phonemes by using / /; sounds will be designated by writing the italicized letter, e.g., *p*.)

Phonetics: Feature Analysis of Phonemes

Phoneticians, researchers who study the physical properties of phonemes, have developed a method of analysis of phonemes using a small set of *articulatory features* based on the ways in which each sound is articulated, or spoken. As an example of how articulatory features are determined, pronounce the sound *p* aloud several times in succession, paying particular attention to the position of your lips. At the same time, hold your hand an inch in front of your mouth as you produce the *p*.

Manner of Articulation

When you say *p*, *p*, *p*, holding your hand in front of your mouth, you will notice that there is no sensation, then a slight explosion of air against your hand. This indicates that the airstream is first blocked, and then comes out in a burst. The general fact that the airstream is interrupted defines the phoneme /p/ as a *consonant*. The difference between consonants and vowels is that consonants are produced by blocking the airstream either partially or completely; vowels are produced with a continuous stream of air. When producing *p*, the airstream is completely blocked, or *stopped*, which defines /p/ as a *stop consonant*. In contrast, *fricatives* (such as /f/, /s/, or /th/) involve sustained turbulence, rather than complete interruption, in the sound stream. The type of interruption in the airstream is called the *manner* of production of the phoneme (see Table 9.3, section A).

Place of Articulation

In saying *p*, the airstream is stopped by bringing the two lips together and then bursting them apart with the air forced up from the lungs. Thus, /p/ is a *bilabial* stop consonant (*bi-labia* means *two lips* in Latin). The specific parts of the mouth used in producing the phoneme, in this case the two lips, are called the *place of articulation*. Other sounds are produced by pressing the tongue against the teeth, such as /th/; such sounds are known as *dental* sounds. *Labiodental* sounds involve contact between the lips and the

Table 9.3 Summary of Phonological Feature Analysis, Showing Features Comprising Several Related Phonemes

		Feature				
		Manner				
	Phoneme	Sound Interrupted	Completely Blocked	Place	Voice	Nasal
A	/p/	Consonant	Stop	Bilabial		
B	/p/	Consonant	Stop	Bilabial	no	
	/b/	Consonant	Stop	Bilabial	yes	
C	/p/	Consonant	Stop	Bilabial	no	no
	/b/	Consonant	Stop	Bilabial	yes	no
	/m/	Consonant	Stop	Bilabial	yes	yes
D	/t/	Consonant	Stop	Velar	no	no
	/d/	Consonant	Stop	Velar	yes	no
	/n/	Consonant	Stop	Velar	yes	yes

teeth, e.g., /f/ or /v/. /H/ is a *glottal* sound, because it is produced by the glottis in the throat.

Voicing

Say *p* and *b* several times with one hand in front of your mouth, as before, but this time put your other hand on your Adam's apple (the voice box). Both sounds involve bringing the two lips together, and expelling air out of one's mouth, so /b/ is also a bilabial stop consonant. The difference between the production of the two sounds is in the *vocal cords*: One feels vibrations in the throat for /b/, but not for /p/. So /b/ is a *voiced* bilabial stop consonant, while /p/ is *voiceless*, as shown in Table 9.3, section B.

Nasality

Now say *p*, *b*, and *m* several times in succession. All three sounds involve bringing the two lips together and then opening them, so all are bilabial stop consonants. Also, both *b* and *m* involve activity in the vocal cords, so they are both bilabial voiced consonants. In addition, however, if you lay a finger like a moustache under your nose as you say *p*, *b*, and *m* several times in succession, you will feel a slight puff of air from your nose as you say *m*. Thus, /m/ is a *nasal* voiced bilabial stop consonant, because the air comes out through the nose, rather than the mouth (Table 9.3, section C).

In conclusion, Table 9.3 presents feature analysis for a family of phonemes, in which the members are related through the possession of overlapping sets of features. Table 9.3, section D also presents another family of phonemes, /t/, /d/, and /n/, which are also stop consonants, but this time the place of articulation involves the tip of the tongue touching the velar ridge, behind the teeth. Except for that component, the analysis parallels exactly that for /p/, /b/, and /m/, respectively, as far as voicing and nasality are concerned.

Implicit Phonological Rules

Now we can return to the question with which we began this section: Why is *bnench* not an acceptable phonological string in English? In English, no word begins with two *stop* consonants such as *b* and *n*. Although some words are *spelled* with two stop consonants at the beginning, such as *knew*, *pneumonia*, and *mnemonics*, the two stop consonants are not both pronounced. One could view this as a phonological rule for forming words in English, because of the high degree of regularity that one finds. All people who know English seem to know that rule implicitly, since no speaker of English produces words that violate it, even though few of us could articulate the rule. English speakers have induced certain phonemic patterns as a result of their exposure to the language, and use them as the basis for word production and for judgments about acceptable sound sequences. Thus, regularities seen in language processing could be explained by the rule-based/computational view as being the result of the person's explicit internalization of rules, or by the emergent perspective as being the result of the person's sensitivity to patterns or high-probability tendencies in the language. This is an example of how the same set of results can be interpreted as evidence for language learning being *rule-governed* versus *pattern-based*.

PROCESSING PHONEMES: STUDIES OF SPEECH PRODUCTION AND PERCEPTION

Categorical Perception of Phonemes

Every day, we are exposed to a multitude of speakers, some with high-pitched voices (such as children), others with deep voices, and those who speak with different dialects or accents. Speech comprehension would be very difficult, indeed, if we processed words or sounds differently based on individual voices. For instance, we perceive the /p/ in *pickle* and *pumpkin* as the same sound, even when spoken by our professor from New York City, and our friend from the South. We carry out *categorical perception* of phonemes, in which we ignore small acoustic differences between phonemes and treat them as members of the same phonemic category. Research on categorical perception has had theoretical implications as to whether language processing is based on a modular system or not.

When a speaker produces a sound stream in the process of speaking, that sound stream is a form of physical energy, which can be represented in a *sound spectrogram*: a visual representation of the distribution of energy of an utterance. Figure 9.3 presents an idealized spectrogram of the energy distribution underlying production of the syllable *ba*. As can be seen, there are two bands of concentrated energy, which are called *formants*. The upper band, *formant$_2$*, corresponds to the burst of energy from the explosion of the stop consonant, which we have already discussed. A rising transition of the first formant (formant$_1$), is correlated with the *voicing* component of the class of voiced stop consonants (Harris, Hoffman, Liberman, DeLattre, & Cooper, 1958), and formant$_1$ also helps determine the specific vowel that we hear. The shape of the formant is based upon the time separating air release and vibration of the vocal cords, which is known as *voice onset time* (or VOT).

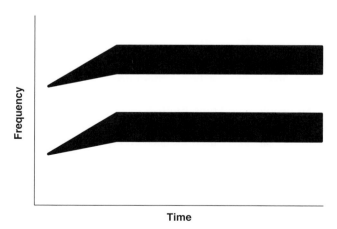

Figure 9.3 Acoustic analysis of speech sounds: Idealized spectrogram of the energy distribution underlying production of the syllable *ba*. Note the two formants (bands of energy) and the fact that both formants begin at the same time.

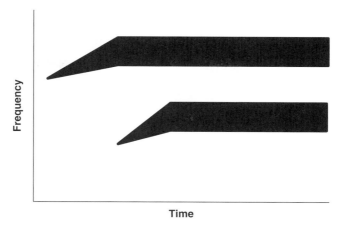

Time

Figure 9.4   Idealized spectrograph for *pa*. Note again the two formants, but this time the lower (voicing) format begins after the other. The time before the voicing begins (voice onset time, VOT) results in hearing a voiceless sound (*pa*) rather than a voiced sound (*ba*).

Figure 9.4 presents the spectrograph for *pa*. As we know from earlier discussion, the main difference between *pa* and *ba* is the absence or presence of the voicing component in the first phoneme (/p/ versus /b/). A comparison of Figures 9.3 and 9.4 shows that the first formant is delayed a significant amount of time in *pa* (e.g., 30–60 milliseconds), which is what gives the consonant its voiceless quality. So an increase in VOT at a given frequency, while formant$_2$ is consistently articulated, results in a change in perception from a voiced bilabial stop consonant to a voiceless one (Lisker, 1975; Abramson & Lisker, 1970; Stevens & Klatt, 1974).

It is possible to manipulate VOT changes artificially using a *speech synthesizer*—a machine that generates sounds—and one can then ask listeners to report what they hear. In Figure 9.5 is a set of artificial spectrographs in which VOT is increased in increments of 20 milliseconds, going from 0 milliseconds (*ba*) to 60 milliseconds (*pa*). One might expect that people's perceptions would gradually shift from one sound to the other, as shown in Figure 9.6. At the middle values of VOT, then, people might perceive mixed versions of the two sounds, or some sound intermediate between *ba* and *pa*.

However, that is not what occurs. As VOT increases over the first few steps, people continue to report hearing *ba*. Then, midway through the VOT series, there is an all-or-none shift in perception, with the voiced sound changing into the voiceless one (see Figure 9.7). Despite minor VOT differences, adults behave as if there are two separate phoneme categories: Short VOTs are perceived as the voiced /b/ sound and longer VOTs as the voiceless /p/. A 20-millisecond change in VOT *within* the category boundary (e.g., from +0 to +20) is not perceived as articulation of a different phoneme, but a 20-millisecond change *across* the boundary (+20 to +40) is significant and results in a differences in speech perception. This categorical perception seems to be different from what occurs in other domains, such as when we listen to music getting louder gradually (rather than in discrete steps). Such results have often been used to

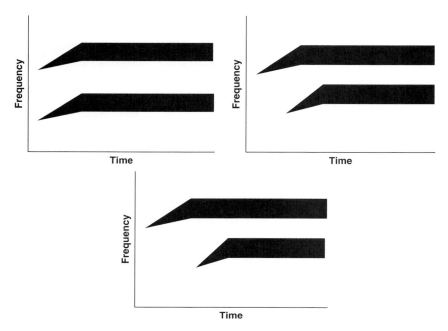

Figure 9.5 Set of spectrographs: VOT increases from the first (*ba*) to the last (*pa*).

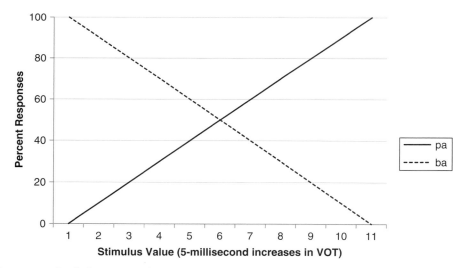

Figure 9.6 Predictions concerning people's perceptions of *pa* versus *ba* in response to an expanded set of stimuli such as those in Figure 9.5, if there is no categorical perception. As VOT increases, there should be a gradual shift from *ba* to *pa* as responses.

support the notion of a language-dedicated module (Liberman, Cooper, Shankweiler, & Studdert-Kennedy, 1967).

Humans' ability to perceive phonemic categories is evident very early in life. In a classic study by Eimas, Siqueland, Jusczyk, and Vigorito (1971), 1- and 4-month-old infants were exposed to repeated speech sounds, in a habituation design (as described

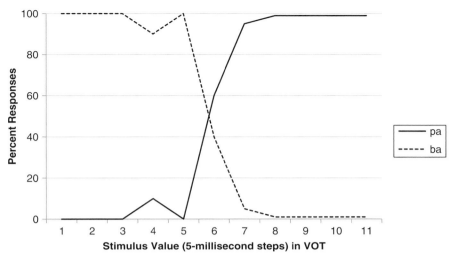

Figure 9.7   Actual perceptual judgments in response to stimuli such as those in Figure 9.5. Perception shifts suddenly from *ba* to *pa*.

in Chapter 6). The infants were given a nipple to suck that triggered a repeated speech sound, such as *ba*. After the infants habituated to, or lost interest in, the sound (e.g., /b/) and stopped sucking, the sound was then changed, with the VOT of the new sound being the critical difference. Half the time, the change in VOT resulted in what adults perceived as a movement across the voiced/voiceless boundary (e.g., *ba* to *pa*; shift of VOT from 20 to 40 milliseconds; 20D in Figure 9.8). Both 1- and 4-month-olds showed dishabituation—an increase in sucking—when the new phoneme was triggered. On the other hand, if the VOT stayed within a category boundary (e.g., +0 milliseconds to +20—*ba*, or +40 to +60 milliseconds—*pa*; 20S in Figure 9.8), the infants continued to show habituation and sucked less because they perceived the same category sound (see Figure 9.8). Thus, very young infants, who had had very limited speech input, nonetheless responded to the same phonological categories as the adults did. Initially, these results seemed to be strong evidence that the categories for speech perception were built into the human perceptual apparatus, consistent with Chomsky's proposal for an innate module for human language.

However, more recent evidence has cast doubt on the modular nature of this language skill (Goldstone & Handrickson, 2009, 2010). For example, categorical perception has also been found in chimps (Kojima, Tatsumi, Kiritani & Hirose, 1989), and chinchillas (Kuhl & Miller, 1975), neither of which has a complex natural language in the manner of humans. Categorization abilities have also been found for general non–speech-based sounds (Cutting, 1982; Cutting & Rosner, 1974; Rosen & Howell, 1981), indicating that the tendency may be a general function of the sound system itself (Kuhl, 1978, 2009), rather than language-specific. Categorical perception can also be found in nonspeech domains, such as when we perceive *bands of separate colors*—red, orange, yellow, and so forth—when we look at a rainbow (even though the rainbow is made up of light rays which form a continuous band of physical energy as they are diffracted through drops of moisture). At the very least, categorical perception is not

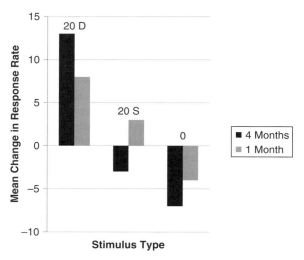

Figure 9.8 Infants' changing response rate to different stimuli.
Adapted from Eimas et al., 1971, Figure 3.

limited to perception of phonemes. In conclusion, studies of categorical perception of phonemes, which showed that infants have the same phoneme boundaries as adults (e.g., Eimas et al., 1971), seemed initially to have provided support for the existence of an innate language-specific processing module in humans. However, subsequent research indicates that this is neither a human-specific nor speech-specific tendency, and thus may not be solely a linguistic skill.

The Multi-Modal Nature of Speech Perception: The McGurk-MacDonald Effect

People clearly use purely acoustic features of phonemes to recognize and categorize sounds. However, people also use visual clues, making much speech perception *multimodal* (where input comes from multiple modalities—e.g., auditory and visual). One phenomenon that illustrates this multimodality is the *McGurk-MacDonald effect* (McGurk & MacDonald, 1976). When a videotape of a man saying *ga* is presented in coordination with an audio of another man saying *ba*, people often perceive the sound as an intermediate *da*. (You can easily find a video of this effect on YouTube.) First listen *and* watch to see what syllable is perceived. Then close your eyes and only listen. Finally, turn off the computer sound and only watch the visual cues as to what is being said. The effect should be clear: What you *see* affects what you *hear*.

This conclusion is supported by studies showing that people perceive speech more easily in ordinary communication situations when they can see the speaker, especially when there is competing noise (MacLeod & Summerfield, 1987). Remez, Fellowes, Pisoni, Goh, and Rubin (1998) asked people to transcribe sentences while only listening to an audiotape of the sentences, or while simultaneously seeing a video of the speaker. The number of syllables transcribed accurately was significantly higher in the audiovisual condition than audio only, again showing that visual language cues contribute to our perception and phonemic analysis of spoken speech. Although both audio and visual information are used in speech perception, the audio may be more important when detecting phonemes (Schmid, Thielmann, & Zigler, 2009), and people can often detect the disconnect between the audio and visual input in the McGurk effect (Soto-Faraco & Alsius, 2009).

Speech Perception: Conclusions

The perception of speech involves processes similar to those found at the core of pattern-recognition as discussed in Chapter 5, including both feature analysis and top-down processes (as illustrated by categorical perception of phonemes). While we can accomplish speech perception based purely on the physical properties of the sounds a person produces (e.g., when we listen to someone talk in the dark), speech comprehension can also be multimodal and knowledge-based. The McGurk effect illustrates that we not only attend to auditory aspects of a speaker's output, but also to the shape of their lips, and other cues such as body language.

INFANTS' SENSITIVITY TO THE SOUND STRUCTURE OF LANGUAGE

Sound Production

We have seen that, many months before they produce their first words, infants are sensitive to the prosody and phonemic structure of the language they hear around them. In production, too, there are precursors to actual language. Infants first begin *cooing*, using mainly vowel sounds and gurgling noises, and then progress to *babbling*, which includes consonant-vowel combinations, such as *dada*, *gege*, and so on. Initially, infants' babbling can include phonemes used in a wide range of languages. With increasing age and exposure to one language, however, the sounds they produce come to resemble more and more the phonemes of the language being spoken around them (Pinker, 1994).

Children's Analysis of Words in Adult Speech

Most people assume that there are pauses between words that allow children to isolate words and acquire them from adult speech. However, we usually do not produce words as separate units, which means that the stream of sound is continuous, like this:

Thestreamofsoundislikethiswithnobreaksbetweencontinuouswords.

How, then, does a child hear separate words in the stream of continuous sound? While the exaggerated enunciation of words and phonemes in motherese/parentese helps (Thiessen, Hill, & Saffran, 2005; Thiessen & Saffran, 2003, 2007), much of our designation of word boundaries is based on top-down processing. Saffran, Aslin, and Newport (1996) studied 8-month-old infants' sensitivity to phonological structure by presenting strings of computer-generated three-syllable nonsense words with consonant-vowel-consonant-vowel-consonant-vowel (CVCVCV) structure, such as *bidaku*, *babupu*, and *golabu*. Strings of the new "words" were presented repeatedly, with no breaks between them, as in this example:

golabubidakubabupubidaku

This situation is similar to what happens in life when children are exposed to language in their typical interactions with other people. Each infant simply heard the strings for two minutes. As can be seen in the just presented example, within each "word," the syllables followed each other in regular order. There is thus a very high probability that, when *bi* is heard, *da* will follow, and that *ku* follows *da*. However, the multisyllabic "words" themselves did not follow each other with regularity.

After the 2-minute exposure to the experimental strings, Saffran et al. (1996) presented the infants with test strings, some of which contained words that had been heard before, and others that contained familiar syllables put together randomly. The infants showed habituation (see Chapter 6), in that they spent less time listening to the "words" from the speech stream and attended more to the novel nonwords. Amazingly, the infants had learned the structure of the strings from a simple, 2-minute exposure. In a second experiment, Saffran et al. confirmed that infants were able to determine word boundaries from statistical regularities in the 2-minute speech stream. Infants paid more attention to syllable combinations composed of the last syllable from one word plus the first syllable of another (e.g., "kuba," because this constituted a novel stimulus) than to syllables from *within* a single word. Simple exposure to a brief speech sample was enough to acquire top-down knowledge about the syllabic structure of new "words."

This research addressed two important questions concerning language comprehension. First, even when speech is continuous, one way to tell when words begin and end is by imposing an organization on the speech spectrum, based on top-down knowledge as to which phonemes and syllables have been heard together before. Secondly, the research of Saffran et al. (1996) indicates that humans are sensitive to statistical probabilities of speech syllables very early in life, and can use that sensitivity to begin to analyze language into word units (see also Lany & Saffran, 2010). This research has been interpreted as supporting an emergent perspective, because general learning principles such as detecting statistical patterns were found to facilitate word learning.

THE PHONEMIC STRUCTURE OF THE FIRST WORDS

At about the end of the first year, a child's babbling changes into recognizable words that clearly seem to *refer* to objects, properties, or actions in the world, such as when a child says *ba* upon seeing a bottle. This does not mean, however, that the first words produced by children are accurate renditions of the words they have heard. Examples of children's early mispronunciations and reductions of words are shown in Table 9.4A. At the level of sounds, consonant clusters in words tend to be reduced—e.g., *black* is pronounced as "b-ack" or *turtle* as "tu-tle." Some phonemes are almost universally difficult for children to pronounce, and are often replaced by other phonemes that tend to be produced earlier in development. For example,

Table 9.4   Children's Early Word Production: Cognitive Bases
for Children's Early Words

A. Examples of children's early words	
Elephant	*EL-fun*
Hippopotamus	*POT-mus*
Giraffe	*RAF*

B. Relation between parental speech and children's first words	
Parental Speech	Child (Pattern Recognition > Memory > Output)
Elephant	*EL – fun*
Hippopotamus	*POT – mus*

the glide sounds /l/ and /r/ are often replaced with /w/ (as in "wabbit" for *rab-bit*). Other sounds, such as /th/ or /v/ may not be mastered until a child is between 4 and 7 years old (International Children's Education, http://www.iched.org/cms/scripts/page.php?site_id=ichedanditem_id=child_speech1). At the level of the syllable, young children are likely to omit first syllables that are unstressed (Demuth & Fee, 1995; Kehoe, 2001) so that *giraffe* becomes '*raffe*); other examples can be seen in Table 9.4.

The systematic mispronunciation of children's first words raises the question of how and why those errors arise. Errors in production of some phonemes cannot explain all patterns. Our discussion of memory, pattern recognition, and attention in Chapters 1–6 can help us understand why young children might only extract certain sorts of information from the speech stream. That is, what a child will say in a situation must depend on what he or she has *stored* and can *retrieve* about what adults said in similar situations (see Table 9.4B). Several factors, such as whether a syllable appears at the beginning, middle, or end of a word, and whether or not it is stressed, may contribute to a particular part of a word being relatively easy to hear and remember. First, in multisyllabic words, some syllables are stressed or emphasized. One example of this is the initial syllable in *elephant* (compare it with the initial un-stressed syllable in *giraffe*). Stressed syllables in English also tend to have longer pronunciation times than unstressed syllables, thus permitting longer processing. In addition, perception of some syllables may be facilitated by their appearing at the beginning or end of words or sentences (similar to a primacy and recency effect in memory).

Echols and Newport (1992) compared words produced by children with those words in standard adult pronunciation. Their summarized results are shown in Table 9.5. They found a serial-position effect in articulation of the children's words: The last syllable is most likely to be produced across all words. In words with three syllables, the first syllable is also very likely to be reproduced by the child and the middle syllable most likely to be left out. Children were also most likely to produce syllables that are stressed in adult speech, that are spoken relatively loudly. For example, one child produced "el-fun" for elephant, thereby omitting the unstressed middle syllable. However, the serial-position effect is seen for both stressed and unstressed syllables. Echols and Newport concluded that two hypotheses were supported by their

Table 9.5 Data on Production of Syllables in Children's Words, from Echols and Newport (1992): Probability That Syllable Is Produced by Child in Spontaneous Speech

| | Position of Syllable in Word | | |
Stress Level of Syllable	Initial	Medial	Final
Unstressed	0.55	0.45	0.90
Stressed	0.90	0.80	1.00

results: (1) Children may be biased to attend to certain syllables in the speech stream (Blasdell & Jensen, 1970; Gleitman, Gleitman, Landau, & Wanner, 1988), or (2) they may *process* all syllables in adult speech—stressed and unstressed, regardless of position—but are most likely to *produce* stressed syllables, especially in final position (Allen & Hawkins, 1980; Gerken, Landau, & Remez, 1990).

The pattern of findings in Table 9.5 points to a close tie between language and the other cognitive processes. Children's production of words can be understood, perhaps not surprisingly, on the basis of their ability to extract information out of the speech stream. Furthermore, that ability seems to be based on general principles of processing that have already been extensively discussed in relation to memory, pattern recognition, and attention.

Development of Word Comprehension

Over the first year of life, infants become better at processing linguistic input, including individual words. Fernald, Marchman, and their colleagues (e.g., Fernald, Perfors, & Marchman, 2006; Hurtado, Marchman, & Fernald, 2008; Marchman & Fernald, 2008) have analyzed the developing infant's capacity to extract information from the sound stream using a *selective looking technique*. An infant is seated in front of two computer-monitor screens. A picture is presented in each monitor—say, a baby and a shoe—and at the same time a voice says "Where's the baby? Do you see it?" A video camera records the infant's eye gaze, allowing the researcher to determine whether or not the infant looks at the picture of the object named in the sentence. Frame-by-frame analysis of the video recordings showed that over the second year of life (from 15 to 25 months of age) infants responded more and more quickly to the label in the spoken sentence, and that the infants were also able to respond correctly to partial words ("Where's the sh . . . ?"), indicating that their developing word-knowledge played a role in processing the linguistic input (Fernald et al., 2006).

In addition, the infants who were more efficient in processing the linguistic message were those whose mothers who talked to them more and who also used more-complex utterances. Thus, infants' abilities are at least in part based on the quality of the speech they hear (Hurtado, Marchman, & Fernald, 2008). Also, language-processing skills in infancy predicted cognitive skills later in life (Marchman & Fernald, 2008). The children who processed words more efficiently at 24 months of age performed better on tests of overall IQ, language production, and working memory at 8 years.

After a child extracts repeating strings of sounds from speech, he or she has to link each of those strings to an event or object in the world. We now turn how the child learns the meanings of words.

Cracking the Semantic Code: Learning the Meanings of Words

Children's first words are usually nouns (*bottle, mommy, daddy*), social phrases (*bye-bye*), adjectives (*wet*), and verbs (*drink, kiss*). Parental input has an effect on the predominant type of words produced: Western parents (as in the United States) tend to emphasize nouns, which is reflected in a noun-bias in their children; Chinese parents are more likely to emphasize verbs, and verbs make up a larger proportion of their children's early vocabulary (Levey & Cruz, 2003). Word learning initially progresses very slowly, but, at around 18 months, children go through a *vocabulary spurt* (though the exact age at which this happens varies greatly from child to child). At this point, the child may learn an average of nine new words per day (Carey, 1978; Dromi, 1987). Pinker (1994) has referred to the children as becoming "vacuum cleaners" for words. Underlying this rapid vocabulary growth is what is called *fast mapping*, in which words and their meanings may be acquired after a single exposure, or only a few. That is, the child quickly *maps* meanings to words. Fast mapping had been thought to occur around 2 years of age, but children as young as 18 months have demonstrated it in the laboratory (Houston-Price, Plunkett, & Harris, 2005).

The Problem of Learning the Meanings of Words

How does a child know to what a new word refers? This connection is not as obvious as it may seem. Imagine that a child and an adult see a white rabbit hopping across a lawn. The adult says "Rabbit!" Presumably, the child has now learned the label for that animal, and will use the word *rabbit* the next time she sees a similar furry creature. However, Quine (1960) pointed out that learning what a word's *reference* is—what the word refers to—is not nearly that simple. How does the child know exactly what "Rabbit!" picks out? The adult might have been referring to the whole scene, including the rabbit hopping its way across the grass on the way to a line of bushes. Alternatively, perhaps the adult was referring to the rabbit's white color; or to the act of hopping; or to the rabbit's ears; or its legs; or its puffy tail. Might "Rabbit" be that animal's proper name? Without some help or guiding principles, the child is reduced to guessing—probably incorrectly—what the label means.

Psychologists have proposed several explanations for the efficiency with which infants and children learn words and their meanings. The *constraints* view holds that the child comes into the world with *processing constraints* that direct the child to focus on relevant aspects of the environment in a word-learning situation (Clark, 1990; Golinkoff, Mervis, & Hirsh-Pasek, 1994; Markman, 1989). In contrast, the *social* theory of word learning argues that social factors, most importantly *the knowledge and intentions of the adult speaker*, assist the child in determining the meanings of words (Akhtar & Tomasello, 1996; Hollich, Hirsh-Pasek, Tucker, & Golinkoff, 2000; Nelson, 1988; Tomasello et al., 1996; Tomasello & Farrar, 1986).

Theories of Word Learning

Constraints View

The constraints view of world learning (e.g., Baldwin, 1989; Clark, 1990; Gleitman, Gleitman, Landau, & Wanner, 1988; Golinkoff et al., 1994; Markman, 1989; Markman & Hutchinson, 1984; Nagy & Gentner, 1990; Waxman & Gelman, 1986) asserts that children are biased toward analyzing the world in ways that increase the likelihood of attaching the right meaning to a word. For instance, the child in the "rabbit" example would only consider the possibility that the parent is referring to the whole object—the rabbit—rather than one or more of its parts or its action. This is called the *whole-object constraint* on word learning. On this view, the mind is so designed that only a few possible meanings are considered to constrain the references for nouns and verbs (Pinker, 1994). This *whole-object* tendency may be due to the perceptual salience of whole objects (Spelke, 1990). When word learning begins, this whole-object tendency combines with a tendency for speakers to refer to whole objects, and results in the child largely producing words that refer to whole objects. A second constraint is children's realization that most words apply to a class of objects (Markman & Hutchinson, 1984). Thus when they learn a new word, e.g., "rabbit," it applies not only to that particular individual animal, but to a larger category of similar animals.

Another constraint that the child uses to maximize word learning is called *mutual exclusivity*. Young children seem to believe that names are *mutually exclusive*: If an object already has a name, then they resist a second name for that object (Markman, 1990). Markman and Wachtel (1988) presented 3-year-olds with two objects—one familiar with a known name (e.g., a *cup*), the other unfamiliar with no known label (e.g., a kitchen gadget for removing pits from cherries). In one condition, the child heard a new word (e.g., "dax"), and was asked to hand the experimenter "the dax." The children assumed that the novel label applied to the object that did not yet have a name (Experiment 1). In another condition, when a second name was produced for a familiar object, children applied the term to a distinctive part of the object which did not already have a label, or to the substance of which it was made—e.g., "pewter," rather than adopt a second label for the whole object (Experiments 2–6).

In summary, the constraints view holds that there must be some constraints on the hypotheses that children entertain during the word-learning situation (Hollich, Hirsh-Pasek, Tucker, & Golinkoff, 2000). Words cannot be learned by mere association, because the label is associated with multiple aspects of the scene—parts of an object, the background, any action that is taking place—and it is impossible to distinguish which aspect of an object or scene was intended by a spoken word. Some researchers believe that these word-learning constraints are universal in all people and specific to a language module (Nagy & Gentner, 1990), and have an innate basis (Carey, 1993; Soja, Carey, & Spelke, 1991; Woodward & Markman, 1991). Alternatively, it might be the case that the whole-object and mutual-exclusivity constraints are simply *lexical principles*, which the child has induced from experience and are useful during language learning (Golinkoff et al., 1994; MacWhinney, 1989). From this latter perspective, the processing constraints are not necessarily based on innate or language-specific guidelines, but on general inductive learning principles; over time a child implicitly realizes which strategies optimize word-learning.

Social-Pragmatic View

Recall from our earlier discussion that a major perspective within emergent theories is the social-pragmatic theory of word learning (Akhtar & Tomasello, 1996; Hollich et al., 2000; Houston-Price, Plunkett, & Duffy, 2006; Nelson, 1988; Tomasello et al., 1996), which emphasizes that, from an early age, infants and children are sensitive to social cues which can help them learn the meanings of words. Furthermore, people supplying the teaching typically attend to what a child is interested in:

> Children do not try and guess what it is that the adult intends to refer to; rather . . . it is the adult who guesses what the child is focused on and then supplies the appropriate word. (Nelson, 1988, pp. 240–241)

One important social-cognitive mechanism affecting word learning is that of *joint attention* (Tomasello & Farrar, 1986). Word learning is optimized when an adult labels an object at which the child is already looking (Tomasello & Farrar, 1986). Joint attention is assumed to involve a child's understanding of the *intentional state* of another person, (i.e., what the other person knows); the child adopts a new label for an object because he or she believes that the object is the target of the attentional focus for another person (Tomasello, 2000). Children as young as 19 months of age look at their parent's eyes to determine the direction of gaze when the parent is labeling an object. Also, infants who are more socially attentive to the adult's direction of gaze during linguistic interaction are more likely to accurately apply the labels they hear around them, and learn words more quickly (Baldwin, 1991, 1993; Tomasello, 1995). In conclusion, young children are aware of social cues in the linguistic environment that indicate the intentional states of other speakers. They then use those cues as a way to map words to objects.

Although social cues are clearly important in learning the meanings of words, given language's important communicative function, they cannot be the whole story. Even if an adult sees a child watching a rabbit hopping across a field, the adult cannot determine exactly what it is about the situation to which the child is attending. Conversely, watching an adult's eye gaze as she labels "dog," for example, will not tell the child if the speaker is referring to the animal versus its leash or its tail, or to the fact that the dog is panting. These examples lead to the conclusion that there must be an additional, nonsocial factor that focuses the child's attention to the aspects of a word's meaning that are not transmitted solely through social cues. This need for an additional factor to explain acquisition of word meanings seems to indicate that some constraints are needed for rapid word learning.

Coalition View

Hollich, Hirsh-Pasek, Tucker, and Golinkoff (2000) have developed a theory of word learning that attempts to reconcile the constraints and social-pragmatic views, bringing them together in a *coalition* model of word learning. The coalition view proposes that learning word meanings depends on a coalition of cues; that is: (1) cues from the object in the environment (e.g., perceptual salience, novelty); (2) constraints that the child uses to confine the possible intended meanings of words; (3) cues from the person talking to the child (e.g., social cues, joint attention); and (4) the verbal message itself are all used by the young child in the learning of meaning of words. Furthermore, the weighting of linguistic versus object-related versus social cues can shift over time. For example, before 18 months of age, new talkers may rely heavily on the perceptual salience of objects to merely associate a word label with its referent; after 18 months, social cues such as the intent of the speaker become more relevant (Hollich, Hirsh-Pasek, Tucker, & Golinkoff, 2000).

LEARNING WORD MEANINGS: CONCLUSIONS

Children are able to acquire meanings of words, often quickly, due to a variety of cues and factors. First, there are constraints in processing information and the kinds of hypotheses children entertain concerning word meanings. Second, the linguistic community is sensitive to the child's capacities, and adults structure the communication situation to maximize the chances that the child will attend to the relevant object as well as to the phonology of a to-be-learned word. Finally, the child utilizes cues about the social/cognitive aspects of language, and adopts strategies that help to optimize word learning.

LEXICAL ACCESS

We have now examined the acquisition of the first words, which form the bricks out of which language is built. As noted earlier, the hypothesized location in memory where words and their meanings are stored is called the *mental lexicon*. Children's word learning is referred to as *lexical acquisition*; when we retrieve or activate words, we engage in *lexical access*. Psychologists have developed several methods to study how the mental lexicon is organized and how we access words and their meanings, including studies of both tip-of-the-tongue states and the processing of ambiguous words in sentences.

The Tip-of-the-Tongue State and Lexical Access

We all experience tip-of-the-tongue (TOT) states, those exasperating situations in which one is trying to recall a word or name, without success, but with the distinct feeling that success is just over the horizon. College students report an average of 1–2 TOT states per week; older adults report 2–4 (Schacter, 2001). The types of words we have trouble retrieving, and the cues that facilitate retrieval, can provide clues as to the organization and functioning of the mental lexicon.

In a classic study, Brown and McNeill (1966) produced TOT states in the lab, by presenting a list of definitions of relatively unfamiliar words, and asking the research participants to produce the word that fit each definition. One such question was: *What is the name of the instrument used by sailors to determine their position based on the positions of the stars?* [Answer: *sextant.*] When participants reported that they were in a TOT state, they were asked to provide any available information on the number of syllables that the word contained; the first letter; any similar-sounding words; or any words of similar meaning that they could retrieve. Of 360 TOT states reported, people were able to retrieve the first letter of the word 57% of the time, and the correct number of syllables 37% of the time. Furthermore, when participants wrote down words related to their intended target, the words were most often related phonologically; for instance, when the target was *caduceus*, similar-sounding words retrieved included *Casadesus*, *Aeschelus*, *cephalus*, and *leucosis*. Brown and McNeill concluded that people often have partial information about target words when in TOT states, and that the retrieval difficulty appears to be at the phonological level.

Brown and McNeill (1966) had proposed that TOT phenomena are due to only *partial activation* of the phonological specification of a word, particularly for the beginning sounds or letters. A more contemporary theory that includes this notion of partial activation is the *transmission deficit model* by Burke, MacKay, Worthley, and Wade (1991; also MacKay & Burke, 1990). The transmission deficit model is built on the *node structure theory*, a connectionist model developed by MacKay (1982, 1987), depicted in Figure 9.9. At the top are *semantic* or *meaning nodes*; during experiments in which a definition is provided, these nodes are already activated. They then send activation down to the *word nodes* (also known as *lemmas*), which contain grammatical information, including word class and gender of nouns in some languages (such as Spanish, French, and Italian), and so forth. Activation then spreads to the phonological level, where the phonemic representation of a word (or *lexeme*) is activated.

The transmission deficit model explains TOTs as being caused by weak connections between the word and phonological levels, typically because only low-frequency words that we rarely use produce tip-of-the-tongue states. Weakened connections may also explain why bilingual people exhibit more TOT states than monolinguals (Colomé, 2001; Ecke, 2004): Dividing speech between two spoken languages may result in lower frequencies for all lexical entries, and thus weakened connections between a word and its phonological representation (Pyers, Gollan, & Emmorey, 2009).

If the transmission deficit model/partial activation theory is correct, then: (a) word-related information about a TOT word should be available, such as the grammatical class of the word, and its masculine or feminine designation of nouns in romance

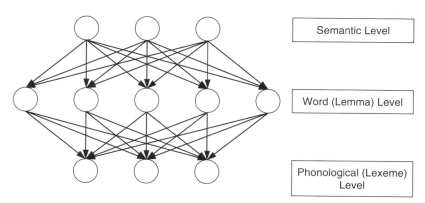

Figure 9.9 Node structure theory: A PDP model that has been proposed as an explanation for tip-of-the-tongue phenomena.

languages; and (b) any extra activation that can accrue at phonological nodes should facilitate retrieval. Phonological hints and similar sounding words should thus lead to resolution of a TOT more than semantic hints or semantically-related words. Research has found that people who speak languages in which nouns are designated as masculine or feminine, such as French or Italian, can retrieve the gender of a word a majority of the time (Ferrand, 2001; Miozzo & Caramazza, 1997).

Phonological Cuing in Resolution of TOT States

Meyer and Bock (1992, Experiment 2) induced TOT states in college students (e.g., what word means *saying little, reserved, uncommunicative*; Answer: *taciturn*), and then provided either a phonological hint (e.g., *tolerant*), a semantically-related hint (e.g., *withdrawn*), or an unrelated hint (e.g., *baby*). Resolution of TOT states was more than twice as likely following a phonological hint than after a semantic hint. Activating the initial phoneme of the target with a phonologically similar cue (which also shared the number of syllables and stress with the target) led to activation of the rest of the target. White and Abrams (2002) also found that same-first-syllable cues (e.g., *ab̲errant* for the target word *abdicate*) were more likely to result in TOT resolution than second- (e.g., *han̲dicap*) or third-syllable primes (e.g., *edu̲cate*) in groups of people aged 18–26 and 60–72. However a group of older participants (aged 73–83) did not significantly benefit from any phonologically similar cues, relative to unrelated prompts. These age-related findings are consistent with the idea that connections among nodes in semantic memory, and transmission from node to node, weaken with age, due perhaps both to the aging process itself and decreased use of low frequency words (Burke, MacKay, Worthley, & Wade, 1991; MacKay & Burke, 1990).

Brain States in TOT

A study by Kikyo, Ohki, and Sekihara (2001) used fMRI to measure brain activity while Japanese people attempted to retrieve proper names of people in the news (e.g., politicians, scientists, heads of companies). An identifying question appeared on a screen (e.g., "Who established SONY?"), and participants pressed button 1 if they knew the target, button 2 if they did not know. TOT states were considered those in which the person took over 6 seconds to correctly retrieve the answer. The researchers found increased activation in the left dorsolateral prefrontal cortex and anterior cingulate gyrus during successful retrieval of TOT targets, while neither site was active when people were unable to retrieve the target. This indicates that these areas in the left hemisphere may be active in word retrieval.

Anomia

A neuropsychological disorder in which people experience chronic TOT states is anomia (meaning *without [a-] name [nomia]*). Anomic people have difficulty producing the names of even common objects. Retrieval is especially impaired for low frequency words (Goodglass, 1980; Martín, Serrano, & Iglesias, 1999; Raymer, Maher, Foundas, Rothi, & Heilman, 2000). This symptom can exist on its own, or as a symptom of aphasia, Alzheimer's disease (Joubert et al., 2008), or temporal-lobe epilepsy (Trebuchon-Da et al., 2009). Although we all experience word-finding difficulties occasionally, such as when we are under stress or fatigued, people with anomia often have more profound problems that render them unable to retrieve the labels of familiar, though often infrequently encountered, objects. During word production, they may often substitute a similar-meaning word for the target (e.g., calling a *beaver* a "chipmunk"), which is a semantic error; or a higher-level category name (e.g., saying "a musical instrument" for *flute*; Martín, Serrano, & Iglesias, 1999). As we saw in Chapter 8, researchers have also found that some categories, such as living creatures, are subject to greater naming difficulties than others (e.g., Goodglass, Wingfield, Hyde, & Theurkauf, 1986; Kolinsky et al., 2002).

There are two major ways in which naming and word-retrieval difficulties may exhibit themselves, which may correspond to activity in different brain areas. Upon being presented with a definition, picture, or object to identify, people with brain damage may have degraded semantic knowledge, and thus may be unable to even place the object in its correct category (e.g., they are unable to say that a spatula is a "utensil") or describe its function (to flip pancakes or hamburgers). This is known as *semantic anomia*, and is typically associated with damage to left or bilateral anterior temporal lobe regions due to progressive dementia (Binder & Price, 2001; Bright, Moss, & Tyler, 2004; D'Esposito et al., 1997; Moore & Price, 1999; Vandenberghe, Price, Wise, Josephs, & Frackowiak, 1996). *Pure anomia*, in contrast, is a condition more like being in a perpetual TOT state, and involves problems with retrieval of phonological information. These patients know the meaning and function of an object (e.g., saying "You sleep on it" for a *hammock*; Antonucci, Beeson, & Rapcsak, 2004), but without a hint, are unable to retrieve its name (Antonucci, Beeson, Labiner, & Rapcsak, 2008; Benson, 1979, 1988; Foundas, Daniels, & Vasterling, 1998; Raymer et al., 1997). Pure anomia is associated with left inferior posterior temporal lobe damage (Binder et al., 1997; Damasio, Grabowski, Tranel, Hichwa, & Damasio, 1996). Thus, when discussing the processes that occur when someone is asked to name a picture, researchers have agreed upon a series of stages: visual processing of the picture, activation of the semantic representation (including activation of the abstract version of the word, known as the *lemma*), and retrieval of the label and its phonological representation (Watamori, Fukusako, Monoi, & Sasanuma, 1991). Semantic anomia is a breakdown at the second stage, while pure anomia occurs at the last stage, during phonological representation of a word (Badecker, Miozzo, & Zanuttini, 1995).

Brain States in Anomia

Levelt, Praamstra, Meyer, Helenius, and Salmelin (1998) studied the time course and brain activation of cognitive steps in picture naming in normal patients using a neuromagnetometer (similar to an EEG, but measuring magnetic fields to determine cortical activation). The average time to name a picture was 538 milliseconds (although pictures with low frequency names, such as *rake* or *sled*, took longer to name than high frequency ones, such as *dog* or *pants*). The researchers proposed lemma activation took place 150–230 milliseconds after picture presentation, and was accomplished by bilateral activity in the occipital and parietal cortex, with some temporal lobe activation (see Figure 9.10). Phonological encoding of the actual verbal label corresponded to activation of left temporal regions in and around Wernicke's area about 200–350 milliseconds after presentation of the target.

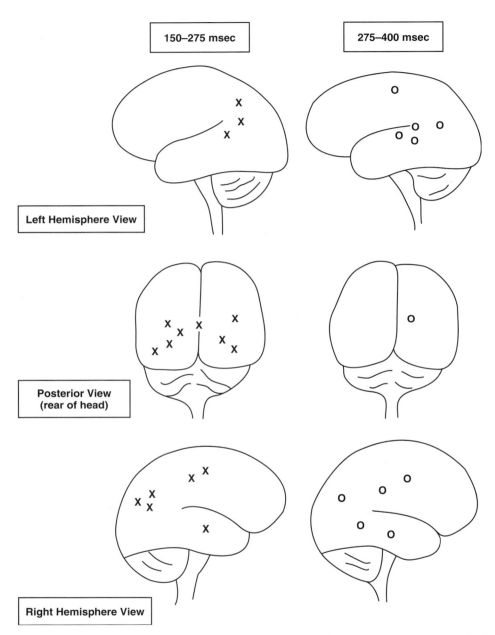

Figure 9.10 Activation of brain areas during lemma selection (X's) and phonological encoding (O's), as depicted in left hemisphere (top), posterior (middle), and right hemisphere (bottom) views, at two time intervals after presentation of word stimuli.
Adapted from Levelt et al., 1998.

Laganaro, Morand, and Schnider (2009) discovered different time courses in lexical retrieval for anomia due to semantic impairments (semantic anomia) versus those due to phonological impairments (pure anomia). They studied EEG data from 16 aphasia patients who were engaged in a picture-naming task. Half of the patients typically produced semantically based errors during naming, the other half produced predominantly phonological errors. Those with lexical-semantic impairments tended to show abnormal EEG patterns relatively soon after presentation of a picture, within 90–200 milliseconds. The lexical-phonologically impaired patients (pure anomics) were more likely to show abnormalities after 300 milliseconds, perhaps as they were retrieving the phonological specification of the word. In conclusion, studies of lexical activation, including research on TOT states and anomia, have provided evidence concerning factors involved in activating words in memory and the brain areas that contribute to lexical retrieval. Further information on word activation comes from studies that have investigated the processing of ambiguous words in sentence contexts, to which we now turn.

Lexical Ambiguity

A standard children's joke asks, "Why was six scared of seven?" Answer: "Because seven eight (ate) nine!" When spoken, the joke hinges on *lexical ambiguity*, because the word pronounced as *ate* is *ambiguous*, or is polysemous (*poly* = many; *semous* = meaning). It can mean both the number eight and the past tense of eat. Appreciating the joke requires that a person access both meanings, and realize that the standard interpretation within the seven, eight, nine sequence is not correct. Someone figuring out the joke might say: "'Because seven, eight, nine'? Huh? Oh! 'Seven *ate* nine.' Now I get it." But what about when your friend says she needs to deposit a check at the bank? You may only be aware of interpreting *bank* as a place for money, but *bank* is also an ambiguous word: *savings* bank and *river* bank. There is evidence that we may sometimes activate *both* meanings when we comprehend a message containing an ambiguous word, even though we are aware of only the meaning that fits the context. Processing of ambiguity has thus provided information on how people access word meanings.

In a pioneering study, Swinney (1979; also Swinney & Hakes, 1976) examined lexical access using a *cross-modal priming* task. Experimental participants listened to a passage that contained an ambiguous word while simultaneously engaging in a visual lexical-decision task, where they had to decide whether a string of visually presented letters formed a word. For instance, people would hear:

> Rumor had it that, for years, the government building had been plagued with problems. The man was not surprised when he found several roaches, spiders, and other _____ in the corner of his room.

In the empty slot, half of the participants heard the ambiguous word *bugs* (which could mean insects *or* spy-related listening devices), the other participants heard the unambiguous word *insects*. As soon as either of those critical words ended, a *visual* target word appeared on the computer screen in front of them. The target word was (a) related to the dominant meaning of the ambiguous word as implied by the sentence

Control Condition (Unambiguous critical word)

AUDIO ⇒ "... he found several roaches, spiders, and other insects"

VIDEO ⇒   SEW

ANT*

SPY

XVL

Experimental Condition (Ambiguous critical word)

AUDIO ⇒   "... he found several roaches, spiders, and other bugs"

VIDEO ⇒   SEW

ANT*

SPY*

XVL

*Word(s) with fastest response time.

Figure 9.11   Outline of Swinney paradigm to study activation of meanings of ambiguous words during sentence processing.

(e.g., ANT); (b) related to the alternate meaning of *bugs* (e.g., SPY); or two control conditions in which the target word was either (c) unrelated to the sentence (e.g., SEW), or (d) not a word (XNR). The task for the participants was to report as quickly as possible whether the target was a word. The entire experimental task is outlined in Figure 9.11.

When the unambiguous word (*insect*) was in the sentence, people were fastest to respond to the word related to its meaning (ANT), as would be expected (Swinney, 1979). When the ambiguous word (*bug*) was in the sentence, however, people were faster to respond to both meanings (ANT and SPY). Based on these and other similar results, a number of researchers have proposed an *exhaustive-access* view of lexical processing (Onifer & Swinney, 1981; Seidenberg, Tanenhaus, Leiman, & Bienkowski, 1982; Swinney, 1979; Tanenhaus, Leiman, & Seidenberg, 1979). According to this view, when a person encounters an ambiguous word, *all* its meanings are activated, regardless of context (Tabossi, 1988). After all meanings have been activated, a second post-access process sways the final interpretation toward the intended meaning, based on the context of the sentence. Evidence suggests that both meanings are not necessarily accessed simultaneously; the dominant meaning of a word, in virtue of its greater frequency (it is the *dominant* meaning because it is the one more frequently used), has a lower threshold, is activated almost immediately (Paul, Kellas, Martin, & Clark, 1992), with the subordinate meaning activated within 100 milliseconds (Simpson & Burgess, 1985, 1988).

However, there is evidence that, under some specific circumstances, only one meaning of an ambiguous word is accessed, and *selective access theories* propose that only the meaning relevant to the sentence context is activated (Glucksberg, Kreuz, & Rho, 1986; Schvaneveldt, Meyer, & Becker, 1976; Simpson, 1981). For example, if one presents an ambiguous word in a linguistic context that highly constrains the dominant meaning, there is no activation of the subordinate meaning (Tabossi, 1988, Experiment 2; Tabossi & Zardon, 1993). A second factor that influences the activation patterns of the meanings of ambiguous words may be whether the two meanings of the term are *balanced* (relatively equal in frequency of usage) or *biased* (where one meaning occurs much more frequently). During reading, people look longer at balanced words (as if trying to resolve which of the two meanings is meant); but they look no longer at biased ambiguous words than they do at control (single-meaning) words (Rayner & Frazier, 1989). Presenting disambiguating information that precedes the ambiguous word (e.g., *kitchen table* versus *statistical table*) can also alter reading patterns. Disambiguating information that supports the subordinate or less-frequent interpretation of a biased ambiguous word increases reading times for that word (Rayner, Cook, Juhasz, & Frazier, 2006). This suggests that, in cases where only the dominant meaning of a word would normally be activated, extra processing time is needed to resolve competition between the dominant and subordinate interpretations when the latter is activated because of the disambiguating information. It should be noted, however, that the research discussed in this section has examined processing of ambiguous nouns. Processing of other types of ambiguous words, such as verbs (e.g., *lie*; Pickering & Frisson, 2001), may involve different activation patterns, based on sentence context.

Conclusion

In summary, there is substantial evidence that multiple meanings are activated when we hear or read ambiguous words. When no context is provided, the dominant meanings of ambiguous words are activated first (Simpson & Burgess, 1985; Simpson & Krueger, 1991), because they may have lower thresholds due to their higher frequency, followed by access of the subordinate meanings of the word. When a context is provided by a sentence or other constraining factor, both meanings are sometimes activated, but the irrelevant meaning may be suppressed in favor of the context-relevant interpretation (Tabossi & Zardon, 1993).

Brain States in Lexical Access

Lexical Activation in Wernicke's Aphasia

Wernicke's aphasia is usually due to damage to the superior temporal gyrus of the left hemisphere. Historically, Wernicke's aphasia was referred to as *receptive aphasia*, because patients' main deficit is in recognizing incoming speech; or as *fluent aphasia*, because Wernicke's patients can speak fluently (i.e., in well-formed sentences), although their sentences are often meaningless. Here are two examples of utterances produced by patients with Wernicke's aphasia.

> I called my mother on the television and did not understand the door. It was too breakfast, but they came from far to near. My mother is not too old for me to be young. (http://atlantaaphasia.org/WhatIsAphasia02.html)

You know that smoodle pinkered and that I want to get him round and take care of him like you want before. (http://www.nidcd.nih.gov/staticresources/health/voice/FactSheetAphasia.pdf)

As can be seen, the spoken utterances of Wernicke's aphasics are peppered with *neologisms* (nonsensical words) and *paraphasias* (errors of various sorts, either *semantic paraphasias*, e.g., word substitutions, or *phonemic paraphasias*, e.g., mispronunciations). The first patient exhibits mainly semantic paraphasias, and the second exhibits more neologisms.

Researchers have proposed that neologisms and paraphasias may be due to overactivation of lexical entries (Milberg, Blumstein, & Dworetsky, 1988); or to a competition among lexical items, in which items that *should* be rejected fail to become deactivated (Janse, 2006). By way of illustration, Yee, Blumstein, and Sedivy (2008) measured eye movements during a picture-finding task. An auditory target word (e.g., "tuba") was presented, along with a three-by-three matrix containing four pictures—one in each corner (see Figure 9.12). Participants were to touch the computer screen on the area where the target picture (*tuba*) appeared. In Experiment 2, the pictures were (a) the target (e.g., *tuba*); (b) a picture whose name began with the same first syllable (e.g., *tulip*), and (c) two control items (e.g., *owl* and *olives*). The participants without aphasia glanced at the nontarget pictures, but then suppressed looking toward the same-first syllable item once they realized that it was not the target. Wernicke's aphasics, on the other hand, fixated longer on the nontarget pictures with similar phonological beginning

Figure 9.12 Stimulus matrix similar to those used by Yee et al. (2008) to examine activation of information in aphasic participants versus non-aphasic participants.

(e.g., *tulip*). This indicated that *phonological competitors* to the auditory target remained activated longer than normal. In Experiment 3, Yee et al. determined that phonological competitors were not only activated, but also spread their activation to semantically associated items; Wernicke's patients who heard *hammock* looked longer at a picture of a nail than at the controls. That result was interpreted as evidence that *hammock* had activated the phonologically related lexical entry for *hammer*, which in turn spread activation to *nail*. Thus, words in the lexical system in Wernicke's aphasics may both become overactivated and spread activation to multiple other words (Yee et al., 2008), resulting in a problem opposite to that suffered during tip-of-the-tongue states.

Harpaz, Levkovitz, and Lavidor (2009) used transcranial magnetic stimulation (TMS) to determine the role of Wernicke's area and its right-hemisphere analogue (the area in the right hemisphere comparable in location to Wernicke's area in the left hemisphere) in activation of the dominant versus subordinate meanings of ambiguous words. In Chapter 1, we reported two uses of TMS—one to functionally paralyze or deactivate parts of the brain. This is typically done by applying low-level frequencies to a region to inhibit performance of that region. The second method was used by Harpaz et al., and involved using a short burst of high-frequency waves to *increase* activity in that area (see also Mottaghy et al., 1999; Sparing et al., 2001). When high-frequency TMS was applied to Wernicke's area in the LH, people were better at making semantic-decision judgments based on the dominant meanings of words; when applied to the corresponding area in the right hemisphere, people were faster at responding to the subordinate meanings of the ambiguous words. This result supports the idea of lateralization of activation of word meanings, with the left hemisphere being best at processing dominant meanings. This result is consistent with early research that reported that right hemisphere damage was most likely to lead to an inability to understand jokes (Gardner, Ling, Flamm, & Silverman, 1975), since jokes often hinge on focusing on the contextually subordinate meaning of an ambiguous word (as in the "seven eight/ate nine" example at the beginning of this section).

Lexical Access: Conclusions

We all suffer from tip-of-the-tongue states occasionally, especially for low frequency words. However, even in TOT states, people often have partial information about a target word available, such as the first or last phoneme or syllable (Brown & McNeill, 1966). With both normal people and pure anomics, the block seems to be at retrieving the phonological representation of the word, which is why phonologically related hints often facilitate retrieval. Research on processing lexical ambiguity indicates that multiple meanings of words are often activated, and then the system utilizes the interpretation that best fits the sentence context. When a context is provided by a sentence or other constraining factor, the irrelevant meaning may be suppressed in favor of the context-relevant interpretation. In this way, a person's mental lexicon can accommodate the multiple meanings of many words, without the meanings of words being in competition with each other indefinitely. In addition, studies of brain functioning in lexical access indicate that there may be lateralization of meanings of ambiguous words. Such studies shed light on lexical storage of words, and psychological processes such as word retrieval.

The Meaning Structure of Words: Morphological Analysis

Many words have a complex internal structure that allows people to use language creatively and to convey subtleties about words and meanings. Consider, for example, the word *untied*, as in *I untied my shoes*. *Untied* has three parts: *tie*, which is a word that has meaning and can stand on its own; and *un-* and *-ed*, both of which are not separate words, but which convey meaning nonetheless. *Un-* tells you that the action being carried out is the opposite of *tie*, and *-ed* tells you the action took place in the past. These small particles of meaning, the smallest units of meaning in a language, are called *morphemes*. *Books* is constructed out of two morphemes—*book* plus the *plural morpheme -s*, which signals that more than one book is being discussed. Morphemes, such as *tie* and *book*—single words that can stand alone—are called *free morphemes*. Morphemes that cannot stand alone, like *un-*, *-s*, and *-ed*, are called *bound morphemes*. The study of the morphemic structure of words is called *morphology*. Specifying the mechanisms through which we combine morphemes into words will help us understand important aspects of language functioning and language development.

Morphological Rules

There is a high degree of regularity in how bound morphemes are combined with free morphemes to create new words. As one example, verbs are made into adjectives in English by adding *suffixes*, or endings, such as *-able*, as in *imaginable*. The suffix *-ism* (as in *Darwinism*, or *Marxism*) makes one kind of noun out of another ("I am not a believer in Marxism"). The suffix *-ian*, as in *Marxian* or *Mozartian*, makes an adjective out of a noun ("That philosophy sounds Marxian"). Similarly, the suffix *-er* makes any verb a noun, as in *writer* and *reader*. There is ample evidence from adult, child, and aphasic data that we access morphemes separately when we speak (e.g., *read* + *er*), and that we decompose multimorphemic words into their components in word recognition, spelling, and other tasks. For example, Laine and Koivisto (1998) determined that multimorphemic words take longer to recognize than single-morpheme words in a lexical decision task.

The most widely used suffixes in English signal pluralization of nouns and the past tense of verbs. These endings, or any alteration to a word to indicate tense, number, person, or case, are called *inflections*. (Note that *inflection* as it is used here is morphological, and not the same as the prosodic aspects of language that we discussed earlier in the chapter.) Most nouns can be made plural by adding the plural morphemes, *-s* or *-es*. A similar phenomenon occurs with verbs. One can take almost any verb and speak about the action having occurred in the past by adding the appropriate inflection—in English it is written as *-ed*. Both these cases seem to indicate application of rules in English.

Development of Morphological Rules: The Wug Test

A groundbreaking study of the potential importance of morphological rules in the child's learning to speak was carried out by Berko (1958). Berko set out to demonstrate that, early in their development as speakers, children were learning rules of language, as demonstrated by how they used morphemes for particular grammatical classes of words. She exposed children to novel nouns and verbs, and studied how the children constructed new plurals and past tenses. For example, a child was presented with a card with a novel animal pictured on it, which was labeled a *wug* by the researcher. The child then saw a new card, with two of the new creatures on it, and the experimenter said: "Here is another one. Now there are two of them. There are two _____." Most children responded with "wugs." They had no difficulty creating the correct plural form for a new noun at the first opportunity. In another condition, a new verb was introduced. A child saw a picture of a girl doing something unfamiliar such as building a structure with sticks, while the experimenter said: "Here is a girl who knows how to rick. She is ricking. She did the same thing yesterday. What did she do yesterday? Yesterday she _____." This time the children responded with *ricked*, the correct past-tense form.

Berko's (1958) study provided clear evidence that young children can generalize to new examples the morphological forms that they have heard. Her results have also been cited as evidence that children are able to learn morphological rules, such as "-*ed* is applied to the end of verbs to indicate past tense," that are then appropriately applied to new words (see Pinker, 1994, Chapter 2). As we shall soon see, these results are still important in theoretical analyses of language processing, especially as to whether children learn morphological rules (Berko, 1958; Pinker, 1994) or merely patterns (McClelland & Rumelhart, 1986; Plunkett & Marchman, 1993, 1996).

GENERATIVITY IN WORD FORMATION: OVERREGULARIZATION

In many languages, such as English, there are a large number of irregular verbs for which the rules for past-tense formation do not apply, such as *do/did*; *come/came*; *think/thought*; *draw/drew*; *be/was*; *see/saw*; and *go/went*. In addition, some verbs do not change at all from past to present, such as *cut*, *set*, *hit*, and *put*. Children sometimes produce *overregularizations*, by adding -ed to the end of irregular verbs to indicate past tense (e.g., *goed*). There are also nouns in English which violate the rule of adding /s/ to form the plural, such *ox/oxen* and *foot/feet*. However, the irregular verbs have been of much more interest to researchers, so we will concentrate on them here. Children's production of regular and irregular verbs has been a testing ground for whether rule learning (Chomsky, 1959; Marcus, 1996; Pinker, 1994) or induction of high-probability patterns underlies language acquisition.

Verbs in English

A recent analysis has examined the frequency of 40 million words in contemporary American English, taken from many different sources: transcripts from spoken language, books—fiction and nonfiction—newspapers, magazines, and so forth (http://www.wordfrequency.info/; retrieved October 8, 2012). If we consider the 5,000 most frequent words from that corpus, the 10 most frequent verbs on the list are: *be, have, do, say, go, can, get, make, know, think*. All of those high-frequency verbs are irregular, and many of their alterations to past tense are unique in the language. That is, once you have learned that the past tense of *say* is pronounced *said*, there is no transfer in form to the past tense of similar root morphemes, such as *pay, stay, or play*. Thus, irregular verbs do not typically permit rule learning; often, one simply has to remember the specific exemplars of the various irregular tenses.

Here is another group of verbs, taken randomly from near the bottom of the top-5,000 list, from positions 4,136–4,189: *tackle, heat, tuck, post, specialize, sail, condemn, unite, equip, exchange*. All those less-frequent verbs are *regular*, which means that the pattern found in one verb can help in forming the past tense of other verbs; once you have learned that the past tense of *post* is *posted*, it can help you to form the past tense of *roast, toast, host*, and *boast*, among others.

Overregularization of the Past Tense

Examination of the development of the past tense in the speech of children shows an intriguing pattern in their use of regular versus irregular forms (Marcus, 2000; Pinker, 1991, 1994; Plunkett & Marchman, 1993). The earliest verbs used by children, usually in the second year, are typically the highly frequent irregular verbs, and they are used correctly: The child says *came, went*, and *did*. Since these verbs are so frequently heard by the child in the speech environment, it is not surprising that they are learned first and used correctly. Shortly thereafter, however, most children begin adding the *regular* ending to *irregular* verbs, producing forms that are never heard in ordinary adult speech: *comed, goed*, and *doed*. This phenomenon is called *overregularization*: The child takes the regular form and uses it in places where it is incorrect. Overregularized forms are found less than 3% of the time when children use past tense (Marcus et al., 1992), but their occurrence does seem to indicate rule learning, since children are unlikely to have heard adults use those overregularized past-tense forms. Later, children produce the correct form of irregular verbs (Cazden, 1968; Ervin & Miller, 1963; Miller & Ervin, 1964; Pinker & Prince, 1988).

Thus, there appears to be a U-shaped form to development of past-tense usage (Marcus et al., 1992). First the child learns each verb separately, by rote, producing correct endings for irregular and regular verbs. Second, the child learns the rule for forming the past tense (add *-ed*), and he or she extends that rule to every verb that is produced, which results in overregularization errors for irregular verbs (Marcus, 1996, 2000). Third, with increasing exposure to irregular verbs, each of them begins to function again as an independent unit and the correct irregular form is retrieved and produced. It is as if a competition arises between the rule and the specific irregular form. Once the irregular form gets strong enough and fast enough, it becomes too fast for the rule to block it, and is correctly produced.

Rules Versus Patterns

As just discussed, the development of overregularizations has been explained by appealing to the child's learning an implicit rule for how to produce the past tense. This perspective is consistent with Chomsky's (1959) proposal that innate, language-specific grammatical rules are triggered in the child, based on the language that the child hears (Pinker, 1991). An alternative explanation that has been considered by researchers does not rely on the notion of linguistic rules, however. This alternative perspective assumes that only one learning mechanism is involved in learning to produce the correct past tenses of all verbs, regular and irregular: Children rely on whatever associations between linguistic elements are strongest at a given time. When the -*ed* to indicate past tense becomes prevalent, they will append -*ed* to both regular and irregular verbs. Then, as they continue to hear the irregular past tense versions of words such as *sing/sang, write/wrote, eat/ate*, those associations will each strengthen, and children will return to the correct forms of those verbs. In this view, there are no "rules," per se, merely strengths of associations among linguistic elements. This perspective has been represented in parallel-distributed processing models of verb learning (e.g., McClelland & Rumelhart, 1986; Plunkett & Marchman, 1993, 1996). As we know from Chapter 1, such models are trained to generalize *patterns* from repeated stimuli, and to use those patterns to assign strengths of connections between stimulus elements, either between a verb and the -*ed* suffix, or, eventually, between an irregular verb and its proper past-tense form.

Plunkett and Marchman (1993, 1996) carried out a series of investigations in which they exposed a PDP model to a vocabulary of verbs, structured similarly to the vocabulary to which a young child might be exposed, to investigate the similarity between the model's output and the productions of children. As the network was being exposed to an increasing number of words, both regular and irregular verbs, the model was subjected to periodic tests, in which both familiar and unfamiliar verbs were presented to see which past tense form the model produced. At first, the network (just like children) produced the irregular verbs correctly, since each one of them had been presented a relatively large number of times, and each verb was relatively unique. With more training, however, and increasing exposure to a wide range of regular verbs, the network began to produce overregularizations of irregular verbs, similar to what occurs with children. Finally, further exposure to the irregular verbs strengthened connections between the present and past tense of those words, and irregular past tenses again were produced correctly.

The important point emphasized by those adopting a PDP perspective (e.g., Plunkett & Marchman, 1996) is that the model simply responds to the *patterns* in the input, rather than either implicit or explicit rules (but see Marcus, 1995, 1996, for a critique). This assumes that there is only one learning mechanism—associationism—operating throughout the process of learning past tense. That is, there is no rote learning, followed by rule development, followed by blocking the application of the past-tense -*ed* rule. Rather, changing associative weights between morphological elements—present-tense and past-tense forms—can explain the early correct use of irregular forms, the later overregulation responses, and the final return to correct use of irregular forms. The evidence from such PDP models has been used to argue against Chomskian claims of an innate language-specific module, because general associative learning principles seemingly explain the U-shaped nature of past-tense verb use in children.

However, Pinker (1991) has maintained that a combination of both the rule-based and associative mechanisms best explains the developmental data: rule-based computation of past tense for regular verbs, and associated memory links between the present and past tense of irregular verbs. On the one hand, Pinker noted that trained neural networks often supply unusual past tense forms which humans themselves do not produce, such as when a neural network produced "wok" as the past tense of "wink" (Pinker, 1994). On the other hand, humans who are confronted with a nonsense verb, or a noun that is to be changed to a verb, usually use the regular -*ed* inflection (as when we tell a classmate, "I *friended* you on Facebook"). Similarly, connectionist models that rely on associative memory are just as likely to spit out "freezled" as the past tense of the nonsense verb *frilj* (Pinker, 1994). Thus, it may be that new verbs and low-frequency verbs are converted to past tense based on rules, whereas only high-frequency verbs are maintained with irregular verb status (Bybee, 1985), because their high frequency permits greater connections that help retrieve the irregular past-tense lexical forms from associative memory (Pinker, 1991).

Lexical Storage: Words or Morphemes?

Children's production of overregularizations and their eventual switch to correct forms of irregular nouns and verbs raises the issue of what counts as a "word" in the lexicon. One possibility is that, even as adults, we store in our mental dictionary roots and morphemes independently, and then combine tenses (-*s*, -*ed*, -*ing*), plurals (e.g., -*s*, -*es*), and so forth as needed during speech (MacKay, 1979; Murrell & Morton, 1974; Smith & Sterling, 1982; Taft, 1981). The alternative is that we have multiple forms of any given word stored (*bed*, *beds*, *bedding*, etc.) and simply retrieve these lexical units directly, much like older children are able to retrieve irregular nouns and verbs (Aitchison, 1987; Monsell, 1985; Sandra, 1990).

Two main techniques have been used to test which theory—roots+morphemes versus multiple lexical forms—is correct. Consider people's possible performance on a lexical-decision task in which multimorphemic words, such as *impartial* or *hunter*, are presented. Based on the roots+morphemes view, people should be slower to respond to multimorphemic words, because two or more morphemes must be activated. However, lexical access times should not differ if words are stored as wholes, in all their various forms. MacKay (1979) found that reaction times to words increased as the number of constituent morphemes increased. Suffixed words, such as *hunter*, also take longer than pseudo-suffixed words, such as *daughter* (which cannot be broken down into a root morpheme, *daught-* and -*er*).

There is evidence that many multimorphemic compound words, such as *teacup*, may also be composed of separate lexical entries (Fiorentino & Poeppel, 2007). As one example, compounds composed of two high-frequency constituents (e.g., *birthday*) are recognized faster than those in which only the first or second constituent is of high frequency (e.g., *birthday* versus *handcuff* or *scrapbook*—in which "hand" and "book" are high frequency, but "cuff" and "scrap" are not). This suggests that *both* component words contribute to recognition (Andrews, 1986; Andrews & Davis, 1999). However, very common compound words, such as *butterfly* or *gingerbread*, may have developed into complete morphological units on their own in the lexicon, so that they are no longer processed as *butter+fly* as we speak or listen (Monsell, 1985; Osgood & Hoosain, 1974; Sandra, 1990). For example, in lexical decision tasks, *bread* semantically primes *butter* (Meyer & Schvanevedlt, 1971); however, *bread* does not prime *butterfly*, indicating that *butterfly* (and other compound words) may be stored as separate representations (Monsell, 1985; Osgood & Hoosain, 1974; Sandra, 1990). Ullman, et al. (1997; also Vannest, Polk, & Lewis, 2005) have provided neuropsychological evidence that supports the idea that two different types of processes are involved in word production. Lexically based retrieval of irregular noun/verb forms relies on medial/temporal lobe activity, while decompositional, rule-based processing of regular forms activates frontal lobes and underlying basal ganglia.

Neuropsychology of Morphology

Evidence from neuropsychology patients also supports a decompositional view of morphology. On a number of tasks—spontaneous speech, picture naming, spelling to dictation, verbal repetition—aphasic patients show an ability to independently access, combine, or substitute morphemes (Badecker & Caramazza, 1987; Miceli, 1994). For example, Romani, Olson, Ward, and Ercolani's (2002) patient, D.W., produced "coatyard" instead of "courtyard," and often added endings to words, even when it did not result in a real word (e.g., "older" became "olders"). Patient F.S., studied by Miceli (1994), produced morphological errors in a repetition task of Italian words, often substituting the wrong gender- and number-based case markers. Badecker (2001) studied an aphasic patient whose picture naming resulted in more errors for compound word targets (e.g., "downpour" became "down storm," and "butterfly" became "butter flower"). The morpheme maintained in compound word errors was usually the one with higher frequency.

Because Finnish is a morphologically rich language that uses multiple cases for pronouns, verb tenses, adjectives, and most forms of speech, interesting data have arisen from Finnish aphasics. One such patient, studied by Laine, Niemi, Koivuselkä-Sallinen, & Hyönä (1995), often made stem+affix errors (see also Kukkonen, 2006). These cases demonstrate that these patients access morphemes independently, even in compound words such as *butterfly*, and can combine morphemes to produce novel (albeit illegal) words, and are not merely accessing multisyllabic words directly from the lexicon.

Morphological Analysis: Conclusions

The two areas in which morphology has been most studied are overregularization of children's verb tenses and the related issue of how words are stored and retrieved from the lexicon. The evidence from both child speech and PDP models suggests that children use rule learning to generate verb tenses, but also rely on associative memory for irregular verbs. Thus, language development appears to rely on both rules and patterns, in partial support of both the rule-based/computational and emergent viewpoints. We will come across similar issues—each view may explain part of the results, rather than one view being *correct* and the other *incorrect*—when we consider the development of sentence production in the next chapter. Research from multimorphemic words—free morphemes plus tenses and plurals—and compound words supports a decompositional approach to the lexicon, with root and bound morphemes stored separately and combined as needed during speech. The exceptions are (a) irregular verb forms, and (b) high-frequency compound words, which may, over time, have earned their own lexical representations.

BRAIN STRUCTURES INVOLVED IN LEXICAL PROCESSING

Modern brain-imaging techniques have made it possible to observe which brain areas are active during processing of words. Petersen, Fox, Posner, Mintun, and Raichle (1988) used PET to isolate areas active in the processing of word meaning. The multilevel task that they used is shown in Figure 9.13, and is based on the subtraction method outlined in Chapter 1. The first task was simply visual presentation of a fixation point. The second task level required passive registration of *words* presented every 1.5 seconds either visually or auditorily (with no action required of the participant beyond looking or listening). The third task introduced word production, as the participants had to repeat or read aloud the words they had heard or seen, respectively. Finally, the fourth task added semantic processing to the components required, as the participants generated a use for the noun they heard or read (e.g., *fork* might lead the person to say "eat"). Thus, subtracting $task_1$ from $task_2$ isolates areas involved in passive word processing; subtracting $task_2$ from $task_3$ isolates areas serving word-production processes; and subtracting $task_3$ from $task_4$ isolates areas serving semantic processing.

A. Peterson et al. tasks:

$Level_1$ Person views fixation point on otherwise blank computer screen

$Level_2$ Visual: Person passively views a word (a noun)

 Auditory: Person passively hears a word (a noun)

$Level_3$ Person reads aloud (visual) or repeats (auditory) the word presented

$Level_4$ Person generates verb in response to noun presented (e.g.: water $\Rightarrow$ "drink")

B. Patterson et al. subtraction study of processing of word meaning

 $Level_2$ (Passive response to visual or auditory words)

− $Level_1$ (Passive response to visual fixation stimulus)
 Passive responding to words

 $Level_3$ (Reading or repeating word)

− $Level_2$(Passive responding to words)
 Production of word

 $Level_4$ (Production of use)

− $Level_3$ (Production of word)
 Finding use (processing meaning of item)

Figure 9.13 Design of study by Peterson et al. (1988) investigating brain areas involved in processing word meaning.

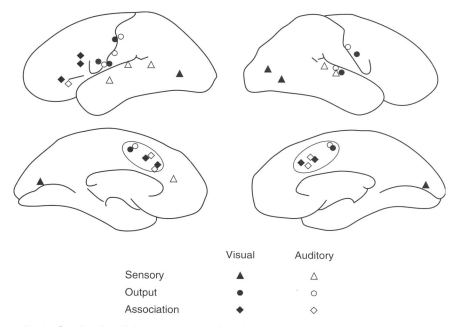

Figure 9.14   Results of study by Peterson et al. (1988). Activation in left hemisphere (left side images) and right hemisphere (right side images), on lateral view of (external) cortex (top images) and inside longitudinal fissure between the hemispheres (bottom images). The key depicts areas most active during visual or auditory presentation of words, in which participants merely recognized the words (Sensory), said the words aloud (Output), or produced a related word (Association).

The diagrams of activity for the various types of processing are shown in Figure 9.14. Passive processing of words (task$_2$ *minus* task$_1$) produced activity in modality-specific primary sensory areas. Viewing of words resulted in activation in the left and right occipital cortex. Passively *listening* to words, on the other hand, produced activity bilaterally in the temporal lobes—in brain areas dedicated to auditory processing, such as Wernicke's area in the LH and its analogous area in the RH. When participants had to *produce* speech in response to the words (to read the visually presented word or to repeat the auditorily presented one), both tasks activated similar *motor* areas of the brain bilaterally, especially areas in the right- and left-motor cortex involved in mouth and tongue movement.

Finally, when the participants had to access the *meaning* of the words by generating a use for them, the areas now involved were similar for both the visual and auditory word tasks. They included left-hemisphere inferior frontal regions known to be involved in semantic association, and the anterior cingulate gyrus, part of the attentional system (see Figure 9.15). In conclusion, this study demonstrates the complexity of the processing that underlies accessing word meaning, with initial modality-specific sensory areas first registering stimuli, and later thought-related areas participating during both visual and auditory presentation of words. Posner and Raichle (1994) commented that the Peterson et al. (1988) study also helped isolate the brain processes underlying conscious thought, because it separated the effects of input processing (passive perception

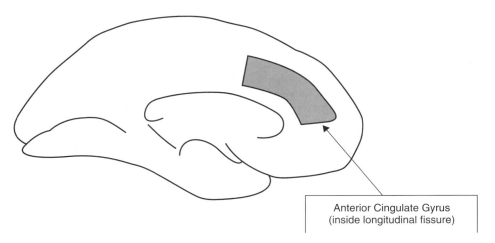

Anterior Cingulate Gyrus
(inside longitudinal fissure)

Figure 9.15 Anterior cingulate gyrus (inside longitudinal fissure; left hemisphere depicted).

of words) and output (speaking in response to words). One could conclude that when task$_3$ is subtracted from task$_4$, what remains are the processes involved in verbal conscious thought.

In another study on the physiological processing of words, Fridriksson, Baker, and Moser (2009) asked aphasia patients and normal control subjects to name aloud 80 colored pictures while undergoing an fMRI scan. Trials on which the pictures were correctly named were compared to those in which the participants made either phonemic or semantic errors. Correct naming in all participants was associated with widespread right hemisphere activation, especially the area in the right hemisphere corresponding to Wernicke's and Broca's areas (which are typically found in the left), plus the right motor cortex. Production of phonemic paraphasias (mispronunciations of a target word) engaged regions in the left inferior parietal lobe—known to be involved in phonological processing—and in the left occipital and posterior inferior temporal lobes. Semantic paraphasias (i.e., word substitutions), on the other hand, were associated with activation of the occipital cortex and posterior inferior temporal gyrus of the right hemisphere. Hickok and Poeppel (2007) have suggested that the left inferior temporal lobe regulates more-specific semantic designations, and the right hemisphere more-general semantic information. Thus, since semantic paraphasias are "in the ballpark" of the target terms (e.g., "horse" for "donkey"), greater RH engagement may only result in close, but not specific, lexical terms.

Sounds and Words: Conclusions

This chapter first introduced you to the different levels of linguistic analysis, and the major theoretical perspectives on language and language development. We then considered the phonological and morphological aspects of words, and how word meanings are acquired. At the level of phonology, important questions centered on how people analyze and process the sounds of language and whether or not that ability is supportive of a language module. Lexical, or word, acquisition was also examined from the perspective of whether innate versus social factors provide the impetus for language learning; much research suggests that *both* factors interact to permit a child's understanding and production of word meanings. Related to word learning is morphology, where the discussion centered on whether people learn word structure through learning of *rules*, or induction of morphological *patterns*. Neuropsychological syndromes have supplemented standard psychological experiments on cognitive processing of speech sounds and words, and have linked the various component skills involved in word use to particular areas of the brain.

REVIEW QUESTIONS

Here are some questions to help you organize your review of this chapter.

1. What are the three main aspects of language that serve as the basis for communication?

2. Summarize evidence for the interaction between production and comprehension during language processing.

3. What are the levels of analysis of language to be examined in this chapter?

4. What are the basic differences between the rule-based/computational and emergent theories of language functioning and development?

5. What are Grice's conversational maxims, and what functions do they serve?

6. What brain area controls prosodic elements of language?

7. What aspects of the prosody of parentese are distinctive?

8. What is *foreign accent syndrome*, and what types of explanations have been offered to explain its occurrence?

9. What are *manner* and *place of articulation* in production of phonemes?

10. What is the reason why *bnench* is not an acceptable sound string in English?

11. What is *categorical perception* of phonemes? How does perception of phonemes change as VOT increases, for example, in the case of /p/ and /b/?

12. What does the McGurk-McDonald effect tell us about the information used in processing language?

13. How are children able to isolate words in speech, when speech is continuous (that is, there are no boundaries between words when we speak)?

14. What are the cognitive bases for the phonemic structure of children's first words?

15. How do infants' word-processing skills develop over the first year?

16. What is *fast mapping* in children's word learning? When does it begin?

17. What *constraints* have been proposed by theorists in explaining how children overcome Quine's problem concerning learning the meaning of words?

18. What is the *social-pragmatic* view's alternative explanation for word-learning?

19. What are TOT states, and what sorts of mechanisms explain their occurrence?

20. What is *anomia*, and what sorts of brain mechanisms play a role in its occurrence?

21. What factors influence whether multiple meanings of ambiguous words are accessed during comprehension of language?

22. What is the lexical and phonological explanation for the language deficits seen in Wernicke's aphasia?

23. What is the *Wug test*? Why is it important in the history of the study of language?

24. What are the *rule-* versus *pattern-learning* explanations for children's overregularizations in forming the past tense?

25. What were the findings of Plunkett and Marchman's study of a PDP network's learning verb past tenses?

26. Why might one say that the study by Peterson, Fox, Posner, Mintun, and Raichle (1988) isolated brain structures underlying conscious thought?

27. What are hemispheric differences in lexical processing?

CHAPTER 10

LANGUAGE II: SENTENCE PROCESSING

Chapter 9 considered the psychology of language at the level of phonemes, inflections, and individual words. In this chapter we consider what is perhaps the most impressive aspect of language: our ability to combine words into sentences. That ability—what Chomsky (1957, 1959) called the *generativity* of language—is what makes language crucially important to us, because our ability to form new sentences as we need them allows us to describe new experiences and express new thoughts. As an example, consider a person who has lost a DVD about the career of artist Pablo Picasso. Several days later, the DVD is found under a pile of papers. If, on finding the DVD, the person says to a companion: "I just found that Picasso DVD that I was looking for," it is unlikely he had ever uttered that sentence before. However, he had no trouble producing the sentence when he found the DVD, and his companion (who had probably never *heard* that sentence before), had no trouble understanding it. Using our knowledge of *grammar*—the combination of syntax and morphology (as shown in Table 10.1)—we are able to assemble words in new ways as needed, so that most of the sentences a person produces during a lifetime are novel. Our ability to produce and understand sentences, and the development of that ability, are the subject of this chapter.

OUTLINE OF CHAPTER 10

This chapter begins with a discussion of sentence structure and of theories about how we process sentences. We then turn to developmental processes in sentence comprehension and production, and examine the debate over whether grammatical aspects of language learning are both innate and subject to a critical period. In the second half of the chapter, we will examine research on the processes that take place when people *understand* discourse, ranging from single sentences to connected passages to metaphors. Evidence about speech production and how it can go wrong, such as when we make speech errors or when people suffer brain damage leading to different subtypes of aphasia, will be shown to be an informative method for studying the mechanisms of speech production.

An important issue in the study of language, as we saw in Chapter 9, has been the degree to which language shows modularity—that is, independence from other cognitive processes. Syntax may be the language component most likely to be relatively independent of other cognitive processes (Pinker, 1994). We saw in Chapter 9 that some aspects of language, such as word learning, are tied to other cognitive skills

Table 10.1   Levels of Analysis in Language

Social Function	Cognitive Rule System		
Pragmatics	Meaning (Semantics)	Syntax (Grammar)	Sound

	Individual Word Meanings
	Sentence Meaning
		Structure of Sentences
		
		Morphology:
		    Structure of Words
			Prosody:
			    Intonation, Pitch, Stress
			Phonology:
			    Sounds of Language
			Phonetics:
			    Production of Phonemes

(Jackendoff & Pinker, 2005). One obvious candidate for a link between language and cognition is the relation between language and our categorical/conceptual knowledge. For instance, we make sense of figurative language utterances like "My job is a jail," by discovering the ways in which jobs and jails might overlap conceptually. Thus, we quickly are able to comprehend that metaphorical statement, by realizing that "jail" here refers to an "abstract" prison, and not to an actual building with bars and prisoners. The *linguistic relativity hypothesis* proposes that the language we use influences how we can think conceptually, and we examine research concerning that view.

ANALYSIS OF SENTENCE STRUCTURE

We typically don't credit a parrot with "language" if all it says is "Hello!" or "Goodbye!" when we enter or leave a room, because it cannot combine words into novel sentences. Furthermore, *sentences* are more than just strings of words: Those words must be organized according to the grammar of a given language, and that organization determines the meaning of the sentence. For example, it means something very different to hear "A dog bit a boy," versus "A dog was bitten by a boy." As occurs with other cognitive processes, we humans process language so effortlessly that we are not consciously aware of the complexities involved in the production and comprehension of sentences. Consider what is involved in understanding sentence (1).

(1) A boy bit a dog.

Sentence (1) contains a *noun-verb-noun* sequence, which are three *content* words. The sentence also contains one *function* or *grammatical* word, repeated twice (the indefinite article, *a*). The three content words tell us about two objects (a *boy* and a *dog*) and an action (*biting*), and the sentence tells us that one of the objects carried out the action on the other. English is a heavily word-order-based language, even young children can understand simple subject-verb-object constructions (Chan, Meints, Lieven, & Tomasello, 2010). In such a sequence, the first noun is interpreted as carrying out the action of the verb, and is the *actor* or *agent*, while the action was carried out on the second noun (the *object* or *patient* or *recipient*).

However, using word order to interpret sentences will not work for passive sentences, such as sentence (2).

(2) A boy was bitten by a dog.

The *was bitten by* in sentence (2) indicates that the first noun should be interpreted as the patient and the second noun as the agent, meaning that the *dog* did the biting, even though *boy* is the first noun mentioned. Thus, in order to analyze how sentences are understood, we must take into account *sentence structure* and the morphemes that contribute to the grammaticality of a sentence (e.g., tenses, auxiliary verbs ("was") etc.; see Chapter 9). Furthermore, a left-to-right word-order strategy of sentence processing does not work with other languages, such as Russian, in which nouns are declined (given specific endings) to indicate the agent versus patient in a sentence. The same word (e.g., *malchik*, which means *boy* in Russian) is pronounced and spelled differently when it is the agent (*malchik*) versus the patient (*malchika*) in a sentence. In a language like Russian, word order is much more flexible than in English, so one cannot rely on word order to understand who did what to whom when someone describes a situation.

In conclusion, one cannot understand how humans process sentences by assuming that we simply work through a sentence from left-to-right to determine its meaning. We must take into account the structure of the sentence. This conclusion leads us to an examination of Chomsky's (1957, 1965, 1995) analysis of the structure of language, which set the stage for much of modern psycholinguistic research.

FORMAL ASPECTS OF SENTENCES

Chomsky (1957, 1965) was one of the first researchers in linguistics to propose a comprehensive analysis of the formal aspects of language, and his views had a strong influence on researchers in other disciplines, especially in psychology (e.g., Miller & Chomsky, 1963). Chomsky believed that one could specify a set of *syntactic* or *grammatical* rules that people use to construct and comprehend sentences. Chomsky's grammatical analysis began with a consideration of the hierarchical, phrase-based structure of sentences, to which we now turn.

Phrase Structure of Sentences

Chomsky (1957, 1965; see also Harris, 1957) proposed that sentences are structured in a hierarchical, rather than left-to-right, manner. Consider sentence (3):

(3) The young artist copied the famous pictures.

The words in sentence (3) form basic units, or *phrases*, that make up its important parts. One piece of evidence for phrase structure is that we can substitute a single word for certain groups of words in the sentence without affecting its grammaticality. As an example, sentence (4) is grammatical, because *the young artist* is a phrase, that is, a unit that can be replaced by a pronoun.

(4) *She* copied the famous pictures.

The young artist is functioning as a *noun phrase* (NP). Similarly, one can substitute a single word for the *verb phrase* (VP), *copied the famous pictures*, as shown in sentence (5):

(5) The young artist *did.*

Thus, the structure of sentence (3) is given by the following syntactical rules (where S = sentence; NP = noun phrase, and VP = verb phrase):

Rule (1) S ⇒ NP + VP

Rule (1) says that the sentence (S) consists of a noun phrase and a verb phrase. The noun phrase and verb phrase themselves can be further broken down:

Rule (2) NP ⇒ (det) + (adj) + N

Rule (3) VP ⇒ V + (NP)

Rules (2) and (3) describe the structure of the NP as a determiner (in this case, *the*), an adjective (*young*) + noun, and the VP as a verb plus a second noun phrase, respectively. The reason that some elements are written inside parentheses is because they are optional, so the sentence *Artists copy pictures* also fits rules (1)–(3). These rules can be used to represent the phrase structure of sentence (3) in a tree diagram (see Figure 10.1). We have illustrated the *phrase structure* of a simple sentence; a complete set of phrase structure rules is called a *phrase-structure grammar*, which specifies the rules that can be used to compose all sentences of a given language.

Increasingly complex sentences can be analyzed using phrase-structure rules, such as sentence (6).

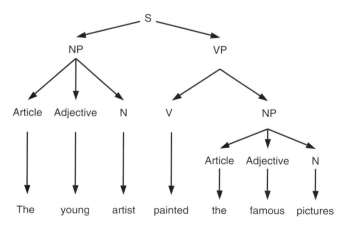

Figure 10.1 Phrase-structure tree for Sentence 3: The young artist painted the famous pictures.

(6) The woman believes **the young artist copied the famous picture**.

Sentence (6) is also made up of an NP and VP, but the VP in sentence (6) contains within it a complete sentence (depicted in bold), which is itself structured as NP + VP. Phrase structure analysis of sentence (6) requires an additional rule (Rule (4)), as shown below.

Rule (1) S ⇒ NP + VP

Rule (2) NP ⇒ (det) + (adj) + N

Rule (3) VP ⇒ V + (NP)

Rule (4) VP ⇒ V + S

The presence of S in the VP in Rule (4) indicates that the VP in a sentence can contain a sentence within it; that is, the symbol S now appears more than once, or *recurs*, in the set of rules. This property of *recursion* means that the same sorts of components can be used again and again, to build increasingly complex structures to communicate compound ideas.

S–Structure, D–Structure, and Trace Theory

Although syntax is clearly tied to the grammatical aspects of language, morphological and semantic aspects are also important to our use of language, since ultimately we seek to convey meaning in language. For example, verbs form a critical part of any sentence. However, simply specifying a verb within a given phrase structure analysis will not necessarily make the sentence grammatical. The type of VP is related to whether the particular verb is *transitive* or *intransitive; intransitive verbs*, such as *cough*, can only take the form VP ⇒ V + (adverb). For example, sentence (7a) is grammatical whereas (7b) is not grammatical, because of the intransitive verb used within the VP. [Nongrammatical sentences are marked by *.]

(7a) The man coughed suddenly.

(7b) *The man coughed the problem.

In contrast, *transitive* verbs *require* a verb phrase of the form VP ⇒ V + NP, as in sentence (8):

(8) The man solved the problem.

Sentence (9) is ungrammatical, because the structure S ⇒ NP + V does not work with a transitive verb:

(9) *The man will solve.

Now consider sentence (10), which is an acceptable English sentence:

(10) That problem the man will solve.

Although sentence (10) ends with the same four-word string that makes up sentence (9), it is grammatical in a way that sentence (9) is not. How can that be? In sentence (10) there is an *implicit* NP in the VP: *That problem* is the object of the transitive verb *solve*, but it has been moved to the beginning of the sentence for emphasis. The sentence can be analyzed by its "invisible" structure, in which *that problem* is part of the VP, versus the actual sentence we see or hear, in which *that problem* appears at the beginning. Chomsky (1957) proposed that every sentence has two structures: (1) a *surface structure* (*s-structure*), which specifies analysis of the sentence as it is produced, and (2) an underlying or *deep* structure (*d-structure*), which specifies all the pieces of information that are important in interpreting the sentence. He assumed that the deep structures of various languages would be nearly identical, even if the surface sentence structure varied widely across languages.

The *s*- and *d*-structures of sentence (10) are shown in Figure 10.2. The *s*-structure shows that the initial NP in the sentence originated in the VP, and was moved to the front (where *t* in the VP stands for the *trace* of the NP in its original location. Producing

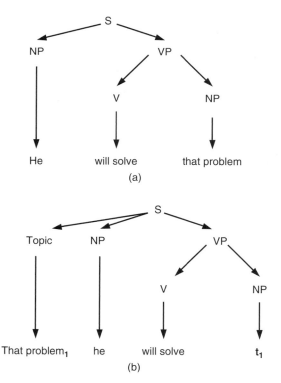

Figure 10.2 Underlying and surface structures of *That problem he will solve*. (a) Underlying structure (*d-structure*). (b) Surface structure (*s-structure*).

an *s*-structure from a *d*-structure requires *transformational rules*, which carry out the function of moving constituents of the *d*-structure. For example, the transformation illustrated in sentence (10) is called *topicalization* (the making of a component, such as an NP within the VP, into the *topic* of a sentence). This move then leaves a trace in the *d*-structure. Other transformations allow us to convert a *d*-structure into a question, or to produce an *s*-structure in the passive form. Chomsky's (1957) theory of language structure was thus known as *Transformational Grammar*.

One important idea within transformational grammar is that syntax is *content-free*—the same syntactic and transformational rules apply, regardless of the ideas expressed within a sentence. Consider the following sentence (Chomsky, 1957):

(11) *Colorless green ideas sleep furiously.*

The sentence is meaningless—how could anything be both colorless and green? Or how could ideas sleep? Syntactically, however, it is consistent with phrase-structure rules of grammar: [NP: Adjective + Adjective + Noun] + [VP: Verb + Adverb] and is perfectly acceptable in English. The morphology in the sentence is also appropriate—an *-s* on the end of a noun (*idea + s*) and an *-ly* on the end of the adverb. In this way, the Chomskian (1957) perspective, which, as noted in the last chapter, is also called the rule-based/computational perspective, proposed that the syntactic aspects of a language are a submodule within the overarching modular framework of language processing, and transformational rules are accomplished by language-specific learning mechanisms.

Transformational Grammar: Conclusions

Sentences have an organization that is often composed of phrases embedded into a more complex structure. Chomsky (1957, 1995) proposed that every sentence can be analyzed at two levels of structure. *S-structure* is made up of the groups of words, or phrases, that serve as functional units in the sentence in speech or writing. *D-structure* specifies all the information needed to interpret the sentence, which sometimes involves information not specified on the surface. The two levels of structure will serve as the basis for a consideration of psychological processes involved in comprehension and production of sentences.

Emergent Perspective on Sentence Processing

In Chapter 9 we contrasted the rule-based theory of word learning with an emergent view, which proposed that word learning came about through the child's use of general—rather than language-specific—learning mechanisms. A similar difference of opinion has arisen concerning the mechanisms involved in sentence processing. In contrast to the Chomskian perspective, the emergent view of language processing proposes that grammar is simply a specific function of the cognitive system (Croft & Cruse, 2004). Syntax is not based on content-free rules, nor is it a separate subcomponent of language. People use their conceptual knowledge about word meanings to separate words into nouns, verbs, and so on. They then use powerful general learning mechanisms to determine statistical regularities in the sentences they hear around them. Those regularities, rather than rules, are used to construct new, and increasingly complex, sentences. We examine evidence relevant to those two views of language later in the chapter. First we turn to an examination of research concerning language processing.

Processing Sentences: Determining Syntactic Structure of a Sentence

When a fluent speaker of a language hears a sentence in a conversation, the first step in interpretation involves *parsing* the sentence into its phrase structure. There are two potential parsing strategies. The first assumes that the listener tries to hold the words in working memory (WM) until the whole sentence has been heard, and then determine the *s*-structure. This strategy would put a large burden on WM, especially for long sentences. The other possible sentence-processing strategy is the *immediacy of interpretation* method (Whitney, 1998), in which a sentence is interpreted immediately, as each word or phrase comes in. In this way, one might be able to parse a sentence while putting a limited burden on working memory, because very few words are held in WM at any given time. The listener continually adds to the syntactic structure he or she has already developed, and words already processed can then be dropped from WM. For example, if you hear *Jim and Mary* ..., you assume that the sentence begins with an NP, so you can turn your attention to the next set of words in the sentence. In addition, one can use one's knowledge about typical sentence structure in a top-down fashion, and assume that a verb phrase will follow (e.g., *Jim and Mary left earl*y.), which may also facilitate processing. We often use expectations about the most likely way a sentence will work out to begin interpretation. Based on this view, sentence processing can be seen as a further example of the role of expectancies and top-down processing in cognitive processing.

Evidence that people process sentences using immediacy of interpretation comes from the study of *garden-path* sentences, which take advantage of our expectations about the most likely way to parse the sentence. Please read sentence (12).

(12) The man whistling tunes pianos.

When you read the first few words, it is tempting to analyze *the man* as an NP that is the subject/agent of the sentence, and *whistling* as the main verb that begins the VP. That interpretation fits when you reach the next word in the sentence, *tunes* (*The man whistling tunes* ...). However, when *pianos* is read, that initial interpretation falls apart. Most people then look back to the beginning of the sentence to gauge where they went wrong. *Whistling*, it turns out, is not the main verb of the sentence, it is the verb of a subordinate clause (*[who is] whistling*), which modifies *the man*. Thus, the correct interpretation of the sentence is:

(13) The man *who is* whistling tunes pianos.

In sentence (13), the word *who* signals the reader that a subordinate clause is beginning, so when *whistling* is seen, it is not interpreted as the main verb, thus making it easier to process *tunes* as the main verb.

Sentence (12) is a *garden-path* sentence, because the beginning of the sentence initially leads the reader "down a garden path" to the wrong interpretation. Garden-path sentences are commonly used to test the use of the immediacy-of-interpretation strategy in processing sentences. If people are parsing and interpreting sentences as they hear/read them, it should take longer to process sentence (12)—a garden path sentence—than sentence (13), which explicitly signals a relative clause with the word *who* or *that*. Just and Carpenter (1992) measured people's eye movements as they read sentences like (12) and (13). Their results indicated that people reading garden-path sentences (12) spent much more time looking at the main verb in the sentence (e.g., *tunes*), presumably because they had to alter their parsing of the sentence to establish the main verb correctly. Thus, Just and Carpenter's results supported use of the immediacy-of-interpretation strategy of processing sentences.

Sentence Processing: Conclusions

Research from garden-path sentences supports the conclusion that people begin parsing and interpreting a sentence as they are hearing it, rather than waiting until the end of the sentence (Whitney, 1998). This immediacy-of-interpretation strategy places less burden on working memory, but it can lead one to begin interpreting a sentence in a way that turns out not to fit the meaning of the complete sentence. We now turn to the question of how children acquire syntactic abilities, including the capacity to comprehend and produce sentences based on their formal characteristics.

DEVELOPMENT OF SYNTAX

At around their first birthday, most children begin to speak, by producing single words. In Chapter 9, we reviewed children's developing phonological awareness and word learning. Before their second birthday, most children have reached the next milestone in the development of language: They produce multiword utterances, beginning with combinations of two words. As we shall see, although those first two-word utterances, may sound primitive to adult ears, they possess many of the characteristics of true sentences (Pinker, 1994).

DEVELOPMENT OF SENTENCE STRUCTURE

One measure of developing syntactic complexity is *mean length of utterance* (*MLU*), which is calculated by determining the average number of morphemes in a child's sentences. Thus, *Mommy drive car* and *Mommy drives car* would count as three and four morphemes, respectively. Once a child begins adding grammatical morphemes, such as tenses, plurals, and possessives, MLU will increase, as shown in Figure 10.3.

Some examples of children's development of multiword utterances are shown in Table 10.2, beginning with the earliest two-word utterances, and progressing over the next several years to longer, more complex utterances, very much like those of adults.

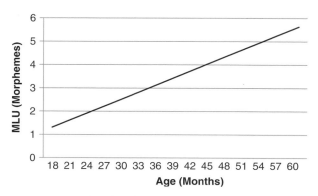

Figure 10.3 Mean length of utterance (MLU) as a function of age.
Adapted from Miller and Chapman, 1981.

Table 10.2 Early Utterances, From 2 Years to 3 Years

Years	Months	Sample Speech Utterances
2	3	Play checkers. Big drum. A bunny-rabbit walk.
2	5	Where wrench go? Now put boots on. What that paper clip doing?
2	7	Going to see kitten. Shadow has hat just like that. Rintin don't fly, Mommy.
2	11	That birdie hopping by Missouri in bag. Why you mixing baby chocolate? I said why not you coming in? We going turn light on so you can't see.
3	1	I like to play with something else. You want to give me some carrots and some beans? Press the button and catch it, sir.

Adapted from Pinker (1994; pp. 269–270).

Although the two- and three-word utterances are obviously not as complex syntactically as adult sentences, the words tend to be uttered in standard or *canonical* order. For instance, English-speaking children will often maintain Subject-Verb-Object order in sentences, even though other function words (e.g., articles, prepositions) are left out (Table 10.3). The fact that children's utterances make sense if one assumes that there is a more-complex "structure" underlying the child's production is one piece of evidence to support the idea that those early strings of words are indeed "sentences."

Table 10.3   Relationship Between 2- and 3-Word Utterances
and Complete Sentences*

Agent	Action	Recipient	Object	Location
Mommy	fix.			
Mommy			pumpkin.	
	put			floor.
I	ride		horsie	
Tractor	go			floor.
	Give	doggie	paper.	
Adam	put		it	box.

*Notice that childhood utterances often follow the standard order of grammatical sentences, but with "filler" words omitted.
Adapted from Pinker (1994; pp. 269–270).

By the time the typical child is 4 years old, he or she is producing sentences of complexity equal to those of adults (Pinker, 1994). One possible mechanism underlying children's grammatical development is that parents, siblings, and teachers reinforce well-formed child speech, and correct ungrammatical utterances. Brown and Hanlon (1970) analyzed transcripts of conversations between young children and their mothers, and found that parents largely tended to respond to the *truth* of what the child said, rather than its grammaticality:

CHILD: Mickey Mouse comes on Tuesday.

PARENT: No, on Thursday.

CHILD: Mommy not a boy, he a girl.

PARENT: That's right.

Thus, although the first utterance is impeccable in its grammar, it was responded to negatively because the child got the day wrong. The second utterance gets the pronoun wrong ("he" for "Mommy") but was responded to positively, because of the truth that is conveyed. Early researchers thus concluded that children's increasing syntactic complexity could not be due to parental feedback.

However, subsequent research has determined that parents do tend to respond to their children's ungrammatical sentences more than to their grammatical ones (Hirsh-Pasek, Treiman, & Schneiderman, 1984; Penner, 1987), but with indirect corrections—typically by *recasting* (or rewording) a child's utterances with only one or two words changed (Bohannon, Padgett, Nelson, & Mark, 1996; Bohannon & Stanowicz, 1988):

CHILD: That be monkey.

ADULT: That *is* a monkey.

Parents also often expand on a child's utterance to produce a more syntactically complex sentence:

CHILD: Monkey climbing.

ADULT: The monkey is climbing to the top of the tree. (examples from Bohannon & Stanowicz, 1988).

Thus, while parents and adult listeners do not *explicitly* point out a child's errors, they may nonetheless supply implicit feedback in the form of recasts and expansions. Research shows that children are sensitive to such subtle negative feedback, and often adjust the grammaticality of their sentences accordingly (Saxton, 2000).

However, several researchers have concluded that the speed with which children develop the ability to produce and comprehend complex sentences cannot be due to parental correction alone, because the pace of syntactic development is more consistent and universal than is the rate of parental negative feedback about ungrammatical utterances (Jackendoff, 1993; Marcus, 1993; Pinker, 1994, 2004). This leads us to the question of whether syntactic development depends on the acquisition of rules, which, as we saw in the discussion of the development of morphology in Chapter 9, is a question that has divided researchers.

Syntactic Development: Acquisition of Rules?

Recent analyses of children's syntactic development have followed a course similar to that of analysis of morphological development, as discussed in Chapter 9. Psycholinguists sympathetic to Chomsky's (1959, 1995) viewpoint (e.g., Pinker, 1994, 2004) have proposed that children formulate *rules* of sentence structure based on a combination of innate, modular grammatical abilities and exposure to the dominant language that they hear. Evidence to support the rule-learning view comes from research showing that preschoolers can implicitly parse sentences into their phrase structure, and use transformations appropriately. Crain and Nakayama (1987) asked 3- to 5-year-old children to convert statements with subject-relative clauses, such as the following, into questions:

The dog who is sleeping is on the blue bench.

One correct answer would be *Is the dog who is sleeping on the blue bench?* If, on the one hand, children have merely learned general patterns for conversion of statements to questions, they might either be tempted to move the first IS in the sentence to the beginning to form a question (e.g., (a) *IS the dog who ___ sleeping is on the blue bench?*), or to move either IS randomly. If, on the other hand, children have implicit knowledge of rules of sentence structure and how to parse a sentence, they should move the main verb IS and leave the IS in the relative clause intact, (b) "*Is the dog who is sleeping ___ on the blue bench?*" Results indicated that not a single child moved a word from the relative clause (as in (a)), although the children's transformations did become more accurate with increasing age. Thus, while children may show individual differences in grammatical production, they appear to be sensitive to the phrase structure of sentences by the late toddler years.

Crain and Nakayama (1987) concluded that their results support the hypothesis that children acquire phrase structure and transformational rules on the basis of an innate tendency to learn language, since a review of the CHILDES speech corpus of recorded conversations between children and adults (Legate & Yang, 2002), found that fewer than 1% of utterances normally spoken to children were in a form similar to those used in the experiment. The CHILDES speech corpus is a large database of children's speech utterances and speech samples spoken *to* children, which is used by research to analyze language production. (It has since been incorporated into the larger TalkBank, which also has speech samples from aphasics, classroom teaching, second language learning, and other sources.)

As an alternative to the rules-learning view, the emergent perspective assumes that children have complex knowledge about the words they learn (including the grammatical class of words, e.g., noun, verb, adjective, preposition). They then use knowledge of those lexical properties, and detection of high-probability sentence structures (e.g., Adj-N-V-possessive-N, as in *Flashing lights grab my attention*), to produce and comprehend sentences (O'Grady, 2005). In contrast to the conclusion that children have acquired *rules* for analyzing sentences, researchers within the emergent perspective have argued that children are adept at discovering statistical regularities within sentence structure. To provide support for the emergent view, Reali and Christiansen (2005) trained a PDP model, designed so that it could keep track of pairs or triplets of words that occur together, to assess whether statistical learning can account for children's detection of sentence structure, such as that exhibited by the children in the experiment by Crain and Nakayama (1987). Reali and Christiansen found that, even when the PDP model was only presented with relatively simple utterances, similar to those that a child is likely to have heard from her mother, this was sufficient for the model to produce utterances that paralleled those of Crain and Nakayama's participants (also see Bannard, Lieven, & Tomasello, 2009). However, even the successful syntax-learning model often produces output that is ungrammatical, and tinkering with a model to correct these errors often requires making the input less similar to speech actually spoken to children (Fitz, 2009). Thus, many researchers believe that an adequate account of sentence development must combine statistical learning and innate constraints (Fitz, 2009; Takahashi & Lidz, 2008), as it is difficult to explain syntactic acquisition purely on the basis of detecting statistical patterns (for further discussion, see Marcus & Berent, 2003).

In sum, we saw in Chapter 9 that statistical regularities may underlie much of phonological and lexical development, and we have seen in this chapter that some progress has been made in devising computer models that use statistical learning as the basis for children's syntactic development. However, the complex nature of the grammatical aspects of language, and children's facility with manipulating syntactic structures (e.g., Crain & Nakayama, 1987; Pinker, 2004), leave open the possibility that implicit rule-based structure-building is occurring as children develop language, and that grammatical development may be partly influenced by innate linguistic predispositions.

Comprehension of Sentences by Children Who Do Not Produce Sentences

As anyone who interacts with young children will attest, children's comprehension of language grows more rapidly than their production. Children may understand words months before they utter their first word; and they may understand simple sentences when they are only producing individual words. This raises the question of how one can determine what not-yet-speaking young children understand. A series of studies by Golinkoff, Hirsh-Pasek, Cauley, and Gordon (1987) used the *selective looking task* to examine infants' comprehension abilities. The task measures the child's attention to one of two visual displays in response to a verbal message (see Figure 10.4). An infant is seated in front of two video monitors, both of which present interactions between characters from Sesame Street. One monitor displays Cookie Monster tickling Big Bird; the other depicts Big Bird tickling Cookie Monster. A voice says, "Look, Big Bird is tickling Cookie Monster." The child's looking time to each of the two monitors is measured.

Sixteen- to 18-month-old infants looked more at the monitor that contained the event that matched the message (Golinkoff et al., 1987). Because reversible sentences were used (either Cookie Monster *or* Big Bird could feasibly be the agent), merely understanding the words alone will not yield a correct interpretation: the child must be sensitive to the grammatical structure of the sentence (in this case, word order) to discern who is the *actor* versus the *object*. Hirsh-Pasek, Golinkoff, and Naigles (1996) have found that older infants (28 months) can discriminate between transitive and intransitive uses of verbs within a sentence frame. They looked longer at a correct screen when they heard, "Big Bird is turning *with* Cookie Monster" versus "Big bird *is turning* Cookie Monster," indicating sensitivity to simple syntactic forms to determine actor/patient roles (Hirsh-Pasek & Golinkoff, 1996).

We saw in Chapter 9 that prosodic cues—intonation and stress information—facilitate phonological processing. Those cues may also provide infants with clues as to segment/phrase boundaries in sentences (Kemler Nelson, Hirsh-Pasek, Jusczyk, & Cassidy, 1989). Infants pay more attention to speech when pauses come between phrase boundaries than in the middle of phrases (Hirsh-Pasek et al., 1987). This may help them to parse the sentence, which then assists interpretation.

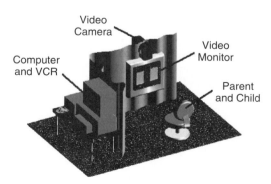

Figure 10.4 Hirsh-Pasek and Golinkoff experimental setup. Infant sits in front of the two video monitors on parent's (typically mother's) lap. Mother is blindfolded, so she cannot affect the child's response to the monitors.

Language Development: Conclusions

Sensitivity to the syntactic structure of sentences is apparent soon after a child's first birthday (Golinkoff et al., 1987). Children are sensitive to subtle feedback about their grammatical errors (Saxton, 2000), and by age 4 show evidence of being able to manipulate increasingly complex sentence forms, such as changing a statement with an embedded clause to a question (Crain & Nakayama, 1987). While such complex abilities have often been taken as evidence of language-specific rule learning (Pinker, 2004), more recent computer models based on statistical learning of grammatical patterns have been able to partially replicate children's development of sentence abilities (Reali & Christiansen, 2005). Thus, it is possible for at least some syntactic rules to be induced through more general learning mechanisms.

THE INNATENESS HYPOTHESIS AND CRITICAL PERIODS FOR LANGUAGE DEVELOPMENT

One addendum to Chomsky's (1957, 1959) proposal that language learning is innate was formulated by Lenneberg (1967), who hypothesized that, similar to other innate behaviors, the grammatical aspects of language—syntax and morphology—should have a *critical period* during which they must develop. He assumed that the period for learning language ended at puberty, when the influx of hormones "cemented" the specializations of the left and right hemispheres. If a first language had not been acquired (typically by a person's left hemisphere) by then, the person would not acquire a full generative ability to produce sentences. The critical-period hypothesis (CPH) has been tested in two ways: through the study of bilingual individuals who acquire their second language after puberty, and through the study of severely neglected children who have not acquired even their first language before puberty.

Acquisition of a Second Language and the Critical Period

The ease and accuracy with which people learn a second language is the most obvious test of the CPH. Johnson and Newport (1989) asked native Chinese and Korean speakers to judge the grammaticality of English sentences. Participants had moved to the United States between ages 3 and 39, and thus differed in their age of acquisition of English as a second language. Results showed that only those who had arrived in the United States between ages 3 and 7 performed equivalently to native speakers, and there was a clear downward trend in performance with age of acquisition (see Figure 10.5). The results from this study have been used to support a critical-period hypothesis, because there was a decline in grammatical abilities with age for those who became immersed in English before puberty; also, very few individuals who attained native language ability were among late arrivers (after age 17).

However, two other empirical findings do not fully support a strong version of the critical-period hypothesis. First, the CPH seems to propose that language-learning ability should drop off sharply after puberty, whereas accuracy at grammaticality judgments tapered off gradually (see Figure 10.5). Secondly, Birdsong and Molis (2001)

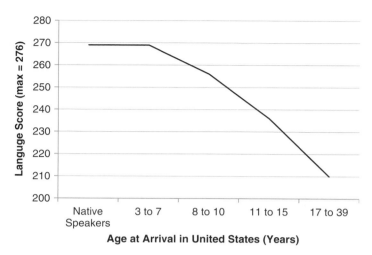

Figure 10.5   Mean scores of nonnative and native speakers of English on a grammaticality task. Adapted from Johnson and Newport, 1989, Table 3.

found much better second-language performance for native Spanish speakers who learned English after puberty, and argued that the similarity of language 1 and language 2 may play a role in acquisition. These results indicate that there might not be a sharply defined critical period for language learning, as Lenneberg (1967) had hypothesized.

Of course, those who learn a second language are already native speakers in a first language, and thus the brain's language centers will have already been stimulated. This may make it easier for subsequent language learning to piggyback onto those regions. A cleaner test of the CPH, then, would be to see if a *first* language could be learned after puberty. Evidence relevant to this test has come from several unfortunate cases where neglected children were prevented from learning language. The most famous case was of a girl from California nicknamed *Genie*, who had been locked in a room without verbal (or any other) stimulation from the time she was 20 months of age until just before her 13th birthday. Curtiss (1977) undertook the task of training Genie to speak, and initially was very optimistic. However, despite Genie's occasional ability to produce grammatical sentences (Jones, 1995), she was unable to systematically use pronouns, negations, the passive tense, or to form questions appropriately (Curtiss, 1977; Fromkin, Krashen, Curtiss, Rigler, & Rigler, 1974). While her word learning was rapid, her syntactic skills in production were approximately at the level of a 2 1/2-year-old child (Fromkin et al., 1974), and her case has largely been used to confirm a critical period for language learning.

Lateralization in Language Learning

Another aspect of the CPH hypothesis involves the lateralization of language function in the brain. If the CPH is valid, then a language learned after the critical period might be represented in the brain differently than a language learned earlier in life. Whether a language is represented in the left or right hemisphere, or bilaterally, can be tested in a number of ways. The Wada test, discussed in Chapter 9, involves the blocking of activity on one side of the brain using sodium amytal. If the person can no longer count or recite a nursery rhyme when one hemisphere has been blocked, that hemisphere is considered to be dominant for language skills. It has been found that 94% of right-handers and 70% of left-handers are left-hemisphere (LH) dominant for language (Bradshaw & Rogers, 1993). Even processing of language based on visual-spatial properties, such as sign language, is largely represented in the LH (Sakai, Tatsuno, Suzuki, Kimura, & Ichida, 2005). When tested, Genie showed an extreme right-hemisphere (RH) dominance for language during dichotic listening tasks (Fromkin, Krashen, Curtiss, Rigler, & Rigler, 1974). Thus, Lenneberg (1967) may have been right that early stimulation of the language areas in the LH is necessary for normal language acquisition, and that these neurons shut down if not specialized before the critical period (thus resulting in the impoverished language that Genie did acquire in her RH).

However, results with normal participants are less clear-cut. If we consider only research on sentence processing, which is an indicator of syntactic abilities, second-language lateralization appears to be dependent on the age of acquisition of language. A meta-analysis of cerebral-lateralization studies found that monolinguals were LH-dominant, and people who learned a second language later in life were LH-dominant for both languages. However, early learners of a second language—during the postulated critical period—showed greater bilateral specialization (Hull & Vaid, 2006). These results are inconsistent with Lenneberg's proposal that the LH is less able to acquire language after puberty, and point to greater participation of the RH in language learning, especially in people exposed to two languages before age 6.

Conclusion: Critical Period Hypothesis

Lenneberg's (1967) hypothesis has stimulated much research, but the support for it has been mixed. On the one hand, the results from Genie's difficulties learning language support the notion of a critical period. On the other hand, evidence from studies of ease of second-language learning and lateralization studies is less supportive of a critical period. The details of how the brain is organized for language development still remain to be worked out.

We have so far in this chapter discussed processing of single sentences. However, much of the speech that we hear involves more than single sentences. In the next section, we consider how people interpret *discourse*—language sequences that extend beyond the single sentence.

BUILDING THE INTERPRETATION OF DISCOURSE: CONSTRUCTING MENTAL SPACES

Sentences are usually heard as part of ongoing streams of conversation, so not only must one determine the meaning of each sentence, but one must also link up the meanings of new sentences with the message that has been heard so far. A number of researchers, in psychology (e.g., Gernsbacher, 1990), linguistics (e.g., Fauconnier, 1994, 1997; Fauconnier & Turner, 2002), and computer science (e.g., Beale, Nirenburg, & Mahesh, 1996; Gawronska & House, 1998), have proposed that interpretation of discourse depends on the listener constructing an internal model, or *mental space*, of the information concerned in a stretch of discourse. A pioneering theory of text comprehension was developed by Kintsch and van Dijk (1978; van Dijk & Kintsch, 1983), who proposed that people develop three levels of mental representations while reading. The first is of the exact text and sentences themselves; the second is a semantic representation based on the meaning of the text, and the third represents the situation represented by the text. If a text is *coherent*, the information that it conveys can be easily transformed into a network of related facts or ideas. Consider the following simple example.

> I saw John and Mary today, and they were getting along well. The last time I saw them, they were fighting, and I was concerned that they might not stay together. I guess I was wrong.

Upon reading this passage, a person will generate a mental representation of two people who are currently affectionate, and contrast this with another representation from the past in which the same two people were arguing. The person would then infer a change in the relational state of the two people. Along similar lines, Gernsbacher (1990, 1991, 1995, 1997) has examined several aspects of what she calls *structure building* during comprehension (see Table 10.4). Gernsbacher's model is proposed as an explanation for comprehension of any sort of language: written, spoken, and, as we shall see, of other sorts as well (for the sake of simplicity, we shall refer to the *listener* within this discussion).

Three Stages of Structure Building

Individual pieces of information in memory, which Gernsbacher (1997) calls *memory nodes*, are activated by an incoming message. These various memory nodes will play a role in building the structure needed for comprehension, as they can either enhance or suppress other related memory nodes. Gernsbacher, Varner, and Faust (1990) proposed three stages of structure building. First, early information leads the individual to build a *foundation* for the structure. Secondly, any additional information that is

Table 10.4 Gernsbacher's Analysis of Sentence Processing

Step	Explanation
Laying a Foundation	Basic framework for understanding the meaning of a text is built.
Mapping and Shifting	Any additional information that is related to, or *coherent with*, information in the foundation is mapped onto it (*mapping*). If a new substructure is started, reader starts to build that framework (*shifting*).
Enhancement and Suppression	Information that fits the general comprehension foundation is enhanced (and more easily remembered). Information that does not fit the foundation is suppressed (and less easily remembered).

related to, or *coherent with*, information in the foundation is mapped onto it. Thirdly, any new information that is not coherent with earlier information signals to the listener to shift and begin building a new foundation. In that way, the listener builds a set of interrelated structures, which capture the meaning transmitted by the complete message. In the remainder of this section, we will review evidence to support this model of discourse processing.

Building a Foundation

Reading Times

Gernsbacher (1997; Gernsbacher, Varner & Faust, 1990) assumes that building a foundational structure takes longer than simply adding information to an already-begun structure. One can test this assumption by presenting a paragraph one sentence at a time, with the reader signaling when he or she is ready to see the next sentence, in order to compare reading times for foundational versus nonfoundational sentences. Within an ordinary paragraph, early sentences take longer to read than do later ones (Greeno & Noreen, 1974; Haberlandt, 1984; Kieras, 1978, 1981), and reading time for the first episode is longer than for later ones (Haberlandt, 1980, 1984; Mandler & Goodman, 1982). (See Figure 10.6.) These results support the idea that information from the early sentences is used to begin the process of structure building. Later-arriving information is easier to attach to the developing structure, and thus is processed faster. Furthermore, in an individual sentence, initial words are read more quickly than later words, even when the identical word is presented at the end versus

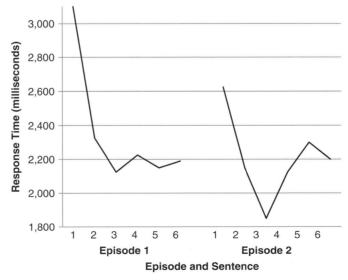

Figure 10.6 Time to process different sentences in two episodes. Responses are slowest overall to the first episode and to the first sentence in each episode.
Adapted from Haberlandt, 1984.

the beginning of the sentence (Aaronson & Ferres, 1983; Aaronson & Scarborough, 1976). Gernsbacher (1990) also showed the same longer-looking times for the initial pictures in wordless picture stories (like a comic strip), so the slower processing of early materials occurs widely in comprehension.

Advantage of First Mention

Information mentioned first in a segment of discourse should, in Gernsbacher's (1990, 1997) view, be easier to access in memory, because the first-mentioned material serves as the foundation or portal through which the listener accesses all subsequent information. This is known as the *advantage of first mention*. Gernsbacher and Hargreaves (1988) presented people with sentences such as (14) and (15), followed by a target probe. Participants were to respond whether the target word was in the sentence.

(14) Tina beat Lisa in the state tennis championship.

   Targets (only one is tested per person): Tina? Lisa?

(15) Lisa beat Tina in the state tennis championship.

   Targets (only one is tested per person): Tina? Lisa?

First-mentioned characters were responded to more quickly, e.g., in sentence (14), *Tina* was responded to faster than *Lisa*. The advantage of first mention is still found if the target words are delayed for 2 seconds after the sentence is presented (Gernsbacher, Hargreaves, & Beeman, 1989; see also Gernsbacher & Hargreaves, 1992).

Memory for Foundational Material

Under the structure-building account, foundational information should be a better cue for remembering discourse than is later, nonfoundational information, since the foundational material serves as the central point for access to the other material. This prediction also has been supported. After reading a story, people recall more of it if they are cued with the first sentence than with a later sentence (Mandler & Goodman, 1982), and they recall more information about a single sentence when cued with the first content word in the sentence (Bock & Irwin, 1980). Access is also enhanced if the first character introduced in a story is mentioned (Gernsbacher, Robertson, Palladino, & Werner, 2004). Thus, initial parts of complex verbal stimuli, that are assumed to serve as the foundation for structure building in comprehension, both take longer to process than later information and are more effective in cueing recall of all the information.

Mapping Coherent Information Onto the Foundation

Once a foundation has been built, new information is processed in relation to that foundation. When new information is *consistent*, or *coherent*, with the foundation, it is *mapped* to the foundation, much like papier-mâché, where strips are attached to the underlying object (e.g., a balloon), so that a more complete and complex object is built up, layer by layer (Gernsbacher, 1997). Just as the newly added paper strips contact the underlying form, new information will activate foundational memory nodes. This process is also outlined in Table 10.4.

Coherence Based on Co-Reference

Coherence is defined by whether new and old information *refer to the same concepts*, which is called *co-reference*. Consider the sentence pairs (16)–(18).

(16) We got some beer out of the trunk.   The beer was warm.

(17) We checked the picnic supplies.   The beer was warm.

(18) Andrew was especially fond of beer.   The beer was warm.

Experimental participants were asked to read those pairs. The question of interest was how long it took to read the second sentence, the target sentence, which was the same in all the pairs. The target was read more quickly in pair (16) than in the other pairs (Haviland & Clark, 1974). The facilitation in processing in sentence pair (16) is presumably brought about because the two sentences are coherent, since they both refer to the same beer.

Coherence Based on Contiguity and Causality

Coherence is also signaled if separate sentences refer to events that happen at about the same time, in the same place, or are causally related. For example, if one is reading a story about a meal in a restaurant, a sentence beginning *Ten minutes later* will be read faster than one starting with *Ten days later* (Anderson, Garrod, & Sanford, 1983). Coherence is fostered as well when sentences are linked because of cause-and-effect relationships between the events they describe. The second sentence in pair (19) is read faster than the same sentence in sentence-pair (20) (Keenan, Baillet, & Brown, 1984).

(19) Joey's big brother punched him again and again. The next day, Joey's body was
      covered in bruises.

(20) Joey went to a neighbor's house to play. The next day, Joey's body was covered
      in bruises.

In pair (19), the bruises can be seen as the result of the beating, which makes the two sentences coherent. This results in the mapping of the second sentence onto the foundation provided by the first, which speeds reading of the second sentence. The bruises have no obvious connection to playing at a neighbor's house, so no mapping occurs in sentence pair (20).

Brain Sites Underlying Mapping

Robertson and colleagues (2000; also Gernsbacher & Robertson, 2004) attempted to isolate brain areas active during this hypothesized mapping process. They used fMRI to measure brain activity as people read sets of sentences that were either coherent or not coherent, through use of definite versus indefinite articles, as in sentence sets (21) versus (22).

(21) A family stopped to rest. The café was almost deserted.

(22) A family stopped to rest. A café was almost deserted.

Set (21), which contains the definite article (*the*), seems more coherent than set (22), which contains the indefinite article (*a*).

To isolate brain areas involved in mapping, activity during processing of both types of sentence sets was compared. Coherent sets of sentences led to increased activity in the right frontal lobe. Robertson et al. (2000) interpreted these findings as indicating that presence of the definite article causes retrieval of the information from the first sentence from episodic memory in order to establish coherent mappings. Secondly, the right hemisphere has been shown to be involved in processing of complex knowledge and word processing (Brownell, Carroll, Rehak, & Wingfield, 1992; Zaidel, Zaidel, Oxbury, & Oxbury, 1995); and third, the right frontal lobe has also been hypothesized to play an important role in direction of internal attention (Knight & Grabowecky, 1995). Thus, use of the definite article encourages coherent mapping through involvement of episodic memory, attention, and overall speech-comprehension processes.

Additionally, van Berkum, Hagoort, and Brown (1999) found brain-wave patterns indicative of more effortful processing when a second sentence was inconsistent with a first (as when a mouse was said to have returned *slowly* to its hole after mention of a cat). Sentences that are incoherent with previous information lead to heightened processing of individual words.

Shifting to a New Structure

When incoming information is not coherent with information presented to that point, the listener or reader needs to shift from the structure he or she has been working with, and begin to build another foundation to incorporate the new information. According to Gernsbacher et al. (2004), shifting occurs because noncoherent information will activate new memory nodes, which will not be connected to the nodes activated by the old structure, thus resulting in formation of a new substructure. Shifting to build a new structure takes effort, which leads to increased time for comprehension. Gernsbacher et al. (2004) presented study participants with an initial paragraph with a single character (say, Grant). Those in the *Re-mention* condition then saw a second paragraph with the same character (Grant), versus a *New* condition in which another character (Alexa) was introduced in the second paragraph. People in the *Neither* condition received a second paragraph in which no character was mentioned. A probe word of either the first character's name (Experiment 1) or an object associated with that character (Experiment 2) appeared either before or after the second paragraph, and participants were asked to respond whether that person/object had been mentioned in the story. As can be seen in Figure 10.7, response times to the first-character probe took longer after the second paragraph had shifted to a second character in the *New* condition, indicating reduced accessibility to the first character.

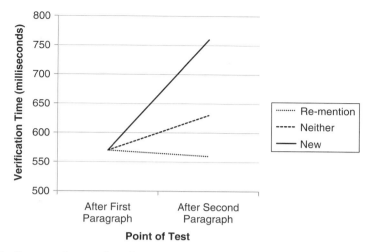

Figure 10.7   Response times to first-character probes before and after second paragraph (in msec). Adapted from Gernsbacher et al., 2004, Experiment 1, Figure 1.

In addition, reading times slow down when new topics, settings, or times are introduced into a passage (e.g., Daneman & Carpenter, 1983; Lesgold, Roth, & Curtis, 1979; Mandler & Goodman, 1982). Presumably, any changes in time, location, or topic result in a shift to or construction of a new structure, which slows down comprehension.

Mechanisms of Processing: Suppression and Enhancement

When memory nodes related to the components of a message are active, they spread activation to other related nodes (see discussion of spreading activation in the section on semantic memory in Chapter 8), which enhances or facilitates those nodes' activation. This enhancement facilitates processing of the related material, and helps to build coherent structures. However, when a topic shift occurs in text or a conversation, then the previously active material is no longer relevant to the structure, and should undergo inhibition or *suppression* so that it does not interfere with processing of the second piece of information. Gernsbacher, and Robertson (1995) found that repeating the same verb within a sentence pair enhanced processing of that verb, but suppressed detection of a related but not-repeated verb. For example, people who saw the sentences, *John ate dinner and watched television. Later he ate dessert*, had enhanced responses to the repeated *ate*, but suppressed processing of the previously mentioned *watched*. We are already familiar with repetition priming (i.e., enhancement) from Chapter 5, and with inhibitory processes (i.e., suppression) from our discussion of *negative priming* (Chapter 6) and inhibition of the meaning of lexically ambiguous words that do not fit a sentence context (Chapter 9).

Individual Differences in Structure Building

Gernsbacher (1997) has proposed that the processes involved in language processing are subject to individual differences in overall cognition. She tested this proposal by developing a general test of comprehension, composed of six stories—two written, two auditory, and two pictorial. When the stories were given to undergraduates, a high correlation ($r = 0.90$) was found among people's comprehension performance on all three types of stories (Gernsbacher, Varner, & Faust, 1990). Differences between high and low comprehenders has also been linked to the efficiency with which they engage in structure building, and in suppression processes. Gernsbacher et al. (1990, Experiments 2 and 3) found that less-skilled comprehenders have trouble accessing previous information because they began to build new substructures when the material did not require that they do so. This resulted in less coherent structures, and poorer comprehension and memory.

Structure Building in Text Processing: Conclusions

There is much experimental evidence to support the idea that comprehension of discourse depends upon construction of mental structures. Those internal representations contain the information necessary to specify all relations among components of discourse. Incoming information is used first to build a foundation for a new mental structure, an operation that requires extensive processing. Later information that is coherent with the foundation is added to it, while noncoherence between the already-constructed foundation and new information results in a new substructure being initiated. Psychological measures of various sorts, ranging from processing times to recall results, support these conclusions. In addition, evidence indicates that differences among people in their ability to comprehend verbal materials may be due at least in part to differences in the efficiencies with which they construct those representations. Based on extensive research, Gernsbacher (e.g., Gernsbacher et al., 1990) has proposed that reading-comprehension skills are heavily interdependent with a variety of other cognitive skills, and she has concluded that her extensive findings do not support a modular view of language-comprehension skills.

We have now considered a number of different aspects of language *comprehension*. *Language production* is the second side of the linguistic coin. We present an overview of speech production and then examine two areas of research carried out by investigators who study the processes involved in language production. We first review research that has analyzed errors made by people in the normal course of speaking. Then we examine neuroscience research on sentence processing in both patients and nonpatients.

STAGES OF SPEECH PRODUCTION

Speech production includes all the processes through which a *meaning* or *idea* ultimately gets translated into spoken language (Dell, 1986; Garrett, 1975). For instance, in Garrett's (1980, 1990) model of speech production, presented in Figure 10.8,

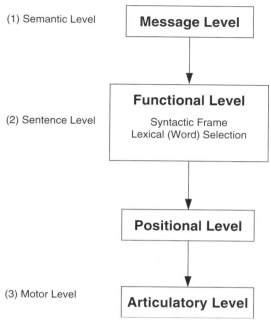

Figure 10.8   Model of speech production by Garrett.
Adapted from Garrett, 1990.

we start (1) with a message or meaning we wish to convey. Then, at level (2), we simultaneously decide on the syntactic structure or *frame* for the sentence that will be used to convey that meaning (e.g., active or passive sentence) *and* the desired words that will fit into that syntactic frame (e.g., *dog*, *canine*, or *German Shepherd*). Morphological elements are then added to the words to indicate details of meaning (e.g., plurals, past tense) and make the sentence grammatical (e.g., subject–verb agreement). Also at this stage, the words are then inserted into the positions in the sentence frame. In the next stage (3), phonological representations of the words and morphemes are activated, which allows the motor system to articulate the phonetic features of the sounds (Levelt, 1983, 1989). In Garret's model of speech, each stage is discreet and feeds into the next level or levels.

Although the general gist of this model is a useful framework, one point of contention among researchers is Garrett's (1975, 1982, 1988) proposal that the levels of production are independent of each other, so that lower levels cannot feed backward to influence higher levels. In contrast, interactionist models, such those by Dell (1986) and Stemberger (1985), have proposed that there can be feedback from lower to higher levels, so that the phonology of a word, for instance, could influence lexical choice. As we will see, there is ample evidence to support an interactionist model of speech production. One source of evidence concerning the processes involved in speech production comes from the errors—slips of the tongue—that all people make during spontaneous speech. We now turn to a review of that research.

WHAT SPEECH ERRORS REVEAL ABOUT LANGUAGE PRODUCTION

Several researchers have collected real-life speech errors, and others have induced speech errors experimentally (e.g., Martin, Weisberg, & Saffran, 1989; Motley, Camden, & Baars, 1983), to analyze the conditions under which mistakes are most often made and what those mistakes tell us about the processes involved in producing speech (Dell, 1995).

Collecting and Analyzing Speech Errors

Dell (1995) reports that a friend told him that then-U.S. President Gerald Ford, hosting a dinner for then-Egyptian President Anwar Sadat, made a toast to Sadat and "the great people of Israel—Egypt, excuse me." Dell's friend then related the incident to him, saying: "I heard Freud made a Fordian slip . . . [laughs]" So we have the original error by President Ford, saying *Israel* for *Egypt*, and another by Dell's friend, who meant to say "*Ford* made a *Freudian* slip." On average, speakers make errors about once or twice per thousand words, which is about once or twice per 5 minutes of speaking (see Table 10.5 for examples).

The speech errors in the *Israel/Egypt* and *Ford/Freud* examples are at the level of *words*, but errors can occur at the sentence, word, morphemic, or phonemic level. Slips of the tongue are not simply random; there are systematic aspects of mistakes that provide a window into normal processes in speech production (Dell, 1986; Fromkin, 1973; Meringer & Mayer, 1895). Similar errors are found in writing (Fromkin, 1973).

In the experimental laboratory, speech errors are induced by having people name pictures or read words under conditions that are designed to optimize mistakes. For example, Baars and Motley (1976) asked people to read aloud word pairs, and found that they could prime transpositions by repeating initial-phoneme patters. For instance, participants were more likely to transpose phonemes and read the target DEAD LEVEL as "LEAD DEVIL" if they had just seen LET DAVID, and LEG

Table 10.5   Examples of Speech Errors

Type of Error	Error Occurs Within a Word or Word Pair	Error Occurs Within a Sentence
Anticipation	"shushi" for *sushi*	"Did you bling any blankets?" for *Did you bring any blankets?*
Perseveration	"Thundercloud Clubs" for *Thundercloud Subs* (a local sandwich shop)	"Your spine has a spurve to it." for *Your spine has a curve to it.*
Substitution	"amphetamines" for *amphibian* (in a vet's office)	"For the research design, I used a Roman circle" for *For the research design, I used a Latin square.*
Transposition	"drain bamage" for *brain damage*	"Put the drawers in the key." for *Put the keys in the drawer.*
Blend	"hilarical" for *hilarious* + *hysterical*	"I was going to take to walk the dogs." For *I was going to take the dogs for a walk,* + *I was going to walk the dogs.*

DANGLE. Researchers can also apply time pressures or alter the difficulty of the speech material in order to encourage laboratory speech errors.

Classifying Errors

Phrase and Sentence Errors

There is evidence that the phrase is the main planning unit of speech production, because many phoneme, morpheme, and word errors tend to stay within phrase boundaries (Boomer & Laver, 1968). Furthermore, word-substitution errors remain syntactically correct: About 95% of the time nouns are substituted or exchanged for nouns, verbs for verbs, and so forth (Bock & Levelt, 1994; Garrett, 1975; Stemberger, 1985). As an example, the error "BRAIN and I were just JIMstorming on the way over here" transposes a proper noun (*Jim*) with a common noun (*brain*) while maintaining the grammaticality of the sentence[1] (MPI error 806). Some errors are simply a different tense or version of the intended utterance, as in "Didn't she beCAME...?" (MPI error 678).

There are some occasions where a verb and a noun appear to switch positions, as in "I ROASTED the COOK" instead of "I cooked the roast" (from Wardlow Lane & Ferreira, 2010). When such a noun-verb switch occurs, at least one of the words is very likely to be syntactically ambiguous—e.g., *roast* and *cook* can function as both verbs AND nouns (Ferreira & Humphreys, 2001). Furthermore, when a verb takes a noun's slot (or vice versa), there is evidence that it takes on the characteristics of that syntactic slot. Ferreira and Humphreys (2001) had people listen to pairs of words and then asked them to verbally insert the words into a utterance frame, such as _____ *the* _____. In order to try to produce speech errors, after the word pair was presented, half the time it was followed by the cue word REPEAT, which meant that the participant should put the words in the frame in the order presented. For example, if the word pair was *tape-record*, they should say "tape the record." On the remaining trials, the cue word was REVERSE, which meant that the participant should reverse the words before inserting them into the frame: for *tape-record*, he or she should say "record the tape." It was hoped that the presence of the reversal condition would result in a tendency to transpose the words in the repeat condition, thereby resulting in a speech error.

To tell whether people altered a verb to a noun in producing an error, or noun to a verb, the researchers used target words whose noun/verb forms used a different stress pattern (for example, for the word *record*, the verb is pronounced *ree-CORD*, the noun, *REH-cord*). The experimental procedure was successful in producing speech errors, and almost every time participants reversed the words, the stress pattern reflected that of the syntactic frame of the error. That is, most people said "ree-CORD the tape" even though they had heard tape-REH-cord (Ferreira & Humphreys, 2001; also Wardlow, Lane, & Ferreira, 2010, Experiment 1). Wardlow, Lane, and Ferreira (2010) concluded

---

[1] Most of the speech error examples used in this section were derived from Victoria Fromkin's corpus of errors (collected over many years) which is now accessible at the Max Planck Institute for Psycholinguistic's website at www.mpi.nl/cgi-bin/sedb/sperco_form4.pl). Speech errors taken from this site are listed by error number; for others, the citation is given.

that these findings support a view in which the syntactic analysis is chosen first, as a *sentence frame*, and the syntactic level then constrains the way words and morphemes are inserted into the sentence frame.

Morpheme and Word Errors

Word and morpheme errors come in a variety of forms. Occasionally, we may activate two words, resulting in a blend, such as "flumsy" for flimsy + clumsy (MPI error 376), or when a psychologist's daughter requested, "please cut my meef"—a combination of meat + beef (Motley, 1985). Within a phrase or sentence, whole words can migrate or trade places, such as the speech error, "a 50-pound DOG of BAG food" (MPI error 306). Again, in most of these cases the earlier-specified syntactic frame constrains which words are transposed, with errors tending to maintain the grammatical class status of the target (e.g., noun ⇔ noun; verb ⇔ verb; adjective ⇔ adjective).

Phonological and Phonemic Errors

Errors of substitution also occur at the sound-related levels of speech production, and include *anticipations*, in which a phoneme shows up earlier in the speech stream than was intended, e.g., "I need to read four or pive pages more before I quit," where the phoneme /p/ replaces the intended *target* phoneme /f/ in *five*. *Perseverations* occur when an already-produced phoneme does not become inhibited after its production and shows up later in the utterance, as in "And you'Ve preVented us . . . presented us with a problem" (MPI error 329). Phonemes are also subject to *deletion*, as in "fore-bain," where the intended /r/ in *brain* was omitted (MPI error 377), or to *addition*, as in "and by allowZing two separate cases" (MPI error 317).

Another type of error occurs when two phonemes switch places, so that both are heard in the error. For instance, Reverend William Spooner, an Oxford professor, chastised a student who had not been coming to class, "You have hissed all my mystery lectures!" The /h/ and /m/ sounds traded places, resulting in "hissed" and "mystery" (in place of "missed" and "history"); this kind of error is known as an *exchange* or *transposition* (see Table 10.5). Because of the frequency with which Rev. Spooner produced those sorts of errors, errors that resulted in legitimate words (and often humorous outcomes), they are referred to as *spoonerisms*.

Another striking fact concerning speech errors is that when phonemes move, their "environments" are often similar in various ways. For example, the words "missed" and "history" in the just-mentioned spoonerism both have a short /i/ as their first vowel, followed by an /s/ sound within the first syllable. The interacting units also usually occupy similar positions within the word (Fromkin, 1971; Meijer, 1997), such as both occurring at the beginning of words. Also, the relevant phonemes usually share phonetic features in terms of their place and manner of articulation (see Chapter 9); e.g., if someone says "fl ee-floating anxiety" instead of "fr ee-floating anxiety," the phonemes /r/ and /l/ are produced similarly (MacKay, 1970; Nooteboom, 2005; Shattuck-Hufnagel & Klatt, 1979).

Lexical Bias in Phonological Speech Errors

A well-documented trend in speech errors is that when phonemic errors occur, many actually form an English word, as in "*flee*-floating anxiety," for *free-floating anxiety*.

In experiments that induce people to make phonological errors, the probability of an error is more likely if the mistake forms a word than if it forms a nonword (Baars, Motley, & MacKay, 1975; Dell & Reich, 1981; Hartsuiker, Corley, & Martensen, 2005; Nooteboom, 2005). Nozari and Dell (2009) proposed that there may be feedback processes from the phonological level to the word/morpheme levels that can function to increase the likelihood of legitimate words in speech errors (Dell, 1986; Dell & Reich, 1981). As nonwords do not activate words or morphemes, their phonological specification will not receive as much activation, decreasing the likelihood of nonword utterances.

Is Speech Production a Serial or Interactive Process?

The lexical bias in phonological speech errors supports a speech-production process in which various levels (such as the word and phoneme levels) interact, rather than the serial, step-by-step production process proposed by Garrett (1990). Further empirical evidence has confirmed that speech errors are most common if they satisfy constraints at, or are influenced by, multiple levels in speech production. Many of the speech-error examples we have presented throughout the chapter clearly show influences from at least two production components (e.g., syntax and phonology).

Freudian Slips? Semantic Influences on Speech Errors

The term *Freudian slip* describes a speech error in which a potentially unconscious message bursts out in an unintended utterance. Motley (1985) related the time when he met another candidate applying for the same job as he, and Motley said "Pleased to beat you," instead of "Pleased to meet you." Freud would have said that the error revealed the underlying thoughts of the speaker (i.e., that the speech error was motivated by Motley's unconscious desires). A more contemporary view would be that the competitive nature of Motley's job search led to a semantically influenced speech error (and note that "beat" also shares phonemic elements with the intended "meet").

Motley and Baars (1976) attempted to induce Freudian slips by asking college men to read word pairs on a computer screen. There were two experimental conditions—one in which people were hooked up to electrodes and threatened with a painful shock if they made any errors; and a second, in which the men first took the Mosher Sex Guilt Inventory and then were administered the word trials by an attractive and provocatively dressed female experimenter. Compared to a control condition, those in the threat-of-shock condition were significantly more likely to make errors on word pairs that resulted in phrases connected to electricity (e.g., to say *damn shock* for SHAM DOCK), whereas those in the sexual-anxiety condition were twice as likely to make errors which led to a sexually-related phrase (e.g., *fast passion* for PAST FASHION). Motley (1985) explained that such seemingly-Freudian slips could be explained by an interaction of semantic, phonological, and contextual factors (such as whether one feared a shock). The interactive nature of speech errors has been confirmed by numerous other studies (e.g., Dell, Martin, & Schwartz, 2007; Dell, Schwartz, Martin, Saffran, & Gagnon, 1997; Martin, Weisberg, & Saffran, 1989).

Speech Errors and Language Production: Conclusions

Speech errors are not random glitches in the production system, but can be used to shed light on language production processes. Both corpus data and laboratory studies have confirmed that errors are almost always units of the same type (word ⇔ word, phoneme ⇔ phoneme, etc.), which indicates that there are separate stages in production of the various levels of units. However, the separate stages do interact with each other to mutually influence the likelihood of speech errors. Verbal mishaps, then, are more likely if an error is both semantically *and* phonologically related to a target, showing that these two levels interact. Additionally, research suggests a greater likelihood of a speech error if the error will result in a legitimate word within that language.

NEUROCOGNITION OF LANGUAGE: BROCA'S APHASIA, OR AGRAMMATISM

As we have already seen in Chapter 9, study of behavioral deficits in various types of aphasia has yielded important information about normal language processes. Just as Wernicke's aphasia and anomia shed light on phonological processing and word retrieval, respectively, *Broca's aphasia* has elucidated how grammatical skills are represented in the brain.

Classical Studies

The most famous early case study of aphasia was Broca's study of a patient called *Tan* (because that was the only utterance he could produce). After Tan's death, Broca carried out an autopsy, and linked Tan's language-production problems to a lesion in the area in the inferior left frontal lobe now known as *Broca's area*, comprising Brodman's areas 44 and 45 (Dronkers, Plaisant, Iba-Zizen, & Cabanis, 2007; see Figure 10.9). Broca postulated that this area in the left hemisphere controls production of speech in right-handed people (and even in most left-handed people). A recent examination of Tan's brain by Dronkers et al. (2007) indicates that his damage was more widespread than the areas now considered to be Broca's area. In particular, Tan suffered damage to the inferior gyrus just in front of Brodman's area 45, the anterior superior temporal gyrus, anterior inferior temporal lobe, and subcortical structures. Thus, Tan's articulation difficulties might have been at least partly due to more widespread damage than Broca's area alone. More recent research also indicates that deeper regions beneath Broca's area may contribute to the language deficits in Broca's aphasia.

Most people classified as Broca's aphasics are not as impaired as Tan was, but they do exhibit impoverished language production, so that their speech is often described as *telegraphic*. As can be seen in the speech sample in Figure 10.9, these patients produce a paucity of verbs, prepositions, articles, and other grammatical aspects of speech. Their sentences are often produced in a halting fashion, and mainly include nouns and catchphrases (e.g., "oh no") so that their meaning is clear, but there is very

A. Map of left-hemisphere speech areas: Broca's area, Wernicke's area, and angular gyrus.

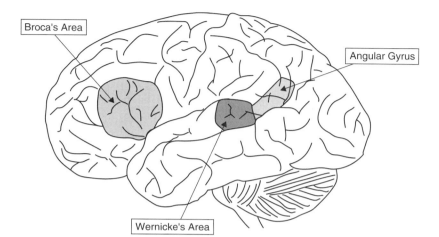

B. Broca's aphasia patient speech; the patient is trying to explain how he came to the hospital for dental surgery:

> Yes ... ah ... Monday ... er ... Dad and Peter H ... (his own name), and Dad .... er ... hospital ... and ah ... Wednesday ... Wednesday, nine o'clock ... and oh ... Thursday ... ten o'clock, ah doctors ... two ... an' doctors ... and er ... teeth ... yah.

C. Wernicke's aphasia patient speech:

> You know that smoodle pinkered and that I want to get him round and take care of him like you want before.

Figure 10.9   Left-hemisphere speech areas and speech samples from language disorders.

little syntactic structure. For this reason, the term *agrammatics* is often preferred to Broca's aphasia (Goodglass & Wingfield, 1997; Zurif, Caramazza, & Myerson, 1972, 1980); we will use both Broca's aphasics and agrammatics interchangeably in our discussion.

The impoverished production of Broca's aphasia differs greatly from the comprehension problems of Wernicke's aphasics (first described by Wernicke in 1879; discussed in Chapter 9). Those differences led to an early model of brain function that proposed that the left frontal inferior gyrus (Broca's area) was responsible for language production, and Wernicke's area (in the left superior posterior temporal region) was responsible for comprehension. This dichotomy of localized areas for speech production and comprehension is too simple, however. First, Wernicke's and Broca's aphasics may suffer deficits in *both* comprehension and production, but for different reasons. As we saw in Chapter 9, Wernicke's aphasia is better explained as a deficit in phonological coding (production) and decoding (comprehension). Agrammatism (Broca's aphasia), on the other hand, is largely due to impairments in grammatical abilities.

Researchers have used comprehension tests to examine the deficits in Broca's aphasia. In one comprehension test, the tester reads a sentence to the patient and asks him or her to pick which one of two pictures fits the sentence. Some types of sentences, such as sentence (23), are difficult for them:

(23) The truck was hit by the car.

If presented with two pictures, one of a car striking a truck and another of a truck striking a car, agrammatics may mistakenly point to the picture of a truck hitting a car for sentence (23). Broca's aphasics *notice* the difference between an active and passive sentence; they "hear" the... *was hit by*... in the passive sentence. However, they cannot perform the necessary transformations to determine that *car*, at the end of the sentence, is still the AGENT. It is as if these patients often interpret sentences by assuming that *any* NP-V-NP string depicts *subject-verb-object*, and then they assign *agent-action-patient* roles accordingly (Caplan & Futter, 1986). While this strategy works for active English sentences, such as *The car hit the truck*, it fails with many others, including passives, such as (23). Broca's aphasics also use nonsyntactic, knowledge-based clues to help them interpret sentences (Schwartz, Saffran, & Marin, 1980; Sherman & Schweikert, 1989; von Stockert & Bader, 1976). For example, they are more likely to correctly comprehend the correct picture depicting sentence (24) than sentence (25), because (24) yields a more plausible scenario.

(24) The bone was eaten by the dog.

(25) The dog was eaten by the bone.

Similar problems show up with production; Broca's aphasics show impoverished speech that is devoid of the grammatical morphemes necessary to produce passive or complex sentences. They are most likely to use simple subject-verb-object sequences to construct sentences in which the most plausible agent appears at the beginning (Saffran, Schwartz, & Marin, 1980; von Stockert & Bader, 1976). Broca's aphasics also have trouble with morphological elements within sentences, such as the use of past tenses appended to verbs. Jonkers and de Bruin (2009) asked Dutch agrammatics to engage in two tasks: (1) a comprehension task, in which they had to choose a correct picture after listening to a sentence illustrating either present or past tense; and (2) a production task, in which they had to articulate the correct form of a verb to match a picture. For example, when shown a picture of a woman who was looking at a completed dinner, they were provided with the sentence frame and correct verb choice (e.g., "cooked") to prompt production of "*This woman cooked the dinner*" (rather than "*This woman cooks the dinner*"). Two findings are of interest: The aphasics' comprehension performance was better than their production, and, in both tasks, patients were more accurate with present- than past-tense verbs (see Figure 10.10).

Linguistic and Cognitive Analysis of Problems in Aphasia

Because agrammatics seem to exhibit parallel deficits in production and comprehension (though their comprehension problems are less obvious and may be most evident in the laboratory), and these problems appear to be tied to the grammatical aspects of language, some researchers have described them as "asyntactic" (Caramazza & Zurif,

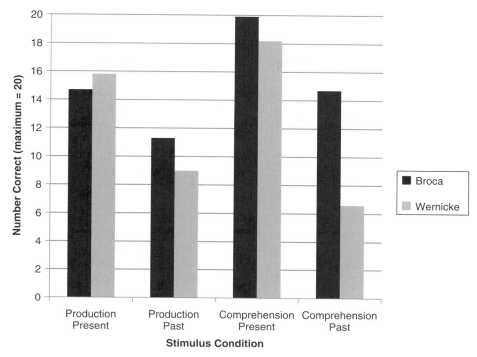

Figure 10.10   Performance of Broca's and Wernicke's patients in various language tasks.
Data from Jonkers and de Bruin, 2009.

1976). It should be noted that, as with all neuropsychological syndromes, there is great individual variation among patients. Several Broca's aphasics have been studied who do not show equivalent deficits in production and comprehension (Caramazza, Basili, Koller, & Berndt, 1981; Kolk & van Grunsven, 1985; Miceli, Mazzucchi, Menn, & Goodglass, 1983; Nespoulous et al., 1988).

One hypothesis developed to explain the language problems exhibited by Broca's aphasics is that their syntactic *module* is damaged. More specifically, Grodzinsky (1989, 1990) has proposed the *deficient-trace theory*, which proposes that sentences in which a *trace* is deleted or moved from its standard place in the sentence lead to the problems that Broca's patients have in comprehension (see Zurif, 1995; see Figure 10.2). For instance, passive sentences shift the object-noun phrase to the left of its position in the d-structure, thus leaving a trace behind (see Figure 10.4). The same thing occurs with what are called *object-gap relative clauses*, as in sentence (26), which many agrammatics fail to comprehend (Hickok, Zurif, & Canseco-Gonzalez, 1993; Mauner, Fromkin, & Cornell, 1993):

(26) It was the truck that the car hit [*trace*].

According to Grodzinsky (1990), Broca's patients are not able to use traces when analyzing or parsing sentences, and therefore cannot correctly interpret sentence (26). The word *truck* must be remembered and then mentally moved to after the main verb *hit* (where it has left a trace), since *truck* is the object of the verb (Grodzinsky, 1986, 1990). If the patients use the NP-V-NP strategy discussed earlier, they are likely either to either assume that the truck did the hitting (since it comes first in sentence (26)), or simply guess at the interpretation, and thus they will be wrong half the time.

In contrast to Grodzinsky's (1995) deficient-trace explanation of the performance of agrammatics, Schwartz, Linebarger, Saffran, and Pate (1987) have proposed a *mapping-deficiency* explanation for agrammatics' difficulties: Agrammatics do not suffer from either a semantic or a syntactic deficit *per se*, but rather have difficulty mapping thematic roles (or cases; Fillmore, 1968) between semantics and syntax. We have discussed those roles—*agent* and *actor* versus *object* and *patient*—earlier in this chapter. Thus, in spontaneous production, agrammatics understand the thematic roles that they want to convey (that is, the speaker has witnessed a situation containing an agent and object), but he or she cannot map those into a grammatical structure. During comprehension, they notice syntactic and morphological elements of the sentence, and can thus distinguish between active and passive (and other) sentences, but cannot exploit the grammatical aspects of a sentence to determine *agent*, *object* status. Under the mapping-deficit view, agrammatics may be able to parse some sentences normally, but still exhibit production and comprehension problems because the psychological mechanism that uses this structural information to *assign* thematic roles is broken (Linebarger, 1995), not that syntactic abilities themselves are impaired (Linebarger, Schwartz, & Saffran, 1983).

One piece of evidence that supports the mapping-deficiency hypothesis is that agrammatics do retain sensitivity to grammatical morphemes and syntactic structure, which indicates that Broca's aphasia is not purely due to a loss of all grammatical knowledge. Linebarger, et al. (1983) presented four Broca's aphasics with grammatical and ungrammatical sentences, such as "I want you to go to the store now," versus "I hope you to go to the store now." The patients only had to judge whether each was a "good" or "bad" sentence. All four of the agrammatics were significantly above chance at separating grammatical from ungrammatical sentences, and three were above 85% accuracy. Thus, they exhibited the ability to judge when a sentence is grammatically correct or not. This indicates that agrammatic aphasics seem not to be able to *exploit* the grammatical aspects of a sentence to determine its meaning. Similar results have been obtained with Italian Broca's aphasics (Wulfeck, Bates, & Capasso, 1991).

Lesion Studies of Aphasia: Conclusions

Research on agrammatism not only sheds light on the component processes used to produce and comprehend grammatical sentences, but also provides insight into the relationship between brain structures and language processes. Although there is some debate as to whether agrammatism is due to a problem with the syntactic aspect of language only (Caramazza & Zurif, 1976; Grodzinsky, 1986, 2000; Zurif, 1995), or to the inability to map between syntactic and semantic aspects of speech (Saffran et al., 1980; Schwartz et al., 1980), the robust influence of plausibility in agrammatic patients' sentence comprehension and production suggests a strong interactive relationship between the conceptual and linguistic systems. However, agrammatic patients' intact semantic system, with impoverished grammar, does suggest some independence of the two levels.

PET and fMRI Studies of Sentence Processing

Analysis of language deficits resulting from lesions has been supplemented by research using PET scans and fMRI, which permit researchers to determine changes in brain activity in normal people during language processing, which confirms the role of Broca's area in syntactic processing. Neuropsychological evidence has indicated that Broca's area is active during processing of syntactically complex sentences (Stromswold, Caplan, Alpert, & Rauch, 1996). In addition, specific parts of Broca's area may control syntactic processing for both spoken and signed languages (Horwitz et al., 2003). Horwitz et al. measured activation levels for Brodman's areas 44 and 45 (BA 44 and BA 45; both considered Broca'a area) during speech tasks. They asked people who were fluent in both English and American Sign Language to: (a) speak about a personal memory; (b) sign a personal memory; (c) make oral movements without any speech; and (d) make hand/arm gestures without any ASL language. The researchers found that BA 44 was active only during oral articulation, but that BA 45 was active during language production of both oral and gestural speech (see Figure 10.11). Thus, parts of Broca's area may supply the motor representation for actual speech, whereas other regions are implicated in syntactic analysis during production and comprehension.

We have now spent some time considering how single sentences and more-complex discourse are processed, including how sentence processing can go awry in aphasia. In the next section, we consider a possible link between language and other cognitive skills, such as reasoning and conceptual thought.

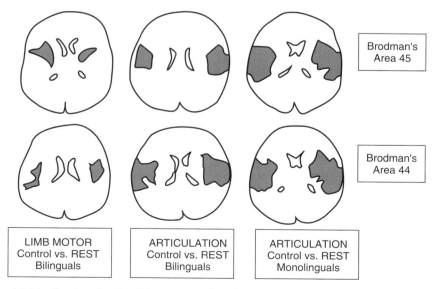

Figure 10.11   Results of study of Horwitz et al. (2003): Activity in Brodman's areas 44 and 45 during oral versus gestural language production in bilinguals (English + ASL) and monolinguals.

THE LINGUISTIC RELATIVITY HYPOTHESIS

As we have seen, one major debate among language researchers has been whether language is *modular*, or functionally independent from other skills, such as categorization or reasoning. There are, however, obvious ways in which language has a direct bearing on other aspects of thinking. For instance, as noted in Chapter 8, it is difficult to conceive of how we could understand and convey such abstract concepts as "justice" or "exponent" without language. Many of us implicitly assume that, although a person who speaks French or Russian or Swahili has a different word for "red," or "happy," or "justice," those speakers when using those words are referring to the same concepts as we do. In contrast to this view, the *linguistic relativity hypothesis* proposes that language and various aspects of thought (such as concepts) are integrally bound and that the language we employ to label and describe the world affects our categories and concepts. This implies that people who speak a different language from us might actually think and understand concepts differently.

The best-known advocate of the linguistic relativity hypothesis was Whorf, an amateur anthropologist (Whorf, 1956; see also Sapir, 1929). A *strong* version of the linguistic relativity hypothesis—that language *dictates* thought—is now often referred to as the *Whorfian hypothesis* (although it is not clear that Whorf himself advocated such a strong stance). Whorf's most famous examples were Inuits' (Eskimos') use of multiple words for snow; and Hopi Indians' distinction between water in a container versus water in a natural location or reservoir. Whorf proposed that the Inuit and Hopi could make more fine-grained perceptual and conceptual distinctions among kinds of snow and water, respectively, than could Americans or Europeans. Because those distinctions were important in each people's culture, they were reflected in their language, which consequently led them to have different perceptions and conceptions of the world.

Whorf's proposal was investigated by Heider (1972), who tested the color perception of members of the Dani tribe of Indonesia. In Dani language, there are only two color terms—those used to indicate dark colors (e.g., blue, black, dark green) and those used to indicate light colors (e.g., white, pink, yellow). According to the Whorfian hypothesis, the Dani should then only be able to perceive differences *between* dark and light colors, but not differences *within* dark colors (or within light colors). Heider (1972, Experiment 3) presented English- and Dani-speakers with samples of different shades of eight different colors (red, yellow, green, blue, pink, orange, brown, and purple). A person was presented with a color sample for 5 seconds, and after a delay of 30 seconds, asked to pick the color they had seen out of 160 color samples. Although the English speakers were more precise in the memory task, the Dani could discriminate between colors such as green and blue, which fell within the same linguistic label within their language. Color perception appeared to be universal across cultures and across languages (at least across the Dani and American college students), which went against the linguistic relativity hypothesis (but see Davidoff, Davies, & Roberson, 1999; and Zhang, He, & Zhang, 2007, for cases in which language was found to influence color memory and color groupings).

Even if we accept Heider's (1972) finding that basic perception is not affected by language, that leaves open the possibilities that: (a) language might influence more *abstract* concepts; and/or (b) a weaker version of the Whorfian hypothesis might hold—language *influences*, but does not dictate, thought or categorization (Boroditsky, 2001). In an intriguing experiment, Boroditsky and her colleagues have found that linguistic traditions influence how people think about objects in the world (Boroditsky, Schmidt, & Phillips, 2003). Fluent speakers of German and Spanish (both which have gender designations for nouns) were asked to list traits associated with particular nouns, such as *bridge*. *Bridge* in German is feminine, whereas it is masculine in Spanish. German speakers were more likely to refer to bridges as *elegant, fragile, slender*, and *pretty*, whereas Spanish speakers produced more answers such as *big, dangerous, strong*, and *sturdy*, consistent with their language's gender classification. It thus appears that the types of words and grammatical devices used within a language may subtly influence how we conceptualize the world and reason about it (see also Boroditsky, Fuhrman, & McCormick, 2011). As a result, it may be difficult to ever fully translate ideas from one language into a radically different language. However, stronger versions of the linguistic relativity hypothesis have not been supported, and even weak effects may be questionable, as not all studies have confirmed Boroditsky's results (e.g., January & Kako, 2007, Tse & Altarriba, 2008).

PROCESSING FIGURATIVE LANGUAGE: COMPREHENSION OF METAPHOR

The research reviewed in the last few sections has, among other things, provided evidence for underappreciated complexity in comprehension of ordinary verbal materials, ranging from single sentences to entire passages. The occurrence of figurative language poses additional problems for language researchers: How do people understand metaphors that are *not* meant to be interpreted literally? We might think that the use of metaphor is restricted to poetry and other artistic language, such as Shakespeare's description in MacBeth of sleep as "death's counterfeit." However, the use of metaphors is ubiquitous in everyday conversation (Cameron, 2003, 2008, 2011). Metaphors are also common in science lessons (Gentner & Grudin, 1985), TV programs (Graesser, Long, & Mio, 1989), sermons (Corts & Meyers, 2002), college lectures (Corts & Pollio, 1999), and literature (Goatly 1997; Semino & Steen, 2008). Even newspaper headlines contain metaphors:

- Government *drops* plans

- Mayor *eases reins* on city's spending

It has been proposed by Lakoff and Johnson (1980, 2003) that much of our language and conceptual system is based on metaphor, because we use our concrete experiences as the basis for understanding and speaking about more-abstract aspects of life. For example, in speaking about *time*, English speakers sometimes use language based on *a journey*: We move through our lives. We say things like: *We are halfway through summer already*. We also talk about time as a physical resource: *We are running out of time. Can you spare me five minutes?* Similarly, we talk about emotions in physical terms: *I felt my anger rising. He is cold*.

As those examples demonstrate, we speak metaphorically in much of our daily speech. We do not literally journey through time, and an emotionally cold person does not have a body temperature less than average. Lakoff and Johnson (1980/2003) propose that our thinking is metaphorical at its base: We use our early concrete experiences (e.g., going on a journey) and the concepts they entail as the basis for our later learning and speaking about more-abstract domains (e.g., the passage of time). If Lackoff and Johnson are correct, then it becomes important to analyze how figurative language is understood and used.

For the cognitive scientist, the intriguing aspect of figurative language is that, even though such language is not literally true, it is still meaningful. Consider sentence (27).

(27) My lawyer is a shark.

This sentence might be uttered admiringly by someone who is impressed with his lawyer's aggressive attempts to achieve victory in a legal matter. However, sentence (27) is false if interpreted literally (as a shark would have trouble passing the bar exam). We immediately realize that the lawyer is only *figuratively* a shark. That is, the lawyer fights tenaciously, relentlessly, and perhaps viciously for the client.

Metaphor is one example of *figurative language*, where one makes a statement using concepts that are not ordinarily brought together to highlight an aspect of one of the concepts. In a metaphorical utterance, one uses one concept, called the *vehicle* (Richards, 1936), to convey information about a second concept, called the *topic*. Thus, in sentence (27), *shark* is the vehicle used to say something about my lawyer—the *topic*. A *simile* is another example of figurative language, which differs from a metaphor in that it makes an explicit comparison between the vehicle and topic (e.g., *My lawyer is like a shark*).

Early theories of metaphor comprehension (e.g., Grice, 1975, Searle, 1979) proposed that people first try to interpret figurative sentences literally; when that proves fruitless (since metaphors are false when taken literally), a metaphorical interpretation is then considered. So, on seeing sentence (27), one would first think about how a lawyer could be an actual shark, which would be unsuccessful. That failure would lead to consideration of a nonliteral interpretation and comprehension of the metaphor. This implies a two-step process, with an attempt at literal interpretation being the first and nonliteral interpretation being the second. However, there is ample evidence that people interpret metaphors directly, without first attempting a literal interpretation (e.g., Glucksberg, Gildea, & Bookin, 1982; see Gibbs, 1994 for a review).

Contemporary Theories of Metaphor Processing

Two contemporary theories have been proposed to account for people's metaphor comprehension. The *structure-mapping* model of metaphors (Bowdle & Gentner, 1997; Gentner & Wolff, 1997) proposes that metaphors and similes are understood as *analogies*. For instance, a teacher may tell a science class, *The atom is like the solar system*, and then proceed to explain correspondences between the two entities. The teacher does this by setting up an *alignment* or *mapping* between corresponding aspects of the two entities: the electrons are like planets, with orbits around a central entity with an attractional force (nucleus/sun, respectively). No school child assumes that superficial traits get transferred: they don't believe that the electrons of an atom are the same size as planets—rather, only higher-level relational properties such as the spatial structure of each are transferred. The structure-mapping theory proposes that both metaphors and similes are functionally equivalent (e.g., *My lawyer is a shark* = *My lawyer is **like** a shark*), and the two forms of figurative language are processed similarly using an alignment of features between the vehicle and topic, with transfer from vehicle to the less-familiar topic.

A different view of metaphor comprehension—the *category* view—was developed by Glucksberg and Keysar (1990), who proposed that metaphors are understood by treating the vehicle of a metaphorical statement as an abstract category. Thus there is no direct comparison process; the topic is subsumed into the metaphorical category. For instance, *My lawyer is a shark* is interpreted by grouping the topic of the sentence (*my lawyer*) as a member of a broader category of PREDATORY THINGS, of which *sharks* are a prototypical member. The conceptualization of *shark*—as the best example of an abstract category—can be constructed at the time a person interprets a metaphoric sentence (similar to Barsalou's [1991, 2009] ad hoc analysis of concepts and categories, discussed in Chapter 8). For familiar metaphors, in contrast, people may already have abstracted a vehicle category.

Glucksberg and Keysar (1990) cite a number of languages in which the name of a prototypical member of a category can be used to refer to the entire category. For example, in American Sign Language, there is no term for *furniture*, rather, the speaker signs *chair+table+bed*. Similarly, in English, we can say something like "When he was just elected President, Bill Clinton was a JFK," where we mean a young, idealistic president. In addition, it is conceivable that, if we learned something that led us to revise downward our opinion of JFK, we could say "JFK was no JFK," and it, too, would be meaningful. Thus, the term JFK is being used in two ways in that sentence: to refer to a person and to refer to a class of young, idealistic, high-achieving people. Even the form that many metaphors take is categorical: *My job IS a jail*, is similar to category statements such as *An apple IS a fruit*.

In the category view (Glucksberg & Keysar, 1990), the property of sharks that is crucial in formation of the new category *shark* is at a higher level, that of *fierce predators*, as shown in Figure 10.12a. According to this analysis, the metaphorical sentence highlights a feature of the *superordinate category PREDATORY THINGS*, which includes sharks as a prototypical member, and which is now being expanded to include lawyers. If this view is correct, then hearing the sentence *My lawyer is a shark* should *not* activate typical properties of sharks, such as the fact that they *have fins*, *have teeth*, and *swim*, because these are not relevant to communicating anything about the lawyer. Rather, the properties that should be activated are those involved in the more abstract category, such as *vicious* and *relentless*. The metaphorical features are directly extracted from the statement, without setting up analogies and carrying out mappings of properties.

Gernsbacher, Keysar, Robertson, and Werner (2001) carried out a test of the category theory of metaphor processing (see Figure 10.12b). They asked participants to read a long list of target sentences, with the task of judging whether or not each

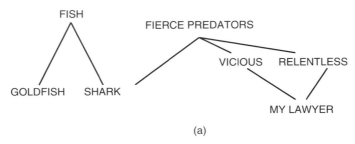

(a)

TARGET SENTENCE	PRIME SENTENCE	
	METAPHOR	LITERAL
Superordinate relevant	That defense lawyer is a shark. Sharks are tenacious.	That large hammerhead is a shark. Sharks are tenacious.
Basic-level relevant	That defense lawyer is a shark. Sharks are good swimmers.	That large hammerhead is a shark. Sharks are good swimmers.

(b)

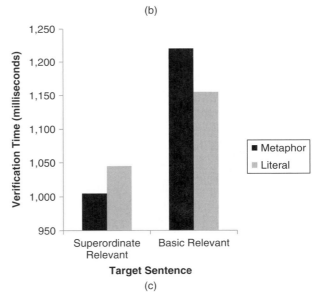

(c)

Figure 10.12 Glucksberg and Keysar's (1990) analysis of the relations underlying comprehension of the sentence "My lawyer is a shark." (a) Analysis. (b) Pairs of sentences from Gernsbacher et al. (2001).

sentence was meaningful. Half the sentences were meaningful. For each target sentence, a priming sentence in the form *X is a Y* appeared first; the priming sentences could be metaphoric (*That defense lawyer is a shark*) or literal (*That large hammerhead is a shark*). The target sentence mentioned a property of the entity that was either relevant to the metaphoric meaning (*Sharks are tenacious*) or the literal meaning (*Sharks are good swimmers*). It was expected that, after reading *metaphoric* primes, people would be quicker to judge as meaningful those sentences that contained other features relevant to the metaphorical interpretation. After a literal prime, they should be faster to respond to target sentences mentioning *literal* traits. The results supported the category view of metaphor: Sentences containing higher-level features relevant to the metaphoric category item (e.g., *tenacious*) were verified as meaningful more quickly than those containing lower-level features of the literal entity (e.g., *good swimmers*). The metaphoric primes led people to activate the metaphoric category meaning, but suppressed more literal traits of the entity.

The Career of Metaphor

We have now examined two views of how metaphors are processed: (1) the structure-mapping theory of Gentner and colleagues (Bowdle & Gentner, 1997; Gentner & Wolff, 1997), which proposes that metaphors are processed as analogies via a comparison process; and (2) the category theory of Glucksberg and Keysar (1990), in which metaphors are processed as category statements. Those two views seem to be in competition, but it has been proposed that they can both explain the data, depending on how familiar a particular metaphor may be. The *career of metaphor* hypothesis, proposed by Bowdle and Gentner (2005), postulates that metaphors are processed as analogies the first few times we hear them, but are processed as categorical statements after they have become familiar. The simile form of figurative sentences lends itself to comparison or analogical comprehension, whereas a metaphor form is more salient for categorical processes. Bowdle and Gentner (2005) presented a list containing figurative sentences, both conventional (e.g., *An opportunity is (like) a doorway*) and novel (e.g., *A mind is (like) a kitchen*) to research participants. Half the time the sentence was presented as a simile (with *like*) and half the time it was presented as a metaphor (without *like*). The participants rated the sentences on a 1 (simile) through 10 (metaphor) scale as to whether they preferred the simile form of a sentence or the metaphorical form. Novel sentences were overwhelmingly preferred in simile form (*X is like Y*; mean rating = 2.81), supporting the idea that they were easier to process as analogical comparisons. However, conventional sentences were more likely to be preferred in categorical *X is Y* form (mean rating = 4.35), showing a tendency toward processing them through categorization. Other research has found that conventionality and familiarity of figurative sentences lead to faster metaphor comprehension times (Blank, 1988; Blasko & Connine, 1993), and has a very large effect on judgments of similarity among the vehicle and topic in metaphors (Bumford & Reeves, 2009). Thus, the "career path" of figurative language starts with comparison/analogical processes and progresses to categorization processes as a metaphor/simile becomes more conventionalized.

Figurative Language: Conclusions

Research on metaphors provides support for the view that use of figurative language is related to our conceptual system, and thus not entirely modular. A number of factors, such as familiarity, conventionality, and level of abstractness, play a role in our comprehension of metaphors. Those factors influence whether metaphors are treated as category statements or whether they undergo a comparison or categorization process. Just as our representations of concepts are constructed to meet our communicative needs (Barsalou, 1983, 1991), our comprehension of metaphorical sentences can be very rapid and conducted online as we listen to a novel figurative sentence.

SENTENCE PROCESSING: CONCLUSIONS

These last two chapters have taken us a long distance, from the first sounds produced by children to the comprehension of complex discourse and the production of sentences. The cognitive science of language is an area in which many different viewpoints come together in attempting to deal with the complexities of the phenomena involved. Linguistic theory (e.g., Chomsky, 1965, 1995; Pinker, 1994) plays a role in providing an understanding of the structure of language, which gives psycholinguistic researchers insight into the phenomena that a theory of language processing must explain. Cognitive researchers (e.g., Nozari & Dell, 2009) have used experimental methods to provide evidence concerning the role of working memory and other processes in comprehension and production of words and sentences. Neurocognitive studies (e.g., Gernsbacher & Robertson, 2004) have examined the role of brain structures in language processing, in normal and patient populations. The study of language thus provides a striking example of the value of multiple perspectives in understanding the complexities of cognitive functioning. In addition, this research area has provided graphic evidence of how modern methods provide means to study underlying cognitive processes, and to formulate and test research hypotheses concerning how internal—mental—processes interact with environmental events to produce behavioral outcomes.

REVIEW QUESTIONS

Here is a set of questions to assist in organizing the material in this chapter.

1. Give some examples of why we cannot assume that humans process sentences in left-to-right order.

2. What is one way to determine if a group of words functions as a phrase in a sentence?

3. What is *recursion* in a phrase-structure grammar and why is it an important property of sentences?

4. What is the difference between *s*- and *d*-structure of sentences?

5. What is the general function of transformational rules in Chomsky's theory?

6. Explain the emergent perspective on sentence processing.

7. How does the study of *garden-path* sentences provide evidence for the *immediacy of interpretation* view of sentence processing?

8. What evidence is there that supports the idea that children's early two- and three-word utterances are sentences?

9. How much of a role does parental correction of children's speech play in syntactic development?

10. Contrast rules-learning versus emergent views of syntactic development.

11. Discuss experimental evidence that children's comprehension precedes their production.

12. Discuss evidence *pro* and *con* the critical-period hypothesis of language development.

13. What does it mean to say that a text is *coherent*?

14. What are the three stages in Gernsbacher's theory of structure building in comprehension?

15. What evidence provides support for the occurrence of building a foundation during comprehension?

16. How is *coherence* signaled during structure building?

17. What brain sites seem to play important roles in mapping?

18. What evidence provides support for the idea of shifting structure during comprehension?

19. What evidence supports the idea that processes involved in comprehension are aspects of general cognitive functioning?

20. Briefly list systematic aspects of different levels of speech errors (i.e., word, morpheme, phoneme).

21. Based on evidence from speech errors, is speech production a serial or an interactive process?

22. What are the *deficient-trace* versus *mapping* explanations of the processing problems exhibited by Broca's aphasics?

23. Discuss evidence for and against the *linguistic-relativity* hypothesis.

24. Explain the differences between *structure-mapping* and *category* views of metaphor comprehension. How are they reconciled by the *career of metaphor* hypothesis?

CHAPTER 11

THINKING I: LOGICAL THINKING AND DECISION MAKING

Before we begin this chapter, please take a look at the questions outlined in Box 11.1.

BOX 11.1 MAKING A DECISION: CHOOSING A MAJOR

What is your major concentration? What factors determined your choice of major? (Interest in the subject matter itself? Friends' opinions? Interest in available courses? Reputations of professors in the department? Research opportunities as an undergraduate? Job prospects after graduation?) Which of those factors (and any others that you might have used) were more versus less important in your final decision? Did you get other information to help make the decision? If so, how did you get that information? If you got it from several sources, did you put more weight on information from one source rather than another?

THINKING AND DECISION MAKING

In the dictionary, the term *thinking* means to have ideas or use the mind. This implies more than a single activity, since using the mind involves a multitude of skills. Within cognitive science, thinking is often used to refer to reasoning, decision making, problem solving, and creativity, all of which are topics of the next three chapters. Each of these activities involves using the mind to produce new ideas.

Making a Decision

At some point in their college careers, most students have to choose a major concentration. In Box 11.1 we raise questions about some factors that might have played a role in such a decision. Imagine that a student who hopes to pursue a career as a professor has narrowed her possible choices of a major to art history or psychology. The factors that play a role in this student's decision, ranging from her initial interest in the two subjects (her interest in art history is higher) to the career prospects for each, are listed in the left-hand column in Table 11.1. Some of her goals—availability of interesting courses and good professors—are short-term, while others—availability of positions in graduate school and prospects for an academic career—are longer-term. The student then gathers evidence concerning how well a major in art history versus psychology will enable her to achieve those goals. She acquires information by talking to other students and professors, searches the Internet for information, contacts

Table 11.1 Choosing a Major: Goals That the Student Wants to Meet in Choosing a Major, and the Results of Research on Each Goal*

Goal Student Wishes to Achieve by Choosing a Major	Possible Majors	
	Psychology	Art History
Initial situation: Area of interest; enjoyable as a potential career	+	++
Interesting courses available	+	+
Quality of teaching	+	+
Scholarly reputation of faculty	++	0
Prospects of entering graduate school (availability of grad-school slots)	+	−
Career prospects; possibility of university position	++	−

*+/0/− in cells indicate how well the two possible majors meet that goal.

potential graduate schools, and looks for reports on availability of faculty positions in those two disciplines.

The two other columns in Table 11.1 show the results of her research: How likely each goal will be met is rated for each major. Based on the information she has gathered, the two possible courses of action change in their relative attractiveness, as shown in Figure 11.1. The student begins with a more-positive feeling toward art history, but switches to psychology as she works through the decision. Most critically, she learns that there are limitations both in numbers of graduate-school slots in art history programs and in numbers of art history faculty positions available. Based on the outcome of her research, this student is likely to choose psychology as a major.

In sum, decisions involve formulating and choosing courses of action, based on one's goals, using any evidence that is available. If this type of thinking is done well

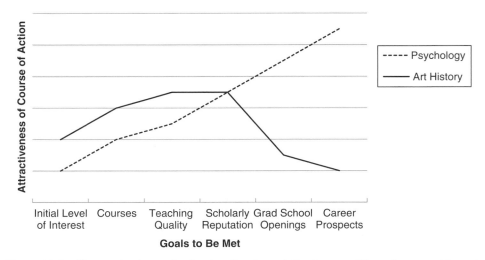

Figure 11.1 Changes in the student's attraction toward the two possible majors as evidence is gathered and considered.

(i.e., systematically), we can call it *rational thinking*, which is thinking that is maximally effective in enabling us to achieve our goals (Baron, 2008). The term *rational thinking* can also be applied to thinking that conforms to the rules of logic or to mathematical or statistical laws. While most of us would hope to carry out rational thinking, there is much evidence that humans often are less-than-rational thinkers. In this chapter, we will consider why humans might sometimes be irrational, and what might be done to make humans more rational.

OUTLINE OF CHAPTER 11

The chapter begins with a brief general consideration of rational versus irrational thinking. We then turn to specific biases people exhibit, and review evidence from the past 40 years that has led many researchers to the conclusion that humans are irrational decision-makers. We begin with a discussion of the factors that are important in gathering, remembering, and evaluating evidence relevant to deciding on a course of action. For example, people sometimes search inefficiently for evidence relevant to possible actions, which may lead us to a decision that is not maximal to achieving our goals. Next, we consider how people draw conclusions from the evidence they gather, and will see that people sometimes make mistakes in drawing conclusions from evidence. Finally, after all the evidence is gathered and assessed, we sometimes do a less-than-perfect job in formulating the alternative courses of action that are available to us, which can result in decision making that does not maximally achieve our goals—a further example of less-than-rational thinking.

Although much of the research to be presented in this chapter is based on a negative premise—that humans are naturally irrational or nonoptimal thinkers—there has been some recent movement away from this relatively gloomy conclusion (e.g., Gigerenzer, 2008; Hart & Mas-Colell, 2003). Researchers have proposed that, even if humans are not for the most part rational thinkers, people can be trained to improve their reasoning skills (e.g., Sedlmeier, 1999), and we will examine this research. Finally, it has been proposed that human reasoning might exhibit *bounded rationality*: We make decisions that, if not optimal, are at least "good enough" (Gigerenzer, 2008; Gigerenzer & Todd, 1999; Simon, 1956, 1978). The chapter will conclude with a review of that research.

THE QUESTION OF HUMAN RATIONALITY

Long before psychologists began to study decision making and reasoning, philosophers, logicians, and mathematicians had discussed the question of how human thinking worked. Most founders of logical systems, such as Aristotle (384–322 B.C.), adopted the general conclusion that ordinary thinking was logical—that is, rational—at its base, and that untutored humans could efficiently make decisions. For example, both Thomas Bayes (1702–1761)—a pioneer in the development of statistics related to making decisions based on the mathematical evidence—and George Boole (1815–1864)—the founder of the Boolean logic system upon which modern digital computers are based—believed that they were only making formal what humans ordinarily did on their own. Rational models of human decision making assume that humans can access relevant information, calculate mathematical probabilities, and arrive at the same conclusions as statisticians and other experts.

One such example of a rational theory that arose out of economic research was *expected value theory* (Pascal, 1670/1995). Expected value theory views every decision as a gamble, and allows one to determine the value of any decision based on the costs versus the probabilities of specific benefits. For example, say a friend offers you a lottery ticket for $1.00 as part of a fundraiser for the charity she belongs to. She tells you that there are two prizes in the lottery, $10 and $5, and the probability of winning each is 0.10 and 0.30, respectively. Based on that information, you could calculate the probability of winning each prize amount added to the probability of losing, to determine the worth—the expected value (EV)—of the ticket:

$$EV = (0.1 \times \$10) + (0.3 \times \$5) + (0.6 \times 0) = \$2.50$$

Based on this calculation, it is worth investing in the ticket, since the expected value of $2.50 is more than the cost of the ticket.

However, expected value theory is *normative*—it illustrates what people *should* do to make rational decisions, not what they actually do. For example, EV predicts that when offered a choice between: (a) $1 million versus (b) a 50% chance of $3 million, people should choose option (b), because a 50% chance of $3 million works out to an expected value of $1.5 million. However, most people prefer the cold hard cash in hand. As we shall see throughout this chapter, people often act in ways that are counter to the logical and statistical conclusions advocated by formal systems.

Questions About Humans as Rational Thinkers

In the 20th century, the view that humans reason rationally (such as by using expected value) was brought into question from several directions. Economists noted that people did not always behave in the ways predicted by models of rational decision making. For one, decisions are often made under conditions of *uncertainty*, where exact probabilities and payoffs are not known. Secondly, there are often extraneous factors, such as emotions or habits, that lead us to make more-subjective judgments than expected-value theory predicts. Led by a series of important investigations by Kahneman and Tversky (1973; Kahneman, Slovic, & Tversky, 1982; Tversky & Kahneman, 1974), psychologists demonstrated that people have difficulties in all aspects of decision making, which has resulted in the general conclusion that humans are often less-than-rational organisms.

The viewpoint developed by Kahneman and Tversky (1973, 1979), often referred to as the *heuristics-and-biases view*, has been very influential. It proposes that people use *heuristics*—general strategies that may facilitate decisions but which do not guarantee success—to help them make decisions. These heuristic methods, which are different than the formal rules of logic and probability theory, can result in people making less-than-optimal—that is, irrational—decisions. In addition, people often show systematic *biases* in their reasoning, another form of irrationality. Much research effort has been expended on understanding the reasons behind this supposed irrationality in human thinking and on developing methods to increase rationality in thinking.

Dysrationalia

Stanovich (1993, 2009; Stanovich & West, 2007) coined the term *dysrationalia*, an analogy to *dyslexia*, as a label for a person's inability to think rationally despite possessing adequate intelligence. In Stanovich's view, thinking rationally is often independent of the type of thinking (i.e., intelligence) that is measured by I.Q. tests. Instead, he thinks of dysrationalia as a deficit in belief formation or in evaluating the consistency of our beliefs, which represents a basic flaw in humans' capacity to carry out rational thinking.

We begin our review of the question of whether humans are rational by examining how people gather and evaluate evidence relevant to the goals they hope to achieve.

THE AVAILABILITY HEURISTIC: RETRIEVABILITY AS A FACTOR IN GATHERING EVIDENCE

Consider the decision faced by a person who wants to drive the safest car possible, and who is trying to decide whether to buy car X or Y. One could read as much as possible about crash-test results, and check surveys in buying guides, to gather evidence to determine which car was safer. Such methods would maximize the chances that the individual would base the decision on the best-available and most-complete evidence. However, we sometimes bypass gathering external evidence, and use what we *remember* about the alternatives as the basis for making a decision. You might remember hearing a neighbor say that car X is very safe, and that memory might influence you to buy that kind of car.

As we know from earlier chapters, memory is fallible, and not all information is remembered equally well. When we rely on memory for evidence during decision making, it can result in erroneous decisions. We have seen that cues can affect the information that a person is able to retrieve, which in turn can affect the decision that the person will make. The *availability heuristic* is the name given to situations in which people rely—perhaps incorrectly—on easily recalled information as the basis for making a decision (Tversky & Kahneman, 1973).

Please carry out the exercise in Box 11.2 before reading further.

Important judgments in real-life situations can be affected by how easily a person can retrieve information, often based on its *salience*. The dramatic or personal nature of some events may lead to their increased retrievability, which is why anecdotal evidence sometimes influences us more heavily than statistics (Bar-Hillel, 1980; Borgida & Nisbett, 1977; Fagerlin, Wang, & Ubel, 2005). Seeing your neighbor's house burn down might provide more of an impetus to invest in a smoke detector than reading a newspaper article about the frequency of house fires in your state. Likewise, people often make negative decisions about whether to swim in the ocean after seeing a shark movie, or about traveling by plane after hearing about a plane accident.

BOX 11.2 ESTIMATES OF FREQUENCY OF VARIOUS CAUSES OF DEATH

For each of the following causes, make an estimate of the probability in a given year that a person will die of that cause. For each million deaths in the population, how many would be expected from each cause?

Cancer (any type)

Flood

Asthma

Firearm accident

Motor vehicle accident (car, truck, bus)

Heart disease

Tornado

Diabetes

Botulism

Suicide

Stroke

All accidents

Adapted from Lichtenstein et al., 1978.

The influence of the availability heuristic was seen in a study in which people were asked to assess the risks of dying from various causes. They often overestimated dangers that have been recently publicized or reported in a dramatic way. Lichtenstein, Slovic, Fischhoff, Layman, and Combs (1978) asked participants to judge the likelihoods of various causes of death and their relative magnitudes, as was done in Box 11.2. For example, if given motor vehicle accident and heart disease, based on the statistical probabilities, one should estimate that heart disease was 14 times more likely to kill a person than a motor vehicle accident (see Table 11.2). However, people were not always accurate in their estimations. The results, a sample of which is presented in Table 11.3, indicated that people (students and members of the League of Women Voters, or LWV, the latter chosen because they are well-informed members of the community) consistently overestimated the least probable dangers and underestimated the most probable. For example, the most overestimated causes of death tended to be dramatic ones that make the news, such as botulism, lightning, tornadoes, homicides, and accidents. The most underestimated causes were nonsensational events such as asthma, tuberculosis, diabetes, strokes, and heart disease. As can be seen in Table 11.3, the same overall pattern of results held for both the students and the LWV members.

Our judgments may derive from our experience with news reports, which emphasize exotic or unusual deaths, and do not report ordinary causes of death. Thus, the unusual deaths become more easily retrieved, resulting in flawed probability estimates, which then influence subsequent decision making. For example, if one were a government official who had to make a decision as to whether to spend money on

Table 11.2   Actual Probabilities of Dying by Various Causes
(frequency of death per 1 million fatalities)

Cause	Deaths per 1 Million Fatalities
Botulism	0.01
Tornado	0.4
Flood	1
Firearms	11
Suicide	120
Diabetes	190
Motor vehicle accident (e.g., car, bus, truck)	270
Stroke	1,020
Heart disease	3,600

Table 11.3   Ways to Die: Paired Comparison Data of Participants
(Students or Members of the League of Women Voters)

Less Likely	More Likely	Ratio More/ Less Likely	% Correct Students	% Correct League of Women Voters
Suicide	Diabetes	1.6	25	31
All accidents	Stroke	1.85	20	23
Diabetes	Motor vehicle accidents	1.42	99	96
Stroke	Cancer	1.57	83	75

trying to protect people from accidents or for research into stroke, a recent experience in an accident might lead one to conclude that risk from accidents is greater, and so prevention of accidents should be funded more. In actuality, however, death from stroke is many times more likely, and so, all other things being equal, should be given higher priority. Thus, one must guard against the possibility that availability has biased one's decision about the frequencies of events.

Research on perceived evaluations of risks in various activities has found that people are overly concerned about certain types of situations, especially those in which large numbers of people might be killed in an unanticipated manner (Slovic, 1987). *Dread risk* is the term used for people's fear about such situations. An example of a hidden negative influence of dread risk has been presented by Gigerenzer (2004), who analyzed the unforeseen consequences of the terrorist attacks of September 11, 2001. As a result of those attacks, many Americans developed a dread of flying, as demonstrated by a decrease in airplane passengers in the last 3 months of 2001 compared to the first 8 months. Gigerenzer compared the numbers of passengers in 2001 with the average of the 4 preceding years, and found that the first 8 months of 2001 were consistent with the flying rates for 1996–2000, but that the figures for October, November, and December, following the attacks, were less than earlier years. A significant number of those avoiding air travel seemed to have switched to automobiles, as there was an increase in driving, especially on rural interstate highways, suggesting that people were using their cars for long-distance travel. However, that additional driving had a negative outcome: more accidents than would have occurred had those people taken planes. Gigerenzer estimated that approximately 350 additional people died in auto accidents in the last 3 months of 2001, which is more than the number of airplane passengers who perished in the terrorist attacks. So, in the attempt to avoid a possible but unlikely catastrophe that filled them with dread, a significant number of people died, in a manner that we all know about and live with, with little dread.

Other researchers have estimated that *dread risk* accounts for about 75% of decision making in risk estimations (Fischhoff, Slovic, Lichtenstein, Read, & Combs, 1978; Slovic, Fischhoff, & Lichtenstein, 1982, 1984, 1985). For example, we judge the probability of things that often cause dramatic consequences or death (e.g., rattlesnakes, death from a terrorist attack) to be more likely than those events or dangers that are more frequent, but are typically associated with only bodily damage or less dramatic deaths (e.g., death from a car crash).

Similar factors can affect other decisions in our lives. For example, people make decisions about where to live based on feelings about the safety of a neighborhood or the quality of the schools. One's feelings about different neighborhoods can be a function of what one remembers concerning them. If one or two stories of crimes make big headlines in the newspapers, we might mistakenly think that one neighborhood is racked by crime, when retrievability of the information is directing our judgment. The availability heuristic has been used to explain decision making in a variety of contexts (e.g., by game show contestants, Matsen & Strøm, 2010; and stock market investors, Kliger & Kudryavtsev, 2010).

The Context of Judgment: Anchoring-and-Adjustment Effects in Gathering Evidence

A different sort of cognitive limitation on processing evidence was shown in a study by Tversky and Kahneman (1974). High-school students were given one of two multiplication problems, and asked to quickly look at their problem and estimate the answer within 5 seconds. They were told not to actually calculate the answer. The two problems were the following.

Problem A: $8 \times 7 \times 6 \times 5 \times 4 \times 3 \times 2 \times 1$

Problem B: $1 \times 2 \times 3 \times 4 \times 5 \times 6 \times 7 \times 8$

As is easily seen, the two problems are mathematically identical and differ only in the order of numbers (which is irrelevant in multiplication), but the median answer for Problem A was 2,250, while for Problem B it was 512 (Tversky and Kahneman, 1974). When carrying out their estimates, people presumably used the first number or the first few numbers in each multiplication problem as an *anchor*, or *reference point*, and that anchor pushed the overall estimate up or down. The responses from *both* groups taken together may also illustrate anchoring; because the multiplication problem uses all single-digit numbers, people's estimates were much lower than the actual answer of 40,320.

Thus, the starting point from which we begin reasoning can affect our thinking. Anchoring can occur even when anchors are completely unrelated to a decision. Ariely, Loewenstein, and Prelec (2003) asked people to write down the last two digits of their Social Security numbers. Despite its irrelevance to the value of a prestigious bottle of wine, when asked, people with lower social security numbers were willing to pay significantly less for a bottle of Côtes du Rhône 1998 than those who had just written down high two-digit numbers. Those with Social Security numbers ending in 80–99 offered prices 200–300% higher than the bids of those with social security numbers ending in 01–20.

Anchoring in Real Life: Harvard Versus Yale, 1968

In 1968, the headline of the Harvard student newspaper, the *Harvard Crimson*, proclaimed, "Harvard beats Yale, 29–29." How could Harvard beat Yale, you might ask, if the score was tied at 29 apiece? Yale was the heavily favored team, with a 16-game winning streak under its belt, and a spectacular quarterback, Brian Dowling. When Yale led 22–6 by halftime, most spectators thought a Yale win was a foregone conclusion. During the second half, Yale fans waved white handkerchiefs at the Harvard fans—the universal sign of surrender—and chanted "We're number 1!"

Yale maintained a decisive lead in the second half, though Harvard continued to inch the score forward until the score was 29–21 in Yale's favor. After a tremendously exciting drive, Harvard scored with only three seconds left on the clock. A two-point conversion tied the score, 29–29, and the Harvard fans went wild.

The anchoring effect can explain the Harvard Crimson headline: Harvard was expected to lose the game. With these lowered expectations, even a tie-game felt like a win, and so they adjusted upwards to "We won!" and stormed the field in joy. Alternately, the players and fans of Yale, whose anchor was the expectation of a win, felt dejected about the tie. As the Yale coach remarked, "It was almost like a nightmare, really.... We feel like we lost it, even though we didn't" (Cozza, 1968, quoted on www.nd.edu/~tmandell/harvard/html). Thus, depending on a person's college affiliation, and whether their team was *expected* to win or lose, a tie was viewed either as a victory (Harvard) or a defeat (Yale).

Anchoring Effects: Conclusions

What these results tell us is that the starting point of a person's reasoning often anchors it, and further adjustments often only deviate slightly from the anchor. This is why salespeople often start the bidding at a high price; when they indicate a willingness to accept a lower price for the car (or a furniture set or an apartment etc.) the customer then views it as a good deal because it is lower than the original anchor.

Cognitive Factors in Gathering Evidence: Conclusions

Before evaluating possible courses of action in some situation, one must consider how one obtained the evidence for and against those courses of action. If the evidence is based on memory—either your own memory or that of someone else—then that evidence may be erroneous or biased. These errors may arise from problems with encoding, when information was not adequately stored in the first place, or during retrieval, as when the cues that were used to remember the information highlight some aspect of the situation over another. In addition, information with a personal tinge (e.g., anecdotal information) may be deemed more relevant than statistical information because of its greater availability.

DIFFICULTIES USING EVIDENCE

Once our hypothetical decision-maker has obtained evidence relevant to several alternative courses of action, he or she must use those pieces of evidence in order to make a decision among those actions. There are two sorts of situations to be considered concerning evaluation of evidence. First is the situation in which people rely on their beliefs, which may make new evidence difficult to accept or to use accurately. One example of this is when people make judgments based on similarity to previous experiences, rather than on the objective evidence, as can be seen in situations involving the *representativeness heuristic*. Another illustration of the tendency to base decisions on our own beliefs is the *confirmation bias* (also known as the *myside bias*) when evaluating evidence (Baron, 2008; Perkins, 1985; Plous, 1993). Secondly, difficulty in decision making can arise when you only have incomplete evidence, which does not point definitively to one conclusion. Sometimes evidence indicates only that one outcome is more *probable* than another, which requires that the person carry out statistical reasoning. People are often not adept at statistical reasoning, which leads to difficulties in making decisions. These two sorts of irrationality are examined next.

Representativeness Heuristic

There are other psychological factors that influence the weight a person assigns to information used to make a decision. Consider the following questions: If you were to flip a coin six times, which of the following sequences do you think is most likely? Which is least likely?

1. H T H T H T
2. H H H T T T
3. H T T H T H
4. H H H H H H

Most people who respond to those sequences think it much less likely that an honest coin would come up HHHHHH than HTTHTH. Their reasoning seems to go something like this: If a coin is honest, then it should generate a random sequence of heads and tails, but the sequence HHHHHH does not look like it was generated by a random process. The HTTHTH (#3) sequence, on the other hand, looks random, so it seems more likely that it would be generated by an honest coin. Thus, our judgment of the likelihood of a result is influenced by our knowledge about how the result was produced. However, *all the sequences are equally likely*. For each coin-flip, the probability of obtaining a head or tail is 0.5. Therefore, the probability of obtaining sequence 1 (HTTHTH) is $0.5 \times 0.5 \times 0.5 \times 0.5 \times 0.5 \times 0.5$, which is *exactly* the same as the probability of obtaining any of the other sequences.

So why do we make a judgment based on how right each sequence looks, rather than the probability of obtaining each sequence? Kahneman and Tversky (1973, Tversky & Kahneman, 1974) suggest that we evaluate each outcome based on how *representative* it is of the process that we believe brought it about. That is, if we are dealing with a random process, then any outcome of that process should look random. Similarly, if we are trying to decide whether a candidate for office is honest, we might focus on her upright posture and open expression as being representative of an honest person (even though evidence suggests we are notoriously bad at accurately judging another person's honesty; DePaulo, Stone, & Lassiter, 1985; Kraut, 1980; Vrij, Edward, Roberts, & Bull, 2000). Kahneman and Tversky concluded that we are often influenced by the *representativeness heuristic*: the tendency to give the greatest weight to occurrences that resemble, or are similar to, high-frequency events from the past.

Garb (1996; see also Garb, 2005) explored the extent to which clinical psychologists exhibited criteria-based judgments (e.g., using the symptom lists from the *Diagnostic and Statistical Manual-III* and *IV*) versus the representativeness heuristic when making diagnoses of patients' mental illnesses. Garb asked clinicians to rate their confidence about a diagnosis of several case studies; and to rate the similarity of each patient to "typical" patients who had obtained that diagnosis. Only 27% of the clinicians made diagnoses that adhered strictly to DSM criteria; the others' diagnoses were better explained by similarity ratings to prototypical patients, thus illustrating the power of the representativeness heuristic even in the face of objective norms (DSM-IV criteria) that could be used.

Confirmation (or Myside) Bias in Evaluating Evidence

We have just seen that memory distortions in gathering evidence may lead people to make decisions that are less than optimal. This is an example of *unintentional* irrational thinking, since the person might not realize that he or she is retrieving biased information from memory. A different sort of irrationality in evaluating evidence has been demonstrated by Stanovich and West (2008a), who have shown that people are more likely to assess evidence positively when it supports their perspective on some issue. Please carry out the exercise in Box 11.3 now.

The two situations in Box 11.3 are identical except for the nationality of the vehicle they refer to. American college students asked to make the judgments requested in Box 11.3 were more likely to agree that the German car should be banned from American roads than that the American vehicle should be banned from German roads (Stanovich & West, 2008b). Thus, the same objective information led to different courses of action for American versus German cars, depending on how it fit the decision-makers' beliefs and values. Information that better confirmed a person's beliefs was weighed more heavily. That confirmation bias manifests itself in several ways (Nickerson, 1998). First, people are most apt to *seek out* information that corroborates their existing position. Second, people are most likely to *weigh* information highly during decision making if it supports their position, and to disregard evidence that goes against their view. In a study by Russell and Jones (1980), believers in extrasensory perception (ESP) who were shown disconfirming evidence about the validity of ESP tended to remember less information, and to remember the evidence less accurately, presumably to maintain their pre-experiment beliefs in ESP. In addition, once people have made a decision, they are more likely to seek out additional information that is consistent with that decision, and to rate consistent information as more credible (Fischer, Jonas, Frey, & Kastenmüller, 2008). Thus, the strength or usefulness of evidence does not depend solely on the information itself: Its value is filtered through the overall beliefs of the individual. This is a clear example of irrationality.

BOX 11.3 CARS ON THE ROAD: AN EXAMPLE OF A BIAS IN REASONING

Read each of the following paragraphs and answer the question at the end of each.

A. Ford Explorer
According to a comprehensive study by the U.S. Department of Transportation, Ford Explorers are 8 times more likely than a typical family car to kill occupants of another car in a crash. The Department of Transportation in Germany is considering recommending a ban on the sale of the Ford Explorer in Germany. Do you think that Germany should ban the sale of the Ford Explorer?

Yes _____   No _____

B. German Car
According to a comprehensive study by the U.S. Department of Transportation, a particular German car is 8 times more likely than a typical family car to kill occupants of another car in a crash. The U.S. Department of Transportation is considering recommending a ban on the sale of this German car.
Should the United States ban the sale of that German car?

Yes _____   No _____

Stanovich and West (2008a, Experiments 1, 2, and 3) demonstrated additional aspects of the *myside bias*. Students were divided on the basis of their answers to one of seven personal questions (e.g., whether they were a smoker/nonsmoker, whether they were in- or out-of-state students, etc.). When asked to indicate their agreement with propositions such as, *The tuition that James Madison University* [the students' university] *charges out-of-state students is too high relative to what it charges in-state students*, out-of-state students were more likely to agree with this statement. Also, people were more likely to judge an argument as well constructed when it was in favor of their own position. The validity of the structure of an argument has nothing to do with the actual position it is advocating, but people were influenced by the position nonetheless. Both these results illustrate a clear myside bias.

Illusory Correlations
A prevalent example of the confirmation bias is when people perceive a relationship between two variables, even when there is no evidence to support that judgment. For example, the vast majority of parents believe that copious amounts of sugar at birthday parties or at Halloween make children hyperactive (Wolraich et al., 1994; Wolraich,

Milich, Stumbo, & Schultz, 1985). However, more than 20 studies have not found any relationship between sugar intake and out-of-control behavior (Ferguson, Stoddart, & Simeon, 1986; Milich & Pelham, 1986; Wolraich et al., 1985; Wolraich et al., 1994; see Rojas & Chan, 2005, for a review); the hyperactivity is more likely due to children's enthusiasm for special events at which sugar is served (e.g., birthday parties). Parents and teachers who begin with the belief that sugar intake causes hyperactivity may be more likely to see evidence in their children's behavior that confirms this view, and to maintain their belief in a correlation which is merely illusory.

Overcoming Confirmation/Myside Bias

One way to try to overcome a myside bias is to see a situation from the other side. For example, in judging whether an American car should be taken off German roads, consider the same question from the perspective of whether a German car should be removed from American roads. If you say yes in the latter case, then, all things equal, you should say yes also in the former case (Stanovich & West, 2008a). Much of the tendency to engage in a confirmation/myside bias is due to selective searching for information that solidifies one's own position. However, when people are explicitly presented with falsifying evidence for a belief they hold, many are able to overcome this bias (Mynatt, Doherty, & Tweney, 1977).

Studies of Statistical Reasoning: Making Decisions Based on Incomplete Evidence

Evidence does not usually come to us in neat summary packages that we can apply to the situations in our lives (Wallsten, Budescu, Rapoport, Zwick, & Forsyth, 1986). For example, a college student trying to decide on a major will not usually suddenly discover a single piece of evidence that encapsulates all aspects of the problem she is facing and directly leads to a specific course of action. Rather, information usually comes to us in pieces from our experiences, and we must determine the general consequences that follow from them. Furthermore, people reason differently, depending on whether they are provided with *a priori* probabilities (e.g., when given in mathematical form) versus when they have personal or anecdotal evidence (Freymuth & Ronan, 2004). Imagine the following exchange.

SUSAN: I am trying to decide on art history or psychology as a major. Do you know anything about the quality of teaching in the two departments?

STEVE: I took intro psych and one other course and both professors were not well organized. I am not taking more psych classes.

How much weight should Susan give to Steve's conclusion?

In this example, Steve presents to Susan a general conclusion concerning the quality of the teaching in the psychology department. Imagine that Steve is at a large university with more than 45 psychology professors. He has had experience with only a small minority of the teachers in that department, and concluded from that experience that *all* psychology professors are poor teachers. Formulating a general conclusion from a *set* or *sample* of specific experiences is called *induction* or *inductive reasoning*. That general conclusion can then serve as evidence in making inferences to new, similar situations. Susan must decide whether she thinks Steve's conclusion is *valid*, that is, whether it follows from the evidence he has.

Much of the reliability of induction is based on the quantity and quality of information that is available when making decisions. Research studying inductive reasoning involves providing people with *statistical evidence*, and asking them to make decisions based on those statistics. You can work through some problems based on statistical evidence in Box 11.4.

BOX 11.4 STATISTICAL EXERCISES

A. Law of Large Numbers: Pieces of Information From Large Versus Small Samples and Which Is to Be Believed

Keith has just arrived in Las Vegas for the first time, and he is eager to win some money at the slots. He stops for gas, and there are two slot machines in the gas station. He watches a woman put two quarters in each machine. The one on the left pays out once, while the other machine does not. He decides to play the machine on the left. As he is about to do so, an elderly man sitting in the station tells him that he has been watching people play those machines for years, and in his experience, the right-hand machine pays out more frequently. Assuming that the man's recollection is accurate and that he is telling the truth, which machine should Keith play?

B. Sample Size and Extreme Values

In a small town nearby, there are two hospitals. Hospital A has an average of 45 births per day. Hospital B is smaller, averaging 15 births per day. On a given day, which hospital has the greater chance of having a proportion of either boys' or girls' births *greater* than 0.60?

Adapted from Fong and Nisbett (1991).

Formulating Inductions: Belief in the Law of Small Numbers

One of the most important determinants of how much faith you should put into an inductive generalization is the *size of the sample of observations*. Small samples do not yield very reliable generalizations. Imagine a child who concludes that all tigers are white on the basis of only being exposed to one albino tiger at the zoo; that would clearly be erroneous. Let's consider a more formal statistical example. Assume that the average height of an adult male in the United States is five-foot-ten. Which is more likely to approximate the average U.S. male height: the mean from a random sample of 3 men, or a random sample of 50 men? It is possible that your sample of 3 men could contain one very short or tall man, which would throw off your average, whereas a few short or tall men in the sample of 50 would not have as much impact on the overall average. Therefore, the answer is that the sample of 50 men would provide a mean height closer to the actual mean height of U.S. males.

This phenomenon is summarized in statistics as the *Law of Large Numbers*, which says that, the larger the sample of observations, the greater the chances that the result will match the true result. Thus, in our psychology-major example, since Steve has taken only two psychology courses, Susan should be skeptical about the accuracy of his conclusion. If Steve had taken classes from 8–10 professors, she could have more confidence in his report concerning the department. However, research studies have demonstrated that people often do not take sample size into account when they gather evidence. People seem to have an inaccurate belief that small sample sizes approximate a population in the same way, and with the same accuracy, as large sample sizes (Tversky & Kahneman, 1971).

Base Rates

Imagine two patients brought into the emergency room complaining of chest pain. If one is an 8-year-old boy, and the other is a 60-year-old man, the physician will be more concerned that the older patient has suffered a heart attack, even if they both share symptoms. Why? Because the doctor's decision-making process will be affected by the probability of heart disease occurring in patients of different age groups, in other words, by the *base rate* of various diseases in different age groups. If the available evidence points to multiple diagnoses, knowing the base rates for specific diagnoses or possibilities can be helpful in making the appropriate decision/diagnosis.

However, people do not always pay attention to base rates when reasoning from statistical information. Evidence suggests that even experts in a field may have inaccurate base-rate expectations. For instance, Maserejian, Lutfey, and McKinlay (2009) asked physicians to: (1) rate the prevalence of coronary heart disease in men versus women, and then (2) make patient diagnoses from videotapes in which actors described symptoms (with the same symptoms presented by male versus female actors). Although heart disease is equally prevalent in men and women, about half of physicians thought it was more prevalent in men. Fortunately, holding biased base rates did not lead to discrepancies in diagnosis: Physicians were able to use the individual symptoms of each case to accurately diagnose patients. However, biased base rates may have been the cause of their greater *confidence* about male diagnoses. That confidence might have arisen as a result of the representativeness heuristic: Men having a heart attack exhibit more prototypical symptoms, such as sudden chest pain, than do women; women's symptoms may present more as fatigue, shortness of breath, or back pain (heartdisease.about.com; www.medicinenet.com).

Based on results such as those just discussed, it seems that base rates are not always taken into account when evaluating evidence, even when such information is directly provided (Kahneman & Tversky, 1982). Often, objective data are overruled by the representativeness heuristic (see Koehler, 1996 for review). As we shall see later in the chapter, people frequently ignore base rates during more complex statistical reasoning (though there are ways to train decision-makers to be sensitive to base rates).

Conjunction Fallacy

A striking example of problems with statistical reasoning comes from demonstrations of the *conjunction fallacy*, presented initially by Tversky and Kahneman (1983). Consider the following description:

> Linda is 31 years old, single, outspoken, and very bright. She majored in philosophy. As a student, she was deeply concerned with issues of discrimination and social justice, and also participated in antinuclear demonstrations.

Based on that information, which is more likely?

(1) Linda is a bank teller.

(2) Linda is a bank teller and is active in the feminist movement.

Tversky and Kahneman (1983) found that 85% of people chose option (2), presumably because the description of Linda seems more representative of (2) than (1). That choice is, however, incorrect, because the probability of two events—Linda being a bank teller *and* being a feminist—occurring together (in what is called a *conjunction* in statistics) can *never* be larger than the probabilities of either of the events occurring alone. As you learned if you have taken a statistics course, the probability of a conjunction of events A and B—that is, of A *and* B occurring together—is determined by multiplying the probabilities of either event occurring alone. Assume that the probability that Linda is a bank teller is 0.8 and the probability that she is a feminist is 0.5. The probability of the conjunction is $0.8 \times 0.5 = 0.4$, which is less than the likelihood of *either* option by itself. No matter what probability you assign to Linda being a feminist, the likelihood that she is *both* a bank teller and feminist cannot be greater than the probability of her being a only bank teller.

Thus, people's intuitions about Linda are inaccurate. One explanation for the occurrence of the conjunction fallacy is that it is due to the representativeness heuristic (Tversky & Kahneman, 1983). Recall from the discussion of the role of folk theories in concepts in Chapter 8—that people are aware of correlations of traits for some categories, such as BIRDs having both feathers and beaks. Thus, we may implicitly store information on when certain traits occur together (such as engineers liking mathematical puzzles) and use that information as the basis for reasoning. In addition, some correlated traits are based on causal relations (e.g., having wings allows birds to fly). This may mean that the use of representativeness is often adaptive in real life, and does not afford the same dysrationalia bias on a daily basis that it does in experimental studies. In fact, Crisp and Feeney (2009) found that the conjunction fallacy was most pronounced when people perceived a strong causal relationship between the two variables.

Nilsson and Andersson (2010) confirmed people's use of the conjunction fallacy in real life. They explored people's bets on single versus multiple outcomes of soccer games in Europe. Assume that each bet on a single game has 2:1 odds. If the odds for the single game bet are 2:1, then the odds for a double-game bet are $2:1 \times 2:1 = 4:1$, and the odds for a triple-game bet are $2:1 \times 2:1 \times 2:1 = 8:1$. When asked to rate their confidence of winning single versus multiple bets, the median confidence for the single bets was higher, indicating that people understood conjunctive bets had a lower probability. However, confidence ratings for two-game and three-game bets were equivalent, showing that bettors clearly failed to realize that three-game bets should have a lower likelihood of being successful than two-game bets.

Statistical Reasoning: Conclusions

Research using a variety of problems indicates that people have difficulties carrying out statistical reasoning. When people carry out inductive reasoning, drawing a general conclusion from specific pieces of data, they are prone to accept a generalization based on a too-small sample. Thus, many people have an incorrect belief in the law of small numbers. We also tend not to take fully into account the base rates of the possible alternate outcomes. Finally, people often fall prey to the conjunction fallacy, perhaps because we use representativeness as the basis for a decision.

CHOOSING POSSIBLE COURSES OF ACTION: FRAMING EFFECTS

We have now reached the last point in making a decision: The individual has accumulated evidence concerning outcomes of possible courses of action and now has to choose among them. A rational person should evaluate possible courses of action solely on the basis of the objective value of the expected outcome of each. Let us say that Action A results in your gaining $10, while Action B results in your gaining $100; if all other things are equal, it seems obvious which action should be chosen. On the other hand, if two actions have the same outcome (e.g., they both result in your gaining $50), then—again, all other things equal—those actions should be equally attractive choices. However, research has shown that possible actions with the same objective outcome can be differentially preferred, depending on how those outcomes are *described* or *framed*. Please work through the exercises in Box 11.5 before reading further.

The four options in Box 11.5 are *equivalent* in terms of probability of numbers of survivors and nonsurvivors. In program A, the certain outcome is that 200 people will be saved, and in program B that is also the outcome that can be expected, given the stated probabilities. That is, the expected outcome in program B is:

$$(1/3 \text{ probability} \times 600 \text{ saved}) + (2/3 \text{ probability} \times 0 \text{ saved})$$
$$= 200 \text{ saved} + 0 \text{ saved} = 200 \text{ saved}$$

Similarly, in both programs C and D, 400 people will die (that is, 200 people will be saved). In C, that is the certain outcome, and in D, it results from the probabilities as follows:

$$(1/3 \text{ probability} \times 0 \text{ die}) + (2/3 \text{ probability} \times 600 \text{ die})$$
$$= 0 \text{ die} + 400 \text{ die} = 400 \text{ die} \ (200 \text{ are saved})$$

However, in Problem 1, the outcomes are *framed* from the point of view of lives being *saved* versus lives *lost*. In that case, participants prefer the outcome where there are guaranteed survivors rather than an option viewed as a gamble in which there is a possibility that everyone will die (see results at the bottom of Box 11.5). So in Problem 1, people prefer the sure-save option A to the risky proposition B, and are thus *risk averse* (Tversky & Kahneman, 1981). In contrast, in Problem 2, the alternatives are framed in a context where the basic assumption is that there definitely will be *deaths*, and now a large majority of people are willing to take a risk and adopt program D, where there is a chance that no one might die rather than choose certain death for 400 in option C (see Box 11.5). Thus, as Problem 2 is framed—certain loss versus a gamble—people are *risk-seeking*.

BOX 11.5 FRAMING EFFECTS AND CHOICE DATA

Please read each scenario and make your choices before examining the results at the bottom of the table.

Problem 1

Imagine that we are preparing for the outbreak of a new disease that has been sweeping the world. It has been determined that the disease will kill 600 people here. Two alternative programs to combat the disease (A and B) have been proposed. Assume that the exact consequences of each proposal are as follows:

A. If proposal A is adopted, 200 people will be saved.

B. If proposal B is adopted, there is a one-third probability that 600 people will be saved, and a two-thirds probability that no people will be saved.

Which proposal (A or B) would you favor?

Problem 2

Imagine that we are preparing for the outbreak of a new disease that has been sweeping the world. It has been determined that the disease will kill 600 people here. Two alternative programs to combat the disease (C and D) have been proposed. Assume that the exact consequences of each proposal are as follows:

C. If proposal C is adopted, 400 people will die.

D. If proposal D is adopted, there is a one-third probability nobody will die and a two-thirds probability that 600 people will die.

Which proposal (C or D) would you favor?

Research Results

Problem 1: Proposal A chosen by 72% of undergraduates; B by 28%.

Problem 2: Proposal C chosen by 22% of undergraduates; D by 78%.

Adapted from Tversky and Kahneman (1981).

Framing effects also influence consumer decision making. Biswas (2009) asked people to make decisions about 14 car features, such as a CD player, security system, and rear-wing spoiler. Some participants started with a base model and *added* features, while others started with a fully loaded model but *deleted* features. When decisions were framed as deletions, people were reluctant to give things up (i.e., they were loss averse), and ended up choosing more car feature options than in the add-features condition.

Conclusion

In sum, the way a course of action is framed can influence the likelihood that it will be chosen. Research on the *framing effect* in decision making indicates that people tend to be risk-averse in positive frames and risk-seeking in negative frames. The robustness of framing effects demonstrates that people are less than completely rational when choosing among objectively equivalent courses of action.

DEDUCTIVE REASONING: MOVING FROM PREMISES TO CONCLUSIONS

We have now examined the processes involved in gathering and evaluating evidence that serves as the basis for drawing conclusions about the courses of action that we have available (e.g., whether to major in art history or psychology, or which public health policy to adopt). Many of the decisions we have discussed this far were inductions or inferences made under conditions of uncertainty. A second sort of reasoning, *deductive reasoning*, or *deduction*, works in a way opposite to induction. In deduction, one assumes first that certain pieces of information—called *premises*—are true and then seeks to determine what conclusions follow from those premises. Two types of deductive reasoning have been studied by logicians and cognitive scientists: *syllogistic* reasoning and *conditional* reasoning. Please work through the examples in Box 11.6.

BOX 11.6 EXAMPLES OF DEDUCTIVE REASONING

A. Syllogistic Reasoning

All trees have roots. This oak is a tree.
Therefore, this oak has roots.
    Is that conclusion true or false?

B. Conditional Reasoning

If it rains on Saturday, then the fair will be canceled.
If the fair is canceled, then our company will lose money.
If our company loses money, then we will have to close our plant.
If we close the plant, then John will lose his job.
It rains.
    Should John apply for unemployment insurance?

C. Informal Syllogistic and Conditional Reasoning

Susan: We are planning to go out tonight to a new club on the river. Would you like to go with us?

Steve: I've been to a couple of those clubs before, and I didn't like them. They were noisy, hot, and expensive. All those clubs on the river are wastes of money. If I think a place is a waste of money, I won't go to it. Will Steve go to the new club?

A *syllogism* (from *reasoning* in Greek) is a set of sentences that serves as the basis for reasoning (see Box 11.6A); the first two sentences are the *premises*, and the third is the *conclusion*. In a well-constructed syllogism, the conclusion follows *necessarily* from the premises. That is, if the premises are true, then the conclusion must be true. When we reason using a syllogism, we produce a conclusion that is not stated directly in the premises, although it logically follows from them.

Conditional reasoning, shown in Box 11.6B, is based on *conditional* sentences of the form *If A, then B*. The *If A* part is known as the *antecedent*, and the *then B* part is the *consequent*. (*Antecedent* means something that comes first, and *consequent* means something that follows from something else.) The first five sentences in Box 11.6A, for example, tell you about various conditions (A) that will produce different effects (B). The last sentence specifies the occurrence of one of those A conditions, and you are to draw a conclusion.

Sometimes both syllogistic and conditional reasoning are used together, as in 11.6C. Completing the argument there requires filling in missing information until you conclude that Steve will not go to the new club. First, we hear him say that all the clubs on the river are wastes of money. Susan has just asked him to go to a club on the river, which should lead her to conclude that he thinks that the new club is a waste of money as well. The syllogism involved here is:

All clubs in the river are wastes of money. This new club is on the river. Therefore, this new club is a waste of money.

There is also conditional reasoning involved in Susan's understanding of Steve's decision. Steve says that *if* he thinks a place is a waste of money, *then* he does not go there. Susan will conclude that he would not want to go to the new club. The informal reasoning in Box 11.6C is closer to that used by us most of the time than are the complete deductive processes outlined in Box 11.6A and B.

Some Rules of Deductive Reasoning

In the fair scenario in Box 11.6B, the conditional premise in the form *If A, then B* is: *If it rains on Saturday, then the fair will be canceled*. The second premise, sentence (5) in Table 11.4, affirms *A*: It rains. We can then conclude that *B*: The fair will be canceled (see Table 11.4B).

The conclusion that the fair will be canceled then becomes a new premise (6), which can become part of the reasoning process (see Table 11.4B), ultimately leading to the conclusion that John should apply for unemployment insurance.

Affirming the *antecedent* (*A*) in the second premise of the fair scenario allows us to conclude that the consequent (*B*) is also true. This type of argument is called in Latin *modus ponens* (*MP*), which simply means the *method (modus) of affirming* (see Table 11.5A). Three other examples of argument types are presented in Table 11.5; reason through those examples before reading further.

Table 11.5B depicts two premises, the already-familiar *IF A – then B* form, and the second premise, *not-B*. According to the rules of logic, we can then conclude *not-A*. In this case, we are first *denying the consequent*, which then allows you to *deny the antecedent*. This type of reasoning is called in Latin *modus tollens* (*MT*), which is the *method* (again, *modus*) *of negating* or *denying*. Both modus ponens and modus tollens are valid arguments, as illustrated by the examples in Table 11.5A and B regarding dogs and mammals. However, people are more apt to accept MP than MT (Evans, 1977; Marcus & Rips, 1979; Markovits, 1988).

Table 11.4   Detailed Reasoning Process Used in Fair Scenario

A. Fair Scenario Outlined

1. If it rains on Saturday, then the fair will be canceled.
2. If the fair is canceled, then our company will lose money.
3. If our company loses money, then we will have to close our plant.
4. If we close the plant, then John will lose his job.
5. It rains.

B. Reasoning Process Specified

Premises 1 + 5 → 6 (Fair will be canceled.)
Premises 2 + 6 → 7 (Company will lose money.)
Premises 3 + 7 → 8 (Plant will be closed.)
Premises 4 + 8 → 9 (John loses his job.)

Table 11.5   Types of Valid and Invalid Conditional Reasoning With Premise 1: *If It Is a Dog, Then It Is a Mammal*

A. Modus Ponens (Affirming the Antecedent)

If A, then B.	A is true.	Conclude that B is true. (Conclusion is valid.)
Example: If this animal is a dog, then it is a mammal.	This animal is a dog.	Conclusion: It is a mammal. (Conclusion is valid.)

B. Modus Tollens (Denying the Consequent)

If A, then B.	B is false.	Conclude that A is false. (Conclusion is valid.)
Example: If this animal is a dog, then it is a mammal.	It is not a mammal.	Conclusion: This animal is not a dog. (Conclusion is valid.)

C. Affirming the Consequent

If A, then B.	B is true.	Cannot conclude that A is true. (Conclusion is invalid.)
Example: If this animal is a dog, then it is a mammal.	It is a mammal.	Conclusion: This animal is a dog. (Conclusion is invalid.)

D. Denying the Antecedent

If A, then B.	A is false.	Cannot conclude that B is false. (Conclusion is invalid.)
Example: If this animal is a dog, then it is a mammal.	This animal is not a dog.	Conclusion: This animal is not a mammal. (Conclusion is invalid.)

Invalid Arguments

Table 11.5C and D depict invalid arguments. The second sentence in 11.5C *affirms the consequent* of the conditional statement; that is, it tells you that *B* is true. If you then assume the antecedent of the conditional is also true, this inference is *invalid*. That is, affirming the consequent does *not* allow you to confirm the antecedent. The conditional sentence simply says that *if* this animal is a dog, then it is a mammal. But if you affirm that the animal is a mammal, it is not necessarily a dog; it could be a horse or a rhinoceros.

In Table 11.5D, the second sentence results in *denying the antecedent*, which leads people to deny the consequent as well. That inference, however, is also invalid. Again, we begin with the conditional statement: If it is a dog, then it is a mammal. If we find out that something is not a dog (deny the antecedent), we cannot validly conclude that it is not a mammal. In research on syllogistic reasoning, people are given the patterns of sentences in Table 11.5 and are asked if the conclusion is valid or invalid. Modus ponens is affirmed by almost all people, modus tollens by very few, and affirming the consequent is accepted more than denying the antecedent (Oberauer, 2006). Thus, some forms of conditional-reasoning arguments result in people accepting invalid conclusions. However, as we shall see in the next section, *what* a problem is about (i.e., the *content* of a problem) may influence reasoning as much as, or more than, the formal nature of a problem.

CONTENT EFFECTS IN DEDUCTIVE REASONING

If you can reason deductively, then you should be able to draw valid conclusions, whether or not you believe the premises, and even if the premises are not true in the real world. After all, we often think about things that we believe are not true, just for the sake of discussion. Research indicates, however, that the content of a problem, and whether its premises and conclusion are true or false in the real world, can interfere with people's ability to reason validly. That is, similarly to the *confirmation bias* discussed earlier, the *meaning* or *content* of a deductive-reasoning problem can affect how well people deal with it. We will consider two *content effects* in reasoning; please work through the examples in Box 11.7.

Belief–Bias in Deductive Reasoning

In one study of the effects of content on reasoning (Klauer, Musch, & Naumer, 2000), college students were given syllogisms such as those in Box 11.7, and were asked to judge whether the conclusion followed from the premises in problems about the addictiveness of cigarettes. Drawing the conclusion that there are some addictive things which are *not* cigarettes (in Box 11.7A and C) fits with the students' beliefs (after all, alcohol, drugs, and other things can also be addictive), but it does *not* logically follow from the premises in the invalid–believable condition (Box 11.7C). However, the invalid–believable condition has the same subject-acceptance rate as the valid–believable condition, and twice the acceptance rate as the valid problem with an unbelievable conclusion (see Box 11.7B). Thus, when an invalid conclusion in a syllogism is supported by our beliefs, we are more likely to commit a fallacy, and accept it as valid. This is called the *belief-bias effect*: Our beliefs bias us into accepting nonvalid conclusions because of their content—what they are about (Evans, Over, & Manktelow, 1993). Belief bias influences judgments of invalid arguments more than valid ones (Evans, Barston, & Pollard, 1983). To see another example of a content effect in reasoning, please work through the problems in Box 11.8 before reading further.

BOX 11.7 SYLLOGISMS USED TO ILLUSTRATE THE BELIEF–BIAS EFFECT

A. Valid, Believable

No cigarettes are inexpensive.

Some addictive things are inexpensive.

Therefore, some addictive things are not cigarettes.

Acceptance rate: 92%

B. Valid, Unbelievable

No addictive things are inexpensive.

Some cigarettes are inexpensive.

Therefore, some cigarettes are not addictive.

Acceptance rate: 46%

C. Invalid, Believable

No addictive things are inexpensive.

Some cigarettes are inexpensive.

Therefore, some addictive things are not cigarettes.

Acceptance rate: 92%

The Selection Task

The answers to the exercises in Box 11.8 are presented in Table 11.6. Although all the problems are formally identical, people are more successful with the concrete problems in Box 11.8A–B than with the abstract problem in Box 11.8C (Griggs and Cox, 1982). In 11.8A, the rule is in *If A, then B format*: *If a person is drinking alcohol, then he or she must be 21*. To determine if the law is being violated, we have to find more information about the cards corresponding to *A* and *not-B*: the person drinking beer (*A*) whose age is unknown, and 16-year old person (*not-B*) who is drinking an unknown beverage. The exercise in Box 11.8B is carried out in the same way: check *A* and *not-B*. The store manager must check the receipt for the check sale over $50 and the nonsigned receipt.

The problem in Box 11.8C also follows the *If A, then B* rule, which means we have to turn over *A* (a card with a vowel) and *not-B* (a card with an odd number); that is, card 2 and card 4. However, fewer than 10% of people pick only those cards (Evans et al., 1993; Wason, 1977). The extreme difference in difficulty of formally identical versions of the selection task is another example of a content effect—that is, irrationality—in deductive reasoning.

BOX 11.8 VARIATIONS ON FOUR-CARD SELECTION TASK

A. Drinking Alcohol/Checking ID Version

You are an inspector for the state liquor control board. It is your job to go into bars and check peoples' identifications, to make sure that no one underage is drinking alcohol in violation of the law. The law is: *If a person is drinking alcohol, he or she must be 21*. You enter a bar and see four people seated around a table. You can see the identifications of two of the people at the table (1 and 2, as indicated below), although you cannot tell what they are drinking. You can also identify from afar the content of two drinks (3 and 4, as noted below), but you cannot determine the age of the people drinking them.

1. Drinking: ?   Age: 16
2. Drinking: ?   Age: 22
3. Drinking: Coke   Age: ?
4. Drinking: Beer   Age: ?

Who has to be checked?

B. Department Store Receipts Version

You are the manager of a department store. The store policy is that if a check sale is over $500, then the department manager must approve and initial it. You are concerned that some check sales have gotten by without department managers' approval. You decide to look to make sure that has not happened. You have before you four receipts from check sales. You can only see one side of each receipt.

1. Front: $750   Back: ?
2. Front: $450   Back: ?
3. Front: ?   Back: Initials
4. Front: ?   Back: Blank

Which of those receipts do you have to examine further in order to see that no nonapproved check sales have slipped by?

C. Four-Card Version

You are given four cards. Each card has a letter printed on one side and a number on the other. You can only see one side of each card. Here are the cards:

Card 1: H
Card 2: E
Card 3: 6
Card 4: 7

Your task is to test whether the following rule is true for this set of four cards: *If a card has a vowel on one side, then it has an even number on the other*. Which of the cards do you have to turn over, to look at the other side, in order to determine whether or not the rule is true or false for this set of cards? See Table 11.6 for answers.

Table 11.6   Correct Answers to Selection Problems in Box 11.8

Question	Correct Answer	Responses
A. Drinking Problem	Answer: 1 and 4; those are the only two who could be violating the law.	Almost everyone is correct.
B. Department Store	Answer 1 and 4.	Almost everyone is correct.
C. Four-Card Task	Cards 2 and 4	Card 2 only: 33% Cards 2 and 3: 46% Cards 2 and 4: 4% All four cards: 7% Other choices: 10%

Content Effects in Deductive Reasoning: Conclusions

There are at least two kinds of content effects in tasks involving deductive reasoning. In syllogistic reasoning, the belief bias leads people to be more likely to accept a conclusion that matches their preexisting beliefs, even when it does not follow from the premises. In conditional reasoning, determining the validity or invalidity of a conditional statement can be dramatically altered by the content in which the problem is presented. We now turn to an examination of theories that have been proposed to explain how content influences people's deductive reasoning.

THEORIES OF DEDUCTIVE REASONING

Psychologists have developed a number of different types of theories to explain the performance of people in situations requiring deductive reasoning. These theories range from the idea that each of us possesses an internal mental logic, which enables us to carry out deductive reasoning, to the idea that reasoning depends on a match between the concrete situation in front of us and our experience.

Formal Rules Theory

Formal rules theory assumes that each of us possesses a *mental logic*, that is, an internal set of abstract logical rules and a set of processes for using them (Braine, 1978; Braine & O'Brien, 1991; O'Brien, 2009; Revlis, 1975; Rips, 1975). Abstract inference rules apply to a wide range of situations, regardless of the specifics of the situation. For example, the rule for modus ponens says that if you see *any* statement of the form *If A, then B*, and if you then learn that A is true, you can assume that B is true. Consider the following set of sentences:

If it rains, then John gets wet. It rains. Therefore?

The first sentence should activate the conditional rule in memory, and then the second sentence affirms part A (the antecedent) so you conclude that B must be true. That is, John gets wet. This is the basis for your ability to carry out modus ponens.

Abstract Rules and Content Effects

The strong content effects often found in deductive reasoning tasks (e.g., Boxes 11.5 and 11.6) raise problems for any theory that assumes that most people use abstract rules to reason logically. According to the abstract-rules theory of reasoning, you should perform equivalently on every task that has a particular logical structure: Either you have the reasoning ability or you do not. However, we have seen that one can perform very differently on different versions of the same logical-reasoning task, such as the four-card task (see Box 11.8), depending on the specific content. According to the mental-logic view, reasoning errors can occur for several reasons: (a) people may misinterpret the premises of a problem (Henle, 1962); (b) the solution requires application of multiple rules, thereby increasing the complexity of the problem (Van der Henst, 2002); (c) some rules are more difficult than others to apply (Van der Henst, 2002); or (d) people may fail to apply the rules of logic equally to all problems. However, the difficulty of matching the empirical findings with the predictions of the mental logic approach has led theorists to propose other possible explanations for people's behavior on deductive-reasoning tasks.

Memory Cuing

Griggs and Cox (1982; Griggs, 1984) proposed that reasoning will be best for specific scenarios that people have stored in memory. Thus, the ability to carry out deductive reasoning depends on how well the content of a problem matches up with one's knowledge. Under this *memory-cuing* interpretation, the four-card task (Box 11.8C) is so difficult because it is presented in abstract terms (unrelated cards, letters, and numbers), which people have difficulty relating to anything they know. The drinking-law problem, on the other hand, can be solved by people simply activating particular episodic memories in which similar premises occurred, and reasoning accordingly. Since experimental participants have presumably had first- or secondhand knowledge of drinking laws and violations of those laws, that makes that form of the four-card task easier to reason about.

However, people's reasoning abilities can extend beyond scenarios with which they have had direct experience. For example, D'Andrade (reported in Rumelhart, 1980) found that people were able to draw the correct conclusions about a problem determining when a manager had to sign retail store receipts, even if a person had never worked in retail sales (see Box 11.8B). Thus, while we may indeed perform better in reasoning about situations that are familiar to us, it is also possible to draw the correct conclusions about problems for which we do not have a direct memory cue. Thus, the memory-cuing view cannot completely explain our ability to reason logically.

Mental Models Theory

Johnson-Laird and his coworkers (e.g., 2001, 2006; García Madruga, Gutiérrez Martínez, Carriedo, Moreno, & Johnson-Laird, 2002; Johnson-Laird & Bara, 1984; Johnson-Laird & Byrne, 1991) have proposed that deductive reasoning, and in fact, many aspects of cognition, are based on use of a *mental model*, which is an internal representation of a state of affairs. Johnson-Laird has proposed that carrying out deductive reasoning depends first of all on construction of mental models in response to the meaning of the premises. Thus, reasoning and drawing inferences are based on the content of a problem, and people's ability to generate corresponding models. As an example, consider the reasoning problem presented in Figure 11.2A, involving spatial relations. The premises serve as the basis for construction of the models shown in Figure 11.2B. The models then are integrated to serve as the basis for drawing the conclusion, as in Figure 11.2C. In deductive reasoning problems such as the drinking problem, even if people themselves have not been exposed to drinking-law violations, they can nonetheless generate a mental model in which someone underage might violate the laws (and then draw the correct conclusions). Thus, the mental-models view can explain how people can reason in situations that the memory-cuing view cannot explain.

A. Syllogism requiring one integrated mental model:

    1. The king is on the right of the queen.
    2. The ace is in front of the king.
    3. The deuce is in front of the queen.

    What is the relation between the deuce and the ace?

B. The premises result in production of the following models:

    1. queen   king

    2. king
       ace

    3. queen
       deuce

C. An integrated model allows one to draw the conclusion to answer the question:

    queen   king
    deuce   ace ⟸ Conclusion: The deuce is to the left of the ace.

D. Syllogism requiring more than one integrated model:

    1. The king is on the right of the queen or the queen is on the right of the king.
    2. The ace is in front of the king.
    3. The deuce is in front of the queen

    What is the relation between the deuce and the ace?

Model 1		Model 2	
queen	king	king	queen
deuce	ace	ace	deuce

Two possible conclusions.

Figure 11.2 Mental models and reasoning.

According to mental-models theory, there can be several reasons why people have problems carrying out deductive reasoning. One possibility is that the content of a problem influences the ease of forming a mental model. Factors such as concreteness or causal connections among premises influence how easy it is to construct a mental model and engage in correct deductive inferences. When participants were given concrete conditional problems (e.g., *I don't drink wine unless I eat meat*), or everyday warnings (e.g., *Don't use a welding torch unless you wear protective eye covering*), people made fewer errors than when the situation was described in abstract terms, such as the four-card problem (Carriedo, García-Madruga, Gutiérrez, & Moreno, 1999).

Also, some reasoning problems allow the construction of more than one set of models, which makes reasoning more difficult (see Figure 11.2D). As an example, Girotto, Mazzoco, and Tasso (1997) found that people were better at deductive reasoning from premises when the consequent is stated first, as in "The plant will grow if it is watered," or "You may see the movie if you finish your homework," compared with "If it is watered, the plant will grow" or "If you finish your homework, you may see the movie." Why? Because people can better generate *modus tollens* (not-B; e.g., "If it is not watered, the plant . . . ") when B comes first, and thus create the relevant mental model. People consistently reason more accurately about problems that permit only one mental model over scenarios that permit multiple models (e.g., compare Figure 11.2B and C; Gutiérrez, Martínez, García Madruga, Johnson-Laird, & Carriedo López, 2002).

In conclusion, Johnson-Laird and his co-workers have been successful in explaining people's performance on propositional and syllogistic reasoning by assuming that mental models serve as the foundation on which cognition is carried out (e.g., Evans, Handley, Harper, & Johnson-Laird, 1999; Johnson-Laird & Bara, 1984; Legrenzi, Girotto, & Johnson-Laird, 1993).

Pragmatic Reasoning Schemas

Cheng and Holyoak (1985; Cheng, Holyoak, Nisbett, & Oliver, 1986; Cheng & Nisbett, 1993) demonstrated that one can facilitate performance on the four-card selection task by embedding it in practical scenarios (as shown in Figure 11.3A). They proposed that people, through their experiences, have induced *pragmatic reasoning schemas* (or *schemata*), which are methods of reasoning that apply to classes of situations. These include such situations as granting permission, understanding cause-and-effect relationships, or taking on an obligation (see Figure 11.3B). *Pragmatic* means that the process is involved in actual everyday aspects of reasoning in domain-specific situations; it is not based on abstract rules that apply everywhere nor necessarily on specific individual experiences. For example, Cheng and Holyoak proposed that we have all experienced situations that involve granting permission in the following form: If you want to do something (X), you must first satisfy some specified conditions (Y). For example, a parent might say to a child, "If you want to see this movie, you must first finish your homework." The inferences that can be made on the basis of the permission schema roughly correspond to those of conditional reasoning. For example, *modus ponens* leads to the inference that if the child saw the movie, she must have finished her homework, whereas *modus tollens* means inferring that if she did *not* finish her homework, then she did *not* see the movie. The fallacy of denying the antecedent

A. Vaccination Version of Selection Task.

You are a public health official at an international airport. Part of your duty is to check that every arriving passenger who wishes to enter the country (rather than just change planes at the airport) has had an inoculation against **cholera**. Every passenger carries a health form. One side of the form indicates whether the passenger is entering or in transit, and the other side of the form lists the inoculations he or she has had in the past 6 months. You can only see one side of the form as the passenger shows it to you. Which of the following forms would you need to turn over to check? Indicate only those forms you would have to check to be sure.

Form 1: Transit
Form 2: Entering
Form 3: Inoculated against: cholera, hepatitis
Form 4: Inoculated against: typhoid

Which forms have to be turned over?

      (a) Forms 2 & 3
      (b) Form 2 only
      (c) Forms 2, 3, & 4
      (d) Forms 2 & 4
      (e) Form 3 only

Answer: (d)

B. Permission and Causal Scenarios

Permission

If you wish to carry out Action A, then you must do B.

Rule 1: If the action is to be taken, then there is a precondition that must be satisfied.
Rule 2: If the action is not to be taken, then the precondition need not be satisfied.
Rule 3: If the precondition is satisfied, then the action may be taken.
Rule 4: If the precondition is not satisfied, then the action must not be taken.

Example: If you want to go outside, you must finish your homework.

Causality

Rule 1: If [the cause] occurs, then [the effect] occurs.
Rule 2: If [the cause] does not occur, then [the effect] does not occur.
Rule 3: If [the effect] occurs, then [the cause] has occurred.
Rule 4: If [the effect] did not occur, then [the cause] has not occurred.

Example: If you are inoculated against typhoid, then you are immune.

Figure 11.3 Two versions of the selection task.

corresponds to claiming that if the child did *not* see the movie, she did *not* finish her homework (although she might have decided to visit a friend instead of seeing the movie after she finished her homework). Affirming the consequent is also invalid—if she finished her homework, then she saw the movie (again, she might have opted to finish her homework but do something else).

According to Cheng and Holyoak, most people are able to deal with the versions of the selection task in Box 11.8A–B because they both involve variations of the permission schema (see Figure 11.3B). The four-card selection task in Box 11.8C, on the other hand, is difficult because it does not fit any pragmatic reasoning schema with which we are familiar. When the context of the four-card task is altered to invoke granting permission, people are more successful in correct reasoning about it (Noveck & O'Brien, 1996). That also explains why people can deal with the traveler/vaccination scenario (see Figure 11.3A): In this variation of the selection task, the abstract materials become part of a permission scenario.

In addition, Cheng, Holyoak, Nisbett, and Oliver (1986) carried out a training study, in which participants were given familiarity with permission and other schemas, such as obligation. An example of an obligation is: *If a worker is injured on the job, the employer must pay medical bills*. Such training facilitated performance on the more abstract four-card selection task, whereas training in rules of formal logic did not produce comparable facilitation.

Conclusion

Pragmatic schemata are neither content-free rules of logic nor merely memories of specific episodes that have been cued by the problem. Rather, they embody types of contractual or social agreements with which we are all familiar (permission, obligation), and knowledge of the general laws and potential violations within each schema allows us to apply them aptly to new situations.

Dual-Process Theories of Reasoning

The various theories of deductive reasoning just reviewed have explained the occurrence of dysrationalia as being due to factors that interfere with the person's ability to carry out the reasoning process as best they can. As an example, reasoning errors may be due to difficulty constructing all the models needed to reason correctly about a situation, or failure to activate the appropriate pragmatic schema. A different explanation for errors in reasoning comes from *dual-process* theories of reasoning, which have been developed by several researchers (e.g., Evans, 2003; Evans & Over, 1996; Kahneman & Frederick, 2005). Dual-process theories propose that there are two systems involved in reasoning, which means that there is more than one way to respond to a reasoning problem. Mistakes can occur if output from the wrong system is used as the basis for responding. Any task that demands logical thinking activates a fast intuitive system which relies on general heuristics, including taking into account context and similarity to previous problems (sometimes called System 1); and a slower, more analytical system that is sensitive to rules (System 2). System 1 makes quick judgments based on a relatively superficial analysis of the situation, so it does not carry out precise and detailed reasoning processes. System 2, in contrast, works more slowly but more precisely, using explicit reasoning processes to work through a problem on a step-by-step basis.

It is normally assumed that: (a) output from the analytical System 2 may override that from intuitive System 1, such as when statisticians, logicians, or economics experts are able to use their formal knowledge to reason optimally about problems that the rest of us often fail; and (b) that System 1 judgment can result in mistakes in reasoning, due to the too-heavy reliance on heuristics and biases, as we saw in many of the studies reviewed earlier. Thus, training on analytical techniques may result in better reasoning. However, recall the example we related in Chapter 1 from the book *Blink* (Gladwell, 2005): Art experts made a quick (and accurate) judgment that the Greek kouros statue was not real, but could not explain how or why they knew this. All the factual data about the age of the stone, its being covered in calcite, and its documentation of authenticity pointed to legitimacy of the statue. Thus, using System 2 information, the Getty Museum bought the kouros for $10 million. In this case, though, the unconscious and automatic judgment of System 1 led to the more rational result: The statue was actually a very clever forgery. This result indicates that not all errors in reasoning are due to incorrect reliance on System 1.

Heit and Rotello (2010) hypothesized that inductive reasoning may be dependent on Type 1 reasoning, whereas deductive reasoning is more influenced by Type 2 reasoning. They asked separate groups of participants to make judgments concerning the strength of inductive arguments or the validity of deductive arguments. They found that similarity to previous problems affected people's decisions about inductive problems, but that logical validity played a bigger role in people's answers to deductive problems. This psychological distinction between the two types of reasoning processes supports the idea that heuristic (System 1) processes are more influential during induction, but analytical (System 2) processes are used more during deductive reasoning.

Theories of Reasoning: Conclusions

A number of different types of theories have been proposed to explain people's performance in situations involving deductive reasoning. Formal rules theory proposes that people possess abstract rules that govern deductive reasoning; whereas the memory-cuing hypothesis predicts that the ability to reason depends on a specific match between information in memory and the situation one is facing. Both mental models and pragmatic reasoning schema use the semantics of reasoning problems—their content—to build representations that allow people to reason. A more-recent theory (Kahneman & Frederick, 2005) proposes that there are two systems involved in reasoning: System 1, a fast-acting intuition-based system that relies on heuristics; and System 2, a slower, more systematic (and logical) processing system. Dual-process theories explain errors in reasoning by assuming that the fast intuitive response, based on factors such as representativeness, sometimes overshadows System 2. The mental-logic view does not account for many of the errors people make during reasoning (Bonatti, 1994), and the memory-cuing view is limited to explaining how people might use specific incidents to reason about very similar examples. Both the mental models and pragmatic schema perspectives have attained empirical support, can explain both people's deductive reasoning successes and errors, and take into account how content can affect reasoning.

ARE HUMANS RATIONAL OR IRRATIONAL?

Taken as a whole, the studies reviewed so far in this chapter do not paint a positive picture of human competence when it comes to making decisions. People show inadequacies in searching for evidence, evaluating evidence, and using statistical evidence;

they often exhibit inabilities to draw valid deductions, and are susceptible to framing effects and other biases. Researchers have had two general types of responses to such results. First, the heuristics-and-biases perspective of Kahneman and Tversky (1973, 1996; Tversky & Kahneman, 1973, 1983) has remained influential, and many researchers (e.g., Stanovich & West, 1998, 2000, 2012; Stanovich, 2008, 2009) have become convinced that human thinking may not be completely rational in many decision-making contexts.

However, other researchers have been reluctant to accept the conclusion that humans are irrational thinkers. There are two lines of argument often used against the irrational-human perspective. The first is that perhaps heuristics and biases are actually adaptive in real life (Gigerenzer & Brighton, 2009; Gigerenzer & Selten, 2002; Rozin & Nemeroff, 2002). That is, outside of the carefully crafted problems of the laboratory, a person's use of stereotypical information (as in the representativeness heuristic) or decision making based on the most salient or dramatic information available (as in the availability heuristic) may actually increase the accuracy and/or speed of many decisions. For example, similarity between two objects or events is typically a useful basis for inference: If one apple tastes good, another of the same type (i.e., one that looks similar) probably tastes good. Thus, representativeness, based on similarity between a current event and past events, is a frequent and useful method of inference.

The second line of argument against irrationality cautions that, before one concludes that humans are irrational, one must determine that there are no other factors that might have affected performance. For example, having too many variables to consider, or focusing on the wrong part of a problem, might lead people to produce incorrect responses on some thinking task, independent of the reasoning process itself. Some researchers (e.g., Stanovich & West, 1998, 2000; Stanovich, 2009, 2012) have investigated whether we can rescue humans from the label *irrational* by showing that factors external to the thinking process might be interfering with a person's demonstrating rational thinking. Let us briefly examine how the optimistic perspective has been tested in the laboratory.

Irrationality Versus Random Error

One possibility concerning poor performance on thinking tasks is that people might sometimes make random errors, due either to cognitive factors (e.g., not paying sufficient attention to the elements of a problem), or because of the content of a problem. However, contrary to the random-error view, there are consistencies in performance on various sorts of reasoning tasks. One finds positive correlations in performance across different kinds of reasoning tasks (Stanovich & West, 2000): A person who makes an error on one sort of reasoning task will tend to make errors on other similar problems, indicating that the error patterns are not random. Thus, one cannot rescue the people-as-rational-thinkers view by appealing to random error.

Irrationality and Cognitive-Processing Limitations

Another proposal that has been made to counter the claim that humans are irrational is that perhaps the breakdown in thinking comes about because the specific task overwhelms the individual's cognitive capacities (Stanovich & West, 2000). As an analogy, you may be able to juggle three balls reasonably well, but if I give you 20 balls and ask you to juggle them, the task may overwhelm your capacity, and I may conclude (incorrectly) that you are unskilled. If this view is correct, then we should find a correlation between measures of cognitive capacity (such as IQ tests) and performance on reasoning and decision-making tasks. That is, people with more cognitive or working-memory capacity should be less likely to fall prey to any excessive cognitive demands of a reasoning problem. Stanovich and West (2008b) used the SAT scores of a group of students as a measure of cognitive capacity, and then administered to those students a set of reasoning and decision-making problems, such as those we have been working through in this chapter. Perhaps surprisingly, even high-SAT participants were subject to framing effects and the conjunction fallacy, and also showed an inability to take base rates into account when solving problems (as seen in Table 11.7A). On

Table 11.7   Stanovich and West (2000) Results

A. Performance of High–Ability (High SAT) Versus Low–Ability (Low SAT) Groups on Reasoning Tasks

Problem	Cognitive Ability	Results	
Framing Effects (Gain/Loss)		Gain Frame*	Loss Frame*
	High SAT	3.00	3.67
	Low SAT	3.11	4.05
Conjunction (Bank Teller)		Bank Teller	Feminist Bank Teller**
	High SAT	2.53	3.46
	Low SAT	2.36	3.73
Base Rate (Engineer/Lawyer)		30 Engineers***	70 Engineers
	High SAT	57	72
	Low SAT	64	74

*Both groups are affected equally by the frame in which the problem is presented.
**Incorrect choice, seen in both groups.
***% choices, High-SAT participants do not choose "engineer" more frequently than Low-SAT people.

B. Correlations Between SAT Scores and Reasoning Tasks. For Some of the Tasks, There Is a Negative Relation Between SAT Scores and Performance (i.e., People With Higher SAT Scores Performed Worse)

Task	Correlation
Syllogisms	.47
Wason Selection Task	.39
Statistical Reasoning	.35
Argument Evaluation	.37
Hypothesis-testing Bias	−.22
Outcome Bias	−.17
If/Only Thinking	−.21

Adapted from Stanovich and West (2008, Table 1).

only one of six problems was there a significant reasoning advantage for the high-SAT group, which suggests that susceptibility to some traditional decision-making biases is not caused by overall intellectual deficits.

Stanovich and West (2008b) did, however, find positive associations between SAT scores and some types of problems, such as probabilistic reasoning, deductive reasoning (as in the Wason four-card selection task), and evaluating logical arguments (see Table 11.7B). This means that a person's overall cognitive capacity, and/or level of quantitative skills (Reyna, Nelson, Han, & Dieckmann, 2009) may play a role in whether that person engages in rational versus irrational thinking on probabilistic and deductive reasoning problems. However, lack of cognitive capacity cannot fully explain susceptibility to heuristics and biases, especially on nonstatistical problems.

Conclusions About Rationality

It is possible to explain away some, but not all, irrational performance on thinking tasks as being the result of random errors, lack of cognitive capacity, lack of understanding of the problem, or differences in interpretation of the problem. Reasoning on some tasks may be tied to domain-specific knowledge or skills (Reyna et al., 2009), and IQ is more likely to be correlated to performance on statistical problems or deductive reasoning than to performance on decisions made under conditions of uncertainty, such as the types of problems Kahneman and Tversky (1973, 1996) studied (Stanovich & West, 2008b). In conclusion, there are clearly individual differences in people's ability to think rationally through the use of logical or statistical reasoning. Given the obvious importance of rational thinking in human affairs, a number of researchers have explored the question of whether there are ways to train people to think more rationally.

TEACHING REASONING AND DECISION MAKING

We have seen that there are situations in which human decision making is less than optimal. Kahneman and Tversky (1973, p. 237) remarked that, "people do not appear to follow the calculus of chance or the statistical theory of prediction." They labeled heuristics and biases "cognitive illusions" that people were largely powerless to overcome (see also Kahneman, 2011), in much the same way as we experience visual illusions, such as the Müller-Lyer illusion, even when we know about its trickery (Kahneman & Tversky, 1996; Tversky & Gilovich, 1989; Tversky & Kahneman, 1974). The *cognitive-illusions view* suggests that there is little or no room for improvement in thinking, but other researchers have shown that people can be trained to improve thinking skills. Optimistic views have been proposed within two camps. First, perhaps people can be trained to think more rationally with sufficient education (e.g., Fong, Krantz, & Nisbett, 1986; Fong & Nisbett, 1991; Lehman, Lempert, and Nisbett, 1988; Nisbett, Fong, Lehmann, & Cheng, 1987). Second, people might reason more rationally if problems were presented in a format that is consistent with everyday, concrete thinking (e.g., Gigerenzer, 1996).

Teaching General Rules of Thinking

There has been a longstanding belief in Western culture that thinking and reasoning are based on general rules or skills, which can be taught through education (Lehman, Lempert, & Nisbett, 1988). Plato, for example, proposed that individuals being groomed to be leaders of society should study arithmetic, because such training would improve general reasoning skills. Training in a *formal discipline*, such as mathematics or syllogistic reasoning, was proposed to have positive effects on thinking in other very different areas (Lehman et al., 1988; Nisbett et al., 1987). Lehman, Lempert, and Nisbett set out to examine directly whether it is possible to train people on abstract rules of thinking, which could then be applied to a multitude of domains. Please work through some examples of their tasks in Box 11.9 now.

BOX 11.9 TRAINING ABSTRACT REASONING: EXAMPLE TEST PROBLEMS FROM LEHMAN, LEMPERT, AND NISBETT (1988)

1. Understanding the Law of Large Numbers

A high school student had to choose between two colleges. The student had several friends who were similar to him in values and abilities at each school. All of his friends at school A liked it on both educational and social grounds; all of them at school B had deep reservations on both grounds. The student visited both schools for a day, and his impressions were the reverse: He liked school B and did not like school A. Which school should he choose?

Answer: The student should choose school A. His one-day visit is less likely to reveal the "true" aspects of the schools than are the much more extensive experiences of his friends. He should go with his friends' opinions.

2. Methodological Reasoning in Everyday Life

The city of Middleopolis has had an unpopular police chief for a year and a half. He is a political appointee who is a crony of the mayor, and he had little previous experience in police administration when he was appointed. The mayor has recently defended the chief in public, announcing that in the time since he took office, crime rates decreased by 12%. Which of the following pieces of evidence would most deflate the mayor's claim that his chief is competent?

a. The crime rates of the two cities closest to Middleopolis in location and size have decreased by 18% in the same period.

b. An independent survey of the citizens of Middleopolis shows that 40% more crime is reported by respondents in the survey than is reported in police records.

c. Common sense indicates that there is little a police chief can do to lower crime rates. These are for the most part due to social and economic conditions beyond the control of officials.

d. The police chief has been discovered to have business contacts with people who are known to be involved in organized crime.

Answer: (a) The information from the two cities similar to Middleopolis indicates that the crime rate in Middleopolis is not low, so the chief cannot take credit for anything.

Lehman et al. (1988) presented graduate students in psychology, chemistry, medicine, and law with tests of methodological, conditional/deductive, and statistical reasoning (see Box 11.9) both at the beginning and in the third year of their graduate careers. Training in law was expected to improve deductive reasoning, because that skill is part of law-school training (see Table 11.8A). Psychology and medical students were expected to improve in probabilistic and statistical reasoning, methodological reasoning, and conditional reasoning, again, because those skills are part of those students' graduate training. Because the structure of the science of chemistry emphasizes law-like rules rather than probabilistic or deductive thinking, it was expected that training in chemistry would not affect conditional, methodological, or statistical reasoning. Students were also given GRE-type verbal-reasoning problems as controls, and it was expected that all groups would show little change on those problems.

As can be seen in Table 11.8B, the predictions were upheld: Graduate training in psychology and medicine had the most profound impact on statistical reasoning and deductive/conditional reasoning, whereas training in law affected mainly deductive/conditional reasoning. While the fact that graduate training led to improvements in thinking supports the notion of formal discipline, the finding that improvement in specific types of reasoning was directly determined by the nature of an individual's graduate training suggests that training did not have the wide-ranging effects assumed by the formal discipline view.

In a second set of studies, Fong and Nisbett (1991) attempted to train undergraduate students directly in the law of large numbers (see Box 11.9), to see if the training would generalize beyond the specific domain in which the material was taught. The extracts that follow present some of the training materials used in the experiment: One

Table 11.8   Lehman et al. (1988) Study of Training in Reasoning

A. Predictions Concerning Graduate Training on Thinking Skills

| | Type of Graduate Training | | | |
| | Probabilistic Sciences | | Deterministic Science | Nonscience |
Type of Reasoning	Psychology	Medicine	Chemistry	Law
Statistical/Methodological	+	+	0	0
Deductive/Conditional	+	+	0	+

B. Training Results: Percent Change in Reasoning Skill from First to Third Year of Postgraduate Training

| | Type of Graduate Training | | | |
| | Probabilistic Sciences | | Deterministic Science | Nonscience |
Type of Reasoning	Psychology	Medicine	Chemistry	Law
Statistical/Methodological	70	27	2	8
Deductive/Conditional	38	33	8	32

set dealt with athletic skills and the second set centered on tests of mental ability (such as IQ tests).

Here are two examples of training material:

Example 1

A major New York law firm had a history of hiring only graduates of large, prestigious law schools. One of the senior partners decided to try hiring some graduates of smaller, less prestigious law schools. Two such people were hired. Their grades and general record were similar to those of people from the prestigious schools hired by the firm. At the end of 3 years, both of them were well above average in the number of cases won and in the volume of law business handled. The senior partner who had hired them argued to colleagues in the firm that, "This experience indicates that graduates of less prestigious schools are at least as ambitious and talented as graduates of the major law schools."

Is the argument basically sound? Does it have weaknesses?

Answer: The senior partner's attitude is quite unwarranted: A larger sample is needed. You cannot draw general claims from a sample of two people.

Example 2

Kevin, a graduate student in psychology, decided to do a research project on "factors affecting performance of major league baseball players" in which he gathered a great amount of demographic data on birthplace, education, marital status, and so forth. Kevin was able to obtain data for some 200 players in the major leagues. One finding that interested Kevin concerned the 110 married players. About 68% of these players improved their performance after getting married, while the remainder had equal or poorer performance. He concluded that marriage is beneficial to a baseball player's performance. Kevin happened to mention his finding to a staff member at Major League Baseball. The staff member listened to Kevin's results and then said, "Your study is interesting, but I don't believe it. I'm sure that baseball performance is worse after a marriage because the ballplayer suddenly has to take on enormous responsibilities: taking care of his spouse and children. Plus, there is the factor of being stressed by having to be on the road so much of the time and therefore away from the family. Because of this he will lose that competitive quality that is necessary for good performance in baseball."

What do you think of the staff member's argument? Is it a sound one or not?

Answer: Kevin's conclusion is based on a relatively large sample, so it is trustworthy. The staff member's argument may have some intuitive appeal, but it should be discounted because it is not supported by any data (at least he did not bring forth any data) and his theory is, in fact, contradicted by Kevin's large sample of 110 players.

After being schooled in how the law of large numbers might apply to that person's training domain (e.g., that a single sports performance in a game is not necessarily indicative of a person's overall skill), participants were given new test problems in the

Table 11.9 Training Use of the Law of Large Numbers: Scores on Reasoning Test After Training

Domain of Training and Test	Time of Test	
	Immediate	Delayed
Same Domain	1.77	1.75
Different Domain	1.75	1.57

Adapted from Figure 2 from Fong and Nisbett, 1991.

same domain (e.g., sports) or the alternate domain (e.g., ability testing). Responses were graded on a 1–3 scale indicating the degree to which the answer invoked statistical explanations, especially concerning the law of large numbers. Results indicated that training did lead to an improvement in overall thinking skills, even in a different domain in which the person had been trained. As can be seen in Table 11.9, performance was as good in the nontrained domain as in the one that was trained. However, after a 2-week delay, performance was best in the *same-domain* condition, which does not fully support the general-rules view (Reeves & Weisberg, 1993a). Thus the results do not indicate that participants in this study actually learned abstract, domain-independent rules.

Frequency Formats

A second approach used to illustrate that humans are logical and can be trained to think rationally argues that evolution has better equipped people to think in terms of concrete frequencies rather than abstract statistical probabilities (Gigerenzer, 1996). For instance, knowing that 3 of 10 friends who went out to dinner together caught the flu is easier to digest cognitively than is hearing, "College students have a 0.30 chance of catching flu this week."

One of the most difficult types of statistical problems within decision making involves Bayesian inference, in which one must mentally juggle several probabilities to infer the statistical likelihood of a given outcome. For instance, imagine a man who was a witness to a hit and run accident at night involving a cab (problem from Gigerenzer & Hoffrage, 1995; Sedlmeier, 1999). The man believes he saw a BLUE cab in the accident, but when tested under dark lighting conditions, he was only 80% accurate at identifying blue versus green. Furthermore, 85% of all cabs in the city are GREEN, whereas only 15% are BLUE. Given this information, the police want to know the likelihood that the cab involved in the accident was actually BLUE. What is your estimate?

Most people estimate that the probability of the cab which caused the accident being blue is usually 80%—about the same as the man's accuracy in identifying cab colors (Kahneman, Slovic, & Tversky, 1982). However, this ignores the low base rate of BLUE cabs in the city (15%); the statistically correct answer is 41.8%. People can be trained to apply a Bayesian formula to such problems, though the benefits to teaching problem-solving using abstract formulae are often very short-lived (Bea & Scholz, 1995). Problems that are mathematically or statistically equivalent are not necessarily *psychologically* equivalent (Feynman, 1967). To this end, Gigerenzer (1994; Gigerenzer & Hoffrage, 1995) and Sedlmeier (1999, 2000; Sedlmeier & Gigerenzer, 2001) have argued that the probability format used in Bayesian reasoning is artificial, and that a more natural way to accrue information is through natural sampling, in which the frequencies of certain events or objects are tallied and represented (as in the college student/flu example above).

We can apply a frequency format to the green and blue cabs problem: Imagine there are 400 cabs in the city, 340 (85%) are green and 60 (15%) are blue. The man who witnessed the hit-and-run accident is only 80% accurate at recognizing the two colors, which means he would correctly recognize 272 (340 × 0.80) of the green cabs and 48 (60 × 0.80) of the blue cabs, as depicted in Figure 11.4a. This means he would *fail* at recognition of 68 green cabs and 12 blue cabs. To determine the probability that a blue cab was actually responsible for the hit-and-run, we need to divide the 48 blue cabs that the man would have accurately recognized by the number of ALL the cabs that he would have thought were blue, rightly (very light gray boxes in Figure 11.4A) and wrongly (darker gray boxes). That number equals 48 + 68, so the probability that he was correct—that is, that a blue cab was *actually* responsible for the crime—equals 48/(48 + 68) or 0.414 (or 41.4%). Frequency format training can be done using either frequency grids (Figure 11.4a) or a frequency tree (see Figure 11.4b).

Being trained to solve problems using natural frequencies also has long-term benefits. Gigerenzer and Hoffrage (1995) found that people trained to solve Bayes's theorem-style problems using frequency formats showed superior solution rates 5 weeks later compared to those trained in standard Bayesian problem solving.

Training Thinking Skills: Conclusions

Lehman et al. (1988) found that graduate training produces improvement in thinking skills, but that the improvement is limited to those skills that are part of the specific training program of a given discipline. Additionally, thinking skills in undergraduates can be improved as a result of exposure to a training program, though most of the benefits are seen either short-term or when tested on problems about the same topic as the training materials (Fong and Nisbett, 1991). Training people to represent problems within frequency formats has resulted in longer-term success in Bayesian (and other) reasoning, perhaps because it is a more natural way of thinking (Gigerenzer & Hoffrage, 1995; Sedlmeier, 1995). Thus, it seems that the extreme pessimism concerning the possibility of teaching thinking skills was unwarranted, although there are constraints on how domain-general the improvement in reasoning skills may be, or whether it is linked to particular kinds of training.

Can Thinking Be Effective Without Being Fully Rational?

Much of this chapter has centered on examination of situations in which human thinking is less than optimal, ranging from demonstrations of framing effects, to errors in statistical reasoning, to inability to carry out deductive reasoning. Research over the past 30 years has been heavily influenced by the heuristics-and-biases approach of

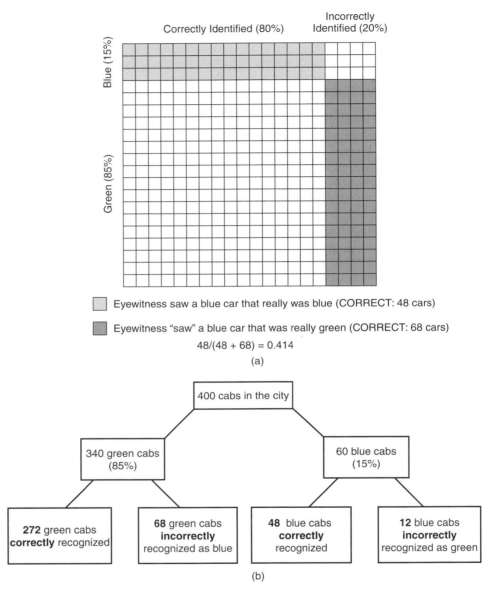

Figure 11.4 (a) Frequency format of cab problem. (b) Frequency tree format for cab problem.

Tversky and Kahneman (1974; Kahneman, 2011) in which people are viewed as less-than-optimal thinkers. However, a number of researchers have proposed that human reasoning doesn't have to be *optimal*, it merely needs to be *adequate*. As an analogy, when making a decision about a career, it may not be critical that you choose the career that makes you the most money (especially if it is a job you wouldn't enjoy), but you do want a career that pays enough for you to live reasonably well. The "good enough" prospective toward decision making was first advocated by Simon (1956, 1957, 1978, 1983), who proposed that human reasoning is based on *bounded rationality*: Decision-making is constrained by limited information, people's sometimes-limited cognitive abilities, and time constraints. This means that humans function in a way which, although perhaps not fully rational according to the rules of probability or formal logic, still allows us to function effectively in our real-world environments. Simon hypothesized that humans do not try to maximize decision-making outcomes, but rather engage in *satisficing*: Setting a decision-making level which is "good enough" for our goals. Satisficing suggests that we will choose a strategy that meets our standards for an adequate (but not necessarily optimum) solution. Thus, some minimal set of criteria must be met, and a person can take into account multiple pieces of information to satisfy those criteria.

More recently, Gigerenzer (2008) and his colleagues (e.g., Gigerenzer & Goldstein, 1996; Gigerenzer & Todd, 1999) have proposed that humans reason on the basis of *fast and frugal heuristics*, which are based on limited information and yet have the potential to outperform decision making based on optimal statistical models (such as Bayes's theorem). Gigerenzer and Goldstein (1996) argued that fast and frugal heuristics could be used to accomplish adequate decision making in a wide range of real-world situations such as: (1) whom to treat first in an emergency room, an elderly heart-attack victim or a teenaged victim of a car accident; (2) whether or not to sell a stock right now, based on a call from a stockbroker who is on the phone with a tip; (3) which answer to choose on a multiple-choice exam. In one experiment, Gigerenzer and Goldstein (1999) asked people to decide which of two cities is larger in population, City X or City Y. If someone does not know the exact populations of the cities in question, then they will need to rely on other information in memory to make a decision. The researchers used computer models to investigate the relative efficiencies of different strategies of searching memory for relevant information.

First, a person must determine if the name of the city is recognized. If not, then the city is probably not very big. Presumably, people also have stored in memory information such as whether a given city is the capital of its state or country, whether it hosts a major sports team, whether it is a university town (see Table 11.10 for relevant facts). Each of those facts has a measure of its *validity* as a basis for predicting that the city is indeed large. The higher the validity, the more useful the cue. For example, in Germany (the study was carried out in Germany and German cities were the stimuli), the capital *is* the largest city, which is why the validity of that cue is 1.0 for that sample of participants. Similarly, all things being equal, having major-league sports teams is useful (but again not perfect) in predicting that German a city is large (validity = 0.87). Gigerenzer and Goldstein (1999) tested traditional statistical models of judgment, which rely on thorough calculation of multiple pieces of information in the database, against fast and frugal heuristics, which are "lazy" and only rely on limited information in the database, to see which search strategy led to most efficient and accurate performance.

First, several complex mathematical calculations were developed, that used all available city facts in the particular database and weighted the validity of each one to statistically compute which city was more likely to be larger. These were designed to optimize correct decision making by taking into account all of the available information. Second,

Table 11.10 Gigerenzer and Goldstein (1996) Study Testing Accuracy of Different Models of Judgment

A. Cues and Their Validity in Predicting the Size of a City (based on German cities)

Cue	Validity
National Capital (Is the city the national capital?)	1.0
Exposition Site (Was the city once an exposition site?)	0.91
Soccer Team (Does the city have a major-league team?)	0.87
Intercity Train (Is the city on the intercity line?)	0.78
State Capital (Is the city a state capital?)	0.77
License Plate (Is the abbreviation for the city one letter long?)	0.75
University (Is the city home to a university?)	0.71
Industrial Belt (Is the city in the industrial belt?)	0.56
East Germany (Was the city in the former East Germany?)	0.51

B. Performance of the Different Decision Rules

Strategy	Accuracy (%)
Take the Best	66
Take the Last	65
Minimalist	65
Complex Statistical Strategy	66

Gigerenzer and Goldstein developed several fast and frugal heuristics that only used partial information or an abbreviated search to make a decision on the relative size of cities (see Table 11.10B). The *take-the-best* heuristic works down the list of cues, starting with the most valid, until it reaches a cue that gives it information that allows a size discrimination between the pair of cities in question. For example, if neither city in a pair is the capital, and both have been sites of international expositions, but one has a soccer team and the other does not, that would be the basis for discriminating between the two cities, and allowing a size decision to be made. The *take-the-best* heuristic ignores all the remaining cues once the best one has been found. In contrast, the *take-the-last* heuristic did not even search the database; it simply started with the cue that had been useful in the previously presented pair (e.g., having a soccer team), and applied it to the next pair of cities. Thus if the soccer-team cue had been useful in deciding that City A was larger than City B, then it was used to determine the relative size of City C versus City D. Finally, the *minimalist* heuristic is the simplest possible: It picks a cue randomly (e.g., "Is the city home to a university?"), and uses it to make a decision on city pairs.

Computer simulations of the different decision-making strategies were tested under varying levels of completeness of information. In some cases, information about various cities was randomly eliminated from the database (analogous to the situation in which a person might not recognize the names of some cities). Secondly, different numbers of city facts were randomly eliminated from the database, simulating the situation in which a person might recognize the name of a city, but not remember that it has a soccer team.

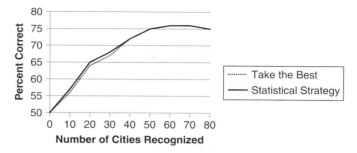

Figure 11.5   Performance of the take-the-best heuristic compared to a more complex rule (Statistical Strategy).

Several interesting findings resulted from this research. First, it turned out that all the heuristics performed about equally: The simple heuristics, using only a subset of the available information, functioned about as well as the complicated formulae that used all available data (see Table 11.10B). Thus, very simple cognitive mechanisms can produce performance that is almost as good as decisions based on much more complex mechanisms. Second, the efficiency of each heuristic was partly dependent on the size of the database used. One might have expected that the highest level of performance would depend on the largest amount of information being available, that is, with the largest database, but that turned out not to be the case. Figure 11.5 shows performance of the *take-the-best* heuristic versus the optimal statistical model as a function of the number of cities recognized. Performance was best when fewer than all the cities were recognized.

Fast and frugal heuristics have been shown to influence a myriad of decision making tasks, from stock market decisions (Borges, Goldstein, Ortmann, & Gigerenzer, 1999), to parent birds' investment as to which baby birds in a nest get fed (Davis & Todd, 1999), to human mate selection (Todd & Miller, 1999).

Bounded Rationality Versus Complete Rationality: Conclusions

The results of Gigerenzer and Goldstein (1996; see also Gigerenzer, 2007; Gigerenzer & Selten, 2002; Gigerenzer & Todd, 1999) lead one to consider the possibility that investigations of thinking (and of other complex behaviors) should concentrate on very simple cognitive mechanisms that work well enough to satisfy the demands placed on us in ordinary environments. We need not be completely rational organisms in a logical-mathematical or statistical sense to function adequately on a daily basis. Perhaps we have evolved so that we can do well enough in the real world through satisficing or the use of fast and frugal heuristics, even though we may perform less than optimally in the psychological laboratory.

NEUROPSYCHOLOGY OF REASONING

Researchers have begun to analyze the brain processes underlying reasoning. For example, Fangmeier, Knauff, Ruff, and Sloutsky (2006) tested neural activity during

Table 11.11 Fangmeier et al. (2006) Example Problem: Spatial Reasoning Task

Premise 1:	V	X
Premise 2:	X	Z
Conclusion:	V	Z
		Conclusion is true.

three postulated stages of deductive reasoning: the premise-processing phase, the premise-integration phase (in which people construct an integrated representation of the sets of premises; Ramnani & Owen, 2004), and the validation phase, in which the proposed conclusion is judged valid or invalid. To avoid confounds from using linguistic stimuli, they used reasoning problems about the spatial relations among a set of three letters. An example problem is presented in Table 11.11. The first premise contains two letters, one on the left and the other on the right. The second premise is then presented, which contains another pair of letters. From the two premises, it is possible to construct the spatial relations among the three different letters (V × Z). The conclusion was then presented, and half the time it matched the information that could be derived from the first two premises and half the time it did not. Participants responded by pressing one of two buttons to indicate whether the conclusion was true or false. In a control/working memory (WM) condition, people were asked to keep the premises in mind, but did not have to make any inferences. For those problems, the participants had to indicate only whether or not the third pair of letters matched either of the other two pairs or not. Brain activity during this task was subtracted from the activity for the reasoning task (see Chapter 1) to determine brain processes due to reasoning alone.

The researchers found that the premise-processing phase mainly produced brain activity because of WM processes. As can be seen in Figure 11.6, there was no independent activation due to premise processing, but the control/working memory condition shows activation of the medial and superior temporal lobe. Bilateral activity in the visual association areas is consistent with use of mental imagery to represent the information in the premises (Knauff, Fangmeier, Ruff, & Johnson-Laird, 2003; Ruff, Knauff, Fangmeier, & Spreer, 2003). The integration phase (reasoning minus working memory) led to enhanced blood flow in the anterior prefrontal cortex. The validation phase of reasoning was associated with activity in the right hemisphere (RH) posterior parietal cortex and bilateral prefrontal cortex. This highlights the role of executive processes (in the PFC) during reasoning, and also the posterior parietal cortex's role in spatially oriented mental models. This study illustrates both the computational processes involved in deductive reasoning and the brain correlates of each subprocess.

Thinking and Decision–Making: Conclusions

Research in the study of thinking over the past several decades has focused on the question of whether humans are rational thinkers, and much of the evidence supports a conclusion that humans are often irrational in all the components of decision making: gathering evidence, drawing conclusions, estimating probabilities, and choosing the best course of action out of several alternatives. In a set of influential papers, Kahneman and Tversky (1973; Tversky & Kahneman, 1974, etc.) proposed that people are less than rational because we are subject to biases and heuristics. While there is ample evidence for people's use of the availability and representativeness heuristics, and for the occurrence of the conjunction fallacy and other biases, recent research has supported the more optimistic conclusion that humans can exhibit high levels of rationality in certain situations, such as when the stimulus materials were made more user-friendly (e.g., when presented in frequency formats). In addition, there is some evidence that even reasoning that falls far short of complete rationality can be good enough in the real world. Rather than dwelling on all the negative results from laboratory investigations, perhaps we should emphasize the overall high level of performance

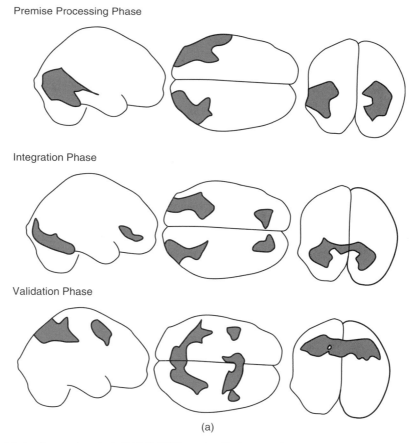

Premise Processing Phase

Integration Phase

Validation Phase

(a)

Figure 11.6 Fangmeier et al. (2006) fMRI results: Brain areas involved in reasoning versus those involved in simple maintenance of information. (a) Reasoning problem. (b) Maintenance problem.
Adapted from Fangmeier, Knauff, Ruff, and Sloutsky, 2006.

Premise Processing Phase

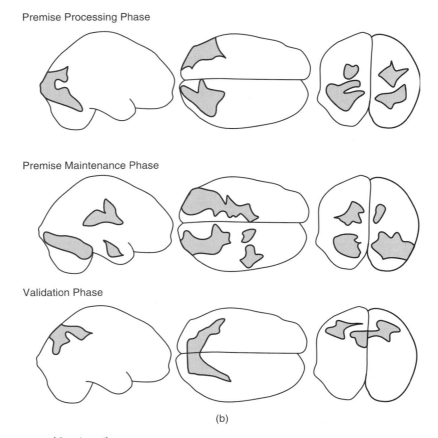

Premise Maintenance Phase

Validation Phase

(b)

Figure 11.6 (*Continued*)

we sometimes achieve. Researchers should then analyze the cognitive processes under-lying those successes, and examine how we could improve performance in situations demanding decision making.

REVIEW QUESTIONS

Here are questions to help you organize the material in the chapter.

1. How did scholars' views of human rationality change during the 20th century?

2. Give an example of the influence of *availability* on decision making.

3. How is "Harvard beats Yale, 29–29" an example of the anchoring heuristic?

4. How do factors involved in gathering evidence contribute to irrationality?

5. How are the *representativeness* heuristic and confirmation or *myside bias* examples of irrationality?

6. How might one overcome myside bias?

7. What is the problem with the reasoning from the "law of small numbers"?

8. Give positive and negative examples of people's use of base rates.

9. Does the conjunction fallacy affect only statistically naïve students?

10. How does framing affect people's tendency to avoid risk?

11. What is a general difference between inductive and deductive reasoning?

12. Briefly summarize valid and invalid types of conditional reasoning.

13. Why is belief bias irrational?

14. How does people's performance on the variations of the selection task (drinking; store receipts; four-cards) demonstrate irrationality?

15. Why do content effects in reasoning raise problems for the abstract-rules theory of reasoning?

16. What research findings raise problems for the memory-cueing theory of reasoning?

17. According to the mental models theory of reasoning, why might people make errors?

18. How has research on training supported the pragmatic schemas theory of reasoning?

19. How do dual-process theories of reasoning account for reasoning errors?

20. Is it possible to rescue people from a verdict of irrationality through postulation of random error and cognitive-processing limitations?

21. Has research on teaching general rules of thinking supported the idea of formal discipline as a way to improve reasoning?

22. How does presenting statistics problems in frequency format support the idea of human rationality?

23. What are *limited rationality* and *satisficing*?

24. Does research support the idea that fast and frugal heuristics are effective?

CHAPTER 12

THINKING II: PROBLEM SOLVING

In this chapter we examine cognition in the broader context of our goals and day-to-day activities. When we try to recall some information, for example, it is usually because that information is relevant to the task we are facing. We might try to remember how to get to a restaurant that we have not been to for a while, or try to remember how to calculate a standard deviation on a statistics test. Similarly, when our attention is drawn to a particular object in the environment, it might be because that object is the keyring we need in order to drive to the market. Much of our cognitive functioning on a daily basis is in the service of *problem solving*. Many professional activities also involve solving problems. Clinical psychologists spend their working days dealing with personal problems brought to them by clients. A corporate lawyer might be faced with the problem of negotiating a successful merger between two companies. One might even say that a painter might be faced with the problem of deciding how to render the appearance of a person on canvas, so as to produce an effective portrait. In sum, there is no doubt that problem solving is central to our cognitive activities (Novick & Bassok, 2005).

Please work through the problems in Box 12.1, which have been used by researchers to study problem solving in the laboratory.

BOX 12.1 SOME DEMONSTRATIONS OF PROBLEM SOLVING

A. General Problem

A small country was ruled from a strong fortress by a dictator. The fortress was situated in the middle of the country, surrounded by farms and villages. Many roads led to the fortress through the countryside. A rebel general vowed to capture the fortress. The general knew that an attack by his entire army would capture the fortress. He gathered his army at the head of one of the roads. The mines were set so that small bodies of men could pass over them safely, since the dictator needed to move his troops and workers to and from the fortress. However, any large force would detonate the mines. Not only would this blow up the road, but it would also destroy many neighboring villages. It therefore seemed impossible to capture the fortress.

What is the solution?

B. Towers of Hanoi

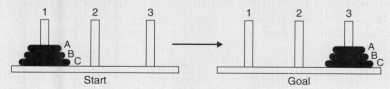

The goal of the problem is to move all three disks from peg 1 to peg 3 so that C is on the bottom, B is in the middle, and A is on top. You may move only one disk at a time, and only to another peg; you may not place a larger disk on top of a smaller one.

C. Missionaries and Cannibals

Three missionaries and three cannibals are traveling together and they come to the bank of a river. The only method of transportation across the river is a boat that will hold at most two people. The missionaries and cannibals hope to use the boat to cross the river, but there is one difficulty: If at any time the cannibals outnumber the missionaries on either bank of the river (including people in the boat at the bank), the outnumbered missionaries will be eaten. How can you get everyone across the river without losing anyone? It will be easier to try to solve the problem on paper, making a diagram.

OUTLINE OF CHAPTER 12

One stream of research on problem solving that we will consider in this chapter—the information-processing or *analytic* perspective—emphasizes the top-down role of knowledge and experience in problem solving (Chase & Simon, 1973; Newell & Simon, 1972; Simon, 1979, 1989; Weisberg, 2006a; see also chapters in Ericsson, Charness, Feltovich, & Hoffman, 2006). In this view, one first analyzes the situation and, based on what one knows about it, develops a solution method. We shall also refer to this view as the *business-as-usual* perspective on problem solving. The analytic perspective assumes that ordinary thinking processes are at play when we attempt problem solving; information from the environment or problem (bottom-up) and our knowledge (top-down processes) are combined to find a solution that meets our problem-solving goals. There is, however, also a tradition within our culture that proposes that problem solving requires that you break away from your past and think outside the box. In cognitive science, this view has focused on the notion that problems can sometimes be solved in a leap of insight—an *Aha!* experience—as one suddenly becomes aware of a new way of approaching a problem. This *insight* or *special-process view* of problem solving minimizes the role of analytic or top-down processes, and contends that solving a problem may require that we break away from what we have learned, in order to find a new perspective. Those differing views on the role of top-down processes in problem solving will serve to anchor the discussion in this chapter.

We begin by defining the important concepts concerning problem solving, after which we examine the information-processing perspective on problem solving. That view, which proposes that problem solving comes about through analysis and search of *problem spaces*, uses the computer metaphor as a way of understanding how humans solve problems (e.g., Anderson, 2010; Newell & Simon, 1972; Novick & Bassock, 2005). We then examine the question of insight in problem solving, taking a historical perspective, and follow the study of insight from its beginnings to the present. Modern researchers use the methods of cognitive science and cognitive neuroscience to collect evidence about how insight may lead to problem solution. The chapter concludes with an examination of research that has indicated that there may not be a sharp distinction between solving problems through analysis versus insight.

QUESTIONS OF DEFINITION: PROBLEMS, PROBLEM SOLVING, AND CREATIVE THINKING

A person has a *problem* when: (1) she is not in the situation she wants to be in, and (2) she does not immediately know how to change the present situation into something more satisfactory. In such circumstances, the person must think about what is to be done (Duncker, 1945; Novick & Bassock, 2005). The unsatisfactory present situation is called the *problem state*. The situation that the individual wants to be in is called the *goal state*. For example, if a student has a research paper due in a week, but has not started the research, that is the problem state. Completing the research paper on time, and to her satisfaction, is the goal state. The activities that she carries out in her attempts to solve the problem are called *operators*, or *moves*. Operators change one state into a different one. Applying the operator of conducting a literature search changes the student's present state (ignorant about the area) into a new one (research has been accomplished; she is prepared to start to write the paper). A series of operators that changes the problem state into the goal is a *solution* to the problem.

Problem Solving, Novelty, and Creative Thinking

A crucial criterion for calling something a problem is that the situation must be *novel*. If the situation that you face is familiar, so that you can simply carry out some action that you performed earlier in a similar situation, then you are simply recalling a solution from the past, rather than solving a problem. Thus, a situation that is a problem for one person may not be a problem for a person with experience in that situation (Novick & Bassock, 2005). The novelty of a problem demands originality, which means that, in solving a problem, you must use *creative thinking*, the type of thinking that results in novel outcomes (Weisberg, 2006a). Examination of laboratory studies of problem solving in this chapter will therefore provide the foundation for an analysis of creative thinking on a broader scale in the next chapter, including production of works of art and scientific theories.

Well- Versus Ill-Defined Problems

In some problems, the problem state, the goal state, and the possible operators are stipulated. Two examples are the Towers of Hanoi problem and Missionaries and Cannibals problem from Box 12.1B and C. In both, you simply have to work out a sequence of legal moves that will transform the problem state into the goal. Such a problem is called a *well-defined* problem. In other problem situations, one or more of the components might not be specified at the beginning, and there may be multiple paths to a solution. For example, let us say that you are a clinical psychologist, and a client comes to you complaining that he is unhappy and wants to change his life. He is not clear about exactly what is bothering him; he just knows that he is not happy. In addition, he does not know how he wants to change his life; he simply wants it to be better than it is now. A problem where at least one component is not specified is called an *ill-defined* problem. The General Problem in Box 12.1A is an example of an ill-defined problem: The goal state is not specified precisely, nor are all the possible operators specified at the beginning. Ill-defined problems require that the problem-solver specify the missing elements before work on a solution can begin. The therapist, for example, must learn specifics about the client's life before beginning to work on how things might be changed for the better.

The Problem Representation

Based on the information presented in a problem, a person will derive an understanding of what the problem requires and what possibilities exist for meeting those require-ments. This understanding is called the individual's *representation* of the problem. When a problem can be represented in multiple ways, the particular representation constructed by an individual determines the types of solution attempts he or she will make, and, ultimately, whether he or she will be successful. An example of the impor-tance of the problem representation in problem-solving performance is provided by the problem in Box 12.2.

BOX 12.2 BUDDHIST MONK PROBLEM

One morning at sunrise a Buddhist monk began to climb a mountain on a narrow path that wound around it. Exactly at sunset, he reached the top where there was a temple and remained there to meditate overnight. At sunrise of the next day he started down the same path, arriving at the bottom of the mountain at sunset. Prove that there must be a spot along the path that he occupied on both trips at exactly the same time of day.

The Buddhist Monk problem initially seems very difficult to solve. Surely the monk's speed of walking would vary greatly on ascent versus descent, as it would seem to be faster to get down the mountain than up it. How could one predict where he will be at a given time on the second day, which seems necessary to solve the problem? However, there is a way of representing the problem that makes it clear that that desired point on the journeys must exist. Imagine the monk and his *avatar* carrying out the upward and downward journeys, respectively, on the *same* rather than different days. So the monk begins his ascent at sunrise, and the avatar begins the descent at that time. Both reach their destinations at sunset, as the problem states. It is obvious that, no matter how quickly or slowly one or the other walks, the monk and the avatar must meet and pass each other at *some point* on the journey. That spot is the one that the problem asks about, so the problem is solved. Thus, by thinking about the problem in a different manner, one can determine the solution. A number of examples in this chapter will show how changing a person's representation of a problem has large effects on performance.

THE INFORMATION-PROCESSING THEORY OF PROBLEM SOLVING: SEARCHING PROBLEM SPACES

One way to begin to understand how people solve problems is to diagram all the possible sequences of moves that one could make in attempting to solve a problem. As an example, Figure 12.1 presents all the possible sequences of moves, or *paths*, that one can take in solving the Towers of Hanoi problem (Box 12.1B). Each sequence of moves in Figure 12.1 will ultimately get you to the goal, in which case you have

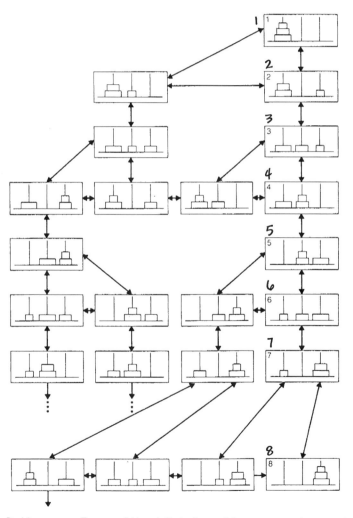

Figure 12.1   Problem space: Towers of Hanoi. Not all possible moves are shown; solution is #8 at bottom right.
From Weisberg, 2006a, Figure 3.6.

solved the problem. This set of all possible paths through a problem—solutions and nonsolutions—is called the *problem space* (Newell & Simon, 1972).

Algorithms Versus Heuristics

For some problems, a specified sequence of moves is available that will guarantee that you will solve the problem. If you are faced with a new arithmetic problem, such as: 37 + 43 + 123 = ?, you can simply apply the rules of addition and, assuming that you make no errors, you will always get the right answer. Presentation of an arithmetic problem to someone who knows the rules of arithmetic results in the correct path through the problem space being chosen. A set of operations that will always produce the correct solution to a problem is called an *algorithm*. Consider the following anagram:

Construct an English word from the letters **R T Y**.

One can solve this problem by searching the problem space completely, or *exhaustively*, by trying out every possible combination of moves. **R T Y**? No. **R Y T**? No. **Y T R**? No. One can continue in this vein (there are only six possible combinations) until **T R Y** is produced.

However, many problems that we face, even simple problems, have problem spaces that are too big for a person to use exhaustive search, and no other algorithms may be available. Consider this anagram:

G M A A N R A S

If you try to solve that anagram through exhaustively searching the problem space, the number of possible paths is large enough that that strategy becomes difficult (there are $8 \times 7 \times 6 \times 5 \times 4 \times 3 \times 2 \times 1 = 40{,}320$ possibilities).

When you are faced with a problem space that is too large to be searched exhaustively, and if you do not have any other algorithm available, then you may be able to use *heuristics*, which are *rules of thumb* that allow you to cut your search down to more manageable size. Heuristics do not guarantee a solution to your problem, but they may facilitate solution (Newell & Simon, 1972; recall our discussion of heuristics in reasoning and decision making from Chapter 11). The use of heuristics in problem solving can be seen if one observes someone trying to solve an anagram. The person might begin by looking for frequent combinations of letters that might begin or end a word. So, in the anagram **G M A A N R A S**, perhaps the solution word begins with **GRA**- or **SAR**-, or ends with -**ANS** or -**AMS**. Thus, the use of heuristics narrows the problem space to allow one to concentrate on a strategy that may yield success. (It turns out that in this situation that heuristic is helpful: The solution word is **ANAGRAMS**, which ends in a frequent letter combination.)

A number of different types of heuristics have been discovered by researchers studying people solving problems (Newell & Simon, 1972; Novick & Bassock, 2005). One method is *hill climbing*: You compare the current state and the goal state and pick an operator that makes progress toward the goal (that is, you are *climbing the hill* toward the goal). So, for example, in the Missionaries and Cannibals (Box 12.1C), you could move two individuals to the other bank, because that move makes most progress toward the goal.

A second heuristic is *working backward*, from the goal to the initial state. This can limit the number of possible moves that must be considered at any point, which cuts down on the space to be searched. Towers of Hanoi, for example, can be solved working backward. Let us say that you are trying to decide on the first move you should make: Should the smallest ring go to the goal peg (C), or the middle peg (B)? Working backward, in the solution the large ring must be at the bottom on the goal peg. Therefore, the goal peg must be empty, so that the large ring can go there. In order to move the large ring to the goal peg, the large ring must have no other rings on it, so the other two rings must be on peg B. Putting those two rings on peg B means that that the middle-sized ring must be on the bottom on that peg. Therefore, the smallest ring must be on the goal peg. So that is the first move: small ring to goal peg. The same method can be repeated for the next move, and so on.

Computer Simulation of Problem Solving

In their pioneering research on problem solving, Newell and Simon (1972) collected data from people trying to solve problems similar to Towers of Hanoi and Missionaries and Cannibals. Two sorts of data were collected: (1) the moves the people made and (2) *verbal protocols*, the speaking-aloud records of their thoughts as they worked. Newell and Simon used those data as the basis for development of a computer program, called the *General Problem Solver* (*GPS*), that was designed to model the human use of heuristic methods to solve problems, for example, the hill-climbing strategy just discussed. The GPS program was able to solve some problems using heuristic methods to search problem spaces, and the general orientation toward problem solving developed by Newell and Simon is still important (e.g., Anderson, 2010; Chronicle, MacGregor, & Ormerod, 2004; Dunbar, 1998; MacGregor, Ormerod, & Chronicle, 2001; Novick & Bassock, 2005; see also chapters in Ericsson et al., 2006, and Holyoak & Morrison, 2005).

To summarize, the information-processing or analytic perspective on problem solving focused on the need to search problem spaces in the solution of problems. For problems with large problem spaces, it may be necessary to use heuristic methods to cut that space down to manageable size.

STRONG METHODS IN PROBLEM SOLVING: STUDIES OF EXPERTISE IN PROBLEM SOLVING

Heuristic methods are very general in their applicability: Each can be applied to many problems a person will encounter. Because of that generality, however, heuristics do not provide detailed information for solving a particular problem. Therefore, they are called *weak methods* (Newell & Simon, 1972). Solving a problem using weak methods involves little in the way of top-down processes, since you are not applying your knowledge very deeply. There are problem situations, however, where success depends on domain-specific information—expertise—that is relevant to the specific problem at hand. An expert is able to apply what have been called *strong* methods to a problem (Luger, 2009), which are directly applicable to the type of problem in question, acquired through extensive experience. Under such circumstances, problem solving becomes a more of a top-down process. The study of expertise in problem solving became the focus of second-generation information-processing research in problem solving (Chase & Simon, 1973; Novick & Bassock, 2005; see chapters in Ericsson et al., 2006).

Expertise and Problem Solving in Chess

A pioneer in the study of expertise in problem solving was de Groot (1965/1978). In Chapter 3 we reviewed de Groot's study of chess masters' extraordinary memory for chess positions. He also explored chess masters' problem-solving strategies. He gave chess players the problem of choosing a move in the middle of a master-level game, using as his stimuli diagrams of the positions of chess pieces from actual master-level tournament games. Chess is a game with such a large problem space that it is impossible for any chess player to search it exhaustively. As an example of the size of that problem space, if you were able to make one move per *second*, it would take you *many centuries* to search through all the possible moves (Beeler, Gosper, & Schroeppel, 1972). De Groot found that, in choosing a move to make, the masters did not necessarily examine more possible moves than did less-skilled players. The masters almost always focused on what turned out to be the best move. Players of lower levels of skill, even though they might be very good players, spent time thinking about moves that the masters never even considered.

De Groot (1965/1978) concluded that many times the master simply looked at the board and *saw* or *recognized* the good moves, based on years of playing chess at a high level. For the chess master, playing chess is at least partially a top-down pattern-recognition task, as discussed in Chapters 3 and 5: Positions are recognized on the basis of knowledge. Once one or two moves have been picked, based on top-down processes, the master then uses his or her chess expertise to analyze the possible outcomes that may arise from each of the selected moves before making a final choice (Ericsson, Krampe, & Tesch-Römer, 1993; see also chapters in Ericsson et al., 2006).

One question that arises from de Groot's work is how the chess master's expertise develops. We can get some idea about that development by again considering chess players' memories for chess games (see Figure 12.2). In an extension of de Groot's memory research, Chase and Simon (1973) tested chess players of varying levels of skill on de Groot's memory-for-chess task. When chess masters were shown chess boards with pieces that had been placed on the board *randomly* (rather than in positions taken from chess games), the chess masters recalled little more than lesser players did. Thus, chess masters have great memories only for master-level chess games. Recall our analysis in Chapters 2 and 3 of top-down processes in memory: Chess masters have available detailed knowledge about the subject matter being tested, which allows

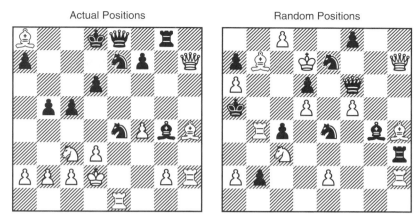

Figure 12.2 De Groot memory task, as modified by Chase and Simon (1973). Chess players of varying levels of ability were shown actual board positions and randomized positions, and asked to recall the locations of the pieces.

them to encode information in a way that makes it easy retrieve (Ericsson, Patel, & Kintsch, 2000).

In analyzing the chess master's knowledge base, Chase and Simon (1973) concluded that one needs to spend at least 10 years deeply immersed in the game in order to reach world-class performance in chess. That time period would be sufficient to allow the chess masters to acquire a depth of knowledge about chess. That conclusion, now known as the *10-year rule*, has been found to hold in many domains, including sports and medicine, as well as several domains that involve creative work, such as musical composition and the writing of poetry (Hayes, 1989; Weisberg, 2006a, 2006b; see chapters in Ericsson et al., 2006). One does not see evidence of world-class performance until the person has been immersed in a domain for years. Those results point to a common top-down thread tying together memory, pattern recognition, problem solving, and creative thinking: Those with more domain-specific knowledge perform better than those with less. That thread will be taken up more fully in the next chapter.

Expertise in Physics

De Groot's study of expertise in chess led to examinations of the influence of expertise in problem solving in many other domains (see chapters in Ericsson et al., 2006). Another area in which novices and experts have been compared is physics; a sample of physics problems is shown in Figure 12.3. Physics problems are of interest to cognitive psychologists because there are two distinct levels of each problem: (1) the surface level, which includes the objects involved (e.g., inclined planes, a pulley), and (2) the underlying principles of physics that are required to solve each of them (e.g., Newton's Second Law of Motion; force = mass × acceleration). Physics novices, who have only taken a physics class or two, often focus on specific objects mentioned, such as a pulley system, an inclined plane, or a spring, to try to solve the problem.

No. 11 (Force Problem)

A man of mass M_1 lowers himself to the ground from a height X by holding onto a rope passed over a massless frictionless pulley and attached to another block of mass M_2. The mass of the man is greater than the mass of the block. What is the tension on the rope?

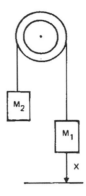

No. 18 (Energy Problem)

A man of mass M_1 lowers himself to the ground from a height X by holding onto a rope passed over a massless frictionless pulley and attached to another block of mass M_2. The mass of the man is greater than the mass of the block. With what speed does the man hit the ground?

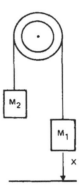

Figure 12.3   Physics problems.

Physics experts, on the other hand, focus on the abstract principles of physics that each problem exemplifies, such as force = mass × acceleration or Newton's Second Law (Chi, Feltovich, & Glaser, 1981). This often leads novices to think that two problems using an inclined plane belong together, even if one is solved via Newton's Second Law and the other via a different physics principle. Furthermore, when asked to remember physics diagrams, novices were less likely to remember the relevant surface details of the diagrams (Feil & Mestre, 2007), which may then lead to less efficient problem solving.

Strong Versus Weak Methods in Problem Solving: Conclusions

In many domains, high-level problem-solving performance demands expertise. The expert is able to pinpoint the crucial elements of a problem, because of the rich database that he or she brings to the situation. Problem solving for the expert becomes at least partly an exercise in pattern recognition. This recognition allows an expert to use past successes and failures to guide present attempts.

USE OF ANALOGIES IN NONEXPERTS: STUDIES OF ANALOGICAL TRANSFER OF KNOWLEDGE IN PROBLEM SOLVING

Strong versus weak methods of problem solving are the ends of a continuum concerning the amount and specificity of knowledge possessed by the person working on a problem. Researchers have also studied intermediate situations, in which a person has some information potentially relevant to a problem, but is not an expert in the domain. Before reading further, please try to solve the problem in Box 12.3.

BOX 12.3 RADIATION PROBLEM

Suppose you are a doctor faced with a patient who has a malignant tumor in his stomach. It is impossible to operate on the patient, but unless the tumor is destroyed the patient will die. There is a kind of ray that can be used to destroy the tumor. If the rays reach it all at once at a sufficiently high intensity, the tumor will be destroyed. Unfortunately, at this intensity the healthy tissue the rays pass through on the way to the tumor will also be destroyed. At lower intensities the rays are harmless to healthy tissue, but they will not affect the tumor, either. What type of procedure might be used to destroy the tumor with the rays and at the same time avoid destroying the healthy tissue?

In a pioneering discussion of heuristics in problem solving, Polya (1945) suggested that, in trying to solve a problem, one might try to find another problem that you have already solved that is *analogous* to the one you are working on. Two situations are analogous when they have the same underlying *structure*, even if the specific objects involved in the two problems—the *surface elements*—are different. For example, the Radiation problem in Box 12.3 is analogous to the General problem in Box 12.1A (see Table 12.1). In both problems, *forces* are trying to overcome a central obstacle, but *the forces cannot be used at full strength*. The two problems are solved by the same method, which could be called *simultaneous convergence*: You must *divide the forces* and send them toward the obstacle, *reuniting the forces at the obstacle*. If you ignore the surface elements—soldiers in the General problem and radiation in the Radiation problem—the solutions are the same.

Table 12.1   Similarities Between General and Radiation Problems

General Problem	Radiation Problem
General	Doctor
Fortress	Tumor
Army	Rays
Using whole army ⇒ exploding mines ⇒ kill innocent people and destroy homes	Using strong rays ⇒ kill healthy tissue ⇒ patient dies
Break up army into small groups, unite simultaneously at fortress: "Simultaneous convergence"	Use weak-intensity rays, unite at tumor: "Simultaneous convergence"

Analogies play many roles in cognitive functioning, some of which were touched on in Chapter 10, where we discussed the use of figurative language—analogies and metaphors—in communication. Analogies have also served to help students understand new concepts. An early description of the structure of the atom was as a solar system, with the nucleus of the atom as the sun, and the electrons as the planets orbiting that sun, with much of the atom made up of empty space. One's knowledge of the solar system assists in understanding the atom. Likewise, we can comprehend the notion of a computer virus based on what we already understand about how viruses infect and weaken organisms. Analogies allow us to transfer information from a familiar situation (e.g., a biological virus) as the basis for understanding a new one (e.g., a destructive computer program). The familiar situation is called the *base*, and the new one, which you do not yet understand, is the *target*. Cognitive scientists say that the base is *applied* to the target. A similar phenomenon can occur in problem solving, where solution to a base problem is used as the basis for solution of a target problem. Using analogies in problem solving may be one of the most common strategies that people use (Dunbar & Blanchette, 2001; Gentner, Holyoak, & Kokinov, 2001; Holyoak, 2005; Holyoak & Thagard, 1997; Klahr & Simon, 1999).

Limitations on Transfer of Knowledge in Problem Solving

Given the analogical relation between the General and Radiation problems, and the importance of analogies in cognition, one might expect that exposure to the former would facilitate solution of the latter. However, experimental research has shown that people who have been exposed to the General problem may not realize that it is relevant when the Radiation problem is presented (Gick & Holyoak, 1980, 1983; Spencer & Weisberg, 1986; see also Reeves & Weisberg, 1993a, b). That is, people may have knowledge available that could be used to solve a novel problem, but they may not retrieve that potentially useful base information and apply it to the new problem.

In a pioneering examination of transfer of knowledge in problem solving, Gick and Holyoak (e.g., 1980, 1983) used the Radiation problem as the target problem (see Box 12.3). The problem is rather difficult, with only about 10% of undergraduates usually solving it using the simultaneous convergence principle. Gick and Holyoak (1980) examined whether performance could be facilitated by providing information concerning how the Radiation problem could be solved, in the form of a potentially useful base analogy. This experiment thus tested *analogical transfer*. Participants were first given exposure to the General problem (the *base*, Box 12.1A), and the researchers then measured whether there was transfer from it to the Radiation problem. Half of those *transfer* participants were told that the General problem might help them solve the Radiation problem (the *Hint* group). The other transfer participants were told nothing about the possible usefulness of the General problem (the *No-Hint* group). A *Control* group was asked to solve the Radiation problem without exposure to any relevant base analogues.

As expected, the Control group performed poorly. In contrast, almost everyone in the Hint condition solved the Radiation problem (Gick & Holyoak, 1980), indicating that the General problem was potentially very useful in solving the Radiation problem. Most importantly, however, only about 30% of the No-Hint participants solved the Radiation problem. Thus, those participants did not spontaneously retrieve the General problem from memory while they were working on the Radiation problem, perhaps due to an inability to see the connection between the base and target without further guidance (see also Catrambone & Holyoak, 1989; Perfetto, Bransford, & Franks, 1983; Spencer & Weisberg, 1986).

Researchers have typically designated three stages in analogical transfer: (1) encoding of base and target analogues, (2) retrieval of the base problem by the target, and (3) application of the base—*mapping* of the base—to the target (Gick & Holyoak, 1983; Holyoak & Koh, 1987; Keane, 1987; Reeves & Weisberg, 1994; Ross, 1987, 1989). Structural versus surface elements of the base and target problems appear to be differentially important at each stage. For example, if the underlying structure can easily be derived from a base problem during encoding of that problem (Holyoak & Koh, 1987; Reeves & Weisberg, 1994), accurate solution is more likely. So, if participants are instructed to summarize the general aspects of the solution method in the base problem, that may lead them to encode the problem in more general or schematic terms, which will make it more likely that the solution method will be transferred from the base to a subsequent target problem.

During retrieval, in contrast, similarity in surface features among problems enhances the likelihood of retrieval of a base analogue (Holyoak & Koh, 1987; Keane, 1987; Ross, 1987), and its subsequent use in problem solving. For instance, Keane (1987) found that inclusion of elements common to the Radiation problem in a base problem (e.g., the base problem described a doctor using radiation in a simultaneous-convergence solution to destroy a *brain* tumor) significantly increased retrieval of the base analogue when people tried to solve the target Radiation problem.

In both adults (Ross, 1989) and children (Gentner & Toupin, 1986), parallels in objects between problems influences mapping of items from base to target analogues. Ross (1989) provided study participants with analogous study and test examples of probability problems (e.g., permutation problems; examples are shown in Table 12.2). As can be seen in the table, the problem domain was the same, but correspondences between objects could be either the same (e.g., mechanics chose cars to work on in both examples) or reversed (e.g., in the base analogue, mechanics chose cars to work on; in the target problem, car owners chose which mechanic would work on their cars). Although the formula was provided with each target problem, similarity of object correspondences between the two problems often guided subjects' mapping, even when such correspondences led to incorrect application of the solution (Ross, 1989, Experiment 1; see also Brookes, Ross, & Mestre, 2011).

Thus, it appears that analogical transfer can be a useful problem solving tool, and that it is greatly facilitated if people understand the underlying or abstract principle exemplified by analogous problems (Gick & Holyoak, 1983; Reeves & Weisberg, 1994). However, people are heavily reliant on the actual surface details of the two problems, both to retrieve a relevant base analogue (Holyoak & Koh, 1987; Keane, 1987) and to map it to a target problem (Brookes et al., 2011; Gentner & Toupin, 1986; Ross, 1989).

Table 12.2 Analogical Transfer in Problem Solving: Three of Ross's Problems

Problem	Description
Study Example	The IBM motor pool has to make sure that the company cars are serviced. On a particular day there are 11 cars and 8 mechanics. The IBM mechanics randomly choose which car they will work on, but the choice is done by seniority. What is the probability that the three most senior mechanics, Al, Bud, and Carl, will choose the cars of the Chairman, President, and Vice-President, respectively?
Same Correspondence (+/+)*	The motor pool at IBM repairs the cars the company salespeople use. The IBM mechanics randomly choose which car to repair, with the best mechanic choosing first, and so forth. There are 16 salespeople who have cars and 5 mechanics. What is the probability that the best mechanic gets to work on the car of the best salesperson and the second best mechanic gets to work on the car of the second best salesperson?
Reversed Correspondence (+/−)*	The motor pool at IBM repairs the cars the company salespeople use. The IBM salespeople randomly choose which mechanic repairs their car, with the best salesperson choosing first, and so forth. There are 14 salespeople who have cars and 16 mechanics. What is the probability that the best mechanic gets to work on the car of the best salesperson and the second best mechanic gets to work on the car of the second best salesperson?

*Note: The first + or − indicates that a similar storyline occurred at study and test, while the second + or − indicates that the correspondences between objects were the same or were reversed.

A Paradox: Analogue Use in Experts Versus Lack of Analogical Transfer in Undergraduates

An interesting puzzle arises when we review the discussion in the last several sections: Effective transfer of information during problem solving is often seen in experts within a given domain, but is much less frequently exhibited by undergraduates in the laboratory (Dunbar, 2001; Dunbar & Blanchette, 2001). On the one hand, experts perform well in problem situations because they have large amounts of knowledge to transfer to a new problem. On the other hand, novices, even when they possess information that is analogous to a new problem, often do not use that information to achieve effective problem solving. Why the discrepancy in effectiveness of transfer of available knowledge?

The difference between experts' versus novices' use of analogies in solving problems may be due to the specificity of the knowledge involved (Ball, Ormerod, & Morley, 2004; Brookes et al., 2011; Christensen & Schunn, 2007; Linsey et al., 2010). The expert's domain-specific knowledge is directly relevant to the problem at hand. A chess master uses chess knowledge to solve chess problems; an expert radiologist uses knowledge about x-rays to read a new x-ray; and so forth. In contrast, in laboratory studies of analogical transfer in which undergraduates are the participants, the relationship between the base and target is not obvious, since the problems typically do not come from the same domain. For example, the relationship between the Radiation and General problems is not apparent simply by looking at the problems (see Boxes 12.1A and 12.3). If the individual has not thought about the base and target situations at a more abstract level (i.e., they both involve *forces*; you have to *divide the forces*; etc.), he or she will not notice their relationship. Thus, one might say that the situation is much more difficult for the undergraduates, since they have no way of knowing that their previously acquired knowledge is relevant to the new problem that they are facing.

Studies of Transfer in Problem Solving: Conclusions

Laboratory studies of transfer, using several different sorts of target problems and different types of base information, have consistently shown a lack of transfer (for review, see Reeves & Weisberg, 1994). Those negative results, although obtained from experiments using laboratory puzzles, may have something general and potentially important to tell us about human thought: We often appear to be heavily dependent on the use of specific related examples to solve problems, rather than using very abstract principles (Ball et al., 2004; Brookes et al., 2011; Christensen & Schunn, 2007; Linsey et al., 2010). For example, retrieving the solution to a problem seems to be tied to the specific domain and/or particular objects that were in the problem (e.g., a general's army), and when a new target problem contains different objects (e.g., a doctor and rays), the new problem will not retrieve potentially useful base information. In other words, the thought processes involved are often rather concrete in nature. When one develops expertise in an area, one is able to deal with problems at a more abstract level, which can result in wider transfer.

In the discussion so far, we have mainly examined laboratory exercises with no direct connection to problem solving in real life. It will be useful to extend the discussion to a domain that is relevant to many of our activities: problem solving in mathematics. Mathematical problem solving is clearly based on top-down processes. Correct calculations require that we have available memorized arithmetical facts, such as basic addition and the multiplication tables. In addition, we become experts through the acquisition of algorithms for carrying out complex operations in addition, subtraction, multiplication, and division. Even in mathematical domains where we are not experts, as when we attempt a new procedure in geometry, calculus, or statistics, we employ heuristics and demonstrate heavy reliance on domain-specific knowledge of numbers and mathematics. In the next section, we consider some of the skills exhibited during mathematical problem solving, and review how data from brain-damaged patients sheds light on how humans process numbers and carry out numerical operations.

MATHEMATICAL PROBLEM SOLVING AND ACALCULIA

Mathematical problem solving occurs on a daily basis, whether it involves making sure we get the right change after buying groceries, looking up the probability of rain on a day we want to have a picnic, or calculating means and standard deviations in a statistics class. Researchers (e.g., McCloskey, Aliminosa, & Sokol, 1991; Sokol & McCloskey, 1991; Warrington, 1982; Whalen, McCloskey, Lindemann, & Bouton, 2002) have proposed three distinct types of mathematical knowledge and related computation skills: (1) *memorized arithmetical facts* which are simply retrieved from memory, such as when a person recalls simple addition sums (e.g., $5 + 2$) or memorized answers within the multiplication tables (e.g., 5×7); (2) *procedural knowledge* about how to carry out mathematical operations, that comes into play when a person calculates the answer to a more complex problem (e.g., 43×56); and (3) *conceptual knowledge* about mathematical laws and operations, which entails being able to provide definitions of mathematical terms and to demonstrate understanding of arithmetical properties, such as knowing that multiplying 8 by 3 is equivalent to adding 3 sets of 8 together.

While there is a large educational and cognitive literature on how children (and adults) develop mathematical skills (e.g., Dehaene, 1997), much interesting knowledge about the cognitive aspects of calculating comes from analyzing the breakdown of mathematical abilities. *Acalculia* is a neuropsychological syndrome in which a person exhibits difficulty in carrying out mathematical calculations (from the Greek *a-*, meaning without, plus *calculare*, to count). It is typically caused by brain damage to the left hemisphere (Jackson & Warrington, 1986; Rosselli & Ardila, 1989), especially the angular gyrus in the parietal lobe, the intraparietal sulcus (Takayama, Sugishita, Akiguchi, & Kimura, 1994), and/or frontal lobes, typically due to a stroke, head trauma, or Alzheimer's disease.

Much of the neuropsychological evidence supports the three-part distinction just laid out between fact retrieval versus procedural skills versus conceptual knowledge. For instance, Rosca (2009) studied a woman, B.D., with a left parietal lobe and thalamic tumor who had lost the ability to calculate exact amounts. The patient was completely accurate at solving single-digit addition, subtraction, and multiplication problems; however, she made errors on all complex calculation problems that she was given involving multiplication, division, addition, and subtraction. Thus, Rosca's patient illustrated intact arithmetic facts but impaired procedures.

In contrast, Cohen and Dehaene (1994) discussed a patient whose impairment was in retrieving basic number facts, although she could carry out multidigit multiplication and division. She would line up problems appropriately, and showed evidence of being able to implement the carrying function and of using correct procedures. However, she could carry out computations only after the experimenter told her basic math facts (e.g., if multiplying 54×36, she needed help with the answer to the initial 4×6 in the ones column). The patient retained conceptual knowledge—she was able to correctly classify numbers as odd or even, for example—and used this knowledge to carry out simple calculations which she was unable to retrieve (e.g., by drawing 5 rows of 5 dots to represent 5×5). There is thus evidence for a double dissociation of math-fact retrieval and mathematical calculations (see also Hittmair-Delazer, Sailer, & Benke, 1995).

Other patients show selective impairment of only some arithmetical operations. Grafman, Kampen, Rosenberg, Salazar, and Boller (1989) studied an Alzheimer's patient who retained the ability to add and subtract, but could not multiply or divide (also see Benson & Weir, 1972). A patient documented by Lampl, Eshel, Gilad, and Sarova-Pinhas (1994) could subtract but not perform any other operations. Such results indicate that those operations may be represented separately both psychologically and in the brain.

Models of Mathematical Knowledge

Several theorists have proposed models of numerical knowledge, to help explain the data both from neuropsychological studies and from research on how people without brain damage accomplish arithmetic tasks and numerical reasoning. McCloskey (1992; Whalen, McCloskey, Lindemann, & Bouton, 2002) has posited that all mathematical calculations are accomplished by a single abstract numerical system, no matter whether the numbers come in verbally or in written Arabic form (i.e., visually). This calculational system is distinct from the single-digit calculation system, which is not based on calculation at all, but, as we have seen, is based on retrieval of arithmetic facts, such as the multiplication tables. Imagine that a person sees a mathematical problem written in numbers, such as 98 × 42. According to McCloskey's model (see Figure 12.4), she would translate those symbols into the abstract numerical system, and the calculation processes would operate on that abstract representation. The problem-solver could then deliver an answer verbally or in numerical form. This model proposes that, no matter the input code or modality of the problem (e.g., verbal vs. numerical), all computation is performed on the same amodal representation. This view is similar to Pylyshyn's (1981) view concerning the amodal nature of the representations manipulated during imagery tasks, which was discussed in Chapter 7.

In contrast to McCloskey's *single-abstract-code* model, Dehaene and colleagues (Berteletti, Lucangeli, Piazza, Dehaene, & Zorzi, 2010; Dehaene, 1997; Dehaene &

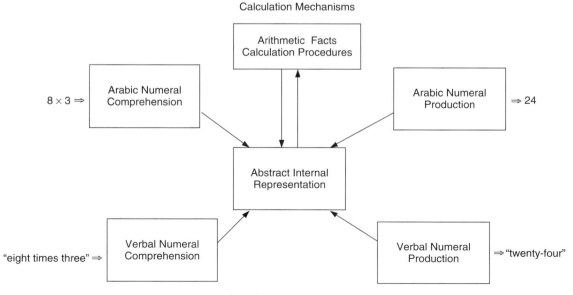

Figure 12.4 McCloskey's (1992) model of numerical processing.

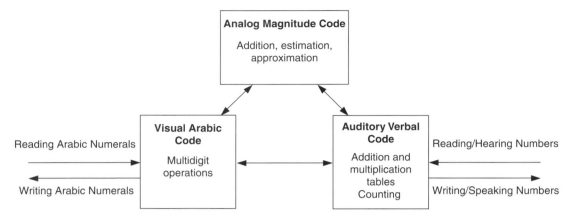

Figure 12.5 Dehaene and Cohen's (1995) model of numerical processing.

Cohen, 1995, 1997; Piazza, 2010; Piazza et al., 2010) have proposed a multiple-code model of numerical representation, which uses three representation codes, each of which can participate in calculations, either by itself or in conjunction with other codes (see Figure 12.5). One code represents numbers in *verbal form* (e.g., "three hundred and fifty-two"), and retrieves math facts, such as memorized answers to one-digit addition and subtraction, plus the multiplication tables. Second, a *visual code* recognizes and represents mathematical information, and carries out calculations, using Arabic number forms. Finally, the *analog magnitude* code is analogous to McCloskey's abstract representation, and can be used for estimation and when making judgments as to which of two numbers is larger (or smaller). It also contains semantic knowledge about numbers and their relative magnitudes, such as that 5 is smaller than 6. Each code can be translated into the other, such as when we see four objects, and say the word "four" or write the number "4." In addition, each system can participate in calculations, either by itself or in conjunction with the other systems.

While the McCloskey model has the advantage of simplicity, the Dehaene and Cohen (1995) model is more flexible, in that it permits computations to be performed in any modality, and it also can explain other aspects of numerical processing, such as estimation and approximate calculation, as well as retrieval of number facts from memory (e.g., simple addition, multiplication tables). In addition, there is both functional and neuroanatomical support for the three-code system (Schmithorst & Brown, 2004): fMRI studies have revealed activation in the bilateral inferior parietal regions during magnitude comparison and numerical approximation tasks (Chochon, Cohen, van de Moortele, & Dehaene, 1999; Dehaene, Spelke, Pinel, Stanescu, & Tsivkin, 1999; Stanescu-Cosson et al., 2000). On the one hand, auditory/verbal number processing, including retrieval of addition and multiplication facts, causes activation in the left perisylvian network (including Broca's and Wernicke's areas; Dehaene, 1997; Houk & Wise, 1995). Manipulation of visual Arabic numerals, on the other hand, has been found to lead to activation in the ventral occipital-temporal lobe in both hemispheres, with greater left hemisphere activity after presentation of words or digits, and greater right hemisphere activation when a person processes Arabic numbers, such as mentally calculating multidigit calculation (Dehaene, 1992, 1997; Piazza, 2010; Piazza et al., 2010).

Use of Analogies in Mathematical Problem Solving

People utilize not only specific mathematical facts and calculation procedures when solving math problems, but also take into account the broader context in which a problem occurs. As one example, when confronted with a new problem in math or statistics, many students may rely on similar problems that they had learned earlier. Reed, Ackinclose, and Voss (1990) investigated how people choose and apply the solution from one math problem to another. For example, a student would be given the following target problem:

> A group of people paid $306 to purchase theater tickets. When seven more people joined the group, the total cost was $425. How many people were in the original group if all tickets had the same price?

This problem can be solved using the following formula:

$$\$306/n = \$425/ \left(n + 7 \right)$$

When asked which of two problems would be more useful in helping them solve the initial problem—either Problem A, a simpler, less inclusive problem that was missing a solution step ($14 = $238/$n$), or Problem B, a more inclusive problem with an *extra* step (e.g., $0.8 \times (\$70/n) = \$120/n + 8$) students did not show a preference for either problem. However, those who chose the more inclusive problem were twice as likely to solve the target problem, indicating that the choice of a more sophisticated example may facilitate successful mathematical problem solving; it is easier to eliminate elements of an equation than to use too simple an equation.

Mathematical Problem Solving: Conclusions

Solving mathematical problems efficiently involves a combination of skills that use both semantic knowledge (e.g., information about numbers, memorization of multiplication tables) and procedural knowledge (knowing how to carry out mathematical operations such as multiplication and division). Patients suffering from acalculia have difficulty with performing mathematical computations, though they may still be able to retrieve numerical facts (such as the product of 8×7). A model of numerical processing by Dehaene and Cohen (1995) proposed three codes in which we can operate on numerical information: an analogue magnitude code, visual code, and verbal form. Their model has received psychological and neuroanatomical support. In addition, we have seen that analogical transfer may facilitate problem solving in mathematics.

ANALYSIS IN PROBLEM SOLVING: SUMMARY AND CONCLUSIONS

In the problem situations we have examined so far, such as Towers of Hanoi, Missionaries and Cannibals, and math problems, the solution occurs in a step-by-step solution process, based on an analysis of the problem. Table 12.3 presents an information-processing model that summarizes the role of top-down processes in analytic problem solving as discussed so far in this chapter. The model assumes that the first step in dealing with any problem involves something like pattern recognition: an attempt to match the situation with the person's knowledge (Weisberg, 2006a, 2006b). If the person possesses expertise in the area (e.g., statistics), there will be a relatively precise match between the problem and that expertise, which will lead to the retrieval of a solution method (e.g., a formula) that relatively precisely fits the problem. This outcome is shown in Stage 1B, and it results in a solution attempt based either on analogical transfer of the problem solution from one example to another, or on application of an abstract solution principle derived from the person's expertise. If the solution transfers successfully, then the problem is solved. If there is no success, then, in Stage 2, the person would attempt to apply weak—i.e., heuristic—methods to the problem. If this stage were successful, then the problem would be solved. If no weak methods were successful, then the person would fail to solve the problem, and would give up or seek more information.

INSIGHT IN PROBLEM SOLVING

We might summarize the discussion so far by saying that the outline in Table 12.3 summarizes *ordinary* or *business-as-usual* problem solving, which we carry out in most

Table 12.3 Top-Down Solution Methods for Analytic Problems

Stage 1: Solution Through Application of Strong Methods

1. Problem presented.	Attempt to match with knowledge.
A. No solution available.	Go to stage 2.
B. Successful match with knowledge.	Transfer solution based on expertise or analogy.
C. If solution transfers successfully.	Problem solved.
D. If solution fails.	Go to stage 2.
Comment:	If no match is made with memory, person goes to Stage 2; if match is made, solution is attempted. Can result in solution of the problem.

Stage 2: Solution Through Application of Weak (Heuristic) Methods

2. Failure at Stage 1A.	Analysis based on weak methods.
A. Analysis successful.	Solution.
B. No solution.	Impasse; problem not solvable.
Comment:	Person works through problem using weak heuristic methods, trying to develop solution; if successful, problem is solved.

circumstances. As noted earlier, however, it has been proposed that there is another kind of problem solving, which depends on *insight*, a set of processes assumed to be very different from the analytic methods discussed so far. Please work through the problems presented in Box 12.4 before reading further.

BOX 12.4 INSIGHT PROBLEMS

Lilies

Water lilies double in area every 24 hours. At the beginning of the summer, there is one water lily on a lake. It takes 30 days for the lake to become completely covered with water lilies. On what day is the lake half covered?

Solution: If the lilies double every 24 hours, then if it takes 30 days for the lake to be fully covered, the lake is half covered on day 29.

Prisoner and Rope

A prisoner was attempting to escape from a tower. He found in his cell a rope that was half long enough to permit him to reach the ground safely. He divided the rope in half and tied the two parts together and escaped. How could he have done this?

Solution: The prisoner divided the rope in half *lengthwise*, by unraveling it, thereby producing enough length for his needs.

Compound–Remote–Associates (CRA) Problems

For each set of three words below, find one other word that, when paired with each individual word, makes a common phrase in English.

1. high / house / district   (answer is *school*: high school; schoolhouse; school district)
2. palm / shoe / house   (answer is *tree*)
3. pie / luck / belly   (answer is *pot*)
4. pine / crab / sauce   (answer is *apple*)

Rebus Problems

Each problem represents a common phrase in visual form. What is the solution phrase for each?

Problem	Solution
1. poPPd	Two peas in a pod
2. you just me	Just between you and me
3. |r|e|a|d|i|n|g|	reading between the lines

Everyone has had the experience of the solution to a problem suddenly flashing into consciousness, out of the blue, in what can be called an *Aha! experience* or *leap of insight*: The proverbial light bulb goes on, and you may be totally surprised to discover that you have solved the problem. You may have had one or more *Aha!* experiences in working through the problems in Box 12.4. For example, an experience of sudden and easy solution of a problem may occur with the Prisoner and Rope, as you puzzle through an impossible situation—*how can one divide a rope in half and make it longer?*—and then suddenly realize that "divides the rope in half" can mean more than one thing.

There is no doubt that solving a problem through insight is very different subjectively from what happens during the solution of analytic problems, such as Towers of Hanoi and Missionaries and Cannibals (Box 12.1), where solutions typically involve incremental progress. A question of interest to researchers is whether that insight experience is brought about by thought processes that are fundamentally different from those that underlie analytical thinking. That question also has relevance to creativity (see Chapter 13), as it is believed that many creative advances are the result of insights accompanied by *Aha!* experiences (e.g., Akin & Akin, 1996; Cunningham, MacGregor, Gibb, & Haar, 2009; Dietrich & Kanso, 2010; Lehrer, 2012b; Novick & Bassok, 2005; Ohlsson, 2011): A creative individual—an artist, inventor, or scientist—suddenly sees some aspect of the world in a new way, leading to a scientific, technological, or artistic advance. Thus, studying insight in the lab might provide an understanding of creative thinking in the world.

Research on insight has a long history, stretching back to early in the 20th century (e.g., Köhler, 1925; Thorndike, 1911). Through the middle of the 20th century, with the development of behaviorism, there was little interest in the topic, but in the past 30 years, there has been renewed interest in insight among cognitive scientists (e.g., Ansburg & Dominowski, 2000; Durso, Rea, & Dayton, 1994; Gilhooly & Fioratou, 2009; Gilhooly, Fioratou, Anthony, & Wynn, 2007; Jung-Beeman et al., 2004; Kaplan & Simon, 1990; Knoblich, Ohlsson, Haider, & Rhenius, 1999; Kounios & Jung-Beeman, 2009; MacGregor, Ormerod, & Chronicle, 2001; Metcalfe, 1987; Metcalfe & Weibe, 1987; Novick & Sherman, 2003; Ohlsson, 1984a, 1984b, 1992, 2011; Perkins, 1981, 2000; Sternberg & Davidson, 1995; Weisberg, 1995, 2006a; Weisberg & Alba, 1981; Wiley & Jarosz, 2012). Over the past century of research in insight, there have emerged two views concerning the processes underlying insight in problem solving. The first view, developed by the Gestalt psychologists early in the 20th century, proposed that solving problems through insight is built on processes basically different from those underlying ordinary problem solving through analysis. We will therefore refer to the Gestalt perspective and the research that grew out of it as the *special process* view of insight (Gilhooly & Fioratou, 2009).

The second view of insight assumes that, even though the subjective experience accompanying insight—the *Aha!* experience—may be very different from that accompanying solution through analysis, that does not mean that the processes involved in insight are different from those underlying analytic problem solving. This view has been called the *business-as-usual* perspective on insight (Ball & Stevens, 2009), because it assumes that solving problems through insight involves the same processes as those involved in ordinary problem solving through analysis (the processes just outlined in Table 12.3), although different subjective experiences are obviously involved. We shall examine the development of those two views from a historical perspective, to try to provide a background for the questions being investigated by modern researchers. We shall first trace the development of the special process view of insight, from the Gestalt psychologists to the present, and then examine the development of the business-as-usual view.

EARLY RESEARCH ON INSIGHT

Research on insight in problem solving began with the study of animals. At the turn of the 20th century, there was a thriving interest in psychological processes in animals. However, most accounts of animal problem solving were based on anecdotes, such as descriptions of how one animal learned to open a locked door (such reports are still seen occasionally in magazines or on television). The writers often claimed that the animals had exhibited intelligence similar to humans, such as the ability to reason and to solve complex problems. In response to unsupported claims about high levels of animal intelligence, Thorndike (1911) undertook a systematic laboratory investigation to determine whether animals were capable of exhibiting intelligence.

Thorndike's Study of Intelligence in Animals: Problem Solving Versus Learning

Thorndike (1911) designed several *puzzle boxes*, each of which was a cage from which a cat could escape by operating a mechanism that opened the door. For example, in one box, the door opened if the animal pushed against a vertical pole in the middle of the cage. However, the mechanism through which the pole was attached to the door was hidden, so that the connection between the pole and the door could not be seen. Straightforward responses like pushing on the door or clawing at it did not result in it opening (see Figure 12.6).

Food was placed outside the hungry animal's cage, in sight but out of reach. Typically, the animals would respond to the sight of the food by reaching toward

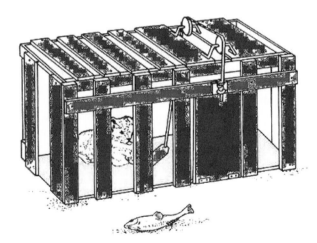

Figure 12.6   A Thorndike puzzle box.

it and scratching the cage door, but those responses were unsuccessful. Thorndike was interested in whether the animals would show anything like insight in figuring out how the door-opening mechanism worked. Evidence for intelligence or reasoning ability would be that the animal would efficiently open the cage once it had figured out how to open the locking mechanism. Thorndike's results showed that his animals did not exhibit insight in his puzzle boxes. They seemed initially to randomly respond in the cage and to stumble on the way to open the door, and only gradually got more efficient at escaping the cage. This slow improvement led Thorndike to the conclusion that the animals only gradually *learned* to escape from the cage; they were not able to exhibit *insight* into how to escape.

THE GESTALT RESPONSE TO THORNDIKE: INTELLIGENCE AND INSIGHT IN APES AND HUMANS

Thorndike's conclusion concerning the lack of intelligence shown by animals was criticized by the Gestalt psychologists, such as Köhler and Wertheimer (e.g., Köhler, 1925; Wertheimer, 1982), who were of the belief that animals were capable of achieving insight or understanding into problems. The Gestalt psychologists, who were well known for their analysis of perceptual phenomena (see Chapter 1), applied analogous concepts to problem solving. In the Gestalt view, a problem situation is like the reversible cube presented in Figure 12.7: More than one interpretation is possible, and, in order for the solution to be produced, the person must see a problem in the correct way.

With the reversible cube, the emergence of a new interpretation of the figure can be called a *restructuring* of the stimulus: One structure suddenly shifts to another. Similarly, solving a problem may necessitate seeing it in a new way, in order to change one's initial less-than-useful representation of the problem to a new one. It follows from this perceptually based analysis of problem solving that, in order for an organism—whether human or chimp—to exhibit insight into a problem, the layout of the whole situation has to be available. Only in this way could the structure of the situation be perceived, so the organism could then produce the insightful solution to the problem. The Gestalt psychologists thus argued that Thorndike never gave his animals a chance to exhibit insight. Thorndike's animals could not see the set-up of

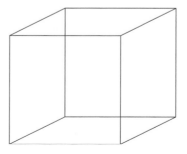

Figure 12.7   Reversible figure: The Necker cube.

the puzzle box, since the operation of the door-opening mechanisms was hidden from view (Weisberg, 2006a). It is not surprising that in such a situation an animal would rely on unintelligent trial-and-error.

Köhler's Investigation of Problem-Solving in Apes

In response to those limitations in Thorndike's work, Köhler (1925) carried out a study designed to demonstrate insight in apes. Köhler's problem situations were designed so that an intelligent animal should be able to solve the problem simply through analysis of the entire situation, thereby demonstrating that they were capable of producing novel responses based on thinking and insight. An example of a problem developed by Köhler is shown in Figure 12.8. The hungry animal is in a cage, and outside, out of reach, is a banana. Lying through the bars is a stick, and the animal quickly picks it up and uses it as a tool to rake in the banana. Once the animal had insight into the structure of the situation, the solution would be produced as an integrated whole, without the fumbling trial and error exhibited by Thorndike's (1911) animals. In support of the idea that perceptual processes were important in problem solving, Köhler found that, in order for the animal to use the stick as a rake, it was crucial that the stick be lying *between* the ape and the banana, so the stick could be perceived as a potential extension of the animal's arm. If the stick were off to the side, so that the banana, stick, and arm could not be seen in one glance, then the stick would not be used.

Köhler (1925) also reported that, sometimes, in the middle of working unsuccessfully on a problem, his animals would sit for a while doing nothing, or might actually walk away from the problem. The animal might then suddenly return to the problem and attempt to carry out a new type of solution. In Köhler's view, the animal had

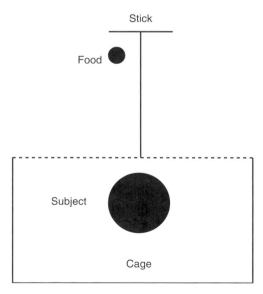

Figure 12.8 Köhler's stick problem.

reached an *impasse*—it had run out of things to do—and this impasse then set off processes that resulted in a sudden restructuring of the problem situation. Restructuring opened the way for the solution by bringing about the rejection of the initial method, which was based on the animal's trying to apply experience to the problem.

Wertheimer: Problem Understanding and Insight in Humans

Wertheimer (1982), another leader of the Gestalt school, investigated insight in problem solving in people, parallel to Köhler's study of apes. Wertheimer also addressed the question of whether problem solving was constructed out of trial-and-error learning, or whether problem solving involved thinking and intelligence, resulting in solutions that were the result of insight based on restructuring a situation. In Wertheimer's terms, thinking and intelligence meant analyzing the situation on its own terms, and determining what it demanded, rather than simply relying on experience and habit. Wertheimer made a distinction between *reproductive* versus *productive* thinking. Reproductive thinking is based on redoing—reproducing—what was done before, and involves using specialized knowledge to solve a problem. Productive thinking, in contrast, goes beyond old responses based on knowledge and habit, and thus results in original and insightful methods for solving problems.

In one of Wertheimer's (1982) problems, he asked people to find the area of a parallelogram (see Figure 12.9). One participant, a young girl, had already learned a method for obtaining the area of a rectangle, by fitting squares inside it, as shown in Figure 12.9a. Faced with the more difficult parallelogram problem, shown in Figure 12.9b, she initially proclaimed, "I certainly don't know how to do *that*." Then, after a moment of silence: "This is *no good here*," pointing to the region at the left end where the squares will not fit, because of the acute angle of the parallelogram; "and *no good here*," pointing to the angled region at the right. After some consideration, suddenly she cried out, "May I have a pair of scissors? What is bad here is just what is needed here. It fits." She took the scissors, cut the figure vertically, and placed the left end at the right (see Figure 12.9c; Wertheimer, 1982, pp. 47–48).

Wertheimer believed that perception of the overall structure of the problem situation was more important than possessing specific knowledge that could be applied to the problem (e.g., how to calculate the area of a rectangle). If one could examine the problem as a whole, to determine what was demanded, one could solve problems without detailed knowledge about the domain, as demonstrated by the girl's figuring out how to determine the area of a parallelogram, about which she had not been taught.

Failure and Fixation in Problem Solving

What is so wrong about using one's (reproductive) knowledge to solve a problem, you might ask? The Gestalt psychologists argued that reliance on reproductive information might result in one's becoming *fixated* on the initial representation of a problem, due to the blind application of experience to the situation (Wertheimer, 1982). In order to find the area of the parallelogram, for example, in Figure 12.9b and c, the child must break away from finding the area of a rectangle. Please work on the Nine-Dot problem in Box 12.5 before reading further.

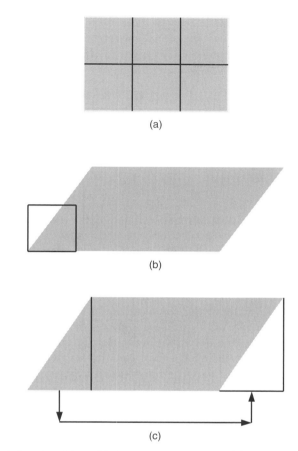

Figure 12.9 Wertheimer's problems. (a) Finding area of rectangle. (b) Parallelogram problem. (c) Girl's solution.

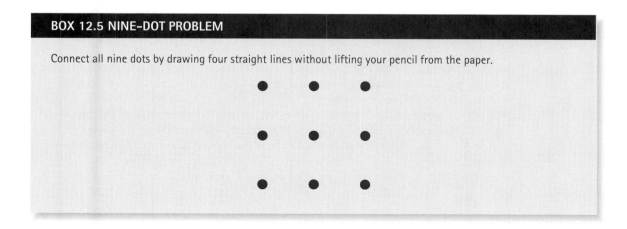

BOX 12.5 NINE–DOT PROBLEM

Connect all nine dots by drawing four straight lines without lifting your pencil from the paper.

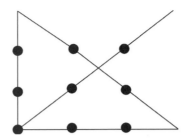

Figure 12.10   Solution to the Nine-Dot problem.

The Nine-Dot Problem

The Nine-Dot problem is one of the most well-known—and most difficult—insight problems in psychology. Several studies have found solution rates of approximately zero in undergraduates (Burnham & Davis, 1969; Kershaw & Ohlsson, 2004; Lung & Dominowski, 1985; Weisberg & Alba, 1981). That low rate of solution is at first glance puzzling, since the basic aspects of the solution are within the grasp of all of us: We all can draw four connected straight lines. According to the Gestalt psychologists, the difficulty of the problem is the result of *fixation* (Novick & Bassok, 2005; Scheerer, 1963): Presentation of the problem results in the person perceiving the dots as a square. The person then keeps the lines within that shape, which makes solution impossible. The 9-Dot problem is the source of the phrase "thinking outside the box," since, as can be seen in Figure 12.10, going outside the box is literally what its solution requires.

Duncker's Study of Functional Fixedness

Another example of fixation was demonstrated by Duncker (1945), a student of Wertheimer and Köhler. Duncker investigated several problems in which seemingly simple solutions were interfered with, again presumably because of fixation. One well-known problem studied by Duncker is the Candle problem, shown in Box 12.6. Please work through that problem before reading further.

Duncker (1945) was particularly interested in the *box solution* to the Candle problem (see Figure 12.11a). When the box is presented filled with tacks (as presented in Box 12.6), people rarely achieve the solution of creating a shelf out of the box for the candle to stand on. However, if the box is presented empty, as in Figure 12.11b, then the box solution is usually given as the first solution (Duncker, 1945; Glucksberg & Weisberg, 1966). Duncker proposed that presenting the box full of tacks highlighted its use as a *container*, and thereby prevented people from seeing that the box can be used as a *platform* or *shelf*. The tendency for the typical function of the object to block the discovery of the function demanded by a problem is known as *functional fixedness* (Duncker, 1945). Functional fixedness is another example of problem solving being interfered with by a too-strong reliance on one's knowledge.

BOX 12.6 CANDLE PROBLEM

Your task is to attach the candle to a wooden wall, so that you can read by its light, using the materials shown in the picture.

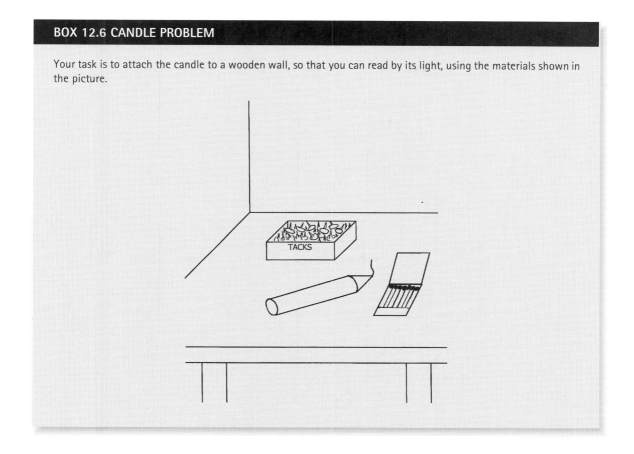

Insight in Problem Solving: Summary

We have now summarized the early development of the Gestalt theory of insight, which we have called the special-process view of insight. In this view, solving a problem through insight exhibits three characteristics (Ohlsson, 1992; Simon, 1986; Weisberg 1995, 2006a). First, the problem is solved suddenly (in an *Aha!* experience). Second, the *Aha!* experience comes about after an impasse (a period of no progress toward solution). Third, the *Aha!* experience comes about as a result of a new way of approaching the problem (a restructuring of the problem), stimulated by the impasse. Restructuring of a problem can be interfered with by fixation on one's experience in similar situations. The Gestalt psychologists' emphasis on the potential negative role of experience—as fixation—led to a widespread belief that productive problem solving, and creative thinking in general, come about only by breaking away from one's experience—by thinking outside the box (e.g., de Bono, 1968; Deitrich & Kanso, 2010; Lehrer, 2012b; Ohlsson, 2011).

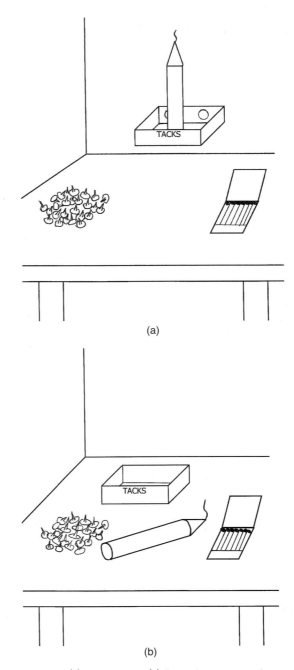

Figure 12.11   Candle problem. (a) Box solution. (b) Empty box presentation.

Modern research has seen a number of advances in the Gestalt perspective, as investigators have attempted to provide support for the special-process view. First of all, Ohlsson (1992, Knoblich et al., 1999) developed *representational change theory*, which elaborated and extended the Gestalt theory of insight, to bring a more modern perspective to it. Second, researchers have carried out studies that have documented the occurrence of *Aha!* experiences in problem solving, and have also used modern methods to demonstrate that solving problems through insight involves different cognitive processes than those involved in analysis. We first examine Ohlsson's extension of Gestalt theory and then review a sample of the research supporting the special-process view.

REPRESENTATIONAL CHANGE THEORY OF INSIGHT

Ohlsson's (1992) *representational change* theory of restructuring and insight was an attempt to bring together the Gestalt notions of restructuring, insight, and fixation with the concept of heuristic methods adapted from the information-processing perspective (Ohlsson, 1984b, 1992; Knoblich et al., 1999; see also Kaplan & Simon, 1990).

Impasse and Insight

As the Gestalt psychologists did, Ohlsson (1992, 2011) emphasized the important role played by impasse in the development of insight.

> Insights occur after the problem-solver has encountered an impasse, i.e., a mental state in which problem-solving has come to a halt; all possibilities seem to have been exhausted and the problem solver cannot think of any way to proceed. Subjectively, his or her mind is "blank." Behaviorally, impasses are characterized by the cessation of problem-solving activity.... Insight, I suggest, is the act of breaking out of an impasse. (1992, p. 4)

That emphasis on insight has been carried forth by present-day researchers (e.g., Dietrich and Kanso, 2010; Jung-Beeman et al., 2004; Lehrer, 2012a; Sandkühler and Bhattacharya, 2008; Sheth, Sandkühler, & Bhattacharya, 2008).

Breaking Out of Impasse: "Switch When Stuck"

In Ohlsson's (1992, 2011) reformulation of the Gestalt view, a person's being in a state of impasse sets in motion special sorts of heuristic methods. Those methods can result in the individual changing the representation of the problem, and thereby restructuring the situation. That restructuring may result in the discovery of a new solution method and an *Aha!* As we saw earlier in this chapter, Newell and Simon (1972) had investigated the heuristic methods that people use to direct the search for new moves *within* the problem space, such as working backward and hill climbing. Ohlsson proposed that heuristically guided search can also occur in insightful problem solving. His representational change theory proposed that, in response to reaching an impasse (meaning that no more moves are available), the individual may attempt to find *a new representation for the whole problem*. That is, the person may try to change the way the problem is analyzed, in the hope that a new method will be found. This heuristic can be called "switch when stuck" (Ohlsson, 1992; see also Kaplan & Simon, 1990): One attempts to switch to a new way of analyzing the problem (to restructure the problem) when one is making no progress (when one is stuck).

Forms of Restructuring

According to Ohlsson (1992), there are several mechanisms through which the *switch when stuck* heuristic can bring about restructuring of a problem. First, the individual may try to find a different way to describe an object or objects in the problem, which could open a new path that leads to solution. This is called *elaboration* of the problem. Second, the individual may decide that some previously ignored object should be included among the objects in the problem, which may lead to new solution methods. This is called *re-encoding* of the problem, since new information is encoded. Finally, the individual may change the way in which he or she thinks about the goal of the problem, or the method to be used in reaching the goal. This is called *relaxing goal constraints*.

As one concrete example of how these ideas might work, Ohlsson (1984b) analyzed a hypothetical example of behavior in the Candle problem (Box 12.6). Initial attempts to solve that problem, typically using the tacks or the melted candle wax as glue, are unsuccessful. Consistent failure would result in an impasse, which would initiate an attempt to restructure the problem. Through Ohlsson's postulated process of *elaboration*, a person might be led to examine the tack-box closely, saying to herself something like: "I did not realize that the box is flat. Is there anything I can do with that? Oh! I can use it as a shelf for the candle." Another possibility for restructuring in the Candle problem, through the process of *re-encoding*, might occur if a person, on reaching an impasse, said something like: "Have I tried to use all the objects in the problem? *Aha*! There's the box holding the tacks. Maybe that can be used to solve the problem." Finally, a person, on reaching an impasse after attempting unsuccessfully to attach the candle to the wall using the tacks, or candle wax as glue, might say: "Is there any other way to get the candle up on the wall? Yes! I can make a candle holder of some sort." That relaxation of the goal constraints of the problem could result in the use of the tack box in a solution.

Switch When Stuck: Bottom-Up Restructuring

One important aspect of Ohlsson's discussion of restructuring (2011, see also Kaplan & Simon, 1990) is that it comes about from bottom-up. Upon reaching an impasse, the individual examines various aspects of the problem and its elements with no overall plan in mind, since he or she is at an impasse, which means that no ideas are available. All that the individual has is the hope that he or she can uncover some new information that will be useful in solving the problem. That perspective is very different from the top-down view that has structured the discussion throughout this book. In the remainder of this chapter we will examine the adequacy of this bottom-up analysis of restructuring and insight and will contrast it with a top-down perspective that is consistent with our earlier discussion of the critical role of knowledge in all our cognitive functioning. We first examine research supporting the bottom-up view.

Constraint Relaxation and Difficulty in Solving Problems

Knoblich, Ohlsson, Haider, and Rhenius (1999; Knoblich, Ohlsson, & Raney, 2001) provided support for Ohlsson's (1992, 2011) analysis of insight through the study of matchstick-arithmetic problems, such as those shown in Box 12.7. Solving matchstick-arithmetic problems requires that one violate rules of arithmetic. Attempt those problems now.

In normal arithmetic, one carries out the same operations to both sides of the equation. Matchstick arithmetic requires that one do something to one side of the equation and something else to the other side. For example, you might take one matchstick away from one side and add it to the other. Thus, in order to carry out such operations, one must *relax the constraints* from arithmetic that one brings to the problem (Ohlsson's third restructuring method). Knoblich et al. (1999) hypothesized that some constraints are more easily relaxed than others.

BOX 12.7 MATCHSTICK ARITHMETIC PROBLEMS

All the lines in the problems below represent matchsticks. Those matchsticks represent Roman numerals. Your goal is to move a single stick so that the initial false statement is transformed into a true arithmetic statement. Only one stick can be moved. A stick cannot be discarded.

Problem	Solution
Problem A: IV = III + III	*Solution*: VI = III + III
Problem B: VI = VII + I	*Solution*: VII = VI + I
Problem C: I = II + II	*Solution*: I = III − II

Adapted from Knoblich et al., 1999.

In order to solve Problem A, the *I* in the *IV* on the left side of the equation must be moved to the other side of the *V*, in order to make it into *VI*. The component *I* can itself be an independent number, which means that the constraint being violated is at a relatively low level, which should make it easy to carry out the required operation. In Problem B, solution requires a similar operation. In Problem C, however, solution requires that the components of the symbol for an arithmetic operation (+) be broken apart; one component must be used as the symbol for a different arithmetic operation (−) and the other component be added to the first number *II* (to turn it into *III*). The destruction of an arithmetic symbol requires the violation of a fundamental or high-level constraint governing arithmetic, which, therefore, should be difficult for the individual to discover.

Knoblich et al. (1999) constructed a set of matchstick-arithmetic problems that varied according to the hypothesized degree of difficulty concerning the constraint that had to be relaxed for solution to occur. They found that, as predicted, problems involving relaxation of lower-level constraints—e.g., moving numbers from one side of an equation to the other—were easier than relaxation of higher-level ones—e.g., changing an arithmetic operation into a number or a number into an arithmetic operation. Those results and others (Öllinger, Jones, & Knoblich, 2006) supported the representational change theory, since the proposed difficulty in relaxing a constraint predicted difficulty in solving a problem.

Representational Change Theory: Summary

Ohlsson's (1992, 2011) representational change theory attempted to formulate an explanation of restructuring within an information-processing framework. He took the notion of heuristics and proposed that, in response to impasse, a switch-when-stuck heuristic could bring about a change in the problem representation and an insightful solution to a problem. A person can discover a new solution path, for example, by considering how to use an object in a new way (*elaboration*), or incorporating a new object into the problem solution (*re-encoding*), or altering the approach or method being taken to solve the problem, through *relaxing goal constraints*. There is some empirical support for Ohlsson's view, especially concerning its prediction of when people should be able to relax constraints on a problem (e.g., Knoblich et al., 1999).

EVIDENCE SUPPORTING THE SPECIAL-PROCESS VIEW

There has been a broad range of recent research that has attempted to provide support for the special-process view of insight, beyond the specific issues addressed by Ohlsson's (1992, 2011) theory. One stream of modern research in support of the special-process view has attempted to demonstrate in various ways that solving problems through insight is different than solving through analysis. First, Metcalfe (1987; Metcalfe & Wiebe, 1987; see also Sheth et al., 2008) developed a laboratory method that provided evidence for the occurrence of experiences of sudden insight—*Aha!* experiences—during some types of problem solving. Those results were taken as support for the Gestalt view of insight brought about through sudden restructuring in response to impasse. Second, researchers provided evidence that the cognitive and brain processes underlying insight were different than those underlying analysis.

Demonstrating *Aha!* Experiences in the Laboratory

In a highly cited set of studies, Metcalfe used a variation on the child's game in which a blindfolded person is searching for something, and we tell them that they are getting *warmer* or *colder* as they move around the environment. Increases in warmth ("You're getting warm, . . . hot, . . . very hot") mean that the person is getting closer and closer to the target, and increases in coldness ("You're getting cold, . . . colder, . . . freezing") mean that he or she is moving away. Metcalfe and Wiebe (1987) asked participants, as they worked to solve each of a set of problems, to provide ratings every 15 seconds of how "warm" they felt, on a 1–7 scale. Those ratings allowed the researchers to obtain a running record of the participants' perceptions of how close they were to solution of the problem.

The warmth ratings obtained by Metcalfe and Wiebe (1987) for insight versus analytic (algebra) problems are shown in Figure 12.12, and they provide evidence for the occurrence of *Aha!* experiences in insight problems. The warmth ratings for the algebra problems showed incremental or gradual progress toward solution. For the insight problems, in contrast, the ratings showed little increase in warmth until just before solution, when there was a rapid increase. These results supported the idea that solution of insight problems occurs suddenly, in a burst of insight, presumably in response to impasse.

Different Cognitive Processes in Insight Versus Analysis

Working Memory and Planning in Insight Versus Analysis

Gestalt theory proposed that insight is the result of a restructuring of the problem that comes about in response to impasse, when the person is at a loss concerning what to do next. It thus follows that planning should play a minimal role in bringing about insight. Indeed, the *Aha!* experience seems the opposite of top-down planning. The occurrence of the solution surprises the very person who produces it. Evidence to support the idea that planning plays little or no role in insight was presented by Lavric, Forstmeier, and Rippon (2000), who asked study participants to solve insight and noninsight problems while carrying out a secondary task—keeping track of numbers presented auditorily—which put a load on working memory (WM).

The basic hypothesis being tested was that overloading WM would interfere with performance on analytic problems, since those problems are solved through planning, and WM is where planning is carried out. In contrast, insight problems should not be affected by WM overload, since planning should play a minor role, if any, in solution of those sorts of problems. Lavric et al. (2000) did find that increasing the load on WM disrupted analytical problem solving more than insight problem solving. Those results supported the view that solving problems through insight was less dependent on WM than was solution through analysis, which suggests that different processes are involved in the two modes of solution.

Verbal Overshadowing of Insight

The finding that WM plays little role in solution of insight problems supports the idea that insight comes about through processes occurring outside of conscious control (i.e., through unconscious processing). A prediction that follows from this perspective is that asking people to think aloud while they are attempting to solve insight problems might be problematic, because conscious verbalization might interfere with those unconscious thought processes needed for insight (Gilhooly, Fioratou, & Henretty, 2010). Schooler, Ohlsson, and Brooks (1993) reported fewer solutions to insight problems (but not to noninsight problems) when people were asked to think aloud as they solved them. This phenomenon has been called *verbal overshadowing* of insight.

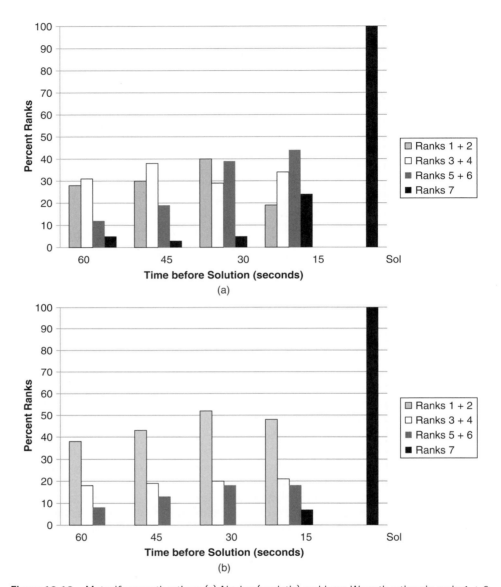

Figure 12.12 Metcalfe warmth ratings. (a) Algebra (analytic) problems. Warmth ratings in ranks 1 + 2 tend to go down, while ratings in ranks 5 + 6 and 7 tend to go up. (b) Insight problems. Warmth ratings change very little until solution, when highest warmth suddenly increases.

Neuroscience of Insight

Recently there has been a movement to unlock the mysteries underlying insight—to "demystify insight" (e.g., Jung-Beeman et al., 2004; Kounios & Beeman, 2009)—through the use of the methods of neuroscience. Studies have been carried out using fMRI and ERP to record activity when people solve Compound-Remote-Associates (CRA) problems (see Box 12.4). People report that solution to those problems can come about in one of two ways: (1) as the result of a systematic search among the associations of the three stimulus words, until a common associate is found (an *analytic* method); or (2) suddenly, without warning, in an *Aha!* experience (i.e., through *insight*; Jung-Beeman et al., 2004; Kounios & Jung-Beeman, 2009). Subtracting the brain regions involved in analysis from those involved in insight would presumably allow one to specify the brain regions related to solving problems with insight. Several researchers have used that subtraction method and have concluded that they have determined the locus of insight in the brain (e.g., Jung-Beeman et al., 2004; Sandkühler & Bhattacharya, 2008; Sheth, Sandkühler, & Bhattacharya, 2008).

In an early study that attempted to provide evidence for where insight came about in the brain, Bowden and Jung-Beeman (1998) presented CRA problems to study participants, and concentrated on problems not solved quickly. If a problem was not solved within 7 seconds, it was followed by one of two words: the solution word (which was not announced as such to the participant) or an unrelated word. That word was presented either to the right visual field (RVF), which provides quicker access to the left hemisphere (rvf-LH), or to the left visual field, which allows for quicker processing by the right hemisphere (lvf-RH). Participants were asked to say the word aloud, and then were queried as to whether the word was the solution to the just-presented CRA problem. The researchers found that decisions as to whether a word was a correct solution to a problem were faster for words presented to the lvf-RH. Bowden and Jung-Beeman concluded that their results supported the idea that the RH carries out *coarse* semantic coding (Beeman & Chiarello, 1998; Chiarello, Burgess, Richards, & Pollock, 1990). Words presented to the RH activate a wide array of associated meanings, including words distantly related to the stimulus word. When a word is presented to the LH, in contrast, the word mainly activates meanings directly connected to it or its close associates. That is, the LH carries out *fine-tuned* semantic processing. Thus, answers to CRA problems are more likely to be found as a result of the diffuse or coarse activation of the RH. This research supports the idea that insightful solutions, at least to CRA problems, come about through mechanisms different than those underlying analytic solutions, which supports the special-process view.

In a further extension of this perspective, Jung-Beeman et al. (2004) more-directly measured brain activity underlying insight. Participants worked on CRA problems while the researchers measured EEG in one study and fMRI in a second. In both studies, the subtraction method was used in an attempt to isolate the brain areas involved in insight. After solving a problem, participants reported whether or not the solution came suddenly, in an Aha! experience (i.e., in a burst of insight). When brain activity underlying analytic solutions was subtracted from that accompanying insight solutions, results from both studies indicated that insight solutions were associated with activity in the anterior superior temporal gyrus in the right temporal lobe. The researchers concluded that restructuring and insight occur in CRA problem solving because, when confronted with an impasse in problem solving, there is a switch to a new mode of search through information in memory (also see Sandkühler & Bhattacharya, 2008; Sheth et al., 2008). The initial unsuccessful search typically involves information in the left hemisphere. This may lead to an impasse and switching to a RH search, which provides more-remote connections among ideas. Those remote associations allow a leap of insight, as a solution worked out through unconscious processing suddenly bursts into consciousness (Jung-Beeman et al., 2004). This analysis of the processes underlying insight is similar to the *switch-when-stuck* heuristic at the core of Ohlsson's (1992) representational change theory.

The postulation of RH coding as being important in insight has not, however, been supported by other studies. In a review of a number of recent studies that have measured the course of brain activity accompanying insight, Dietrich and Kanso (2010) concluded that the results were not supportive of RH importance in insight. Some studies have found activation in the LH rather than the RH, and other studies have found activation in both hemispheres. Also, the activation in the RH should, according to the theory of Jung-Beeman and colleagues, be more important later in the solution process, since activity is assumed to switch from the LH to the RH as the individual breaks out of impasse, which should occur later rather than earlier in the solution process. However, again, studies have not consistently found later activation in the RH as insight occurs. At present, the evidence does not support the idea that coarse semantic coding in the RH is critical for insight.

Insight as a Special Process: Summary

The special-process view of insight proposes that some problems are difficult because they require restructuring—breaking away from the past—in order for solution to occur. Support for the special-process view has come from studies that have demonstrated that insight occurs suddenly (Metcalfe, 1987; Metcalfe & Wiebe, 1987), as well as from studies that have indicated that different processes are involved in solution through insight versus analysis. Researchers have also used neuroscience methods to try to determine brain areas underlying insightful problem solving. One hypothesis that has been studied is that solving CRA problems through insight depends on right-hemisphere processing of distant semantic relations, but that hypothesis has not received strong support (Dietrich & Kanso, 2010). The coming years will surely bring about a surge in neuroscience research examining insight and related phenomena. In the next chapter we shall review research concerning brain processes involved in creativity.

INSIGHT AS BUSINESS-AS-USUAL

Although the initial development of Gestalt theory took place early in the 1900s, the question of insight in problem solving has, as we have seen, fascinated researchers and laypeople into the 21st century (e.g., Lehrer, 2012a; Ohlsson, 2011). Much of the recent interest in insight came about as the result of challenges to the Gestalt view. Questions were raised concerning whether it was necessary to postulate insight as a special mode of problem solving. As noted, this skeptical perspective toward insight as a special process has been called the *business-as-usual* view of insight (Ball & Stevens, 2009; Jung-Beeman et al., 2004). Researchers who supported the business-as-usual view reported research findings that raised challenges for the special-process view.

First, research indicated that insight might be much more dependent on experience than the Gestalt psychologists realized (Birch, 1945; Harlow, 1949). Contrary to the special-process view, insight might depend on knowledge, rather than on the rejection of knowledge. Second, research results indicated that insight was brought about through ordinary cognitive processes, rather than through some special insight process triggered by impasse (Jung-Beeman et al., 2004; Ohlsson, 1992). Third, questions were raised about the notion of fixation in problem solving, the idea that difficulty in solving some problems—for example, the Nine-Dot problem or the Candle problem—was the result of a too-strong reliance on past strategies or knowledge. Finally, research has demonstrated that the fact that a problem is solved in a sudden *Aha!* does not mean that no progress has been made before the *Aha!* That result also raises questions about the importance of impasse in insight. Together, those findings raised the more general question of whether it was useful to talk about insight as a distinct process in problem solving. We will review some of the results that have raised questions about the special-process view of insight and then discuss a synthesis of the special-process and business-as-usual views on insight.

Knowledge and Insight in Köhler's Apes

Köhler (1925) played down the role of experience in his apes' performance on the insight problems he investigated. However, one potential difficulty with Köhler's conclusions, as he knew, stemmed from the fact that most of his animal participants had been captured at various ages and brought to the colony, and thus their experience with sticks and other objects was unknown. Birch (1945) carried out a study very similar to Köhler's, also using the stick problem (see Figure 12.8). In contrast to Köhler's wild-born animals, however, Birch's animals were raised in captivity from birth, so he was sure that they had had no exposure to sticks before seeing the problem. Birch tested four naïve animals on the stick problem, and his results did not support the Gestalt view: Without prior use of sticks, only one of the animals attempted to use the stick to rake in the fruit. That single chimp first by accident pushed the stick while trying to reach the food, causing it to move the banana. That discovery stimulated the animal to attempt to move the banana with the stick, and he was eventually successful at retrieving the food. However, his success appears to have been predicated upon accident, rather than planning or insight.

After those failures on the stick problem, Birch's (1945) animals were returned to their compound, and sticks were left there by the experimenters. As the animals came across those new objects, they picked them up and began manipulating them, eventually using them to poke things, as extensions of their arms. After several days of free play with the sticks, the problem was presented again, and now all the previously unsuccessful animals quickly solved it. It thus seems that experience with sticks is necessary before an animal will have the insight of using a stick as a rake. Thus, solving even a relatively simple three-step problem (pick up stick, use as a rake, retrieve banana) requires a certain amount of expertise on the part of the animal.

Ordinary Processes in Insight

A second challenge to the Gestalt theory of insight came from research demonstrating that solution of insight problems came about through ordinary thought processes (i.e., through "business as usual" as far as thinking is concerned). In an early examination of the processes underlying insight, Perkins (1981) presented the Antique-Coin problem to people:

> A dealer in antique coins got an offer to buy a beautiful bronze coin. The coin had an emperor's head on one side and the date 544 B.C. stamped on the other. The dealer examined the coin, but instead of buying it, he called the police. Why?

The solution to the problem is that the man is a swindler, trying to sell the dealer a fake coin: How could a coin have the date *B.C.* on it? The maker of the coin would have to have been able to predict when Christ would be born. That is, presumably, impossible, so the coin must be fake.

When one of Perkins's participants solved the problem, he or she was asked to report immediately on the thoughts that had led up to solution. Two of Perkins's participants' reports are presented here:

Perkins's Two Protocols From the Antique-Coin Problem

Abbott

1. Couldn't figure out what was wrong after reading through once.

2. Decided to read problem over again.

3. Asked himself, do architects dig up coins? Decided yes.

4. Asked himself, could the problem have something to do with bronze? Decided no.

5. Saw the word "marked." This was suspicious. Marked could mean many different things.

6. Decided to see what followed in the text.

7. Saw 544 B.C. (Imagined grungy coin in the dirt; had an impression of ancient times.)

8. Immediately realized–"it snapped"–that B.C. was the flaw.

Binet

1. Thought perhaps they didn't mark coins with the date then.

2. Thought they didn't date at all—too early for calendar. (Image of backwards man hammering 544 on each little bronze coin.)

3. Focused on 544 B.C.

4. Looked at B.C.

5. Realized "B.C.—that means Before Christ."

6. Rationalized that it couldn't be before Christ since Christ hadn't been born yet.

7. Saw no possible way to anticipate when Christ was going to be born.

8. Concluded "Fake!"

The two people solved the problem differently, with one (whom Perkins called Abbott) reporting that the solution "just snapped" together in a leap of insight; the other (Binet) worked out the solution through analysis, in a logical series of steps. When Perkins examined the two reports, however, he concluded that the thought processes carried out by Abbott and Binet were very similar, which raised questions about whether Abbott's leap of insight was as special as it might seem to be.

First, neither Abbott nor Binet reached an impasse, meaning that impasse was not necessary for insight, which contradicts the special-process view (see also Fleck & Weisberg, 2004). Second, both Abbott and Binet focused on, or *recognized*, the date as the crucial piece of information, and thus Abbott's *Aha!* experience did not come out of nothing. Third, there was no restructuring of the problem on Abbott's part: The date was available from the beginning. Fourth, Abbott's leap turned out to have required only a couple of steps of reasoning on Binet's part; that is, the insight process did not do much in the way of cognitive work. What was required was that the thinker *realize* the impossibility of the coin maker's knowing that Christ would be born at some later date.

Perkins (1981) proposed that we could understand *Aha!* experiences as being the result of ordinary cognitive processes, such as *recognizing* or *realizing* that something is true or false, without assuming the operation of extraordinary thought processes, such as leaps of insight in response to an impasse. Abbott's supposed leap of insight was simply due to the ordinary process of realizing that something was impossible, and seeing what followed from that. Perkins drew an analogy between insight and our understanding of jokes: Sometimes we can get a joke directly, as soon as we hear the punchline (similar to Abbott's insight), while other times we have to have the logic of the joke explained to us (similar to Binet's solving the problem in a series of small steps). The research of Perkins is one of several studies that have shown that the same sorts of processes are at work in insight and analysis (Chein, Weisberg, Streeter, & Kwok, 2010; Chronicle et al., 2004; Fleck & Weisberg, 2004; Gilhooly et al., 2010). Such results indicate that there may not be a need to assume that insight is a special mode of solving problems.

The Question of Fixation in Problem Solving

The Gestalt psychologists and their followers developed the notion of *fixation* in order to explain why people were not able to solve seemingly simple problems (e.g., the Nine-Dot and Candle problems). As one example, most people do not use the tack-box in a solution to the Candle problem, although that would appear to be a simple and elegant solution. Similarly, the Gestalt interpretation of the Nine-Dot problem (e.g., Scheerer, 1963) proposed that it is not very difficult in and of itself—after all, we can all draw four connected straight lines—but solution is interfered with by people's fixation on the shape of the square. However, there is evidence that both the Candle and Nine-Dot problems are solved in ways that do not support Gestalt theory. In both cases, impasse and fixation play roles that are much less important that the special-process view assumes.

Restructuring and Insight Without Impasse in the Candle Problem
We have examined Ohlsson's discussion of how *representational change theory* (Ohlsson, 1992) might be applied to explain people's behavior on the Candle problem. Impasse

would activate the *switch-when-stuck* heuristic, which might lead to using the tack box as a platform or shelf. Fleck and Weisberg (2004) tested Ohlsson's analysis of performance on the Candle problem by collecting verbal protocols, which provided detailed information concerning the processes underlying solution. Of 34 people whom they tested, a total of 8 (24%) produced the box solution to the problem. That result was consistent with earlier results: Most people do not produce the insightful solution to the problem.

Fleck and Weisberg's (2004) collection of protocols enabled them to test the prediction that insightful solutions should be the result of a response to an impasse. The results did not support that prediction: Of those eight box-solvers, almost all solved the problem *without* impasse. That is, those people restructured the problem without first encountering impasse. These findings provide another example of Perkins's (1981) finding that solution to insight problems can occur without impasse (see also Weisberg & Suls, 1973). Fleck and Weisberg also found that restructuring in the Candle problem did not come about in the manner hypothesized by Ohlsson (1992). Most of the participants tested by Fleck and Weisberg restructured the problem in response to new information that they acquired as they worked on the problem. For example, they might try to tack the candle to the wall, which typically failed: The tacks were too short. That failure led to the realization that they needed to find a way to hold the candle up. That restructuring—changing the goal constraints from attaching the candle to the wall to fabricating something to hold the candle up—could be called *top-down restructuring*, because the information from the failed solution was used by the participants as the basis for a reanalysis of the problem (see also Weisberg & Suls, 1973). Thus, one can have a restructuring in response to new information from the problem, rather than solely in a bottom-up response to impasse, as postulated by Ohlsson's (1992) constraint-relaxation theory.

However, as noted, a small minority of individuals did solve the problem after an impasse, and they did so in a bottom-up manner, supporting Ohlsson (1992). As an example, one person first tried to attach the candle to the wall using tacks, and succeeded in doing so after combining the tacks with wax-glue obtained by melting the candle. She was then asked if she could produce another solution, but was unable to think of anything else, meaning that she had reached impasse. On a further request by the experimenter to try to think of something else, she said, "Okay, what objects have I not yet used? Can I use the box from the tacks? Maybe I can. . . ." Thus, she restructured the problem by examining objects not thought about earlier (what Ohlsson referred to as *elaboration*), in an attempt to find something new that she could do, without any overall plan. In sum, it seems that impasse and bottom-up restructuring (switch when stuck) is much less important in restructuring and insight than Ohlsson (1992) and the Gestalt psychologists assumed.

Fixation Versus Expertise and Heuristics in Solving the Nine-Dot Problem

The Gestalt interpretation of the difficulty in the Nine-Dot problem—as arising from fixation on the shape of the square—suggests that removing the constraint surrounding the boundaries of the square should lead to immediate solution. In order to test this view, Weisberg and Alba (1981) gave college students the Nine-Dot problem with a hint: In order to solve the problem, they had to draw lines outside the square. Contrary to predictions of the Gestalt view, that out-of-the-box hint was not very effective in

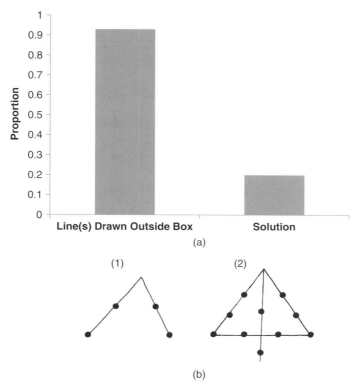

Figure 12.13   Results from Weisberg and Alba's (1981) study of the Nine-Dot Problem. (a) Effects of an "outside-of-the-box" hint on Nine-Dot problem performance. (b) Weisberg and Alba practice problems. Drawing lines outside dot pattern is necessary for solution. Problem (1): Connect four dots with two lines; Problem (2): Connect dots with four lines.

producing solutions, although it did result in breaking fixation, as everyone drew lines beyond the boundaries of the square (see Figure 12.13a). Also, those people who did solve the problem after the *out-of-the-box* hint did not do so in a sudden burst of insight. Rather, it took multiple tries before they were able to solve the problem. In another experiment, Weisberg and Alba (1981) gave undergraduates training solving simple connect-the-dots problems in which they had to draw lines outside the shape defined by the dots (see Figure 12.13b). This experience facilitated performance on the Nine-Dot problem, although not nearly all the participants solved it (see also Chein et al., 2010).

Those results indicated that, contrary to the Gestalt view, the Nine-Dot problem might be difficult because it requires knowledge or previous practice that most people do not possess. Similar results were reported by Lung and Dominowski (1985): Extensive experience solving simpler versions of connect-the-dots problems was necessary before solution to the Nine-Dot problem occurred. Weisberg and Alba (1981), like Perkins (1981), raised questions about whether fixation and insight play a critical role when people attempt to solve the Nine-Dot problem. That perspective was extended further by MacGregor, Ormerod, & Chronicle (2001; Chronicle, MacGregor, &

Ormerod, 2004; see also Chein et al., 2010), who proposed an analysis of solution of the Nine-Dot problem formulated in business-as-usual terms, to which we now turn.

Analytic Methods in Insight: An Information-Processing Model of Performance on the Nine-Dot Problem

One reason that researchers maintained a distinction between insight and analysis as methods of solving problems is because information-processing models had not been developed to deal with insight problems (for an exception, see Weisberg & Suls, 1973). However, that situation changed not very long ago, when MacGregor, Ormerod, and Chronicle (2001; see also Chronicle, MacGregor, & Ormerod, 2004) proposed an information-processing model—the progress-monitoring theory—to explain people's behavior on the Nine-Dot and several similar problems. The model assumes that a hill-climbing heuristic is used on the Nine-Dot problem: In choosing a move (i.e., what line to draw next), the person will draw that line that will cover the maximum number of dots that remain unconnected. That type of move gets you climbing up the hill toward solution. As an example, on beginning the problem, the person has nine dots to connect with four lines, meaning that each line must connect on average $9/4 =$ 2.25 dots. So any line that connects more than two dots will be considered.

In order to determine the specific line to draw, the person attempts in imagination to extend as many lines as he or she can from a given line, to determine the ultimate outcome of drawing a given line. The number of lines that a person can contemplate is limited by the person's capacity for *lookahead* (i.e., by the person's visual-WM capacity [Chein et al., 2010]). One difficulty posed by the Nine-Dot problem, in this view, is that most people's capacity for lookahead does not enable them to see, until it is too late, the consequences of the line sequences that they initiate. On each solution attempt, they begin by covering the number of dots required by the hill-climbing heuristic (e.g., three dots with a single line), and they continue to do so until they realize that they have exhausted the four lines but have not solved the problem.

One prediction that follows from this analysis is that people with larger visual-WM capacities will perform better on the Nine-Dot problem. Chein et al. (2010) measured people's visual- and verbal-WM capacities and found that people with larger visual-WM capacity were more likely to draw lines outside the box formed by the dots, and were also more likely to solve the problem. Verbal-WM capacity, on the other hand, was unrelated to performance on the problem. If we can assume that larger visual-WM capacity indicates a larger capacity for planning in the visual-spatial domain, then the results of Chein and colleagues indicate that planning might be important in solution of the Nine-Dot problem. This result supports the information-processing model of MacGregor and colleagues (Chronicle et al., 2004; MacGregor et al., 2001). Thus, there is reason to believe that the business-as-usual view can deal with performance on the Nine-Dot problem.

Insight as Business–as–Usual: Conclusions

Several questions were raised about the Gestalt theory of insight in problem solving. First, evidence was presented that experience plays an important role in problem solution in both humans and chimps. Second, there is evidence that "insight" can be brought about by ordinary processes, the same as those involved in analytic methods. Finally, questions were raised about the notion of fixation in problem solving, (i.e., the idea that solution to many problems is interfered with by a too-strong reliance on top-down processes). Even when a hint is provided that should enable people to overcome any fixation, solution does not necessarily occur (e.g., Weisberg & Alba, 1981). In addition, many people achieve solution of insight problems without a period of fixation (Fleck & Wiesberg, 2004).

THE STATUS OF INSIGHT: A HYBRID MODEL

There is no doubt that some problems are solved with an *Aha!* experience (Metcalfe, 1986; Metcalfe & Wiebe, 1987). However, on the basis of research discussed in the last section of this chapter, questions can be raised about the sharp distinction between analysis and insight postulated by the special-process view. There is evidence that restructuring in problem solving can be brought about in a top-down fashion, without impasse, as a result of new information arising out of failed solution attempts (e.g., Fleck & Weisberg, 2004; Perkins, 1981). It is also true, however, that people can sometimes solve problems through bottom-up restructuring in response to impasse (switch when stuck), as postulated by Ohlsson (1992), although that phenomenon seems to occur relatively infrequently (Fleck & Weisberg, 2004). A task facing researchers is to specify more exactly the characteristics of those situations in which insight occurs; to determine when insight depends on knowledge versus when it does not; and when it occurs after an impasse versus more incrementally.

In order to help us understand the set of findings just summarized, we can expand a bit on the information-processing model presented earlier for analytic problems (see Table 12.4). Additions to the model to deal with the findings concerning restructuring and insight are presented in Stages 3 and 4. If, in Stage 1, an unsuccessful solution results in the discovery of some new information (Stage 1D), the individual uses that information as the basis for a new attempt to solve the problem (Stage 3). The problem-solving process begins again: A new memory search is carried out, with the difficulty that arose from the unsuccessful solution as a new problem to solve. This new information can lead to top-down restructuring of the problem and to its solution based on a new perspective. If there is no new information arising from the failed solution (Stage 1E), then the person would try to solve the problem through the application of weak methods (Stage 2). If Stage 2 fails, the person is at an impasse. Bottom-up restructuring in response to impasse (switch-when-stuck) is added as Stage 4 in the expanded model.

With this model, we can begin to understand all the major phenomena associated with insight in problem solving. Furthermore, we can incorporate the business-as-usual view (Stages 1–3) and the special-process view (Stage 4) into one single model, which indicates that the two views are not necessarily antagonistic, but, in some ways at least, are complementary.

Table 12.4 Elaboration of Stages in Solving a Problem Through Analysis (Including Top-Down and Bottom-Up Restructuring in Response to Impasse)

Stage 1—Solution Through Application of Strong Methods

---

1. Problem presented ⇒ Attempt to match with knowledge
   A. No solution available ⇒ Stage 2
   B. Successful match with knowledge ⇒ Transfer solution based on analogy or expertise
   C. If solution transfers successfully ⇒ Problem solved (problem is familiar ⇒ no Aha!)
   D. If solution fails, but new information arises ⇒ Stage 3
   E. If solution fails and no new information arises ⇒ Stage 2
   Comment: If no match is made with memory, person goes to Stage 2; if match is made, solution is attempted. Can result in direct solution of the problem; no restructuring. New information arising from unsuccessful solution leads to Stage 3.

Stage 2—Solution Through Application of Weak Methods

---

2. Failure at Stage 1A ⇒ Analysis based on weak methods
   A. Analysis successful ⇒ Solution
   B. No solution ⇒ Impasse ⇒ Stage 4
   Comment: Person works through problem using weak heuristic methods, trying to develop solution; if successful, problem solved without restructuring; however, Aha! is possible.

Stage 3—Top-Down Restructuring Based on Analysis: Repairing a Failed Solution

---

3. Attempt to match with knowledge any new information from failure at Stage 1C
   A. New match with knowledge ⇒ New Method (Restructuring). If new method leads to solution ⇒ Problem solved.
   B. If new method leads to failure, but more new information arises from the failure ⇒ Stage 3A
   C. If new method fails and no new information arises ⇒ Impasse ⇒ Stage 4
   Comment: Restructuring based on feedback from problem; Aha! possible.

Stage 4—Bottom-Up Restructuring in Response to Impasse

---

4. Impasse ⇒ "Switch when stuck"
   A. If bottom-up restructuring leads to new information ⇒ Stage 3
   B. If no new information ⇒ stop
   Comment: attempt to acquire new information from bottom up, through re-encoding, elaboration, and constraint relaxation, may result in restructuring; and perhaps Aha!

PROBLEM SOLVING: CONCLUSIONS

This chapter has reviewed psychological research on problem solving. We began with an analysis of well- versus ill-defined problems, and examined the concept of the problem space. Algorithms and heuristic methods of solving problems were then considered, which led to an examination of the role of expertise in solving problems. We also examined the use of analogies in problem solving, and explored studies demonstrating difficulties experienced by nonexperts in the transfer of knowledge in problem solving. We then turned to a consideration of the notion of leaps of insight in problem solving. Over the course of the past 100 years there has been a cycling of opinion concerning the importance of experience in insight. Beginning with Thorndike (1911), one viewpoint has emphasized the importance of knowledge for effective problem solving. A second view, originating with the Gestalt psychologists (Köhler, 1925; Wertheimer, 1982), has proposed that human thinking can function productively in the absence of specific experience, and that people can solve problems through insight, in response to impasse. According to this view, human thought can go considerably beyond the past, so long as we do not become fixated on what we have done before (Duncker, 1945; Wertheimer, 1982).

However, the Gestalt-based insight view has been called into question by several different sorts of results. First, investigators have found that relatively specific experience is necessary before animals or humans exhibit insight into several different types of problems (Birch, 1945; Harlow, 1949; Lung & Dominowski, 1985; Weisberg & Alba, 1981). In addition, there is evidence that the cognitive processes underlying leaps of insight are the same as those underlying more ordinary activities (Chein et al., 2010; Fleck & Weisberg, 2004; Perkins, 1981). An information-processing or analytic model of problem solving was outlined which could explain those findings.

One general conclusion that can be drawn from this discussion is that problem solving in many cases is an active, top-down process, which depends on the application of one's knowledge to the situation in which one finds oneself, whether that knowledge is procedural (as in the use of mathematical computations) or content-based (as when a chess expert uses her knowledge of chess to solve new problems). Whether or not such top-down processes are dominant in all problem-solving situations, however, is still being worked out by researchers. As we shall see in the next chapter, similar issues have arisen in the study of creativity in the arts and sciences, as researchers have attempted to determine the role of top-down processes (i.e., knowledge and experience) in those activities.

REVIEW QUESTIONS

Here is a set of questions to help you organize your review of this chapter.

1. How do cognitive scientists define *a problem*? What are its important components?

2. What is the relation between problem solving and creative thinking?

3. What are the differences between well- and ill-defined problems?

4. What is the *problem representation*? Give an example of how the problem representation can affect how difficult it is to solve a problem.

5. Define the *problem space*, and give examples of algorithms versus heuristics as different ways of searching problem spaces.

6. What are the differences between *weak* and *strong* methods of solving problems?

7. Describe de Groot's results on chess masters' performance in choosing a move in chess. How do Chase and Simon (1973) use the 10-year rule to explain the results found by de Groot?

8. Describe the stage of analogical transfer in problem solving postulated by researchers and discuss limitations on the occurrence of transfer of knowledge during problem solving.

9. Compare single-abstract-code versus multiple-code models of numerical representation.

10. Summarize the *special-process* versus *business-as-usual* views concerning the processes underlying insight in problem solving.

11. Summarize Thorndike's early research on insight and Köhler's Gestalt response to Thorndike.

12. Describe Wertheimer's research on insight in humans.

13. What is *fixation* in problem solving?

14. Describe Duncker's studies of functional fixedness in problem solving.

15. Describe the *representational-change* theory of insight.

16. What forms of restructuring does the representational-change theory postulate?

17. Summarize results supporting the representational-change theory of insight, including studies of brain mechanisms underlying insight.

18. Describe results from studies of animals and humans that have raised problems for the special-process view of insight.

19. What questions have been raised about the concept of fixation in problem solving, based on study of the Nine-Dot problem?

20. Summarize results that support the business-as-usual perspective on insight.

CHAPTER 13

THINKING III: CREATIVE THINKING

In Chapter 12, we explored how the cognitive processes function in solving a problem. Solving problems involves creativity, since, by definition, the solution to a problem is novel. In this chapter we extend the discussion to the study of creative thinking in all its manifestations. Understanding creativity is potentially of great importance: Our lives have been shaped by the accomplishments of creative thinkers (see Figure 13.1). All of modern technology—computers; the cell phone, social networking, and other modes of communication; the automobile; the airplane; electrical appliances large and small—all are the result of the creative work of inventors and scientists. Creative scientists in medicine and related areas have contributed to our ever-longer and increasingly healthy lives. Artistic creativity—painting and sculpture, music, drama, literature, poetry—has made our lives richer. We bestow honors, such as Nobel Prizes, on our most creative individuals and their stories fill our libraries. Creative thinking is also a big business: Our largest and most prestigious corporations, as well as the largest government agencies, are constantly searching for ways to be more innovative, and they pay handsome fees to consultants who promise to help them achieve new levels of innovation. Articles about how to increase creativity in business appear regularly in newspapers (e.g., Segal, 2010). There are debates in educational circles concerning the best way to structure our educational system so that children come out as young adults who are able to think creatively.

Problem Solving and Creativity

Examination of research on problem solving in Chapter 12 indicated that the themes that we have used to structure the discussion earlier in the book—most important, top-down processing—also served to help us understand the role of cognition in problem solving. In many experiments, the specificity of the knowledge an individual possessed determined the way in which a problem would be approached. Expertise in an area allows a problem-solver to bring *strong methods* to the problem; that is, specific solution methods that relatively precisely fit the problem at hand. If an individual does not possess problem-specific expertise, then he or she might need to apply heuristic methods—*weak methods*—to the problem. Heuristic methods, such as hill climbing and working backward, do not provide detailed information concerning how one might solve the specific problem in front of you, but may point one in the right direction and increase the likelihood of a solution. In this chapter, the top-down perspective will be brought to the study of creative thinking.

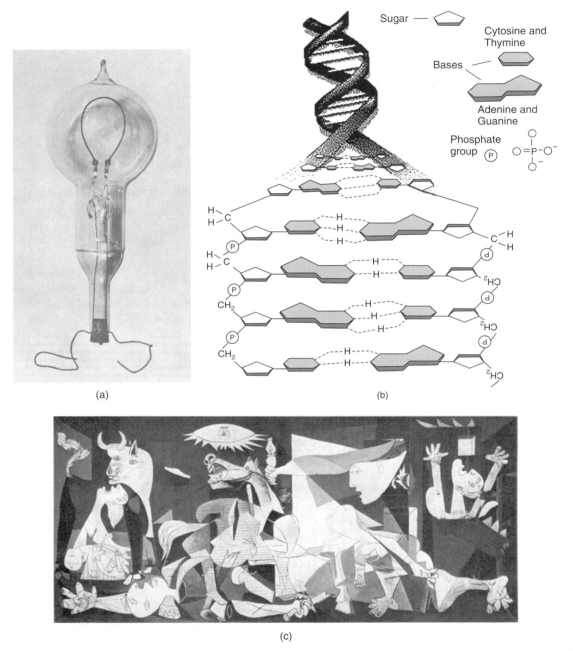

Figure 13.1 Examples of results of creative thinking. (a) Edison's lightbulb. (b) Structure of DNA. (c) Picasso's *Guernica*.

BARRIERS TO THE STUDY OF CREATIVITY

Important though creativity may be, there are two attitudes held by many in our society that make it difficult for them to accept an analysis of creative thinking based on the top-down perspective taken in this book. First, some people believe that the topic of creativity cannot be studied by the methods of cognitive science because it is a completely subjective experience, in which ideas well up from deep within the souls of a few gifted individuals. Even the creators cannot tell us where their ideas come from, so how can we even begin to understand that process using our "objective" scientific methods? Second, even if we could begin to understand creativity, many people believe that the top-down perspective that we bring to the topic misses the critical aspect of creativity. There is in our culture a generally accepted idea that the creative process involves *thinking outside of the box* (a phrase we first encountered in Chapter 12 in connection with the Gestalt view of problem solving). This means rejecting top-down processes, because one is supposed to "let go" of knowledge and strategies. Thus, it would seem that any cognitive analysis of creativity based on top-down processes is doomed to fail.

However, in this chapter we propose that the idea that creativity depends on thinking outside the box is incorrect. Instead we present an alternate view that creative thinking does *not* depend on thinking outside the box or breaking away from what we know. Rather, creative thinking builds on one's expertise in an area, using the cognitive processes we have already discussed in this book. Most importantly, creative thinking is a top-down process.

OUTLINE OF CHAPTER 13

As the first step in examining creativity, this chapter begins with the definition of creativity and related concepts. We then examine two case studies of creative achievements at the highest level, one in science—Watson and Crick's discovery of the double helix of DNA—and one in art—the development of Picasso's great painting *Guernica* (see Figure 13.1). Those case studies provide an introduction to how we can study creativity and will also serve as background for the remainder of the discussion. We then turn to the psychological study of creative thinking, presenting first the *information-processing* view of creativity, introduced in the discussion of problem solving in Chapter 12. This section examines research that demonstrates that large-scale, real-world creative thinking—in science *and* the arts—is based on ordinary cognitive processes, plus expertise in the domain in which you are working (rather than on thinking outside the box).

After presenting the idea that the creative process depends on ordinary top-down thinking, we then examine research that claims creativity is due to extraordinary thought processes, including (a) whether creative thought is dependent on a certain degree of psychopathology ("genius and madness"), and (b) the possible role of unconscious thinking in creativity. We then turn to an important area in creativity research that examines how we might develop tests to measure creativity, a stream of research that evolved out of the intelligence-testing movement. This area is called *psychometrics of creativity*; psychometrics refers to mental (*psycho-*) testing or measurement

(-*metrics*). Finally, since creativity is of such great importance in society, we examine research centering on the question of whether it is possible to facilitate creative thinking.

The study of creativity extends beyond the examination of creative *thinking*, as researchers have investigated, for example, whether certain personality characteristics play a role in creative accomplishment. Researchers have also examined the possible role of environmental factors in creativity. Since this book is concerned with cognitive processes, in this chapter we concentrate on creative thinking. For broader reviews of creativity, see Runco (2007), Sawyer (2012), and Weisberg (2006a).

QUESTIONS OF DEFINITION: CREATIVE PRODUCTS, CREATIVE THINKING, AND CREATIVITY

The critical element in calling some outcome *creative* is that it be *new*. That novel outcome can be a physical object, such as a work of art or an invention, or a psychological product, such as a new theory about how a certain kind of cancer develops. Boden (1990, 2004, 2010) has made a distinction between *personal* versus *historical* creativity (*P*- versus *H*-creativity; see also Weisberg, 1986, 2006a). Personal creativity means that the idea or product is new for the person, but it might or might not be new for the society as a whole. Historical creativity means that the product is new for society (i.e., new for everyone). A student reported that she was reading an assignment, and she got an idea for a new experimental study, only to turn the page and find, much to her disappointment, that the study had already been carried out. Was the student creative in thinking of her study? Yes, because the idea was novel *for her*. Thus she has exhibited P-creativity, but not H-creativity.

Creative Accidents? Intention in Creativity

Let us say that, while working, a painter accidentally spills paint on a partially finished canvas, leaving a large stain that, in the painter's opinion, renders the canvas unusable. The painter is visited by the director of a museum, who sees the stained canvas and loves it, not realizing that it is the result of an accident. The director purchases the canvas and puts it on display in the museum. Was the painter creative in producing that painting? No: The stain was an accident, and someone is creative only when a novel product is produced intentionally. Similarly, if you ask a person who suffers from schizophrenia to try to solve a problem, he or she may produce a novel response, such as a stream of free-associations that you will not be able to understand and which will not be relevant to the problem. Is that product creative? Again, the answer is no: Someone in the grip of schizophrenia would not be able to direct his or her thought processes toward the problem at hand, so no creativity would be possible. In sum, creativity is the intentional production of novelty.

The Question of Value in the Definition of Creativity

Most researchers who study creativity define the concept a bit differently than we do: in order to be labeled creative, a creative product must be novel and also be *of value* (see, e.g., Boden, 2010; Dietrich & Kanso, 2010; Runco, 2007; Sawyer, 2012). An invention must carry out the task for which it was designed; a scientific theory must increase our understanding of some phenomenon; a work of art must be appreciated by an audience. If a product is not valued by others, then, according to this definition, it is not creative, even if it is novel and produced intentionally.

It is our view that one should separate the creativity of a product from its value. One difficulty in using value as part of the definition of creativity is that value can change over time. For example, the work of the Impressionist painters is now among the most beloved and historically important in all of painting. However, their paintings were ridiculed by art critics when first put on exhibit in Paris more than 135 years ago (Rewald, 1946, 1986). As another example, the first printing of Melville's *Moby Dick* did not even sell 3,000 copies, and the author died penniless. That book is now read by many high school and college students in the United States as a major piece of literature.

If we used value as part of the definition of creativity, we would have to say that a person could *become* creative after death (Csikszentmihalyi, 1988, 1999) if others came to appreciate his or her works. Do we really want to say that Melville or the Impressionists became creative after they died? This position seems to miss a critical aspect of creativity: Whether or not something is creative does not depend on whether anyone likes or values it. It is totally reasonable to say of something: "I see that it is creative, but I hate it." It thus seems more straightforward to keep separate the creativity of a product from its value, and to say that a novel product, if it is produced intentionally, is creative. If the world's opinion of a work changes, then we can say that the work has become more or less *valued* or *appreciated*, but not that the work—or the person who created it—has become more or less creative.

Defining Creativity: Conclusions

In conclusion, creative thinking occurs when a person intentionally produces something that is novel for them. Sometimes those novel products are valued highly by society, and sometimes they are not, but all of them are creative products. Accidental accomplishments, and those of people who cannot focus intentionally on the situation, do not count as creative.

We begin the discussion of the cognitive processes underlying creative thinking by examining two cases of seminal creative accomplishment. These case studies will show how creativity at the highest level can be studied and will also set the stage for the discussion in the rest of the chapter.

TWO CASE STUDIES IN CREATIVITY

Creativity in Science: Discovery of the Double Helix

In 1953, James Watson and Francis Crick published the double-helix model of the structure of DNA, which has had revolutionary effects on our understanding and control over genetic processes. Geneticists, biologists, and other scientists, including Watson and Crick's teachers, had for more than 50 years been pursuing the question of the composition and structure of the genetic material (Judson, 1979; Olby, 1994; Weisberg, 2006a). Watson and Crick succeeded in formulating a model of the structure of DNA after approximately $1^1/_2$ years of work. Other research groups were at that time also working on the structure of DNA, and Watson and Crick were not the first to publish a possible structure, but theirs was ultimately judged to be correct.

Preliminary Decisions

Watson and Crick's collaboration began in autumn, 1951, when Watson, with a recent PhD in genetics, came to Cambridge University, where Crick was working on his PhD in biology. Shortly after meeting, Watson and Crick realized that they both were interested in solving the problem of the structure of DNA, and they decided to collaborate. Watson and Crick made two early decisions concerning the direction of their work that were important in setting them on the path to success: (1) they decided to try to build a *model* of the structure of DNA, and (2) they assumed that DNA would be in the shape of a *helix*. Other researchers studying DNA had not made those decisions, and therefore were slowed down in finding the structure (Weisberg, 2006a).

Where did Watson and Crick get those two critical ideas? Both of those critical assumptions were based on the work of Linus Pauling, a world-famous chemist, who had recently proposed a model of the structure of the protein alpha-keratin (Olby, 1994; Watson, 1968). Alpha-keratin, like DNA, is a large organic molecule—a macromolecule; it forms many bodily structures, among them hair and fingernails. Pauling had proposed that alpha keratin was helical in shape, and he had built a model of the structure to show how all the atoms in the molecule fit together. Watson and Crick adopted Pauling's basic idea concerning the importance of helical structures in organic macromolecules, as well as his model-building method.

The use of information from Pauling's alpha-helix by Watson and Crick can be seen as an example of *analogical transfer* in problem solving, as discussed in Chapter 12, since DNA and alpha-keratin are analogous in several ways. Both are organic macromolecules made up of small units that repeat again and again to form the large molecule. Those small units in both alpha-keratin and in DNA are linked together by means of identical chemical bonds. In the Crick and Watson case, then, new ideas came about through the adoption of already-existing ideas that had been developed by someone else; there was no breaking away from what was known, no leap outside of the box.

Adopting Pauling's perspective and method did not settle all the issues facing Watson and Crick, however. Experimental evidence, based primarily on x-ray pictures of DNA taken by other investigators, indicated that DNA might be a helix, but it did not specify how many *strands* or *backbones* made up the helix. We now know that DNA contains two strands (it is a *double* helix), but when Watson and Crick started working, evidence indicated only that the molecule was thicker than a single strand. There might have been two, three, or four strands, for example, as shown in Figure 13.2a. A further decision faced by Watson and Crick concerned where to put the *bases*, which are four different compounds (abbreviated A, T, C, and G) that form the "rungs" of the "spiral staircase" of DNA (see Figure 13.2b)—the specific sequence of bases that determines the genetic code. When Watson and Crick started their work, they were unsure if the

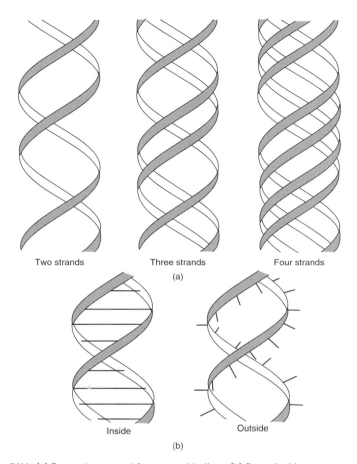

Two strands   Three strands   Four strands

(a)

Inside   Outside

(b)

Figure 13.2   DNA. (a) Two-, three-, and four-strand helices. (b) Bases inside versus outside.

bases were inside the helix or protruding toward the outside (as shown in the possible models in Figure 13.2b).

The Triple Helix

Based on discussions with other investigators, Watson and Crick first built a *triple helix*, a three-stranded model of DNA, with the bases on the *outside*. Thus, they made two incorrect assumptions, although both of those choices were scientifically reasonable at the time. For example, available evidence concerning the density of DNA supported the idea of three strands, although that evidence was shown later to be incorrect. One reason Watson and Crick put the bases on the outside of the helical backbones was because they could not figure out how to fit them inside. Since the bases are of different sizes, to fit base pairs inside the helix, the backbones would have to ripple back and forth. This would not make for a rigid structure, which they knew that DNA was. Putting the bases outside eliminated this problem.

Thus, as is true with many initial attempts at producing creative work (e.g., Edison's light bulb; the Wright brothers' airplane), Watson and Crick's first attempt to solve their problem was a failure (Weisberg, 2006a). It took more than a year before they formulated the correct model of DNA. During that time, they acquired new information that directed them to two backbones, as well as other information that led them to the conclusion that the bases must be inside the structure. For example, Watson and Crick learned that when DNA was exposed to moisture, it increased in length by 20%. That information allowed Watson to deduce that two strands were involved, not three.

Double Helix

By early 1953, Watson and Crick had built part of a model with two backbones, but which had no bases inside, because they were still unsure how to get them to fit. They then began to consider specific possible arrangements of the bases inside the backbones. Watson first tried pairs of the same bases, that is, A with A, C with C, and so forth, as the rungs of the staircase, a scheme that was called *like-with-like*, or *like-like*. That idea came from several sources, including research done by Watson's graduate school professors. Like-like pairing did not work, however, because of the different sizes of the four bases, so Watson then set out to try to find different pairings that would fit. Those would be *complementary pairings*, where different bases fit together and complement each other. On a Saturday morning in February 1953, Watson used cardboard models of the bases to try to figure out how they might fit together in the center of the helix, like pieces in a jig-saw puzzle. Following is his account of what happened (Watson, 1968, pp. 123–125).

> When I got to our still-empty office... [t]hough I initially went back to my like-like prejudices, I saw all too well that they led nowhere.... [I] began shifting the bases in and out of various other pairing possibilities. Suddenly I became aware that an [A–T] pair held together by two hydrogen bonds was identical in shape to a [G–C] pair held together by at least two hydrogen bonds. All the hydrogen bonds seemed to form naturally; no fudging was required to make the two types of base pairs identical in shape.... Upon his arrival Francis [Crick] did not get more than halfway through the door before I let loose that the answer to everything was in our hands.

DNA: Conclusions

Watson and Crick's model of DNA was one of the great discoveries in 20th-century science, which has had profound effects on our lives in many ways, including paving the way for the mapping of the human genome. However, as far as cognitive processes are concerned, the discovery was relatively straightforward, as Watson and Crick used the available evidence to build a candidate model of DNA. First, they used Pauling's work as the foundation for their own, in an example of analogical transfer. Second, when their first model proved incorrect, they began testing new hypotheses and acquired new information that allowed them to ultimately produce the correct double helix structure.

This example of creative thinking at the highest level in science seems to be comprehensible in a straightforward manner. However, perhaps that comprehensibility is due to the fact that the example comes from science, which is a structured domain. Creativity in art might be a much "messier" and open-ended situation, and, therefore, harder to deal with on a cognitive level. In addition, artistic creativity might be more dependent on thinking outside of the box. We therefore now turn to creativity in the arts, to demonstrate that similar top-down cognitive processes are involved there as well.

Artistic Creativity: Picasso's *Guernica*

Pablo Picasso (1881–1973) was legendary for his precocity; his radical remaking of art several times during the 20th century; and his long, very productive, and sometimes tumultuous life (Richardson & McCully, 2007). One of Picasso's greatest paintings, *Guernica* (see Figure 13.1c), commemorates the bombing of the town of Guernica, in northern Spain, on April 27, 1937, during the Spanish Civil War. The town seems to have had no strategic value, and the bombing therefore was seen as an act designed to terrorize the population (Chipp, 1988). Reports of the bombing quickly reached Paris, where Picasso lived, and stimulated him to drop another project and create a painting in response. He began work on *Guernica* on May 1, and within 6 weeks had produced a work that has been universally hailed as one of the great antiwar documents of modern times. It is striking to note that there is no actual depiction of war in the painting: There are several people (all women, except for a baby and a male statue), and several animals, but no soldiers. Picasso makes us feel that something terrible has happened, but does not present the event directly. A second noteworthy aspect of the painting is that it has no color; it is painted in black, white, and shades of gray. The physical darkness in the painting serves to present a psychological mood of darkness, highlighted by a few bright objects, to which our attention is drawn. The painting is also massive in size, measuring more than 11-by-25 feet, which serves to add to the dramatic effect that it has on viewers.

Development of Guernica

Painters often carry out preliminary work, thinking about what they might do, and producing sketches of various sorts, before they start to work on the actual painting. Picasso dated and numbered some 45 sketches for *Guernica*. In his first 2 days of preliminary work, he produced mainly sketches of the overall composition of the painting; two sketches produced on the first day are shown in Figure 13.3a. As can be seen, Picasso had the overall structure in mind from the beginning, although some working out of the details still had to occur (Weisberg, 2004; Weisberg & Hass, 2007). As shown in Figure 13.3b, Picasso also worked on the specific characters in the painting, producing drawings of horses, bulls, women with and without children, and so forth. Thus, even though Picasso had most of the final characters in mind from the beginning, he was not sure how he wanted to portray them.

New Ideas in Painting

The essence of *Guernica* can be seen in the first sketches, which might lead one to conclude that Picasso made a great creative leap, in which he produced this great work from nothing, in a burst of inspiration. However, the overall idea for *Guernica* was produced so quickly because it was developed by Picasso out of his own work. The organization of the painting, and the cast of characters, can be seen in many other works by Picasso in the mid-1930s, one of which, the etching *Minotauromachy*, is shown in

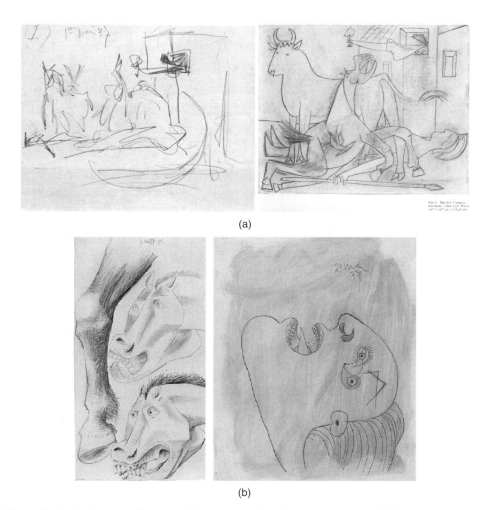

Figure 13.3   Sketches for *Guernica*. (a) Two composition sketches from May 1. (b) Character sketches.

Figure 13.4a. The name *Minotauromachy* is a combination of two words: *minotaur*, the half-man, half-bull from Greek mythology, and *tauromachy*, a Greek word meaning *bullfight*. The characters in *Minotauromachy* are similar to those in *Guernica*: a bull, a horse, a young woman holding a light, a dead person, a woman overlooking the scene from a window, a bird, and a vertical person at one end. In addition, when one considers how an etching is made, the match between *Guernica* and *Minotauromachy* becomes even closer. An etching is printed on paper from a printing plate, on which the artist first draws the image. When you print an image from a plate, the picture is reversed from left to right. Therefore, Picasso actually drew the version shown in Figure 13.4b. We now see a correspondence between the various characters and also in their arrangement in the composition. Thus, either Picasso based *Guernica* directly on *Minotauromachy* or both works were developed out of a common set of ideas that

Minotauromachy

(a) Bull (Minotaur)
(b) Horse (attitude)
(c) Dead person
(d) Sword
(e) Women observing
(f) Women with light
(g) Birds
(h) Vertical man fleeing

(a)

Guernica

(a) Bull
(b) Horse (attitude)
(c) Dead person (Statue)
(d) Sword
(e & f) Women observing
        Holding light
(g) Birds
(h) Vertical woman falling

(b)

Figure 13.4   (a) Picasso's *Minotauromachy*. (b) Minotauromachy reversed. Letters on items in left-hand column depict correspondences between *Minotauromachy* and *Guernica*.

Picasso used in many works. In conclusion, the reason that Picasso so quickly arrived at the structure of *Guernica* was because it was a variation on work he had done in the past (see also Damian & Simonton, 2011; Doyle, 2008). Picasso did not think outside the box in producing the overall structure of *Guernica*.

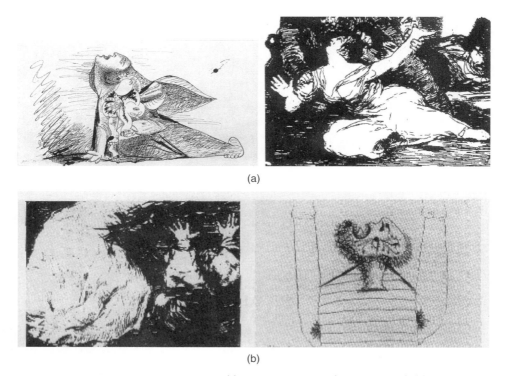

Figure 13.5 Comparing Goya and Picasso. (a) Woman on ground (Picasso on left). (b) Man in grave (Picasso on right).

In addition to having direct connections to work by Picasso, *Guernica* also has links to works by other artists, only one of whom will be mentioned here. Picasso had much admiration for the great Spanish artist Francisco de Goya (1746–1828), whose influence can be seen in many of Picasso's works (Chipp, 1988). In Figure 13.5 are two of Goya's works, and one can see similarities between these works and *Guernica* that seem to be too close to be coincidence, especially given the Spanish connection between the two artists. The works of Goya depicted in Figure 13.5 are part of a group called *Disasters of War*, produced by Goya in response to brutal events brought about by Napoleon's invasion of Spain early in the 19th century. Given the wartime event that stimulated *Guernica*, it is not surprising that Picasso might think of those compositions by Goya while he was working. Again, Picasso's thinking was not outside the box.

Guernica: *Conclusions*

This discussion has shown that the development of *Guernica* followed a path similar to that seen in the discovery of the DNA double helix. As did Watson and Crick, Picasso built his work on the foundation of earlier work, in this case, his own work. In addition, as with DNA, the work of others also contributed to the development of the new work, and that work of others was closely related to—perhaps even analogous to—the work that Picasso was trying to create.

Case Studies in Creativity: Conclusions

These two case studies have given us, in very abbreviated form, an introduction to the psychological study of creative achievement at the highest level (for further discussion, see Weisberg, 2006a, Chapters 1 and 5). Examination of such case studies removes some of the mystery from creativity, as we see that one can trace the development of great creative achievements. One may be surprised at the seemingly straightforward manner in which these two extraordinary products developed. From a cognitive perspective, there was no evidence of extraordinary thinking—no leaps outside of the box—involved in bringing them about, even if the outcomes were exceptional. We will have occasion to refer back to these case studies as we work through the discussion in this chapter. Most importantly, they will provide information that we can refer to as we review research and theory concerning the creative process. We now begin that review by examining the information-processing analysis of creativity.

THE INFORMATION-PROCESSING PERSPECTIVE ON CREATIVITY

In the last chapter, we discussed the information-processing view of problem solving, as developed by Newell and Simon (1972) and elaborated by subsequent researchers (e.g., Anderson, 2010; Chase & Simon, 1973; Fugelsang, Stein, Green, & Dunbar, 2004; Weisberg, 2006a, 2006b). Newell and Simon also discussed creative thinking more generally, and the basic viewpoint that they adopted toward creative thinking was that it was also heuristic-based problem solving (Newell, Shaw, & Simon, 1962; also see Boden, 2004, 2010; Perkins, 1981; Weisberg, 1986, 2006a). This perspective on creative thinking has developed in several ways over the years. First, analysis of heuristics in thinking has been extended to the study of creative thinking (e.g., Dunbar, 1995; Fugelsang, Stein, Green, & Dunbar, 2004). Second, in a parallel to research on expertise in problem solving, there has also been investigation of the role of expertise in creative thinking in the arts, sciences, and invention (Weisberg, 2006b; see chapters in Ericsson, Charness, Feltovich, & Hoffman, 2006). We now turn to a discussion of those two specific aspects of the information-processing perspective applied to creativity. This discussion will tie research on creativity to research on problem solving discussed in the last chapter, as well as to the cognitive processes more generally.

HEURISTICS IN SCIENTIFIC THINKING: OBSERVING SCIENTISTS AT WORK

Direct observation of the possible role of heuristics in the creative process in science comes from research done by Dunbar (1995; also see Baker & Dunbar, 2000; Dunbar & Fugelsang, 2005; Fugelsang et al., 2004), who spent time as a "fly on the wall" in four high-level research laboratories in molecular biology. These laboratories were working on such questions as how HIV infects a host organism. The lab directors gave Dunbar permission to observe all lab activities, including lab meetings, and to interview the scientists working in the labs, read all reports, and so forth. This access allowed Dunbar to observe firsthand a number of significant scientific discoveries, to assess the thought processes of scientists, and to observe in general how progress in science is brought about.

Different sets of heuristics were activated in response to the outcome of an experiment, depending on whether it produced positive (or expected) results versus negative (or unexpected) results. For example, a scientist's lab might be studying conditions that facilitate a virus's infecting a host organism (so that they could later interfere with the process of infection). When an experiment produced a result that was expected, the researcher then went on to the next preplanned phase of the research (e.g., the scientist might vary an aspect of the environment, to see if it affected the ability of the virus to infect the host). Alternatively, the scientist might vary a characteristic of the host, to determine if that changed the susceptibility of the host to infection. Those responses to the initial positive result can be looked upon as a set of heuristic methods designed to allow a researcher to go beyond an obtained result that was expected. Those heuristics facilitate scientific reasoning by generating a set of responses to an expected experimental outcome that takes the researcher down one solution path through the "problem space" of possibilities concerning the research being carried out.

In the lab meetings that Dunbar attended, however, over half the results that were reported turned out to contradict the initial hypotheses formulated by the scientists. That negative evidence typically set off another set of heuristics, which played an important role in getting the scientists to discard a hypothesis they had been testing. This rejection of formerly held hypotheses then might lead them down a different solution pathway, to the development of a new way of analyzing the phenomenon of interest. In other words, negative evidence played a large role in stimulating a set of heuristics that resulted in a *conceptual change* in science, which led to subsequent experiments that had not been previously planned. However, this conceptual change typically did not occur quickly or easily.

When negative evidence was first discovered, the investigators would first try to explain it away, by assuming that there was a flaw in the design of the experiment. Thus, the first set of heuristics brought into play by an unexpected finding were what could be called *repair-the-experiment* heuristics, which involve methods that scientists acquire during their training. If the scientist was convinced that the unexpected result was real, that is, not due to experimental error, the next step centered on the hypothesis that the researcher was working with. In such a situation, the scientist would try to change specific aspects of the hypothesis, while keeping the overall hypothesis. This response, based on what could be called *repair-the-hypothesis* heuristics, resulted in little conceptual change on the investigator's part.

The most important outcome occurred when an unexpected finding resulted in questions being raised about the whole overall hypothesis the researcher was working with. Typically, in presenting the results to the other members of the lab, the researcher might initially try to preserve the overall hypothesis, but it would become evident to the other researchers that tinkering with the hypothesis would not be sufficient. Others in the lab meeting then either offered new hypotheses or forced the researcher to develop new ones—we could call this *change-the-hypothesis* heuristics— that sometimes resulted in the researcher changing his or her way of conceptualizing the problem and, in the process, discovering a new way to understand the previously confusing results. Thus, a critically important heuristic seen in science is changing one's hypothesis in the face of unexpected results, which often happens in a social setting, such as a lab meeting.

As we have just seen, Dunbar (1995; Dunbar & Fugelsang, 2005) has found that strategies and heuristics that led to scientific discoveries often involved a social process, as other scientists stimulated a colleague to develop a new interpretation for unpredicted data. Dunbar also found that professional scientists rely on both domain-specific knowledge and the social context of a lab to avoid making many of the reasoning errors often found among novices in laboratory studies of reasoning, as discussed in Chapter 10. One important finding by Dunbar (1995) is that highly experienced investigators were more likely than were less-experienced investigators to give up their hypothesis in response to negative evidence. Those with less scientific background were more subject to a falsification bias (continuing to accept a hypothesis even when the evidence did not support it). Indeed, Dunbar found that experienced scientists sometimes gave up a hypothesis too easily, perhaps because of a history of being wrong. Such an individual would be more willing to give up cherished ideas that the evidence did not support, and thus would be more likely to develop theories that would match with reality. Based on Dunbar's results, it seems that flexibility of thinking in response to negative results—which is the result of the operation of the sets of heuristics that we have been discussing—may be a domain-specific effect of previous failures, rather than being something that young people bring with them into the scientific enterprise.

Computational Approach to Creativity

As we have noted before, the information-processing approach to cognition has been based on the adoption of the modern computer as a model of how human cognition might be carried out. Thus, Newell and Simon's (1972) analysis of cognition involved developing programs that could solve simple problems in logic, for example, by using heuristic methods of the sort we have discussed in this chapter and in others. That perspective has been applied to creativity on the broader scale. Boden (2004) has summarized research demonstrating that creativity may be carried out by computational processes and she has been an advocate of the view that it should be possible to create a program that could create works of art or symphonies.

Computational Models of Scientific Creativity

Early research on computational models of scientific creativity was carried out Langley, Simon, Bradshaw, and Zytkow (1987; see also Kulkarni & Simon, 1988). That research focused on developing computer programs that were able to make discoveries in several scientific disciplines, when the program was given data that a scientist might encounter. As an example, the BACON program was able to re-create an important advance in the history of astronomy—Johannes Kepler's discovery of his third law of planetary motion. Kepler (1571–1630) made several discoveries concerning the motions of the planets, which are summarized in Kepler's three *Laws of Planetary Motion*. Kepler's laws were important in the history of astronomy because they paved the way for Newton's analysis of the orbits of the planets.

Table 13.1 BACON Program's Development of Kepler's Third Law of Planetary Motion

Planet	D	P	Term 1 (D/P)	Term 2 (D²/P)	Term 3 (D³/P²)
A	1	1	1	1	1
B	4	8	0.5	2	1
C	9	27	0.33	3	1

Kepler took data from observations of the planets that had been collected by astronomer Tycho Brahe (1546–1601), for whom Kepler had served as an assistant, and found ways to summarize those data in a particularly elegant form (see the D and P columns in Table 13.1 for the data). The third of Kepler's laws states that, for any planet orbiting the sun, there is a regular relationship between the *period* of orbit (P; the time it takes the planet to go around the sun) and the distance (D) between the planet and the sun. That relation is expressed in the following formula:

$$D^3/P^2 = 1$$

That is, the cube of the distance divided by the square of the period equals 1.

The BACON program analyzed the numbers in the first two columns in Table 13.1 using several heuristic methods, which were part of the program. Those heuristics are general methods for manipulating numbers.

1. If the values of a term are constant, then assume that the term always has that value.

2. If the values of two numerical terms increase together, then consider their ratio.

3. If the values of one numerical term increase as those of another decrease, consider their product.

Those heuristics are both very simple and very general, since they do not apply to specific terms or domains. Most important, they are not relevant directly to astronomy and planetary motion. That lack of domain-specific content makes them weak methods, of the sort that we have already discussed.

BACON first examined the two columns of numbers, and determined that heuristic 2 was relevant. It then produced the quantity D/P, which is shown in column 4 in Table 13.1 (labeled *Term 1*). The values of Term 1 are not equal, so the program keeps working. Heuristic 3 can be applied to columns 2 and 4 (D and Term 1), so that is the next step. That results in Term 2 in Table 13.1. Heuristic 3 is now relevant to the data in the fourth and fifth columns (Term 1 decreases while the values of Term 2 are increasing), so it is applied. Multiplying one by the other produces Term 3, which equals one for all the values, so the program stops, drawing the conclusion that the relationship between D and P for this set of measures is $D^3/P^2 = 1$, which is Kepler's Third Law.

Thus, with a few simple arithmetic-based heuristics, which, it should be noted, were available to Kepler, BACON carried out a series of calculations that resulted in production of a formula that is equivalent to Kepler's Third Law of Planetary Motion.

Langley and colleagues (1987) concluded that BACON's success supported the idea that Kepler's creative process might have involved the same sorts of heuristic methods, which are within the grasp of most high-school students.

Computer Artists

Concerning the possibility of computer generation of art, one can program a computer with both general and specific knowledge, with rules and heuristics that can provide novel combinations of elements, resulting in a creative work (thus providing an example of *generativity*—being able to generate an infinite number of artworks from a finite set of program rules, similar to producing novel sentences from a finite set of grammatical rules such as we discussed in Chapter 10). One such program has been created, which produced the drawings shown in Figure 13.6. Harold Cohen, who

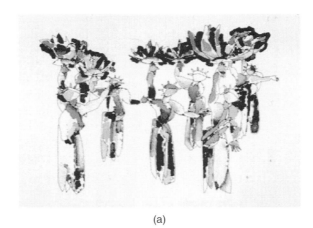

(a)

(b)

Figure 13.6 Two works by AARON, a computer program. (a) *Liberty and Friends*, 1985 (based on descriptions of the Statue of Liberty). (b) *Two Friends with Potted Plant*, 1991.

began life as an abstract artist, became interested in programming computers to create novel artistic works. He developed a program, called AARON, providing it with general knowledge (e.g., information about how to distinguish a figure from ground, how to provide a sense of perspective, and how to simulate some aspects of dimensionality), plus more-specific information about the shape and relation of parts of the human figure and plant life. As can be seen in Figure 13.6, the program can produce novel visual works.

AARON did not initially have color information, and the works in Figure 13.6 are early works and so were not drawn in color. In order to enable the program to produce works in color, Cohen had to analyze how he, as an artist, used color in his work, so that he would be able to write the computer code that would produce colored artworks. In papers available on his website (http://crca.ucsd.edu/~hcohen/), Cohen recounts AARON's development, which as indicated was a journey of analysis and discovery for Cohen as well. Cohen's writings are recommended to anyone who is interested in the question of creativity in art. Although one might argue that the artistic products of AARON do not parallel those of the great artists, Cohen has shown it possible to computationally produce novel artistic works through the use of specifiable processes.

Computer-based advances have been made in other creative domains, such as Cope's Emi program (*E*xperiments in *M*usical *I*ntelligence), which creates classical music in the style of Bach, or any other composer, after being exposed to a sample of the composer's works (http://artsites.ucsc.edu/faculty/cope/). The program is able to abstract the style of the composer from the sample of compositions and use that style information to produce compositions that sound as if they were created by the composer. Cope (2005) has used Emi as the basis for a discussion of how human musical creativity works.

Heuristic Methods in Creativity: Conclusions

The research just reviewed has provided support for the first component of the information-processing view of creativity, that is, the importance of heuristic methods in creative thinking. Dunbar's studies of scientific creativity in research laboratories (Dunbar, 1995; Dunbar & Fuglesang, 2005) support the notion that simple heuristic methods, such as changing hypotheses in response to unexpected results, are important in scientific thinking (for additional discussion of heuristics in creativity, see Carlson & Gorman, 1992). The development of computer programs that use heuristics and rules derived from some artistic or scientific domain to generate novel products in that domain provides further evidence concerning the potential importance of heuristic methods in creative thinking. Those programs also raise the possibility that at some point computers will be able to exhibit creativity on a scale that might rival that of humans (Boden, 2010).

As noted earlier, the second important component of the information-processing orientation to problem solving is the emphasis on the role of expertise and top-down processes in world-class problem-solving performance. We now turn to the question of the role of expertise in world-class creativity.

EXPERTISE IN CREATIVE THINKING:
THE 10-YEAR RULE IN CREATIVITY

One important component of the information-processing perspective on problem solving discussed in Chapter 12 was an emphasis on the positive role in problem solving of expertise, encapsulated as the *10-year rule* (Chase & Simon, 1973). In an extension of that viewpoint to creativity, Hayes (1989) demonstrated that the 10-year rule is relevant to creative achievement in musical composition, painting, and poetry. He found that even the most outstanding individuals required many years of preparation before they began to produce great works.

Composers

Hayes (1989) examined the biographies of 76 eminent composers, including J. S. Bach, Beethoven, Haydn, Brahms, and Tchaikovsky, to determine when they began to study music. He then calculated the length of time between a composer's introduction to musical instruction and the production of that individual's first notable work or masterwork. A masterwork was defined by Hayes as a composition with at least five recordings available in record catalogs. More than 500 masterworks were produced by his sample of 76 composers, and only 3 of those works were composed before year 10 of the composer's career, and those 3 were composed in years 8 or 9. The average pattern of career productivity began with what Hayes called 10 years of silence before the first masterwork. Even Mozart, perhaps the most precocious and undoubtedly one of the most prolific of all composers, fit this profile (see also Kozbelt, 2005). Mozart's father, a professional musician, began giving the young Mozart music lessons when the boy was very young (reportedly at the boy's insistence). Mozart's first musical compositions were produced at age 6 or so, but they are not played or recorded very frequently today. Mozart's first masterwork was his "Piano Concerto #9," which was written in 1777, 10-plus years into his career, when he was over 20. Thus, although Mozart began his career very early, he still required a significant amount of time before he made his mark.

Weisberg (2006a) found a similar pattern in the development of the Beatles (i.e., John Lennon and Paul McCartney) as songwriters. They had been working together for several years before writing their first hit, and their major works (*Revolver, Rubber Soul*, and *Sgt. Pepper*) were produced almost 10 years into their collaboration. Other composers showing similar patterns of development were discussed by Hass and Weisberg (2009; Hass, Weisberg, & Choi, 2010) and Kozbelt (2004).

Painters

Hayes's (1989) analysis of the career development of 131 painters, including Picasso and Monet, showed the same pattern as that found in the musicians: There was an initial period with no masterworks, where a masterwork was defined as a work that appeared in books on the history of art. Here, too, this description fit the careers of even the most precocious and productive individuals, such as Picasso, who began to paint at about age 9, under the tutelage of his father (also a painter). Picasso's first notable works were produced at about age 15. Picasso proclaimed that he painted like the great painter Raphael (1483–1520) from the very beginning, meaning that he did not need to develop as a painter, but this does not seem to be true (Pariser, 1987; Richardson, 1991). Picasso also had to grapple with the problems that all developing artists must go through before they can accurately represent objects through drawing and painting.

Scientists

Raskin (1936) reviewed the careers of eminent scientists of the time. After several years of training, they produced their first publication at age 25.2 years. However, their most important papers were published just over 10 years later, at age 35.4. Simonton (2007) has corroborated those findings using a wider sample of scientists. Similar results have been found in related domains such as mathematics (Gustin, 1985) and medicine (Patel & Groen, 1991). Bloom and his colleagues (Bloom, 1985) and Gardner (1993) have also provided evidence to support the importance of the 10-year rule in creative development.

The 10–Year Rule in Creative Thinking: Conclusions

Hayes's (1989) groundbreaking results showed that composers and painters required significant periods of time to acquire sufficient knowledge and skills to perform at world-class levels in their fields. Hayes's basic conclusions have been supported by similar findings reported by other investigators (e.g., Bloom, 1985; Gardner, 1993; Kozbelt, 2004; Weisberg, 2006a). In sum, years of commitment to a discipline are required for creative achievement.

DEVELOPMENT OF CREATIVE CAPACITY: TALENT VERSUS PRACTICE

Hayes's (1989) analysis and the research that has supported it leave us with the question of what is happening as people are developing their skill, before those individuals are producing masterworks. That is, how does world-class creative capacity develop? On the one hand, it is typically assumed that *talent*—an innate capacity to function well within some domain—must play a critical role in the development of any creative skill (Norton et al., 2005). We say of people who produce great art or music or science that they are *talented* or *gifted*. However, recent years have seen the development of a viewpoint that proposes that *deliberate practice*—repeating again and again the to-be-mastered components of a skill under the supervision of a teacher or coach—may play a critical role in the development of world-class skills, including skills in domains demanding creativity (Ericsson, Roring, & Nandagopal, 2007; Ericsson & Ward, 2007).

Talent

It has long been believed that certain individuals are genetically prepared to succeed in certain domains; we say that such people have a *talent* for the domain, or are *gifted* (Baker, 2007; Coleman, 2007; Ericsson, Roring, & Nandagopal, 2007; Gagné, 2007). Talent is assumed to show itself relatively early in life, and it allows a person to achieve very high levels of performance. Without talent, all the practice in the world will be of little help in trying to become truly world class in some domain. Evidence for the existence of innate talent comes from studies of *autistic savants* (or *savants*), extraordinary individuals who may be severely disabled psychologically and yet are able to perform at an extremely high level in some restricted domain, such as architecture, sculpture, music, or mathematical calculation (Baron-Cohen, 2009). Most interesting for the present discussion are savants who show exceptional ability in some artistic domain (i.e., savants who can draw with remarkable skill, or play music beautifully, without formal instruction). Savants are presumably able to do what they do because they have an innate talent, which is isolated from the other aspects of their development. It is assumed that the savant is an extreme case of what happens in any person who develops into a world-class performer: An innate talent provides the basis for development.

Deliberate Practice and the Development of Expert Performance

In opposition to the talent view, Ericsson and coworkers have proposed that the ability to perform at world-class levels in any domain is the result of very large amounts of *deliberate practice*, which can overcome whatever innate differences may exist among us (e.g., Ericsson, Krampe, & Tesch-Römer, 1993; Ericsson, Roring, & Nandagopal, 2007; Ericsson & Ward, 2007; see also Bloom, 1985; Sloboda, Davidson, Howe, & Moore, 1996; and chapters in Ericsson et al., 2006). Top-performing individuals—in athletic, academic, or artistic domains—repeat, again and again, the specific parts of the skill that require improvement. This practice is performed first under the eye of a teacher or coach, and then the person engages in further work or practice alone. Ericsson and colleagues proposed that there is essentially no limit to the level of performance a healthy individual can reach in any skill. If the person is capable of carrying out the activity, then, with sufficient deliberate practice over years, he or she can reach the highest level of performance. On average, the 10-year rule will apply (although it may take longer than this if the person begins deliberate practice in early childhood; Hayes, 1989).

In support of this view, Ericsson et al. (1993) studied four groups of musicians of different levels of skill, and measured the amount of practice and other activities in which they engaged. One group was made up of elite professional violinists, members of world-class symphony orchestras; the other three groups were student violinists at a prestigious music school, classified at three different levels of skill, based on teacher assessments and student performance. All the violinists, professionals and students, were interviewed concerning their activities, musical and otherwise, and all of the students were asked to keep diaries of their activities over a week.

The professional violinists spent more time practicing than the students did, and also more time sleeping; this supported the idea that practice was effortful, and necessitated sleep for recovery from the effort expended (it may also have allowed better memory consolidation—see Chapter 4—as sleep prevents interference from other activities). The better student violinists had begun study of the violin earlier in life than the other students and had practiced more throughout their careers. For instance, the highest-level student violinists had accumulated more than 10,000 hours of practice from the time they had begun study until the age of 20, compared with approximately 8,000 hours for the good violinists, and 4,000 hours for those of lowest skill. (It should be kept in mind that all the students were exceptional violinists, since the music school was one of the best.) A second study, of high-level pianists, found similar results (Ericsson et al., 1993; see also Bloom, 1985). Hyllegard and his colleagues (e.g., Hyllegard & Bories, 2008, 2009; Hyllegard & Yamamoto, 2007) demonstrated that people learning new skills, in a variety of domains, rate practice as useful but effortful and not particularly pleasurable. This supports the theory of deliberate practice, and suggests that achieving world-class levels of achievement in any domain requires that a person be motivated to put forth the years of hard work necessary. Not everyone is so motivated, and thus will not put in the requisite study or practice time, resulting in less-than-outstanding performance.

One issue that is not addressed directly by the Ericsson et al. (1993) study of musical achievement is the issue of talent. One might argue, in response to the results reported by Ericsson et al., that the best violinists achieved the high levels that they did because they had talent for the violin. They made best use of their practice because of the capacities that they brought to music. A study by Sloboda, Davidson, Howe, and Moore (1996) tried to separate the effects of practice from those of talent. They studied a group of young people in England who were enrolled in music education courses. These students were all training under a standard curriculum, and were required to take a set of performance examinations that determine the student's progress. If it is true that the best students—those who ultimately reached exceptional levels of accomplishment—did so on the basis of an innate talent, one should see exemplary performance from a young age on the progress examinations. In addition, the talented students should require less practice time to achieve and maintain their high-level performance, while the lower-achieving students should not show the same level of progress, even if they practice as much as the talented students.

Sloboda et al. (1996) had the students keep records of how much time they spent practicing over the course of their music training, and the results did not support the hypotheses of the "talent" position. The amount of practice needed to go from one competence level to the next was *constant* for all groups. In other words, if it took the lower-achieving group 200 hours of practice to go from level x to level $x + 1$, it took the higher-achieving students the same number of practice hours. That is, the better students did not progress to the next skill level on fewer overall hours of practice. The only difference between the higher- and lower-achieving students was that the better students worked more *intensely*: They carried out those hours of practice in a shorter period of time and thus moved to the next skill level sooner. Thus, the Sloboda et al. (1996) results provide no support for the idea that high levels of achievement depend on talent.

Talent and Practice in Creativity: Remaining Questions

Although a number of research results point to the central importance of practice and accumulated expertise in the development of world-class creative skill, other researchers have proposed that talent should not be ignored in trying to understand the development of high levels of achievement (e.g., Baker, 2007; Coleman, 2007; Freeman, 2007; Gagné, 2007; Sternberg, 1988, 2003; Subotnik, Jarvin, & Rayhack, 2007; Winner, 1996; Ziegler, 2007). According to the advocates of the talent view, initial talent is still necessary for the development of world-class creative skill, because, for one thing, a person will not commit to years of deliberate practice in a domain unless he or she possesses talent (i.e., an innate skill) in that domain. In other words, genetic abilities interact with environmental factors, such as practice and seeking out top-notch mentors, to optimize performance in an activity. Scarr and McCartney (1983) have proposed that gene-environment interactions can take several forms. In *niche-picking*, people with a biologically based talent may be more likely to seek out activities that are consistent with that talent. So a child with innate talent for music might be drawn to the piano during a sibling's lessons. *Evocative* interactions occur when other people treat an individual differently because of his or her innate predispositions or abilities (e.g., a parent may spend more time and money taking a child who shows violin talent to lessons; Ericsson et al., 1993; Moore, Burland, & Davidson, 2003). According to those who hold the talent view, Ericsson and coworkers have only answered the question of *how* someone achieves world-class skill; they have not answered *why*, which is where talent and innate predispositions can supply the answer.

At present there is no definitive way to distinguish the relative importance of innate talent versus practice in accomplishing world-class performance in fields that require creativity. As we have seen, this is an area of active interest among researchers, because of the potential importance of the findings, so there should be much in the way of new developments here in the near future.

THE INFORMATION–PROCESSING VIEW OF CREATIVITY: SUMMARY

We have now laid out the components of the information-processing view of creativity, which proposes that creative thinking builds on the past, is dependent on expertise, and advances in small steps rather than through great leaps outside the box. We now turn to two areas of research that assume—contrary to the information-processing view—that creative ideas come about through the operation of extraordinary thought processes. The two ideas that we will discuss are: first, that creativity depends on psychopathology (genius and madness), and, second, that creativity depends on unconscious processes.

GENIUS AND MADNESS

In the thousands of years before the development of modern scientific methods for studying cognitive processes, people developed various nonscientific explanations concerning how creative ideas came about. For example, the Greeks worshipped the

Muses, nine daughters of Zeus, each of whom ruled a different area of activity: poetry, dance, music, history, astronomy, and so forth. During creative production, it was assumed that the person was *possessed* by the Muse: The ideas came from her, and were simply transmitted through the person (Becker, 1978). Thus, ideas literally came from *outside* of one's mind; that is, one was out of one's mind when producing creative ideas. In more modern times, the idea that one is out of one's mind during creative work led to the idea that insanity—psychopathology—might facilitate creative thinking.

In an early study of the relationship between psychopathology and creativity, Andreasen and Powers (1975) tested mentally-ill people—schizophrenics and manic-depressives—on various laboratory thinking tasks, and their performance was compared to that of creative individuals who did not exhibit psychopathology. The schizophrenics and manic-depressives were hospital patients, and the creative individuals were writers at the University of Iowa Writers' Workshop, which is renowned for attracting important writers. One task that was used was an object-sorting task, to illuminate the structure of a person's concepts. The individual is given a set of seemingly randomly chosen objects (a red ball, a candy cigar, a lock, a bicycle bell, a plate, a red paper circle, a pipe, a knife and fork, a candle, pliers, a key, a toy dog, a bell, etc.) and is asked to place them into groups that fit together. The objects one puts together are evidence for an underlying concept. Results showed that the object-sorting performance of the creative individuals was similar to that of people suffering from manic-depression. Researchers therefore turned to the possible role of manic-depression, also known as *bipolar disorder*, in the creative-thinking process. (For discussion of the possible relation between schizophrenia and creativity, see Sass, 2000–2001.)

Bipolarity and Creativity

In bipolar disorder, a person alternates between periods of great elation and energy (mania) and depression (Goodwin & Jamison, 1990; Jamison, 1993). During the manic period, a person can work almost without sleep, and may feel that he or she can do anything—overcome any obstacle, accomplish any goal. Unfortunately, a person in the throes of mania also has a tendency to undertake grandiose schemes without planning, such as investing all of one's savings in extremely risky business ventures, or marrying someone they have just met. The manic person feels that ideas flow very easily, which has led some theorists to postulate that mania may facilitate creative thinking (Andreasen, 2005; Jamison, 1993).

Jamison (1993) studied the lives of world-famous creative individuals in art and literature, and concluded that many of them—about 50% of poets, 38% of musicians, and roughly 20% of painters and sculptors—were bipolar, all rates far above the 1% rate of the disorder in the general population. Two examples are the poets Lord Byron (1788–1824), who led a turbulent life, in which many episodes had the out-of-control, up-and-down aspects of bipolar disorder (with one contemporary describing him as "mad, bad, and dangerous to know"); and Sylvia Plath (1932–1963), who was hospitalized for mental illness and later committed suicide. Studies by Andreasen (e.g., 1987) and Richards and coworkers (e.g., Richards, Kinney, Lunde, Benet, & Merzel, 1988) presented evidence that bipolar individuals and their close relatives tend to be more creative (as measured by lifetime creative achievements, such as publishing poetry), and that creative people tend to have bipolarity in their family histories. Based on results such as these, it has been suggested that being in a manic state facilitates creative thinking, by producing connections among ideas that would not occur during normal states (Kraepelin, 1921; Jamison, 1993).

The Question of Causality

Let us assume that there is indeed a *relationship* or *correlation* between manic-depression and creativity; that is, assume that many creative people tend to suffer from manic-depression, and sufferers of manic-depression tend to be creative. That set of results alone does not, however, show a *causal* link between bipolarity and creativity. The fact that bipolarity and creativity are correlated could mean several things. First, bipolarity might indeed increase creativity of thinking (e.g., Jamison, 1993); however, the opposite might also be true: Perhaps being creative makes one bipolar. For example, success and failure in one's creative endeavors might drive one from the highs of mania to the depths of depression (Johnson et al., 2000). It might also be the case that bipolarity and creativity are both related to something else, and are not related to each other (e.g., there might be some set of experiences in childhood that lead to adults who are both creative and bipolar). Finally, another possibility, raised by Ludwig (1995), is similar to the *niche-picking* hypothesis advanced earlier in connection with talent: creative people who have bipolar or other disorders may feel most at home in the arts (e.g., music, poetry, or literature). In this case also there would be no direct connection between bipolarity and the creativity of one's thought processes. It is typically assumed in our society that madness is causally related to genius (i.e., that bipolarity, for example, facilitates creative thinking; Jamison, 1993). However, as we have just seen, specifying the exact relationship between genius and madness turns out to be a difficult problem.

In order to provide a more direct test of the hypothesis that being in a manic state increases creativity of thinking, Weisberg (1994) carried out an analysis of the creative productivity of classical composer Robert Schumann (1810–1856), who is generally believed to have suffered from bipolar disorder (Jamison, 1993; Slater & Meyer, 1959). Schumann experienced periods of manic elation, followed by bleak periods, in which he tried more than once to commit suicide. He spent time in asylums, as did other members of his immediate family (bipolar disorder has been long known to have a genetic component and to run in families), and he died in an asylum of what may have been self-induced starvation. Slater and Meyer presented evidence that Schumann's disorder affected the quantity of his work, as shown in Figure 13.7a, which displays the number of compositions Schumann completed in each year of his career, and the diagnosis of his prevailing mood state for that year. As is summarized in Figure 13.7b, Schumann was approximately 5 times more productive during his manic years, so there seems to be no doubt that Schumann's output increased greatly during his highs.

However, the results in Figure 13.7b do not say anything about whether Schumann was producing *better* compositions during his manic years; they only show that he was producing more of them. Weisberg (1994) examined whether Schumann's changing mood states affected the quality of compositions. As a measure of the quality of a composition, Weisberg used Hayes's (1989) measure: The number of recordings

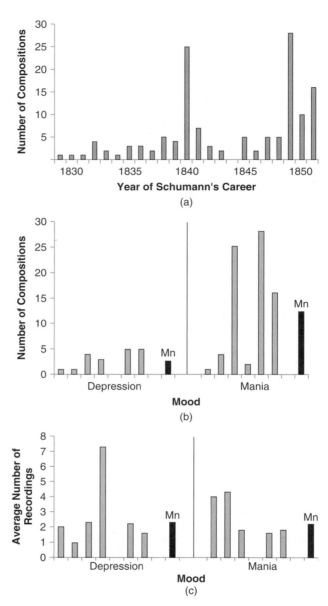

Figure 13.7 Bipolarity and creativity: Robert Schumann. (a). Schumann's productivity over his career. (b) Quantity summarized for manic versus depressive years; productivity as a function of mood. (c) Quality for manic versus depressive years.

available for a given musical composition was used as an indicator of quality of work. If Schumann's periods of mania made him a more effective composer, then compositions produced during his manic years should be recorded more frequently, on average, than compositions produced during the depressive years. This hypothesis was not supported, as shown in Figure 13.7c: Compositions from Schumann's manic years were not, on average, recorded more frequently than those from depressive years. Obviously, a single study of one individual cannot settle an issue as complicated as this, but these results support the conclusion that in Schumann's case the creative thought process was not changed by bipolar disorder (see also Ramey & Weisberg, 2004).

Genius and Madness: Conclusions

The question of the relation of genius and madness, an issue of interest to the ancient Greeks (Becker, 1978; see also Eysenck, 1995), still has resonance today. There seems to be no doubt that the extreme mood changes experienced by bipolar individuals affect their motivation to work, and mania may increase output. However, as evidenced by the case of Schumann and his bipolarity, the quality of the work may not change, meaning that the thought processes are not necessarily changed by mental illness (Weisberg, 1994). We now turn to a second possibility concerning extraordinary thinking processes in creativity: the unconscious.

UNCONSCIOUS THINKING AND INCUBATION IN CREATIVITY

Many researchers who study creative thinking have proposed that unconscious thought processes play a role in bringing about new ideas (e.g., Csikszentmihalyi, 1996; Kounios & Jung-Beeman, 2009; Simonton, 1999). The unconscious can carry out a stream of thinking separate from our conscious thought, which can sometimes result in an idea popping into consciousness. A second aspect of the unconscious stems from Freud (1910), who proposed that unconscious thought can link ideas that conscious thinking cannot. For example, Freud proposed that Leonardo painted the *Mona Lisa* with that hint of a smile because Leonardo lost his mother as a boy (Stannard, 1980). Therefore, he painted women looking as if they were slightly out of reach, although he himself may not have known why he did so. Much of the evidence for the role of the unconscious in creative thought comes from anecdotal evidence from great thinkers or artistic individuals, who have provided subjective evidence for the role of the unconscious in creative productions. Such reports have convinced researchers (see, e.g., Georgsdottir, Lubart, & Getz, 2003) of the functioning of the unconscious in creativity.

Poincaré's Reports of His Unconscious Creative Processes

The most-cited report concerning unconscious processes in creative thinking was produced by the mathematician and scientist Henri Poincaré (1854–1912), who carried out world-class creative work in a variety of fields, including mathematics, physics, and geology (Miller, 1996). Although not a psychologist, Poincaré (1908/1954) developed a theory of the creative-thinking process, and presented detailed reports concerning how several of his most important mathematical breakthroughs had occurred to him. His ideas in this area have had widespread effects on the psychological study of creativity and are still cited by researchers. We will examine one of Poincaré's reports.

The first critical segment of Poincaré's mathematical work involved his attempt to prove that a certain sort of mathematical function could not exist (Miller, 1996; it is not necessary that we nonmathematicians understand the mathematics here). He worked without success for 15 days on this task. One night, after a typically unsuccessful day, he drank black coffee and could not sleep.

> Ideas rose in crowds; I felt them collide until pairs interlocked, so to speak, making a stable combination. By the next morning I had established the existence of a class of [those] functions. . . . I had only to write out the results, which took but a few hours. (p. 36)

During this sleepless night, Poincaré established that one example of the presumed-impossible functions could be shown to exist. Because he felt himself to be merely an observer of what was happening, he concluded that he had been observing the workings of his own unconscious.

Poincaré then went to a geological conference (Miller, 1996), a previously scheduled trip that interrupted his mathematical work. While at this conference, in the midst of a conversation having nothing to do with mathematics, he had the realization that the recently discovered functions were potentially important.

> The incidents of travel made me forget my mathematical work. . . . [W]e entered an omnibus to go some place or other. At the moment when I put my foot on the step, the idea [about the importance of those functions] came to me, without anything in my former thoughts seeming to have paved the way for it. . . . I did not verify the idea; I should not have had time, as, upon taking my seat in the omnibus, I went on with a conversation already commenced, but I felt a perfect certainty. On my return [home], for conscience' sake, I verified the result at my leisure. (p. 37)

In order to explain this experience, Poincaré (1908/1954) concluded that he must have been thinking about those functions all along, on an unconscious level. Poincaré proposed that creative thinking is carried out in two cycles. First, conscious work on the problem serves to activate potentially relevant ideas. If the thinker is not successful (i.e., reaches an impasse), he or she ultimately gives up conscious work. The unconscious then takes over, producing combination after combination of those previously activated ideas. If a combination hit upon by the unconscious has relevance to a problem recently thought about, that idea comes barging into consciousness as an *Aha!* experience. We see here a connection between creativity and the discussion of insight in problem solving in Chapter 12.

Stages in Creative Thinking

Wallas (1926) elaborated on Poincaré's analysis of the cognitive unconscious, postulating four separate stages in the production of a creative leap: (1) *preparation*;

(2) *incubation*; (3) *illumination*; and (4) *verification*. The *preparation* stage occurs when the person begins to work on the problem, and serves to activate ideas that will be used later by the unconscious. We saw that stage when Poincaré worked without success on his problem for many sessions. When Poincaré dropped his work on the problem and left for his geological conference, the *incubation* stage began: Like an embryo that is developing invisibly in an egg, the problem was being worked on at an unconscious level. Occasionally, a combination of ideas will be produced in the unconscious that has potential relevance to an unresolved problem. The person will then experience a sudden *illumination*, an *Aha!* experience, as the idea bursts into consciousness. Such incubation effects are accepted by modern researchers, as they were by Poincaré, as direct evidence for the functioning of the unconscious. In Wallas's final stage, *verification*, the illumination must be shown to be correct, or *verified*, as Poincare reported doing.

Modern Analyses of Unconscious Processes in Creative Thinking

Modern researchers (e.g., Csikszentmihalyi, 1996; Miller, 1996; Simonton, 1995, 2011a) include the incubation process as part of their discussions of creative thinking. The basic idea is that problems that require creative thinking are often very complex, with many possible combinations of ideas. If we did not do much of the work in the unconscious, then we would never get anything accomplished (Simonton, 1995, p. 472). As noted earlier, it has also been assumed that the unconscious can bring together ideas that would not have been linked in ordinary conscious thinking (Koestler, 1964). "Only by falling back on this less disciplined resource can the creator arrive at insights that are genuinely profound" (Simonton, 1995, p. 472). Csikszentmihalyi (1996, p. 100) and coworkers interviewed a large number of individuals who have carried out lifetimes of creative work in a wide variety of fields. Those individuals, ranging from chemists to investment bankers, often reported that they used unconscious processes to assist them in their work. They structure their workdays to have a period of idle time, working in the garden, say, during which they believe incubation is taking place.

Questions About Unconscious Thinking in Creativity

When individuals of the highest repute provide the information about their thought processes, it seems that we can learn much (Ghiselin, 1954). However, contrary to that optimistic conclusion, Poincaré's report and those of others may have little value as evidence for unconscious processes in creative thinking. There are two problems with such accounts. First, introspection does not necessarily provide valid or accurate accounts of one's information processing. For instance, as we saw in Chapter 5, there is psychological and neuropsychological evidence that we process individual features of letters before we recognize whole letters (recall Hubel and Wiesel's [1959] *simple cells*). Yet introspection does not provide this information, as we are not conscious of this stage. Second, the only support that Poincaré provided for his assumption of unconscious thinking was his *Aha!* experience after breaking away from a problem. However, the fact that an *Aha!* experience occurs does not, by itself, tell us how cognitive processes work; we need independent evidence, beyond a report of the *Aha!* experiences. The evidence provided by the people interviewed by Csikszentmihalyi (1996) suffers from the same problem: All they know is that they had a creative idea while working in the garden, say. They (and we) have no direct evidence concerning the structure of their thought processes, or, more specifically, that unconscious processing was involved.

Unconscious Thinking in Creativity: Conclusions

Postulation of unconscious thinking in creativity depends on subjective reports concerning *Aha!* experiences, which are not objective scientific evidence for unconscious thinking in creativity. What we need now are some creative methods for producing objective evidence for unconscious thinking processes (for some possibilities, see the discussion of unconscious processing in Chapter 5). Until then, the unconscious must remain a fascinating but as yet unsupported possibility. Furthermore, there is evidence, which we will now review, that one can explain incubation effects without assuming that unconscious processing has occurred.

INCUBATION AND ILLUMINATION WITHOUT THE UNCONSCIOUS

One of the reasons for postulating unconscious processes in creative thinking is the occurrence of incubation effects (*Aha!* experiences). In more neutral terms, we can say that *incubation* is a name for a situation in which solution to a problem occurs, sometimes suddenly, after the individual has taken a break from the problem. Many years ago, Woodworth (1938; see also Simon, 1986) proposed that positive effects of breaking away from a problem might simply be due to forgetting of incorrect approaches during the time away. In addition, a break might allow retrieval of new information. In Woodworth's analysis, there is nothing useful occurring during the incubation period, either consciously or unconsciously, except the forgetting of the old method.

Evidence to support this forgetting explanation comes from research by S. Smith and colleagues (e.g., Kohn & Smith, 2009; Smith & Blankenship, 1991) and C. Smith and her colleagues (Smith, Bushouse, & Lord, 2010). Smith and Blankenship used *rebus* problems as stimulus material in order to test the forgetting hypothesis. In a rebus problem, a visual configuration represents a familiar phrase, and the person's task is to decipher the phrase. Here are two examples of rebus problems. For each one, what phrase is represented?

---

(1) print   (Answer: "small print")
(2) STA4NCE   (Answer: "For Instance"; that is "4" *in* "STANCE" = "For instance")

Smith and Blankenship presented rebus problems with hints. Some of the hints were purposely designed to be not helpful (see Figure 13.8), so the people were unable

Example: you just me

Clue: between

Solution: Just between you and me.

Test Problem 1:

Helpful clues

Clues: between; lines

Solution: *Reading between the lines*

Test Problem 2:

Non-helpful clues

fly night

Clues: paper; over

Solution: *Fly by night*

(a)

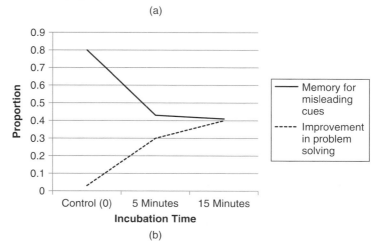

Incubation Time

(b)

Figure 13.8   (a) Rebus problems, with helpful or misleading clues presented for each. (b) Smith and Blankenship (1989) results. Proportion rebus problems solved and cues forgotten over time. Over time, cues are forgotten and problems are solved.

to solve the problems and were led to an impasse. Smith then gave people different amounts of time away from the problems before giving them a second chance to solve them. That time away from the problems corresponded to Poincaré's incubation break. Results indicated that second-chance solutions increased with longer breaks. Smith also asked the participants to try to remember the (misleading) hints that had originally been presented with the unsolved problems. The participants tended to forget the misleading hints over the break, and increased forgetting of the incorrect hint was related to *better* performance on the problems. In other words, taking a break from problem solution helped because it resulted in the decay of erroneous or misleading information (in the misleading hint condition), and thus changed the information that was retrieved by the problem. Thus, one does not have to assume that unconscious processes are operative during a break in order to understand why taking a break can help problem solvers. This view has been supported by other studies (e.g., Kohn & Smith, 2009; Smith et al., 2009; Vul & Pashler, 2007).

Another possible explanation for positive effects of taking a break from a problem is that an external stimulus encountered during the break might cue solution to the problem. There is experimental evidence that an external stimulus can sometimes cue the solution to a problem, and the person may not be aware that cuing had taken place (Seifert, Meyer, Davidson, Patalano, & Yaniv, 1995; Smith, 1995). Therefore, the person might assume it was because of unconscious thought processes, but that would be incorrect. A classic study by Maier (1931) demonstrated that people's problem-solving performance can be affected by environmental events or new information of which they are not aware. He tested people on the Two-String problem, shown in Figure 13.9, which asks people to tie together two strings hanging from the ceiling. The problem seems straightforward, until the person grasps one string and reaches for the other, only to find that the string-in-hand is too short to be able to hold it and grasp the other. How can one reach the second string while holding the first?

Maier was interested in the solution of setting one string swinging like a pendulum, grasping the second string, and waiting for the "pendulum" string to swing back to you, so it can be grasped and tied to the second. In one condition, after the participant had worked unsuccessfully on the problem, the experimenter walked past

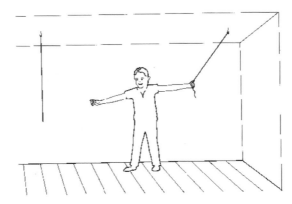

Figure 13.9 Two-String problem: How can he tie the strings together?

one string, casually pushing it aside and setting it into swinging motion, without indicating that that had anything to do with the problem. This hint was effective, with 75% of previously unsuccessful people solving the problem shortly thereafter. Most interestingly, several of those solvers reported no awareness of the experimenter's having set the string into swinging motion. Those individuals also reported that the solution had suddenly come to them as a whole. Other people solved the problem in several steps: They first thought about setting the string to swinging, and then realized that that could be used to solve the problem. Those latter people tended to acknowledge that they had seen the string in motion. So what may have happened to some of the former (unconscious) participants was that the realization of the solution interfered with their memory for the event that had triggered the process. Extending this analysis to incubation effects, a break from a problem makes possible encounters with environmental stimuli that may cue solution. This is another explanation for incubation that does not involve unpredictable, unconscious thinking.

Conclusions: Unconscious Processes in Creative Thinking?

At present, evidence for unconscious processes in creative thinking is based on fascinating personal reports concerning the experiences of people who do creative work. However, those reports do not, by themselves, offer independent support for occurrence of unconscious processes. As we have seen in other endeavors (e.g., mental imagery, Chapter 7), introspective accounts are not necessarily a reliable method for cognitive science. Other explanations have been proposed for incubation that do not assume unconscious processing of a solution, but instead are based on forgetting of incorrect methods and cuing of solutions by external events. In sum, at this time, evidence for unconscious processes in creative thinking is not very strong.

We have now examined the information-processing perspective on creativity and have also reviewed two perspectives that assume that creative thinking is based on extraordinary processes: genius and madness; and unconscious thinking. We now turn to a different viewpoint on creativity, the psychometric view, which came out of the mental-testing movement. This view began with the question of how one might measure people's potential for creativity.

THE PSYCHOMETRIC PERSPECTIVE: TESTING FOR CREATIVE ABILITY

In 1950, J. P. Guilford, the president of the American Psychological Association, used his presidential address to propose that psychology take up the study of creativity. Guilford was a psychometrician: His area of expertise was mental testing, specifically I.Q. testing. He laid out methods that could be used to test people for their capacity to think creatively, just as we test people for their capacity to think intelligently. Box 13.1 presents several types of items used to measure creative-thinking potential. Please work through those exercises before reading further.

The exercises in Box 13.1 serve to flesh out Guilford's conception of how the creative process works. In order to get the creative process started, the thinker must see deficiencies in some aspect of the world. Only then will he or she spend time contemplating what might be done to correct those problems, which is the first step in producing a creative outcome. Thus, the creative person must be *sensitive to problems* (see also Petroski, 1992). Exercises A and B in Box 13.1 allow one to measure a person's sensitivity to problems.

BOX 13.1 EXAMPLES OF CREATIVE-THINKING TESTS

A. Suppose that humans suddenly began to be born with six fingers on each hand, instead of five. List all the consequences that you can think of that would arise. (Give yourself 5 minutes.)

B. List all the problems or difficulties you can think of with the present-day toaster (5 minutes).

C. List all the white edible things that you can (3 minutes).

D. List all the words you can think of in response to *Mother* (3 minutes).

E. List all the uses you can think of for a *brick* (3 minutes).

Once a problem has been identified, the person must then begin to think about how it can be overcome. It seemed obvious to Guilford (1950) that the more ideas a person can produce, the greater the chance that he or she will produce a useful one. Therefore, Guilford proposed that *fluency of thought*, the capacity to produce a large number of ideas in a given period of time, would be one characteristic of the creative thinker. In order to test for fluent thought, one can give people a task that requires that they produce multiple ideas, such as exercises C and D in Box 13.1.

In addition to being *fluent* in idea production, the creative thinker must also be a *flexible* thinker. According to Guilford, creative thinking requires that one break away from one's habitual ways of thinking, and strike out in new directions (similar to out-of-the-box thinking and the how Gestalt psychologists emphasized productive over reproductive thinking, as discussed in Chapter 12). One can score exercises C and D in Box 13.1 for flexibility of thought, by determining whether a person tends to stay within a category when generating ideas, or whether he or she tends to switch from one category to another. For example, in producing names of white edible things, a person who says *milk*, *cottage cheese*, *sour cream*, *vanilla ice cream*, and *vanilla frozen yogurt* would be relatively inflexible, because those items are all white dairy foods. A flexible person might say *milk*, *carob-covered raisins*, *white corn*, *white wine*, *tofu*, and *lobster*, where each item comes from a different category of food.

The creative thinker will also produce *original ideas*, those not produced by many other people. One can score the exercises in Box 13.1 for originality of ideas. Consider the *Unusual-Uses Test* (Box 13.1E). If a student lists a use for a brick that most students also list (e.g., doorstop), then there would be little originality in that idea; however, if he or she listed a use for a brick that no one else thought of (e.g., a way to bake hollow bread loaves), that would be a highly original idea.

Guilford (1950) took measures of fluency, flexibility, and originality and combined them into a score for *divergent thinking*. Divergent thinking enables the person to produce ideas that *diverge*, or move away, from the usual. Those ideas then can serve as the basis for a creative outcome. Divergent thinking is out-of-the-box thinking, and is contrasted with *convergent* thinking, which occurs when one uses available information to converge on a single answer that solves a problem. In a situation demanding a creative response, Guilford theorized that one would first use divergent thinking to produce many possible ideas. Convergent thinking would then be used to narrow down those ideas to something potentially useful. Guilford believed that each person is to some degree capable of creative thinking. People who produce great creative advances possess the divergent-thinking capacities to a greater degree, but we all have some of that ability.

Testing the Tests: The Validity of Creative-Thinking Tests

Guilford's ideas concerning how to develop tests to measure divergent thinking have been very influential (for discussion, see Runco, 2007). A number of different batteries of tests were developed, by Guilford (1950) and by other researchers (e.g., Torrance, 1974; Wallach & Kogan, 1965). Those tests, especially several developed by Torrance (1974), have been used hundreds of thousands of times, in many different settings, from schools, where they are used in screening children for gifted programs; to industry, where they are used in hiring decisions; to laboratory research settings, where they are used to select creative participants for research studies. However, even though divergent-thinking tests have been used for over 50 years, there is still controversy concerning whether they are useful as measures of creative thinking ability (Baer, 2011a, b; Kim, 2011a, b). Most important is the question of whether scores on the tests are related to real-world creativity, or, in other words, whether the tests are *valid*. Several studies have found that people who score high in divergent thinking do not necessarily score highly on creativity based on such measures as ratings by teachers or job supervisors, or their creative accomplishments (for reviews, see Runco, 2007; Sawyer, 2012; Weisberg, 2006a). Some studies find little or no relation between test performance and creative accomplishment while other studies do find a relationship. The results are not as clear as one might hope, which means that divergent-thinking tests have limited use in predicting creativity.

The Case Studies in Creativity and Divergent Thinking

We have already seen in the case studies of DNA and *Guernica* that those creative advances, one in science and one in art, were solidly based on work that had come earlier, both by the people themselves and others in the field. Those thinkers used information and ideas that were already available, rather than creating something based on a leap of divergent thinking. Therefore, in those cases the process of creative thought was not based on divergent thinking, contrary to Guilford (1950). It therefore would not be surprising if the tests did not predict who would be creative (for additional discussion, see Dietrich & Kanso, 2010; Weisberg, 2006a).

Psychometrics of Creativity: Conclusions

The psychometric viewpoint has been valuable in stimulating much research concerning divergent thinking. However, Guilford's basic idea, that creative thinking is based on divergent thinking, has received mixed support from studies of real-world creative thinking. Based on these results, one could say that creativity is not based on some special sort of divergent thinking process.

THE DARWINIAN THEORY OF CREATIVITY: BLIND VARIATION AND SELECTIVE RETENTION AS A MODEL OF CREATIVE THOUGHT

We have so far in this chapter concentrated on creative thinking, since this is a book on cognition, and creative thinking involves cognitive processes. However, as noted earlier, the study of creativity is broader than the study of creative thinking, since it is believed that additional aspects of the person, such as personality characteristics and environmental factors, play a role in whether or not a person will produce creative outcomes. A number of *confluence models of creativity* have been proposed in recent years (e.g., Amabile, 1983, 1996; Csikszentmihalyi, 1999; Rubenson & Runco, 1995; Sternberg & Lubart, 1996). Those models assume that creative production is the result of the coming together, or confluence, of a number of factors, including cognitive processes, personality characteristics, and family and other social factors. We will examine one prominent confluence model, Simonton's (e.g., 1988, 1995, 2003, 2011a) Darwinian theory of creativity, to demonstrate the breadth of those models. As noted earlier, however, due to the focus of this book, we will provide only an introduction to this literature.

Simonton's (1988, 1995, 2011a) theory of creativity is based on that of Campbell (1960), who proposed that the processes underlying creative thinking were analogous to the processes underlying evolution in Darwin's theory of natural selection. One can specify three stages in natural selection. The first stage involves random or *blind* changes in the genetic material from one generation to the next. The organism has no say in or control over the occurrence of those variations, which is why they are blind. Sometimes one of those blind changes results in an organism that is more likely to survive, and therefore that change will be selected, which is the second stage. In stage 3, that change must be retained, and passed down to the next generation (in the genome).

The same argument was applied by Campbell (1960) to creative thought, which also involves three stages. First is a blind idea-generation process. That is, an individual producing ideas—possible solutions in response to a problem, say—has no way of knowing which, if any, will be successful, so one can describe the process as "blind." Of those blind variations on old ideas, one may happen to solve the problem at hand. That is, that idea will be selected by the problem (stage 2) and will be retained in memory for future use (stage 3). In Simonton's (1995, 2003, 2011a, b) elaboration of Campbell's view, the blind generation of new ideas is brought about either through unconscious thinking (adopted from Poincaré) or as the result of a chance encounter with an environmental event (Seifert et al., 1995).

A number of different sorts of evidence are brought forth by Simonton (1999, 2011a) to support his theory. First, he quotes several thinkers of renown, including Poincaré and Einstein, whose reports on their thought processes are interpreted as supporting the Darwinian view. We have already discussed Poincaré's beliefs about creativity being due to ideas set in motion, which then randomly come together. Along similar lines, Einstein said that "combinatorial play seems to be the essential feature in productive thought" (Einstein, in Hadamard, 1954, p. 142). That quote is taken by Simonton as additional evidence for the random or blind combination of ideas. Guilford's (1950, 1959) notion of divergent thinking is also discussed by Simonton as one possible basis for idea generation. Simonton (2007; Damian & Simonton, 2011) has also carried out several case studies of creative accomplishments, including Galileo's studies of the planets, and has interpreted the results from the perspective of the Darwinian perspective.

Simonton discusses one example of blindness in creative thinking with which we are already familiar: Watson's attempts to determine how the bases might be paired between the backbones of DNA. As noted earlier, he used cardboard models of the bases, which he moved around on his desktop into possible configurations, to work through possible pairings. Simonton noted that the structure of that activity indicated that Watson at that point was working from the bottom up, rather than from the top down, as we have emphasized in this book. It should be noted, however, that the configuration of the bases was the last step in the determination of the structure of DNA, and the more-important first steps taken by Watson and Crick (i.e., the decision to assume that DNA was helical and that modeling would be the strategy they would pursue) were clearly driven from the top down (Olby, 1994; Weisberg, 2006a).

Going beyond the analysis of cognitive processes involved in creative thinking, Simonton (1999, Ch. 3) also reviewed research on personality characteristics of creative people, and concluded that several psychological characteristics typical of creative individuals might be important in facilitating the random production of ideas. Creative individuals typically report having a wide range of interests, which in Simonton's view would provide the wide-ranging associative background that would support random connections among ideas. Similarly, highly creative individuals are often found to be introverted, which would result in their spending time alone, which would allow the long periods needed for "the long sequences of free association" necessary for production of creative ideas (Simonton, 1999, p. 91). Simonton also discusses the possible link between genius and madness, and proposed that a touch of madness might help the creative thought process become more free-associative.

Thirdly, Simonton also proposed that social and environmental factors, both small-scale and large-scale, can affect creative production. For example, birth order may influence creative accomplishment (Simonton, 1999). Evidence indicates that first-borns are more likely to engage in creative pursuits (Sulloway, 1996). However, first-borns may be less likely to produce revolutionary creative advances than later-born individuals (for additional discussion, see Sulloway, 1996, 2009). Also, based on a study ranging over two millennia, Simonton (1976, 2011b) has concluded that occurrence of war affects creative output: War in one generation (as determined by historical records) results in less creative accomplishment in the next one (as determined by patent records and other historical information).

In sum, Simonton (1988, 1995, 1999, 2003, 2011a) has developed a wide-ranging theory of creativity based on Darwin's theory of evolution (Campbell, 1960). The theory incorporates cognitive aspects (blind production of ideas), as well as personality components and social factors. Simonton's evidence includes reports of renowned thinkers concerning the operation of their creative process, as well as personality research. He has also examined the influence of social and environmental factors on creative production. This is one example of how the study of creativity can go beyond the examination of creative thinking, which is the focus of this chapter. Further discussion of confluence models of creativity can be found in Runco (2007), Sawyer (2012), and Weisberg (2006a).

YOU TOO CAN BE CREATIVE!

We have now completed a review of a wide range of research on creativity, much of which has been concerned with creativity at the highest levels. We now turn to the opposite end of the scale, to examine the question of whether one's creativity can be increased. Given the importance of creative thinking in modern society, it is not surprising that there is much interest in the question of whether the creativity of us ordinary folks can be increased. If you Google "creativity," you will find many websites that promise to unleash your creative thinking power. Each site claims to have a unique simple insight into how the creative process works, which they will teach to you, for a fee. However, usually missing from those sites is concrete evidence that the methods being touted actually work. Given what we now know about expertise and the 10-year rule in creative development, it would seem to be a waste of time and effort (and money) to learn a simple method that proposes to increase your ability to produce new ideas, without taking into account the data-base of the domain.

However, Finke, Ward, and Smith (1992; also Smith, Ward, & Finke, 1995) have developed a method of facilitating creative thinking that is based on cognitive theorizing and which, in contrast to most of the self-help methods, has been tested with success in controlled scientific studies. Finke et al. base their training program on their *Geneplore* model of creativity. The term *geneplore* comes from a combination of *generate* and *explore*, and it assumes that creative thinking comes about in two phases: One first *generates* novel ideas, and then *explores* their possibilities. The process involved here is bottom-up in nature, since the person is generating objects without any specific goal idea in mind. Finke and co-workers have shown that structured use of generation-plus-exploration in a laboratory setting can facilitate production of creative products.

In one study, student participants were shown drawings of simple forms (see Figure 13.10a); they were instructed to take three forms, randomly chosen by the experimenter, and use imagery to combine them into an interesting-looking new object that might be useful in some way. The resulting forms are called *preinventive forms*, because they do not yet have any use (see Figure 13.10b). Thus, the first step in this method is based on what one could call guided imagery. The second step of the process centers on exploring the potential usefulness of the forms. After the participants generated a preinventive form, they were given the name of one of eight object categories, shown in Figure 13.10, and were asked to think of a way that the preinventive form could be used within that category. Fitting the preinventive form into the category changes it from a preinventive form into an invention (see Figure 13.10c and 13.10d).

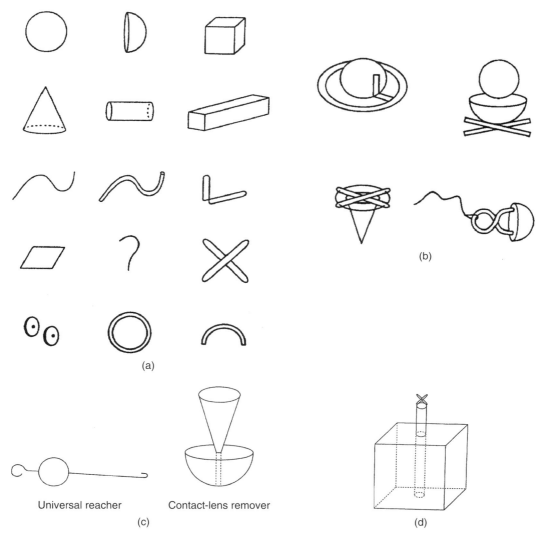

Figure 13.10 Finke et al.'s guided-imagery creative-production task. (a) Some examples of components given to participants. Three were chosen at random for each attempt to produce an invention. (b) Some examples of preinventive forms (combinations of forms produced by participants). Examples of object-category names: (1) furniture; (2) tools and utensils; (3) toys and games. (c) Some inventions, made by combining components into preinventive forms and interpreting those forms on the basis of the category names. Concept names: 1. Architecture: Concepts in building design; 2. Medicine: Mechanisms of infection; 3. Political science: forms of government. (d) Example of a conceptual interpretation of a preinventive form. The student producing this invention interpreted as an example of the concept of "viral cancellation." Two viruses attacking a cell at the same time might cancel out each other's effects. A preinventive form is interpreted in an abstract conceptual manner.

In one study, participants were given a total of 360 attempts at producing an invention, and 65 of the products were judged as creative inventions, with potential use.

Using Guided Imagery to Stimulate Creative Thinking

The research of Finke et al. (1992; Smith et al., 1995) provides a method that might be useful if one were an inventor trying to produce some new device, and if one had no specific object type in mind. In such a situation, one might simply carry out the structured task shown in Figure 13.10a, and one might be successful. However, such a method might be less useful if you were assigned the task of improving your company's line of lawnmowers, say. Similarly, if one were a novelist, trying to develop a plot line from scratch, the method might be helpful; but what if one were trying to develop a specific scene? In conclusion, the research of Finke, Ward, and Smith (1992; Smith et al., 1995) is of interest because it provides a method for generating creative products that has withstood testing under strict laboratory conditions. However, until now, the method has been applied to a limited range of situations. In the future, as this model stimulates further research into processes involved in generating new ideas, we will learn more about the limitations, if any, in our ability to facilitate creative thinking.

TOWARD A NEUROSCIENCE OF CREATIVITY

The 21st century has seen the beginnings of a neuroscience of creativity, as researchers have tried to isolate brain areas underlying creative production. In Chapter 12 we discussed neuroscience research designed to isolate brain areas related to insight (*Aha!* experiences) in problem solving. Researchers have also tried to examine creative thinking in other domains. As one example, people have been tested on the unusual-uses test and other divergent-thinking tests (Box 13.1) while brain activity is measured, through fMRI or EEG (Dietrich & Kanso, 2010). The results have been difficult to interpret, as different studies have found different patterns of activation, making it difficult to draw firm conclusions.

Methodologically, it is challenging to obtain measures of creative activity in the fMRI apparatus or using EEG measures, which require that people be relatively still during the procedure. As an example, if one is interested in creativity in the visual arts, one must develop a method that would allow one to measure brain activity while an artist, say, was drawing. Similarly, in studying creativity in musical composition, one would like to have a composer producing new melodies while lying in the fMRI apparatus. Researchers have been very clever in developing methods to enable them to examine creative activity in a variety of domains. As one example, creative thinking in music has been studied by having jazz pianists improvise—create new music—by using a keyboard while they are lying in the fMRI apparatus (Limb & Braun, 2008). Brain activity in that condition was compared with activity in a control condition in which the musicians played well-known musical sequences, and so were not involved in creating music. The comparison of the brain activity in the two conditions indicated that the prefrontal cortex played an important role during musical improvisation.

In another study (Solso, 2001; see also Miall, Gowen, & Tchalenko, 2009), a visual artist with many years' experience drawing portraits was placed in an fMRI apparatus set up so that he could draw. He was asked to create a picture (sketch a portrait based on a photo presented to him). In another condition, he copied a geometric form that was presented to him. A nonartist carrying out the same tasks served as a control. The fMRI recordings indicated that creating a new portrait led to activity in the parietal lobe—the visual-processing areas—in the novice, but not in the artist. The artist's extensive experience might have allowed him to quickly go beyond the visual-spatial aspects of the face. Similarly, the artist exhibited more activity in the frontal cortex, which may indicate planning on his part as he organized the portrait.

While the designs of such studies are impressive, the research so far has been difficult to interpret (Dietrich & Kanso, 2010), because the results are not consistent. First of all, there is considerable variability in the results across studies designed to investigate creativity in the same domain, such as musical creativity. In addition, diverse brain areas are active in different types of creative activities, indicating that there is little support for some general neuropsychological circuitry underlying creativity in all domains. As Dietrich and Kanso note, one difficulty facing researchers studying the neuroscience of creativity is that different researchers work under very different conceptions concerning how the creative process works, which leads them to design very different sorts of studies. Those design differences make it difficult to make comparisons of results across studies. While there is no doubt that there will soon be great advances in our understanding of the brain circuitry underlying creativity, those advances may have to wait until we have a more general agreement concerning how the creative process operates at the level of cognitive processes. Then researchers will be able to determine the brain structures and processes underlying creativity. It is also likely that the neuropsychology of creativity will turn out to be domain-specific, with different parts of the cortex contributing to creative ventures in art versus music versus scientific discoveries.

CONCLUSIONS ABOUT CREATIVE THINKING: ORDINARY PROCESSES PRODUCING EXTRAORDINARY OUTCOMES

A basic assumption of those who have studied creative thinking, from antiquity to the present, is that new ideas are the product of extraordinary thought processes. It is assumed that ordinary conscious thinking cannot bring about the sometimes radically new ideas that form the basis for many of humanity's greatest achievements. The research reviewed in this chapter has supported the opposite conclusion, that there is nothing extraordinary about the cognitive processes underlying creative thinking (although those thought processes may result in extraordinary products). We began with an examination of two case studies, DNA and *Guernica*, which served as a basis for anchoring the discussion. We then considered the information-processing view (Boden, 1990, 2004; Ericsson et al., 1993; Newell, Shaw, & Simon, 1958; Weisberg, 1986, 2006a, b), which assumes that creative thinking is ordinary problem solving, based on expertise within the domain. This view was supported by the case studies of real-life creative thinking. We then examined two variations on the idea that creative thinking depends on extraordinary processes: madness and the unconscious. However, little support was found at present for either possibility. Similarly, the psychometric view, that creative thinking is based on divergent thinking, was also not strongly supported. We also briefly reviewed research examining the neuroscience of creativity, and concluded that it might be too early to expect strong conclusions concerning brain involvement in creativity.

This discussion of creativity has served as a useful conclusion to out exploration of the cognitive processes, as it indicates that the cognitive processes that we discussed earlier in the book—memory, working memory, pattern recognition, attention, imagery, concepts, reasoning—are relevant to the analysis of human functioning at the highest levels.

REVIEW QUESTIONS

Here is a set of questions to guide your study and review of this chapter.

1. According to the introduction in this chapter, what are some barriers to the study of creativity from the perspective taken in this book?

2. How is *creativity* defined in this book? How is that definition different from that held by most researchers?

3. Watson and Crick made two critical decisions in beginning their work on DNA. What were those decisions and what was their basis?

4. Describe how the bases in the double helix are arranged and how Watson discovered that arrangement.

5. Where did the basic idea for *Guernica* come from? What evidence supports that conclusion?

6. Give examples of the use of heuristics in scientific thinking, as discovered by Dunbar.

7. Summarize the computational approach to creativity and some evidence in support of it.

8. What is the 10-year rule in creative development and what are Hayes's 10 years of silence concerning composers of music?

9. Summarize the *deliberate-practice* view of development of expert performance and contrast it with the *talent* view.

10. What objections have been raised to the *deliberate-practice* view?

11. Summarize evidence supporting the idea that bipolar disorder is related to creativity.

12. What evidence raises questions concerning the causal role of bipolarity in creative productivity?

13. Summarize Poincaré's theory of creative thinking.

14. According to Wallas, what are the stages in creative thinking?

15. What questions can be raised about the role of the unconscious in creativity?

16. Summarize evidence supporting the idea that *incubation* can occur without unconscious processing.

17. Summarize the components in Guilford's analysis of creativity.

18. Summarize evidence for and against the validity of creative-thinking tests.

19. Summarize the Darwinian theory of creativity.

20. Describe why a creator's "hit ratio" is important in the Darwinian theory and summarize evidence concerning hit ratios for and against the Darwinian view.

21. Discuss Finke, Smith, and Ward's program for facilitating creativity.

22. Summarize results from studies of brain imaging during creative activity.

REFERENCES

Aaronson, D., & Ferres, S. (1983). A model for coding lexical categories during reading. *Journal of Experimental Psychology: Human Perception and Performance*, *9*, 700–725.

Aaronson, D., & Scarborough, H. S. (1976). Performance theories for sentence coding: Some quantitative evidence. *Journal of Experimental Psychology: Human Perception and Performance*, *2*, 56–70.

Abramson, A., & Lisker, L. (1970). Discrimination along the voicing continuum: Cross-language tests. *Proceedings of the 6th International Congress of the Phonetic Sciences*, Prague, 1967 (pp. 569–573). Prague, Czech Republic: Academia.

Acha, J., & Perea, M. (2008). The effects of length and transposed-letter similarity in lexical decision: Evidence with beginning, intermediate, and adult readers. *British Journal of Psychology*, *99*, 245–264.

Aggleton, J. P., Vann, S. D., Denby, C., Dix, S., Mayes, A. R., Roberts, N., & Yonelinas, A. P. (2005). Sparing of the familiarity component of recognition memory in a patient with hippocampal pathology. *Neuropsychologia*, *43*, 1810–1823.

Ainsworth, K. A., and Baumann, R. (1995). The effect of appropriate context on comprehension and recall. *Unpublished manuscript*, Carleton College, Northfield, MN.

Aitchison, J. (1987). Reproductive furniture and extinguished professors. In R. Steele & T. Threadgold (Eds.), *Language topics: Essays in honour of Michael Halliday* (Vol. 2, pp. 3–14). Amsterdam, The Netherlands: John Benjamins.

Akhlaghi, A., Jahangiri, N., Azarpazhooh, M. R., Elyasi, M., & Ghale, M. (2011). Foreign accent syndrome: Neurolinguistic description of a new case. In *Proceedings of 2011 International Conference on Language, Literature and Linguistics*, Dubai, United Arab Emirates.

Akhtar, N., & Tomasello, M. (1996). Twenty-four-month-old children learn words for absent objects and actions. *British Journal of Developmental Psychology*, *14*, 79–93.

Akin, O., & Akin, C. (1996). Frames of reference in architectural design: Analysing the hyper-acclamation (A-h-a-!). *Design Studies*, *17*, 341–361.

Alba, J. W., & Hasher, L. (1983). Is memory schematic? *Psychological Bulletin*, *93*, 203–231.

Allen, G. D., & Hawkins, S. (1980). Phonological rhythm: Definition and development. *Child Phonology*, *1*, 227–256.

Allen, S. W., & Brooks, L. R. (1991). Specializing the operation of an explicit rule. *Journal of Experimental Psychology: General*, *120*, 3–19.

Amabile, T. M. (1983). *The social psychology of creativity*. New York, NY: Springer-Verlag.

Amabile, T. M. (1996). *Creativity in context*. Boulder, CO: Westview.

American Psychological Association. (1995). *Questions and answers about memories of childhood abuse*. http://www.apa.org/topics/trauma/memories.aspx

Ammerlaan, T. (1997). "Corrosion" or "loss" of emigrant Dutch in Australia: An experiment on first language attrition. In S. Kroon & J. Klatter-Folmer (Eds.), *Dutch Overseas: Studies in maintenance, shift and loss of Dutch as an immigrant language* (pp. 69–985). Amsterdam: Tilburg University Press, 69–985.

Amy Kuo, M. L., & Hooper, S. (2004). The effects of visual and verbal coding mnemonics on learning Chinese characters in computer-based instruction. *Journal of Technology Research and Development*, *52*(3), 23–38.

Anderson, A., Garrod, S., & Sanford, A. J. (1983). The accessibility of pronominal antecedents as a function of episode shifts in narrative text. *Quarterly Journal of Experimental Psychology*, *35A*, 427–440.

Anderson, J. R. (1974). Retrieval of prepositional information from long-term memory. *Cognitive Psychology*, *6*, 451–474.

Anderson, J. R. (1976). *Language, memory, and thought*. Hillsdale, NJ: Erlbaum.

Anderson, J. R. (1983). *The architecture of cognition*. Cambridge, MA: Harvard University Press.

Anderson, J. R. (2010). *Cognitive psychology and its implications* (7th ed.). New York, NY: Worth.

Anderson, J. R., & Bower, G. H. (1973). *Human associative memory*. Washington, DC: Winston.

Anderson, J. R., & Schooler, L. J. (1991). Reflections of the environment in memory. *Psychological Science*, *2*, 396–408.

Andrade, J., & Baddeley, A. (2011). The contribution of phonological short-term memory to artificial grammar learning. *Quarterly Journal of Experimental Psychology*, *64*(5), 960–974.

Andreasen, N. C. (1987). Creativity and mental illness: Prevalence rates in writers and their first-degree relatives. *American Journal of Psychiatry*, *144*, 1288–1292.

Andreasen, N. C. (2005). *The creating brain: The neuroscience of genius*. New York, NY: Dana Press.

Andreasen, N. J. C., & Powers, P. S. (1975). Creativity and psychosis: An examination of conceptual style. *Archives of General Psychiatry*, *32*(1), 70–73.

Andrews, S. (1986). Morphological influences on lexical access: Lexical or nonlexical effects? *Journal of Memory and Language*, *25*, 726–740.

Andrews, S., & Davis, C. (1999). Interactive activation accounts of morphological decomposition: Finding the trap in mousetrap? *Brain and Language*, *68*, 355–361.

Angelone, B. L., Levin, D. T., & Simons, D. J. (2003). The roles of representation and comparison failures in change blindness. *Perception*, *32*, 947–962.

Ansburg, P. I., & Dominowski, R. L. (2000). Promoting insightful problem solving. *Journal of Creative Behavior*, *34*, 30–60.

Antonucci, S. M., Beeson, P. M., Labiner, D. M., & Rapcsak, S. Z. (2008). Naming and semantic knowledge in patients with left inferior temporal lobe lesions. *Aphasiology*, *22*(3), 281–304.

Antonucci, S. M., Beeson, P. M., & Rapcsak, S. Z. (2004). Anomia in patients with left inferior temporal lobe lesions. *Aphasiology*, *18*, 543–554.

Ardila, A., Rosselli, M., & Ardila, O. (1987). Foreign accent: An aphasic epiphenomenon? *Aphasiology*, *2*, 493–499.

Ariely, D., Loewenstein, G., & Prelec, D. (2003). Coherent arbitrariness: Stable demand curves without stable preferences. *Quarterly Journal of Economics*, *118*, 73–105.

Ariely, D., Loewenstein, G., & Prelec, D. (2006). Tom Sawyer and the construction of value. *Journal of Economic Behavior & Organization*, *60*, 1–10.

Armstrong, S. L., Gleitman, L. R., & Gleitman, H. (1983). What some concepts might not be. *Cognition*, *13*, 263–308.

Ashcraft, M. H. (1978). Property dominance and typicality effects in property statement verification. *Journal of Verbal Learning and Verbal Behavior*, *11*, 155–164.

Assal, G., Favre, C., & Anderes, J. (1984). Nonrecognition of familiar animals by a farmer: Zooagnosia or prosopagnosia for animals. *Revue Neurologique* (Paris), *140*, 580–584.

Atkinson, R. C., & Shiffrin, R. M. (1968). Human memory: A proposed system and its control processes. In K. W. Spence & J. T. Spence (Eds.), *The psychology of learning and motivation* (Vol. 2, pp. 89–195). New York, NY: Academic Press.

Atkinson, R. C., & Shiffrin, R. M. (1971). The control of short-term memory. *Scientific American*, *224*, 82–90.

Atran, S. (1998). Folk biology and the anthropology of science: Cognitive universals and cultural particulars. *Behavioral and Brain Sciences*, *21* (4), 547–569.

Atran, S. (1999). Folkbiology. In R. Wilson & F. Keil (Eds.), *The MIT encyclopedia of the cognitive sciences* (pp. 316–317). Cambridge, MA: MIT Press.

Atran, S., & Medin, D. L. (2008). *The native mind and the cultural construction of nature*. Cambridge, MA: MIT Press.

Atran, S., Medin, D. L., & Ross, N. (2002). Thinking about biology: Modular constraints on categorization and reasoning in the everyday life of Americans, Maya, and scientists. *Mind and Society*, *3* (2), 31–63.

Awh, E., Jonides, J., Smith, E. E., Schumacher, E., Koeppe, R. A., & Katz, S. (1996). Dissociation of storage and rehearsal in verbal working memory: Evidence from positron emission tomography. *Psychological Science*, 7, 25–31.

Baars, B. J., & Motley, M. T. (1976). Spoonerisms as the result of conflict between sequencers: Evidence from artificially elicited slips of the tongue. *American Journal of Psychology*, *89* (3), 467–484.

Baars, B. J., Motley, M. T., & MacKay, D. (1975). Output editing for lexical status in artificially elicited slips of the tongue. *Journal of Verbal Learning & Verbal Behavior*, *14*, 382–391.

Baddeley, A. D. (1966a). The influence of acoustic and semantic similarity on long-term memory for word sequences. *Quarterly Journal of Experimental Psychology*, *18*, 302–309.

Baddeley, A. D. (1966b). Short term memory for word sequences as a function of acoustic, semantic and formal similarity. *Quarterly Journal of Experimental Psychology*, *18*, 362–365.

Baddeley, A. D. (1986). *Working memory*. Oxford, UK: Oxford University Press.

Baddeley, A. D. (1990). *Human memory: Theory and practice*. London, UK: Erlbaum.

Baddeley, A. D. (2000). The episodic buffer: A new component of working memory? *Trends in Cognitive Science*, *4*, 417–423.

Baddeley, A. D. (2007). *Working memory, thought, and action*. Oxford, UK: Oxford University Press.

Baddeley, A. D., Allen, R. J., & Hitch, G. J. (2010). Investigating the episodic buffer. *Psychologica Belgica*, *50*, 223–243.

Baddeley, A. D., & Hitch, G. L. (1974). Working memory. In G. A. Bower (Ed.), *The psychology of learning and motivation: Advances in research and theory* (Vol. 8, pp. 47–89). New York, NY: Academic Press.

Baddeley, A. D., & Hitch, G. L. (1994). Developments in the concept of working memory. *Neuropsychology*, *8*, 485–493.

Baddeley, A. D., Lewis, V., & Vallar, G. (1984). Exploring the articulatory loop. *Quarterly Journal of Experimental Psychology*, *36A*, 233–252.

Baddeley, A. D., & Salame, P. (1986). The unattended speech effect: Perception or memory? *Journal of Experimental Psychology: Learning, Memory, and Cognition*, *12*, 525–529.

Baddeley, A. D., Thomson, N., & Buchanan, M. (1975). Word length and the structure of short-term memory. *Journal of Verbal Learning and Verbal Behavior*, *14*, 575–589.

Badecker, W. (2001). Lexical composition and the production of compounds: Evidence from errors in naming. *Language and Cognitive Processes*, *16* (4), 337–366.

Badecker, W., & Caramazza, A. (1987). The analysis of morphological errors in a case of acquired dyslexia. *Brain and Language*, *32*, 278–305.

Badecker, W., Miozzo, M., & Zanuttini, R. (1995). The two-stage model of lexical retrieval: Evidence from a case of anomia with selective preservation of grammatical gender. *Cognition*, *57*, 193–216.

Baer, J. (2011a). How divergent thinking tests mislead us: Are the Torrance Tests still relevant in the 21st century? *Psychology of Aesthetics, Creativity, and the Arts*, *5*(4), 309–313.

Baer, J. (2011b). Four (more) arguments against the Torrance Tests. *Psychology of Aesthetics, Creativity, and the Arts*, *5*(4), 316–317.

Bahrick, H. P. (1984). Semantic memory content in permastore: Fifty years of memory for Spanish learned in school. *Journal of Experimental Psychology: General*, *113*, 1–37.

Bahrick, H. P., Bahrick, L. E., Bahrick, A. S., & Bahrick, P. O. (1993). Maintenance of foreign language vocabulary and the spacing effect. *Psychological Science*, *4*, 316–321.

Bahrick, H. P., Bahrick, P. O., & Wittlinger, R. P. (1975). Fifty years of memory for names and faces: A cross-sectional approach. *Journal of Experimental Psychology: General*, *104*, 54–75.

Bahrick, H. P., & Phelps, E. (1987). Retention of Spanish vocabulary over eight years. *Journal of Experimental Psychology: Learning, Memory, and Cognition*, *13*, 344–349.

Baker, J. (2007). Nature and nurture interact to create expert performers. *High Ability Studies*, *18*(1), 57–58.

Baker, L. M., & Dunbar, K. (2000). Experimental design heuristics for scientific discovery: The use of baseline and known controls. *International Journal of Human Computer Studies*, *53*, 335–349.

Baldwin, D. A. (1989). Priorities in children's expectations about object label reference: Form over color. *Child Development*, *60*(6), 1291–1306.

Baldwin, D. A. (1991). Infants' contribution to the achievement of joint reference. *Child Development*, *62*(5), 875–890.

Baldwin, D. (1993). Early referential understanding: Infants' ability to understand referential acts for what they are. *Developmental Psychology*, *29*, 832–843.

Ball, L. J., Ormerod, T. C., & Morley, N. J. (2004). Spontaneous analogising in engineering design: A comparative analysis of experts and novices. *Design Studies*, *25*, 495–508.

Ball, L. J., & Stevens, A. (2009). Evidence for a verbally-based analytic component to insight problem solving. In N. Taatgen & H. van Rijn (Eds.), *Proceedings of the Thirty-First Annual Conference of the Cognitive Science Society*. Austin, TX: Cognitive Science Society.

Bannard, C., Lieven, E., & Tomasello, M. (2009). Modeling children's early grammatical knowledge. *Proceedings of the National Academy of Sciences, USA*, *106*(41), 17284–17289.

Bar, M., & Biederman, I. (1998). Subliminal visual priming. *Psychological Science*, *9*, 464–469.

Bar-Hillel, M. (1980). The base-rate fallacy in probability judgments. *Acta Psychologica*, *44*, 211–233.

Barclay, C., & Wellman, H. (1986). Accuracies and inaccuracies in autobiographical memories. *Journal of Memory and Language*, *25*, 93–103.

Barker, A. T., Jalinous, R., & Freeston, I. L. (1985). Non-invasive magnetic stimulation of human motor cortex. *The Lancet*, *325*(8437), 1106–1107.

Baron, J. (2008). *Thinking and deciding* (4th ed.). Cambridge, UK: Cambridge University Press.

Baron-Cohen, S. (2009). Autism: The empathizing-systemizing (E-S) theory. *Annals of the New York Academy of Sciences*, *1156*, 68–80.

Barsalou, L. W. (1982). Context-independent and context-dependent information in concepts. *Memory & Cognition*, *10*, 82–93.

Barsalou, L. W. (1983). Ad hoc categories. *Memory & Cognition*, *11*, 211–227.

Barsalou, L. W. (1987). The instability of graded structure: Implications for the nature of concepts. In U. Neisser (Ed.), *Concepts and conceptual development: Ecological and intellectual factors in categorization* (pp. 101–140). Cambridge, UK: Cambridge University Press.

Barsalou, L. W. (1989). Intraconcept similarity and its implications for interconcept similarity. In S. Vosniadou & A. Ortony (Eds.), *Similarity and analogical reasoning* (pp. 76–121). Cambridge, UK: Cambridge University Press.

Barsalou, L. W. (1991). Deriving categories to achieve goals. In G. H. Bower (Ed.), *The psychology of learning and motivation: Advances in research and theory* (Vol. 27, pp. 1–64). San Diego, CA: Academic Press.

Barsalou, L. W. (1993). Flexibility, structure, and linguistic vagary in concepts: Manifestations of a compositional system of perceptual symbols. In A. C. Collins, S. E. Gathercole, & M. A. Conway (Eds.), *Theories of memory* (pp. 29–101). London, UK: Erlbaum.

Barsalou, L. W. (2005a). Abstraction as dynamic interpretation in perceptual symbol systems. In L. Gershkoff-Stowe & D. Rakison (Eds.), *Building object categories* (pp. 389–431). Carnegie Symposium Series. Mahwah, NJ: Erlbaum.

Barsalou, L. W. (2005b). Continuity of the conceptual system across species. *Trends in Cognitive Sciences*, *9*, 309–311.

Barsalou, L. W. (2009). Simulation, situated conceptualization, and prediction. *Philosophical Transactions of the Royal Society of London: Biological Sciences*, *364*, 1281–1289.

Barsalou, L. W., & Sewell, D. R. (1984). Constructing representations of categories from different points of view. *Emory Cognition Project Technical Report #2*. Atlanta, GA: Emory University.

Barsalou, L. W., Sewell, D. R., & Ballato, S. M. (1986). *Assessing the stability of category representations with graded structure*. Unpublished manuscript.

Barsalou, L. W., Spindler, J. L., Sewell, D. R., Ballato, S. M., & Gendel, E. M. (1987). *Assessing the stability of category representations with property generation*. (Unpublished manuscript). Emory University, Atlanta, GA.

Bartlett, F. C. (1923). *Psychology and primitive culture*. Cambridge, UK: Cambridge University Press.

Bartlett, F. C. (1932). *Remembering: A study in experimental and social psychology*. Cambridge, UK: Cambridge University Press.

Bartlett, F. C. (1958). *Thinking: An experimental and social study*. London, UK: George Allen & Unwin.

Basden, B. H., Basden, D. R., & Gargano, G. J. (1993). Directed forgetting in implicit and explicit memory tests: A comparison of methods. *Journal of Experimental Psychology: Learning, Memory, and Cognition*, *19*, 603–616.

Basso, A., Capitani, E., & Laiacona, M. (1988). Progressive language impairment without dementia: A case with isolated category specific semantic defect. *Journal of Neurology, Neurosurgery, & Psychiatry*, *51*, 1201–1207.

Bates, E. (1997). On language savants and the structure of the mind: A review of Neil Smith and Ianthi-Maria Tsimpli, *The mind of a savant: Language learning and modularity*. *International Journal of Bilingualism*, *1*(2), 163–179.

Bates, E., Kintsch, W., Fletcher, C., & Giuliani, V. (1980). On the role of pronominalization and ellipsis in texts: Some memory experiments. *Journal of Verbal Learning and Verbal Behavior*, *19*, 121–134.

Bates, E., Masling, M., & Kintsch, W. (1978). Recognition memory for aspects of dialogue. *Journal of Experimental Psychology: Human Learning and Memory*, *4*, 187–197.

Battig, F. B., & Montague, W. E. (1969). Category norms for verbal items in 56 categories: A replication and extension of the Connecticut category norms. *Journal of Experimental Psychology Monograph*, *80*, 1–46.

Bayes, T. (1763). An essay towards solving a problem in the doctrine of chances. *Philosophical Transactions*, *53*, 370–418.

Bayley, P. J., Hopkins, R. O., & Squire, L. R. (2006). The fate of old memories after medial temporal lobe damage. *Journal of Neuroscience*, *26*, 13311–13317.

Baylis, G. C., Rolls, E. T., & Leonard, C. M. (1987). Functional subdivisions of the temporal lobe neocortex. *Journal of Neuroscience*, *7*, 330–342.

Bazhenova, O. V., Stroganova, T. A., Doussard-Roosevelt, J. A., Posikera, L. A., & Porges, S. W. (2007). Physiological responses of 5-month-old infants to smiling and blank faces. *International Journal of Psychophysiology*, *63*, 64–76.

BBC News (producer) & English, G. (director). (1987). The foolish wise ones. United Kingdom.

Bea, W., & Scholz, R. (1995). Graphische Modelle bedingter Wahrscheinlichkeiten im empirisch-didaktischen Vergleich. *Journal für Mathematik-Didaktik*, *16*, 299–327.

Beale, S., Nirenburg, S., & Mahesh, K. (1996). Hunter-Gatherer: Three search techniques integrated for natural language semantics. In *Proceedings of* AAAI-96, Portland, Oregon.

Becker, G. (1978). *The mad genius controversy*. London, UK: Sage.

Becker, J. T., MacAndrew, D. K., & Fiez, J. A. (1999). A comment on the functional localization of the phonological storage subsystem of working memory. *Brain and Cognition*, *41*(1), 27–38.

Beeler, M., Gosper, R. W., & Schroeppel, R. (1972). *HAKMEM*. Cambridge, MA: MIT Artificial Intelligence Laboratory, Memo AIM-239, p. 35, February 1972. http://www.inwap.com/pdp10/hbaker/hakmem/proposed.html#item95

Beeman, M. J., & Chiarello, C. (1998). Complementary right and left hemisphere language comprehension. *Current Directions in Psychological Science*, *7*, 2–8.

Behrmann, M., Moscovitch, M., & Winocur, G. (1994). Intact mental imagery and impaired visual perception: Dissociable processes in a patient with visual agnosia. *Journal of Experimental: Psychology Human Perception and Performance*, *20*, 1068–1087.

Behrmann, M., & Tipper, S. P. (1999). Attention accesses multiple reference frames: Evidence from visual neglect. *Journal of Experimental Psychology: Human Perception and Performance*, *25*(1), 83–101.

Belli, R. F. (1989). Influences of misleading postevent information: Misinformation interference and acceptance. *Journal of Experimental Psychology: General*, *118*, 72–85.

Bennamoun, M., & Boashash, B. (1997). A structural-description–based vision system for automatic object recognition. In *IEEE transactions on systems, man, and cybernetics. Part B, Cybernetics : a publication of the IEEE Systems, Man, and Cybernetics Society*, *27* (6), 893–906.

Benson, D. F. (1979). Neurologic correlates of anomia. In H. Whitaker (Ed.), *Studies in neurolinguistics* (Vol. 4, pp. 293–328). New York, NY: Academic Press.

Benson, D. F. (1988). Classical syndromes of aphasia. In F. G. Boller (Ed.), *Handbook of neuropsychology* (Vol. 1, pp. 267–280). Amsterdam, The Netherlands: Elsevier Science Publishers.

Benson, D. F., & Greenberg, J. P. (1969). Visual form agnosia. *Archives of Neurology*, *20*, 82–89.

Benson, D. F., & Weir, W. F. (1972). Acalculia: Acquired anarithmetia. *Cortex*, *8*, 465–472.

Berbaum, K., Bever, T., & Chung, C. S. (1983). Light source position in the perception of object shape. *Perception*, *12*(4), 411–416.

Bergman, E., & Roediger, H. L. (1999). Can Bartlett's repeated reproduction experiments be replicated? *Memory & Cognition*, *27*, 937–947.

Berko, J. (1958). The child's learning of English morphology. *Word*, *14*, 150–177.

Berlin, B. (1978). Ethnobiological classification. In E. Rosch & B. B. Lloyd (Eds.), *Cognition and categorization* (pp. 9–26). Hillsdale, NJ: Erlbaum.

Bernstein, L. J., & Robertson, L. C. (1998). Independence between illusory conjunctions of color and motion with shape following bilateral parietal lesions. *Psychological Science*, *9*, 167–175.

Berteletti, I., Lucangeli, D., Piazza, M., Dehaene, S., & Zorzi, M. (2010). Numerical estimation in preschoolers. *Developmental Psychology*, *46*(2), 545–551.

Biederman, I. (1987). Recognition-by-components: A theory of human image understanding. *Psychological Review*, *94*, 115–147.

Biederman, I. (1995). Visual object recognition. In S. F. Kosslyn and D. N. Osherson (Eds.), *An Invitation to Cognitive Science: Vol. 2. Visual Cognition* (2nd ed., pp. 121–165). Cambridge, MA: MIT Press.

Biederman, I., Glass, A. L., & Stacy, E. W., Jr., (1973). Searching for objects in real-world scenes. *Journal of Experimental Psychology*, *97*, 22–27.

Biederman, I., & Ju, G. (1988). Surface vs. edge-based determinants of visual recognition. *Cognitive Psychology*, *20*, 38–64.

Biederman, I., Ju, G., & Clapper, J. (1985). *The perception of partial objects*. (Unpublished manuscript), State University of New York at Buffalo.

Biederman, I., & Kalocsai, P. (1997). Neurocomputational bases of object and face recognition. *Philosophical Transactions of the Royal Society of London: Biological Sciences*, *352*, 1203–1219.

Binder, J. R. (2007). Effects of word imageability on semantic access: Neuroimaging studies. In J. Hart & M. A. Kraut (Eds.), *Neural basis of semantic memory* (pp. 149–181). Cambridge, UK: Cambridge University Press.

Binder, J. R., Frost, J. A., Hammeke, T. A., Cox, R. W., Rao, S., & Prieto, T. (1997). Human brain language areas identified by functional magnetic resonance imaging. *Journal of Neuroscience*, *17*, 353–362.

Binder, J. R., & Price, C. (2001). Functional imaging of language. In R. Cabeza & A. Kingstone (Eds.), *Handbook of functional neuroimaging of cognition* (pp. 187–251). Cambridge, MA: MIT Press.

Birch, H. (1945). The relation of previous experience to insightful problem solving. *Journal of Comparative Psychology*, *38*, 367–383.

Birdsong, D., & Molis, M. (2001). On the evidence for maturational constraints in second-language acquisition. *Journal of Memory and Language*, *44*, 235–249.

Bisiach, E., & Luzzatti, C. (1978). Unilateral neglect of representational space. *Cortex*, *14*, 129–133.

Biswas, D. (2009). The effects of option framing on consumer choices: Making decisions in rational versus experiential processing modes. *Journal of Consumer Behavior*, *8*, 284–299.

Bjork, E. L., & Bjork, R. A. (1996). Continuing influences of to-be-forgotten information. *Consciousness and Cognition*, *5*, 176–196.

Bjork, E. L., & Bjork, R. A. (2003). Intentional forgetting can increase, not decrease, the residual influences of to-be-forgotten information. *Journal of Experimental Psychology: Learning, Memory, and Cognition*, *29*, 524–531.

Bjork, E. L., Bjork, R. A., & Anderson, M. C. (1998). Varieties of goal-directed forgetting. In J. M. Golding & C. MacLeod (Eds.), *Intentional forgetting: Interdisciplinary approaches* (pp. 103–137). Hillsdale, NJ: Erlbaum.

Blank, G. D. (1988). Metaphors in the lexicon. *Metaphor and Symbolic Activity*, *3*, 21–36.

Blasdell, R., & Jensen, P. (1970). Stress and word position as determinants of imitation in first language learners. *Journal of Speech and Hearing Research*, *13*, 193–202.

Blasko, D. G., & Connine, C. M. (1993). Effects of familiarity and aptness on metaphor processing. *Journal of Experimental Psychology: Learning, Memory and Cognition*, *19*, 295–308.

Bliss, T. V. P., & Gardner-Medwin, A. R. (1973). Long-lasting potentiation of synaptic transmission in the Dentate Area of the unanaesthetised rabbit following stimulation of the perforant path. *Journal of Physiology*, *232*, 357–374.

Bloom, B. S. (Ed.). (1985). *Developing talent in young people*. New York, NY: Ballantine.

Bloom, P., & Gelman, S. A. (2008). Psychological essentialism in selecting the 14th Dalai Lama. *Trends in Cognitive Sciences*, *12*, 243.

Blumstein, S. E., & Kurowski, K. (2006). The foreign accent syndrome: A perspective. *Journal of Neurolinguistics*, *19*, 346–355.

Bock, J. K. (1986). Syntactic persistence in language production. *Cognitive Psychology*, *18*, 355–387.

Bock, J. K., & Irwin, D. E. (1980). Syntactic effects of information availability in sentence production. *Journal of Verbal Learning and Verbal Behavior*, *19*, 467–484.

Bock, J. K., & Levelt, W. J. M. (1994). Language production: Grammatical encoding. In M. Gernsbacher (Ed.), *Handbook of psycholinguistics* (pp. 945–984). San Diego, CA: Academic Press.

Boden, M. (1990). *The creative mind: Myths and mechanisms*. London: Weidenfeld and Nicolson.

Boden, M. (2004). *The creative mind: Myths and mechanisms* (2nd ed.). New York, NY: Routledge.

Boden, M. (2010). *Creativity in art: Three types of surprise*. New York, NY: Oxford.

Bohannon, J. N. (1988). Flashbulb memories for the Space Shuttle disaster: A tale of two theories. *Cognition*, *29*, 179–196.

Bohannon, J. N., Padgett, R. J., Nelson, K. E., & Mark, M. (1996). Useful evidence on negative evidence. *Developmental Psychology*, *33*, 551–555.

Bohannon, J. N., & Stanowicz, L. (1988). The issue of negative evidence: Adult responses to children's language errors. *Developmental Psychology*. *24*, 684–689.

Bonatti, L. (1994). Propositional reasoning by model? *Psychological Review*, *101*(4), 725–733.

Boomer, D. S., & Laver, J. D. M. (1968). Slips of the tongue. *British Journal of Disorders of Communication*, *3*(1), 2–12.

Bor, D., & Owen, A. M. (2007). A common prefrontal-parietal network for mnemonic and mathematical recoding strategies within working memory. *Cerebral Cortex*, *17*(4), 778–786.

Borges, B., Goldstein, D. G., Ortmann, A., & Gigerenzer, G. (1999). Can ignorance beat the stock market? In G. Gigerenzer, P. M. Todd, & the ABC Research Group (Eds.), *Simple heuristics that make us smart*. New York, NY: Oxford University Press.

Borgida, E., & Nisbett, R. E. (1977). The differential impact of abstract vs. concrete information on decisions. *Journal of Applied Social Psychology*, *7*, 258–271.

Boring, E. G. (1953). A history of introspection. *Psychological Bulletin*, *50*, 169–189.

Boroditsky, L. (2001). Does language shape thought? English and Mandarin speakers' conceptions of time. *Cognitive Psychology*, *43*, 1–22.

Boroditsky, L., Fuhrman, O., & McCormick, K. (2011). Do English and Mandarin speakers think about time differently? *Cognition*, *118*(1), 123–129.

Boroditsky, L., Schmidt, L., & Phillips, W. (2003). Sex, syntax, and semantics. In D. Gentner & S. Goldin-Meadow (Eds.), *Language in mind: Advances in the study of language and cognition* (pp. 61–80). Cambridge, MA: MIT Press.

Bowden, E. M., & Jung-Beeman, M. J. (1998). Getting the right idea: Semantic activation in the tight hemisphere my help solve insight problems. *Psychological Science*, *9*, 435–440.

Bowdle, B. F., & Gentner, D. (1997). Informativity and asymmetry in comparisons. *Cognitive Psychology*, *34*, 244–286.

Bowdle, B. F., & Gentner, D. (2005). The career of metaphor. *Psychological Review*, *112*(1), 193–216.

Bower, G. H. (1970). Imagery as a relational organizer in associative learning. *Journal of Verbal Learning and Verbal Behavior*, *9*, 529–533.

Bower, G. H., Black, J. B., & Turner, T. J. (1979). Scripts in memory for texts. *Cognitive Psychology*, *11*, 177–220.

Bower, G. H., & Clark, M. (1969). Narrative stories as mediators for serial learning. *Psychonomic Science*, *14*, 181–182.

Bower, G. H., & Karlin, M. B. (1974). Depth of processing pictures of faces and recognition memory. *Journal of Experimental Psychology*, *103*, 751–757.

Bower, G. H., & Rinck, M. (2001). Selecting one among many referents in spatial situation models. *Journal of Experimental Psychlogy: Learning, Memory, and Cognition*, *27*, 81–98.

Bradshaw, J. L., & Rogers, L. (1993). *The evolution of lateral asymmetries, language, tool use and intellect*. San Diego, CA: Academic Press.

Brady, N., & Field, D. J. (2000). Local contrast in natural images: Normalization and coding efficiency. *Perception*, *29*(9), 1041–1055.

Braine, M. D. S. (1978). On the relation between the natural logic of reasoning and standard logic. *Psychological Review*, *85*, 1–21.

Braine, M. D. S., & O'Brien, D. P. (1991). A theory of *If*: A lexical entry, reasoning program, and pragmatic principles. *Psychological Review*, *98*, 182–203.

Brainerd, C. J., & Reyna, V. F. (1998). Fuzzy-trace theory and children's false memories. *Journal of Experimental Child Psychology*, *71*, 81–129.

Branigan, H. P., Pickering, M. J., MacLean, J. F., & Stewart, A. J. (2006). The role of local and global syntactic structure in language production: Evidence from syntactic priming. *Language and Cognitive Processes*, *21* (7–8), 974–1010.

Bransford, J. D., Franks, J. J., Morris, C. D., & Stein, B. S. (1979). Some general constraints on learning and memory research. In L. S. Cermak & F. I. M. Craik (Eds.), *Levels of processing in human memory* (pp. 331–355). Hillsdale, NJ: Erlbaum.

Bransford, J. D., & Johnson, M. K. (1972). Contextual prerequisites for understanding: Some investigations of comprehension and recall. *Journal of Verbal Learning and Verbal Behavior*, *11*, 717–726.

Bransford, J. D., & Johnson, M. K. (1973). Considerations of some problems of comprehension. In W. C. Chase (Ed.), *Visual information processing* (pp. 383–438). New York, NY: Academic Press.

Brewer, W. F. (1986). What is autobiographical memory? In D. Rubin (Ed.), *Autobiographical memory* (pp. 25–49). Cambridge, UK: Cambridge University Press.

Brewer, W. F. (1988). Memory for randomly sampled autobiographical events. In U. Neisser & E. Winograd (Eds.), *Remembering reconsidered: Ecological and traditional approaches to the study of memory* (pp. 21–90). Cambridge, UK: Cambridge University Press.

Brewer, W. F. (2000a) Bartlett, functionalism, and modern schema theories. *Journal of Mind and Behavior*, *21* (1–2), 37–44.

Brewer, W. F. (2000b). Bartlett's concept of the schema and its impact on theories of knowledge representation in contemporary cognitive psychology. In A. Saito (Ed.), *Bartlett, culture and cognition* (pp. 115–134). Hove, UK: Psychology Press.

Brewin, C. R., Andrews, B., & Gotlib, I. H. (1993). Psychopathology and early experience: A reappraisal of retrospective reports. *Psychological Bulletin*, *113*, 82–98.

Brigham, F. J., & Brigham, M. M. (1998). Using keyword mnemonics in general music classes: Cognitive psychology meets music history. *Journal of Research and Development in Education*, *31*, 205–213.

Bright, P., Buckman, J., Fradera, A., Yoshimasu, H., Colchester, A. C. F., & Kopelman, M. D. (2006). Retrograde amnesia in patients with hippocampal, medial temporal, temporal lobe or frontal pathology. *Learning and Memory*, *13*, 545–547.

Bright, P., Moss, H. E., & Tyler, L. K. (2004). Unitary versus multiple semantics: PET studies of word and picture processing. *Brain & Language*, *89* (3), 417–432.

Broadbent, D. E. (1958). *Perception and communication*. New York, NY: Pergamon Press.

Broadbent, D. E., & Broadbent, M. H. (1987). From detection to identification: Response to multiple targets in rapid serial visual presentation. *Perception & Psychophysics*, *42*, 105–113.

Broca, P. P. (1861). Loss of speech, chronic softening and partial destruction of the anterior left lobe of the brain. *Bulletin de la Société Anthropologique*, *2*, 235–238. English translation available at: http://psychclassics.yorku.ca/Broca/perte-e.htm

Brockmole, J. R., & Henderson, J. M. (2008). Prioritizing new objects for eye fixation in real-world scenes: Effects of object-scene consistency. *Visual Cognition*, *16*, 375–390.

Brookes, D. T., Ross, B. H., & Mestre, J. P. (2011). Specificity, transfer, and the development of expertise. *Physical Review Special Topics—Physics Education Research 2011*, *7*(1), 010105-1-010105-8.

Brooks, L. R. (1968). Spatial and verbal components of the act of recall. *Canadian Journal of Psychology*, *22*, 349–368.

Brooks, L. R. (1978). Nonanalytic concept formation and memory for instances. In E. Rosch & B. B. Lloyd (Eds.), *Cognition and categorization* (pp. 169–211). Hillsdale, NJ: Erlbaum.

Brooks, L. R., Norman, G. R., & Allen, S. W. (1991). Role of specific similarity in a medical diagnostic task. *Journal of Experimental Psychology: General*, *120*, 278–287.

Brown, B. B. (1966). Specificity of EEG photic flicker responses to color as related to visual imagery ability. *Psychophysiology*, *2*(3), 197–207.

Brown, G. D. A., Neath, I., & Chater, N. (2007). A temporal ratio model of memory. *Psychological Review*, *114*, 539–576.

Brown, J. (1958). Some tests of the decay theory of immediate memory. *Quarterly Journal of Experimental Psychology*, *10*, 12–21.

Brown, R. (1958). How shall a thing be called? *Psychological Review*, *65*(1), 14–21.

Brown, R., & Hanlon, C. (1970). Derivational complexity and order of acquisition in child speech. In R. Hayes (Ed.), *Cognition and the development of language*. New York, NY: Wiley.

Brown, R., & Kulik, J. (1977). Flashbulb memories. *Cognition*, *5*, 73–99.

Brown, R., & McNeill, D. (1966). The "tip of the tongue" phenomenon. *Journal of Verbal Learning and Verbal Behavior*, *5*, 325–337.

Brownell, H. H., Carroll, J. J., Rehak, A., & Wingfield, A. (1992). The use of pronoun anaphora and speaker mood in the interpretation of conversational utterances by right hemisphere brain-damaged patients. *Brain and Language*, *43*(1), 121–147.

Bruce, K. R., & Pihl, R. O. (1997). Forget "drinking to forget": Enhanced consolidation of emotionally charged memory by alcohol. *Experimental Clinical Psychopharmacology*, *5*, 242–250.

Bruce, V., & Young, A. (1986). Understanding face recognition. *The British Journal of Psychology*, *77*, 305–327.

Bruck, M., Ceci, S. J., Francoeur, E., & Barr, R. (1995). "I hardly cried when I got my shot!": Influencing children's reports about a visit to their pediatrician. *Child Development*, *66*, 193–208.

Bruck, M., Ceci, S. J., & Hembrooke, H. (1997). Children's false reports of pleasant and unpleasant events. In D. Read & D. S. Lindsay (Eds.), *Recollections of trauma: Scientific research and clinical practice* (pp. 199–219). New York, NY: Plenum Press.

Bruck, M., Ceci, S. J., & Hembrooke, H. (2002). The nature of children's true and false narratives. *Developmental Review*, *22*(3), 520–554.

Bruner, J., Goodnow, J., & Austin, A. (1956). *A study of thinking*. New York, NY: Wiley.

Bruyer, R., Laterre, C., Seron, X., Feyereisen, P., Strypstein, E., Pierrard, E., & Rectem, D. (1983). A case of prosopagnosia with some preserved covert remembrance of familiar faces. *Brain and Cognition*, *2*, 257–284.

Bumford, D., & Reeves, L. (2009). Effects of grammatical form and familiarity on metaphor comprehension. Paper presented at The Metaphor Festival, Stockholm University, Sweden, September 9–11, 2009.

Burgess, C., Livesay, K., & Lund, K. (1998). Explorations in context space: Words, sentences, discourse. *Discourse Processes*, *25*, 211–257.

Burgess, C., & Lund, K. (1997). Modeling cerebral asymmetries of semantic memory using high-dimensional semantic space. In M. Beeman & C. Chiarello (Eds.), *Right hemisphere language comprehension: Perspectives from cognitive neuroscience* (pp. 61–66). Hillsdale, NJ: Erlbaum.

Burke, D. M., MacKay, D. G., Worthley, J. S., & Wade, E. (1991). On the tip of the tongue: What causes word finding failures in young and older adults? *Journal of Memory and Language*, *30*, 542–579.

Burnham, C. A., & Davis, K. G. (1969). The nine-dot problem: Beyond perceptual organization. *Psychonomic Science*, *17*, 321–323.

Burns, D. J., & Gold, D. E. (1999). An analysis of item gains and losses in retroactive interference. *Journal of Experimental Psychology: Learning, Memory, and Cognition*, *25*, 978–985.

Burtt, H. E. (1931). *Legal psychology*. New York, NY: Prentice-Hall.

Bybee, J. (1985). *Morphology*. Amsterdam, The Netherlands: John Benjamins.

Cabeza, R., Dolcos, F., Graham, R., & Nyberg, L. (2002). Similarities and differences in the neural correlates of episodic memory retrieval and working memory. *Neuroimage*, *16*, 317–330.

Cabeza, R., & Nyberg, L. (2000). Imaging cognition II: An empirical review of 275 PET and fMRI studies. *Journal of Cognitive Neuroscience*, *12*(1), 1–47.

Cabeza, R., Rao, S. M., Wagner, A. D., Mayer, A. R., & Schacter, D. L. (2001). Can medial temporal lobe regions distinguish true from false? An event-related functional MRI study of veridical and illusory recognition memory. *Proceedings of the National Academy of Sciences, USA*, *98*, 4805–4810.

Cameron, L. (2003). *Metaphor in educational discourse*. London, UK: Continuum.

Cameron, L. (2008). Metaphor and talk. In R. Gibbs (Ed.), *The Cambridge handbook of metaphor and thought* (pp. 197–211). Cambridge: Cambridge University Press.

Cameron, L. (2011). Metaphor in spoken discourse. In J. P. Gee & M. Handford (Eds.), *The Routledge handbook of discourse analysis* (pp. 342–355). London, UK: Routledge.

Campbell, D. T. (1960). Blind variation and selective retention in creative thought as in other knowledge processes. *Psychological Review*, *67*, 380–400.

Campion, J., & Latto, R. (1985). Apperceptive agnosia due to carbon monoxide poisoning. An interpretation based on critical band masking from disseminated lesions. *Behavioral Brain Research*, *15*, 227–240.

Campo, P., Maestú, F., Capilla, A., Morales, M., Fernández, S., del Río, D., & Ortiz, T. (2008). Temporal dynamics of parietal activity during word-location binding. *Neuropsychology*, *22*, 85–99.

Campos, L., & Alonso-Quecuty, M. L. (2006). Remembering a criminal conversation: Beyond eyewitness testimony. *Memory*, *14*, 27–36.

Caplan, D., & Futter, C. (1986). Assignment of thematic roles to nouns in sentence comprehension by an agrammatic patient. *Brain and Language*, *27*(1), 117–134.

Caramazza, A., Basili, A. G., Koller, J. J., & Berndt, R. S. (1981). An investigation of repetition and language processing in a case of conduction aphasia. *Brain & Language*, *14*(2), 235–271.

Caramazza, A., & Shelton, J. R. (1998). Domain-specific knowledge systems in the brain: The animate-inanimate distinction. *Journal of Cognitive Neuroscience*, *10*, 1–34.

Caramazza, A., & Zurif, E. (1976). Dissociation of algorithmic and heuristic processes in language comprehension: Evidence from aphasia. *Brain and Language*, *3*, 572–582.

Cardoso-Leite, P., & Gorea, A. (2010). On the perceptual/motor distinction: A review of concepts, theory, experimental paradigms and data interpretations. *Seeing and Perceiving*, *23*, 89–151.

Carey, S. (1978). The child as word learner. In J. Bresnan, G. Miller, & M. Halle (Eds.), *Linguistic theory and psychological reality* (pp. 264–293). Cambridge, MA: MIT Press.

Carey, S. (1993). Speaking of objects, as such. In G. Harman (Ed.), *Conceptions of the mind: Essays in honor of G. A. Miller* (pp. 139–159). Hillsdale, NJ: Erlbaum.

Carlson, W. B., & Gorman, M. E. (1992). A cognitive framework to understand technological creativity: Bell, Edison, and the telephone. In R. J. Weber & D. N. Perkins (Eds.), *Inventive minds: Creativity in technology* (pp. 48–79). New York, NY: Oxford University Press.

Carney, R. N., & Levin, J. R. (1998a). Do mnemonic memories fade as time goes away? Here's looking anew! *Contemporary Educational Psychology*, *23*, 276–297.

Carney, R. N., & Levin, J. R. (1998b). Coming to terms with the keyword method in introductory psychology: A "neuromnemonic" example. *Teaching Psychology*, *25*, 132–134.

Carney, R. N., & Levin, J. R. (2001). Remembering the names of unfamiliar animals: Keywords as keys to their kingdom. *Applied Cognitive Psychology*, *15*(2), 133–143.

Caron, R. F., & Caron, A. J. (1968). The effects of repeated exposure and stimulus complexity on visual fixation in infants. *Psychonomic Science*, *10*, 207–208.

Carriedo, N., García-Madruga, J. A., Gutiérrez, F., & Moreno, S. (1999). How does content affect "unless" conditional reasoning? In *Proceedings of the European Conference on Cognitive Science* (pp. 271–277), Siena, Italy.

Castel, A. D., McCabe, D. P., Roediger, H. L., & Heitman, J. L. (2007). The dark side of expertise: Domain-specific memory errors. *Psychological Science*, *18*, 3–5.

Catrambone, R., & Holyoak, K. J. (1989). Overcoming contextual limitations on problem solving transfer. *Journal of Experimental Psychology: Learning, Memory, and Cognition*, *15*, 1147–1156.

Cavaco, S., Anderson, S. W., Allen, J. S., Castro-Caldas, A., & Damasio, H. (2004). The scope of preserved procedural memory in amnesia. *Brain*, *127*, 1853–1867.

Cave, C. B., & Kosslyn, S. M. (1993). The role of parts and spatial relations in object identification. *Perception*, *22*, 229–248.

Cazden, C. B. (1968). The acquisition of noun and verb inflections. *Child Development*, *39*, 433–448.

Ceci, S. J. (1995). Memory distortions in children. *Journal of the Neurological Sciences*, *134*, 1–8.

Ceci, S. J., Loftus, E. F., Leichtman, M., & Bruck, M. (1994). The role of source misattributions in the creation of false beliefs among preschoolers. *International Journal of Clinical and Experimental Hypnosis*, *62*, 304–320.

Cepeda, N. J., Pashler, H., Vul, E., Wixted, J. T., & Rohrer, D. (2006). Distributed practice in verbal recall tasks: A review and quantitative synthesis. *Psychological Bulletin*, *132*, 354–380.

Chalmers, K. A., Humphreys, M. S., & Dennis, S. (1997). A naturalistic study of the word frequency effect in episodic recognition. *Memory & Cognition*, *25*, 780–784.

Chambers, D., & Reisberg, D. (1985). Can mental images be ambiguous? *Journal of Experimental Psychology: Human Perception and Performance*, *11*, 317–328.

Chan, A., Meints, K., Lieven, E., & Tomasello, M. (2010). Young children's comprehension of English SVO word order revisited: Testing the same children in act-out and intermodal preferential looking tasks. *Cognitive Development*, *25*(1), 30–45.

Chase, W. G., & Ericsson, K. A. (1981). Skilled memory. In J. R. Anderson (Ed.), *Cognitive skills and their acquisition* (pp. 141–189). Hillsdale, NJ: Erlbaum.

Chase, W. G., & Simon, H. (1973). Perception in chess. *Cognitive Psychology*, *1*(1), 33–81.

Chein, J., Weisberg, R., Streeter, N., & Kwok, S. (2010). Working memory and insight in the nine-dot problem. *Memory & Cognition*, *38*(7), 883–892.

Cheng, P. W., & Holyoak, K. J. (1985). Pragmatic reasoning schemas. *Cognitive Psychology*, *17*, 391–416.

Cheng, P. W., Holyoak, K. J., Nisbett, R. E., & Oliver, L. M. (1986). Pragmatic versus syntactic approaches to training deductive reasoning. *Cognitive Psychology*, *18*, 293–328.

Cheng, P. W., & Nisbett, R. E. (1993). Pragmatic constraints on causal deduction. In R. E. Nisbett (Ed.), *Rules for reasoning* (pp. 207–227). Hillsdale, NJ: Erlbaum.

Cherry, E. C. (1953). Some experiments on the recognition of speech, with one and with two ears. *Journal of Acoustic Society of America*, *25*, 975–979.

Chi, M. T. H., Feltovich P. J., & Glaser, R. (1981). Categorization and representation of physics problems by experts and novices. *Cognitive Science*, *5*, 121–152.

Chiarello, C., Burgess, C., Richards, L., & Pollock, A. (1990). Semantic and associative priming in the cerebral hemispheres: Some words do, some words don't . . . sometimes, some places. *Brain and Language*, *38*, 75–104.

Chipp, H. B. (1988). *Picasso's "Guernica": History, transformations, meanings*. Berkeley: University of California Press.

Chomsky, N. (1957). *Syntactic structures*. The Hague, The Netherlands: Mouton.

Chomsky, N. (1959). A review of B. F. Skinner's *Verbal behavior. Language*, *35*(1), 26–58.

Chomsky, N. (1965). *Aspects of the theory of syntax*. Cambridge, MA: MIT Press.

Chomsky, N. (1995). *The minimalist program*. Cambridge, MA: The MIT Press.

Christensen, B. T., & Schunn, C. D. (2007). The relationship of analogical distance to analogical function and pre-inventive structure: The case of engineering design. *Memory & Cognition*, *35*(1), 29–38.

Chronicle, E. P., MacGregor, J. N., & Ormerod, T. C. (2004). What makes an insight problem? The roles of heuristics, goal conception and solution recoding in knowledge-lean problems. *Journal of Experimental Psychology: Learning, Memory, and Cognition*, *30*, 14–27.

Ciaramelli, E. (2008). The role of ventromedial prefrontal cortex in navigation: A case of impaired wayfinding and rehabilitation. *Neuropsychologia*, *46*(7), 2099–2105.

Cimpian, A., Gelman, S. A., & Brandone, A. C. (2010). Theory-based considerations influence the interpretation of generic sentences. *Language and Cognitive Processes*, *25*(2), 261–276.

Claeys, K. G., Dupont, P., Cornette, L., Sunaert, S., Van Hecke, P., De Schutter, E., & Orban, G. A. (2004). Color discrimination involves ventral and dorsal stream visual areas. *Cerebral Cortex*, *14*, 803–822.

Clarapède, E. (1911). Recognition et moïté. *Archives of Psychology*, *11*, 79–90. (Reprinted in D. Rapaport (Ed.). *Organization and pathology of thought*. New York, NY: Columbia University Press, 1951.)

Clark, A. (1993). *Associative engines: Connectionism, concepts, and representational change*. Cambridge, MA: MIT Press.

Clark, E. V. (1990). On the pragmatics of contrast. *Journal of Child Language*, *17*, 417–443.

Clark, R. E., Broadbent, N. J., Zola, S. M., & Squire, L. R. (2002). Anterograde amnesia and temporally-graded retrograde amnesia for a nonspatial memory task following lesions of hippocampus and subiculum. *Journal of Neuroscience*, *22*, 4663–4669.

Clark, R. E., Manns, J. R., & Squire, L. R. (2002). Classical conditioning, awareness, and brain systems. *Trends in Cognitive Sciences*, *6*, 524–531.

Cocchini, G., Bartolo, A., & Nichelli, P. (2006). Left ipsilesional neglect for visual imagery: A mental image generation impairment? *Neurocase*, *12*(3), 197–206.

Coelho, C., & Robb, M. (2001). Acoustic analysis of foreign accent syndrome: An examination of three explanatory models. *Journal of Medical Speech-Language Pathology*, *9*, 227–242.

Coenen, A. M. L., & Van Luijtelaar, E. L. J. M. (1997). Effects of benzodiazepines, sleep and sleep deprivation on vigilance and memory. *Acta Neurologica Belgica*, *97*, 123–129.

Cofer, C. N., & Musgrave, B. S. (Eds.). (1961). *Verbal learning and verbal behavior*. New York, NY: McGraw-Hill.

Cofer, C. N., & Musgrave, B. S. (Eds.). (1963). *Verbal behavior and learning: Problems and processes*. New York, NY: McGraw-Hill.

Cohen, L. B., & Cashon, C. H. (2001). Do 7-month-old infants process independent features or facial configurations? *Infant and Child Development*, *10*, 83–92.

Cohen, L., & Dehaene, S. (1994). Amnesia for arithmetic facts: A single case study. *Brain and Language*, *47*, 214–232.

Cohen, N. J., Eichenbaum, H., Deacedo, B. S., & Corkin, S. (1985). Different memory systems underlying acquisition of procedural and declarative knowledge. *Annals of the New York Academy of Sciences*, *444*, 54–71.

Coleman, L. J. (2007). Parts do not make a whole. Lumping expertise into one whole. *High Ability Studies*, *18*(1), 63–64.

Collins, A. M., & Loftus, E. F. (1975). A spreading-activation theory of semantic processing. *Psychological Review*, *82*(6), 407–428.

Collins, A. M., & Quillian, M. R. (1969). Retrieval time from semantic memory. *Journal of Verbal Learning and Verbal Behavior*, *8*, 240–247.

Colomé, A. (2001). Lexical activation in bilinguals' speech production: Language-specific or language-independent? *Journal of Memory and Language*, *45*, 721–736.

Connor, C. (2005). The neural space of visual shape perception. In L. Albertazzi (Ed.). *Visual thought* (pp. 105–114), in series *Advances in Consciousness Research*, *67*. Amsterdam, The Netherlands: John Benjamins Publishing Company.

Conrad, C. (1972). Cognitive economy in semantic memory. *Journal of Experimental Psychology*, *92*(2), 149–154.

Conrad, R. (1964). Acoustic confusions in immediate memory. *British Journal of Psychology*, *55*, 75–84.

Conrad, R., & Hull, A. J. (1964). Information, acoustic confusion and memory span. *British Journal of Psychology*, *55*, 429–432.

Conway, M. A., Cohen, G., & Stanhope, N. (1991). On the very long-term retention of knowledge acquired through formal education: Twelve years of cognitive psychology. *Journal of Experimental Psychology: General*, *120*, 395–409.

Cooper, E. E., & Wojan, T. J. (1996). Differences in the coding of spatial relations in faces and objects. *Investigations in Ophthalmologic and Visual Science*, *37*, 842.

Cooper, E. E., & Wojan, T. J. (2000). Differences in the coding of spatial relations in face identification and basic-level object recognition. *Journal of Experimental Psychology: Learning, Memory, and Cognition*, *26*, 470–488.

Cooper, J., & Strayer, D. (2008). Effects of simulator practice and real-world experience on cell-phone-related driver distraction. *Human Factors*, *50*, 893–902.

Cooper, L. A., & Shepard, R. N. (1973). Chronometric studies of the rotation of mental images. In W. G. Chase (Ed.), *Visual information processing* (pp. 75–176). New York, NY: Academic Press.

Cooper, L. M. (1966). Spontaneous and suggested posthypnotic source amnesia. *International Journal of Clinical and Experimental Hypnosis*, *14*, 180–193.

Cope, D. (2005). *Computer models of musical creativity*. Cambridge, MA: MIT Press.

Corbetta, M., Kincade, J. M., & Shulman, G. L. (2002). Neural systems for visual orienting and their relationship to spatial working memory. *Journal of Cognitive Neuroscience*, *14*, 508–523.

Corbetta, M., Patel, G. H., & Shulman, G. L. (2008). The reorienting system of the human brain: From environment to theory of mind. *Neuron*, *58*, 306–324.

Corkin, S. (1968). Acquisition of motor skill after bilateral medial temporal-lobe excision. *Neuropsychologia*, *6*, 255–265.

Corkin, S. (1984) Lasting consequences of bilateral medial temporal lobectomy: Clinical course and experimental findings in H.M. *Seminars in Neurology*, *4*, 252–262.

Corkin, S. (2002). What's new with the amnesic patient H.M.? *Nature Reviews Neuroscience*, *3*, 153–160.

Cortese, M. J., & Fugett, A. (2004). Imageability ratings for 3,000 monosyllabic words. *Behavior Research Methods, Instruments, & Computers*, *36*, 384–387.

Corts, D. P., & Meyers, K. (2002). Conceptual clusters in figurative language production. *Journal of Psycholinguistic Research*, *31*(4), 391–408.

Corts, D. P., & Pollio, H. R. (1999). Spontaneous production of figurative language and gesture in college lectures. *Metaphor and Symbol*, *14*(2), 81–100.

Cowan, N. (2001). The magical number 4 in short-term memory: A reconsideration of mental storage capacity. *Behavioral and Brain Sciences*, *24*, 87–114.

Cowan, N. (2008). Sensory memory. In H. L. Roediger, III, (Ed.), *Cognitive psychology of memory* (pp. 23–32). Vol. 2 of J. Byrne (Ed.), *Learning and memory: A comprehensive reference*. Oxford, UK: Elsevier.

Cowan, N., Beschin N., & Della Sala, S. (2004). Verbal recall in amnesiacs under conditions of diminished retroactive interference. *Brain*, *127*, 825–834.

Craik, F. I. M., & Lockhart, R. S. (1972). Levels of processing: A framework for memory research. *Journal of Verbal Learning and Verbal Behavior*, *11*, 671–684.

Crain, S., & Nakayama, M. (1987). Structure dependence in grammar formation. *Language*, *63*, 522–543.

Cree, G. S., & McRae, K. (2003). Analyzing the factors underlying the structure and computation of the meaning of chipmunk, cherry, chisel, cheese and cello (and many other such concrete nouns). *Journal of Experimental Psychology: General*, *132*(2), 163–201.

Crisp, A. K., & Feeney, A. (2009). Causal conjunction fallacies: The roles of causal strength and mental resources. *Quarterly Journal of Experimental Psychology*, *62*(12), 2320–2337.

Croft, W., & Cruse, D. A. (2004). *Cognitive linguistics*. Cambridge, UK: Cambridge University Press.

Csikszentmihalyi, M. (1988). Society, culture, and person: A systems view of creativity. In R. J. Sternberg (Ed.), *The nature of creativity: Current psychological perspectives* (pp. 325–339). Cambridge, UK: Cambridge University Press.

Csikszentmihalyi, M. (1996). *Creativity: Flow and the psychology of discovery and invention*. New York, NY: HarperCollins.

Csikszentmihalyi, M. (1999). Implications of a systems perspective for the study of creativity. In R. J. Sternberg (Ed.), *Handbook of creativity* (pp. 313–335). Cambridge, UK: Cambridge University Press.

Cultice, J. C., Somerville, S. C., & Wellman, H. M. (1983). Preschoolers' memory monitoring: Feeling-of-knowing judgments. *Child Development*, *54*, 1480–1486.

Cunningham, J. B., MacGregor, J. N., Gibb, J., & Haar, J. (2009). Categories of insight and their correlates: An exploration of relationships among classic-type insight problems, rebus problems, remote associates, and esoteric analogies. *Journal of Creative Behavior*, *43*(1), 1–22.

Curtiss, S. (1977). *Genie: A psycholinguistic study of a modern-day "wild child."* Boston, MA: Academic Press.

Cutting, J. E. (1982). Plucks and bows are categorically perceived, sometimes. *Perception & Psychophysics*, *31*, 462–476.

Cutting, J. E., & Rosner, B. S. (1974). Categories and boundaries in speech and music. *Perception & Psychophysics*, *16*, 564–570.

Damasio, H., Grabowski, T. J., Tranel, D., Hichwa, R. D., & Damasio, A. R. (1996). A neural basis for lexical retrieval. *Nature*, *380*, 499–505.

Damian, R. I., & Simonton, D. K. (2011). From past to future art: The creative impact of Picasso's 1935 *Minotauromachy* on his 1937 *Guernica*. *Psychology of Aesthetics, Creativity and the Arts*, *5*, 360–369.

Daneman, M., & Carpenter, P. A. (1983). Individual differences in integrating information between and within sentences. *Journal of Experimental Psychology: Learning, Memory, and Cognition*, *9*, 561–584.

Darwin, C. J., Turvey, M. T., & Crowder, R. G. (1972). An auditory analogue of the Sperling partial report procedure: Evidence for brief auditory storage. *Cognitive Psychology*, *3*, 255–267.

Daum, I., & Ackermann, H. (1994). Frontal-type memory impairment associated with thalamic damage. *International Journal of Neuroscience*, *77*, 187–198.

Davachi, L., Maril, A., & Wagner, A. D. (2001). When keeping in mind supports later bringing to mind: Neural markers of phonological rehearsal predict subsequent remembering. *Journal of Cognitive Neuroscience*, *13*(8), 1059–1070.

Davidoff, J. , Davies, I., & Roberson, D. (1999). Colour categories in a stone-age tribe. *Nature*, *398*, 203–204.

Davidson, P. S. R., Cook, S. P., Glisky, E. I., Verfaellie, M., & Rapcsak, S. Z. (2005). Source memory in the real world: A neuropsychological study of flashbulb memory. *Journal of Clinical and Experimental Neuropsychology*, *27*(7), 915–929.

Davis, J., & Todd, P. M. (1999). Parental investment by simple decision rules. In G. Gigerenzer, P. M. Todd, & the ABC Research Group (Eds.), *Simple heuristics that make us smart* (pp. 309–326). New York, NY: Oxford University Press.

de Bono, E. (1968). *New think*. New York, NY: Basic.

deCasper, A. J., & Fifer, W. P. (1980). Of human bonding: newborns prefer their mothers' voices. *Science*, *208*, 1174–1176.

Deese, J. (1959). Influence of inter-item associative strength upon immediate free recall. *Psychological Reports*, *5*, 305–312.

de Groot, A. D. (1978). *Thought and choice in chess*. The Hague, The Netherlands: Mouton. (Original work published 1965)

de Haan, M., & Nelson, C. A. (1997). Recognition of the mother's face by six-month-old infants: A neurobehavioral study. *Child Development*, *68*, 187–210.

Dehaene, S. (1997). *The number sense*. New York, NY: Oxford University Press.

Dehaene, S., & Cohen, L. (1995). Towards an anatomical and functional model of number processing. *Mathematical Cognition*, *1*, 83–120.

Dehaene, S., & Cohen, L. (1997). Cerebral pathways for calculation: Double dissociation between rote verbal and quantitative knowledge of arithmetic. *Cortex*, *33*, 219–250.

Dell, G. S. (1986). A spreading activation theory of retrieval in sentence production. *Psychological Review*, *93*, 283–321.

Dell, G. S. (1995). Speaking and misspeaking. In L. Gleitman & M. Liberman (Eds.), *Invitation to cognitive science, Part I, Language* (pp. 183–208). Cambridge, MA: MIT Press.

Dell, G. S., Martin, N., & Schwartz, M. F. (2007). A case-series test of the interactive two-step model of lexical access: Predicting word repetition from picture naming. *Journal of Memory and Language*, *56*, 490–520.

Dell, G. S., & Reich, P. A. (1981). Stages in sentence production: An analysis of speech error data. *Journal of Verbal Learning and Verbal Behavior*, *20*, 611–629.

Dell, G. S., Schwartz, M. F., Martin, N., Saffran, E. M., & Gagnon, D. A. (1997). Lexical access in aphasic and nonaphasic patients. *Psychological Review*, *104*, 801–838.

DeLong, K. A., Urbach, T. P., & Kutas, M. (2005). Probabilistic word pre-activation during language comprehension inferred from electrical brain activity. *Nature Neuroscience*, *8*(8), 1117–1121.

Delvenne, J. F., Seron, X., Coyette, F., & Rossion, B. (2004). Evidence for perceptual deficits in associative visual (prosop)agnosia: A single-case study. *Neuropsychologia*, *42*, 597–612.

DeMarie, D., Miller, P. H., Ferron, J., & Cunningham, W. R. (2004). Path analysis tests of theoretical models of children's memory performance. *Journal of Cognition and Development*, *5*, 461–492.

Demuth, K., & Fee, E. J. (1995). Minimal words in early phonological development. (Unpublished manuscript). Brown University, Providence, RI, and Dalhousie University, Halifax, Nova Scotia, Canada.

Denis, M. (2008). Assessing the symbolic distance effect in mental images constructed from verbal descriptions: A study of individual differences in the mental comparison of distances. *Acta Psychologica*, *127*, 197–210.

Dennett, D. (1991). *Consciousness explained*. New York, NY: Penguin.

De Paulo, B. M., Stone, J. I., & Lassiter, G. D. (1985). Deceiving and detecting deceit. In B. R. Schlenker (Ed.), *The self and social life* (pp. 323–370). New York, NY: McGraw-Hill.

DePrince, A. P., Allard, C. B., Oh, H., & Freyd, J. J. (2004). What's in a name for memory errors? Implications and ethical issues arising from the use of the term "false memory" for errors in memory for details. *Ethics and Behavior*, *14*, 210–233.

de Renzi, E., Liotti, M., & Nichelli, P. (1987). Semantic amnesia with preservation of autobiographic memory. A case report. *Cortex*, *23*, 575–597.

de Renzi, E., & Lucchelli, F. (1994). Are semantic systems separately represented in the brain? The case of living category impairment. *Cortex*, *30*, 3–25.

de Renzi, E., & Nichelli, P. (1975). Verbal and non-verbal short-term memory impairment following hemispheric damage. *Cortex*, *11*(4), 341–354.

D'Esposito, M., Aguirre, G. K., Zarahn, E., Ballard, D., Shin, R. K., & Lease, J. (1998). Functional MRI studies of spatial and nonspatial working memory. *Cognitive Brain Research*, *7*, 1–13.

D'Esposito, M., Detre, J. A., Alsop, D. C., Shin, R. K., Atlas, S., & Grossman, M. (1995). The neural basis of the central executive system of working memory. *Nature*, *378*, 279–281.

D'Esposito, M., Detre, J. A., Auguirre, G. K., Stallcup, M., Alsop, D. C., Tippet J. L., & Farah, M. J. (1997). A functional MRI study of mental image generation. *Neuropsychologia*, *35*(5), 725–730.

D'Esposito, M., & Postle, B. R. (1999). The dependence of span and delayed-response performance on prefrontal cortex. *Neuropsychologia*, *37*, 1303–1315.

Deutsch, J. A., & Deutsch, D. (1963). Attention: Some theoretical considerations. *Psychological Review*, *70*, 80–90.

Devlin, J. T., Russell, R. P., Davis, M. H., Price, C. J., Moss, H. E., Fadili, M. J., & Tyler, L. K. (2002). Is there an anatomical basis for category-specificity? Semantic memory studies in PET and fMRI. *Neuropsychologia*, *40*(1), 54–75.

Diamond, R., & Carey, S. (1986). Why faces are and are not special: An effect of expertise. *Journal of Experimental Psychology: General*, *115*, 107–117.

Diana, R. A., Yonelinas, A. P., & Ranganath, C. (2007). Imaging recollection and familiarity in the medial temporal lobe: A three-component model. *Trends in Cognitive Science*, *11*(9), 379–386.

Diesendruck, G., & Gelman, S. A. (1999). Domain differences in absolute judgments of category membership: Evidence for an essentialist account of categorization. *Psychonomic Bulletin and Review*, *6*, 338–346.

Dietrich, A., & Kanso, R. (2010). A review of EEG, ERP, and neuroimaging studies of creativity and insight. *Psychological Bulletin*, *136*, 822–848.

Di Gennaro, G., Grammaldo, L. G., Quarato, P. P., Esposito, V., Mascia, A., Sparano, A., . . . Picardi, A. (2006). Severe amnesia following bilateral medial temporal lobe damage occurring on two distinct occasions. *Neurological Sciences*, *27*(2), 129–133.

DoBeS project on Taa language, http://www.mpi.nl/DOBES/projects/taa/

Donders, F. C. (1868/1969). Over de snelheid van psychische processen [On the speed of psychological processes]. (W. Koster, Trans.). In W. Koster (Ed.), *Attention and performance: II* (pp. 412–431). Amsterdam, The Netherlands: North-Holland. (Original work published 1868.)

Downing, P. E. (2000). Interactions between visual working memory and selective attention. *Psychological Science*, *11*, 467–473.

Doyle, C. (2008). Exploring the creation of Picasso's *Guernica*: Composition studies, chance, metaphors, and expertise. *Creativity Research Journal*, *20*(4), 445–450. doi: 10.1080/10400410802391918

Drews, F., Pasupathi, M., & Strayer, D. (2008). Passenger and cell phone conversations in simulated driving. *Journal of Experimental Psychology: Applied*, *14*, 392–400.

Driskill, J., & Morgan, J. (1996). Interviewing young children about body touch and handling. *Monographs of the Society for Research in Child Development*, *61* (4–5), 1–186.

Dromi, E. (1987). *Early lexical development*. London, UK: Cambridge University Press.

Dronkers, N. F., Plaisant, O., Iba-Zizen, M. T., & Cabanis, E. A. (2007). Paul Broca's historic cases: High resolution MR imaging of the brains of Leborgne and Lelong. *Brain*, *130*, 1432–1441.

Duchaine, B., Yovel, G., Butterworth, E., & Nakayama, K. (2006). Prosopagnosia as an impairment to face-specific mechanisms: Elimination of the alternative hypotheses in a developmental case. *Cognitive Neuropsychology*, *23*, 714–747.

Dunbar, K. (1995). How scientists really reason: Scientific reasoning in real-world laboratories. In R. J. Sternberg & J. E. Davidson (Eds.). *The nature of insight* (pp. 365–395). Cambridge, MA: MIT Press.

Dunbar, K. (1998). Problem solving. In W. Bechtel & G. Graham (Eds.), *A companion to cognitive science* (pp. 289–298). London, UK: Blackwell.

Dunbar, K. (2001). The analogical paradox: Why analogy is so easy in naturalistic settings, yet so difficult in the psychology laboratory. In D. Gentner, K. J. Holyoak, & B. Kokinov (Eds.), *Analogy: Perspectives from cognitive science* (pp. 313–334). Cambridge, MA: MIT Press.

Dunbar, K., & Blanchette, I. (2001). The *in vivo/in vitro* approach to cognition: The case of analogy. *Trends in Cognitive Sciences*, *5*, 334–339.

Dunbar, K., & Fugelsang, J. (2005). Scientific thinking and reasoning. In K. J. Holyoak & R. Morrison (Eds.), *Cambridge Handbook of Thinking & Reasoning* (pp. 705–726). Cambridge, UK: Cambridge University Press.

Duncker, K. (1945). On problem solving. *Psychological Monographs*, *58* (5) (Whole No. 270).

Dunlosky, J., & Metcalfe, J. (2009). *Metacognition*. Thousand Oaks, CA: Sage.

Durso, F. T., Rea, C. B., & Dayton, T. (1994). Graph-theoretic confirmation of restructuring during insight. *Psychological Science*, *5*, 94–98.

Duthie, J. K., Nippold, M. A., Billow, J. L., & Mansfield, T. C. (2008). Mental imagery of concrete proverbs: A developmental study of children, adolescents, and adults. *Applied Psycholinguistics*, *29*, 151–173.

Duysens, J., Orban, G. A., Cremieux, J., & Maes, H. (1985). Visual cortical correlates of visible persistence. *Vision Research*, *25* (2), 171–178.

Easterbrook, M. A., Kivilesky, B. S., Muir, D. W., and LaPlante, D. P. (1999). Newborns discriminate schematic faces from scrambled faces. *Canadian Journal of Experimental Psychology/Revue canadienne de psychologie expérimentale*, *53* (3), 231–241.

Ebbinghaus, H. (1885/1964). *Memory: A contribution to experimental psychology*. New York, NY: Dover.

Echols, C. H., & Newport, E. L. (1992). The role of stress and position in determining first words. *Language Acquisition*, *2*, 189–220.

Ecke, P. (2004). Words on the tip of the tongue: A study of lexical retrieval failures in Spanish–English bilinguals. *Southwest Journal of Linguistics*, *23*, 1–31.

Egly, R., Driver, J., & Rafal, R. D. (1994). Shifting visual attention between objects and locations: Evidence from normal and parietal lesion subjects. *Journal of Experimental Psychology: General*, *123* (2), 161–177.

Eich, E., Reeves, J., Jaeger, B., & Graff-Radford, S. (1985). Memory for pain: Relation between past and present pain intensity. *Pain*, *223*, 375–379.

Eimas, P. D., Siqueland, E. R., Jusczyk, P., & Vigorito, J. (1971). Speech perception in infants. *Science*, *171*, 303–306.

Ekstrom, A. D., & Bookheimer, S. Y. (2007). Spatial and temporal episodic memory retrieval recruit dissociable functional networks in the human brain. *Learning and Memory*, *14*, 645–654.

Ellis, A. (1982). Modality-specific repetition priming of auditory word recognition. *Current Psychological Research*, *2*, 123–128.

Ellis, H. D. (1986). Face recall: A psychological perspective. *Human Learning: Journal of Practical Research & Applications*, *5*(4), 189–196.

Erickson, M. A., & Kruschke, J. K. (1998). Rules and exemplars in category learning. *Journal of Experimental Psychology: General*, *127*, 107–140.

Ericsson, K. A., Charness, N., Feltovich, P. J., & Hoffman, R. R. (Eds.). (2006). *The Cambridge handbook of expertise and expert performance*. Cambridge, UK: Cambridge University Press.

Ericsson, K. A., Chase, W. G., & Faloon, S. (1980). Acquisition of a memory skill. *Science*, *208*, 1181–1182.

Ericsson, K. A., Krampe, R. T., & Tesch-Römer, C. (1993). The role of deliberate practice in the acquisition of expert performance. *Psychological Review*, *100*, 363–406.

Ericsson, K. A., Patel, V. L., & Kintsch, W. (2000). How experts' adaptations to representative task demands account for the expertise effect in memory recall: Comment on Vicente and Wang (1998). *Psychological Review*, *107*, 578–592.

Ericsson, K. A., Roring, R. W., & Nandagopal, K. (2007). Giftedness and evidence for reproducibly superior performance: An account based on the expert-performance framework. *High Ability Studies*, *18*(1), 3–56.

Ericsson, K. A., & Simon, H. A. (1980). Verbal reports as data. *Psychological Review*, *87*, 215–251.

Ericsson, K. A., & Ward, P. (2007). Capturing the naturally occurring superior performance of experts in the laboratory: Toward a science of expert and exceptional performance. *Current Directions in Psychological Science*, *16*, 346–350.

Eriksen, C. W., & Collins, J. F. (1967). Some temporal characteristics of visual pattern perception. *Journal of Experimental Psychology*, *74*, 476–484.

Ervin, S. M., & Miller, W. (1963). Language development. *National Society for the Study of Education Yearbook*, 108–143.

Estes, W. K. (1955). Statistical theory of spontaneous recovery and regression. *Psychological Review*, *62*, 145–154.

Estes, W. K. (1990). William James symposium [Special Issue]. *Psychological Science*, *1*(3), 149–150.

Evans, F. J., & Thorne, W. A. F. (1966). Two types of posthypnotic amnesia: Recall amnesia and source amnesia. *International Journal of Clinical and Experimental Hypnosis*, *14*, 162–179.

Evans, J. St. B. T. (1977). Toward a statistical theory of reasoning. *Quarterly Journal of Experimental Psychology*, *29*, 297–306.

Evans, J. St. B. T. (2003). In two minds: Dual-process accounts of reasoning. *Trends in Cognitive Sciences*, *7*(10), 454–459.

Evans, J., St. B. T., Barston, J. L., & Pollard, P. (1983). On the conflict between logic and belief in syllogistic reasoning. *Memory & Cognition*, *11*, 295–306.

Evans, J. St. B. T., Handley, S. J., Harper, C. N. J., & Johnson-Laird, P. N. (1999). Reasoning about necessity and possibility: A test of the mental model theory of deduction. *Journal of Experimental Psychology: Learning, Memory, and Cognition*, *25*(6), 1495–1513.

Evans, J. St. B. T., & Over, D. E. (1996). *Rationality and reasoning*. London, UK: Psychology Press.

Evans, J. St. B. T., Over, D. E., & Manktelow, K. I. (1993). Reasoning, decision making, and rationality. *Cognition*, *49*, 165–187.

Eysenck, H. J. (1995). *Genius: The natural history of creativity*. New York, NY: Cambridge University Press.

Fadiga, L., Craighero, L., Buccino, G., & Rizzolatti, G. (2002). Speech listening specifically modulates the excitability of tongue muscles: A TMS study. *European Journal of Neuroscience*, *15*, 399–402.

Fagan, J. F. (1970). Memory in the infant. *Journal of Experimental Child Psychology*, *9*, 217–226.

Fagerlin, A., Wang, C., & Ubel, P. A. (2005). Reducing the influence of anecdotal reasoning on people's health care decisions: Is a picture worth a thousand statistics? *Medical Decision Making*, *25*(4), 398–405.

Fangmeier, T., Knauff, M., Ruff, C. C., & Sloutsky, V. (2006). fMRI evidence for a three-stage model of deductive reasoning. *Journal of Cognitive Neuroscience 18*(3), 320–334.

Fantz, R. L. (1961). The origin of form perception. *Scientific American*, *204*, 66–72.

Fantz, R. L. (1964). Visual experience in infants: Decreased attention to familiar patterns relative to novel ones. *Science*, *164*, 668–670.

Farah, M. J. (1984). The neurological basis of mental imagery: A componential analysis. *Cognition*, *18*, 245–272.

Farah, M. J. (1985). Psychophysical evidence for a shared representational medium for mental images and percepts. *Journal of Experimental Psychology: General*, *114*, 91–103.

Farah, M. J. (1990). *Visual agnosia: Disorders of object recognition and what they tell us about normal vision*. Cambridge, MA: MIT Press.

Farah, M. J. (1992). Is an object an object an object? Cognitive and neuropsychological investigations of domain specificity in visual object recognition. *Current Directions in Psychological Science*, *1*(5), 164–169.

Farah, M. J., Hammond, K. H., Levine, D. N., & Calvanio, R. (1988). Visual and spatial mental imagery: Dissociable systems of representation. *Cognitive Psychology*, *20*, 439–462.

Farah, M. J., & McClelland, J. L. (1991). A computational model of semantic memory impairment: Modality-specificity and emergent category-specificity. *Journal of Experimental Psychology: General*, *120*, 339–357.

Farah, M. J., Soso, M. J., & Dasheiff, R. M. (1992). Visual angle of the mind's eye before and after unilateral occipital lobectomy. *Journal of Experimental Psychology: Human Perception and Performance*, *18*(1), 241–246.

Farah, M. J., Weisberg, L. L., Monheit, M., & Peronnet, F. (1989). Brain activity underlying mental imagery: Event–related potentials during mental image generation. *Journal of Cognitive Neuroscience*, *4*, 302–316.

Fauconnier, G. (1994). *Mental spaces*. New York, NY: Cambridge University Press.

Fauconnier, G. (1997). *Mappings in thought and language*. Cambridge, UK: Cambridge University Press.

Fauconnier, G., & Turner, M. (2002). *The way we think: Conceptual blending and the mind's hidden complexities*. New York, NY: Basic.

Feil, A., & Mestre, J. (2007). Expert–novice differences on a recognition memory test of physics diagrams. In L. Hsu, C. Henderson, & L. McCullough (Eds.), *Proceedings of the 2007 Physics Education Research Conference* (pp. 100–103). Melville, NY: American Institute of Physics.

Ferguson, H. B., Stoddart, C., & Simeon, J. G. (1986). Double-blind challenge studies of behavioral and cognitive effects of sucrose-aspartame ingestion in normal children. *Nutrition Reviews*, *44*, 144–150.

Fernald, A. (1985). Four-month-old infants prefer to listen to motherese. *Infant Behavior and Development*, *8*, 181–195.

Fernald, A. (1992). Human maternal vocalizations to infants as biologically relevant signals. In J. Barkow, L. Cosmides, & J. Tooby (Eds.), *The adapted mind: Evolutionary psychology and the generation of culture* (pp. 391–428). Oxford, UK: Oxford University Press.

Fernald, A. (1993). Approval and disapproval: Infant responsiveness to vocal affect in familiar and unfamiliar languages. *Child Development*, *64*, 657–674.

Fernald, A., & Kuhl, P. (1987). Acoustic determinants of infant preference for motherese speech. *Infant Behavior and Development*, *10*, 279–293.

Fernald, A., Perfors, A., & Marchman, V. A. (2006). Picking up speed in understanding: Speech processing efficiency and vocabulary growth across the second year. *Developmental Psychology*, *42*, 98–116.

Ferrand, L. (2001). Grammatical gender is also on the tip of French tongues. *Current Psychology Letters: Behaviour, Brain & Cognition*, *5*, 7–20.

Ferreira, V. S., & Humphreys, K. R. (2001). Syntactic influences on lexical and morphological processing. *Journal of Memory and Language*, *44*, 52–80.

Fiez, J. A., Petersen, S. E., & Raichle, M. E. (Unpublished manuscript, cited in Posner & Raichle, 1994/1997).

Fillmore, C. J. (1968). The case for case. In E. Bach & R. T. Harms (Eds.), *Universals in linguistic theory* (pp. 1–88). New York, NY: Holt, Rinehart, and Winston.

Finke, R. A. (1989). *Principles of mental imagery*. Cambridge, MA: MIT Press.

Finke, R. A., Pinker, S., & Farah, M. (1989). Reinterpreting visual patterns in mental imagery. *Cognitive Science*, *13*, 51–78.

Finke, R. A., Ward, T. B., & Smith, S. M. (1992). *Creative cognition*. Cambridge, MA: MIT Press.

Fiorentino, R., & Poeppel, D. (2007). Processing of compound words: An MEG study. *Brain and Language*, *103*, 18–19.

Fischer, P., Jonas, E., Frey, D., & Kastenmüller, A. (2008). Selective exposure and decision framing: The impact of gain and loss framing on confirmatory information search after decisions. *Journal of Experimental Social Psychology*, *44*, 312–320.

Fischhoff, B., Slovic, P., Lichtenstein, S., Read, S., & Combs, B. (1978). How safe is safe enough? A psychometric study of attitudes towards technological risks and benefits. *Policy Sciences*, *8*, 127–152.

Fisher, R. P., & Craik, F. I. M. (1977). Interaction between encoding and retrieval operations in cued recall. *Journal of Experimental Psychology: Human Learning and Memory*, *3*, 701–707.

Fitz, H. (2009). *Neural syntax*. (PhD dissertation). University of Amsterdam, The Netherlands.

Flavell, J. H. (1970). Developmental studies of mediated memory. In H. W. Reese & L. P. Lipsitt (Eds.), *Advances in child development and behavior* (Vol. 5, pp. 217–247). New York, NY: Academic Press.

Flavell, J. H. (1976). Metacognitive aspects of problem solving. In L. B. Resnick (Ed.), *The nature of intelligence* (pp. 231–236). Hillsdale, NJ: Erlbaum.

Flavell, J. H., Beach, D. R., & Chinsky, J. M. (1966). Spontaneous verbal rehearsal in a memory task as a function of age. *Child Development*, *37*, 283–299.

Fleck, J. I., & Weisberg, R. W. (2004). The use of verbal protocols as data: An analysis of insight in the candle problem. *Memory & Cognition*, *32*, 990–1006.

Fletcher, P. C., & Henson, R. N. (2001). Frontal lobes and human memory: Insights from functional neuroimaging. *Brain 124* (Pt 5), 849–881.

Fodor, J. (1983). *The modularity of mind: An essay on faculty psychology*. Cambridge, MA: MIT Press.

Foer, J. (2011). *Moonwalking with Einstein: The art and science of remembering everything*. London, UK: Penguin Press.

Fong, G. T., Krantz, D. H., & Nisbett. R. E. (1986). The effects of statistical training on thinking about everyday problems. *Cognitive Psychology*, *18*, 253–292.

Fong, G. T., & Nisbett, R. E. (1991). Immediate and delayed transfer of training effects in statistical reasoning. *Journal of Experimental Psychology: General*, *120*, 36–45.

Forster, K. I., & Chambers, S. (1973). Lexical access and naming time. *Journal of Verbal Learning and Verbal Behavior*, *12*, 627–635.

Forster, K. I., & Davis, C. (1984). Repetition priming and frequency attenuation in lexical access. *Journal of Experimental Psychology: Learning, Memory, and Cognition*, *10*, 680–698.

The 44 sounds (phonemes) of English, Retrieved from http://www.dyslexia–speld.com/LinkClick.aspx?fileticket=Kh7hycbitgA%3D&tabid=92&mid=500&language=en–AU

Foundas, A. L., Daniels, S. K., & Vasterling, J. J. (1998). Anomia: Case studies with lesion localization. *Neurocase*, *4*, 35–43.

Frawley, T. J. (2008). Gender schema and prejudicial recall: How children misremember, fabricate, and distort gendered picture book information. *Journal of Research in Childhood Education*, *22*, 291–303.

Frazor, R. A., & Geisler, W. S. (2006). Local luminance and contrast in natural images. *Vision Research*, *46*, 1585–1598.

Fredrikson, J. R., & Kroll, J. F. (1976). Spelling and sound: Approaches to the internal lexicon. *Journal of Experimental Psychology: Human Perception and Performance*, *2*, 361–379.

Freeman, J. (2007). If you can't measure it—it doesn't exist. *High Ability Studies*, *18*, 65.

Freud, S. (1891). *Zur Auffassung der Aphasien. Leipzig: Deuticke*. [Available in English as *On aphasia: A critical study*. Translated by E. Stengel, International Universities Press, 1953, or (in extract) in K. H. Pribram (Ed.), *Brain and Behaviour 4: Adaptation*. (1969). Harmondsworth: Penguin.

Freud, S. (1910). The origin and development of psychoanalysis. *American Journal of Psychology*, *21*, 181–218.

Freymuth, A. K., & Ronan, G. F. (2004). Modeling patient decision-making: The role of base-rate and anecdotal information. *Journal of Clinical Psychology in Medical Settings*, *11*, 211–216.

Fridriksson, J., Baker, J. M., & Moser, D. (2009). Cortical mapping of naming errors in aphasia. *Human Brain Mapping*, *30*(8), 2487–2498.

Fromkin, V. A. (1971). The non-anomalous nature of anomalous utterances. *Language*, *47*(1), 27–52.

Fromkin, V. A. (Ed.). (1973). *Speech errors as linguistic evidence*. The Hague, The Netherlands: Mouton.

Fromkin, V. A., Krashen, S., Curtiss, S., Rigler, D., & Rigler, M. (1974). The development of language in Genie: A case of language acquisition beyond the "critical period." *Brain and Language*, *1*, 81–107.

Fugelsang, J., Stein, C., Green, A., & Dunbar, K. (2004). Theory and data interactions of the scientific mind: Evidence from the molecular and the cognitive laboratory. *Canadian Journal of Experimental Psychology*, *58*, 132–141.

Funahashi, S., Bruce, C. J., & Goldman-Rakic, P. S. (1989). Mnemonic coding of visual space in the monkey's dorsolateral prefrontal cortex. *Journal of Neurophysiology*, *61*(2), 331–349.

Gabrieli, J. D. E., Cohen, N. J., & Corkin, S. (1988). The impaired learning of semantic knowledge following bilateral medial temporal-lobe resection. *Brain and Cognition*, *7*, 157–177.

Gabrieli, J. D. E., Corkin, S., Mickel, S. F., & Growdon, J. H. (1993). Intact acquisition and long-term retention of mirror-tracing skill in Alzheimer's disease and in global amnesia. *Behavioral Neuroscience*, *107*, 899–910.

Gabrieli, J. D. E., Desmond, J. E., Demb, J. B., Wagner, A. D., Stone, M. V., Vaidya, C. J., & Glover, G. H. (1996). Functional magnetic resonance imaging of semantic memory processes in the frontal lobes. *Psychological Science*, *7*, 278–283.

Gabrieli, J. D. E., Fleischman, D. A., Keane, M. M., Reminger, S. L., & Morrell, F. (1995). Double dissociation between memory systems underlying explicit and implicit memory in the human brain. *Psychological Science*, *6*, 76–82.

Gaffan, D., & Heywood, C. A. (1993). A spurious category-specific visual agnosia for living things in normal human and nonhuman primates. *Journal of Cognitive Neuroscience*, *5*, 118–128.

Gagné, F. (2007). Predictably, an unconvincing second attempt. *High Ability Studies*, *18*(1), 67–69.

Gaillard, A., Urdapilleta, I., Houix, O., & Manetta, C. (2011). Effects of task and category membership on representation stability. *Psicológica*, *32*, 31–48.

Gainotti, G., Messerli, P., & Tissot, R. (1972). Qualitative analysis of unilateral spatial neglect in relation to laterality of cerebral lesions. *Journal of Neurology, Neurosurgery, and Psychiatry*, *35*, 545–550.

Gainotti, G., Silveri, M. C., Daniele, A., & Giustolisi, L. (1995). Neuroanatomical correlates of category-specific semantic disorders: A critical survey. *Memory*, *3*, 247–264.

Gall, F. J., & Spurzheim, J. G. (1809). Recherches sur le système nerveux en général, et sur celui du cerveau en particulier; Mmoire pr sent l'Institut de France, le 14 mars, 1808; suivi d'observations sur le Rapport qui en t fait cette compagnie par ses Commissaires.

Gall, F. J., & Spurzheim, J. G. (1810). Anatomie et physionomie du système nerveux en général et du cerveau en particulier. Premier volume. Anatomie et physiologie du système nerveux en général et anatomie du cerveau en particulier. Paris, France: F. Schoell.

Gallo, D. A., Roberts, M. J., & Seamon, J. G. (1997). Remembering words not presented in lists: Can we avoid creating false memories? *Psychonomic Bulletin & Review*, *4*, 271–276.

Galper, R. E. (1970). Recognition of faces in photographic negative. *Psychonomic Science*, *19*, 207–208

Galton, F. (1883). *Enquiries into human faculty and its development*. London, UK: J. M. Dent & Co.

Ganis, G., Thompson, W. L., & Kosslyn, S. M. (2004). Brain areas underlying visual mental imagery and visual perception: An fMRI study. *Cognitive Brain Research*, *20*, 226–241.

Garb, H. N. (1996). The representativeness and past–behavior heuristics in clinical judgment. *Professional Psychology: Research and Practice*, *27*, 272–277.

Garb, H. N. (2005). Clinical judgment and decision making. *Annual Review of Clinical Psychology*, *1*, 67–89.

García Madruga, J. A., Gutiérrez Martínez, F., Carriedo, N., Moreno, S., & Johnson-Laird, P. (2002). Mental models in deductive reasoning. *The Spanish Journal of Psychology*, *5*(2), 90–101.

Gardner, H. (1993). *Creating minds: An anatomy of creativity seen through the lives of Freud, Einstein, Picasso, Stravinsky, Eliot, Graham, and Gandhi*. New York, NY: Basic Books.

Gardner, H., Ling, P. K., Flamm, L., & Silverman, J. (1975). Comprehension and appreciation of humorous material following brain damage. *Brain*, *98*(3), 399–412.

Gardner, M. K., Rothkopf, E. Z., Lapan, R., & Lafferty, T. (1987). The word frequency effect in lexical decision: Finding a frequency-based component. *Memory & Cognition*, *15*, 24–28.

Garoff-Eaton, R. J., Kensinger, E. A., & Schacter, D. L. (2007). The neural correlates of conceptual and perceptual false recognition. *Learning & Memory*, *14*(10), 684–692.

Garoff-Eaton, R. J., Slotnick, S. D., & Schacter, D. L. (2006). Not all false memories are created equal: The neural basis of false recognition. *Cerebral Cortex*, *16*, 1645–1652.

Garrett, M. F. (1975). The analysis of sentence production. In G. H. Bower (Ed.), *Psychology of learning and motivation* (Vol. 9, pp. 133–177). New York, NY: Academic Press.

Garrett, M. F. (1980). Levels of processing in sentence production. In B. Butterworth (Ed.), *Language production* (Vol. 1, pp. 177–220). Orlando, FL: Academic Press.

Garrett, M. F. (1982). Production of speech: Observations from normal and pathological language use. In A. Ellis (Ed.), *Normality and pathology in cognitive functions* (pp. 19–76). London, UK: Academic Press.

Garrett, M. F. (1988). Processes in language production. In F. J. Newmeyer (Ed.), *Language: Psychological and biological aspects*. New York, NY: Cambridge University Press.

Garrett, M. F. (1990). Sentence processing. In D. N. Osherson & H. Lasnik (Eds.), *An invitation to cognitive science: Vol. 1. Language* (pp. 133–175). Cambridge, MA: MIT Press.

Gauthier, I., Behrmann, M., & Tarr, M. J. (1999). Can face recognition really be dissociated from object recognition? *Journal of Cognitive Neuroscience*, *11*, 349–370.

Gauthier, I., Skudlarski, P., Gore, J. C., & Anderson, A. W. (2000). Expertise for cars and birds recruits brain areas involved in face recognition. *Nature Neuroscience*, *3*, 191–197.

Gauthier, I., Tarr, M. J., Anderson A. W., Skudlarski, P., & Gore, J. C. (1999). Activation of the middle fusiform "face area" increases with expertise recognizing novel objects. *Nature Neuroscience*, *2*, 568–573.

Gawronska, B., & House, D. (1998). Information extraction and text generation of news reports for a Swedish-English bilingual spoken dialogue system. In R. H. Mannell & J. Robert-Ribes (Eds.), *ICSLP (5th International Conference on Spoken Language Processing) '98 Proceedings* (Vol. 4, pp. 1139–1142). Sydney, Australia.

Gazzaniga, M. S., Ivry, R., & Mangun, G. R. (1998). *Fundamentals of cognitive neuroscience*. New York, NY: Norton.

Geisler, W. S. (2008). Visual perception and the statistical properties of natural scenes. *Annual Review of Psychology*, *59*, 167–192.

Geisler, W. S., & Kersten, D. (2002). Illusions, perception and Bayes. *Nature Neuroscience*, *5*, 508–510.

Gelman, A., Carlin, J. B., Stern, H. S., & Rubin, D. B. (2003). *Bayesian data analysis* (2nd ed.). London, UK: CRC Press.

Gelman, S. A. (2004). Psychological essentialism in children. *Trends in Cognitive Sciences*, *8*, 404–409.

Gelman, S. A., & Markman, E. M. (1986). Categories and induction in young children. *Cognition*, *23*, 183–209.

Gelman, S. A., & Markman, E. M. (1987). Young children's inductions from natural kinds: The role of categories over appearances. *Child Development*, *58*, 1532–1541.

Gelman, S. A., & Wellman. H. M. (1991). Insides and essences: Early understandings of the non-obvious. *Cognition*, *38*, 213–244.

Gentner, D., & Grudin, J. (1985). The evolution of mental metaphors in psychology: A 90-year retrospective. *American Psychologist*, *40*, 181–192.

Gentner, D., Holyoak, K. J., & Kokinov, B. N. (Eds.). (2001). *The analogical mind: Perspectives from cognitive science*. Cambridge, MA: MIT Press.

Gentner, D., & Toupin, C. (1986). Systematicity and surface similarity in the development of analogy. *Cognitive Science*, *10*, 277–300.

Gentner, D., & Wolff, P. (1997). Alignment in the processing of metaphor. *Journal of Memory and Language*, *37*, 331–355.

Georgsdottir, A. S., Lubart, T. I., & Getz, I. (2003). The role of flexibility in innovation. In L. V. Shavinina (Ed.), *International handbook on innovation* (pp. 180–190). Amsterdam, The Netherlands: Elsevier Science.

Gerken, L. A., Landau, B., & Remez, R. (1990). Function morphemes in young children's speech perception and production. *Developmental Psychology*, *27*, 204–216.

Gernsbacher, M. A. (1990). *Language comprehension as structure building*. Hillsdale, NJ: Erlbaum.

Gernsbacher, M. A. (1991). Cognitive processes and mechanisms in language comprehension: The structure building framework. In G. H. Bower (Ed.), *The psychology of learning and motivation* (pp. 217–263). New York, NY: Academic Press.

Gernsbacher, M. A. (1995). The Structure Building Framework: What it is, what it might also be, and why. In B. K. Britton & A. C. Graesser, (Eds.), *Models of text understanding* (pp. 289–311). Hillsdale, NJ: Erlbaum.

Gernsbacher, M. A. (1997). Two decades of structure building. *Discourse Processes*, *23*, 265–304.

Gernsbacher, M. A., & Hargreaves, D. (1988). Accessing sentence participants: The advantage of first mention. *Journal of Memory and Language*, *27*, 699–717.

Gernsbacher, M. A., & Hargreaves, D. (1992). The privilege of primacy: Experimental data and cognitive explanations. In D. L. Payne (Ed.), *Pragmatics of word order flexibility* (pp. 83–116). Philadelphia, PA: John Benjamins.

Gernsbacher, M. A., Hargreaves, D., & Beeman, M. (1989). Building and accessing clausal representations: The advantage of first mention versus the advantage of clause recency. *Journal of Memory and Language*, *28*, 735–755.

Gernsbacher, M. A., Keysar, B., Robertson, R. R. W., & Werner, N. K. (2001). The role of suppression and enhancement in understanding metaphors. *Journal of Memory and Language*, *45*, 433–450.

Gernsbacher, M. A., & Robertson, D. A. (2004). Watching the brain comprehend discourse. In A. Healy (Ed.), *Experimental cognitive psychology and its applications*. Washington, DC: APA Publications.

Gernsbacher, M. A., & Robertson, R. R. W. (1995). Reading skill and suppression revisited. *Psychological Science*, *6*, 165–169.

Gernsbacher, M. A., Robertson, R., Palladino, P., & Werner, N. K. (2004). Managing mental representations during comprehension. *Discourse Processes*, *37*, 145–164.

Gernsbacher, M. A., Varner, K. R., & Faust, M. (1990). Investigating differences in general comprehension skill. *Journal of Experimental Psychology: Learning, Memory, and Cognition*, *16*, 430–445.

Gershberg, E. B., & Shimamura, A. P. (1995). The role of the frontal lobes in the use of organizational strategies in free recall. *Neuropsychologia*, *13*, 1305–1333.

Ghatan, P. H., Hsieh, J. C., Petersson, K. M., Stone-Elander, S., & Ingvar, M. (1998). Coexistence of attention-based facilitation and inhibition in the human cortex. *NeuroImage*, *7*, 23–29.

Ghiselin, B. (1954). *The creative process: A symposium*. Berkeley, CA: University of California Press.

Gibbs, R. W., Jr., (1994). *The poetics of mind: Figurative thought, language, and understanding*. Cambridge, UK: Cambridge University Press.

Gick, M. L., & Holyoak, K. J. (1980). Analogical problem solving. *Cognitive Psychology*, *12*, 306–355.

Gick, M. L., & Holyoak, K. J. (1983). Schema induction and analogical transfer. *Cognitive Psychology*, *15*(1), 1–38.

Gigerenzer, G. (1994). Why the distinction between single-event probabilities and frequencies is important for psychology (and vice versa). In G. Wright & P. Ayton (Eds.), *Subjective probability* (pp. 129–161). Chichester, UK: Wiley.

Gigerenzer, G. (1996). On narrow norms and vague heuristics: A reply to Kahneman and Tversky. *Psychological Review*, *103*(3), 592–596.

Gigerenzer, G. (2004). Dread risk, September 11, and fatal traffic accidents. *Psychological Science*, *15*(4), 286–287.

Gigerenzer, G. (2008). *Rationality for mortals: How people cope with uncertainty*. New York, NY: Oxford University Press.

Gigerenzer, G., & Brighton, H. (2009). Homo heuristicus: Why biased minds make better inferences. *Topics in Cognitive Science*, *1*, 107–143.

Gigerenzer, G., & Goldstein, D. (1996). Reasoning the fast and frugal way: Models of bounded rationality. *Psychological Review*, *103*(4), 650–666.

Gigerenzer, G., & Goldstein, D. G. (1999). Betting on one good reason: The take the best heuristic. In G. Gigerenzer, P. M. Todd, & the ABC Research Group. *Simple heuristics that make us smart* (pp. 75–95). New York, NY: Oxford University Press.

Gigerenzer, G., & Hoffrage, U. (1995). How to improve Bayesian reasoning without instruction: Frequency formats. *Psychological Review*, *102*, 684–704.

Gigerenzer, G., & Selten, R. (Eds.). (2002). *Bounded rationality: The adaptive toolbox*. Cambridge, MA: MIT Press.

Gigerenzer, G., Todd, P. M., & the ABC Research Group. (1999). *Simple heuristics that make us smart*. New York, NY: Oxford University Press.

Gilboa, A., Winocur, G., Rosenbaum, R. S., Poreh, A., Gao, F., Black, S. E.,. . . . Moscovitch, M. (2006). Hippocampal contributions to recollection in retrograde and anterograde amnesia. *Hippocampus*, *16*(11), 966–980.

Gilhooly, K. J., & Fioratou, E. (2009). Executive functions in insight versus non-insight problem solving: An individual differences approach. *Thinking & Reasoning*, *15*(4), 355–376.

Gilhooly, K. J., Fioratou, E., Anthony, S., & Wynn, V. (2007). Divergent thinking: Strategies and executive involvement in generating novel uses for familiar objects. *British Journal of Psychology*, *98*, 611–625.

Gilhooly, K. J., Fioratou, E., & Henretty, N. (2010). Verbalization and problem solving: Insight and spatial factors. *British Journal of Psychology*, *101*, 81–93.

Girotto, V., Mazzocco, A., & Tasso, A. (1997). The effect of premise order in conditional reasoning: A test of the mental model theory. *Cognition*, *63*, 1–28.

Gladwell, M. (2005). *Blink: The power of thinking without thinking*. New York, NY: Little, Brown and Co.

Gladwell, M. (2011). *Outliers: The story of success*. New York, NY: Back Bay Books.

Glanzer, M., & Cunitz, A. R. (1966). Two storage mechanisms in free recall. *Journal of Verbal Learning and Verbal Behavior*, *5*, 351–360.

Glaze, J. A. (1928). The association value of non-sense syllables. *Pedagogical Seminary and Journal of Genetic Psychology*, *35*, 255–269.

Gleitman, L. R., Gleitman, H., Landau, B., & Wanner, E. (1988). Where learning begins: Initial representations for language learning. In F. J. Newmeyer (Ed.), *Linguistics: The Cambridge survey*, *Vol. 3. Language: Psychological and biological aspects* (pp. 150–193). New York, NY: Cambridge University Press.

Glenberg, A. M. (1979). Component-levels theory of the effects of spacing of repetitions of recall and recognition. *Memory & Cognition*, *7*, 95–112.

Glenberg, A. M., Smith, S. M., & Green, C. (1977). Type I rehearsal: Maintenance and more. *Journal of Verbal Learning & Verbal Behavior*, *16*, 339–352.

Glezer, V. D., Leushina, L. I., Nevskaya, A. A., & Prazdnikova, N. V. (1973). Studies on visual pattern recognition in man and animals. *Vision Research*, *14*(7), 555–583.

Glisky, E. L., & Schacter, D. L. (1987). Acquisition of domain-specific knowledge in organic amnesia: Training for computer-related work. *Neuropsychologia*, *25*, 893–906.

Glisky, E. L., Schacter, D. L., & Tulving, E. (1986). Learning and retention of computer related vocabulary in memory impaired patients: Method of vanishing cues. *Journal of Clinical and Experimental Neuropsychology*, *8*, 292–312.

Glucksberg, S., Gildea, P., & Bookin, H. B. (1982). On understanding nonliteral speech: Can people ignore metaphors? *Journal of Verbal Learning and Verbal Behavior*, *21*, 85–98.

Glucksberg, S., & Keysar, B. (1990). Understanding metaphorical comparisons: Beyond similarity. *Psychological Review*, *97*, 3–18.

Glucksberg, S., Kreuz, R. J., & Rho, S. H. (1986). Context can constrain lexical access: Implications for models of language comprehension. *Journal of Experimental Psychology: Learning, Memory, and Cognition*, *12*, 323–335.

Glucksberg, S., & Weisberg, R. (1966). Verbal behavior and problem solving: Some effects of labeling in a functional fixedness task. *Journal of Experimental Psychology*, *71*, 659–664.

Goatly, A. (1997). *The language of metaphors*. London, UK: Routledge.

Godden, D. R., & Baddeley, A. D. (1975). Context-dependent memory in two natural environments: on land and underwater. *British Journal of Psychology*, *66*, 325–331.

Gold, J. J., & Squire, L., (2006). The anatomy of amnesia: Neurohistological analysis of three new cases. *Learning & Memory*, *13* (6), 699–710.

Goldenberg, G., Steiner, M., Podreka, I., & Deecke, L. (1992). Regional cerebral blood flow patterns related to verification of high and low imagery sentences. *Neuropsychologia*, *30*, 1081–1092.

Golding, J. M., & Long, D. L. (1998). There's more to intentional forgetting than directed forgetting: An integrative review. In J. M. Golding & C. M. MacLeod (Eds.), *Intentional forgetting: Interdisciplinary approaches* (pp. 59–102). Mahwah, NJ: Erlbaum.

Goldmann, R. E., Sullivan, A. L., Droller, D. B. J., Rugg, M. D., Curran, T., Holcomb, P. J., . . . Budson, A. E. (2003). Late frontal brain potentials distinguish true and false recognition. *NeuroReport: For Rapid Communication of Neuroscience Research*, *14* (13), 1717–1720.

Goldstone, R. L., & Hendrickson, A. T. (2009). Categorical perception. *Interdisciplinary Reviews: Cognitive Science*, *1* (1), 69–78.

Golinkoff, R. M., Hirsh-Pasek, K., Cauley, K., & Gordon, L. (1987). The eyes have it: Lexical and syntactic comprehension in a new paradigm. *Journal of Child Language*, *14*, 23–46.

Golinkoff, R. M., Mervis, C. B., & Hirsh-Pasek, K. (1994). Early object labels: The case for a developmental lexical principles framework. *Journal of Child Language*, *21*, 125–155.

Good, I. J. (1980). Some history of the hierarchical Bayesian methodology. In J. M. Bernardo, M. H. DeGroot, D. V. Lindley, & A. F. M. Smith (Eds.), *Bayesian statistics* (pp. 489–519). Valencia, Spain: Valencia University Press.

Goodale, M. A., & Milner, A. D. (1992). Separate visual pathways for perception and action. *Trends in Neurosciences*, *15*, 20–25.

Goodale, M. A., & Milner, A. D. (2004). *Sight unseen: An exploration of consciousness and unconscious vision*. New York, NY: Oxford University Press.

Goodale, M. A., Milner, A. D., Jakobson, L. S., & Carey, D. P. (1991). A neurological dissociation between perceiving objects and grasping them. *Nature*, *349*, 154–156.

Goodglass, H. (1980). Disorders of naming following brain injury. *American Scientist*, *68* (6), 647–655.

Goodglass, H., & Wingfield, A. (1997). Word-finding deficits in aphasia: Brain-behavior relations and clinical symptomatology. In H. Goodglass & A. Wingfield (Eds.), *Anomia: Neuroanatomical and cognitive correlates*. (pp. 3–27). San Diego, CA: Academic Press.

Goodglass, H., Wingfield, A., Hyde, M. R., & Theurkauf, J. C. (1986). Category-specific dissociations in naming and recognition in aphasic patients. *Cortex*, *22*, 87–102.

Goodwin, F., & Jamison, K. R. (1990). *Manic-depressive illness*. New York, NY: Oxford University Press.

Gordon, B. N., Ornstein, P. A., Nida, R. E., Follmer, A., Crenshaw, M. C., & Albert, G. (1993). Does the use of dolls facilitate children's memory of visits to the doctor? *Applied Cognitive Psychology*, 7, 459–474.

Gould, J. L. (1986). The locale map of honey bees: Do insects have cognitive maps? *Science*, *232*, 861–863.

Gould, J. L., & Gould, C. G. (2012). *Nature's compass: The mystery of animal navigation*. Princeton, NJ: Princeton University Press.

Governors Highway Safety Association. (n.d.). *Cell phone and texting laws*. Retrieved from www.ghsa.org/html/stateinfo/laws/cellphone_laws.html

Graesser, A., Long, D., & Mio, J. (1989). What are the cognitive and conceptual components of humorous texts? *Poetics*, *18*, 143–164.

Graf, P., & Schacter, D. L. (1985). Implicit and explicit memory for new associations in normal and amnesic subjects. *Journal of Experimental Psychology: Learning, Memory, and Cognition*, *11*, 501–518.

Graf, P., Squire, L. R., & Mandler, G. (1984). The information that amnesic patients do not forget. *Journal of Experimental Psychology: Learning, Memory, and Cognition*, *10*, 164–178.

Grafman, J., Kampen, D., Rosenberg, J., Salazar, A., & Boller, F. (1989). Calculation abilities in a patient with a virtual left hemispherectomy. *Behavioral Neurology*, *2*, 183–194.

Green, J. T. (1997). Using numerosity judgments to determine what is learned during automatization. *Journal of Experimental Psychology: Learning, Memory, and Cognition*, *23*, 1046–1052.

Greeno, J. G., & Noreen, D. L. (1974). Time to read semantically related sentences. *Memory & Cognition*, *2*, 117–120.

Grice, P. (1975). Logic and conversation. In P. Cole & J. Morgan (Eds.), *Syntax and semantics: Vol. 3. Speech acts* (pp. 41–58). New York, NY: Academic Press.

Griggs, R. A. (1984). Memory cueing and instructional effects on Wason's selection task. *Current Psychological Research and Reviews*, *3*, 3–10.

Griggs, R. A., & Cox, J. R. (1982). The elusive thematic-materials effect in Wason's selection task. *British Journal of Psychology*, *73*, 407–420.

Grill-Spector, K., Knouf, N., & Kanwisher, N. (2004). The fusiform face area subserves face perception, not generic within-category identification. *Nature Neuroscience*, *7*, 555–562.

Grimes, J. (1996). On the failure to detect changes in scenes across saccades. In K. Akins (Ed.), *Vancouver studies in cognitive science: Vol. 2. Perception* (pp. 89–110). New York, NY: Oxford University Press.

Grodzinsky, Y. (1986). Language deficits and the theory of syntax. *Brain and Language*, *27*(1), 135–159.

Grodzinsky, Y. (1989). Agrammatic comprehension of relative clauses. *Brain and Language*, *31*, 480–499.

Grodzinsky, Y. (1990). *Theoretical perspectives on language deficits*. Cambridge, MA: MIT Press.

Grodzinsky, Y. (1995). A restrictive theory of agrammatic comprehension. *Brain and Language*, *50*(1), Special issue: Linguistic representational and processing analyses of agrammatism, 27–51.

Grodzinsky, Y. (2000). The neurology of syntax: Language use without Broca's area. *Behavioral and Brain Sciences*, *23*(1), 1–71.

Gross, M. M. (1972). Hemispheric specialization for processing of visually presented verbal and spatial stimuli. *Perception & Psychophysics*, *12*(4), 357–363.

Guilford, J. P. (1950). Creativity. *American Psychologist*, *5*, 444–454.

Guilford, J. P. (1959). Traits of creativity. In H. H. Anderson (Ed.), *Creativity and its cultivation* (pp. 142–161). New York, NY: Harper & Row.

Gur, M., & Snodderly, D. M. (2007). Direction selectivity in V1 of alert monkeys: Evidence for parallel pathways for motion processing. *Journal of Physiology*, *585*, 383–400.

Gustin, W. C. (1985). The development of exceptional research mathematicians. In B. S. Bloom (Ed.), *Developing talent in young people* (pp. 270–331). New York, NY: Ballantine.

Gutiérrez Martínez, F., García Madruga, J. A., Johnson-Laird, P. N., & Carriedo López, N. (2002). Razonamiento con condicionales múltiples. *La perspectiva de los modelos mentales. Anuario de Psicología*, *33*(1), 3–24.

Haberlandt, K. (1980). Story grammar and reading time of story constituents. *Poetics*, *9*, 99–118.

Haberlandt, K. (1984). Components of sentence and word reading times. In D. E. Kieras & M. A. Just (Eds.), *New methods in reading comprehension research* (pp. 3–11). Hillsdale, NJ: Erlbaum.

Hadamard, J. (1954). *The psychology of invention in the mathematical field*. New York, NY: Dover.

Hahn, U., & Chater, N. (1997). Concepts and similarity. In K. Lamberts & D. Shanks (Eds.), *Knowledge, concepts, and categories* (pp. 43–92). Hove, UK: Erlbaum.

Haley, K. L., Roth, H. L., Helm-Estabrooks, N., & Thiessen, A. (2010). Foreign accent syndrome due to conversion disorder: Phonetic analyses and clinical course. *Journal of Neurolinguistics*, *23*, 28–43.

Halpern, A. R., & Zatorre, R. J. (1999). When that tune runs through your head: A PET investigation of auditory imagery for familiar melodies. *Cerebral Cortex*, *9*, 697–704.

Halpern, A. R., Zatorre, R. J., Bouffard, M., & Johnson, J. A. (2004). Behavioral and neural correlates of perceived and imagined timbre. *Neuropsychologia*, *42*, 1281–1292.

Halpern, D. F., & Wai, J. (2007). The world of competitive Scrabble: Novice and expert differences in visuospatial and verbal abilities. *Journal of Experimental Psychology: Applied*, *13(2)*, 79–94.

Hamann, S. B., Squire, L. R., & Schacter, D. L. (1995). Perceptual thresholds and priming in amnesia. *Neuropsychology*, *9*, 3–15.

Harlow, H. F. (1949). The formation of learning sets. *Psychological Review*, *56*, 51–65.

Harpaz, Y., Levkovitz, Y., & Lavidor, M. (2009). Lexical ambiguity resolution in Wernicke's area and its right homologue. *Cortex*, *45*(9), 1097–1103.

Harries, M., & Perrett, D. (1991). Visual processing of faces in temporal cortex: Physiological evidence for a modular organization and possible anatomical correlates. *Journal of Cognitive Neuroscience*, *3*, 9–24.

Harris, K. S., Hoffman, H. S., Liberman, A. M., Delattre, P. C., & Cooper, F. S. (1958). Effect of third–formant transitions on the perception of the voiced stop consonants. *Journal of the Acoustical Society of America*, *30*, 122–126.

Harris, Z. (1957). Co-occurrence and transformation in linguistic structure. *Language*, *33*, 322–337.

Hart, J., & Gordon, B. (1992). Neural subsystems for object knowledge. *Nature*, *359*, 60–64.

Hart, S., & Mas-Colell, A. (2003). Regret-based continuous-time dynamics. *Games and Economic Behavior*, *45*(2), 375–394.

Hartsuiker, R. J., Corley, M., & Martensen, H. (2005). Object attraction in subject-verb agreement construction. *Journal of Memory and Language*, *45*, 546–572.

Harvey, M., Milner, A. D., & Roberts, R. C. (1995). Differential effects of line length on bisection judgments in hemispatial neglect. *Cortex*, *31*, 711–722.

Hasher, L., Stoltzfus, E. R., Zacks, R. T., & Rypma, B. (1991). Age and inhibition. *Journal of Experimental Psychology: Learning, Memory, and Cognition*, *17*, 163–169.

Hasher, L., & Zacks, R. T. (1979). Automatic and effortful processes in memory. *Journal of Experimental Psychology: General*, *108*, 356–388.

Hasher, L., & Zacks, R. T. (1984). Automatic processing of fundamental information: The case of frequency of occurrence. *American Psychologist*, *39*, 1372–1388.

Hasher, L., & Zacks, R. T. (1988). Working memory, comprehension, and aging: A review and a new view. In G. H. Bower (Ed.), *The Psychology of Learning and Motivation* (Vol. 22, pp. 193–225). New York, NY: Academic Press.

Hasher, L., Zacks, R. T., Rose, K. C., & Sanft, H. (1987). Truly incidental encoding of frequency information. *American Journal of Psychology*, *100*, 69–91.

Hass, R., & Weisberg, R. W. (2009). Career development in two seminal American songwriters: A test of the equal-odds rule. *Creativity Research Journal*, *21*, 183–190.

Hass, R. W., Weisberg, R. W., & Choi, J. (2010). Quantitative case-studies in musical composition: The development of creativity in popular-songwriting teams. *Psychology of Music*, *38*(4), 463–480.

Haueisen, J., & Knösche, T. R. (2001). Involuntary motor activity in pianists evoked by music perception. *Journal of Cognitive Neuroscience*, *13*(6), 786–792.

Hauser, M. D., Chomsky, N., & Fitch, W. T. (2002). The faculty of language: What is it, who has it, and how did it evolve? *Science*, *298*, 1569–1579.

Haviland, S. E., & Clark, H. H. (1974). What's new? Acquiring new information as a process in comprehension. *Journal of Verbal Learning and Verbal Behavior*, *13*, 512–521.

Haxby, J. V., Grady, C. L., Ungerleider, L. G., & Horwitz, B. (1991). Mapping the functional neuroanatomy of the intact human brain with brain work imaging. *Neuropsychologia*, *6*, 539–555.

Haxby, J. V., Horwitz, B., Ungerleider, L. G., Maisog, J. M., Pietrini, P., & Grady, C. L. (1994). The functional organization of human extrastriate cortex: A PET–rCBF study of selective attention to faces and locations. *Journal of Neuroscience*, *14*, 6336–6353.

Hayama, H., & Rugg, M. D. (2009). Right dorsolateral prefrontal cortex is engaged during post-retrieval processing of both episodic and semantic information. *Neuropsychologia*, *47* (12), 2409–2416.

Hayes, J. R. (1989). *The complete problem solver*. Mahwah, NJ: Erlbaum.

Hayward, W. G. (1998). Effects of outline in object recognition. *Journal of Experimental Psychology: Human Perception and Performance*, *24*, 427–440.

Hebb, D. O. (1949). *The organization of behavior: A neuropsychological theory*. New York, NY: Wiley.

Heider, E. A. (1972). Probabilities, sampling, and ethnographic method: The case of Dani colour names. *Man*, *7*, 448–466.

Heider, E. A., & Olivier, D. C. (1972). The structure of the color space for naming and memory in two languages. *Cognitive Psychology*, *3*, 337–354.

Heilman, K. M., & Valenstein, E. (1979). Mechanisms underlying hemispatial neglect. *Annals of Neurology*, *5*, 166–170.

Heit, E., & Rotello, C. M. (2010). Relations between inductive reasoning and deductive reasoning. *Journal of Experimental Psychology: Learning, Memory, and Cognition*, *36*, 805–812.

Henke, K., Schweinberger, S., Grigo, A., Klos, T., & Sommer, W. (1998). Specificity of face recognition: Recognition of exemplars of non-face objects in prosopagnosia. *Cortex*, *34*, 289–296.

Henle, M. (1962). On the relation beween logic and thinking. *Psychological Review*, *69*, 366–378.

Henson, R. N. (2003). Neuroimaging studies of priming. *Progress in Neurobiology*, *70*, 53–81.

Henson, R. N., Hornberger, M., & Rugg, M. D. (2005). Further dissociating processes in recognition memory using fMRI. *Journal of Cognitive Neuroscience*, *17*, 1058–1073.

Henson, R. N., Shallice, T., & Dolan, R. J. (1999). The role of right prefrontal cortex in episodic retrieval: An fMRI test of the monitoring hypothesis. *Brain*, *122*, 1367–1381.

Herrera, A., & Macizo, P. (2008). Cross-notational semantic priming between symbolic and non-symbolic numerosity. *Quarterly Journal of Experimental Psychology*, *61*, 1538–1559.

Herrnstein, R. J., & Murray, C. (1994). *The bell curve: Intelligence and class structure in American life*. New York, NY: The Free Press.

Hickok, G., & Poeppel, D. (2007). The cortical organization of speech processing. *Nature Reviews Neuroscience*, *8* (5), 393–402.

Hickok, G., Zurif, E., & Canseco-Gonzalez, E. (1993). Structural description of agrammatic comprehension. *Brain and Language*, *45*, 249–303.

Hill, H., & Bruce, V. (1996). Effects of lighting on the perception of facial surfaces. *Journal of Experimental Psychology: Human Perception and Performance*, *22*, 986–1004.

Hillis, A. E., & Caramazza, A. (1991). Category-specific naming and comprehension impairment: A double dissociation. *Brain*, *114*, 2081–2094.

Hintzman, D. L. (1974). Theoretical implications of the spacing effect. In R. L. Solso (Ed.), *Theories in cognitive psychology: The Loyola symposium* (pp. 77–97). Potomac, MD: Erlbaum.

Hintzman, D. L. (1976). Repetition and memory. In G. H. Bower (Ed.), *The psychology of learning and motivation* (Vol. 10, pp. 47–91). New York, NY: Academic Press.

Hintzman, D. L. (1986). "Schema Abstraction" in a multiple-trace memory model. *Psychological Review*, *93* (4), 411–428.

Hintzman, D. L. (1988). Judgments of frequency and recognition memory in a multiple-trace memory model. *Psychological Review*, *95*, 528–551.

Hintzman, D. L., Block, R. A., & Inskeep, N. R. (1972). Memory for mode of input. *Journal of Verbal Learning & Verbal Behavior*, *11*, 741–749.

Hintzman, D. L., Summers, J. J., Eki, N. T., & Moore, M. D. (1975). Voluntary attention and the spacing effect. *Memory & Cognition*, *3*, 576–580.

Hirsh-Pasek, K. & Golinkoff, R. (1996). *The origins of grammar*. Cambridge, MA: MIT Press.

Hirsh-Pasek, K., Golinkoff, R., & Naigles, L. (1996). Young children's ability to use syntactic frames to derive meaning. In K. Hirsh-Pasek & R. Golinkoff (Eds.). *The origins of grammar: Evidence from early language comprehension* (pp. 123–158). Cambridge, MA: MIT Press.

Hirsh-Pasek, K., Kemler Nelson, D. G., Jusczyk, P. W., Cassidy, K. W., Druss, B., & Kennedy, L. (1987). Clauses are perceptual units for young infants. *Cognition*, *26*, 269–286.

Hirsh-Pasek, K., Treiman, R., & Schneiderman, M. (1984). Brown & Hanlon revisited: Mothers' sensitivity to ungrammatical forms. *Journal of Child Language*, *11*(1), 81–89.

Hirst, W., & Volpe, B. T. (1988). Memory strategies with brain damage. *Brain and Cognition*, *8*, 379–408.

Hitch, G. J., & Baddeley, A. D. (1976). Verbal reasoning and working memory. *Quarterly Journal of Experimental Psychology*, *28*, 603–621.

Hittmair-Delazer, M., Sailer, U., & Benke, T. (1995). Impaired arithmetic facts but intact conceptual knowledge—A single case study of dyscalculia. *Cortex*, *31*, 139–147.

Hollich, G. J., Hirsh-Pasek, K., & Golinkoff, R. M. (2000). Breaking the language barrier: An emergentist coalition model for the origins of word learning. *Monographs of the Society for Research in Child Development*, *65*(3, Serial No. 262).

Hirsh-Pasek, K., Golinkoff, R., & Naigles, L. (1996). Young children's ability to use syntactic frames to derive meaning. In K. Hirsh-Pasek & R. Golinkoff (Eds.). *The origins of grammar: Evidence from early language comprehension* (pp. 123–158). Cambridge, MA: MIT Press.

Hollingworth, A. (2003). Failures of retrieval and comparison constrain change detection in natural scenes. *Journal of Experimental Psychology: Human Perception and Performance*, *29*, 388–403.

Hollingworth, A., & Henderson, J. M. (2000). Semantic informativeness mediates the detection of changes in natural scenes. *Visual Cognition*, *7*, 213–235.

Holmes, G. (1918). Disturbances of visual orientation. *British Journal of Ophthalmology*, *2*, 449–468.

Holyoak, K. J. (2005). Analogy. In K. J. Holyoak & R. G. Morrison (Eds.), *The Cambridge handbook of thinking and reasoning* (pp. 117–142). Cambridge, UK: Cambridge University Press.

Holyoak, K. J., & Koh, K. (1987). Surface and structural similarity in analogical transfer. *Memory & Cognition*, *15*, 323–340.

Holyoak, K. J., & Morrison, R. G. (Eds.). (2005). *The Cambridge handbook of thinking and reasoning*. Cambridge, UK: Cambridge University Press.

Holyoak, K. J., & Thagard, P. (1997). The analogical mind. *American Psychologist*, *52*, 35–44.

Hopfinger, J. B., & Mangun, G. R. (1998). Reflexive attention modulates processing of visual stimuli in human extrastriate cortex. *Psychological Science*, *9*, 441–447.

Horwitz, B., Amunts, K., Bhattacharyya, R., Patkin, D., Jeffries, K., Zilles, K., & Braun, A. R. (2003). Activation of Broca's area during the production of spoken and signed language: A combined cytoarchitectonic mapping and PET analysis. *Neuropsychologia*, *41*(14), 1868–1876.

Houston-Price, C., Plunkett, K., & Duffy, H. (2006). The use of social and salience cues in early word learning. *Journal of Experimental Child Psychology*, *95*(1), 27–55.

Houston-Price, C., Plunkett, K., & Harris, P. L. (2005). Word learning "wizardry" at 1;6. *Journal of Child Language, 32*, 175–189. In K. Pezdek and W. P. Banks (Eds.), *The recovered memory/false memory debate* (pp. 197–210). San Diego, CA: Academic Press.

Howarth, C. I., & Ellis, R. (1961). The relative intelligibility threshold for one's own name compared with other names. *Quarterly Journal of Experimental Psychology, 13*, 236–239.

Huang, L., & Pashler, H. (2007). Working memory and the guidance of visual attention: Consonance-driven orienting. *Psychonomic Bulletin & Review, 14*, 148–153.

Hubel, D. H., & Wiesel, T. N. (1959). Receptive fields of single neurones in the cat's striate cortex. *Journal of Physiology, 148*, 574–591.

Hubel, D. H., & Wiesel, T. N. (1962). Receptive fields, binocular interaction and functional architecture in the cat's visual cortex. *Journal of Physiology, 160*, 106–154.

Hubel, D. H., & Wiesel, T. N. (1968). Receptive fields and functional architecture of monkey striate cortex. *Journal of Physiology, 195*, 215–243.

Hue, C., & Ericsson, J. R. (1988). Short-term memory for Chinese characters and radicals. *Memory and Cognition, 16*, 196–205.

Huettel, S., Song, A. W., & McCarthy, G. (2004). *Functional magnetic resonance imaging*. Sunderland, MA: Sinauer Associates.

Hull, R., & Vaid, J. (2006). Laterality and language experience. *Laterality, 11*, 436–464.

Hummel, J. E., & Holyoak, K. J. (2001). A process model of human transitive inference. In M. Gattis (Ed.), *Spatial schemas in abstract thought* (pp. 279–305). Cambridge, MA: MIT Press.

Humphrey, G. (1951). *Thinking: An introduction to its experimental psychology*. London, UK: Methuen.

Humphreys, G. W., & Forde, E. M. E. (2001). Category-specific deficits: A major review and presentation of the hierarchical interactive theory (HIT). *Behavioral and Brain Sciences, 24*, 453–465.

Humphreys, G. W., & Riddoch, M. J. (1987). *To see but not to see: A case study of visual agnosia*. London, UK: Erlbaum.

Humphreys, J. T. (1986). Measurement, prediction, and training of harmonic audiation and performance skills. *Journal of Research in Music Education, 34*, 192–199.

Hunt, R., & Elliott, J. (1980). The role of nonsemantic information in memory: Orthographic distinctiveness effects on retention. *Journal of Experimental Psychology: General, 109*, 49–74.

Hurtado, N., Marchman, V. A., & Fernald, A. (2008). Does input influence uptake? Links between maternal talk, processing speed and vocabulary size in Spanish-learning children. *Developmental Science, 11*(6), F31–F39.

Hutchins, S., & Palmer, C. (2008). Repetition priming in music. *Journal of Experimental. Psychology: Human Perception and Performance, 34*, 693–707.

Hyde, T. S., & Jenkins, J. J. (1969). Differential effects of incidental tasks on the organization of recall of a list of highly associated words. *Journal of Experimental Psychology, 82*, 472–481.

Hyde, T. S., & Jenkins, J. J. (1973). Recall for words as a function of semantic, graphic, and syntactic orienting tasks. *Journal of Verbal Learning and Verbal Behavior, 12*, 471–480.

Hyllegard, R., & Bories, T. L. (2008). Deliberate practice theory: Relevance, effort, and inherent enjoyment of music practice. *Perceptual and Motor Skills, 107*(2), 439–448.

Hyllegard, R., & Bories, T. L. (2009). Deliberate practice theory: Perceived relevance, effort, and inherent enjoyment of music practice: Study II. *Perceptual and Motor Skills, 109*(2), 431–440.

Hyllegard, R., & Yamamoto, M. (2007). Testing assumptions of deliberate practice theory: Relevance, effort, and inherent enjoyment of practice with a novel task: Study II. *Perceptual and Motor Skills, 105*(2), 435–446.

Hyman, I., Boss, S., Wise, B., McKenzie, K., & Caggiano, J. (2009). Did you see the unicycling clown? Inattentional blindness while walking and talking on a cell phone. *Applied Cognitive Psychology*, *24*, 597–607.

Innocence Project. (n.d.). Retrieved from www.innocenceproject.org

Insurance Corporation of British Columbia. (2007). *ICBC Information Request Response* 2007.2 RR IBC.103.1.1.

Intraub, H., Bender, R. S., & Mangels, J. A. (1992). Looking at pictures but remembering scenes. *Journal of Experimental Psychology: Learning, Memory, and Cognition*, *18*, 180–191.

Intraub, H., Gottesman, C. V., Bills, A. (1998). Effects of perceiving and imagining scenes on memory for pictures. *Journal of Experimental, Psychology: Learning, Memory and Cognition*, *24*, 186–201.

Intraub, H., & Nicklos, S. (1985). Levels of processing and picture memory: The physical superiority effect. *Journal of Experimental Psychology: Learning, Memory, and Cognition*, *11*, 284–298.

Intraub, H., & Richardson, M. (1989). Wide-angle memories of close-up scenes. *Journal of Experimental Psychology: Learning, Memory, and Cognition*, *15*, 179–187.

Irwin, D. I., & Lupker, S. J. (1983). Semantic priming of pictures and words: A levels of processing approach. *Journal of Verbal Learning and Verbal Behavior*, *22*, 45–60.

Isurin, L. (2000). Deserted island or a child's first language forgetting. *Bilingualism: Language and Cognition*, *3*, 151–166.

Isurin, L., & McDonald, J. L. (2001). Retroactive interference form translation equivalents: Implications for first language forgetting. *Memory & Cognition*, *29*, 312–319.

Jackendoff, R. (1993). *Patterns in the mind: Language and human nature*. New York: Harvester Wheatsheaf.

Jackendoff, R., & Pinker, S. (2005). The nature of the language faculty and its implications for evolution of language (Reply to Fitch, Hauser, & Chomsky). *Cognition*, *97*(2), 211–225.

Jackson, M., & Warrington, E. K. (1986). Arithmetic skills in patients with unilateral cerebral lesions. *Cortex*, *22*, 611–620.

Jacoby, L. (1975). Physical features vs. meaning: A difference in decay. *Memory & Cognition*, *3*, 247–251.

James, W. (1890/1950). *The principles of psychology* (2 Vols.). New York, NY: Dover Publications.

James, W. (1892). *Text-book of psychology*. London: Macmillan and Co.

Jamison, K. R. (1993). *Touched with fire: Manic-depressive illness and the artistic temperament*. New York, NY: The Free Press.

Jankowiak, J., Kinsbourne, M., Shalev, R. S., Bachman, D. L. (1992). Preserved visual imagery and categorization in a case of associative visual agnosia. *Journal of Cognitive Neuroscience*, *4*(2), 119–131.

Janowsky, J. S., Shimamura, A. P., & Squire, L. R. (1989). Memory and metamemory: Comparisons between patients with frontal lobe lesions and amnesic patients. *Psychobiology*, *17*, 3–11.

Janse, E. (2006). Lexical competition effects in aphasia: Deactivation of lexical candidates in spoken word processing. *Brain and Language*, *97*, 1–11.

January, D., & Kako, E. (2007). Re-evaluating evidence for the linguistic relativity hypothesis: Response to Boroditsky (2001). *Cognition*, *104*(2), 417–426.

Jasper, H., & Penfield, W. (1951/1954). *Epilepsy and the functional anatomy of the human brain* (2nd ed.). New York, NY: Little, Brown and Co.

Jenkins, J. C., & Dallenbach, K. M. (1924). Obliviscence during sleep and waking. *American Journal of Psychology*, *35*, 605–612.

Johnson, H. M. (1994). Processes of successful intentional forgetting. *Psychological Bulletin*, *116*(2), 274–292.

Johnson-Laird, P. N. (2001). Mental models and deduction. *Trends in Cognitive Sciences*, *5*, 434–442.

Johnson-Laird, P. N. (2006). *How we reason*. Oxford, UK: Oxford University Press.

Johnson-Laird, P. N., & Bara, B. G. (1984). Syllogistic inference. *Cognition 16*, 1–61.

Johnson-Laird, P. N., & Byrne, R. M. J. (1991). *Deduction*. Hove, UK: Erlbaum.

Johnson, M. H., Dziurawiec, S., Ellis, H., & Morton, J. (1991). Newborn preferential tracking of face-like stimuli and its subsequent decline. *Cognition*, *40*, 1–19.

Johnson, M. H., & Morton, J. (1991). *Biology and cognitive development. The case of face recognition*. Oxford, UK: Blackwell.

Johnson, J. S., & Newport, E. L. (1989). Critical period effects in second language learning: The influence of maturational state on the acquisition of English as a second language. *Cognitive Psychology*, *21* (1), 60–99.

Johnson, S. C., & Solomon, G. (1997). Why dogs have puppies and cats have kittens: Young children's understanding of biological origins. *Child Development*, *68* (3), 404–419.

Johnson, S. L., Sandrow, D., Meyer, B., Winters, R., Miller, I., Solomon, D., & Keitner, G. (2000). Increases in manic symptoms after life events involving goal attainment. *Journal of Abnormal Psychology*, *109*, 721–727.

Johnston, A., Hill, H., & Carman, N. (1992). Recognising faces: Effects of lighting direction, inversion, and brightness reversal. *Perception*, *21*, 365–375.

Johnston, J. C., & McClelland, J. L. (1980). Experimental tests of a hierarchical model of word identification. *Journal of Verbal Learning and Verbal Behavior*, *19*, 503–524.

Johnston, M. (1997). *Spectral evidence: The Ramona case. Incest, memory, and truth on trial in Napa Valley*. Boston, MA: Houghton Mifflin.

Johnston, W. A., & Uhl, C. N. (1976). The contributions of encoding effort and variability to the spacing effect on free recall. *Journal of Experimental Psychology: Human Learning & Memory*, *2*, 153–160.

Jonides, J., Smith, E. E., Koeppe, R. A., Awh, E., Minoshima, S., & Mintun, M. A. (1993). Spatial working memory in humans as revealed by PET. *Nature*, *363*, 623–625.

Jonkers, R., & de Bruin, A. (2009). Tense processing in Broca's and Wernicke's aphasia. *Aphasiology*, *23* (10), 1252–1265.

Joslyn, S. L., & Oakes, M. A. (2005). Directed forgetting and autobiographical events. *Memory and Cognition*, *33*, 577–587.

Joubert, S., Felician, O., Barbeau, E. J., Didic, M., Poncet, M., & Ceccaldi, M. (2008). Patterns of semantic memory impairment in mild cognitive impairment. *Behavioural Neurology*, *19* (1–2), 35–40.

Judson, H. F. (1979). *The eighth day of creation: Makers of the revolution in biology*. New York, NY: Simon & Schuster.

Jung-Beeman, M., Bowden, E. M., Haberman, J., Frymaire, J., Arambel-Liu, S., Greenblatt, R., . . . Kounios, J. (2004). Neural activity when people solve verbal problems with insight. *PloS Biology*, *2*, 1–11.

Just, M. A., & Carpenter, P. A. (1987). *The psychology of reading and language comprehension*. Boston, MA: Allyn & Bacon.

Just, M. A., & Carpenter, P. A. (1992). A capacity theory of comprehension: Individual differences in working memory. *Psychological Review*, *99*, 122–149.

Justice, E. M., Baker-Ward, L., Gupta, S., & Jannings, L. R. (1997). Means to the goal of remembering: Developmental changes in awareness of strategy use-performance relations. *Journal of Experimental Child Psychology*, *65*, 293–314.

Kahneman, D. (1973). *Attention and effort*. Englewood Cliffs, NJ: Prentice-Hall.

Kahneman, D. (2011). *Thinking, fast and slow*. New York, NY: Farrar, Straus and Giroux.

Kahneman, D., & Frederick, S. (2005). A model of heuristic judgment. In K. J. Holyoak & R. G. Morrison (Eds.), *The Cambridge handbook of thinking and reasoning* (pp. 267–293). Cambridge, UK: Cambridge University Press.

Kahneman, D., Slovic, P., & Tversky, A. (Eds.). (1982). *Judgment under uncertainty: Heuristics and biases*. New York, NY: Cambridge University Press.

Kahneman, D., & Tversky, A. (1973). On the psychology of prediction. *Psychological Review*, *80*, 237–257.

Kahneman, D., & Tversky, A. (1979). Prospect theory: An analysis of decision under risk. *Econometrica*, *47*(2), 263–292.

Kahneman, D., & Tversky, A. (1982). On the study of statistical intuitions. In D. Kahneman, P. Slovic, & A. Tversky (Eds.), *Judgment under uncertainty: Heuristics and biases* (pp. 493–508). New York, NY: Cambridge University Press.

Kahneman, D., & Tversky, A. (1996). On the reality of cognitive illusions: A reply to Gigerenzer's critique. *Psychological Review*, *103*, 582–591.

Kalakoski, V. (2007). Effect of skill level on recall of visually presented patterns of musical notes. *Scandinavian Journal of Psychology*, *48*(2), 87–96.

Kalish, C. W. (2002). Essentialist to some degree: The structure of natural kind categories. *Memory & Cognition*, *30*, 340–352.

Kane, M. J., May, C. P., Hasher, L., Rahhal, T., & Stoltzfus, E. R. (1997). Dual mechanisms of negative priming. *Journal of Experimental Psychology: Human Perception and Performance*, *23*, 632–650.

Kanske, P., & Kotz, S. A. (2007). Concreteness in emotional words: ERP evidence from a hemifield study. *Brain Research*, *1148*, 138–148.

Kanwisher, N. G. (1987). Repetition blindness: Type recognition without token individuation. *Cognition*, *27*, 117–143.

Kanwisher, N. G. (2006). What's in a face? *Science*, *311*, 617.

Kanwisher, N. G., McDermott, J., & Chun, M. (1997). The fusiform face area: A module in human extrastriate cortex specialized for the perception of faces. *Journal of Neuroscience*, *17*, 4302–4311.

Kanwisher, N., Yin, C., & Wojciulik, N. (1999). Repetition blindness for pictures: Evidence for the rapid computation of abstract visual descriptions. In V. Coltheart (Ed.), *Fleeting memories* (pp. 119–150). Cambridge, MA: MIT Press.

Kaplan, C. A., & Simon, H. A. (1990). In search of insight. *Cognitive Psychology*, *22*, 374–419.

Karremans, J. C., Stroebe, W., & Claus, J. (2006). Beyond Vicary's fantasies: The impact of subliminal priming and brand choice. *Journal of Experimental Social Psychology*, *42*, 792–798.

Kay, P. (1979). *The role of cognitive schemata in word meaning: Hedges revisited*. Berkeley: University of California, Department of Linguistics.

Keane, M. (1987). Cognitive theory of analogy. In J. T. E. Richardson, M. Eysenck, & D. Warren-Piper (Eds.), *Student learning: Research in cognitive psychology and education*. Guilford, UK: Open University Press.

Keenan, J. M., Baillet, S. D., & Brown, P. (1984). The effects of causal cohesion on comprehension and memory. *Journal of Verbal Learning and Verbal Behavior*, *23*, 115–126.

Kehoe, M. (2001). Prosodic patterns in children's multisyllabic word patterns. *Language, Speech, and Hearing Services in Schools*, *32*, 284–294.

Keil, F. C. (1983). On the emergence of semantic and conceptual distinctions. *Journal of Experimental Psychology: General*, *112*, 357–385.

Keil, F. C. (1989). *Concepts, kinds, and cognitive development*. Cambridge, MA: Harvard University Press.

Keil, F. C. (1992). The origins of an autonomous biology. In M. R. Gunnar and M. Maratsos (Eds.), *Modularity and constraints in language and cognition* (pp. 103–137). Hillsdale, NJ: Lawrence Erlbaum Associates.

Keil, F. C., & Batterman, N. (1984). A characteristic-to-defining shift in the development of word meaning. *Journal of Verbal Learning and Verbal Behavior*, *23*, 211–236.

Kelemen, W. L., & Creeley, C. E. (2003). State-dependant memory effects using caffeine and placebo do not extend to metamemory. *Journal of General Psychology*, *130*, 70–86.

Kemler Nelson, D. G., Hirsh-Pasek, K., Jusczyk, P. W., & Cassidy, K. W. (1989). How the prosodic cues in motherese might assist language learning. *Journal of Child Language*, *16*(1), 55–68.

Kendler, H. H. (1987). *Historical foundations of modern psychology*. Chicago, IL: Dorsey Press.

Kennedy, K. M., Rodrigue, K. M., & Raz, N. (2007). Fragmented pictures revisited: Long-term changes in repetition priming, relation to skill learning, and the role of cognitive resources. *Gerontology*, *53*, 148–158.

Kensinger, E. A., & Corkin, S. (2000). Retrograde memory in amnesia: A "famous faces" study with the amnesic patient H.M. *Society for Neuroscience Abstracts*, *26*, 463.1.

Keppel, G. (1964). Facilitation in short- and long-term retention of paired associates following distributed practice in learning. *Journal of Verbal Learning and Verbal Behavior*, *3*, 91–111.

Keppel, G. (1967). A reconsideration of the extinction-recovery theory. *Journal of Verbal Learning and Verbal Behavior*, *6*, 476–487.

Keppel, G., & Underwood, B. J. (1962). Proactive inhibition in short-term retention of single items. *Journal of Verbal Learning & Verbal Behavior*, *1*, 153–161.

Kershaw, T. C., & Ohlsson, S. (2004). Multiple causes of difficulty in insight: The case of the nine-dot problem. *Journal of Experimental Psychology: Learning, Memory, and Cognition*, *30*(1), 3–13.

Kersten, D., Mamassian, P., & Yuille, A., (2004). Object perception as Bayesian inference. *Annual Reviews of Psychology*, *55*, 271–304.

Keysers, C., Xiao, D. K., Földiák, P., & Perrett, D. I. (2005). Out of sight but not out of mind: The neurophysiology of iconic memory in the superior temporal sulcus. *Cognitive Neuropsychology*, *22*, 316–332.

Kieras, D. (1978). Beyond pictures and words: Alternative information processing models for imagery effects in verbal memory. *Psychological Bulletin*, *85*, 532–554.

Kieras, D. (1981). Component processes in the comprehension of simple prose. *Journal of Verbal Learning and Verbal Behavior*, *20*, 1–23.

Kikyo, H., Ohki, K., & Sekihara, K. (2001). Temporal characterization of memory retrieval processes: An fMRI study of the tip of the tongue phenomenon. *European Journal of Neuroscience*, *14*, 887–892.

Kim, H. (2011). Neural activity that predicts subsequent memory and forgetting: A meta-analysis of 74 fMRI studies. *Neuroimage 54*, 2446–2461.

Kim, K. H. (2011a). The APA 2009 Division 10 debate: Are the Torrance Tests of Creative Thinking still relevant in the 21st century? *Psychology of Aesthetics, Creativity, and the Arts*, *5*(4), 302–308.

Kim, K. H. (2011b). Proven reliability and validity of the Torrance Tests of Creative Thinking (TTCT). *Psychology of Aesthetics, Creativity, and the Arts*, *5*(4), 314–315.

Kim, Y. (2008). The effect of improvisation-assisted desensitization, and music-assisted progressive muscle relaxation and imagery on reducing pianists' music performance anxiety. *Journal of Music Therapy*, *45*, 165–191.

Kimball, D. R., & Bjork, R. A. (2002). Influences of intentional and unintentional forgetting on false memories. *Journal of Experimental Psychology: General*, *131*, 116–130.

King-Sears, M. E., Mercer, D. D., & Sindelar, P. T. (1992). Toward independence with keyword mnemonics: A strategy for science vocabulary instruction. *Remedial and Special Education*, *13*, 22–33.

Kinney, G. C., Marsetta, M. Y., & Showman, D. J. (1966). *Studies in display symbol legibility, XII: The legibility of alphanumeric symbols for digitalized television*. Bedford, MA: The MITRE Corporation, TR-66–117.

Kinsbourne, M., & Warrington, E. K. (1962). A disorder of simultaneous form perception. *Brain*, *85*, 461–486.

Kintsch, W., & van Dijk, T. A. (1978). Toward a model of text comprehension and production. *Psychological Review*, *85*, 363–943.

Kirchhoff, B. A., Wagner, A. D., Maril, A., & Stern, C. E. (2000). Prefrontal-temporal circuitry for episodic encoding and subsequent memory. *Journal of Neuroscience*, *20*(16), 6173–6180.

Klahr, D., & Simon, H. A. (1999). Studies of scientific discovery: Complementary approaches and convergent findings. *Psychological Bulletin*, *125*(5), 524–543.

Klauer, K. C., Musch, J., & Naumer, B. (2000). On belief bias in syllogistic reasoning. *Psychological Review*, *107*(4), 852–884.

Kliger, D., & Kudryavtsev, A. (2008). Reference point formation by market investors. *Journal of Banking and Finance*, *32*, 1782–1794.

Kliger, D., & Kudryavtsev, A. (2010). The availability heuristic and investors' reaction to company–specific events. *Journal of Behavioral Finance*, *11*(1), 50–65.

Knauff, M., Fangmeier, T., Ruff, C. C., & Johnson-Laird, P. N. (2003). Reasoning, models, and images: Behavioral measures and cortical activity. *Journal of Cognitive Neuroscience*, *15*(4), 559–573.

Knight, R. T., & Grabowecky, M. F. (1995). Escape from linear time: Prefrontal cortex and conscious experience. In M. S. Gazzaniga (Ed.), *The cognitive neurosciences* (pp. 1357–1371). Cambridge, MA: MIT Press.

Knoblich, G., Ohlsson, S., Haider, H., & Rhenius, D. (1999). Constraint relaxation and chunk decomposition in insight problem solving. *Journal of Experimental Psychology: Learning, Memory, and Cognition*, *25*, 1534–1556.

Knoblich, G., Ohlsson, S., & Raney, G. (2001). An eye movement study of insight problem solving. *Memory & Cognition*, *29*, 1000–1009.

Knowlton, B. J. (1997). Declarative and nondeclarative knowledge: Insights from cognitive neuroscience. In K. Lamberts & D. Shanks (Eds.), *Knowledge, concepts, and categories* (pp. 215–246). East Sussex, UK: Psychology Press.

Knowlton, B. J., & Forde, K. (2008). Neural representations of nondeclarative memories. *Current Directions in Psychological Science*, *17*, 107–111.

Knowlton, B. J., & Squire, L. R. (1993). The learning of natural categories: Parallel memory systems for item memory and category-level knowledge. *Science*, *262*, 1747–1749.

Knox, A. V. (2001). Functional magnetic resonance imaging of inhibitory processes during directed forgetting. *Dissertation Abstracts International: Section B: The Sciences and Engineering*, *61*(7-B), 3872.

Koehler, J. J. (1996). The base rate fallacy reconsidered: Normative, descriptive and methodological challenges. *Behavioral and Brain Sciences*, *19*, 1–53.

Koestler, A. (1964). *The act of creation*. London, UK: Hutchinson & Co.

Köhler, W. (1925). *The mentality of apes*. New York, NY: Harcourt, Brace and Co.

Kohn, N., & Smith, S. M. (2009). Partly vs. completely out of your mind: Effects of incubation and distraction on resolving fixation. *Journal of Creative Behavior*, *43*(2), 102–118.

Kojima, S., Tatsumi, I. F., Kiritani, S., & Hirose, H. (1989). Vocal-auditory functions of the chimpanzee: Consonant perception. *Human Evolution*, *4*, 403–416.

Kolers, P. A., & Roediger, H. L. (1984). Procedures of mind. *Journal of Verbal Learning and Verbal Behavior*, *23*, 425–449.

Kolinsky, R., Fery, P., Messina, D., Peretz, I., Evinck, S., Ventura, P., & Morais, J. (2002). The fur of the crocodile and the mooing sheep: A longitudinal study of a patient with category-specific impairment for biological things. *Cognitive Neuropsychology*, *19*, 301–342.

Kolk, H. H. J., & van Grunsven, M. M. F. (1985). Agrammatism as a variable phenomenon. *Cognitive Neuropsychology*, *2*, 347–384.

Konen, C., & Kastner, S. (2008). Two heirarchically organized neural systems for object information in human visual cortex. *Nature Neuroscience*, *11*(2), 224–231.

Koriat, A. (1993). How do we know that we know? The accessibility model of the feeling of knowing. *Psychological Review*, *100*, 609–639.

Koriat, A., Goldsmith, M., & Pansky, A. (2000). Toward a psychology of memory accuracy. *Annual Review of Psychology*, *51*, 481–537.

Kosslyn, S. M. (1973). Scanning visual images: Some structural implications. *Perception & Psychophysics*, *14*, 90–94.

Kosslyn, S. M. (1975). Information representation in visual images. *Cognitive Psychology*, *7*, 341–370.

Kosslyn, S. M. (1976). Can imagery be distinguished from other forms of internal representation? Evidence from studies of information retrieval time. *Memory & Cognition*, *4*, 291–297.

Kosslyn, S. M. (1980). *Image and mind*. Cambridge, MA: Harvard University Press.

Kosslyn, S. M. (2003). What shape are a German Shepherd's ears? In J. Brockman (Ed.), *The new humanists: Science at the edge* (pp. 125–143). New York, NY: Barnes & Noble Books.

Kosslyn, S. M., & Alper, S. N. (1977). On the pictorial properties of visual images: Effects of image size on memory for words. *Canadian Journal of Psychology*, *31*, 32–40.

Kosslyn, S. M., Alpert, N. M., Thompson, W. L., Maljkovic, V., Weise, S. B., Chabris, C. F., . . . Buonanno, F. S. (1993). Visual mental imagery activates topographically organized visual cortex: PET investigations. *Journal of Cognitive Neuroscience*, *5*, 263–287.

Kosslyn, S. M., Ball, T. M., & Reiser, B. J. (1978). Visual images preserve metric spatial information: Evidence from studies of image scanning. *Journal of Experimental Psychology: Human Perception and Performance*, *4*(1), 47–60.

Kosslyn, S. M., Behrmann, M., & Jeannerod, M. (1995). The cognitive neuroscience of mental imagery. *Neuropsychologia*, *33*(11), 1335–1344.

Kosslyn, S. M., Cave, C. B., Provost, D. A., & Von Gierke, S. (1988). Sequential processes in image generation. *Cognitive Psychology*, *20*, 319–343.

Kosslyn, S. M., & Chabris, C. F. (1993). The mind is not a camera, the brain is not a VCR. *Aldus Magazine*, *4*, 33–36.

Kosslyn, S. M., & Koenig, O. (1995). *Wet mind: The new cognitive neuroscience*. New York, NY/Toronto, Canada: The Free Press.

Kosslyn, S. M., Maljkovic, V., Hamilton, S. E., Horwitz, G., & Thompson, W. L. (1995). Two types of image generation: Evidence for left- and right-hemisphere processes. *Neuropsychologia*, *33*, 1485–1510.

Kosslyn, S. M., Reiser, B. J., Farah, M. J., & Fliegel, S. L. (1983). Generating visual images: Units and relations. *Journal of Experimental Psychology: General*, *112*, 278–303.

Kosslyn, S. M., Segar, C., Pani, J., & Hillger, L. A. (1990). When is imagery used in everyday life? A diary study. *Journal of Mental Imagery*, *14*, 131–152.

Kosslyn, S. M., Thompson, W. L., & Alpert, N. M. (1997). Neural systems shared by visual imagery and visual perception: A positron emission tomography study. *NeuroImage*, *6*, 320–334.

Kosslyn, S. M., Thompson, W. L., & Ganis, G. (2006). *The case for mental imagery*. Oxford, UK: Oxford University Press.

Kosslyn, S. M., Thompson, W. L., Kim, I. J., & Alpert, N. M. (1995). Topographical representations of mental images in primary visual cortex. *Nature*, *378*, 496–498.

Kosslyn, S. M., Thompson, W. L., Sukel, K. E., & Alpert, N. (2005). Two types of image generation: Evidence from PET. *Cognitive, Affective, & Behavioral Neuroscience*, *5*, 41–53.

Kounios, J., & Jung-Beeman, M. (2009). Aha! The cognitive neuroscience of insight. *Current Directions in Psychological Science*, *18*, 210–216.

Kourtzi, Z., & Kanwisher, N. (2000). Cortical regions involved in perceiving object shape. *The Journal of Neuroscience*, *20*(9), 3310–3318.

Kovács, G., Vogels, R., & Orban, G. A. (1995). Cortical correlate of pattern backward masking. *Proceedings of the National Academy of Sciences of the United States of America*, *92*, 5587–5591.

Kozbelt, A. (2004). Reexamining the equal-odds rule in classical composers. In J. P. Frois, P. Andrade, & J. F Marques. (Eds.), *Art and science. Proceedings of the XVIII Congress of the International Association of Empirical Aesthetics* (pp. 540–543). Lisbon, Portugal: IAEA.

Kozbelt, A. (2005). Factors affecting aesthetic success and improvement in creativity: A case study of the musical genres of Mozart. *Psychology of Music*, *33*, 235–255.

Kraemer, D. J. M., Macrae, C. N., Green, A. E., & Kelley, W. M. (2005). Musical imagery: Sound of silence activates auditory cortex. *Nature*, *434*, 158.

Kraepelin, E. (1921). *Manic-depressive insanity and paranoia*. Edinburgh, UK: E. & S. Livingstone.

Krakow, B. (2004). An emerging interdisciplinary sleep medicine perspective on the high prevalence of co-morbid sleep-disordered breathing and insomnia. *Sleep Medicine*, *5*, 431–433.

Krakow, B., Hollifield, M., Schrader, R., Koss, M., Tandberg, D., Lauriello, J., . . . Kellner, R. (2000). A controlled study of imagery rehearsal for chronic nightmares in sexual assault survivors with PTSD: A preliminary report. *Journal of Traumatic Stress*, *13*(4), 589–609.

Kraut, R. (1980). Humans as lie detectors: Some second thoughts. *Journal of Communications*, *30*, 209–216.

Kreigeskorte, N., Formisano, E., Sorber, B., & Goebel, B. (2007). Individual faces elicit distinct response patterns in human anterior temporal cortex. *PNAS Proceedings of the National Academy of Sciences of the United States of America*, *104*(51), 20600–20605.

Kreutzer, M. A., Leonard, C., & Flavell, J. H. (1975). An interview study of children's knowledge about memory. *Monographs of the Society for Research in Child Development*, *40*(1, Serial No. 159).

Kuhl, P. K. (1978). Predispositions for the perception of speech–sound categories: A species-specific phenomenon? In F. D. Minifie & L. L. Lloyd (Eds.), *Communicative and cognitive abilities: Early behavioral assessment* (pp. 229–255). Baltimore, MD: University Park Press.

Kuhl, P. K. (2009). Early language acquisition: Phonetic and word learning, neural substrates, and a theoretical model. In B. Moore, L. Tyler, & W. Marslen-Wilson (Eds.), *The perception of speech: From sound to meaning* (pp. 103–131). Oxford, UK: Oxford University Press.

Kuhl, P. K., Andruski, J. E., Chistovich, I. A., Chistovich, L. A., Kozhevnikova, E. V., Ryskina, V. L., . . . Lacerda, F. (1997). Cross-language analysis of phonetic units in language addressed to infants. *Science*, *277*, 684–686.

Kuhl, P. K., & Miller, J. D. (1975). Speech perception by the chinchilla: Voiced-voiceless distinction in alveolar plosive consonants. *Science*, *190*, 69–72.

Kukkonen, P. (2006). Aphasic errors for the mental organization of morphology. *A Man of Measure: Festschrift in Honour of Fred Karlsson. Special supplement to SKY Journal of Linguistics*, *19*, 209–218.

Kulkarni, D., & Simon, H. A. (1988). The processes of scientific discovery: The strategy of experimentation. *Cognitive Science*, *12*, 139–175.

Külpe, O. (1901). *Outline of psychology based on the results of experimental investigation*. New York, NY: Macmillan.

Kvavilashvili, L., Mirani, J., Schlagman, S., & Kornbrot, D. (2003). Comparing flashbulb memories of September 11 and the death of Princess Diana: Effects of time delays and nationality. *Applied Cognitive Psychology*, *17*, 1017–1031.

Kwantes, P. J. (2005). Using context to build semantics. *Psychonomic Bulletin and Review*, *12*, 703–710.

Labov, W. (1973). The boundaries of words and their meanings. In C.-J. N. Bailey & R. W. Shuy (Eds.), *New ways of analysing variation in English* (pp. 340–373). Washington, DC: Georgetown University Press.

Laeng, B., & Teodorescu, D-S. (2002). Eye scanpaths during visual imagery reenact those of perception of the same visual scene. *Cognitive Science*, *26*, 207–231.

Laganaro, M., Morand, S., & Schnider, A. (2009). Time course of evoked-potential changes in different forms of anomia in aphasia. *Journal of Cognitive Neuroscience*, *21*(8), 1499–1510.

Laiacona, M., Capitani, E., & Barbarotto, R. (1997). Semantic category dissociations: A longitudinal study of two cases. *Cortex*, *33*, 441–461.

Laiacona, M., Capitani, E., & Caramazza, A. (2003). Category-specific semantic deficits do not reflect the sensory-functional organization of the brain: A test of the "sensory-quality" hypothesis. *Neurocase*, *9*, 221–231.

Laine, M., & Koivisto, M. (1998). Lexical access to inflected words as measured by lateralized visual lexical decision. *Psychological Research*, *61*, 220–229.

Laine, M., Niemi, J., Koivuselkä-Sallinen, P., & Hyönä, J. (1995). Morphological processing of polymorphemic nouns in a highly inflecting language. *Cognitive Neuropsychology*, *12*(5), 457–502.

Lakoff, G. (1982). *Categories and cognitive models*. Series A, No. 96. Trier, Germany: Linguistic Agency, University of Trier.

Lakoff, G., & Johnson, M. (1980). *Metaphors we live by*. Chicago, IL: University of Chicago Press.

Lakoff, G., & Johnson, M. (2003). *Metaphors we live by* (2nd ed.). Chicago, IL: University of Chicago Press.

Lakoff, R. (1972). Language in context. *Language*, *48*, 907–927.

Lambert, S., Sampaio, E., Scheiber, C., & Mauss, Y. (2001). Imagerie mentale "tactilo-kinesthésique" chez l'aveugle: Une étude par IRMf. *Neuropsychologie de la Langue Française*, *11*, 126.

Lampl, Y., Eshel, Y., Gilad, R., & Sarova-Pinhas, I. (1994). Selective acalculia with sparing of the subtraction process in a patient with left parietotemporal hemorrhage. *Neurology*, *44*, 1759–1761.

Landau, B., Hoffman, J. E., & Kurz, N. (2006). Object recognition with severe spatial deficits in Williams syndrome: Sparing and breakdown. *Cognition*, *100*, 1–28.

Landauer, T. K., & Dumais, S. T. (1997). A solution to Plato's problem: The latent semantic analysis theory of the acquisition, induction, and representation of knowledge. *Psychological Review*, *104*, 211–240.

Landauer, T., McNamara, D., Dennis, S., & Kintsch, W. (Eds.). (2007). *Handbook of latent semantic analysis*. Mahwah, NJ: Erlbaum.

Laney, C., & Loftus, E. F. (2008). Emotional content of true and false memories. *Memory*, *16*(5), 500–516.

Lang, A. J., Craske, M. G., Brown, M., & Ghaneian, A. (2001). Fear-related state dependent memory. *Cognition & Emotion*, *15*, 695–703.

Langheim, F. J., Callicott, J. H., Mattay, V. S., Duyn, J. H., & Weinberger, D. R. (2002). Cortical systems associated with covert music rehearsal. *Neuroimage*, *16*(4), 901–908.

Langley, P., Simon, H. A., Bradshaw, G. L., & Zytkow, J. M. (1987). *Scientific discovery: Computational explorations of the creative process*. Cambridge, MA: MIT Press.

Lany, J., & Saffran, J. R. (2010). From statistics to meanings: Infant acquisition of lexical categories. *Psychological Science*, *21*, 284–291.

Lassaline, M. E., & Logan, G. D. (1993). Memory-based automaticity in the discrimination of visual numerosity. *Journal of Experimental Psychology: Learning, Memory, and Cognition*, *19*, 561–581.

Lau, E., Stroud, C., Plesch, S., & Phillips, C. (2006). The role of structural prediction in rapid syntactic analysis. *Brain and Language*, *98*(1), 74–88.

Laughlin, S. (1981). A simple coding procedure enhances a neuron's information capacity. *Zeitschrift für Naturforsch*, *36*, 910–912.

Lavric, A., Forstmeier, S., & Rippon, G. (2000). Differences in working memory involvement in analytical and creative tasks. *Neuroreport: For Rapid Communication of Neuroscience Research*, *11*, 1613–1618.

Lazar, R. M., Festa, J. R., Geller, A. E., Romano, G. M., & Marshall, R. S. (2007). Multitasking disorder from right temporoparietal stroke. *Cognitive and Behavioral Neurology*, *20*(3), 157–162.

Lazarus, A. A., & Abramovitz, A. (2004). A multimodal behavioral approach to performance anxiety. *Journal of Clinical Psychology*, *60*, 831–840.

Leahey, T. H. (1992). The mythical revolutions of American psychology. *American Psychologist*, *47*, 308–318.

Leder, H., & Bruce, V. (2000). When inverted faces are recognised: The role of configural information in face recognition. *Quarterly Journal of Experimental Psychology*, *53A*, 513–536.

LeDoux, J. E. (1996). *The emotional brain*. New York, NY: Simon & Schuster.

Lee, T. S. (2002). Top-down influence in early visual processing: A Bayesian perspective. *Physiology & Behavior*, *77*(4–5), 645–650.

Legate, J. A., & Yang, C. (2002). Empirical reassessments of poverty of stimulus arguments. *Linguistic Review*, *19*, 151–162.

Legrenzi, P., Girotto, V., & Johnson-Laird, P. N. (1993). Focusing in reasoning and decision making. *Cognition*, *49*, 37–66.

Lehky, S. R., & Sereno, A. B. (2007). Comparison of shape encoding in primate dorsal and ventral visual pathways. *Journal of Neurophysiology*, *97*, 307–319.

Lehman, D. R., Lempert, R. O., & Nisbett, R. E. (1988). The effects of graduate training on reasoning: Formal discipline and thinking about everyday-life events. *American Psychologist*, *43*, 431–442.

Lehrer, J. (2012a). The eureka hunt. *The New Yorker* (July 28, 2008), 40–45.

Lehrer, J. (2012b). *Imagine: How creativity works*. Boston, MA: Houghton Mifflin Harcourt.

Leichtman, M. D., & Ceci, S. J. (1995). The effects of stereotypes and suggestions on preschoolers' reports. *Developmental Psychology*, *31*, 568–578.

Lenneberg, E. H. (1967). *Biological foundations of language*. New York, NY: Wiley.

Leo, M. A., & Lieber, C. S. (1989). Alcohol and vitamin A. *Alcohol Health and Research World*, *13*, 250–254.

Leopold, W. (1939). *Speech development of a bilingual child: A linguist's record: Vol. I. Vocabulary growth in the first two years*. Evanston, IL: Northwestern University Press.

Lesgold, A. M., Roth, S. F., & Curtis, M. E. (1979). Foregrounding effects in discourse comprehension. *Journal of Verbal Learning and Verbal Behavior*, *18*, 291–308.

Levelt, W. J. M. (1983). Monitoring and self-repair in speech, *Cognition*, *14*, 41–104.

Levelt, W. J. M. (1989). *Speaking: From intention to articulation*. Cambridge, MA: MIT Press.

Levelt, W. J. M., Praamstra, P., Meyer, A. S., Helenius, P., & Salmelin, R. (1998). An MEG study of picture naming. *Journal of Cognitive Neuroscience*, *10*, 553–567.

Levey, S., & Cruz, D. (2003). The first words produced by bilingual Mandarin-Chinese/English speaking children. *Communication Disorders Quarterly*, *24*(3), 129–136.

Levick, W. R., & Sacks, J. L. (1970). Responses of the cat retinal ganglion cells to brief flashes of light. *Journal of Physiology*, *206*, 677–700.

Levin, D. T., & Simons, D. J. (1997). Failure to detect changes to attended objects in motion pictures. *Psychonomic Bulletin and Review*, *4*, 501–506.

Levin, D. T., Simons, D. J., Angelone, B. L., & Chabris, C. F. (2002). Memory for centrally attended changing objects in an incidental real-world change detection paradigm. *British Journal of Psychology*, *93*, 289–302.

Levine, D. N., Warach, J., & Farah, M. J. (1985). Two visual systems in mental imagery: Dissociation of "what" and "where" in imagery disorders due to bilateral posterior cerebral lesions. *Neurology*, *35*, 1010–1018.

Levy, J., Pashler, H., & Boer, E. (2006). Central interference in driving: Is there any stopping the psychological refractory period? *Psychological Science*, *17*, 228–235.

Li, W., Paller, K., & Zinbarg, R. (2008). Conscious intrusion of threat information via unconscious priming in anxiety. *Cognition & Emotion*, *22*, 44–62.

Liberman, A. M., Cooper, F. S., Shankweiler, D. P., & Studdert-Kennedy, M. (1967). Perception of the speech code. *Psychological Review*, *74*, 431–461.

Lichtenstein, S., Slovic, P., Fischhoff, B., Layman, M., & Combs, B. (1978). Judged frequency of lethal events. *Journal of Experimental Psychology: Human Learning and Memory*, *4*, 551–578.

Limb, C. J., & Braun, A. R. (2008). Neural substrates of spontaneous musical performance: An fMRI study of jazz improvisation. *PloS ONE*, *3*(2), e1679.

Lindsay, D. S. (1990). Misleading suggestions can impair eyewitnesses' ability to remember event details. *Journal of Experimental Psychology: Learning, Memory, and Cognition*, *16*, 1077–1083.

Linebarger, M. (1995). Agrammatism as evidence about grammar. *Brain and Language*, *50*, 52–91.

Linebarger, M. C., Schwartz, M. F., & Saffran, E. M. (1983). Sensitivity to grammatical structure in so-called agrammatic aphasics. *Cognition*, *13*, 361–92.

Linsey, J., Tseng, I., Fu, K., Cagan, J., Wood, K., & Schunn, C. D. (2010). A study of design fixation, its mitigation and perception in engineering design faculty. *Journal of Mechanical Design*, *132*(041003), 1–12.

Linton, M. (1975). Memory for real-world events. In D. A. Norman & D. E. Rumelhart (Eds.), *Explorations in cognition* (pp. 376–404). San Francisco, CA: Freeman.

Linton, M. (1986). Ways of searching and the contents of memory. In D. C. Rubin (Ed.), *Autobiographical memory* (pp. 50–67). Cambridge, UK: Cambridge University Press.

Lisker, L. (1975). Is it VOT or a first-formant transition detector? *Journal of the Acoustical Society of America*, *57*, 1547–1551.

Lissauer, H. (1890). Ein fall von Seelenblindheit nebst einem Beitrage zur Theorie derselben. *Arch Psychiat Nervkrankh*, *21*, 222–270.

Livingston, R. B. (1967). Reinforcement. In G. Quarton, T. Melnechuk, & F. Schmitt (Eds.), *The neurosciences: A study program* (pp. 514–576). New York, NY: Rockefeller Press.

Locke, J. (1690). An essay concerning human understanding. In W. Dennis (Ed., 1948). *Readings in the history of psychology. Century psychology series* (pp. 55–68). East Norwalk, CT: Appleton-Century-Crofts.

Loess, H. (1967). Short-term memory, word class, and sequence of items. *Journal of Experimental Psychology*, *74*, 556–561.

Loftus, E. F. (1979). *Eyewitness testimony*. Cambridge, MA: Harvard University Press.

Loftus, E. F., Donders, K., Hoffman, H. G., & Schooler, J. W. (1989). Creating new memories that are quickly assessed and confidently held. *Memory and Cognition*, *17*, 607–616.

Loftus, E. F., Doyle, J. M., & Dysert, J. (2008). *Eyewitness testimony: Civil & Criminal* (4th ed.). Charlottesville, VA: Lexis Law Publishing.

Loftus, E. F., & Hoffman, H. G. (1989). Misinformation and memory: The creation of memory. *Journal of Experimental Psychology: General*, *118*, 100–104.

Loftus, E. F., & Loftus, G. R. (1980). On the permanence of stored information in the human brain. *American Psychologist*, *35*, 409–420.

Loftus, E. F., Miller, D. G., & Burns, H. J. (1978). Semantic integration of verbal information into a visual memory. *Human Learning and Memory*, *4*, 19–31.

Loftus, E. F., & Palmer, J. C. (1974). Reconstruction of automobile destruction: An example of the interaction between language and behavior. *Journal of Verbal and Learning Behavior*, *13*, 585–589.

Loftus, E. F., & Pickrell, J. E. (1995). The formation of false memories. *Psychiatric Annals*, *25*, 720–725.

Logan, G. D. (1988). Toward an instance theory of automatization. *Psychological Review*, *95*, 492–527.

Logan, G. D. (1992). Shapes of reaction time distributions and shapes of learning curves: A test of the instance theory of automaticity. *Journal of Experimental Psychology: Learning, Memory, and Cognition*, *18*, 883–914.

Logan, G. D. (2002). An instance theory of attention and memory. *Psychological Review*, *109*, 376–400.

Logan, G. D., & Etherton, J. L. (1994). What is learned during automatization? The role of attention in constructing an instance. *Journal of Experimental Psychology: Learning, Memory, and Cognition*, *20*, 1022–1050.

Logie, R. H. (1986). Visuo-spatial processing in working memory. *Quarterly Journal of Experimental Psychology*, *38A*, 229–247.

Logie, R. H., Della Sala, S., Wynn, V., & Baddeley, A. D. (2000). Visual similarity effects in immediate serial recall. *Quarterly Journal of Experimental Psychology*, *53A*, 626–646.

Longuet-Higgins, H. C. (1973). Comments on the Lighthill Report and the Sutherland Reply. In *Artificial intelligence: A paper symposium* (pp. 35–37). London: Science Research Council.

Lopez, A., Atran, S., Coley, J. D., Medin, D. L., & Smith, E. E. (1997). The tree of life: Universal and cultural features of folkbiological taxonomies and inductions. *Cognitive Psychology*, *32*, 251–295.

Lorge, I. (1930). Influence of regularly interpolated time intervals upon subsequent learning. *Contributions to Education* (Whole No. 438).

Lowe, D. G. (1985). Further investigation of inhibitory mechanisms in attention. *Memory & Cognition*, *13*, 74–80.

Lowe, G. (1988). State-dependent retrieval effects with social drugs. *British Journal of Addiction*, *83*, 99–103.

Ludwig, A. M. (1995). *The price of greatness: Resolving the creativity and madness controversy*. New York, NY: Guilford Press.

Luger, G. F. (2009). *Artificial intelligence: Structures and strategies for complex problem solving* (6th ed.). Boston, MA: Addison-Wesley.

Lund, K., & Burgess, C. (1996). Producing high-dimensional semantic spaces from lexical co-occurrence. *Behavior Research Methods, Instrumentation, and Computers*, *28*, 203–208.

Lung, C. T., & Dominowski, R. L. (1985). Effects of strategy instructions and practice on nine-dot problem solving. *Journal of Experimental Psychology: Learning, Memory, and Cognition*, *11*, 804–811.

Lupker, S. J. (1988). Picture naming: an investigation of the nature of categorical priming. *Journal of Experimental Psychology: Learning, Memory, and Cognition*, *14*, 444–455.

Luria, A. R. (1968). *Mind of a mnemonist: A little book about a vast memory*. New York, NY: Cape.

Lyon, T. D., & Flavell, J. F. (1993). Young children's understanding of forgetting over time. *Child Development*, *64*, 789–800.

MacArthur, R. H., & Pianka, E. R. (1966). On the optimal use of a patchy environment. *American Naturalist*, *100*, 603–609.

MacGregor, J. N., Ormerod, T. C., & Chronicle, E. P. (2001). Information-processing and insight: A process model of performance on the nine-dot and related problems. *Journal of Experimental Psychology: Learning, Memory and Cognition*, *27*, 176–201.

Mack, A., Pappas, Z., Silverman, M., & Gay, R. (2002). What we see: Inattention and the capture of attention by meaning. *Consciousness and Cognition*, *11*, 488–506.

Mack, A., & Rock, I. (1998). *Inattentional blindness*. Cambridge, MA: MIT Press.

MacKay, D. G. (1970). Spoonerisms: The structure of errors in the serial order of speech. *Neuropsychologia*, *8*, 323–350.

MacKay, D. G. (1979). Lexical insertion, inflection and derivation: Creative processes in word production. *Journal of Psycholinguistic Research*, *8*, 477–498.

MacKay, D. G. (1982). The problem of flexibility, fluency and speed-accuracy trade-off in skilled behavior. *Psychological Review*, *89*(5), 483–506.

MacKay, D. G. (1987). *The organization of perception and action: A theory for language and other cognitive skills*. Berlin, Germany: Springer-Verlag.

MacKay, D. G., & Burke, D. M. (1990). Cognition and aging: A theory of new learning and the use of old connections. In T. Hess (Ed.), *Aging and cognition: Knowledge organization and utilization* (pp. 213–263). Amsterdam, The Netherlands: North Holland.

MacLeod, A., & Summerfield, Q. (1987). Quantifying the contribution of vision to speech perception in noise. *British Journal of Audiology*, *21*, 131–141.

MacLeod, C. M. (1998). Directed forgetting. In J. M. Golding & C. M. MacLeod (Eds.), *Intentional forgetting: Interdisciplinary approaches* (pp. 1–57). Mahwah, NJ: Erlbaum.

MacWhinney, B. (1989). Making words make sense: Commentary on "The mutual exclusivity bias in children's word learning" by W. Merriman and L. Bowman. *Monographs of the Society for Research in Child Development*, *220*, 124–129.

Maier, N. R. F. (1930). Reasoning in humans. I. On direction. *Journal of Comparative Psychology*, *12*, 115–143.

Maier, N. R. F. (1931). Reasoning in humans: II. The solution of a problem and its appearance in consciousness. *Journal of Comparative & Physiological Psychology*, *12*, 181–194.

Malt, B. C. (1994). Water is not H_2O. *Cognitive Psychology*, *27*, 41–70.

Mandler, J. M., & Goodman, M. (1982). On the psychological validity of story structure. *Journal of Verbal Learning and Verbal Behavior*, *21*, 507–523.

Mandler, J. M., & Mandler, G. (1964). *Thinking: From association to Gestalt*. New York, NY: Wiley.

Maravita, A., Spadoni, M., Mazzucchi, A., & Parma, M. (1995). A new case of retrograde amnesia with abnormal forgetting rate. *Cortex*, *31*, 653–667.

Marchman, V. A., & Fernald, A. (2008). Speed of word recognition and vocabulary knowledge in infancy predict cognitive and language outcomes in later childhood. *Developmental Science*, *11*, F9–F16.

Marcus, G. F. (1993). Negative evidence in language acquisition. *Cognition*, *46*, 53–85.

Marcus, G. F. (1995). The acquisition of inflection in children and multilayered connectionist networks. *Cognition*, *56*, 271–279.

Marcus, G. F. (1996). Why do children say "breaked"? *Current Directions in Psychological Science*, *5*, 81–85.

Marcus, G. F. (2000). Pa bi ku and ga ti ga: Two mechanisms children could use to learn about language and the world. *Current Directions in Psychological Science*, *9*, 145–147.

Marcus, G. F., & Berent, I. (2003). Are there limits to statistical learning? *Science*, *300*, 53–55.

Marcus, G. F., Pinker, S., Ullman, M., Hollander, M., Rosen, T. J., & Xu, F. (1992). Overregularization in language acquisition. *Monographs of the Society for Research in Child Development*, *57* (4, Serial No. 228).

Marcus, S., & Rips, L. (1979). Conditional reasoning. *Journal of Verbal Learning and Verbal Behavior*, *18*, 199–223.

Markman, A. B., & Ross, B. (2003). Category use and category learning. *Psychological Bulletin*, *129*, 592–613.

Markman, A. B., & Wisniewski, E. J. (1997). Similar and different: The differentiation of basic level categories. *Journal of Experimental Psychology: Learning, Memory, and Cognition*, *23*(1), 54–70.

Markman, E. M. (1989). *Categorization and naming in children: Problems of induction*. Cambridge, MA: MIT Press.

Markman, E. M. (1990). Constraints children place on word meanings. *Cognitive Science*, *14*, 154–173.

Markman, E. M., & Hutchinson, J. (1984). Children's sensitivity to constraints on word meaning: Taxonomic versus thematic relations. *Cognitive Psychology*, *16*, 1–27.

Markman, E. M., & Wachtel, G. F. (1988). Children's use of mutual exclusivity to constrain the meaning of words. *Cognitive Psychology*, *20*, 121–157.

Markovits, H. (1988). Conditional reasoning, representation and empirical evidence on a concrete task. *Quarterly Journal of Experimental Psychology*, *40A*(3), 483–495.

Markus, G. B. (1986). Stability and change in political attitudes: Observed, recalled, and "explained." *Political Behavior*, *8*(1), 21–44.

Marr, D. (1982). *Vision*. San Francisco, CA: W. H. Freeman.

Marr, D., & Nishihara, H. K. (1978). Representation and recognition of the spatial organization of three-dimensional shapes. *Proceedings of the Royal Society of London, Series B*, *200*, 269–294.

Marschark, M., & Hunt, R. R. (1989). A reexamination of the role of imagery in learning and memory. *Journal of Experimental Psychology: Learning, Memory, and Cognition*, *15*(4), 710–720.

Marshall, J. C., & Halligan, P. W. (1988). Blindsight and insight in visuo-spatial neglect. *Nature*, *336*(6201), 766–767.

Marslen-Wilson, W., & Teuber, H.-L. (1975). Memory for remote events in retrograde amnesia: Recognition of public figures from newsphotographs. *Neuropsychologia*, *13*, 353–364.

Martin, C. B., & Deutscher, M. (1966). Remembering. *Philosophical Review*, *75*, 161–196.

Martin, K. M., & Aggleton, J. P. (1993). Contextual effects on the ability of divers to use decompression tables. *Applied Cognitive Psychology*, *7*, 311–316.

Martin, N., Weisberg, R. W., & Saffran, E. M. (1989). Variables influencing the occurrence of naming errors: Implications for models of lexical retrieval. *Journal of Memory and Language*, *28*, 462–485.

Martín, P., Serrano, J. M., & Iglesias, J. (1999). Phonological/semantic errors in two Spanish-speaking patients with anomic aphasia. *Aphasiology*, *13*, 225–236.

Maschke, M., Gomez, C. M., Tuite, P. J., & Konczak, J. (2003). Dysfunction of the basal ganglia, but not of the cerebellum, impairs kinaesthesia. *Brain*, *126*, 2312–2322.

Maserejian, N. N., Lutfey, K. E., & McKinlay, J. B. (2009). Do physicians attend to base rates? Prevalence data and statistical discrimination in the diagnosis of coronary heart disease. *Health Services Research*, *44*(6), 1933–1949.

Mast, F. W., & Kosslyn, S. M. (2002). Visual mental images can be ambiguous: Insights from individual differences in spatial transformation abilities. *Cognition*, *86*, 57–70.

Matsen, E., & Strøm, B. (2010). Dominated choices in a simple game with large stakes. *Experimental Economics*, *13*(1), 99–119.

Matsumura, N., Nishijo, H., Tamura, R., Eifuku, S., Endo, S., & Ono, T. (1999). Spatial- and task-dependent neuronal responses during real and virtual translocation in the monkey hippocampal formation. *Journal of Neuroscience*, *19*, 2381–2393.

Mauner, G., Fromkin, V. A., & Cornell, T. L. (1993). Comprehension and acceptability judgments in agrammatism: Disruptions in the syntax of referential dependency and the two-chain hypothesis. *Brain and Language*, *45*, 340–370.

May, C. P., Kane, M. J., & Hasher, L. (1995). Determinants of negative priming. *Psychological Bulletin*, *118*, 35–54.

McAuliffe, J., & Pratt, J. (2005). The role of temporal and spatial factors in covert orienting of visual attention tasks. *Psychological Research*, *69*, 285–291.

McCarthy, R., & Warrington, E. (1988). Evidence for modality-specific meaning systems in the brain. *Nature*, *334*(4), 428–430.

McCarthy, R. A., & Warrington, E. K. (1990). *Cognitive neuropsychology: A clinical introduction*. San Diego, CA: Academic Press.

McClelland, J. L., Botvinick, M. M., Noelle, D. C., Plaut, D. C., Rogers, T. T., Seidenberg, M. S., & Smith, L. B. (2010). Letting structure emerge: Connectionist and dynamical systems approaches to understanding cognition. *Trends in Cognitive Sciences*, *14*, 348–356.

McClelland, J. L., & Rumelhart, D. E. (1981). An interactive activation model of context effects in letter perception: Part 1. An account of Basic Findings. *Psychological Review*, *88*, 375–407.

McClelland, J. L., Rumelhart, D. E., and the PDP Research Group. (1986). *Parallel distributed processing: Explorations in the microstructure of cognition* (Vol. I). Cambridge, MA: MIT Press.

McCloskey, M. (1991). Networks and theories: The place of connectionism in cognitive science. *Psychological Science*, *2*, 387–395.

McCloskey, M. (1992). Cognitive mechanisms in numerical processing: Evidence from acquired dyscalculia. *Cognition*, *44*, 107–157.

McCloskey, M., Aliminosa, D., & Sokol, S. (1991). Facts, rules, and procedures in normal calculation: Evidence from multiple single-patient studies of impaired arithmetic fact retrieval. *Brain and Cognition*, *17*, 154–203.

McCloskey, M., Wible, C. G., & Cohen, N. J. (1988). Is there a special flashbulb memory mechanism? *Journal of Experimental Psychology: General*, *117*, 171–181.

McCloskey, M., & Zaragoza, M. (1985). Misleading postevent information and memory for events: Arguments and evidence against memory impairment hypotheses. *Journal of Experimental Psychology: General*, *114*, 3–18.

McConnell, J., & Quinn, J. G. (2000). Interference in visual working memory. *Quarterly Journal of Experimental Psychology: Human Experimental Psychology*, *53*, 53–67.

McDaniel, M. A., & Einstein, G. O. (1986). Bizarre imagery as an effective memory aid: The importance of distinctiveness. *Journal of Experimental Psychology: Learning, Memory, and Cognition*, *12*(1), 54–65.

McDaniel, M. A., Einstein, G. O., DeLosh, E. L., May, C. P., & Brady, P. (1995). The bizarreness effect: It's not surprising, it's complex. *Journal of Experimental Psychology: Learning, Memory, and Cognition*, *21*(2), 422–435.

McGeoch, J. A. (1931). Forgetting and the law of disuse. *Psychological Review*, *39*, 352–370.

McGlinchey-Berroth, R., Milberg, W. P., Verfaellie, M., Alexander, M., & Kilduff, P. T. (1993). Semantic processing in the neglected visual field: Evidence from a lexical decision task. *Cognitive Neuropsychology*, *10*, 79–108.

McGurk, H., & MacDonald J. (1976). Hearing lips and seeing voices. *Nature*, *264*, 746–748.

Medin, D. L., Goldstone, R. L., & Gentner, D. (1993). Respects for similarity. *Psychological Review*, *100* (2), 254–278.

Medin, D. L., Lynch, E. B., Coley, J. D., & Atran, S. (1997). Categorization and reasoning among tree experts: Do all roads lead to Rome? *Cognitive Psychology*, *32*, 49–96.

Medin, D. L., & Ortony, A. (1989). Psychological essentialism. In S. Vosniadou & A. Ortony (Eds.), *Similarity and analogical reasoning* (pp. 179–195). New York, NY: Cambridge University Press.

Medin, D. L., & Schaffer, M. M. (1978). Context theory of classification learning. *Psychological Review*, *85*, 207–238.

Meijer, P. J. A. (1997). What speech errors can tell us about word-form generation: The roles of constraint and opportunity. *Journal of Psycholinguistic Research*, *26*, 141–158.

Menzel, R., Geiger, K., Müller, U., Joerges, J., & Chittka, L. (1998). Bees travel novel homeward routes by integrating separately acquired vector memories. *Animal Behavior*, *55*, 139–152.

Meringer, R., & Mayer, C. (1895). *Versprechen und Verlesen: Eine psychologisch-linguistiche Studie*. Stuttgart, German: G. J. Göschen.

Mesulam, M. M. (1985). *Principles of behavioral neurology*. Philadelphia, PA: Davis.

Metcalfe, J. (1986). Premonitions of insight predict impending error. *Journal of Experimental Psychology: Learning, Memory, and Cognition*, *12* (4), 623–634.

Metcalfe, J. (1987). Premonitions of insight predict impending error. *Journal of Experimental Psychology: Learning, Memory, and Cognition*, *12*, 623–634.

Metcalfe, J. (2009). Metacognitive judgments and control of study. *Current Directions in Psychological Science*, *18*, 159–163.

Metcalfe, J., & Finn, B. (2008). Familiarity and retrieval processes in delayed judgments of learning. *Journal of Experimental Psychology: Learning, Memory, and Cognition*, *34*, 1084–1097.

Metcalfe, J., & Wiebe, D. (1987). Intuition in insight and non-insight problem solving. *Memory & Cognition*, *15*, 238–246.

Meyer, A. S., & Bock, K. (1992). The tip-of-the-tongue phenomenon: Blocking or partial activation? *Memory & Cognition*, *20*, 715–726.

Meyer, D. E., & Schvaneveldt, R. W. (1971). Facilitation in recognizing pairs of words: Evidence of a dependence between retrieval operations. *Journal of Experimental Psychology*, *90* (2), 227–234.

Miall, R. C., Gowen E., & Tchalenko, J. (2009). Drawing cartoon faces—a functional imaging study of the cognitive neuroscience of drawing. *Cortex*, *45* (3), 394–406.

Miceli, G. (1994). Morphological errors and the representation of morphology in the lexical-semantic system. *Philosophical Transactions of the Royal Society of London, B*, *346*, 79–87.

Miceli, G., Mazzucchi, A., Menn, L., & Goodglass, H. (1983). Contrasting cases of Italian agrammatic aphasia without comprehension disorder. *Brain and Language*, *19*, 65–97.

Milberg, W. P., Blumstein, S. E., & Dworetzky, B. (1988). Phonological processing and lexical access in aphasia. *Brain and Language*, *34* (2), 279–293.

Milich, R., & Pelham, W. E. (1986). Effects of sugar ingestion on the classroom and playgroup behavior of attention deficit disordered boys. *Journal of Consulting and Clinical Psychology*. *54*, 714–718.

Mill, J. (1829). *Analysis of the phenomenon of the human mind* (Vol. 1 & 2). Cambridge, MA: Baldwin & Craddock.

Mill, J. S. (1843). *A system of logic: Ratiocinative and inductive*. New York: Harper and Brothers.

Miller, A. I. (1996). *Insights of genius: Imagery and creativity in science and art*. New York, NY: Springer-Verlag.

Miller, G. A. (1956). The magical number seven, plus or minus two: Some limits on our capacity for processing information. *Psychological Review*, *63*, 81–97.

Miller, G. A., & Chomsky, N. (1963). Finitary models of language users. In D. R. Luce, R. R. Bush, & E. Galanter (Eds.), *Handbook of mathematical psychology* (Vol. 2, pp. 419–491). New York, NY: Wiley.

Miller, G. A., Galanter, E., & Pribram, K. H. (1960). *Plans and the structure of behavior*. New York, NY: Holt, Rinehart & Winston.

Miller, K. D., & MacKay, D. J. C. (1994). The role of constraints in Hebbian learning. *Neural Computation*, *6*, 100–126.

Miller, W., & Ervin, S. (1964). The development of grammar in child language. In U. Bellugi & R. Brown (Eds.), *The acquisition of language. Monographs of the Society for Research in Child Development* (pp. 9–34). Lafayette, IN: Child Development Publications of the Society for Research in Child Development.

Milner, A. D., & Goodale, M. A. (1995). *The visual brain in action*. New York, NY: Oxford University Press.

Milner, A. D., & Goodale, M. A. (2006). *The visual brain in action* (2nd ed. with new epilogue). Oxford: Oxford University Press.

Milner, A. D., & Goodale, M. A. (2008). Two visual systems reviewed. *Neuropsychologia*, *46*, 774–785.

Milner, A. D., Perrett, D. I., Johnston, R. S., Benson, P. J., Jordan, T. R., Heeley, D. W.,...Davidson, D. L. W. (1991). Perception and action in visual form agnosia. *Brain*, *114*, 405–428.

Milner, B. (1962). Les troubles de la memoire accompagnent des lesion hippocampiques bilaterales. [Disturbance of memory accompanying bilateral hippocampal lesions.] In P. Passouant (Ed.), *Physiologie de l'hippocampe* (pp. 247–272). Paris, France: Centre Nationale de La Recherche Scientifique.

Milner, B., Corkin, S., & Teuber, H. L. (1968). Further analysis of the hippocampal amnesic syndrome: Fourteen year follow-up study of H.M. *Neuropsychologia*, *6*, 215–234.

Miozzo, M., & Caramazza, A. (1997). Retrieval of lexical-syntactic features in tip-of-the tongue states. *Journal of Experimental Psychology: Learning, Memory, and Cognition*, *23*(6), 1410–1423.

Mishkin, M., Ungerleider, L. G., & Macko, K. A. (1983). Object vision and spatial vision: Two cortical pathways. *Trends in Neurosciences*, *6*, 414–417.

Mitchell, P. J., & Redman, J. R. (1992). Effects of caffeine, time of day and user history on study-related performance. *Psychopharmacology*, *109*, 121–126.

Moely, E., Olson, F. A., Hawles, T. G., & Flavell, J. H. (1969). Production deficiency in young children's clustered recall. *Developmental Psychology*, *1*, 26–34.

Moen, I. (2000). Foreign accent syndrome: A review of contemporary explanations. *Aphasiology*, *14*(1), 5–15.

Monrad-Krohn, G. H. (1947). Dysprosody or altered 'melody of language'. *Brain*, *70*, 405–415.

Monsell, S. (1985). Repetition and the lexicon. In A. W. Ellis (Ed.), *Progress in the psychology of language* (Vol. 2, pp. 147–195). London, UK: Erlbaum.

Moore, B. A., & Krakow, B. (2007). Imagery rehearsal therapy for acute posttraumatic nightmares among combat soldiers in Iraq. [Research Letter] *American Journal of Psychiatry*, *164*(4), 683–684.

Moore, C. J., & Price, C. J. (1999). Three distinct ventral occipitotemporal regions for reading and object naming. *Neuroimage*, *10*(2), 181–192.

Moore, D. G., Burland, K., & Davidson, J. W. (2003). The social context of musical success: A development account. *British Journal of Psychology*, *94*(4), 529–549.

Moray, N. (1959). Attention in dichotic listening: Affective cues and the influence of instructions. *Quarterly Journal of Experimental Psychology*, *11*, 55–60.

Moray, N., Bates, A., & Barnett, I. (1965). Experiments on the four-eared man. *Journal of the Acoustical Society of America*, *38*, 196–201.

Morris, C. D., Bransford, J. D., & Franks, J. J. (1977). Levels of processing versus transfer appropriate processing. *Journal of Verbal Learning & Verbal Behavior*, *16*, 519–533.

Morris, R. (1984). Developments of a water-maze procedure for studying spatial learning in the rat. *Journal of Neuroscience Methods*, *11*, 47–60.

Moscovitch, M., Winocur, G., & Behrmann, M. (1997). What is special about face recognition? Nineteen experiments on a person with visual object agnosia and dyslexia but normal face recognition. *Journal of Cognitive Neuroscience*, *9*, 555–604.

Moss, H. E., & Tyler, L. K. (2000). A progressive category-specific semantic deficit for non-living things. *Neuropsychologia*, *38*, 60–82.

Motley, M. T. (1985). Slips of the tongue. *Scientific American*, *253*, 116–127.

Motley, M. T., & Baars, B. J. (1976). Laboratory induction of verbal slips: A new method for psycholinguistic research. *Communication Quarterly*, *24*, 28–34.

Motley, M. T., Camden, C. T., & Baars, B. J. (1983). Polysemantic lexical access: Evidence from laboratory induced double entendres. *Communication Monographs*, *50*, 193–205.

Mottaghy, F. M., Shah, N. J., Krause, B. J., Schmidt, D., Halsband, U., Jancke, L., & Muller-Gartner, H. W. (1999). Neuronal correlates of encoding and retrieval in episodic memory during a paired-word association learning task: A functional magnetic resonance imaging study. *Experimental Brain Research*, *128*, 332–342.

Müller, G. E. (1911). Analyse der Gedächtnistätigkeit und des Vorstellungsverlaufes. Vol. 1. *Zeitschrift fur Psychologic*, Supplement no. 5.

Müller, G. E., & Pilzecker, A. (1900). Experimentelle Beiträge zur Lehre vom Gedächtniss. *Zeitschrift für Psychologie. Ergänzungsband 1*, 1–300.

Müller, M., & Wehner, R. (1988). Path integration in desert ants, *Cataglyphis fortis*. *Proceedings of the National Academy of Sciences, USA*, *85*, 5287–5290.

Murphy, G. L., & Medin, D. L. (1985). The role of theories in conceptual coherence. *Psychological Review*, *92*(3), 289–316.

Murphy, G. L., & Ross, B. H. (2007). Use of single or multiple categories in category-based induction. In A. Feeney & E. Heit (Eds.), *Inductive reasoning. Experimental, developmental, and computational approaches* (pp. 205–225). Cambridge, UK: Cambridge University Press.

Murphy, G. L., & Shapiro, A. M. (1994). Forgetting of verbatim information in discourse. *Memory & Cognition*, *22*(1), 85–94.

Murrell, G. A., & Morton, J. (1974). Word recognition and morphemic structure. *Journal of Experimental Psychology*, *102*, 963–968.

Mynatt, C. R., Doherty, M. E., & Tweney, R. D. (1977). Confirmation bias in a simulated research environment: An experimental study of scientific inference. *The Quarterly Journal of Experimental Psychology*, *29*(1), 85–95.

Nachson, I., & Zelig, A. (2003). Flashbulb and factual memories: The case of Rabin's assassination. *Applied Cognitive Psychology*, *17*, 519–531.

Nagy, W., & Gentner, D. (1990). Semantic constraints on lexical categories. *Language and Cognitive Processes*, *5*, 169–201.

Nakamura, T., Wright, A. A., Katz, J. S., Bodily, K. D., & Sturz, B. R. (2009). Abstract-concept learning carryover effects from the initial training set. *Journal of Comparative Psychology*, *123*, 79–89.

Naveh-Benjamin, M. (1988). Recognition of spatial location information: Another failure to support automaticity. *Memory and Cognition*, *16*, 437–445.

Navon, D. (1977). Forest before trees: The precedence of global features in visual perception. *Cognitive Psychology*, *9*, 353–383.

Nederhouser, M., Yue, X., Mangini, M. C., & Biederman, I. (2007). The deleterious effect of contrast reversal on recognition is unique to faces, not objects. *Vision Research*, *47*, 2134–2142.

Nee, D. E., Berman, M. G., Moore, K. S., & Jonides, J. (2008). Neuroscientific evidence about the distinction between short- and long-term memory. *Current Directions in Psychological Science*, *17*, 102–106.

Neill, W. T., & Westberry, R. L. (1987). Selective attention and the suppression of cognitive noise. *Journal of Experimental Psychology: Learning, Memory, and Cognition*, *13*, 327–334.

Neisser, U. (1963). Decision time without reaction time: Experiments in visual scanning. *American Journal of Psychology*, *36*, 376–385.

Neisser, U. (1967). *Cognitive psychology*. Englewood Cliffs, NJ: Prentice-Hall.

Neisser, U. (1976). *Cognition and reality: Principles and implications of cognitive psychology*. San Francisco, CA: Freeman.

Neisser, U. (1982). Snapshots or benchmarks? In U. Neisser (Ed.), *Memory observed: Remembering in natural contexts* (pp. 43–48). San Francisco, CA: Freeman.

Neisser, U., & Becklen, R. (1975). Selective looking: Attending to visually specified events. *Cognitive Psychology*, *7*, 480–494.

Nelson, K. (1988). Constraints on word learning? *Cognitive Development*, *3*, 221–246.

Nespoulous, J.-L., Dordain, M., Perron, C., Ska, B., Bub, D., Caplan, D., . . . Lecours, A.-R. (1988). Agrammatism in sentence production without comprehension deficits: Reduced availability of syntactic structures and/or of grammatical morphemes? A case study. *Brain and Language*, *33*, 273–295.

Newell, A. J., Shaw, C., & Simon, H. A. (1958). Chess-playing programs and the problem of complexity. *IBM Journal of Research and Development*, *2*, 320–325.

Newell, A. J., Shaw, C., & Simon, H. A. (1962). The processes of creative thinking. In H. E. Gruber, G. Terrell, & M. Wertheimer (Eds.), *Contemporary approaches to creative thinking* (pp. 153–189). New York, NY: Pergamon.

Newell, A. J., & Simon, H. A. (1972). *Human problem solving*. Englewood Cliffs, NJ: Prentice-Hall.

Newman, E. L., Caplan, J. B., Kirschen, M. P., Korolev, I. O., Sekuler, R., & Kahana, M. J. (2007). Learning your way around town: How virtual taxicab drivers learn to use both layout and land-mark information. *Cognition*, *104*, 231–253.

Nickerson, R. S. (1998). Confirmation bias: A ubiquitous phenomenon in many guises. *Review of General Psychology*, *2*(2), 175–220.

Nigro, G., & Neisser, U. (1983). Point of view in personal memories. *Cognitive Psychology*, *15*, 467–482.

Nilsson, H., & Andersson, P. (2010). Making the seemingly impossible appear possible: Effects of conjunction fallacies in evaluations of bets on football games. *Journal of Economic Psychology*, *3*, 172–180.

Nilsson, L.-G., & Bäckman, L. (1991). Encoding dimensions of subject-performed tasks. *Psychological Research*, *53*, 212–218.

Nisbett, R. E., Fong, G. T., Lehman, D. R., & Cheng, P. W. (1987). Teaching reasoning. *Science*, *238*, 625–631.

Nisbett, R., & Wilson, T. (1977). Telling more than we can know: Verbal reports on mental processes. *Psychological Review*, *84*, 231–259.

Noble, C. E. (1961). Measurements of association value (a), rated associations (a1), and scaled meaningfulness (m1) for the 2100 CVC combinations of the English alphabet. *Psychological Reports*, *8*, 487–521.

Nooteboom, S. G. (2005). Lexical bias revisited: Detecting, rejecting and repairing speech errors in inner speech. *Speech Communication*, *47*, 43–58.

Norman, D. (1968). Toward a theory of memory and attention. *Psychological Review*, *75*, 522–536.

Norrick, N. R. (2009). Interjections as pragmatic markers. *Journal of Pragmatics*, *41*, 866–891.

Norton, A., Winner, E., Cronin, K., Overy, K., Lee, D. J., & Schlaug, G. (2005). Are there pre-existing neural, cognitive, or motoric markers for musical ability? *Brain and Cognition*, *59(2)*, 124–134.

Nosofsky, R. M., Gluck, M., Palmeri, T. J., McKinley, S. C., & Glauthier, P. (1994). Comparing models of rule-based classification learning: A replication and extension of Shepard, Hovland, and Jenkins (1961). *Memory & Cognition*, *22*, 352–369.

Nosofsky, R. M., & Palmeri, T. J. (1997). An exemplar-based random walk model of speeded classification. *Psychological Review*, *104*, 266–300.

Nosofsky, R. M., & Zaki, S. R. (1998). Dissociations between categorization and recognition in amnesic and normal individuals: An exemplar-based interpretation. *Psychological Science*, *9*, 247–255.

Noveck, I. A., & O'Brien, D. P. (1996). To what extent do pragmatic reasoning schemas affect performance on Wason's selection task? *Quarterly Journal of Experimental Psychology*, *49A (2)*, 463–489.

Novick, L. R., & Bassok, M. (2005). Problem solving. In K. J. Holyoak & R. G. Morrison (Eds.), *Cambridge handbook of thinking and reasoning* (pp. 321–349). New York, NY: Cambridge University Press.

Novick, L. R., & Sherman, S. J. (2003). On the nature of insight solutions: Evidence from skill differences in anagram solution. *The Quarterly Journal of Experimental Psychology*, *56A*, 351–382.

Nozari, N., & Dell, G. S. (2009). More on lexical bias: How efficient can a "lexical editor" be? *Journal of Memory and Language*, *60*, 291–307.

Nyberg, L., Cabeza, R., & Tulving, E. (1996). PET studies of encoding and retrieval: The HERA Model. *Psychonomic Bulletin & Review*, *3*, 134–147.

Nyberg, L., McIntosh, A. R., Cabeza, R., Habib, R., Houle, S., & Tulving, E. (1996). General and specific brain regions involved in encoding and retrieval of events: What, where, and when. *Proceedings of the National Academy of Sciences, USA*, *93*, 11280–11285.

Oberauer, K. (2006). Reasoning with conditionals: A test of formal models of four theories. *Cognitive Psychology*, *53*, 238–283.

O'Brien, D. (2009). Human reasoning requires a mental logic. *Behavioral and Brain Sciences*, *32*, 96–97.

O'Craven, K., & Kanwisher, N. (2000). Mental imagery of faces and places activates corresponding stimulus-specific brain regions. *Journal of Cognitive Neuroscience*, *12*, 1013–1023.

O'Grady, W. (2005). *Syntactic carpentry: An emergentist approach to syntax*. Mahwah, NJ: Erlbaum.

Ohlsson, S. (1984a). Restructuring revisited. I. Summary and critique of the Gestalt theory of problem solving. *Scandinavian Journal of Psychology*, *25*, 65–78.

Ohlsson, S. (1984b). Restructuring revisited. II. An information processing theory of restructuring and insight. *Scandinavian Journal of Psychology*, *25*, 117–129.

Ohlsson, S. (1992). Information-processing explanations of insight and related phenomena. In M. T. Keane & K. J. Gilhooly (Eds.), *Advances in the psychology of thinking* (Vol. 1, pp. 1–44). New York, NY: Harvester Wheatsheaf.

Ohlsson, S. (2011). *Deep learning: How the mind overrides experience*. Cambridge, MA: MIT Press.

Oien, K. M., & Goernert, P. N. (2003). The role of intentional forgetting in employee selection. *Journal of General Psychology*, *130*, 97–110.

Ojemann, J. G., Ojemann, G. A., & Lettich, E. (1992). Neuronal activity related to faces and matching in human right nondominant temporal cortex. *Brain*, *115*, 1–13.

O'Keefe, J., & Dostrovsky, J. (1971). The hippocampus as a spatial map: Preliminary evidence from unit activity in the freely moving rat. *Brain Research*, *31*, 573–590.

Olby, R. (1994). *The path to the double helix. The discovery of DNA*. New York, NY: Dover.

Öllinger, M., Jones, G., & Knoblich, G. (2006). Heuristics and representational change in two-move matchstick arithmetic tasks. *Advances in Cognitive Psychology*, *2*, 239–253.

Olshtain, E., & Barzilay, M. (1991). Lexical retrieval difficulties in adult language attrition. In H. Seliger & R. Vago (Eds.), *First language attrition* (pp. 139–150). Cambridge, UK: Cambridge University Press.

Olton, D. S., & Samuelson, R. J. (1976). Remembrance of places past: Spatial memory in rats. *Animal Behaviour Processes*, *2*, 97–116.

Onifer, W., & Swinney, D. (1981). Accessing lexical ambiguities during sentence comprehension: Effects of frequency-of-meaning and contextual bias. *Memory and Cognition*, *9*(3), 225–236.

Ophir, E., Nass, C. I., & Wagner, A. D. (2009). Cognitive control in media multitaskers. *Proceedings of the National Academy of Sciences, USA*, *106*, 15583–15587.

O'Regan, J. K., & Noë, A. (2001a). A sensorimotor account of vision and visual consciousness. *Behavioral and Brain Sciences*, *24*, 939–1031.

O'Regan, J. K., & Noë, A. (2001b). What it is like to see: A sensorimotor theory of visual experience. *Synthèse*, *129*, 79–103.

Ornstein, P. A., Naus, M. J., & Liberty, C. (1975). Rehearsal and organizational processes in children's memory. *Child Development*, *46*, 818–830.

Osgood, C. E., & Hoosain, R. (1974). Salience of the word as a unit in the perception of language. *Perception and Psychophysics*, *15*, 168–192.

Ost, J., & Costall, A. (2002). Misremembering Bartlett: A study in serial reproduction. *British Journal of Psychology*, *93*, 243–255.

Owen, A. M., Doyon, J., Petrides, M., & Evans, A. C. (1995). Planning and spatial working memory: A positron emission tomography study in humans. *European Journal of Neuroscience*, *8*, 353–364.

Paap, K. R., McDonald, J. E., Schvaneveldt, R. W., & Noel, R. W. (1987). Frequency and pronounceability in visually presented naming and lexical-decision tasks. In M. Coltheart (Ed.), *Attention and performance XII* (pp. 221–243). Hillsdale, NJ: Erlbaum.

Paivio, A. (1963). Learning of adjective-noun paired associates as a function of adjective-noun word order and noun abstractness. *Canadian Journal of Psychology*, *17*, 370–379.

Paivio, A. (1965). Abstractness, imagery, and meaningfulness in paired-associate learning. *Journal of Verbal Learning and Verbal Behavior*, *4*, 32–38.

Paivio, A. (1971). *Imagery and verbal processes*. New York, NY: Holt, Rinehart, and Winston.

Paivio, A. (1975). Perceptual comparisons through the mind's eye. *Memory & Cognition*, *3*, 635–647.

Paivio, A. (1991). *Images in mind: The evolution of a theory*. Sussex, UK: Harvester Wheatsheaf.

Paivio, A. (2006). *Mind and its evolution: A dual coding theoretical approach*. Mahwah, NJ: Erlbaum.

Paivio, A., Yuille, J. C., & Madigan, S. A. (1968). Concreteness, imagery, and meaningfulness values for 925 nouns. *Journal of Experimental Psychology*, *76*, 1–25.

Papagno, C., Valentine, T., & Baddeley, A. D. (1991). Phonological short-term memory and foreign-language vocabulary learning. *Journal of Memory and Language*, *30*, 331–347.

Pariser, D. (1987). The juvenile drawings of Klee, Toulouse-Lautrec, and Picasso. *Visual Arts Research*, *13*, 53–67.

Pascual-Leone, A. (2003). The brain that plays music and is changed by it. In I. Peretz & R. Zatorre (Eds.), *The cognitive neuroscience of music* (pp. 396–412). Oxford, UK: Oxford University Press.

Pashler, H., & Johnston, J. C. (1998). Attentional limitations in dual-task performance. In H. Pashler (Ed.), *Attention* (pp. 155–189). Hove, UK: Erlbaum.

Pashler, H., Johnston, J. C., & Ruthruff, E. (2001). Attention and performance. *Annual Review of Psychology*, *52*, 629–651.

Pashler, H., & Shiu, L. P. (1999). Do images involuntarily trigger search? A test of Pillsbury's hypothesis. *Psychonomic Bulletin & Review*, *6*, 445–448.

Patel, V. L., & Groen, G. J. (1991). The general and specific nature of medical expertise: A critical look. In K. A. Ericsson & J. Smith (Eds.), *Toward a general theory of expertise: Prospects and limits* (pp. 93–125). New York, NY: Cambridge University Press.

Patten, B. M. (1972). The ancient art of memory: Usefulness in treatment. *Archives of Neurology*, *26*, 26–31.

Paul, S. T., Kellas, G., Martin, M., & Clark, M. B. (1992). The influence of contextual features on the activation of ambiguous word meanings. *Journal of Experimental Psychology: Learning, Memory, and Cognition*, *18*, 703–717.

Paulesu, E., Frith, C. D., & Frackowiak, R. S. J. (1993). The neural correlates of the verbal component of working memory. *Nature*, *362*, 342–345.

Pavese, A., Coslett, H. B., Saffran, E. M., & Buxbaum, L. J. (2002). Limitations of attentional orienting: Effects of abrupt visual onsets and offsets on naming two objects in a patient with bilateral posterior lesions. *Neuropsychologia*, *40*, 1097–1103.

Pendergrast, M. (1996). *Victims of memory: Sex abuse accusations and shattered lives* (2nd ed.). Hinesburg, VT: Upper Access.

Penfield, W., & Perot, P. (1963). The brain's record of auditory and visual experience. A final summary and discussion. *Brain*, *86*, 595–696.

Penner, S. (1987). Parental responses to grammatical and ungrammatical child utterances. *Child Development*, *58*, 376–384.

Perenin, M., & Vighetto, A. (1988). Optic ataxia: A specific disruption in visuomotor mechanisms. *Brain*, *111*(3), 643–674.

Perfetto, G. A., Bransford, J. D., & Franks, J. J. (1983). Constraints on access in a problem solving context. *Memory and Cognition*, *11*, 24–31.

Perkins, D. N. (1981). *The mind's best work*. Cambridge, MA: Harvard University Press.

Perkins, D. N. (1985). Postprimary education has little impact on informal reasoning. *Journal of Educational Psychology*, *77*, 562–571.

Perkins, D. N. (2000). *The eureka effect: The art and logic of breakthrough thinking*. New York, NY: Norton.

Perky, C. (1910). An experimental study of imagination. *American Journal of Psychology*, *21*, 422–452.

Péruch, P., Chabanne, V., Nesa, M.-P., Thinus-Blanc, C., & Denis, M. (2006a). Comparing distances in mental images constructed from visual experience or verbal descriptions: The impact of survey versus route perspective. *Quarterly Journal of Experimental Psychology*, *59*, 1950–1967.

Péruch, P., Chabanne, V., Nesa, M.-P., Thinus-Blanc, C., & Denis, M. (2006b). Comparing distances in mental images constructed from visual experience or verbal descriptions: A study of individual differences in the mental comparison of distances. *Acta Psychologica*, *127*.

Pessoa, L., Gutierrez, E., Bandettini, P. A., & Ungerleider, L. G. (2002). Neural correlates of visual working memory: fMRI amplitude predicts task performance. *Neuron*, *35* 975–987.

Petersen, S. E., Fox, P. T., Posner, M. I., Mintun, M., & Raichle, M. E. (1988). Positron emission tomographic studies of the cortical anatomy of single-word processing. *Nature*, *331*, 585–589.

Peterson, L. R., & Peterson, M. J. (1959). Short-term retention of individual verbal items. *Journal of Experimental Psychology*, *58*, 193–198.

Peterson, L. R., Wampler, R., Kirkpatrick, M., & Saltzman, D. (1963). Effect of spacing presentations on retention of a paired associate over short intervals. *Journal of Experimental Psychology*, *66*, 206–209.

Petrides, M. (2000). Dissociable roles of mid-dorsolateral prefrontal and anterior inferotemporal cortex in visual working memory. *The Journal of Neuroscience*, *20*(19), 7496–7503.

Petrides, M., Alivisatos, B., Meyer, E., & Evans, A. C. (1993). Functional activation of the human frontal cortex during the performance of verbal working memory tasks. *Proceedings of the National Academy of Sciences, USA*, *90*, 878–882.

Petroski, H. (1992). *To engineer is human: The role of failure in successful design*. New York, NY: Vintage Books.

Pezdek, K. (2001). A cognitive analysis of the recovered memory/false memory debate. *Journal of Aggression, Maltreatment, and Trauma*, *4*, 73–85.

Pezdek, K. (2003). Event memory and autobiographical memory for the events of September 11, 2001. *Applied Cognitive Psychology*, *17*, 1033–1045.

Pezdek, K., Finger, K., & Hodge, D. (1997). Planting false childhood memories: The role of event plausibility. *Psychological Science*, *8*, 437–441.

Pezdek, K., & Lam, S. (2007). What research paradigms have cognitive psychologists used to study "false memory," and what are the implications of these choices? *Consciousness and Cognition*, *16*, 2–17.

Pezdek, K., Maki, R., Valencia-Laver, D., Whetstone, T., Stoeckert, J., & Dougherty, T. (1988). Picture memory: Recognizing added and deleted details. *Journal of Experimental Psychology: Learning, Memory and Cognition*, *14*, 468–476.

Pezdek, K., & Roe, C. (1996). Memory for childhood events: How suggestible is it?

Pezdek, K., & Roe, C. (1997). The suggestibility of children's memory for being touched: Planting, erasing, and changing memories. *Law and Human Behavior*, *21*, 95–106.

Phillips, W. A. (1974). On the distinction between sensory storage and short-term visual memory. *Perception & Psychophysics*, *16*, 283–290.

Piazza, M. (2010). Neurocognitive start-up tools for symbolic number representations. *Trends in Cognitive Science*, *14*(12), 542–551.

Piazza, M., Facoetti, A., Trussardi, A. N., Berteletti, I., Conte, S., Lucangeli, D., Dehaene, S., & Zorzi, M. (2010). Developmental trajectory of number acuity reveals a severe impairment in developmental dyscalculia. *Cognition*, *116*(1), 33–41.

Pickering, M. J., & Frisson, S. (2001). The semantic processing of verbs: Evidence from eye movements. *Journal of Experimental Psychology: Learning, Memory, and Cognition*, *27*, 556–573.

Pickering, M. J., & Garrod, S. (2004). Toward a mechanistic psychology of dialogue. *Behavioral and Brain Sciences*, *27*(2), 169–226.

Pickering, M. J., & Garrod, S. (2007). Do people use language production to make predictions during comprehension? *Trends in Cognitive Sciences*, *11*(3), 105–110.

Pietrini, V., Nertempi, P., Vaglia, A., Revello, M. G., Pinna, V., & Ferro-Milone, F. (1988). Recovery from herpes simplex encephalitis: Selective impairment of specific semantic categories with neuroradiological correlation. *Journal of Neurology, Neurosurgery & Psychiatry*, *51*, 1284–1293.

Pillsbury, W. B. (1908). *Attention*. London, UK: Sonnenschein.

Pillsbury, W. B. (1911). *The Essentials of psychology*. London, UK: Macmillan.

Pinker, S. (1991). Rules of language. *Science*, *253*, 530–535.

Pinker, S. (1994). *The language instinct: How the mind creates language*. New York, NY: Harper Collins.

Pinker, S. (1999). *Words and rules*. New York: Harper Perennial.

Pinker, S. (2004). Clarifying the logical problem of language acquisition. *Journal of Child Language*, *31*, 949–953.

Pinker, S., & Prince, A. (1988). On language and connectionism: Analysis of a parallel distributed processing model of language acquisition. *Cognition*, *28*, 73–193.

Plous, S. (1993). *The psychology of judgment and decision making*. New York, NY: McGraw-Hill.

Plunkett, K., & Marchman, V. A. (1993). From rote learning to system building: Acquiring verb morphology in children and connectionist nets. *Cognition*, *48* (1), 21–69.

Plunkett, K., & Marchman, V. A. (1996). Learning from a connectionist model of the acquisition of the English past tense. *Cognition*, *61* (3), 299–308.

Podgorny, P., & Shepard, R. N. (1978). Functional representations common to visual perception and imagination. *Journal of Experimental Psychology: Human Perception and Performance*, *4*, 21–35.

Poincaré, H. (1908/1954). Mathematical creation. In B. Ghiselin (Ed.), *The creative process: A symposium* (pp. 33–42). New York, NY: Mentor.

Poldrack, R. A., and Wagner, A. D. (2004). What can neuroimaging tell us about the mind? Insights from prefrontal cortex. *Current Directions in Psychological Science*, *13* (5), 177–181.

Poldrack, R. A., Wagner, A. D., Prull, M. W., Desmond, J. E., Glover, G. H., & Gabrieli, J. D. E. (1999). Functional specialization for semantic and phonological processing in the left inferior frontal cortex. *NeuroImage*, *10*, 15–35.

Polya, G. (1945). *How to solve it*. Princeton, NJ: Princeton University Press.

Posner, M. I., Boies, S. J., Echelman, W. H., & Taylor, R. L. (1969). Retention of visual and name codes of single letters. *Journal of Experimental Psychology*, (*79*, I Pt. 2).

Posner, M. I., & Cohen, Y. (1984). Components of visual orienting. In H. Bouma & D. Bonwhuis (Eds.), *Attention and performance X: Control of language processes* (pp. 551–556). Hillsdale, NJ: Erlbaum.

Posner, M. I., Nissen, M. J., & Ogden W. C. (1978). Attended and unattended processing modes: The role for spatial location. In H. L. Pick & I. J. Saltzman (Eds.), *Modes of perceiving and processing information* (pp. 137–157). Hillsdale, NJ: Erlbaum.

Posner, M. I., & Petersen, S. E. (1990). The attention system of the human brain. *Annual Review of Neuroscience*, *13*, 25–42.

Posner, M. I., & Raichle, M. (1994/1997). *Images of mind*. New York, NY: Scientific American Library. (Original work published 1994)

Postle, B. R., & Corkin, S. (1998). Impaired word-stem completion priming but intact perceptual identification priming with novel words: Evidence from the amnesic patient *H.M. Neuropsychologia*, *36*, 421–440.

Pratt, J., & Abrams, R. A. (1995). Inhibition of return to successively cued spatial locations. *Journal of Experimental Psychology: Human Perception and Performance*, *21*, 1343–1353.

Pratt, J., & McAuliffe, J. (2002). Inhibition of return in visual masking? The importance of the inter-stimulus interval and type of search task. *Visual Cognition*, *9*, 869–888.

Pressley, M., & Levin, J. R. (1977). Task parameters affecting the efficacy of a visual imagery learning strategy in younger and older children. *Journal of Experimental Child Psychology*, *24*, 53–59.

Principe, G., & Ceci, S. J. (2002). I saw it with my own ears: The effects of peer conversations on preschoolers' reports of nonexperienced events. *Journal of Experimental Child Psychology*, *83*, 1–25.

Puce, A., Allison, T., Asgari, M., Gore, J. C., & McCarthy, G. (1996). Differential sensitivity of human visual cortex to faces, letter strings, and textures: A functional magnetic resonance imaging study. *Journal of Neuroscience*, *16*, 5205–5215.

Pyers, J., Gollan, T., & Emmorey, K. (2009). Bimodal bilinguals reveal the source of tip of the tongue states. *Cognition*, *112*, 323–329.

Pylyshyn, Z. W. (1973). What the mind's eye tells the mind's brain. *Psychological Bulletin*, *80*, 1–24.

Pylyshyn, Z. W. (1981). The imagery debate: Analogue media versus tacit knowledge. *Psychological Review*, *88*, 16–45.

Pylyshyn, Z. W. (2003). *Seeing and visualizing: It's not what you think*. Cambridge, MA: MIT Press.

Pylyshyn, Z. W. (2007). *Things and places: How the mind connects with the world*. Cambridge, MA: MIT Press.

Quine, W. V. O. (1960). *Word and object*. Cambridge, MA: MIT Press.

Quinn, J. G., & McConnell, J. (1996). Irrelevant pictures in visual working memory. *Quarterly Journal of Experimental Psychology*, *49A*, 200–215.

Quinn, P. C. (1987). The categorical representation of visual pattern information by young infants. *Cognition*, *27*, 145–179.

Quiroga, R., Reddy, L., Kreiman, G., Koch, C., & Fried, I. (2005). Invariant visual representation by single-neurons in the human brain. *Nature*, *435*, 1102–1107.

Rabbitt, P. M. A. (1997). *Theory and methodology in executive function research: Methodology of frontal and executive function*. East Sussex, UK: Psychology Press.

Rafal, R., Smith, J., Krantz, J., Cohen, A., & Brennan, C. (1990). Extrageniculate vision in hemianopic humans: Saccade inhibition by signals in the blind field. *Science*, *250*, 118–121.

Ramey, C. J., & Weisberg, R. W. (2004). The "poetical activity" of Emily Dickinson: A further test of the hypothesis that affective disorders foster creativity. *Creativity Research Journal*, *16*, 173–185.

Ramnani, N., & Owen, A. M. (2004). Anterior prefrontal cortex: Insights into function from anatomy and neuroimaging. *Nature Reviews Neuroscience*, *5*(3), 184–194.

Ranganath, C., & Blumenfeld, R. S. (2005). Doubts about double dissociations between short- and long-term memory. *Trends in Cognitive Sciences*, *9*(8), 374–380.

Ranganath, C., & D'Esposito, M. (2001). Medial temporal lobe activity associated with active maintenance of novel information. *Neuron*, *31*, 865–873.

Raposo, A., Moss, H. E., Stamatakis, E. A., & Tyler, L. K. (2006). Repetition suppression and semantic enhancement: An investigation of the neural correlates of priming. *Neuropsychologia*, *44*(12), 2284–2295.

Raskin, E. A. (1936). Comparison of scientific and literary ability: A biographical study of eminent scientists and men of letters of the nineteenth century. *Journal of Abnormal and Social Psychology*, *31*, 20–35.

Ratneshwar, S., Barsalou, L. W., Pechmann, C., & Moore, M. (2001). Goal derived categories: The role of personal and situational goals in category representation. *Journal of Consumer Psychology*, *10*, 147–157.

Raymer, A. M., Foundas, A. L., Maher, L. M., Greenwald, M. L., Morris, M., Rothi, L. J. G., & Heilman, K. M. (1997). Cognitive neuropsychological analysis and neuroanatomic correlates in a case of acute anomia. *Brain and Language*, *58*(1), 137–156.

Raymer, A. M., Maher, L. M., Foundas, A. L., Rothi, A. L., & Heilman, K. M. (2000). Analysis of lexical recovery in an individual with acute anomia. *Aphasiology*, *14*(9), 901–910.

Raymond, J. E., Shapiro, K. L., & Arnell, K. M. (1992). Temporary suppression of visual processing in an RSVP task: An attentional blink? *Journal of Experimental Psychology: Human Perception and Performance*, *18*, 849–860.

Rayner, K. (1998). Eye movements in reading and information processing: 20 years of research. *Psychological Bulletin*, *124*, 372–422.

Rayner, K., & Frazier, L. (1989). Selection mechanisms in reading lexically ambiguous words. *Journal of Experimental Psychology: Learning, Memory, and Cognition*, *15*, 779–790.

Rayner, K., Cook, A. E., Juhasz, B. J., & Frazier, L. (2006). Immediate disambiguation of lexically ambiguous words during reading: Evidence from eye movements. *British Journal of Psychology*, *97*, 467–482.

Rayner, K., & Pollatsek, A. (1989). *The psychology of reading*. Englewood Cliffs, NJ: Prentice-Hall.

Reali, F., & Christiansen, M. H. (2005). Uncovering the richness of the stimulus: Structural dependence and indirect statistical evidence. *Cognitive Science*, *29*, 1007–1028.

Redelmeier, D. A., & Tibshirani, R. J. (1997). Association between cellular-telephone calls and motor vehicle collisions. *New England Journal of Medicine*, *336*, 453–458.

Reder, L. M., & Ritter, F. E. (1992). What determines initial feeling of knowing? *Journal of Experimental Psychology: Learning, Memory, and Cognition*, *18*, 435–451.

Reed, S. K. (1974). Structural descriptions and the limitations of visual images. *Memory & Cognition*, *2*, 329–336.

Reed, S. K., Ackinclose, C. C., & Voss, A. A. (1990). Selecting analogous problems: Similarity versus inclusiveness. *Memory & Cognition*, *18*(1), 83–98.

Reed, S. K., & Johnsen, J. A. (1975). Detection of parts in patterns and images. *Memory & Cognition*, *3*, 569–575.

Reeves, L. M., & Weisberg, R. W. (1993a). Abstract versus concrete information as the basis for transfer in problem solving: Comment on Fong and Nisbett (1991). *Journal of Experimental Psychology: General*, *122*, 125–128.

Reeves, L. M., & Weisberg, R. W. (1993b). On the concrete nature of human thinking: Content and context in analogical transfer. *Educational Psychology*, *13*, 245–258. (Invited paper; part of special issue on thinking)

Reeves, L. M., & Weisberg, R. W. (1994). Models of analogical transfer in problem solving. *Psychological Bulletin*, *116*, 381–400.

Reicher, G. M. (1969). Perceptual recognition as a function of meaningfulness of stimulus material. *Journal of Experimental Psychology*, *81*, 275–280.

Reinvang, I., Nielsen, C. S., Gjerstad, L., & Bakke, S. J. (2000). Isolated retrograde amnesia: Evidence for preservation of implicit memory. An event-related potential investigation. *Neurocase*, *6*, 423–433.

Reitman, J. S. (1971). Mechanisms of forgetting in short-term memory. *Cognitive Psychology*, *2*, 185–195.

Remez, R. E., Fellowes, J. M., Pisoni, D. B., Goh, W. D., & Rubin, P. E. (1998). Multimodal perceptual organization of speech: Evidence from tone analogs of spoken utterances. *Speech Communication*, *26*, 65–73.

Remondes, M., & Schuman, E. M. (2004). Role for a cortical input to hippocampal area CA1 in the consolidation of a long-term memory. *Nature*, *431*, 699–703.

Rempel-Clower, N. L., Zola-Morgan, S. M., Squire, L. R., & Amaral, D. G. (1996). Three cases of enduring memory impairment after bilateral damage limited to the hippocampal formation. *Journal of Neuroscience*, *16*, 5233–5255.

Rensink, R. A. (2000). Seeing, sensing, and scrutinizing. *Vision Research*, *40*, 1469–1487.

Rensink, R. A. (2002). Change detection. *Annual Review of Psychology*, *53*, 245–277.

Rensink, R. A., O'Regan, J. K., & Clark, J. J. (1997). To see or not to see: The need for attention to perceive changes in scenes. *Psychological Science*, *8*, 368–373.

Revlis, R. (1975). Syllogistic reasoning: Logical decisions from a complex data base. In R. J. Falmagne (Ed.), *Reasoning: Representation and process in children and adults* (pp. 93–133). Hillsdale, NJ: Erlbaum.

Rewald, J. (1946). *The history of Impressionism*. New York, NY: Museum of Modern Art.

Rewald, J. (1986). *Studies in Post-Impressionism*. I. Gordon & F. Weitzenhoffer (Eds.). New York, NY: Harry N. Abrams.

Reyna, V. F., Nelson, W., Han, P., & Dieckmann, N. F. (2009). How numeracy influences risk comprehension and medical decision making. *Psychological Bulletin*, *135*, 943–973.

Rhodes, M., & Gelman, S. A. (2009). Five-year-olds' beliefs about the discreetness of category boundaries for animals and artifacts. *Psychonomic Bulletin and Review*, *16*, 920–924.

Richards, I. A. (1936). *The philosophy of rhetoric*. Oxford, UK: Oxford University Press.

Richards, R., Kinney, D. K., Lunde, I., Benet, M., & Merzel, A. P. C. (1988). Creativity in manic-depressives, cyclothymes, their normal relatives, and control subjects. *Journal of Abnormal Psychology*, *97*, 281–288.

Richardson, J. (2007). *A life of Picasso: The prodigy, 1881–1906*. New York: Knopf.

Richardson, J., Engle, R., Hasher, L., Logie, R., Stoltzfus, E., & Zacks, R. (1996). *Working memory and human cognition*. New York, NY: Oxford University Press.

Richardson, J., & McCully, M. (1991). *A life of Picasso: Vol. 1*. 1881–1906. New York, NY: Random House.

Richardson, J., & McCully, M. (2007). *A life of Picasso: The triumphant years, 1917–1932* (Vol. 3). New York: Knopf.

Riddoch, M. J., Humphreys, G. W., Akhtar, N., Allen, H., Bracewell, R., Martyn Schofield, A. J. (2008). A tale of two agnosias: Distinctions between form and integrative agnosia. *Cognitive Neuropsychology*, *25* (1), 56–92.

Riddoch, M. J., Humphreys, G. W., Blott, W., Hardy, E., & Smith, A. D. (2003). Visual and spatial short-term memory in integrative agnosia. *Cognitive Neuropsychology*, *20*, 641–671.

Riddoch, M. J., Humphreys, G. W., Gannon, T., Blott, W., & Jones, V. (1999). Memories are made of this: The effects of time on stored visual knowledge in a case of visual agnosia. *Brain*, *122*, 537–559.

Riddoch, M. J., Johnston, R. A., Bracewell, M., Boutsen, B., & Humphreys, G. W. (2008). Are faces are special? A case of pure prosopagnosia. *Cognitive Neuropsychology*, *25*, 3–26.

Rips, L. J. (1975). Inductive judgments about natural categories. *Journal of Verbal Learning and Verbal Behavior*, *14*, 665–681.

Rips, L. J. (1989). Similarity, typicality and categorization. In S. Vosniardou & A. Ortony (Eds.), *Similarity and analogical reasoning* (pp. 21–59). New York, NY: Cambridge University Press.

Rips, L. J., Shoben, E. J., & Smith, F. E. (1973). Semantic distance and the verification of semantic relations. *Journal of Verbal Learning and Verbal Behavior*, *14*, 665–681.

Rittenhouse, D. (1786). Explanation of an optical deception. *Transactions of the American Philosophical Society*, *9*, 578–585.

Rivers, W. H. R. (1905). Observations on the senses of the Todas. *British Journal of Psychology* *1*, 321–396.

Roberts, K., & Horowitz, F. D. (1986). Basic level categorization in seven- and nine-month-old infants. *Journal of Child Language*, *13*, 191–208.

Robertson, D. A., Gernsbacher, M. A., Guidotti, S. J., Robertson, R. W. R., Irwin, W., Mock, B. J., & Campana, M. E. (2000). Functional neuroanatomy of the cognitive process of mapping during discourse comprehension. *Psychological Science*, *11*, 255–260.

Robertson, I. H., & Halligan, P. W. (1999). *Spatial neglect: A clinical handbook for diagnosis and treatment*. Hove, UK: Erlbaum.

Robins, R. W., Gosling, S. D., & Craik, K. H. (1999). An empirical analysis of trends in psychology. *American Psychologist*, *54*, 117–128.

Roediger, H. L., & Guynn, M. J. (1996). Retrieval processes. In E. L. Bjork & R. A. Bjork (Eds.), *Human memory* (pp. 197–236). San Diego, CA: Academic Press.

Roediger, H. L., & McDermott, K. B. (1995). Creating false memories: Remembering words not presented in lists. *Journal of Experimental Psychology: Learning, Memory, and Cognition*, *21*, 803–814.

Rofé, Y. (2008). Does repression exist? Memory, pathogenic, unconscious, and clinical evidence. *Review of General Psychology* *12* (1), 63–85.

Rogers, T. T., & McClelland, J. L. (2004). *Semantic cognition: A parallel distributed processing approach*. Cambridge, MA: MIT Press.

Rogers, T. T., & McClelland, J. L. (2008). Précis of *Semantic cognition: A parallel distributed processing approach*. *Behavioral and Brain Sciences*, *31*, 689–749.

Rohrer, D., & Taylor, K. (2006). The effects of overlearning and distributed practice on the retention of mathematics knowledge. *Applied Cognitive Psychology*, *20*, 1209–1224.

Rojas, N. L., & Chan, E. (2005). Old and new controversies in the alternative treatment of attention-deficit hyperactivity disorder. *Mental Retardation and Developmental Disabilities: Research Reviews*, *11*, 116–130.

Rolls, E. T., Robertson, R. G., & Georges-François, P. (1997). Spatial view cells in the primate hippocampus. *European Journal of Neuroscience*, *9*, 1789–1794.

Rolls, E. T., & Tovée, M. J. (1994). Processing speed in the cerebral cortex, and the neurophysiology of backward masking. *Proceedings of the Royal Society of London B*, *257*, 9–15.

Romani, C., Olson, A., Ward, J., & Ercolani, M. G. (2002). Formal lexical paragraphias in a single case study: How "masterpiece" can become "misterpieman" and "curiosity" "suretoy." *Brain and Language*, *83*, 300–334.

Rosca, E. C. (2009). Arithmetic procedural knowledge: A cortico-subcortical circuit. *Brain Research*, *1302*, 148–156.

Rosch, E. H. (1973). Natural categories. *Cognitive Psychology*, *4*(3), 328–350.

Rosch, E. H. (1975). Cognitive representation of semantic categories. *Journal of Experimental Psychology*, *104*(3), 192–233.

Rosch, E. H. (1978). Principles of Categorization. In E. Rosch & B. B. Lloyd (Eds.), *Cognition and categorization* (pp. 27–48). Hillsdale, NJ: Erlbaum.

Rosch, E. H., & Mervis, C. B. (1975). Family resemblances: Studies in the internal structure of categories. *Cognitive Psychology*, *7*(4), 573–605.

Rosch, E. H., Mervis, C. B., Gray, W. D., Johnson, D. M., & Boyes-Braem, P. (1976). Basic objects in natural categories. *Cognitive Psychology*, *8*(3), 382–439.

Rose, D. (1996). Some reflections on (or by?) grandmother cells. *Perception*, *25*, 881–886.

Rosen, S. M., & Howell, P. (1981). Plucks and bows are not categorically perceived. *Perception & Psychophysics*, *30*(2), 156–168.

Ross, B. H. (1987). This is like that: The use of earlier problems and the separation of similarity effects. *Journal of Experimental Psychology: Learning, Memory, and Cognition*, *13*, 629–639.

Ross, B. H. (1989). Distinguishing types of superficial similarity: Different effects on the access and use of earlier problems. *Journal of Experimental Psychology: Learning, Memory, and Cognition*, *15*, 456–468.

Ross, B. H., & Spalding, T. L. (1994). Concepts and categories. In R. Sternberg (Ed.), *Handbook of perception and cognition: Vol. 12. Thinking and problem solving* (pp. 119–148). San Diego, CA: Academic Press.

Ross, E., Edmondson, J. A., Seibert, G. B., & Homan, R. W. (1988). Acoustic analysis of affective prosody during right-sided Wada test: A within-subjects verification of the right hemisphere's role in language. *Brain and Language*, *33*, 128–145.

Ross, J., & Lawrence, K. (1968). Some observations on memory artifice. *Psychonomic Science*, *13*, 107–108.

Rosselli, M., & Ardila, A. (1989). Calculation deficits in patients with right and left hemisphere damage. *Neuropsychologia*, *27*, 607–618.

Rothmayr, C., Baumann, O., Endestad, T., Rutschmann, R. M., Magnussen, S., & Greenlee, M. W. (2007). Dissociation of neural correlates of verbal and non-verbal visual working memory with different delays. *Behavioral and Brain Functions*, *3*, 56.

Rozin, P., & Nemeroff, C. (2002). Sympathetic magical thinking: The contagion and similarity "heuristics." In T. Gilovich, D. Griffin, & D. Kahneman (Eds.), *Heuristics and biases. The psychology of intuitive judgment* (pp. 201–216). Cambridge, UK: Cambridge University Press.

Rubenson, D. L., & Runco, M. A. (1995). The psychoeconomic view of creative work in groups and organizations. *Creativity and Innovation Management*, *4*(4), 232–241.

Rubin, D. C., & Kozin, M. (1984). Vivid memories. *Cognition*, *16*, 81–95.

Ruderman, D. L. (1994). The statistics of natural images. *Network*, *5*, 517–548.

Rueckl, J. G., Cave, K. R., & Kosslyn, S. M. (1989). Why are "what" and "where" processed by separate cortical visual systems? A computational investigation. *Journal of Cognitive Neuroscience*, *1*, 171–186.

Ruff, C. C., Knauff, M., Fangmeier, T., & Spreer, J. (2003). Reasoning and working memory: Common and distinct neuronal processes. *Neuropsychologia*, *41*(9), 1241–1253.

Rugg, M. D., & Allan, K. (2000). Event-related potential studies of long-term memory. In E. Tulving & F. I. M. Craik (Eds.), *The Oxford handbook of memory* (pp. 521–537). Oxford, UK: Oxford University Press.

Rugg, M. D., Allan, K., & Birch, C. S. (2000). Electrophysiological evidence for the modulation of retrieval orientation by depth of study processing. *Journal of Cognitive Neuroscience*, *12*(4), 664–678.

Rugg, M. D., Henson, R. N., & Robb, W. G. (2003). Neural correlates of retrieval processing in the prefrontal cortex during recognition and exclusion tasks. *Neuropsychologia*, *41*(1), 40–52.

Rumelhart, D. E. (1980). Schemata: The building blocks of cognition. In R. J. Spiro, B. C. Bruce, & W. F. Brewer (Eds.), *Theoretical issues in reading comprehension* (pp. 33–58). Hillsdale, NJ: Erlbaum.

Rumelhart, D. E., McClelland, J. L., and the PDP Research Group. (1986). *Parallel distributed processing: Explorations in the microstructure of cognition* (Vol. II). Cambridge, MA: MIT Press.

Runco, M. A. (2007). *Creativity theories and themes: Research, development, and practice*. New York, NY: Elsevier.

Rundus, D. (1971). Analysis of rehearsal processes in free recall. *Journal of Experimental Psychology*, *89*, 63–77.

Rundus, D., & Atkinson, R. C. (1970). Rehearsal processes in free recall: A procedure for direct observation. *Journal of Verbal Learning and Verbal Behavior*, *9*, 99–105.

Russell, D., & Jones, W. H. (1980). When superstition fails: Reactions to disconfirmation of paranormal beliefs. *Personality and Social Psychology Bulletin*, *6*(1), 83–88.

Russell, R., Sinha, P., Biederman, I., & Nederhouser, M. (2006). Is pigmentation important for face recognition? Evidence from contrast negation. *Perception*, *35*, 749–759.

Ruthruff, E., Johnston, J. C., & Van Selst, M. V. (2001). Why practice reduces dual-task interference. *Journal of Experimental Psychology: Human Perception and Performance*, *27*, 3–21.

Sacchett, C., & Humphreys, G. W. (1992). Calling a squirrel a squirrel but a canoe a wigwam: A category-specific deficit for artifactual objects and body parts. *Cognitive Neuropsychology*, *4*, 131–185.

Sacks, O. (1985). *The man who mistook his wife for a hat, and other clinical tales*. New York, NY: Summit Books.

Saffran, E. M., Schwartz, M. F., & Marin, O. S. (1980). The word order problem in agrammatism: II. *Production. Brain and Language*, *10*(2), 263–280.

Saffran, J. R., Aslin, R. N., & Newport, E. L. (1996). Statistical learning by 8-month-old infants. *Science*, *274*, 1926–1928.

Sakai, K. L., Tatsuno, Y., Suzuki, K., Kimura, H., & Ichida, Y. (2005). Sign and speech: Amodal commonality in left hemisphere dominance for comprehension of sentences. *Brain: A Journal of Neurology*, *128*(6), 1407–1417.

Salame, P., & Baddeley, A. D. (1982). Disruption of short-term memory by unattended speech: Implications for the structure of working memory. *Journal of Verbal Learning and Verbal Behavior*, *21*, 150–164.

Salame, P., & Baddeley, A. D. (1989). Effects of background music on phonological short-term memory. *Quarterly Journal of Experimental Psychology*, *41A*, 107–122.

Salame, P., & Baddeley, A. D. (1990). The effects of irrelevant speech on immediate free recall. *Bulletin of the Psychonomic Society*, *28*, 540–542.

Sandkühler, S., & Bhattacharya, J. (2008). Deconstructing insight: EEG correlates of insightful problem solving. *PLoS One*, *3*(1), e1459.

Sandra, D. (1990). On the representation and processing of compound words: Automatic access to constituent morphemes does not occur. *Quarterly Journal of Experimental Psychology A: Human Experimental Psychology*, *42*, 529–567.

Sanes, J. N., Dimitrov, B., & Hallett, M. (1990). Motor learning in patients with cerebellar dysfunction. *Brain*, *113*, 103–120.

Sangha, S., Scheibenstock, A., Martens, K., Varshney, N., Cooke, R., & Lukowiak, K. (2005). Impairing forgetting by preventing new learning and memory. *Behavioral Neuroscience*, *119*, 787–796.

Sapir, E. (1929). The status of linguistics as a science. *Language*, *5*, 207–214.

Sartori, G., & Job, R. (1988). The oyster with four legs: A neuropsychological study on the interaction of visual and semantic information. *Cognitive Neuropsychology*, *5*(1), Special issue: The cognitive neuropsychology of visual and semantic processing of concepts, 105–132.

Sartori, G., Job, R., Miozzo, M., Zago, S., & Marchiori, G. (1993.) Category-specific form knowledge deficit in a patient with herpes simplex encephalitis. *Journal of Clinical and Experimental Neuropsychology*, *12*, 280–299.

Sass, L. (2000–2001). Eccentricity, conformism, and the primary process. *Creativity Research Journal*, *13*, 37–44.

Saufley, W. H., Otaka, S. R., & Bavaresco, J. L. (1985). Context effects: Classroom tests and context independence. *Memory & Cognition*, *13*, 522–528.

Sawyer, R. K. (2012). *Explaining creativity: The science of human innovation* (2nd ed.). New York, NY: Oxford University Press.

Saxton, M. (2000). Negative evidence and negative feedback: Immediate effects on the grammaticality of child speech. *First Language*, *20*(3), 221–252.

Scarr, S., & McCartney, K. (1983). How people make their own environments: A theory of genotype-environment effects. *Child Development*, *54*, 424–435.

Schacter, D. (1996). *Searching for memory: The brain, the mind, and the past*. New York, NY: Basic Books.

Schacter, D. L. (2001). *The seven sins of memory: How the mind forgets and remembers*. Boston, MA: Houghton Mifflin.

Schacter, D. L., Buckner, R. L., Koutstaal, W., Dale, A. M., & Rosen, B. R. (1997). Late onset of anterior prefrontal activity during true and false recognition: An event-related fMRI study. *NeuroImage*, *6*, 259–269.

Schacter, D. L., Church, B., & Treadwell, J. (1994). Implicit memory in amnesic patients: Evidence for spared auditory priming. *Psychological Science*, *5*, 20–25.

Schacter, D. L., Harbluk, J. L., & McLachlan, D. R. (1984). Retrieval without recollection: An experimental analysis of source amnesia. *Journal of Verbal Learning and Verbal Behavior*, *23*, 593–611.

Schank, R., & Abelson, R. (1977). *Scripts, plans, goals, and understanding: An inquiry into human knowledge structure*. Hillsdale, NJ: Erlbaum.

Scheerer, M. (1963). On problem-solving. *Scientific American*, *208*, 118–128.

Schenk, T., & Milner, A. D. (2006). Concurrent visuomotor behavior improves form discrimination in a patient with visual form agnosia. *European Journal of Neuroscience*, *24*, 1495–1503.

Schmid, G., Thielmann, A., & Ziegler, W. (2009). The influence of visual and auditory information on the perception of speech and non-speech oral movements in patients with left hemisphere lesions. *Clinical Linguistics and Phonetics*, *23*(3), 208–221.

Schneider, G. (1969). Two visual systems: Brain mechanisms for localization and discrimination are dissociated by tectal and cortical lesions. *Science*, *163*, 895–902.

Schneider, W., & Bjorklund, D. F. (1998). Memory. In W. Damon, R. S. Siegler, & D. Kuhn (Eds.), *Handbook of child psychology* (5th ed., Vol. 2, pp. 467–521). New York, NY: Wiley.

Schneider, W., & Pressley, M. (1997). *Memory development between 2 and 20* (2nd ed.). Hillsdale, NJ: Erlbaum.

Schneider, W., & Shiffrin, R. M. (1977). Controlled and automatic human information processing: I. Detection, search, and attention. *Psychological Review*, *84*, 1–66.

Schneider, W., & Sodian, B. (1997). Memory strategy development: Lessons from longitudinal research. *Developmental Review*, *17*, 442–461.

Scholl, B. J. (2005). Innateness and (Bayesian) visual perception: Reconciling nativism and development. In P. Carruthers, S. Laurence, & S. Stich (Eds.), *The innate mind: Structure and contents* (pp. 34–52). New York, NY: Oxford University Press.

Schon, K., Hasselmo, M. E., Lopresti, M. L., Tricarico, M. D., & Stern, C. E. (2004). Persistence of parahippocampal representation in the absence of stimulus input enhances long-term encoding: A functional magnetic resonance imaging study of subsequent memory after a delayed match-to-sample task. *Journal of Neuroscience*, *24*, 11088–11097.

Schooler, J. W., Ohlsson, S., & Brooks, K. (1993). Thoughts beyond words: When language overshadows insight. *Journal of Experimental Psychology: General*, *122*, 166–183.

Schunn, C. D., Reder, L. M., Nhouyvanisvong, A., Richards, D. R., & Stroffolino, P. J. (1997). To calculate or not calculate: A source activation confusion (SAC) model of problem-familiarity's role in strategy selection. *Journal of Experimental Psychology: Learning, Memory, and Cognition*, *23*, 3–29.

Schvaneveldt, R. W., Meyer, D. E., & Becker, C. A. (1976). Lexical ambiguity, semantic context, and visual word recognition. *Journal of Experimental Psychology: Human Perception and Performance*, *2*, 243–256.

Schwartz, B. L. (2008). Working memory load differentially affects tip-of-the-tongue states and feeling-of-knowing judgment. *Memory & Cognition*, *36*, 9–19.

Schwartz, M., Linebarger, M., Saffran, E., and Pate, D. (1987). Syntactic transparency and sentence interpretation in aphasia. *Language and Cognitive Processes*, *2*, 85–113.

Schwartz, M. F., Saffran, E. M., & Marin, O. S. (1980). The word order problem in agrammatism: I. Comprehension. *Brain and Language*, *10*, 249–262.

Scoville, W. B. (1968). Amnesia after bilateral mesial temporal-lobe excision: Introduction to case H. M. *Neuropsychologica*, *6*, 211–213.

Scoville, W. B., & Milner, B. (1957). Loss of recent memory after bilateral hippocampal lesions. *Journal of Neurology, Neurosurgery, and Psychiatry*, *20*, 11–21.

Seamon, J. G., Schlegel, S. E., Hiester, P. M., Landau, A. M., & Blumenthal, B. F. (2002). Misremembering pictured objects: People of all ages demonstrate the boundary extension illusion. *American Journal of Psychology*, *115*, 151–167.

Searle, J. R. (1979). Metaphor. In A. Ortony (Ed.), *Metaphor and thought* (pp. 92–123). New York, NY: Cambridge University Press.

Sedlmeier, P. (1999). *Improving statistical reasoning: Theoretical models and practical implications*. Mahwah, NJ: Erlbaum.

Sedlmeier, P. (2000). How to improve statistical thinking: Choose the task representation wisely and learn by doing. *Instructional Science*, *28*, 227–262.

Sedlmeier, P., & Gigerenzer, G. (2001). Teaching Bayesian reasoning in less than two hours. *Journal of Experimental Psychology: General*, *130*, 380–400.

Segal, D. (2010). Just manic enough: Seeking perfect entrepreneurs. *New York Times*, September 19, 2010, BU1.

Segal, S. J., & Fusella, V. (1970). Influence of imaged pictures and sounds on the detection of visual and auditory signals. *Journal of Experimental Psychology*, *83*, 458–464.

Segall, M. H., Campbell, D. T., & Herskovits, M. J. (1963). Cultural differences in the perception of geometric illusions. *Science*, *139*(3556), 769–771.

Segall, M. H., Campbell, D. T., & Herskovits, M. J. (1966). *The influence of culture on visual perception*. Indianapolis, IN: Bobbs-Merrill.

Seidenberg, M. S., Tanenhaus, M. J., Leiman, J. M., & Bienkowski, M. (1982). Automatic access of the meanings of ambiguous words in context: Some limitations of knowledge-based processing. *Cognitive Psychology*, *14*, 538–559.

Seifert, C. M., Meyer, D. E., Davidson, N., Patalano, A. J., & Yaniv, I. (1995). Demystification of cognitive insight: The prepared-mind perspective. In R. J. Sternberg & J. Davidson (Eds.), *The nature of insight* (pp. 65–124). Cambridge, MA: MIT Press.

Seiffert, A. E., & Di Lollo, V. (1997). Low-level masking in the attentional blink. *Journal of Experimental Psychology: Human Perception and Performance*, *23*, 1061–1073.

Semino, E., & Steen, G. (2008). Metaphor in literature. In R. Gibbs (Ed.), *Cambridge handbook of metaphor and thought* (pp. 232–246). Cambridge, UK: Cambridge University Press.

Sergent, J., Ohta, S., & MacDonald, B. (1992). Functional neuroanatomy of face and object processing: A positron emission tomography study. *Brain*, *115*, 15–36.

Sergent, J., & Signoret, J. (1992). Varieties of functional deficits in prosopagnosia. *Cerebral Cortex*, *2*, 375–388.

Service, E. (1992). Phonology, working memory, and foreign-language learning. *Quarterly Journal of Experimental Psychology*, *45A*, 21–50.

Servos, P., & Goodale, M. (1995). Preserved visual imagery in visual form agnosia. *Neuropsychologia*, *33*, 1383–1394.

Shallice, T. (1988). *From neuropsychology to mental structure*. Cambridge, UK: Cambridge University Press.

Shapiro, B., & Danly, M. (1985). The role of the right hemisphere in the control of speech prosody in propositional and affective contexts. *Brain and Language*, *25*, 19–36.

Shapiro, K., Driver, J., Ward, R., & Sorensen, R. E. (1997). Priming from the attentional blink: A failure to extract visual tokens but not visual types. *Psychological Science*, *8*(2), 95–100.

Shattuck-Hufnagel, S., & Klatt. D. H. (1979). The limited use of distinctive features and markedness in speech production: Evidence from speech error data. *Journal of Verbal Learning and Verbal Behavior 18*, 41–55.

Shaughnessy, J. J., Zimmerman, J., & Underwood, B. J. (1972). The spacing effect in learning word pairs and components of word pairs. *Memory & Cognition*, *2*, 742–748.

Shelton, P., Bowers, D., Duara, R. J., & Heilman, K. M. (1994). Apperceptive visual agnosia. *Brain & Cognition*, *25*, 1–23.

Shepard, R. N. (1967). Recognition memory for words, sentences, and pictures. *Journal of Verbal Learning and Verbal Behavior*, *6*, 156–163.

Shepard, R. N. (1978). Externalization of mental images and the act of creation. In B. S. Randhawa & W. E. Coffman (Eds.), *Vision, thinking and communication* (pp. 133–189). New York, NY: Academic Press.

Shepard, R. N., & Metzler, J. (1971). Mental rotation of three dimensional objects. *Science*, *171*(972), 701–703.

Sherman, J., & Schweikert, J. (1989). Syntactic and semantic contributions to sentence interpretation in agrammatism. *Brain and Language*, *37*, 419–439.

Sheth, B. R., Sandkühler, S., & Bhattacharya, J. (2008). Posterior beta and anterior gamma oscillations predict cognitive insight. *Journal of Cognitive Neuroscience*, *21*(7), 1269–1279.

Shiffrin, R. M., & Atkinson, R. C. (1969). Storage and retrieval processes in long-term memory. *Psychological Review*, *76*, 179–193.

Shiffrin, R. M., & Schneider, W. (1977). Controlled and automatic human information processing: II. Perceptual learning, automatic attending, and a general theory. *Psychological Review*, *84*, 127–190.

Shomstein, S., & Yantis, S. (2004). Control of attention shifts between vision and audition in human cortex. *Journal of Neuroscience*, *24*, 10702–10706.

Shtulman, A. (2006). Qualitative differences between naïve and scientific theories of evolution. *Cognitive Psychology*, *52*, 170–194.

Siddle, D. A., & Packer, J. S. (1987). Stimulus omission and dishabituation of the electrodermal orienting response: The allocation of processing resources. *Psychophysiology*, *24*, 181–190.

Silverman, M. E., & Mack, A. (2006). Change blindness and priming: When it does and does not occur. *Consciousness and Cognition*, *15*, 409–422.

Simon, H. A. (1956). Rational choice and the structure of the environment. *Psychological Review*, *63*(2), 129–138.

Simon, H. A. (1957). *Models of man*. New York, NY: Wiley.

Simon, H. A. (1974). How big is a chunk? *Science*, *183*, 482–488.

Simon, H. A. (1978). Rationality as a process and product of thought. *American Economic Review*, *68*, 1–16.

Simon, H. A. (1979). *Models of thought* (Vols. 1 and 2). New Haven, CT: Yale University Press.

Simon, H. A. (1980). Information-processing explanations of understanding. In P. W. Jusczyk & R. M. Klein (Eds.), *The nature of thought: Essays in honor of D. O. Hebb* (pp. 37–50). Hillsdale, NJ: Erlbaum.

Simon, H. A. (1983). *Reason in human affairs*. Palo Alto, CA: Stanford University Press.

Simon, H. A. (1986). The information-processing explanation of Gestalt phenomena. *Computers in Human Behavior*, *2*, 241–255.

Simon, H. A. (1989). The information-processing explanation of Gestalt phenomena. In H. A. Simon (Ed.), *Models of thought* (Vol. 2, pp. 481–493). New Haven, CT: Yale University Press.

Simons, D. J. (1996). In sight, out of mind: When object representations fail. *Psychological Science*, *7*, 301–305.

Simons, D. J., Chabris, C. F., Schnur, T. T., & Levin, D. T. (2002). Evidence for preserved representations in change blindness. *Consciousness and Cognition*, *11*, 78–97.

Simons, D. J., & Levin, D. T. (1997). Change blindness. *Trends in Cognitive Science*, *1*, 261–267.

Simonton, D. K. (1976). The causal relation between war and scientific discovery: An exploratory cross-national analysis. *Journal of Cross-Cultural Psychology*, *7*, 133–144.

Simonton, D. K. (1988). Creativity, leadership, and chance. In R. J. Sternberg (Ed.), *The nature of creativity: Contemporary psychological perspectives* (pp. 386–426). New York, NY: Cambridge University Press.

Simonton, D. K. (1995). Foresight in insight? A Darwinian answer. In R. J. Sternberg & J. E. Davidson (Eds.), *The nature of insight* (pp. 465–494). Cambridge, MA: MIT Press.

Simonton, D. K. (1999). *Origins of genius: Darwinian perspectives on creativity*. New York, NY: Oxford University Press.

Simonton, D. K. (2003). Scientific creativity as constrained stochastic behavior: The integration of product, process, and person perspectives. *Psychological Bulletin*, *129*, 475–494.

Simonton, D. K. (2007). Achievement. In J. E. Birren (Ed.), *Encyclopedia of gerontology* (2nd ed., Vol. 1, pp. 20–29). San Diego, CA: Academic Press.

Simonton, D. K. (2011a). Creativity and discovery as blind variation and selective retention: Multiple-variant definitions and blind-sighted integration. *Psychology of Aesthetics, Creativity, and the Arts*, *5*, 222–228.

Simonton, D. K. (2011b). War. In M. A. Runco & S. Pritzker (Eds.), *Encyclopedia of creativity* (2nd ed., Vol. 2, pp. 509–514). Oxford, UK: Elsevier.

Simpson, G. B. (1981). Meaning dominance and semantic context in the processing of lexical ambiguity. *Journal of Verbal Learning & Verbal Behavior*, *20*(1), 120–136.

Simpson, G. B., & Burgess, C. (1985). Activation and selection processes in the recognition of ambiguous words. *Journal of Experimental Psychology: Human Perception and Performance*, *11*, 28–39.

Simpson, G. B., & Burgess, C. (1988). Lexical ambiguity and its implication for models of word recognition. In S. L. Small, G. W. Cottrell, & M. K. Tanenhaus (Eds.), *Lexical ambiguity resolution in the comprehension of human language* (pp. 271–288). Los Altos, CA: Morgan Kaufmann.

Simpson, G. B., & Krueger, M. A. (1991). Selective access of homograph meanings in sentence context. *Journal of Memory & Language*, *30*, 627–643.

Sinha, P., Balas, B. J., Ostrovsky, Y., & Russell, R. (2006a). Face recognition by humans: 19 results all computer vision researchers should know about. *Proceedings of the IEEE*, *94*(11), 1948–1962.

Sinha, P., Balas, B. J., Ostrovsky, Y., & Russell, R. (2006b). Face recognition by humans. In *Face Recognition: Advanced Modeling and Methods*. New York, NY: Academic Press.

Skinner, B. F. (1938). *The behavior of organisms: An experimental analysis*. New York, NY: D. Unwin.

Skinner, B. F. (1957). *Verbal behavior*. New York, NY: Appleton-Century-Crofts.

Slater, E., & Meyer, A. (1959). Contributions to a pathography of the musicians: 1. Robert Schumann. *Confinia Psychiatrica*, *2*, 65–94.

Sloboda, J. A., Davidson, J. W., Howe, M. J. A., & Moore, D. G. (1996). The role of practice in the development of performing musicians. *British Journal of Psychology. 87*, 287–309.

Sloman, S. A. (1993). Feature-based induction. *Cognitive Psychology*, *25*, 231–280.

Slotnick, S. D., & Schacter, D. L. (2004). A sensory signature that distinguishes true from false memories. *Nature Neuroscience*, *7*(6), 664–672.

Slovic, P. (1987). Risk perception. *Science*, *236*, 280–285.

Slovic, P., Fischhoff, B., & Lichtenstein, S. (1982). Why study risk perceptions? *Risk Analysis*, *2*, 83–93.

Slovic, P., Fischhoff, B., & Lichtenstein, S. (1984). Modeling the societal impact of fatal accidents. *Management Science*, *30*, 464–474.

Slovic, P., Fischhoff, B., & Lichtenstein, S. (1985). Regulation of risk: A psychological perspective. In R. Noll (Ed.), *Regulatory policy and the social sciences* (pp. 241–278). Berkeley, CA: University of California Press.

Small, D. M., Gitelman, D. R., Gregory, M. D., Nobre, A. C., Parrish, T. B., & Mesulam, M. M. (2003). The posterior cingulate and medial prefrontal cortex mediate the anticipatory allocation of spatial attention. *NeuroImage*, *18*(3), 633–641.

Smith, C. M., Bushouse, E., & Lord, J. (2010). Individual and group performance on insight problems: The effects of experimentally induced fixation. *Group Processes & Intergroup Relations*, *13*, 91–99.

Smith, E. E., & Jonides, J. (1995). Working memory in humans: Neuropsychological evidence. In M. S. Gazzaniga (Ed.), *The cognitive neurosciences* (pp. 1009–1020). Cambridge, MA: MIT Press.

Smith, E. E., & Jonides, J. (1997). Working memory: A view from neuroimaging. *Cognitive Psychology*, *33*: 5–42.

Smith, E. E., & Jonides, J. (1999). Storage and executive processes in the frontal lobes, *Science*, *283* (5408), 1657–1661.

Smith, E. E., Shoben, E. J., & Rips, L. J. (1974). Structure and process in semantic memory: A featural model for semantic decisions. *Psychological Review*, *81* (3), 214–241.

Smith, E. R. (1998). Mental representation and memory. In D. Gilbert, S. Fiske, & G. Lindzey (Eds.), *Handbook of social psychology* (4th ed., Vol. 1, pp. 391–445). New York, NY: McGraw-Hill.

Smith, E. R., & Conrey, F. R. (2007). Agent-based modeling: A new approach for theory-building in social psychology. *Personality and Social Psychology Review*, *11*, 87–104.

Smith, L. B., & Samuelson, L. K. (1997). Perceiving and remembering: Category stability, variability and development. In K. Lamberts and D. Shanks (Eds.), *Knowledge, concepts and categories* (pp. 161–195). Cambridge, MA: The MIT Press.

Smith, M. C., Bibi, U., & Sheard, D. (2003). Evidence for the differential impact of time and emotion on personal and event memories for September 11, 2001. *Applied Cognitive Psychology*, *17*, 1047–1055.

Smith, P. T., & Sterling, C. M. (1982). Factors affecting the perceived morphemic structure of written words. *Journal of Verbal Learning and Verbal Behavior*, *21*, 704–721.

Smith, S. M. (1979). Remembering in and out of context. *Journal of Experimental Psychology: Human Learning and Memory*, *5* (5), 460–471.

Smith, S. M. (1995). Fixation, incubation, and insight in memory, problem solving, and creativity. In S. M. Smith, T. B. Ward, & R. A. Finke (Eds.), *The creative cognition approach* (pp. 135–155). Cambridge, MA: MIT Press.

Smith, S. M., & Blankenship, S. E. (1991). Incubation and the persistence of fixation in problem solving. *American Journal of Psychology*, *104*, 61–87.

Smith, S. M., Ward, T. B., & Finke, R. A. (Eds.) (1995). *The creative cognition approach*. Cambridge, MA: MIT Press.

Soja, N. N., Carey, S., & Spelke, E. S. (1991). Ontological categories guide young children's inductions of word meaning: Object terms and substance terms. *Cognition*, *38* (2), 179–211.

Sokol, S. M., & McCloskey, M. (1991). Cognitive mechanisms in calculation. In R. J. Sternberg & P. A. Frensch (Eds.), *Complex problem solving: Principles and mechanisms* (pp. 85–116). Hillsdale, NJ: Erlbaum.

Sokolov, E. N. (1975). The neuronal mechanisms of the orienting reflex. In E. N. Sokolov & O. S. Vinogradova (Eds.), *Neuronal mechanisms of the orienting reflex* (pp. 217–235). Hillsdale, NJ: Erlbaum.

Solso, R. L. (2001). Brain activities in a skilled versus a novice artist: An fMRI study. *Leonardo 34*, 31–34.

Solso, R. L., & Short, B. A. (1979). Color recognition. *Bulletin of the Psychonomic Society*, *14*, 275–277.

Soto, D., & Blanco, M. J. (2004). Spatial attention and object-based attention: A comparison within a single task. *Vision Research*, *44* (1), 69–81.

Soto-Faraco, S., & Alsius, A. (2009). Deconstructing the McGurk-MacDonald illusion. *Journal of Experimental Psychology: Human Perception and Performance*, *35* (2), 580–587.

Sparing, R., Mottaghy, F. M., Hungs, M., Bruègmann, M., Foltys, H., Huber, W., & Toèpper, R. (2001). Repetitive transcranial magnetic stimulation effects on language function depend on the stimulation parameters. *Journal of Clinical Neurophysiology*, *4*, 326–330.

Sparks, D. L. (1986). Translation of sensory signals into commands for control of saccadic eye movements: Role of primate superior colliculus. *Physiological Review*, *66*, 118–171.

Spelke, E., Hirst, W., & Neisser, U. (1976). Skills of divided attention. *Cognition*, *4*, 215–230.

Spelke, E. S. (1990). Principles of object perception. *Cognitive Science*, *14*(1), 29–56.

Spencer, R. M., & Weisberg, R. W. (1986). Context-dependent effects on analogical transfer during problem solving. *Memory & Cognition*, *14*, 442–449.

Sperling, G. (1960). The information available in brief visual presentations. *Psychological Monographs*, *74* (11, Whole No. 498).

Springer, K. (1996). Young children's understanding of a biological basis for parent–offspring relations. *Child Development*, *67*, 2841–2856.

Squire, L. R., & Alvarez, P. (1995). Retrograde amnesia and memory consolidation: A neurobiological perspective. *Current Opinion in Neurobiology*, *5*, 169–177.

Squire, L. R., & Bayley, P. J. (2007). The neuroscience of remote memory. *Current Opinion in Neurobiology*, *17*, 185–196.

Squire, L. R., & Knowlton, B. J. (1995). Learning about categories in the absence of memory. *Proceedings of the National Academy of Sciences, USA*, *92*, 12470–12474.

Squire, L. R., Shimamura, A., & Graf, P. (1885). Independence of recognition memory and priming effects: Neuropsychological analysis. *Journal of Experimental Psychology: Learning, Memory, and Cognition*, *11*, 37–44.

Squire, L. R., Stark, C. E. L., & Clark, R. E. (2004). The medial temporal lobe. *Annual Review of Neuroscience*, *27*, 279–306.

Stalnaker, R. (2002). Common ground. *Linguistics and Philosophy*, *25*, 701–721.

Standing, L. (1973). Learning 10000 pictures. *Quarterly Journal of Experimental Psychology*, *25*, 207–222.

Stankiewicz, B. J., & Kalia, A. A. (2007). Acquisition of structural versus object landmark knowledge. *Journal of Experimental Psychology: Human Perception and Performance*, *33*, 378–390.

Stannard, D. E. (1980). *Shrinking history: On Freud and the failure of psychohistory*. New York, NY: Oxford University Press.

Stanovich, K. E. (1993). Dysrationalia: A new specific learning disability. *Journal of Learning Disabilities*, *26*(8), 501–515.

Stanovich, K. E. (2009). The thinking that IQ tests miss. *Scientific American Mind*, *20*(6), 34–39.

Stanovich, K. E. (2012). On the distinction between rationality and intelligence: Implications for understanding individual differences in reasoning. In K. Holyoak & R. Morrison (Eds.), *The Oxford handbook of thinking and reasoning* (pp. 343–365). New York, NY: Oxford University Press.

Stanovich, K. E., & West, R. F. (1998). Individual differences in rational thought. *Journal of Experimental Psychology: General*, *127*, 161–188.

Stanovich, K. E., & West, R. F. (2000). Individual differences in reasoning: Implications for the rationality debate? *Behavioral and Brain Sciences*, *23*, 645–665.

Stanovich, K. E., & West, R. F. (2007). Natural myside bias is independent of cognitive ability. *Thinking & Reasoning*, *13*(3), 225–247.

Stanovich, K. E., & West, R. F. (2008a). On the failure of intelligence to predict myside bias and one-sided bias. *Thinking & Reasoning*, *14*, 129–167.

Stanovich, K. E., & West, R. F. (2008b). On the relative independence of thinking biases and cognitive ability. *Journal of Personality and Social Psychology*, *94*, 672–695.

Steblay, N., Hosch, H., Culhane, S. E., & McWethy, A. (2006). The impact on juror verdicts of judicial instruction to disregard inadmissible evidence: A meta-analysis. *Law and Human Behavior*, *30*(4), 469–542.

Stein, B. S. (1978). Depth of processing reexamined: The effects of the precision of encoding and test appropriateness. *Journal of Verbal Learning & Verbal Behavior*, *17*(2), 165–174.

Stemberger, J. P. (1985). An interactive activation model of *language* production. In A. Ellis. (Ed.), *Progress in the psychology of language* (Vol. 1, pp. 143–186). Hillsdale, NJ: Erlbaum.

Stepankova, K., Fenton, A. A., Pastalkova, E., Kalina, M., & Bohbot, V. D. (2004). Object-location memory impairment in patients with thermal lesions to the right or left hippocampus. *Neuropsychologia*, *42*, 1017–1028.

Sternberg, R. J. (1988). *The triarchic mind: A new theory of human intelligence*. New York, NY: Viking Penguin.

Sternberg, R. J. (2003). Giftedness according to the theory of successful intelligence. In N. Colangelo & G. Davis (Eds.), *Handbook of gifted education* (88–99). Boston, MA: Allyn & Bacon.

Sternberg, R. J., & Davidson, J. E. (Eds.). (1995). *The nature of insight*. Cambridge, MA: MIT Press.

Sternberg, R. J., & Lubart, T. (1996). Investing in creativity. *American Psychologist*, *51*(7), 677–688.

Sternberg, S. (1966). High-speed scanning in human memory. *Science*, *153*, 652–654.

Stevens, K. N., & Klatt, D. H. (1974). Role of formant transitions in the voiced-voiceless distinction for stops. *Journal of the Acoustical Society of America*, *55*, 653–659.

Steward, M. S., Steward, D. S., Farquhar, L., Myers, J. E. B., Reinhart, M., Welker, J., & . . . Morgan, J. (1996). Interviewing young children about body touch and handling. *Monographs of the Society for Research in Child Development*, *61*(4–5), 1–186.

Steward, M. S., Steward, D. S., Farquhar, L., Myers, J. E. B., Reinhart, M., Welker, J., & . . . Svoboda, E. (2007, February 13). Faces, faces everywhere. *New York Times*. Retrieved from http://www.nytimes.com/2007/02/13/health/psychology/13face.html?pagewanted=all&_r=0

Steyvers, M., Griffiths, T. L., & Dennis, S. (2006). Probabilistic inference in human semantic memory. *Trends in Cognitive Sciences*, *10*, 327–334.

Stolz, J. A. (1996). Exogenous orienting does not reflect an encapsulated set of processes. *Journal of Experimental Psychology: Human Perception and Performance*, *22*, 187–201.

Stolz, J. A. (1999). Word recognition and temporal order judgments: Semantics turns back the clock. *Canadian Journal of Experimental Psychology*, *53*, 316–322.

Stone, B., Dennis, S., & Kwantes, P. J. (2011). Comparing methods for single paragraph similarity analysis. *Topics in Cognitive Science*, *3*(1), 92–122.

Stone, S. P., Halligan, P. W., & Greenwood, R. J. (1993). The incidence of neglect phenomena and related disorders in patients with an acute right or left hemisphere stroke. *Age & Ageing*, *22*, 46–52.

Storms, G., De Boeck, P., & Ruts, W. (2000). Prototype and exemplar-based information in natural language categories. *Journal of Memory & Language*, *42*, 51–73.

Strayer, D. L., & Drews, F. (2007). Cell-phone-induced driver distraction. *Current Directions in Psychological Science*, *16*, 128–131.

Strayer, D. L., Drews, F. A., & Crouch, D. (2006). A comparison of the cell-phone driver and the drunk driver. *Human Factors*, *48*, 381–391.

Strayer, D. L., & Johnston, W. A. (2001). Driven to distraction: Dual-task studies of simulated driving and conversing on a cellular phone. *Psychological Science*, *12*, 462–466.

Stromswold, K., Caplan, D., Alpert, N., & Rauch, S. (1996). Localization of syntactic comprehension by positron emission tomography. *Brain and Language*, *52*(3), 452–473.

Stroop, J. R. (1935). Studies of interference in serial verbal reactions. *Journal of Experimental Psychology*, *18*, 643–662.

Subotnik, R. F., Jarvin, L., & Rayhack, K. (2007). Exploring the implications of putting the expert performance framework into practice. *High Ability Studies*, *18*, 85.

Sulloway, F. J. (1996). *Born to rebel: Birth order, family dynamics, and revolutionary genius*. New York, NY: Pantheon.

Sulloway, F. J. (2009). Sources of scientific innovation: A meta-analytic Approach (Commentary on Simonton, 2009). *Perspectives on Psychological Science*, *4*, 455–459.

The Sunday Times. (2010, April). Migraine left woman with Chinese accent. http://www.perthnow.com.au/news/breaking-news/migraine-left-woman-with-chinese-accent/story-e6frg12u-1225855831038

Suzuki, M., Johnson, J. D., & Rugg, M. D. (2011). Decrements in hippocampal activity with item repetition during continuous recognition: An fMRI study. *Journal of Cognitive Neuroscience*, *23*(6), 1522–1532.

Swinney, D. (1979). Lexical access during sentence comprehension: (Re)consideration of context effects. *Journal of Verbal Learning and Verbal Behavior*, *18*, 645–660.

Swinney, D., & Hakes, D. (1976). Effects of prior context upon lexical access during sentence comprehension. *Journal of Verbal Learning and Verbal Behavior*, *15*, 681–689.

Symonds, C., & Mackenzie, I. (1957). Bilateral loss of vision from cerebral infarction. *Brain*, *80*(4), 415–455.

Tabossi, P. (1988). Accessing lexical ambiguity in different types of sentential contexts. *Journal of Memory & Language*, *27*, 324–340.

Tabossi, P., & Zardon, F. (1993). Processing ambiguous words in context. *Journal of Memory and Language*, *32*, 359–372.

Tadmor, Y., & Tolhurst, D. J. (2000). The difference-of-Gaussians receptive-field model and the contrast in natural scenes. *Vision Research*, *40*, 3145–3157.

Taft, M. (1981). Prefix stripping revisited. *Journal of Verbal Learning and Verbal Behavior*, *20*, 289–297.

Takahashi, E., & Lidz, J. (2008). Beyond statistical learning in syntax. In A. Gavarró & M. João Freitas (Eds.), *Proceedings of generative approaches to language acquisition (GALA) 2007* (pp. 446–456). Newcastle-upon-Tyne, UK: Cambridge Scholars Publishing.

Takayama, Y., Sugishita, M., Akiguchi, I., & Kimura, J. (1994). Isolated acalculia due to left parietal lesion. *Archives of Neurology*, *51*, 286–291.

Talmi, D., Grady, C. L., Goshen-Gottstein, Y., & Moscovitch, M. (2005). Neuroimaging the serial position curve: A test of single-store versus dual-store models. *Psychological Science*, *16*(9), 716–723.

Tam, H., Jarrold, C., Baddeley, A. D., & Sabatos-DeVito, M. (2010). The development of memory maintenance: Children's use of phonological rehearsal and attentional refreshment in working memory tasks. *Journal of Experimental Child Psychology*, *107*, 306–324.

Tanaka, J. W., & Farah, M. J. (1993). Parts and wholes in face recognition. *Quarterly Journal of Experimental Psychology*, *46A*, 225–245.

Tanenhaus, M. K., Leiman, J. M., & Seidenberg, M. S. (1979). Evidence for multiple stages in the processing of ambiguous words in syntactic contexts. *Journal of Verbal Learning and Verbal Behavior*, *18*, 427–441.

Tapp, P. D., Siwak, C. T., Head, E., Cotman, C. W., Murphey, H., Muggenburg, B. A., . . . Milgram, N. W. (2004). Concept abstraction in the aging dog: Development of a protocol using successive discrimination and size concept tasks. *Behavioral and Brain Research*, *153*, 199–210.

Taylor, M. G., Rhodes, M., & Gelman, S. A. (2009). Boys will be boys; cows will be cows: Children's essentialist reasoning about gender categories and animal species. *Child Development*, *79*, 1270–1287.

Tenenbaum, J. B., Griffiths, T. L., & Kemp, C. (2006). Theory-based Bayesian models of inductive learning and reasoning. *Trends in Cognitive Sciences*, *10*, 309–318.

Teuber, H.-L., Milner, B., & Vaughan, H. G., Jr., (1968). Persistent anterograde amnesia after stab wound of the basal brain. *Neuropsychologia*, *6*, 267–282.

Thiessen, E. D., Hill, E., & Saffran, J. R. (2005). Infant-directed speech facilitates word segmentation. *Infancy*, *7*, 53–71.

Thiessen, E. D., & Saffran, J. R. (2003). When cues collide: Statistical and stress cues in infant word segmentation. *Developmental Psychology*, *39*, 706–716.

Thiessen, E. D., & Saffran, J. R. (2007). Learning to learn: Infants' acquisition of stress-based strategies for word segmentation. *Language Learning & Development*, *3*, 73–100.

Thomas, M. H., & Wang, A. Y. (1996). Learning by the keyword mnemonic: Looking for long-term benefits. *Journal of Experimental Psychology: Applied*, *2*, 330–342.

Thomas, N. J. T. (2008). Mental imagery. In Zalta, E. N. (Ed.). *The Stanford encyclopedia of philosophy*. Stanford, CA: CSLI. Retrieved from http://plato.stanford.edu/entries/mental-imagery/

Thompson, C. P., & Cowan, T. (1986). Flashbulb memories: A nicer interpretation of a Neisser recollection. *Cognition*, *22*, 199–200.

Thompson, P. (1980). Margaret Thatcher: A new illusion. *Perception*, *9*, 483–484.

Thorndike, E. L. (1898). Animal intelligence. *Psychological Review Monograph Supplement*, *2*(4), 1–8.

Thorndike, E. L. (1911). *Animal Intelligence*. New York, NY: Macmillan.

Thornton, B., Haskell, H., & Libby, L. (2006). A comparison of learning styles between gifted and non-gifted high school students. *Individual Differences Research*, *4*, 106–110.

Tienson, J. L. (1988). An introduction to connectionism. *Southern Journal of Philosophy*, *26*(S1), 1–16.

Till, R. E., & Jenkins, J. J. (1973). The effects of cued orienting tasks on the free recall of words. *Journal of Verbal Learning and Verbal Behavior*, *12*, 489–498.

Tlauka, M., Donaldson, P. K., & Wilson, D. (2008). Forgetting in spatial memories acquired in a virtual environment. *Applied Cognitive Psychology*, *22*, 69–84.

Todd, J. J., & Marois, R. (2004). Capacity limit of visual short-term memory in human posterior parietal cortex. *Nature*, *428*(6984), 751–754.

Todd, J. J., & Marois, R. (2005). Posterior parietal cortex activity predicts individual differences in visual short-term memory capacity. *Cognitive, Affective, and Behavioral Neuroscience*, *5*(2), 144–155.

Todd, P. M., & Miller, G. (1999). From pride and prejudice to persuasion: Realistic heuristics for mate search. In G. Gigerenzer, P. M. Todd, & ABC Research Group (Eds.), *Simple heuristics that make us smart* (pp. 287–308). New York, NY: Oxford University Press.

Tolman, E. C. (1932). *Purposive behavior in animals and men*. New York, NY: Century.

Tolman, E. C. (1948). Cognitive maps in rats and men. *Psychological Review*, *55*, 189–208.

Tomasello, M. (1995). Joint attention as social cognition. In C. Moore & P. Dunham (Eds.), *Joint attention: Its origins and role in development* (pp. 103–130). Hillsdale, NJ: Erlbaum.

Tomasello, M. (2000). *The cultural origins of human cognition*. Cambridge, MA: Harvard University Press.

Tomasello, M. (2006). Acquiring linguistic constructions. In D. Kuhn & R. Siegler (Eds.), *Handbook of child psychology: Cognition, perception, and language* (5th ed., Vol. 2, pp. 255–298). Hoboken, NJ: Wiley.

Tomasello, M., & Akhtar, N. (1995). Two-year-olds use pragmatic cues to differentiate reference to objects and actions. *Cognitive Development*, *10*, 201–224.

Tomasello, M., & Farrar, M. J. (1986). Joint attention and early language. *Child Development*, *57*, 1454–1463.

Tomasello, M., Strosberg, R., & Akhtar, N. (1996). Eighteen-month-old children learn words in non-ostensive contexts. *Journal of Child Language*, *22*, 1–20.

Torrance, E. P. (1974). *Torrance tests of creative thinking*. Bensenville, IL: Scholastic Testing Service.

Toth, L. J., & Assad, J. A. (2002). Dynamic coding of behaviourally relevant stimuli in parietal cortex, *Nature*, *415* (6868), 165–168.

Trebuchon-Da, F. A., Guedj, E., Alario, F. X., Laguitton, V., Mundler, O., Chauvel, P., & Liegeois-Chauvel, C. (2009). Brain regions underlying word finding difficulties in temporal lobe epilepsy. *Brain*, *132* (Pt 10), 2772–2784.

Treisman, A. (1960). Contextual cues in selective listening. *Quarterly Journal of Experimental Psychology*, *12*, 242–248.

Treisman, A. (1964). Selective attention in man. *British Medical Bulletin*, *20*, 12–16.

Treisman, A. (1969). Strategies and models of selective attention. *Psychological Review*, *76*, 282–299.

Treisman, A. (1993). The perception of features and objects. In A. Baddeley & L. Weiskrantz (Eds.), *Attention: Selection, awareness and control. A tribute to Donald Broadbent* (pp. 5–35). Oxford, UK: Clarendon Press.

Treisman, A. (1996). The binding problem. *Current Opinion in Neurobiology*, *6* (2), 171–178.

Treisman, A., & Geffen, G. (1967). Selective attention: Perception or response? *Quarterly Journal of Experimental Psychology*, *19*, 1–17.

Treisman, A., & Gelade, G. (1980). A feature integration theory of attention. *Cognitive Psychology*, *12*, 97–136.

Treisman, A., & Gormican, S. (1988). Feature analysis in early vision: Evidence from search asymmetries. *Psychological Review*, *95*, 15–48.

Treisman, A., & Schmidt, H. (1982). Illusory conjunctions in the perception of objects. *Cognitive Psychology*, *14*, 107–141.

Trout-Ervin, E. D. (1990). Application of keyword mnemonics to learning terminology in a college classroom. *Journal of Experimental Education*, *59*, 31–41.

Tsao, D. Y., Freiwald, W. A., Knutsen, T. A., Mandeville, J. B., & Tootell, R. B. H. (2003). The representation of faces and objects in macaque cerebral cortex. *Nature Neuroscience*, *6*, 989–995.

Tsao, D. Y., Freiwald, W. A., Tootell, R. B. H., & Livingstone, M. S. L. (2006). A cortical region consisting entirely of face cells. *Science*, *311*, 670–674.

Tse, C. S., & Altarriba, J. (2008). Evidence against linguistic relativity in Chinese and English: A case study of spatial and temporal metaphors. *Journal of Cognition and Culture*, *8*, 335–357.

Tulving, E. (1962). Subjective organization in free recall of unrelated words. *Psychological Review*, *69*, 344–354.

Tulving, E. (1983). *Elements of episodic memory*. New York, NY: Oxford University Press.

Tulving, E. (2002). Episodic memory: From mind to brain. *Annual Review of Psychology*, *53*, 1–25.

Tulving, E., & Pearlstone, Z. (1966). Availability versus accessibility of information in memory for words. *Journal of Verbal Learning & Verbal Behavior*, *5*, 381–391.

Tulving, E., Schacter, D. L., McLachlan, D. R., & Moscovitch, M. (1988). Priming of semantic autobiographical knowledge: A case study of retrograde amnesia. *Brain Cognition*, *8* (1), 3–20.

Tulving, E., & Thomson, D. M. (1971). Retrieval processes in recognition memory: Effects of associative context. *Journal of Experimental Psychology*, *87*, 116–124.

Tulving, E., & Thomson, D. M. (1973). Encoding specificity and retrieval processes in episodic memory. *Psychological Review*, *80*, 352–373.

Tversky, A., & Gilovich, T. (1989). The "hot hand": Statistical reality or cognitive illusion? *Chance 2* (4), 31–34.

Tversky, A., & Kahneman, D. (1971). Belief in the law of small numbers. *Psychological Bulletin*, *76* (2), 105–110.

Tversky, A., & Kahneman, D. (1973). Availability: A heuristic for judging frequency and probability. *Cognitive Psychology*, *5* (2), 207–232. doi:10.1016/0010–0285(73)90033–9

Tversky, A., & Kahneman, D. (1974). Judgment under uncertainty: Heuristics and biases. *Science*, *185* (4157), 1124–1131. doi:10.1126/science.185.4157.1124

Tversky, A., & Kahneman, D. (1981). The framing of decisions and the psychology of choice. *Science*, *211*, 453–458.

Tversky, A., & Kahneman, D. (1983). Extensional versus intuitive reasoning: The conjunction fallacy in probability judgment. *Psychological Review*, *90* (4), 293–315.

Tye, M. (1991). *The imagery debate*. Cambridge, MA: MIT Press, Bradford Books.

Ullman, M. T., Corkin, S., Coppola, M., Hickok, G., Growdon, J. H., Koroshetz, W. J., & Pinker, S. (1997). A neural dissociation within language: Evidence that the mental dictionary is part of declarative memory, and that grammatical rules are processed by the procedural system. *Journal of Cognitive Neuroscience*, *9*, 266–276.

Uncapher, M. R., & Wagner, A. D. (2009). Posterior parietal cortex and episodic encoding: Insights from fMRI subsequent memory effects and dual attention theory. *Neurobiology of Learning and Memory*, *91* (2), 139–154.

Underwood, B. J. (1957). Interference and forgetting. *Psychological Review*, *64*, 49–60.

Ungerleider, L. G., & Mishkin, M. (1982). Two cortical visual systems. In D. J. Ingle, M. A. Goodale, & R. J. W. Mansfield (Eds.), *Analysis of visual behavior* (pp. 549–586). Cambridge, MA: MIT Press.

Valentine, T., & Bruce, V. (1986). The effects of distinctiveness in recognising and classifying faces. *Perception*, *15*, 525–535.

Van Berkum, J. J. A., Hagoort, P., & Brown, C. M. (1999). Semantic integration in sentences and discourse: Evidence from the N400. *Journal of Cognitive Neuroscience*, *11* (6), 657–671.

Vandenberghe, R., Price, C., Wise, R., Josephs, O., & Frackowiak, R. S. J. (1996). Functional anatomy of a common semantic system for words and pictures. *Nature*, *383*, 254–256.

Van der Henst, J. B. (2002). Mental model theory versus the inference rule approach in relational reasoning. *Thinking and Reasoning*, *8*, 193–205.

Van der Linden, M., Brédart, S., Depoorter, N., & Coyette, F. (1996). Semantic memory and amnesia: A case study. *Cognitive Neuropsychology*, *13*, 391–413.

Van Dijk, T. A., & Kintsch, W. (1983). *Strategies of discourse comprehension*. New York, NY: Academic Press.

van Doorn, H., van der Kamp, J., & Savelsbergh, G. J. P. (2007). Grasping the Müller-Lyer illusion: The contributions of vision for perception in action. *Neuropsychologia*, *45*, 1939–1947.

Vannest, J., Polk, T. A., & Lewis, R. L. (2005). Dual-route processing of complex words: New fMRI evidence from derivational suffixation. *Cognitive, Affective, & Behavioral Neuroscience*, *2005*, *5* (1), 67–76.

Van Selst, M. V., Ruthruff, E., & Johnston, J. C. (1999). Can practice eliminate the Psychological Refractory Period effect? *Journal of Experimental Psychology: Human Perception and Performance*, *25*, 1268–1283.

Van Til, R. (1997). *Lost daughters: Recovered memory therapy and the people it hurts*. Grand Rapids, MI: Eerdmans.

Vogt, S. E., & Magnussen, S. (2007a). Expertise in pictorial perception: Eye movement patterns and visual memory in artists and laymen. *Perception*, *36*, 91–100.

Vogt, S. E., & Magnussen, S. (2007b). Long-term memory for 400 pictures on a common theme. *Experimental Psychology*, *54*, 298–303.

von Stockert, T. R., & Bader, L. (1976). Some relations of grammar and lexicon in aphasia. *Cortex*, *12* (1), 49–60.

Voss, J., Vesonder, G., & Spilich, G. (1980). Text generation and recall by high-knowledge and low-knowledge individuals. *Journal of Verbal Learning and Verbal Behavior*, *19*, 651–667.

Vrij, A. (2008). *Detecting lies and deceit: Pitfalls and opportunities*. Chichester, UK: Wiley.

Vul, E., & Pashler, H. (2007). Incubation benefits only after people have been misdirected. *Memory & Cognition*, *35*, 701–710.

Wagner, A. D., & Davichi, L. (2001). Cognitive neuroscience: Forgetting of things past. *Current Biology*, *11* (23), R964–R967.

Wallace, W. H., Turner, S. H., & Perkins, C. (1957). Preliminary studies of human information storage. Signal Corps Project No. 1320, Institute for Cooperative Research, University of Pennsylvania. Cited in: Paivio, A. (1965). Abstractness, imagery, and meaningfulness in paired-associate learning. *Journal of Verbal Learning and Verbal Behavior*, *4*, 32–38.

Wallach, M. A., & Kogan, N. (1965). *Modes of thinking in young children: A study of the creativity-intelligence distinction*. New York, NY: Holt, Rinehart & Winston.

Wallas, G. (1926). *The art of thought*. New York, NY: Harcourt Brace.

Walsh, D. A., & Jenkins, J. J. (1973). Effects of orienting tasks on free recall in incidental learning: "Difficulty," "effort," and "process" explanations. *Journal of Verbal Learning and Verbal Behavior*, *12*, 481–488.

Wallsten, T. S., Budescu, D. V., Rapoport, A., Zwick, R., & Forsyth, B. (1986). Measuring the vague meanings of probability terms. *Journal of Experimental Psychology: General*, *115*, 348–365.

Wang, A. Y., Thomas, M. H., & Ouellette, J. A. (1992). The keyword mnemonic and retention of second language vocabulary. *Journal of Educational Psychology*, *84*, 520–528.

Warburton, D. M. (1995). Effects of caffeine on mood without caffeine abstinence. *Psychopharmacology*, *119*, 66–70.

Wardlow Lane, L., & Ferreira, V. S. (2010). Abstract syntax in sentence production: Evidence from stem-exchange errors. *Journal of Memory and Language*, *62*, 151–165.

Warren, R. M., & Sherman, G. L. (1974). Phonemic restorations based on subsequent context. *Perception & Psychophysics*, *16*, 150–156.

Warren, R. M., & Warren, R. P. (1970). Auditory illusions and confusions. *Scientific American*, *223*, 30–36.

Warrington, E. K. (1982). The fractionation of arithmetical skills: A single case study. *Quarterly Journal of Experimental Psychology 1982*, *34A*, 31–51.

Warrington, E. K., & McCarthy, R. A. (1983). Category specific access dysphasia. *Brain*, *106*, 859–878.

Warrington, E. K., & McCarthy, R. A. (1987). Categories of knowledge: Further fractionations and an attempted integration. *Brain*, *110*, 1273–1296.

Warrington, E. K., & McCarthy, R. A. (1994). Multiple meaning systems in the brain: A case for visual semantics. *Neuropsychologia*, *32* (12), 1465–1473.

Warrington, E. K., & Shallice, T. (1984). Category-specific semantic impairments. *Brain*, *107*, 829–854.

Warrington, E. K., & Taylor, A. M. (1973). Visual discrimination in patients with localized cerebral lesions. *Cortex*, *9* (1), 82–93.

Wason, P. C. (1977). Self-contradictions. In P. N. Johnson-Laird & P. C. Wason (Eds.), *Thinking: Readings in cognitive science* (pp. 114–128). Cambridge, UK: Cambridge University Press.

Watamori, T. S., Fukusako, Y., Monoi, H., & Sasanuma, S., (1991). Confrontation naming in dementia and aphasia. *Clinical Aphasiology*, *20*, 211–221.

Watkins, K., & Paus, T. (2004). Modulation of motor excitability during speech perception: The role of Broca's area. *Journal of Cognitive Neuroscience*, *16*, 978–987.

Watkins, K. E., Strafella, A. P., & Paus, T. (2003). Seeing and hearing speech excites the motor system involved in speech production. *Neuropsychologia*, *41*, 989–994.

Watkins, O. C., & Watkins, M. J. (1977). Serial recall and the modality effect: Effects of word frequency. *Journal of Experimental Psychology: Human Learning and Memory*, *3*, 712–718.

Watson, J. B. (1913). Psychology as the behaviorist views it. *Psychological Review*, *20*, 158–177.

Watson, J. B. (1919). *Behaviorism*. New York, NY: Lippincott.

Watson, J. B. (1930). *Behaviorism*. Chicago, IL: University of Chicago Press.

Watson, J. D. (1968). *The double helix: A personal account of the discovery of the structure of DNA*. New York, NY: New American Library.

Watson, J. D., & Crick, F. H. C. (1953). A structure for deoxyribose nucleic acid. *Nature*, *171*, 737–738.

Waugh, N. C., & Norman, D. A. (1965). Primary Memory. *Psychological Review*, *72*, 89–104.

Waxman, S. R., & Gelman, R. (1986). Preschoolers' use of superordinate relations in classification and language. *Cognitive Development*, *1*, 139–156.

Waxman, S., Medin, D., & Ross, N. (2007). Folkbiological reasoning from a cross-cultural developmental perspective: Early essentialist notions are shaped by cultural beliefs. *Developmental Psychology*, *43*, 294–308.

Weingardt, K. R., Loftus, E. F., & Lindsay, D. S. (1995). Misinformation revisited: New evidence on the suggestibility of memory. *Memory & Cognition*, *23*(1), 72–82.

Weir, W. (1984). Another look at *subliminal* "facts." *Advertising Age*, October 15, 46.

Weisberg, R. W. (1986). *Creativity: Genius and other myths*. New York, NY: Freeman.

Weisberg, R. W. (1994). Genius and madness? A quasi-experimental test of the hypothesis that manic-depression increases creativity. *Psychological Science*, *5*, 361–367.

Weisberg, R. W. (1995). Prolegomena to theories of insight in problem solving: Definition of terms and a taxonomy of problems. In R. J. Sternberg, & J. E. Davidson (Eds.), *The nature of insight* (pp. 157–196). Cambridge, MA: MIT Press.

Weisberg, R. W. (2004). On structure in the creative process: A quantitative case-study of the creation of Picasso's *Guernica*. *Empirical Studies in the Arts*, *22*, 23–54.

Weisberg, R. W. (2006a). *Creativity: Understanding innovation in problem solving, science, invention, and the arts*. Hoboken, NJ: Wiley.

Weisberg, R. W. (2006b). Modes of expertise in creative thinking: Evidence from case studies. In K. A. Ericsson, N. Charness, P. Feltovich, & R. R. Hoffman (Eds.), *Cambridge handbook of expertise and expert performance* (pp. 761–787). Cambridge, UK: Cambridge University Press.

Weisberg, R. W., & Alba, J. W. (1981). An examination of the alleged role of "fixation" in the solution of several "insight" problems. *Journal of Experimental Psychology: General*, *110*, 169–192.

Weisberg, R. W., & Hass, R. (2007). We are all partly right: Comment on Simonton. *Creativity Research Journal*, *19*, 345–360.

Weisberg, R. W., & Suls, J. M. (1973). An information-processing model of Duncker's candle problem. *Cognitive Psychology*, *4*, 255–276.

Weiskrantz, L. (1986). *Blindsight: A case study and implications*. Oxford, UK: Oxford University Press.

Welch, M. J. (1974). Infants' visual attention to varying degrees of novelty. *Child Development*, *45*, 344–350.

Wellman, H. M. (1977). Tip of the tongue and feeling of knowing experiences: A developmental study of memory monitoring. *Child Development*, *48*, 13–21.

Wertheimer, M. (1923). Laws of organization in perceptual forms. First published as Untersuchungen zur Lehre von der Gestalt II, in *Psycologische Forschung*, *4*, 301–350. Translation published in Ellis, W. (1938). *A source book of Gestalt psychology* (pp. 71–88). London, UK: Routledge & Kegan Paul.

Wertheimer, M. (1959). *Productive thinking* (enlarged ed.). New York, NY: Harper & Row.

Wertheimer, M. (1982). *Productive thinking* (enlarged ed.). Chicago: University of Chicago Press.

Westen, D. (1998). The scientific legacy of Sigmund Freud: Toward a psychodynamically informed psychological science. *Psychological Bulletin*, *124*, 333–371.

Whalen, J., McCloskey, M., Lindemann, M., & Bouton, G. (2002). Representing arithmetic table facts in memory: Evidence from acquired impairments. *Cognitive Neuropsychology*, *19*, 505–522.

Wheeler, D. D. (1970). Processes in word recognition. *Cognitive Psychology*, *1*, 59–85.

Wheeler, M. A., Stuss, D. T., & Tulving, E. (1997). Toward a theory of episodic memory: The frontal lobes and autonoetic consciousness. *Psychological Bulletin*, *121*, 331–354.

White, K. K., & Abrams, L. (2002). Does priming specific syllables during tip-of-the-tongue states facilitate word retrieval in older adults? *Psychology and Aging*, *17*, 226–235.

Whitney, P. (1998). *Psychology of language*. New York, NY: Houghton Mifflin.

Whorf, B. L. (1956/1997). In J. B. Caroll (Ed.), *Language, thought, and reality: Selected Writings* Cambridge, MA: MIT Press.

Wickens, C. D. (1984). Processing resources in attention. In R. Parasuraman & R. Davies (Eds.), *Varieties of attention* (pp. 63–102). New York, NY: Academic Press.

Wickens, D. D., Born, D. G., & Allen, C. K. (1963). Proactive inhibition and item similarity in short term memory. *Journal of Verbal Learning and Verbal Behavior*, *2*, 440–445.

Wickens, D. D., Clark, S. E., Hill, F. A., & Wittlinger, R. P. (1968). Grammatical class as an encoding category in short-term memory. *Journal of Experimental Psychology*, *78*, 599–604.

Wiggs, C. L., & Martin, A. (1998). Properties and mechanisms of perceptual priming. *Current Opinion in Neurobiology*, *8*, 227–233.

Wiley, J., & Jarosz, A. F. (2012). How working memory capacity affects problem solving. *Psychology of Learning and Motivation*, *56*, 185–227.

Willingham, D. B., Koroshetz, W. J., & Peterson, E. (1996). Motor skill learning has diverse neural bases: Spared and impaired skill acquisition in Huntington's disease. *Neuropsychology*, *10*, 315–321.

Wilson, B. A., & Baddeley, A. D. (1988). Semantic, episodic and autobiographical memory in a post-meningitic amnesic patient. *Brain and Cognition*, *8*, 31–46.

Wilson, B. A., Green, R., Teasdale, T., Beckers, K., Della Sala, S., Kaschel, R., . . . Weber, E. (1996). Implicit learning in amnesic subjects: A comparison with a large group of normal control subjects. *The Clinical Neuropsychologist*, *10*, 279–292.

Winner, E. (1996). The rage to master: The decisive case for talent in the visual arts. In K. A. Ericsson (Ed.), *The road to excellence: The acquisition of expert performance in the arts and sciences, sports and games* (pp. 271–301). Hillsdale, NJ: Erlbaum.

Winograd, E. (1981). Elaboration and distinctiveness in *memory* for faces. *Journal of Experimental Psychology: Human Learning and Memory*, *7*, 181–190.

Wittgenstein, L. (1953). *Philosophical investigations* (G. E. M. Anscombe, trans.). Oxford, UK: Basil Blackwell.

Wixted, J. T. (2004). The psychology and neuroscience of forgetting. *Annual Review of Psychology*, *55*, 235–269.

Wixted, J. T. (2005). A theory about why we forget what we once knew. *Current Directions in Psychological Science*, *14*, 6–9.

Wollen, K. A., Weber, A., & Lowry, D. H. (1972). Bizarreness versus interaction of mental images as determinants of learning. *Cognitive Psychology*, *3*, 518–523.

Wolraich, M. L., Lindgren, S. D., Stumbo, P. J., Stegink, L. D., Appelbaum, M. I., & Kiritsy, M. C. (1994). Effects of diets high in sucrose or aspartame on the behavior and cognitive performance of children. *New England Journal of Medicine*, *330*(5), 301–307.

Wolraich, M. L., Milich, R., Stumbo, P., & Schultz, F. (1985). The effects of sucrose ingestion on the behavior of hyperactive boys. *Pediatrics*, *106*(4), 657–682.

Wood, N., & Cowan, N. (1995). The cocktail party phenomenon revisited: Attention and memory in the classic selective listening procedure of Cherry (1953). *Journal of Experimental Psychology: General*, *124*, 243–262.

Woodruff-Pak, D. S. (1993). Eyeblink classical conditioning in H. M.: Delay and trace paradigms. *Behavioral Neuroscience*, *107*, 911–925.

Woodward, A. L., & Markman, E. M. (1991). Constraints on learning as default assumptions: Comments on Merriman and Bowman's "The mutual exclusivity bias in children's word learning." *Developmental Review*, *11*, 137–163.

Woodworth, R. S. (1938). *Experimental psychology*. New York, NY: Holt.

Woodworth, R. S., & Schlosberg, H. (1954). *Experimental psychology*. New York, NY: Henry Holt.

Wright, G., & Ayton, P. (Eds.). (1994). *Subjective probability*. Chichester, UK: Wiley.

Wu, J., Mai, X., Chan, C. C. H., Zheng, Y., & Luo, Y. (2006). Event-related potentials during mental imagery of animal sounds. *Psychophysiology*, *43*, 592–597.

Wulfeck, B., Bates, E., & Capasso, R. (1991). A cross-linguistic study of grammaticality judgments in Broca's aphasia. *Brain and Language*, *41*, 311–336.

www.brainconnection.com

www.recordholders.org

Wylie, G. R., Foxe, J. J., & Taylor, T. L. (2008). Forgetting as an active process: An fMRI investigation of item–method–directed forgetting. *Cerebral Cortex*, *18*(3), 670–682.

Xing, J., & Bailey, L. L. (2005). Attention and memory in air traffic control tasks. *Journal of Vision*, *5*(8), 427.

Xu, Y. (2005). Revisiting the role of the fusiform face area in visual expertise. *Cerebral Cortex*, *15*, 1234–1242.

Xu, Y., & Chun, M. M. (2006). Dissociable neural mechanisms supporting visual short-term memory for objects. *Nature*, *440*(7080), 91–95.

Yarmey, A. D., & O'Neill, B. J. (1969a). S-R and R-S paired-associate learning as a function of concreteness imagery, specificity, and association value. *Journal of Psychology: Interdisciplinary and Applied*, *71*(1), 1969, 95–109.

Yarmey, A. D., & O'Neill, B. J. (1969b). S-R and R-S paired-associate learning as a function of word order and noun abstractness. *Canadian Journal of Psychology*, *17*, 370–379.

Yates, F. (1966). *The art of memory*. Chicago, IL: University of Chicago Press.

Yee, E., Blumstein, S. E., & Sedivy, J. C. (2008). Lexical-semantic activation in Broca's and Wernicke's aphasia: Evidence from eye movements. *Journal of Cognitive Neuroscience*, *20*, 592–612.

Yik, W. F. (1978). Short-term memory for Chinese words. *Quarterly Journal of Experimental Psychology*, *30*, 487–494.

Yin, R. K. (1969). Looking at upside-down faces. *Journal of Experimental Psychology*, *81*(1), 141–145.

Young, A., Hellawell, D., & Hay, D. (1987). Configurational information in face perception. *Perception*, *16*, 747–759.

Yue, X., Tjan, B., & Biederman, I. (2006). What makes faces special? *Vision Research*, *46*, 3802–3811.

Yuille, A., & Kersten, D. (2006). Vision as Bayesian inference: Analysis by synthesis? *Trends in Cognitive Sciences*, *10*, 301–308.

Yussen, S. R., & Levy, V. (1975). Developmental changes in predicting one's own span of short term memory. *Journal of Experimental Child Psychology*, *19*, 502–508.

Yussen, S. R., Mathews, S. Huang, T., & Evans, R. (1988). The robustness and temporal course of the story schema's influence on recall. *Journal of Experimental Psychology: Learning, Memory, and Cognition*, *14*, 171–179.

Zabrucky, K., & Ratner, H. H. (1986). Children's comprehension monitoring and recall of inconsistent stories. *Child Development*, *57*, 1401–1418.

Zacks, R. T., & Hasher, L. (1994). Directed ignoring: Inhibitory regulation of working memory. In D. Dagenbach & T. H. Carr (Eds.), *Inhibitory mechanisms in attention, memory, and language* (pp. 241–264). New York, NY: Academic Press.

Zaidel, D. W., Zaidel, E., Oxbury, S. M., & Oxbury, J. M. (1995). The interpretation of sentence ambiuity in patients with uilateral focal brain surgery. *Brain and Language*, *51*(3), 458–468.

Zanini, S. (2008). Generalised script sequencing deficits following frontal lobe lesions. *Cortex*, *44*, 140–149.

Zaragoza, M. S., & Lane, S. M. (1994). Source misattributions and the suggestibility of eye-witness memory. *Journal of Experimental Psychology: Learning, Memory, and Cognition*, *20*, 934–945.

Zatorre, R. J., & Halpern, A. R. (2005). Mental concerts: Musical imagery and auditory cortex. *Neuron*, *47*, 9–12.

Zatorre, R. J., Halpern, A. R., Perry, D. W., Meyer, E., & Evans, A. C. (1996). Hearing in the mind's ear: A PET investigation of musical imagery and perception. *Journal of Cognitive Neuroscience*, *8*, 29–46.

Zechmeister, E. B., & McKillip, J. (1971). Recall of place on a page. *Journal of Educational Psychology*, *63*, 446–453.

Zhang, Q., He, X., & Zhang, J. (2007). A comparative study on the classification of basic color terms by undergraduates from Yi nationality, Bai nationality and Naxi nationality. *Acta Psychologica Sinica*, *39*(1), 18–26.

Zhao, W., Chellappa, R., Rosenfeld, A., & Phillips, P. J. (2003). Face recognition: A literature survey. *ACM Computing Surveys*, 399–458.

Zhong, C., & DeVoe, S. E. (2010). You are how you eat: Fast food and impatience. *Psychological Science*, *21*, 619–622.

Zhong, C. B., Dijksterhuis, A., & Galinsky, A. D. (2008). The merits of unconscious thought in creativity. *Psychological Science*, *19*, 912–918.

Ziegler, A. (2007). Ericsson's three challenges of giftedness research. *High Ability Studies*, *18*(1), 93–95.

Zola-Morgan, S. M., & Squire, L. R. (1986). Memory impairment in monkeys following lesions limited to the hippocampus. *Behavioral Neuroscience*, *100*, 155–160.

Zola-Morgan, S. M., & Squire, L. R. (1990). The primate hippocampal formation: Evidence for a time-limited role in memory storage. *Science*, *250*(4978), 288–290.

Zola-Morgan, S., Squire, L. R., & Amaral, D. G. (1986). Human amnesia and the medial temporal region: Enduring memory impairment following a bilateral lesion limited to field CA1 of the hippocampus. *The Journal of Neuroscience*, *6*, 2950–2967.

Zurif, E. B. (1980). Language mechanisms: A neuropsychological perspective. *American Scientist*, *68*, 305–311.

Zurif, E. B. (1995). Brain regions of relevance to syntactic processing. In L. Gleitman & M. Liberman (Eds.), *Invitation to cognitive sciences* (Vol. I, 2nd ed., pp. 381–398). Cambridge, MA: MIT Press.

Zurif, E. B., Caramazza, A., & Myerson, R. (1972). Grammatical judgments of agrammatic aphasics. *Neuropsychologia*, *10*(4), 405–417.

AUTHOR INDEX

Cherry, E. C., 262, 263, 265, 270, 271
Chi, M. T. H., 524
Chiarello, C., 551
Chinsky, J. M., 69
Chipp, H. B., 571, 574
Chittka, L., 199
Chochon, 532
Choi, J., 581
Chomsky, N., 15–16, 17, 19, 40, 42, 379, 383, 393, 413, 414, 423, 425, 428, 429, 434, 437, 464
Christensen, B. T., 528, 529
Christiansen, M. H., 435, 437
Chronicle, E. P., 521, 536, 555, 557, 558
Chun, M., 224, 225
Chun, M. M., 80
Chung, Chan Sup, 185
Church, B., 90
Ciaramelli, E., 201
Cimpian, A., 348
Claeys, K. G., 198
Claparède, É., 90, 91, 122
Clapper, J., 212, 213–214
Clark, A., 368, 399
Clark, E. V., 400
Clark, H. H., 443
Clark, J. J., 259, 260
Clark, M., 295–296, 298
Clark, M. B., 408
Clark, R. E., 91
Clark, S. E., 63
Claus, J., 238, 240
Cocchini, G., 321
Coelho, C., 387
Coenen, A. M. L., 155
Cofer, C. N., 10, 156
Cohen, A., 251
Cohen, G., 146, 150
Cohen, L., 530, 532, 533
Cohen, L. B., 220

Cohen, N. J., 85, 86, 163, 165, 166
Cohen, Y., 248
Coleman, L. J., 583, 585
Coley, J. D., 362, 364
Collins, A. M., 354, 355, 356, 359, 360, 362, 376
Collins, J. F., 53
Combs, B., 472, 474
Connine, C. M., 463
Conrad, R., 63
Conrey, F. R., 368, 369
Conte, S., 532, 533
Conway, M. A., 146–147, 150
Cook, A. E., 409
Cook, S. P., 166
Cooper, E. E., 221
Cooper, F. S., 390, 392
Cooper, J., 267, 268
Cooper, L. A., 300–301, 302, 304, 307
Cooper, L. M., 85
Cope, D., 580
Coppola, M., 417
Corkin, S., 85, 86–87, 89, 90, 91, 417
Corley, M., 451
Cornell, T. L., 455
Cornette, L., 198
Cortese, M. J., 296
Corts, D. P., 459
Coslett, H. B., 257
Cowan, N., 52, 85, 266
Cowan, T., 165
Cox, J. A., 492
Cox, J. R., 489
Cox, R. W., 405
Coyette, F., 85, 88, 89, 191
Cozza, 475
Craighero, L., 381
Craik, F. I. M., 68
Craik, K. H., 3, 23, 68
Crain, S., 434–435, 437

Cree, G. S., 373–374, 375, 376
Creeley, C. E., 150
Cremieux, J., 55
Crenshaw, M. C., 175
Crick, F., 35, 565, 567–570, 574, 599
Crisp, A. K., 482
Croft, W., 383, 429
Cronin, K., 582
Crouch, D., 4, 267
Crowder, R. G., 55–56
Cruse, D. A., 383, 429
Cruz, D., 398
Csikszentmihalyi, M., 567, 589, 591, 592, 598
Culhane, S. E., 160
Cunitz, A. R., 68
Cunningham, J. B., 536
Cunningham, W. R., 69
Curtis, M. E., 445
Curtiss, S., 438, 439
Cutting, J. E., 393

Dale, A. M., 170
Dallenbach, K. M., 155
Damasio, A. R., 370, 372, 405
Damasio, H., 85, 87, 370, 372, 405
Damian, R. I., 573, 599
D'Andrade, 492
Daneman, M., 445
Daniele, A., 370
Daniels, S. K., 405
Danly, M., 386
Darwin, C. J., 55–56
Dashieff, R. M., 318
Daum, I., 91
Davachi, L., 81, 185
Davidoff, J., 458
Davidson, D. L. W., 189, 190
Davidson, J. E., 536
Davidson, J. W., 583, 584, 585

SUBJECT INDEX

Page numbers in *italic* type indicate boxes, figures, and tables